# THE
# LEGEND
# OF
# HENRY FORD

# THE
# LEGEND
# OF
# HENRY FORD

BY

KEITH SWARD

*with a new preface by William Greenleaf*

*New York*   **ATHENEUM**   1968

Published by Atheneum
Reprinted by arrangement with Holt, Rinehart & Winston Co., Inc.
Copyright 1948 by Keith Sward
Preface copyright © 1968 by William Greenleaf
All rights reserved
Library of Congress catalog card number 68-16412
Manufactured in the United States of America by
The Murray Printing Company, Forge Village, Massachusetts
Published in Canada by McClelland & Stewart Ltd.

# ACKNOWLEDGMENT

In the research which the preparation of this biography entailed, I incurred an unpayable debt to J. W., Joe Brown and his associates, the late Thomas Beer, and especially Kurt Anderson. J. T., R. G., M. B., R. M. S. and John S. Lamont in particular were most helpful in reviewing the manuscript and giving it the benefit of their disinterested criticism. Without the wholehearted assistance of a number of other people—each of whom greatly eased my labors—I might never have carried the work to completion. In this category fall D. R., H. V., J. L. O., E. O. R., and D. F. M.

KEITH SWARD.

# Preface

## by William Greenleaf

PETER F. DRUCKER astutely characterized Ford as "the last Populist."
Historians are still debating the precise meaning of the term, but if
Populism is understood as an agrarian middle-class movement to safeguard the individualism of the small businessman against powerful
monopolies, banks, corporations, railroads, absentee owners, speculators,
and middlemen, one finds here a legacy whose rhetoric Ford was able
to exploit in his lifelong identification with untrammeled individualism
and open competition.

In considerable measure, Ford's popularity was based on his success
in epitomizing the middle-class creed whose matrix was a village and
yeoman outlook that extolled hard and useful work, self-reliance, and
thrift. That creed was a commitment to the values of competitive individualism, the free marketplace, the legitimacy of a reasonable profit on
a socially useful commodity or service, the promotion of progress
through technological efficiency, and the broadest possible diffusion of
material abundance in a society without extremes of poverty and wealth.
In the decades that saw the United States shifting from an agrarian to
an industrial base, this ethos remained generally unchanged despite successive adjustments to the realities of an economy dominated by big
business. It prevailed during the Progressive era, when innovations in
public policy, accompanied by an eager acceptance of a host of technological advances, outstripped a social outlook that traced back to the
nineteenth century. In *Middletown* (1929), the Lynds found that the
overlay of an industrial culture energized by machine technology had
not really affected social attitudes still rooted in an agrarian experience.
This kind of setting was hospitable to a flourishing Ford legend.

The farmers esteemed Ford and for many years were his best customers. Today, when the automobile has become inseparable from urbanization, it is easy to overlook how important the rural market was to the early commercial success of the motor car. After 1898 a depressed staple agriculture entered upon a period of sustained prosperity—the so-called "golden age" of American farming—that lasted until 1920. As early as 1905 it was clear that whoever could meet the growing rural demand for a relatively cheap and mechanically reliable car adapted to poor country roads would reap a fortune and earn a reputation as a public benefactor. At this time the city worker was not a factor in the automobile market. In 1909, when the price of the Model T touring car, originally set at $850, was advanced to $950, the average annual earnings of workers in manufacturing industries was $518. Ford satisfied the demand for reliable utility transportation in the rural markets, especially in the Midwest and in the Northern Plains states. By 1916 the price of the Model T touring car had been reduced to $360. After World War I, the advent of installment buying in the motor car trade brought the city worker into the new car market. Without the brisk farm demand of 1909–1920, however, it is doubtful whether large-scale urbanization stimulated by the automobile would have come so soon after the war. Until the passing of the Model T in 1927, the car retained its sizable following in the small-town market, which helped give Ford his record sales years from 1923 to 1925. In 1924 the Lynds found that 2,578 of the 6,221 cars in Middletown were Fords, accounting for 41 percent.

Both in the hinterland and in the city, Ford was admired because his business success was regarded as exemplary. For a time Ford held a virtual monopoly in the cheap car field—in 1913, for example, he made 96 percent of all cars priced at $600 or less—but no one ever accused him of being a monopolist. He never used the devices of a Standard Oil to win his supremacy in the automotive industry. His fortune never aroused the cries of "tainted wealth" that had been touched off by the Rockefeller riches. To many, Ford was synonymous with the social benefits of price reductions resulting from factory economies stemming from technological progress. As late as 1958 the Kefauver Committee observed in its report on administered prices: "Perhaps the outstanding example in our history of the administration of price in an economically desirable manner was the repeated reduction by Henry Ford of the price of the Model T."

Ford's stature as an individualist cast in the mold of the middle-class creed was reinforced by his independence of finance capitalism and his neo-Populist denunciations of "Wall Street bankers." The early history of the Ford company reads almost like an idealized version of the precept that small enterprise is the creative wellspring of the American business system. The establishment of the company in 1903 with a paid-in capital of $28,000 coincided with the end of the first great wave of mergers in our history. The company thrived despite a continuing tendency toward consolidation in the industrial economy. The Ford Motor Company, which never borrowed an outside dollar to finance its expansion, grew by reinvesting its earnings; and although Ford went to an Eastern financial syndicate in 1919, when he bought out his minority stockholders, he quickly repaid his obligations. Ford's personal control of his company and his vaunted freedom from "Wall Street domination" counted for even more after 1920, when increasing consolidation in the auto industry sharply reduced the number of independent firms and raised bankers to a commanding position. To those who cherished the virtues of individualism, it did not greatly matter that the installation of banker control at General Motors in 1920 led to a system of management far more effective than the one-man rule of Henry Ford. To the small-town mind suspicious of organized wealth and resentful of the large impersonal corporation, the image of Ford as a captain of industry beholden to no one was far more attractive and compelling.

In 1914 Ford's doctrine of high wages, low prices, and technological efficiency made him the prophet of a consumer-oriented society geared to the mass production of durable goods. He early became a world-wide symbol of the promise of material abundance for the industrializing societies of this century, as witnessed by his profound impact on the Soviet Union, where Ford techniques were widely admired, studied, and adapted from the time of Lenin on into the 1930's. Ford himself looked forward to the day when the developing nations would no longer be dependent upon the more advanced technology of the West. If the promise of universal plenty is ever realized, it will doubtless owe much to the concept of mass production as a method for organizing labor, power, machines, and materials. As a Michigan farm boy, Ford became intrigued with the possibilities of shifting the burden of work from men to machines, and he pursued this task almost until the end. Ford never invented anything, not even the moving assembly line, but succeeding generations will most likely remember him as a point in history where the forces of technology converged to produce a new and epochal result.

In the grand perspectives of world history, Ford stands as a symbol of man's mastery of his material environment. But in setting him against the span of universal history, it is well to guard against the habitual temptation to reduce world figures to abstractions. The readers of *The Legend of Henry Ford* will find here the man behind the myth—complex, paradoxical, a genius and an ignoramus.

As a social critic, Mr. Sward discerns that the fundamental reasons
for the power and persistence of the Ford legend are to be found less
in the contrivances of press-agentry than in the values of American
society during the heyday of Ford's reputation. A transitional figure,
Ford was a link between the small-town culture of the late nineteenth
century and the urban-corporate order of our own time. The transportation revolution of the cheap mass-produced motor car wrought far-
reaching social change; the Model T probably did more than any other
contemporary force to break down rural isolation and to destroy the
culture of the hinterland. Yet Ford himself nostalgically turned his gaze
backward, away from the restless motor age to the past he resurrected
and preserved in his museum at Dearborn. Even as a multimillionaire
industrialist, he never cut himself off from the sources of the small-town
way of life he had known in his Michigan youth. His public image
bespoke a simplicity and lack of ostentation flavored with the democ-
ratizing tendencies of a farm-and-village society. He strengthened that
image by uniquely adapting the lexicon of Populism to his own uses
as an industrial tycoon.

The publication of *The Legend of Henry Ford* in 1948 was a pioneer
contribution to the enormous literature on the most celebrated of American industrialists; it set a new standard for the treatment of its important
and complex subject. Before the book appeared, no systematically re-
searched and documented account of Ford's many-sided career as an
auto-maker and a public figure existed. Mr. Sward's comprehensive and
engrossing narrative met this need. Its absolute candor made it a turning point for subsequent writers on Ford and his company.

The intensive cultivation of Ford history in the two decades since
the book was first published has elaborated and added many details to
a story unrivaled in the annals of American industrial enterprise. The
Ford Motor Company Archives, opened to researchers and historians in
1951, have challenged Mr. Sward's findings only on a few minor points.*
Mr. Sward's absorbing study, with its critical realism and keenly per-
ceptive judgments, remains the best one-volume portrayal of Henry
Ford and the industrial empire he helped to build and almost destroyed.
Like the Model T in its own day, and like the Model A still in daily use,
Mr. Sward's work is durable. It should command the interest of all who
would like to understand the thrust of the forces which carried the

* See Allan Nevins and Frank Ernest Hill, *Ford: The Times, the Man, the
Company* (New York, 1954), and *Ford: Expansion and Challenge* (New York,
1957). These are the first two panels in a three-volume history which takes the
story up to 1962. The interested reader may be referred to the controverted points
by consulting the index of these two volumes under the entry, "Sward, Keith."

agrarian American society of the late nineteenth century into the industrial and urban order of the twentieth century.

The creation of the Ford legend began in January, 1914, when Henry Ford suddenly rocketed to fame with the announcement of the Five Dollar Day. For more than thirty years his deeds and utterances became the stock-in-trade of American and world journalism. Much of this first phase of myth-making centered on Ford's social idealism: the spectacular and short-lived labor policies of the Five Dollar Day; the knight-errantry of the Peace Ship episode; the Senate race Ford made in Michigan at the behest of President Woodrow Wilson; the serio-comic ordeal of the *Chicago Tribune* libel suit; and Ford's astonishing but unredeemed pledge to return to the government his share of company profits on World War I military contracts. Up to 1914, his name had been the impersonal trade label of a well-known, low-priced automobile. After the war, it was a household word. Within a brief span of five years, Ford had become a public personage renowned for his liberalism and humanitarianism, and closely identified with Wilsonian idealism at its crest in 1918–1919. Although outwardly laconic and humble in manner, Ford did not for long remain indifferent to the uses of indiscriminate publicity.

The second phase began in 1920, shortly after Ford bought out his minority stockholders and won complete control of his industrial empire. Possibly as the reaction of an ill-educated man to adverse comment on his puerile performance on the witness stand in the *Chicago Tribune* trial, Ford retreated from his humanitarianism into the social pathology of anti-Semitism. In the pages of his journal, the *Dearborn Independent,* where he had at first supported the Wilsonian program of world reconstruction, Ford mounted a virulent anti-Semitic campaign that made him a controversial and, in some quarters, a much-admired figure.

Despite the pitiless exposure of Ford's intellectual inadequacies in the *Chicago Tribune* trial and the irresponsibility of his anti-Semitic tirades, his popularity was not seriously impaired. The early 1920's, after all, saw a tidal surge of national xenophobia and immigration restriction. And Ford, as always, exerted a potent hold on the village mind, even among those who did not share his extreme prejudices. Early in 1923 both major parties boomed Ford for President, and in a poll conducted by *Collier's Weekly* he ran ahead of President Warren G. Harding by 8 to 5, leading Harding even in the President's home state of Ohio.

In the immediate postwar era, Ford encouraged a deliberate and concerted effort to make him the central figure of a massive campaign of self-advertisement conducted by a diversified publicity apparatus operating from the Dearborn offices of the Ford Motor Company. This apparatus consisted of aides and associates like Ernest G. Liebold and William J. Cameron, ghost writers like Samuel Crowther, fulsome "court" biographers like Sarah T. Bushnell and William R. Stidger, and complaisant newspapermen who accepted at face value the glowing testimonials drawn up at company headquarters. The output of this extensive machinery of publicity, and the chain reaction it triggered in the press, was truly staggering. As early as January, 1924, the journalist and historian Arthur Pound wrote: "In a newspaper morgue the envelope filed under 'Ford, Henry,' bulks larger than that devoted to any other private citizen."

That Ford eagerly accepted the credibility of the legend was abundantly clear in *My Life and Work* (1922). This authorized account, told in first person, was actually written by Samuel Crowther, who is identified on the title page as Ford's "collaborator." Unquestionably the book provides valuable insights into Ford's industrial policies and social views, but it is an unreliable presentation of his career.

But even as this calculated image was taking shape, a literature critical of Ford was finding its way into print. The liberal-minded Edwin G. Pipp, a former Detroit newspaperman who edited the *Dearborn Independent* in its early days, broke with Ford and brought out a little-known and ephemeral Detroit journal, *Pipp's Weekly,* an authoritative and richly informative source that would later be forgotten until Mr. Sward mined it with exceptional skill. The Rev. Samuel S. Marquis, the dean of St. Paul's Cathedral in Detroit, and former head of the Sociological Department which Ford had organized in conjunction with the Five Dollar Day, published in 1923 his illuminating *Henry Ford: An Interpretation.* Eastern journalists like Robert Littell and William Hard, writing for the *New Republic* and the *Nation* in the early 1920's, furnished incisive analyses. Such estimates, ranging from critical to hostile, did not reach a wide public. They were overshadowed by the sheer mass of the generally favorable publicity which Ford continued to enjoy well into the 1930's. Ford's reputation was at its height until about 1925; its ensuing decline was gentle, partly because it was so protracted.

By 1925, however, there was substantial evidence of a disparity between the public image of Ford as a machine-age innovator, far-seeing benefactor, folk hero, and culture symbol, and, on the other side, the comparatively unfamiliar reality of Ford as an industrial despot and a pathetically ill-informed bigot in many fields outside his immediate interests.

Over the years, the legend took on more ample dimensions. Occasionally there appeared a work on Ford refreshingly free of hero-

worship. Such was *And Then Came Ford* (1929), by Charles Merz, the
first attempt to deal with Ford as a social phenomenon of the automobile age. This was followed by *The Tragedy of Henry Ford* (1932), by
Jonathan Norton Leonard, a profoundly hostile study that was essentially a savage caricature. Its circus-poster portrait of Ford as a country
bumpkin of the machine age was too one-sided to be credible. By this
time, Ford was approaching his seventieth year. His major achievements
were behind him. Plainly, there was room for a balanced critical assessment based on the voluminous sources in print, but it was clear that a
serious researcher would have to pick his way through a maze of conflicting evidence full of pitfalls for the unwary investigator.

It was at this point, the first and most bitter years of the Great
Depression, that Keith Sward found his subject. Against a background
of bank failures, idle factories, breadlines, and Hoovervilles, the viewpoint of *The Legend of Henry Ford* was influenced by pervasive dis-
enchantment with American business leadership. In Detroit, where
automotive production in 1932 was down 75 percent from the peak year
of 1929, the relief rolls were clogged with jobless Ford workers. Ford,
who disapproved of charity, refused to contribute to private community efforts to alleviate the plight of the needy. His homilies on the state
of the national economy became progressively irrelevant to the grim
facts. In the summer of 1932, unemployment stood at approximately
13,000,000. Ford counseled workers to abandon the cities and "return
to the land." In October, 1932, he said: "If we could only realize it, these
are the best times we ever had."

Keith Sward was living in Pittsburgh, then a city of silent mills and
jobless men. Born in Oakland, Nebraska, in 1903, he was raised in a
conventional middle-class household in St. Paul, Minnesota. In his youth
he did not question the accepted Midwestern stereotype of Ford as a
liberal and a humanitarian. Mr. Sward took his doctorate in clinical and
social psychology at the University of Minnesota, pursued post-doctoral
study at Leland Stanford University, and settled in Pittsburgh to engage
in private practice as a clinical psychologist. In Pittsburgh, Mr. Sward
observed more than the malfunctioning of industrial capitalism. He saw
also at first hand the beginnings of a new era in organized labor destined
to produce the Steel Workers' Organizing Committee and to stimulate
the genesis of the CIO. Pittsburgh had been the center of the unsuccessful steel strike and organizing drive of 1919–1920, and was one of
the citadels of the "American Plan," a highly effective campaign for the
open shop that spread to many industries. In the 1920's a number of
factors, including welfare capitalism and the conservatism of the Amer-

ican Federation of Labor, combined to leave huge sectors of the basic industries unorganized. The false dawn of enforceable collective bargaining under Section 7a of the National Industrial Recovery Act only compounded labor's bitterness and frustration, and even after the passage of the Wagner National Labor Relations Act in 1935 it took at least four more years before most of the battles for union recognition in the basic industries were won. The Ford Motor Company, the last holdout among the "Big Three," did not sign a contract with the United Automobile Workers until 1941.

In 1932 the workers in the steel mills of Pittsburgh and in the automotive plants of Detroit were the underdogs of the most technologically advanced domains of American industry. Today no employee in the most backward sectors of our industrial economy would tolerate the conditions which prevailed in those shops throughout the 1920's and much of the '30's. The unorganized workers in steel and autos were subjected to speed-ups, harassment, intimidation, labor espionage, and arbitrary dismissal. There was no institutionalized job security or job seniority. The Ford plants had the worst labor relations in the automobile industry. The rough discipline enforced on and off the factory floor by the Ford Service Department under Harry Bennett was an oppressive horror worthy of the nightmare vision of a Hieronymus Bosch or a Goya. "Big labor" had not yet arisen to redress the excessive power of a generally backward management.

In this book Mr. Sward's sympathies are with labor, but they flow from a broad concern with human dignity and the quest of the disadvantaged for social justice, not from a parochial identification with trade unionism or with a particular union. Ford spoke much of the dignity of labor. "Work is our sanity, our self-respect, our salvation," he said. "...Work is the greatest blessing." But he treated his workers with contempt, and when he wrote, "A great business is really too big to be human," he said more than he intended.

In writing *The Legend of Henry Ford*, Sward followed no particular model or "school" of historical interpretation. The book stands on its own merits. It is distinguished for its expert marshaling and shrewd assessment of a wide range of information gleaned with discriminating judgment from government documents, court proceedings, newspaper files, and little-known periodicals such as the long-overlooked *Pipp's Weekly* and the invaluable *Detroit Saturday Night*. A glance at the twenty-page bibliography attests that, by the time this book was published, Mr. Sward had become the outstanding authority on Henry Ford.

Mr. Sward acknowledges Ford's contribution to our industrial civilization, but he insists on setting the record straight. In Ford's case, this almost always involved the "conflict between fact and pretension," as Mr. Sward characterizes it—a conflict generated by the contrast between reality and myth. Thus, where accounts sponsored or authorized by the Ford publicity apparatus ignored the efforts of others in building the company, Mr. Sward takes pains to portray the developing enterprise as an associative achievement. Given the complexities of modern industrial technology, it could not have been otherwise. Some of the most exciting and instructive pages of the book tell of that time of headlong innovation and expansion culminating in the feat of the moving final assembly line in 1913–1914. It was a time when almost every day seemed to bring its crop of new problems and fresh solutions, and when Couzens, Sorensen, Wills, Carl Emde, Charles Morgana, Clarence W. Avery, William S. Knudsen, and many others pushed the company along the path to greatness. Nowhere in the existing literature on Ford had there been anything to compare with this.

Ford's role was scaled down, but Mr. Sward does not underestimate it. As he points out, the "driving force" behind these achievements was Henry Ford. On the whole, the Ford of these early days is portrayed in a very favorable light. Nor is the performance of James Couzens overlooked. Mr. Sward applauds him as "the business genius of the Ford concern" and sets forth in explicit detail his signal contributions to those extraordinarily fruitful years before Couzens departed in 1915.

Like those other great entrepreneurs, Carnegie and Rockefeller, Ford had a marked ability to attract and hold able lieutenants in the years before he conducted his first great purge in 1919–1921. The men he chose were not wedded to any rigid or exclusive system. They were the proponents of a flexible and pragmatic method which did not accept any technical solution as final, but regarded each advance as a point of departure for another solution. The vast innovative energies of the Ford enterprise began to run down when Ford became the prisoner of his growing isolation and hardening prejudices. In time, after a lengthy power struggle raised Harry Bennett to the regency, the Ford enterprise was brought to the edge of ruin. The years of decline at Ford underscore the perils of one-man rule in the large corporation. One of the reasons why General Motors overtook Ford was the superior pattern of corporate management introduced by Alfred P. Sloan, Jr., between 1921 and 1925. The negative example of Henry Ford as a company despot teaches us that his methods are inimical to the rational governance of big business and incompatible with the obligations of private economic power in a democratic society.

# CONTENTS

## PART ONE: On the Assembly Line

## PART FIVE: Modern Times

# On the Assembly Line

Machinery is the new Messiah.—*Henry Ford*

# One

## HORSELESS CARRIAGE

### 1

THREE TURNS of history set the stage for the career of Henry Ford, the most celebrated Yankee mechanic of his age. These events were the invention of the automobile in France, the readiness with which the North American continent embraced the new invention, and the fact that Ransom E. Olds, the first American to bring the automobile into mass production, did his work in Michigan, not far from the farm where Henry Ford was born two years before the American Civil War had run its course.

For the original conception of the automobile, mankind is indebted to Gottlieb Daimler, the inventor of the high-speed, internal-combustion gasoline engine, as well as the first man to apply this new power plant to a self-propelled vehicle. Opening a new epoch in history, Daimler demonstrated a crude gasoline motor car on the streets of Paris in 1886, seventeen years before the founding of the Ford Motor Co. His labors were duplicated almost immediately by Carl Benz of Mannheim. Then, using Daimler's patents, the French firm of Panhard and Levassor evolved the basic design of the automobile as we know it today. This company's engineers conceived the fundamentals of the modern motor car, placing the engine forward, and adding the refinements of clutch, gear-box and transmission system. Panhard and Levassor had the further distinction of being the first practical manufacturers in the field.

At the outset, consequently, France was the world's first automotive center. She added the words "automobile," "garage" and "chauffeur" to the language of nations. For more than a decade she was to lead the world in the production of motor cars. Her output for 1903—the last year of her supremacy and the year in which the

Ford Motor Co. was founded—exceeded that of the United States by a margin of 5000 cars.

At the turn of the century, however, France had to cede her leadership to Yankee machinists, to men like Olds and Ford and Studebaker. Not that her own mechanics and industrialists were less apt or less enterprising than the American "automobileer." She lost out simply because for the purpose of exploiting the motor car, the new world was more richly endowed than the old. By contrast with France, the United States had a superior technology, a larger potential market, and an infinitely greater wealth of material resources.

Once the automobile caught on in the 90's, it found its perfect medium on the North American continent. Here, all the basic industries of the nation were ripe and ready to supply the wants of the rising automobile manufacturer. The developed resources of the country were limitless. The land was rich in steel and oil. Rockefeller's work was all but finished. Ten years earlier, S. F. Bowser had invented a self-measuring oil pump, the forerunner of the modern filling station. By 1890 the United States was producing more than one-third of the world's annual tonnage of iron and steel. The 90's brought Andrew Carnegie's career to a close. Likewise in this decade the pioneers of the American automobile could draw on the experience of a mature rubber industry. Goodyear had vulcanized rubber twenty years before the Civil War. Hard rubber tires had been used on horse-drawn vehicles since the 50's. And the principle of the pneumatic valve, which made possible the air-filled tire of the American bicycle of the 90's, had been conceived by August Schroeder half a century before the invention of the automobile.

The first American builders of the automobile had a further advantage over their French rivals in that they had access to a richer experience in the arts of mass production. Most of the fundamental factory appliances like the jig and the crane, and most of the basic machine tools—the pneumatic drill, the air-hammer, the turret lathe and other power machinery for molding and milling and grinding— had become standard equipment in the more advanced machine shops of the new world. Correspondingly, there were more Americans than Frenchmen who had had a first-hand acquaintance with machinery and mechanical work. The Americans of the 90's had only finished conquering a continent with the use of their hands and elementary tools. They could boast a small army of artisan-mechanics, already at work in the railroad shops, in the plants which were making bicycles and carriages, and, above all, in the machine shops of the eastern seaboard. For their first lessons in precision manufacturing—without which mass production of the automobile would have been impossible—America's automotive pioneers had no need to leave their native soil. They had only to apply to a new product the arts of production which had been worked out a generation earlier in the American munitions factories, in the domestic manufacture of sewing machines, and in the foremost machine shops of New England.

Among the assets which made America, of all the semi-industrialized nations, best suited for the development of the automobile was the most extensive railroad system in the world, the largest self-contained population—hence, the largest body of potential users of the automobile and the greatest reaches of sheer space. At the close of the 80's, seven transcontinental railway lines connected the coastal limits of North America. By this time the United States had laid one-half of the world's trackbed, and of the 76,000,000 people within her continental borders in 1890, 21,000,000 lived west of the Mississippi, in states and territories where there were fewer than ten inhabitants to the square mile. The invention of the automobile was perfectly timed, therefore, to meet the needs of the expanding American West and Middle West.

## 2

At the outset the American motor car made enemies as well as friends. It was too noisy and too fast for a generation that was geared to the quiet and easy tempo of a horse age. It antagonized the farmer because it threw his teams into a panic. Moreover, the first American cars, built entirely by hand, were so expensive they were beyond the reach of the average citizen. Thus for a decade the automobile failed to displace the horse because, as Duryea once put it, "Oats were too cheap." Furthermore, the early models were utterly undependable. Breakdowns were the rule. The enterprising "automobileer" had to harden himself to the jeering of lookers-on and passers-by.

The antagonisms toward America's first gasoline buggies are reflected in the laws and journals of the period. In 1899 the town of San Rafael, California, had an ordinance which required the driver of an automobile to come to a dead stop within three hundred feet of every passing horse. A year later Vermont was enforcing a statute which compelled every motorist in motion to employ "a person of mature age" to walk ahead of him one-eighth of a mile, bearing a red flag in his hand. The speed limit within the city limits of Savannah,

Cincinnati and of San Francisco in 1902 was eight miles per hour. By act of city council, motorists at this time were barred from the parkways of most of the country's larger cities. An "automobileer" who defied such an ordinance in Chicago in 1902 was arrested for "riot, disturbance and breach of the peace." He had made bold to take his machine onto Michigan Boulevard, traveling at a moderate rate of speed but over a course reserved for horse-drawn vehicles. The farmers of the nation, meanwhile, were bitter in their denunciations of the "devil wagon."

All in all, it took ten years to wean the American public from its original prejudice against the motor car. By 1905 or thereabouts, most of the country was willing to concede what Thomas Edison had foreseen a decade earlier. In discussing the future of the automobile, Edison had remarked with finality in 1895, "The horse is doomed!"

All that America was waiting for in 1900, so far as automobiles were concerned, was a car that would run and one that it could afford to buy. The nation was marking time until someone had the genius to carry the new product from the field of invention into the realm of practical manufacturing. That transition took place in the city of Detroit. It occurred there rather than in some other center of the United States because of a series of social "accidents" and because of the direct influence of two outstanding personalities: Ransom E. Olds and Henry M. Leland.

The first of the social "accidents" that was to make Detroit the automobile capital of the world was the fact that, before the rise of the motor car, the bicycle and carriage manufacturers of the country had concentrated their operations in Michigan and Ohio. By the time it became feasible to manufacture automobiles, both of these older trades had begun to slip. The "bicycle bubble" exploded in the 90's. Simultaneously the timber reserves of Michigan were getting thinned, and the carriage-makers of the State, stripped of a natural advantage in their basic raw material, had begun to cast about for new fields of enterprise. Thus Studebaker, Nash, Durant and the seven Fisher brothers went over to the automobile trade direct from the wagon and carriage shops. The migrants from the defunct bicycle business included men like Alexander Winton, John Willys, W. E. Metzger, Charles Duryea, Barney Oldfield and the Dodge brothers. Long before they made the shift, these promoters and manufacturers had a sound basic knowledge of factory method. Those who had worked in the carriage plants of Flint led the country in advanced assembly methods of production.

Certain other economic conditions made Detroit ripe for its work of incubating the automobile. Many of its mechanics and industrialists were already familiar with the gasoline motor. They had been making marine engines since the 80's. The city had, in addition, a large reservoir of machine shops and of metal-working establishments. When the need arose, it could solicit labor from the adjoining Province of Ontario into which skilled machinists had migrated from the factory towns of England and Scotland. Finally, the city enjoyed a favored location on the Great Lakes waterway.

But before it could comprehend either its own industrial destiny or the potentialities of the automobile, Detroit required the example of Ransom E. Olds. Olds appeared on the scene in 1899 when the company which he managed, the Olds Motor Works, began to produce the original Oldsmobile.

Olds and his associates started out on a shoestring. Their plant, located on East Jefferson Avenue some distance from the heart of Detroit, was small. The money behind their venture could have been raised by any small-town banker. Their undertaking succeeded where others failed, however, in that it was guided by an excellent business sense and a degree of genius.

To begin with, Olds made the job easier by farming out most of his work. The Dodge brothers who ran a thriving machine shop were placed under contract to build his engines. His transmissions were made by the Lelands, father and son. Olds concentrated on the job of final assembly. For that work a miniature factory was adequate. The "merry Oldsmobile" was soundly put together; Olds made a cheaper car and a better product than any other pioneer in the business because he was the first to bring the automobile into quantity production. Small as it was, the factory on East Jefferson was the model of its day. It was the first plant in the United States specifically designed and laid out for the manufacture of motor cars. In five years' time the growth of factory methods at the Olds Works was so remarkable that Olds is remembered to this day as the "father" of automotive mass production. When the industry finally became entrenched in the city of Detroit for good, more than a hundred of its prominent executives were former associates or employes of the original Olds group.

In their haste to get a footing in the new field and because they were green at the job, most of Olds' imitators and Olds himself had one major fault in common. Their factory methods were raw, and their cars were correspondingly crude and unreliable. The man who best understood this basic shortcoming and who pointed the way to its correction was Henry M. Leland, one of Olds' suppliers.

Unlike most of his fellow-pioneers in the automobile business, Leland was a craftsman from the very beginning. When he entered the industry, he was already expert in four of the fields which contributed to the rise of the automobile. Having worked in the federal arsenal at Springfield, Massachusetts, during the Civil War, and later at the Colt arms plant, he had had his first exposure to precision-machine work in the munitions industry. He had an intimate knowledge of the best factory practices of New England from having worked for one of the foremost tool-making firms of the East in the 70's and 80's. Moreover, he was thoroughly familiar with two products which were immediate forerunners of the American motor car. Throughout the 90's he had made marine engines and bicycle parts in a factory of his own in Detroit.

From the day he began making automobile parts for Olds in 1899, Leland was the foremost artisan of the trade. The gears which he built for the first Oldsmobile were models of workmanship. They gave this car much of its reputation for smooth and dependable performance. The following year, in 1900, Leland became a manufacturer in his own right. He designed the Cadillac and began his notable career as production manager of the Cadillac Motor Car Co.

Six years later, Leland made a dramatic experiment that could have been duplicated by none of his fellow-manufacturers in America and, perhaps, by no other car-maker in the world. He took three Cadillacs to London, and in the presence of impartial experts, he had the cars disassembled and their parts scrambled so that none could tell which pieces had come from which car. Then, from this hodge-podge of parts, workmen proceeded to reconstruct three new automobiles on the spot. Once reassembled, the Cadillacs not only ran but they succeeded in passing as well a rigorous 500-mile speed test. This brilliant performance was the first demonstration that precision techniques had been successfully applied to the manufacture of the motor car and that a producer of the automobile had mastered the principle of "interchangeability of parts."

Meanwhile, it was Leland's personal achievement in the arts of production, along with Olds' example, that made Detroit the birthplace of the American automobile industry. Because of his influence, Detroit clinched its primacy in the new field; it perfected its techniques of manufacturing more quickly than any other factory center in the country.*

## 3

Such was the state of the feverish young industry when Henry Ford and a small group of his associates founded the Ford Motor Co. in 1903. Ford himself was forty at the time. Although he was destined to become Leland's and Olds' most distinguished disciple, his background was as ordinary as that of hundreds of other mechanics who had been enthralled by the spectacle of the "horseless carriage."

Born in Michigan near the township of Dearborn in 1863, Henry Ford was the son of a moderately successful farmer. He sprang from a line of early American settlers. His mother's people were Pennsylvania Dutch. His father's father was an Irish immigrant.

As Ford has told us in his autobiography, written when he was fifty-nine, he detested farm work from the moment he put his hand to it. As a boy he rebelled against the continual round of chores and the long hours of dreary, sweating labor. The only thing that made life at all bearable on his father's acres, he recalled in later life, was the fact that now and then he had a chance to fiddle with machinery. Here, if nowhere else, young Ford had been at home down on the farm. He was the born tinkerer. When he was still in grammar school he developed the knack of keeping his father's farm machinery in repair. When all the appliances were in working order on his father's place, he would scurry about to see if any of the neighbors had implements or machines that needed "fixing." He was barely in his teens when he began to putter with old clocks and watches, pulling them apart and mending them by trial and error. So pronounced was this youngster's passion for mechanical work that it drove him off the farm altogether at an age when the interests of the average boy are only half formed. At sixteen he resolved to follow the machinist's trade. With that end in mind, he overrode his father's objections and set out for the nearby city of Detroit.

In 1879, the year in which Ford left the farm, Detroit was a busy lake port and a rising manufacturing center with a population of

* Although he was nearly sixty when he produced the first Cadillac, Leland was to remain in the trade for twenty years to come. Selling out to General Motors in 1909, he continued to manage GM's Cadillac unit for the next eight years. Then at the close of the first World War, Leland and his son, Wilfred, made a fresh start. They designed the Lincoln and founded the Lincoln Motor Car Co. This enterprise, in turn, was to be absorbed by the Ford Motor Co.

100,000. It had a place for zealous young men who were quick with their hands. Ford hired out at once as a machinist's apprentice in a shop that was building marine engines for the lake trade. His habits of work at the time have been described by one of his co-workers who was interviewed on the subject years later by a Detroit newspaperman. According to this former fellow-worker, Henry Ford, the apprentice of 1880, was apt and diligent at the bench, but he never worked "too hard;" he was continually "wandering about the shop" to see what the other man was doing. Several years later, in the middle of the 80's, Ford had an even wider opportunity to see what the "other fellow" was up to. By this time a full-fledged journeyman, he was hired by a manufacturer to travel along the waterfront and to the larger farms, installing and repairing steam and gasoline engines.

At the age of twenty-four, after having devoted eight years to the craft of his choice, Ford reversed himself. He went back to the farm. Whether he was following his own wishes or the desires of his family, he acted as if he had come back to stay. For he immediately accepted from his father the present of a threshing machine and a forty-acre strip of ground. The prodigal son settled on the land, apparently for good. A year later he married Clara Bryant, the daughter of a prosperous neighboring farmer.

As long as he remained in Dearborn, Ford was only learning all over again what he had the wit to grasp when he was a farmhand in his youth. Once more he found that he had no real hankering for the farm. During this adult trial on the land, he was in his element only in the fall, when he could make the rounds with his mechanical thresher, taking it from one place to the next for a price. But for the most part, the tinkerer was perpetually at war with the farmer. While his neighbors tilled their soil with reins in hand, Ford was devoting a good share of his time to an experiment in "horseless" plowing. Convincing his father and other farmers in the locality that he had "wheels in his head" for certain, he pieced together bits of discarded barnyard equipment in a fruitless effort to make a steam locomotive that would displace the horse. After two years of such conflict, with his feet on the land and his heart in the shop, Ford deserted the farm for good. In 1888, turning twenty-six, he took his young bride to Detroit, intent on earning his living in a trade that was more to his liking.

Transported to a more congenial environment, Ford readily found his niche. He went to work as a mechanical engineer at the Edison Illuminating Co., the concern that supplied the city of Detroit with light and power. Here he remained for eleven years. He was a highly regarded Detroit-Edison employe in 1892, four years after his second desertion from the farm, when Charles Duryea startled the new world by inventing the first American automobile.

Like many another mechanic, Ford was bewitched by Duryea's feat. He devoured reports on the subject which appeared in the newspapers and popular magazines of the day. Straightway he settled down to the job of making a car of his own. Once fired by such a desire, Ford hung on for the next seven years, laboring against odds that would have sidetracked all but the most dogged. Throughout this period he was, of necessity, still tied to a full-time job at the power company; his laborious experiments had to be sandwiched in during leisure hours. His tools were crude and inadequate; he did most of his work by hand; the workshop which he set up in a small shed behind his home on Bagley Avenue was a primitive affair. Pioneering car-builders like himself had the scantiest precedent behind them. Their work was largely uncharted; it was a case of try-and-try-again in a new line of endeavor in which failure was far more common than success. Moreover, in resolving to follow in Duryea's footsteps, Ford had to persist in the face of widespread social disapproval. As a rule, amateur inventors in this field were objects of ridicule. They were still popularly regarded as a queer and impractical lot.

Before he had carried his first car much beyond the blueprint stage, Ford had the good fortune to meet Charles B. King. King was a versatile fellow-townsman who was then hard at work on an automobile of his own. When these two began to fraternize for the purpose of exchanging ideas, King was unquestionably the more advanced member of the pair. He was an established marine engineer; he was widely read in the field of automotive invention; he was corresponding with car-builders and scientific societies all over Europe; and the motor car which he was building was farther along than Ford's. At the same time Ford was a stimulating mechanic in his own right; he was full of ideas; he was curious and hard-working; he had a flair for picking up ideas in conversation; and in this particular field that obsessed him he was an easy and lively talker.

While fraternizing with Ford, King brought his motor car to completion. This automobile, the first in Detroit, was given a secret trial run one night in 1894. And shortly thereafter King decided to go to Paris to make a study of the French automobile industry. Before he left the country, convinced of the fact that his own handiwork had been outmoded by French inventions, he called in his friend Henry

Ford and made him a present of the parts and designs of the car which he had demonstrated with success in 1894.*

Stimulated by his contacts with King and rewarded by his own mastery of the subject, Ford was prepared in the spring of 1896 to conduct a trial performance of the "horseless carriage" that he himself had built.† After spending the better part of two days and nights in a last effort to put his machine in working order, he took to the road at two in the morning. It was raining at the time, and his wife, crouched under an umbrella, came out to see him off. Ford's patient labors were crowned with success. Jerking and sputtering, the car ran. Its happy inventor, worn with fatigue, rode into the night, picking his way over the dark, cedar-block pavement with the aid of a dangling kerosene lamp.

This first work of Ford's was a gasoline "quadricycle," its chassis a buggy frame mounted on four bicycle wheels. Its air-cooled motor had two cylinders which Ford had made by hand from the exhaust pipe of a steam engine. Having no reverse gear, the vehicle could move forward but not backward. The power from its motor was transmitted to the rear wheels by a revolving leather belt.

From the standpoint of mechanics or design, the car had no novel features. It was like most of the other automotive models of the period. It represented no departure in principle from the work of King or Duryea or from the original invention which Daimler had demonstrated in Paris ten years earlier. The significance of the Ford model of 1896, as Arthur Pound points out in his book *Detroit, Dynamic City,* is the fact that it worked and that it encouraged Ford to go ahead.

Heartened by his first success but still dependent on the job at the electric light works, Ford began living for the day when he could give himself over completely to the automobile. Whenever time allowed, he continued to hug the bench in the shed on Bagley Avenue, and within the next several years he brought out two more experimental cars. Meanwhile his test rides, like those of other contemporary car-builders, became more and more public. In trying out this or that

* King was an artist as well as an inventor and engineer. When he reached Paris, he switched careers; he dropped the automobile and took up painting instead.

† Ford later dated the appearance of his first car by remarking in his autobiography, "I was running it when the bobolinks came to Dearborn and they always come on April 2nd." This 1896 model was not, as he further contended in his autobiography, "the only car in Detroit for a long time." King's car appeared in the city two years earlier than his own. And three years after the initial demonstration of Ford's first automobile, the Oldsmobile was in production.

model, Ford ventured onto the streets of Detroit in full daylight, exposing both his person and his machines to an element of risk. As long as his cars were still a novel sight, he was cursed and often threatened by draymen and teamsters. Eventually he appealed to the mayor of the city for protection and was given a special street permit which allowed him to proceed with his daylight rides, unmolested. On other occasions it was the car rather than the man that was subject to hazards. There were times when Ford had to desert one or another of his models in a strange neighborhood while he took off on foot to fetch a tool or a missing part. When that happened, he took the precaution of chaining the abandoned vehicle to the nearest lamp post so that no youngster or bicycle rider could make off with it in his absence.

By 1899 Ford was a recognized pioneer in the business. He had three cars to his credit, and his work had received the personal blessing of the great inventor, Thomas A. Edison. Ford and Edison had met in the East in the course of a conference given over to the affairs of the Detroit Edison Co. After listening to a first-hand account of Ford's hobby, Edison, who had already pronounced that "the horse" was "doomed," gave warm encouragement to the efforts of his young visitor from Detroit.

Ford's increasing stature in Detroit proper is indicated by the caliber of the men who collected about him. His personal circle included at the time such figures as Tom Cooper, a retired bicycle racing champion who was relatively well-to-do, and C. Harold Wills, a gifted young draftsman and engineer.

While pooling his talents with those of Wills and Cooper, Ford had his first big chance in the field that concerned him most. He was approached by a group of local capitalists who wanted to go into the business of making and selling cars. These financiers invited Ford to join them, and he accepted. Having filled the role of amateur experimenter for the better part of seven years, he was more than willing to try his hand as manufacturer. The organization with which he joined forces in the double capacity of part owner and "chief engineer" was the Detroit Automobile Co. The year was 1899. Simultaneously and under almost identical circumstances, Ransom Olds started in at the Olds Motor Works.

But while Olds made a brilliant start in the business, Ford's efforts at the Detroit Automobile Co. failed from the beginning. Within a year's time Ford was out of a job; and in the course of reorganizing —this time as founders of the Cadillac Motor Car Co.—his erstwhile directors were hunting for a new production manager. The man selected to fill Ford's place was Henry M. Leland.

As to the primary reason for Ford's failure, all the reputable early commentators of the trade are in agreement.[1] These authorities hold that the product manufactured by the Detroit Automobile Co. was utterly unsalable. They say that as "chief engineer" undergoing his first trial as manufacturer, Ford exhausted a sizable budget in an effort to perfect a high-priced racing model that had no commercial value whatsoever. According to Ford's autobiographical account of this period, it was his directors who were responsible for missing the mass market by so wide a margin. When he was powerless to make them see the light, he later contended, he resigned of his own accord.

If such were Ford's thwarted intentions in 1900, he gave no indication of the fact, or he was once more overruled against his better judgment when he reentered the business the following year. For during his second effort as a manufacturer, after he began to function under a new set of promoters in 1901 as manager of the Ford Automobile Co., he repeated the mistake that he had made two years earlier. Still wide of the market, he squandered his time and his resources on another unsalable commodity, an expensive high-powered racer designed in collaboration with Tom Cooper and C. H. Wills.[2] Consequently the Ford Automobile Co., like the concern which Ford had managed previously, lasted but a single year. It was dissolved in 1902.

Still bent on having a career in the automobile business, Ford concentrated as never before on the very interest that had defeated his first practical effort in the field. Working privately with Wills and Cooper and operating on Cooper's money, he continued to develop his flair for racing models. What concerned him at this period was not so much a passion for racing, but rather the hope that his engineering exploits and his performance on the dirt track would command attention and give him still another opportunity in the manufacturing field. Other car builders of the day, men like Pierce, Winton, Packard and Chevrolet, were courting financial backers in the same manner. They were distinguishing themselves as either racers or long-distance drivers.

For some time Ford himself took to the track to demonstrate the cars that issued from his work with Wills and Cooper. At the wheel of these models that became ever faster and more powerful, he made an outstanding record. His first notable success took place at a racing event held in the fashionable Detroit suburb of Grosse Pointe, before a group of spectators whom the Detroit *News* described as "society folk" from Cleveland and Detroit. When he reached the finish line on this occasion, his appearance must have amused the well-groomed members of the audience; he was daubed with oil from head to foot; "his tie looked as though it had been cooked in lard." But he led the field. In taking stock of the event, the Detroit *News* remarked that the performance of the two-cylindered Ford-Wills-Cooper car was so "wonderful," it had lifted Ford into the "front rank of American chauffeurs." Other similar feats followed. Before long, reports of Ford's prowess as a "speed demon" began to appear in the columns of the widely circulated trade journal *Horseless Age*. In one dispatch *Horseless Age* announced that over a half-mile course laid out along a residential boulevard inside the city limits of Detroit, Ford had driven one of his racing machines at a speed of seventy miles per hour. In another column, the magazine printed an open challenge to the effect that Henry Ford, the "Detroit chauffeur," was willing to race against any "foreign mechanic," provided the contest be held on an American track.

In the summer of 1902, however, Ford thought it prudent to withdraw from active participation in racing events. By this time he had produced his most famous racer, the "999." The "999" was a big red car that shot flames from its motor. It was so fast that neither Ford nor either of his principal associates cared to risk his life trying it out at full speed. To find a candidate for the job, the three co-builders of the car were forced to extend their circle. Cooper found the man they were looking for. He succeeded in enlisting as a driver Barney Oldfield, an old friend who, like himself, was a former bicycle racing champion. Deft and reckless, Oldfield began where Ford left off and in the same locality. He entered the "999" in a widely publicized three-mile race held at Grosse Pointe in October, 1902, and he finished half a mile in front of his closest competitor. Among the cars which had had to trail behind him was the celebrated "Bullet," driven by Alexander Winton.

In the process of launching his own career as one of the pioneer "daredevils" of the American track, Oldfield helped to put Henry Ford back on his feet. For one of the closest followers of the "999"'s career was Alex Y. Malcomson, a prosperous local coal dealer who was on the point of investing a modest fortune in the automobile business. Malcomson was already convinced of the wisdom of making such an investment; he had studied the rise of the Olds Motor Works. What he lacked for the fulfillment of his plans in the fall of 1902 was some trustworthy automotive inventor and shop man who was still without a backer.

Checking into the facts, he decided that Ford was his man. From what he could gather, Ford was the leading spirit of the group which produced the "999;" he already had a name in the field; he was an able mechanic; he had no other business commitments; and he was surrounded by a group of talented co-workers. Within a month after Barney Oldfield's spectacular performance at Grosse Pointe, Malcomson sought out Ford and the two men began the negotiations that led to the founding of the Ford Motor Co.

# Two

## BIRTH OF THE MODEL T

### 1

AFTER SEVERAL meetings, Malcomson and Ford decided to join forces permanently. They resolved to enter the automobile business, acting as co-founders of the Ford Motor Co., and spent the next seven months laying the groundwork for their project. In the meantime it was Ford's job to build a suitable specimen car, one that would enable the company to gauge its first business commitments, and one that could stand up in competition with Cadillac, Oldsmobile and the other favorite models of the day. In this endeavor Ford collaborated once more with his friend C. H. Wills. Malcomson was busy, meanwhile, with the financial and organizational problems of the proposed corporation.

The two founders of the Ford organization were hampered at the outset by a lack of capital. The "Ford" articles of incorporation as drafted by Malcomson's lawyers, called for an issue of stock with a par value of $100,000. Such an investment greatly exceeded the combined personal wealth of Ford and his patron. Ford had little money. Malcomson, though the owner of a flourishing coal business, was only moderately well-to-do, and after he had mustered all the cash he could spare from his own business, additional funds had to be raised from outside sources.

The job of soliciting some minority shareholders fell, naturally, to

Malcomson. The coal dealer had the necessary financial connections. He was an able and magnetic businessman. He, rather than Ford, had something to offer in the way of security. In his quest for investors he had an established business which he was willing to pledge to the limit.

So far as their own interests were concerned, Ford and Malcomson agreed to share and share alike in the fortunes of their venture. Each was to get 25½ per cent of the company's stock. Both were to sit on the board of directors, and the two men arrived at an understanding as to their administrative functions, once the company became a going concern. Malcomson, as holder of the purse strings, was to serve as treasurer. Ford, as top man in the factory, was to be vice-president and general manager at a salary of $3000 a year.

Among the outsiders for whom a place had to be made in the Ford organization, the largest investor was John S. Gray, a Detroit banker and manufacturer. Wholly on the strength of his confidence in Malcomson, Gray consented to make a loan of $10,000 to the Ford Motor Co. In return for his risk, the banker was named director and president of the corporation. Ten per cent of the Ford stock was issued in his name. The security for his loan was a personal note signed by Malcomson.

A second, and very minor, interest in the company went to Albert Strelow, a carpenter who ran a small wood-working business in a two-story frame building on Mack Avenue, close to the central business district of Detroit. Carried away by Malcomson's glowing account of the future prospects of the automobile business, Strelow agreed to exchange his property for a small block of Ford shares. The result of this arrangement was that the Ford Motor Co. got a plant without having to pay for it in cash. Such as it was, the Strelow shop became the first Ford factory.

It was in his negotiations with John and Horace Dodge that Malcomson did most to give the Ford Motor Co. an auspicious beginning. The Dodge brothers were retained by him to serve as the chief suppliers of the Ford business. It was to be their job to build the motors and other key parts of the first Ford car. By entering into such an arrangement, Malcomson not only enlarged the plant facilities of the Ford company without having to spend his own funds, but he succeeded, as well, in capturing two top-notch executives who were already seasoned hands in the business. Up until the time they combined their interests with Ford's, the Dodges had been making parts for Olds in a good-sized machine shop of their own. Under the terms of their contract with the Ford Motor Co., they were to retain the ownership of their machine shop, John Dodge was to become a Ford director, and each of the brothers was awarded 5 per cent of the Ford shares. In breaking off their former connections, the Dodges, like banker Gray, were giving a vote of confidence to Malcomson, content with the fact that their contract bore Malcomson's signature. With that guarantee they began to retool their shop to meet the specifications of the Ford-Wills car, a full month before the actual incorporation of the Ford Motor Co.

In the course of mortgaging his former business in order to found a new one, Malcomson was nettled by the fact that any direct supervision of the daily affairs of the Ford venture on his part would be out of the question. By the nature of things, his function was to protect his own credit and to look to the credit of the Ford Motor Co. by concentrating on the coal business as never before. He determined, therefore, to make himself felt in the front office of the Ford company by proxy. For this purpose he selected James Couzens, one of his own employes whom he considered bright and energetic. By the time the Ford organization was ready to start operating, Couzens was installed as its secretary and business manager. His salary was set at $208 a month. While he was at it, Malcomson contrived to give his young "watchdog" of thirty-one a personal stake in the business. At his instigation, Couzens was allotted 2½ per cent of the company's stock.

Finally, and again at Malcomson's insistence, two Detroit lawyers, John W. Anderson and Horace H. Rackham, were admitted into the circle of Ford shareholders. Rackham and Anderson were the attorneys who had drawn up the "Ford" papers of incorporation, having received for this service a fee of $25. Each was awarded a 5 per cent interest in the Ford Motor Co., and apparently neither man had to pay cash for his shares at the time they were set aside in his name. In using his influence to arrange such a concession, Malcomson may have been making only a friendly gesture, dropping a plum in the laps of two of his old business acquaintances. Rackham and Anderson were his personal attorneys. By giving preference to this pair, he was at the same time assured of getting free legal advice and of consolidating his own position at the Ford Motor Co., for Anderson was promptly elected to a seat on the board.

Inasmuch as Malcomson paid the piper, he also seems to have called the tune in that the plans of the Ford corporation made no provision for rewarding any of Ford's friends or business associates.

Thus no stock interest and no key executive post was reserved either for Tom Cooper, who had subsidized the "999" and helped to establish Ford's reputation by taking the "999" on tour, or for C. H. Wills, the co-designer of the car which Ford and Malcomson were about to manufacture. In the latter case, Ford had cause for some alarm. He was particularly anxious to retain Wills' services as a draftsman and engineer. Wills was eager to work for him, but only on condition that he be given a stake in the company. What Ford hit on eventually, either out of necessity or as a matter of choice, was a private profit-sharing agreement. By word of mouth, he offered to split with Wills on a fixed percentage basis whatever personal profits he was to take out of the business. On the strength of this oral assurance, Wills agreed to go along.

Largely at Malcomson's dictation, then, the executive roster of the Ford Motor Co. was drawn up in full shortly after the company's incorporation in June, 1903. The directors of the corporation were Gray, Anderson, John Dodge, Ford and Malcomson. The company's principal officers were Gray, president; Couzens, secretary and business manager; Malcomson, treasurer; and Ford, vice-president and general manager.

When the company finally opened its doors for business, its cash on hand was but a fraction of the $100,000 that represented the full nominal worth of the Ford securities. This discrepancy had several explanations. Fifteen per cent or more of the shares of the corporation had been withheld for future sale. Little or no cash had come from the minority stockholders who obtained their shares on credit, or for whom stock was set aside with the understanding that it could be paid for out of future earnings. Another set of Ford investors had paid for their holdings in kind rather than in cash. Strelow had given the corporation a factory; the Dodge brothers provided the benefit of their experience and the use of their machine shop; Ford gave his name, certain patent rights and the working model of a car. Thus it was chiefly from Gray and Malcomson that the company recruited its only liquid capital. This investment, representing the bulk of the issued Ford shares that were paid for in actual cash at the outset, was only $28,000.

## 2

In January 1904, Ford underwent his last and most famous trial as a racer. This time, however, he was no longer the amateur mechanic

on the lookout for a financial sponsor, but rather, an established manufacturer who wanted to advertise his wares after the fashion of the
period. The car Ford chose for the purpose was, again, the "999."
The course over which he proposed to race against time was a straight,
cindered path laid out on the ice of Lake St. Clair. On this occasion
Ford arranged to carry a passenger. He had had mechanical trouble
with the device that controlled the supply of gasoline, and he was
afraid that the throttle might freeze in position with the motor wide
open, so he had Ed (Spider) Huff, one of his employes, lie on the
running board with instructions to shut off the carburetor by hand once
the car had passed the finish mark.

Speeding over the ice together, Ford and Huff established an
unofficial world's record. Traveling faster than 90 miles per hour
they covered the distance of one mile in 39 2/5ths seconds. Ford and
his companions then celebrated their feat on the spot. They built
a fire on the ice, cooking and devouring with relish a muskrat dinner.

Meanwhile the Ford Motor Co. had introduced its first product,
the automobile designed by Ford and Wills. This car, unlike the
racing models that Ford had fancied earlier, was eminently practical
and relatively inexpensive. It was priced at $850. Its make-up was
pictured in a piece of advertising matter which Couzens inserted in
the *Motor World* late in 1903. "The most reliable machine in the
world," read Couzens' advertisement. "A two-cylinder car of ample
power for the steepest hills and the muddiest roads, built to stand
the severest strains. The same genius which conceived the world's
record maker—the '999'—has made possible the production of a
thoroughly practical car at a moderate price."

According to plan it was the Dodge brothers who were responsible for the actual construction of the first Ford cars. The motors
and most of the parts that went into these models were assembled in
their machine shed and then loaded into hay wagons for delivery to
the Ford plant on Mack Avenue. All that was added at the Ford
Motor Co. proper for a year or more were the tires and the finishing
touches on the body.

In the meantime, Ford and Couzens hewed to the business pattern which Olds had laid down. They made every effort to shorten
the process of final assembly, while working insofar as possible on
the other fellow's money. Like Olds, they took full advantage of the
thirty- to sixty-day credit extended by their suppliers. Before long,
while waiting for their suppliers' bills to fall due, they were in a
position to meet their labor costs with the funds provided by their

customers and dealers. So great was the demand for every make of car and for the Ford car in particular, that salesmen began to place their orders by flocking to the very doors of the Ford Motor Co., in many cases making cash deposits with the company in advance of actual delivery.

One of these enthusiastic dealers who became Ford's first sales agent in New York City was John Wanamaker, the department store magnate. Though no offense was intended, when Wanamaker first introduced the Ford car to his customers he put the new line of merchandise under the supervision of a clerk who up until that time had served the Wanamaker store as manager of its toy department.

Operating intelligently in a seller's market and offering the public a reasonably priced and well-made car, the Ford Motor Co. succeeded from the very beginning. In the first fifteen months of its existence, the company sold more than 1700 cars. At this point, after allowing for taxes and for such sums as were needed to expand the business, the Ford directors declared a cash dividend of $100,000. Their first profits, consequently, represented a return of more than 100 per cent on an original issue of stock, two-thirds of which had never been paid for in cash originally.

One result of such unforeseen prosperity was that two of Ford's stockholders promptly lost their heads. First it was Strelow, the carpenter who had provided the company with its original factory site. Seized by a desire to speculate, Strelow disposed of his Ford holdings in 1905. He sold out to Couzens for $25,000 and reinvested his money in a gold mine in British Columbia.*

Then Malcomson, reputedly a sage man of affairs, went off the deep end. He was so excited by his first quick success that, while retaining his Ford connection and continuing to operate a coal business with one hand, he tried to promote still another automobile simultaneously. He failed in the attempt. He overreached himself to a point where his creditors closed in.

Under duress and in order to stave off bankruptcy, in 1906 Malcomson had to sacrifice his Ford holdings. Ford and Couzens bought out his quarter-interest at a price of $175,000. In its fourth year, the Ford business was so highly regarded that the buyers had no difficulty in financing the transaction. At the bank where they borrowed the amount of the purchase price, Couzens and Ford

* His fortune was wiped out in this enterprise. Years later, according to the New York *Times*, Strelow was seen outside the employment office of the Ford Motor Co., waiting his turn in the hopes of being taken on as a Ford laborer.[1]

endorsed one another's notes. Dipping into profits, they retired their loan within the next nine months.

Thus, largely as a result of the Malcomson deal, control of the Ford Motor Co. passed into the hands of Ford and Couzens. Having raised his share from 25½ to 58½ per cent, Ford was now the company's dominant stockholder. During the same process of readjustment, Couzens' minority interest in the corporation had increased fourfold, from 2½ to 10 per cent.

This shift of power was accentuated, meanwhile, by the removal of still another of the original Ford investors. The year of Malcomson's withdrawal was marked by the death of John S. Gray. None of the remaining stockholders was able to absorb Gray's share at the time, and the banker's heirs had no desire to sell. But in the course of filling Gray's vacancy, Ford and Couzens tightened their hold on the managerial reins of the company. The presidency went to Ford. John Dodge was moved up to take Ford's place as vice-president. Couzens, taking over the post vacated by Malcomson, was named secretary-treasurer.

Before the year 1906 had run its course, the remaining stockholders of the Ford Motor Co. had every reason for hugging their investment. With Ford in the shop and Couzens in the front office, the business was excellently managed. The demand for the Ford product was so great that the company had been forced to expand its plant, moving into a new three-story building located at the intersection of Piquette Street and Beaubien. Having sold more than 5000 cars in a single season, the corporation had entrenched itself as one of the leading producers of the trade. It was fast becoming, in addition, a prodigious money-maker. Taken at their face value, the Ford securities had shown a net return of 310 per cent. Within a four-year period they had yielded cash dividends amounting to $310,000.

## 3

As yet, however, the Ford Motor Co. was only on the fringes of its great success. For the company was still undecided as to the type of car which it considered best suited for the market. It was here that Henry Ford was to make his fortune as well as his greatest single contribution to modern times.

In the process of choosing between this or that possible model, the Ford management had to reckon with the customs of the period. It was the tradition of the trade at this time to cater, almost exclusively, to the relatively well-to-do. As a result the new automobile of 1906 was, without exception, a "luxury" product. It was heavy and cumbersome, often custom-built, and too expensive for the average person. With such a market, every automobile manufacturer in Europe and America seemed content. Dozens of motor car companies were rolling in money. To all appearances, there were enough wealthy buyers to go around.*

During the first five years of its existence, the Ford company experimented with eight different models. Each was designated by a different letter of the alphabet. Diverse in design, these cars were equally dissimilar in price. The original Ford model of 1903 sold, as Couzens had advertised, "at a modest price." It had cost a hundred dollars more than the cheapest Oldsmobile.

Three years later, however, the company ordered an about-face. It tried its fortunes in the "luxury" field. During the season of 1905-1906, the cheapest Ford car cost $1000; the most expensive one, $2000. The effect on sales was disastrous. Business fell away sharply. The season's profits dropped to $100,000, to one-third of the figure they had reached the previous year.

Alarmed by this falling off of trade, the company hurriedly reversed its course. It lowered prices the following year. The effect on the business was magical. In the second half of 1906 and throughout the year 1907—despite the onset of a nation-wide panic—there were more Ford buyers than ever before. When other businesses had to close their doors, Ford made a net profit of one and one-quarter million dollars. Most of the credit for ordering such a successful and timely

* From the very first the American automobile was widely regarded as a rich man's plaything. This notion was evident in the fastidious design of some of the early models. Thus, early in the century, the Detroit *Saturday Night* told of a young man of fashion who had ordered a car equipped for the convenience of his female passengers, with cream and powder jars, atomizers, electric hair curlers and a complete manicuring set. Likewise, the well-to-do were frequently singled out as the exclusive sponsors of the automobile. In noting the fact that some millionaires had taken their cars to a select eastern summer resort in 1899, *Horseless Age,* then the leading journal of the trade, paid its respects to the "gracious patronage" of "our American aristocracy." In this day the rich themselves thought of the automobile as a luxury reserved for the few. In 1901 a group of wealthy businessmen living in Westchester County, New York, formed a club for the purpose of building a chain of private gasoline depots and service stations. It was understood at the same time that the plain people of the country were to function as the tenders and repairers of the motor car. Guided by such a conviction, the Detroit *Saturday Night* said in 1909 that the best chauffeurs were to be recruited from the ranks of former coachmen. Such drivers, observed the *Saturday Night,* were dutiful members of the "servant class" who could be counted on to know "exactly what is expected of them by their masters."

retreat from the "luxury" field must go to Ford. At any rate, the directors of the company were so gratified by their prosperity during a year of business depression that, in December 1907, they voted to raise the salary of their president and general manager from $300 to $3000 a month.

Early the following year Ford had the great inspiration of his life. At his insistence the company announced that henceforth it would limit its efforts to the production of a single, standardized, relatively inexpensive car. As Couzens was to relate years later, this epochal decision at the Ford Motor Co.—to take up where Olds and Renault had left off—was Ford's own. According to Couzens, Ford arrived at the idea on impulse and was just as abrupt in demanding its adoption as future company policy.[2]

Actually, however, the new program had been taking shape in Ford's mind for months, if not for years. For one thing it had already proved itself in dollars and cents. From 1905 through 1907 the company had demonstrated beyond any question that the lower the price, the higher would be the earnings. The shift to a uniform, popularly-priced model was fundamentally, therefore, common sense; it was an attempt to make a permanent thing of a combination that had worked best in the past from the standpoint of sales and profits.

In grasping this point ahead of his associates, Ford was not only the astute merchant; he was at the same time giving expression to his temperament both as a mechanic and as a one-time farmer. Here the best commentary comes from John Anderson, one of the co-founders of the company. Testifying at the Couzens' tax hearings of 1927, Anderson read into the record some excerpts from a diary that he had kept during the formative years of the Ford Motor Co. Among other things this journal was a record of what Ford talked about when his plans for a "universal" automobile were coming to a jell.

From these notes it appears that the concept of a standardized car of relatively simple design developed as a matter of course during Ford's struggle to bring order out of chaos in the shop. Well before 1908 he told Anderson that their company could never hope to make a go of large-scale production until all its products were made as much alike as "pins or matches." Further, when Ford arrived at the idea of making a car for the masses, he was unquestionably influenced by his origins; he was thinking of his product, not from the standpoint of rich and sporting patrons, but in terms of his own people. Some-time before 1908 he confided to Anderson how he hoped to make a motor car that the farmer could afford, a vehicle with a removable

engine that could be applied "universally." As Ford then envisioned
the automobile, it was to be an all-purpose machine, capable of getting
the farmer to market and of being used incidentally to saw wood,
pump water, run farm machinery and do the churning.

Such was the Model T, the end-product of Ford's dreams and
of his company's quest for a market. As Norval Hawkins, Ford's first
sales manager, described the vehicle in the course of testifying at
the Couzens' tax hearings, it was "practically a farmer's car." There
was nothing ornate or fancy about the T. It was what Ford had
hoped for, 100 per cent utility. It was light and sturdy, built for
performance rather than looks, a tough, plain, black oblong box
mounted on wheels, and the commoner could afford to own one.
Stripped of all accessories, the original Model T's, almost as much
alike as "pins or matches," sold for $850.

In designing his all-purpose machine, Ford relied to some extent
on the experience of other manufacturers. His engineers had borrowed
from the Oldsmobile and the Cadillac. As early as 1905 they had
imported one of Renault's models and "torn it down" for inspection.*
But by and large, the Model T was an original Ford product.

The over-all concept of the car was Ford's.† This or that Ford
technician had worked up the details of the machine. The car's ignition
system, which consisted of a magneto built in as an integral part of
the motor, was perfected by "Spider" Huff, the man who had helped
to pilot the "999" over the ice of Lake St. Clair. Other mechanics in
the Ford organization gave the T its system of "splash" lubrication,
its rear axle of unique design and its principle of three-point suspension. From C. H. Wills, Ford's foremost early designer, the car got
its planetary transmission and the alloy steel for which it was to
become justly famous. It was also Wills who at this time had Ford's
name written out in longhand and adopted as the company's trade-
mark. The script used for the purpose was not, as many have since
believed, a copy of Ford's signature. On the contrary, it had been

* The practice of buying a car produced by one's competitor and taking it
apart to see what made it tick was perfectly orthodox. Some inventors and manufacturers, however, went even further. They tried to ferret out the ideas of a rival
before he had succeeded in reaching the production stage. In many cases, the
exhibitor or contestant who took part in early road tests and automobile shows
hired guards to stand watch over his machine.
† Neither at the dawn of the industry nor later was Ford ever credited with any
specific outstanding invention. For a listing of the American landmarks of automotive invention, see New York *Times*, January 1, 1914; January 10, 1932; Federal
Trade Commission, *Report on Motor Vehicle Industry*, 1939; *Fortune*, December,
1931; Arthur Pound, *Turning Wheel*.

made from a childhood printing set which Wills found stored away in his attic.

Once in production the Model T won immediate favor. It sold itself, and the reasons for its popularity were self-evident. More than any automobile in circulation at the time, it matched the farmer's purpose and the pocketbook of the man in the street. Its mechanical principles were so simple that with a little time and patience they could be readily mastered by any amateur. And no contemporary car was so well adapted to what the world in general and the United States in particular had to offer in the way of roads and thoroughfares.

In its native environment the first Model T and every other motor car of the period had to conquer a roadbed that had been handed down from the horse age. Few tougher proving grounds can be imagined. Vast sections of the American hinterland were without well-defined highways of any kind. Treacherous passes were the rule in the Rocky Mountain states. In the settled farming sections of the Mississippi Valley the typical roadway was a narrow, unimproved dirt track, ground to powder in the dry season, and all but impassable when it rained or snowed.

But whereas the perilous backroad and the gumbo of the plain states were too much for the average car, they were the making of the Model T. By contrast with other models of the day, Ford's car of 1908 was tough, compact and feather-light. Because of its high-riding chassis, it could pass over stretches of rock and quagmire like a man on stilts. To be sure, the vehicle shook and rattled with the rest. It was all bone and muscle with no fat on its frame. But as soon as it took to the road it proceeded to prove that it was built to get there, despite hell and high water.

One of the first notable demonstrations of the fact that the American highway had found its master occurred in the summer of 1909 when the Ford Motor Co. entered a car in the transcontinental race from New York to Seattle. The contest was sponsored by the Automobile Club of America. The Ford driver who made the trip had no picnic. It took him twenty-two hours to cover a single four-mile stretch of open country in the state of Utah. But after an exhausting drive that lasted twenty days and fifty-two minutes, he came in first. Five months later, however, the winner's prize was awarded to another contestant. On second thought the judges of the contest decided that Ford's man had violated one of the rules. Having motor trouble somewhere along the way, he had changed engines on the sly.[3] But despite this particular dubious performance, the evidence was overwhelming that as master of sand and muck and mudhole the Model T had no peer.

Rain or shine, the car held up under the wear and tear of the farm. In 1912 a Model T won the distinction of being the first automobile to conquer the Grand Canyon of the Colorado. The driver who was responsible for this feat had coped with the heat by draping wet bags over his motor and gasoline tank. He had to use dynamite to blast the rocks out of his path. That same year the owner of another Ford car won first honors in a publicized farm-and-ranch run, driving between Dallas and San Antonio over open country. Competitive hill-climbs, one of the favorite early methods of trying out a car, were won by the Model T time and time again.

While this plain but sterling little performer was winning friends in the small towns and on the farms, it came as close as it could to fulfilling Ford's dream of general utility. Before long one of the trade journals began to advertise a "Ford attachment" that could be hooked up to a Model T for the purpose of operating belt-driven farm machinery.

Meanwhile the soundness of Ford's preference for a cheap car was borne out by the earnings of the Ford Motor Co. In one year's time the Model T established itself as the trade's best seller and leading money-maker, and Ford sold 11,000 cars, outstripping every other producer in both sales and profits. Taking stock of such a phenomenal increase in business, the directors of the corporation decided to expand the scale of their enterprise. They increased their capitalization from $150,000 to $2,000,000 and the number of outstanding shares from 1000 to 20,000. To effect this internal reorganization, the seven remaining shareholders of the company voted themselves a stock dividend amounting to 1000 per cent.

### 4

But despite the impressive early record of the Model T, the Ford Motor Co. came within an inch of losing its separate identity in the industry, first in 1908, and again in 1909. While they were pioneering with a cheap car, Ford and Couzens twice entered into negotiations for the purpose of selling their stock to an interested outside bidder. The buyer with whom they dealt on both occasions was W. C. Durant, the dashing and brilliant promoter of General Motors, forerunner of the General Motors Corporation.

When Durant first raised the matter with Ford and Couzens in

1908, he was already a commanding figure in the field. He had welded together a combine that included Buick, Cadillac, Oakland and Oldsmobile. What he proposed to Ford was a merger. He wanted the Ford organization for a fifth subsidiary of General Motors. The negotiators were in accord as to the estimated value of the Ford interests. Durant put the price at $3,000,000, and Ford agreed to sell at that figure, but not on Durant's terms. Ford wanted cash on the line. Durant, the super-salesman, was peddling GM stock for the most part. The deal fell through.

In the following year GM came forward with a second proposal. This time, in view of the remarkable showing of the Model T, the purchase price was more attractive. It was to be $8,000,000. Ford again agreed to sell, but once more on his own terms. Speaking for himself and all his minority stockholders, he demanded immediate payment of the full $8,000,000 in hard cash. It was the opinion of the GM board at the time, however, that the Ford business was "not worth that much." So the best Durant could offer by way of a counterproposal was part payment in cash, the rest in securities. With Ford it was still "gold on the table" or nothing. Consequently this deal, like the negotiations of the previous year, came to nothing.[4]

The abortive meetings with Durant revealed, incidentally, what was going on in the minds of Couzens and Ford shortly after the birth of the Model T. In consenting to step out of the picture for $8,000,000 in 1909, it would seem that both men had failed to grasp the full significance of their car for the masses, that neither was then motivated by a long-range concept of what he was about. Instead, they were following in the footsteps of their former sponsor Alex Malcomson. They were on the point of picking the fruit before it was ripe, awed by the prospect of getting rich quick. Had the sale to General Motors gone through, Couzens would have retired a near-millionaire at the age of thirty-seven; Ford, a multi-millionaire at forty-six. But as long as the company remained in their hands (from 1906 on they owned 68½ per cent of the Ford stock between them), Ford and Couzens meant to hold their own. They gave proof of that fact from 1909 to 1911 when they collided with the rest of the industry over the merits of a famous patent.

The controversy in question revolved about the legal rights of George B. Selden, a lawyer and amateur inventor to whom the federal government had issued an automotive patent so broad in scope that it appeared to cover every type of "road locomotive" in existence. The insights embodied in the Selden patent were evidently genuine and highly original. In point of time they antedated Charles Duryea's invention of the first American automobile. Yet for some reason Selden made no effort to apply his ideas; he never so much as built a car of his own. Instead, he simply nursed along his "paper invention" by filing one application after another at the federal patent office. When it became clear that the motor car had commercial possibilities, he signed over his rights to a group of New York financiers.

Selden's assignees set out at once to exploit what looked like a sure thing. They organized the Association of Licensed Automobile Manufacturers. This trade body in turn proposed to limit the manufacture of motor cars in the United States only to those producers who acknowledged the validity of the Selden patent. Each manufacturer who applied for a license was expected to pay into the ALAM treasury an annual royalty amounting to 1 per cent of the retail value of his total sales for the year.

By the time the Ford Motor Co. introduced the Model T, 90 per cent of the trade's producers were doing business as licensees of the ALAM. As yet, none had dared to make a court test of the sweeping Selden claims, nor had the practices of the ALAM given special cause for any such action. No manufacturer who applied for a license had been turned away. Aside from having to pay a royalty, each licensee had been free to go his own way. Moreover, the ALAM had actually given its members something for their money. To a large extent it had functioned like the present-day Automobile Manufacturers Association. The bulk of its income had been devoted to promoting the interests of the trade as a whole. Only a fraction of its funds had been drained off at the top by the ALAM promoters.*

Among the few concerns which were still outside the fold in 1908, the largest and the most successful was the Ford Motor Co. As Ford and Couzens took stock of the ALAM, it was a budding trust, nurtured by Wall Street for the sole purpose of getting something for nothing. From the start they simply ignored its existence. Eventually, however, they did consent to sit in on an ALAM conference held at the old Russell House in Detroit. What took place at this gathering was later described by Theodore F. MacManus, one of the reliable early chroniclers of the trade.[5]

According to MacManus, the conversations at the Russell House were brief and fiery. A spokesman for the ALAM began to stress the

* From the time they founded the ALAM until 1911 when their rights were invalidated by court action, the holders of the Selden patent took a profit of only $150,000.

merits of "getting together." He went on to assert that in order to enforce the Selden claims his organization was prepared to go the limit. Couzens, very much in character, is supposed to have cut the speaker short by retorting, "Selden can take his patent and go to hell with it." All Ford said was, "Couzens has answered you." An ALAM official promptly declared that he would file suit at once. In the meantime, he vowed, his colleagues would do their utmost to put the Ford Motor Co. out of business. Then Ford hit the ceiling. He jumped out of his chair, shook a finger at his threatener and shouted, "Let them try it!" At this point the conferees stalked out of the room.

Their next meeting occurred in a Federal courtroom where Ford had to answer the charge that he was guilty of patent infringement. In the first round of the battle, Ford was the loser. Passing on the dispute in 1909, the bench ruled that the Selden patent was valid and, therefore, applicable to the Ford Motor Co. and to all other companies engaged in the production of motor cars. Ford counsel met this reverse by taking the case into a court of appeal.

While the appeal was pending, the litigants waged war in the public prints. For its part the ALAM tried to browbeat Ford by running advertisements in which it threatened to prosecute any and all persons who dared to buy Ford cars. Couzens fought back with counter-publicity. One of his retaliatory advertisements which appeared in 1910 dubbed the ALAM "a Divine Executive Committee;" it ridiculed the Selden patent as "a freak among alleged inventions." While he was at it, Ford's belligerent but clever business manager put in a word for the Model T. With such a car on the market, he said in the same copy, was it possible for any person who enjoyed the full use of his faculties to "fall" for the inferior models turned out by other manufacturers in some "71 varieties" and at "extravagant prices?"[6]

To reassure the customer who might have shied away from a Model T for fear of "buying a lawsuit," Ford's legal advisers thought up a shrewd expedient. With every sale the company offered to post a bond to protect the buyer in the event of future prosecution by the ALAM. John Wanamaker, who was handling Ford sales in New York City and Philadelphia, made a similar standing offer to all his personal customers.

In the end Ford managed to beat the ALAM without any outside assistance, other than the supporting action of John Wanamaker. In 1911 a federal court of appeal declared that the Selden patent did not apply to the Model T, nor to any other type of car made in the

United States. Emboldened by this turn of events, most of the manufacturers who had never questioned the Selden claim bolted from the ranks. And for want of funds and a supporting membership, the ALAM promptly went to pieces.

As it worked out, the Selden suit was a blessing in disguise for all concerned, except for the insiders of the ALAM. For the trade as a whole soon organized itself to prevent a recurrence of similar disputes in the future. All but a few automotive manufacturers, with Ford and Packard the chief exceptions, banded together to form a patent pool. As a result of this voluntary combination, the industry was to be, henceforth, notably free of patent litigation.

From the standpoint of Ford's business, the fight against Selden had been all to the good. During the life of the action, from 1909 to 1911, only fifty of Ford's customers ever asked for a bond when they bought their Model T's.[7] During that same interval, the company sold 18,000 cars. In looking back on the Selden suit years later, Ford said it was one of the best advertising media he had ever enjoyed. In his opinion, he said, it had called attention to the Ford Motor Co. at the expense of all its competitors.

But throughout the period in question and for the next two decades, the real key to Ford's stunning success was the fact that the public liked his product. From 1908 on, as Couzens took occasion to remark ten years later, Ford cars were "not sold;" they were "simply handed over the counter."

When the Model T was only beginning to catch on here, there and everywhere, one of the neatest symbols of its triumph was an illuminated signboard which the Ford Motor Co. placed in 1908 on the roof of the old Detroit Opera House on Cadillac Square. When the lights were turned on at night, this display pictured a Ford car in motion; it reproduced a Model T with turning wheels; it portrayed as one of the car's passengers a woman with a neck scarf that danced and streamed over her shoulder. Here E. LeRoy Pelletier, Ford's first advertising man, could exhibit his prowess as a phrase-maker. Over the glittering Ford sign on Cadillac Square there appeared for the first time Pelletier's pat and happy slogan, "Watch the Fords Go By."

# Three

## THE NEW MESSIAH

### 1

WITH THE ADVENT of the Model T, the managers of the Ford Motor Co. quickly discovered that they were ill-equipped to satisfy the demand for their popular product, for as yet the precipitous rise in Ford sales had invoked no corresponding change in Ford's methods of production. In fact, when the company brought out the Model T in 1908, its assembly techniques were much the same as they had been in Strelow's carpenter shed five years earlier.

At Ford's and in all other shops in Detroit, the process of putting an automobile together still revolved about the versatile mechanic, who was compelled to move about in order to do his work. Ford's assemblers were still all-around men. Their work was largely stationary, yet they had to move on to the next job on foot as soon as the car-in-the-making at their particular station had been taken the whole distance—from bare frame to finished product. To be sure, time had added some refinements. In 1908 it was no longer necessary for the assembler to leave his place of work for trips to the tool crib or the parts bin. Stock-runners had been set aside to perform this function. Nor was the Ford mechanic himself in 1908 quite the man he had been in 1903. In the intervening years the job of final assembly had been split up ever so little. In place of the jack-of-all-trades who formerly "did it all," there were now several assemblers who worked over a particular car side by side, each one responsible for a somewhat limited set of operations.

Aware of the fact that their manufacturing methods called for revision, Ford and Couzens late in 1908 decided to call in Walter E. Flanders. Flanders was then recognized as a foremost factory expert. He agreed to work for Ford on condition that he name his own salary and that he be given a free hand in his approach to the production problem. Both conditions were granted. Flanders was made production manager of the Ford Motor Co., and in meeting his salary demands Ford and Couzens went him one better. They promised to pay him a bonus of $20,000 if he succeeded in turning out 10,000 cars in twelve months' time, something no one else had ever done before.[1]

Working day and night on a job that fascinated him, and with his prestige at stake, Flanders left a profound imprint on the Ford organization. He turned the Ford factory inside out, rearranging old equipment and installing new in a tireless effort to streamline the operations of the company's thousand employes. The production quota for the year, 10,000 cars, was met with only two days to spare. At this point Flanders resigned in order to become a partner in the E.M.F. Co., a new automobile enterprise that took its name from the last initials of its three co-founders—Everitt, Metzger and Flanders. In the meantime Ford had been given the benefit of the best technical advice that money could buy. Thanks to Flanders, a near-genius at mechanization, the Ford company was now equipped with the essentials of scientific mass production. It was apparent, meanwhile, that the Ford plant at Piquette and Beaubien, though only three years old, was already overcrowded and out of date.

Consequently, steps were taken to get into larger and more modern quarters. Agents of the Ford Motor Co. quietly invaded the Detroit suburb of Highland Park for the purpose of buying up a great tract of cheap land. Simultaneously, architects were engaged to design a new office and factory structure. Built along lines suggested by what Ford and Couzens had learned from Flanders and by what they had picked up on their own, the trim, well-lighted and spacious plant at Highland Park began to operate in 1910. It was here that Ford's assembly methods underwent really radical transformation. Needless to say, these subsequent production changes came about neither suddenly nor easily. They were evolved the hard way, in the course of ten or twelve years of laborious trial-and-error.

Ford and his engineers made their first notable strides in production merely by reorganizing again and again the various departments of their new plant that were given over to the making of parts. In these feeder shops that supplied the final assemblers stood small forests of tools and machinery. Had the company laid out this vast array of equipment along old-fashioned lines, it would have grouped each *class* of machinery in a department by itself. Like machines would have gone with like—the lathes here, the power drills there, and so on. But the Ford technicians had already done away with such rutted modes of factory layout. They were applying in their own way, instead, the theory of line production which Frederick W. Taylor, the "father" of scientific management, had worked out several years earlier in the American steel industry.*

* Taylor anticipated all the production methods that were to take Detroit by storm. A report of his epochal efforts to rationalize the steel industry appeared in print eight years before the incorporation of the Ford Motor Co. One of his early

This meant that Ford and his production experts were now ever on the move, building a factory method as well as a car, and building it as they went, wholly in terms of the job to be done. For one thing they were breaking down into ever-smaller units every mechanical operation required for the making of each automotive part. It was this job analysis which they bore in mind in deciding just what machine was to go where at Highland Park. What Ford now strove for was straight line production; he was arranging his equipment in orderly sequences, laying it out insofar as possible in continuous parallel lines. Under this system a grinding tool might be placed at the start of any given production line, next to a heat-treating furnace, then a boring machine, or whatever was needed so that each consecutive tool would fall into its "natural" position in the line. The layout which Ford stuck to in any case was the one that worked, the one that permitted the work in hand to "flow" from one machine to the next with the fewest possible interruptions and with the least amount of waste motion and cross-hauling along the way. By 1910 the Ford people had achieved spectacular success with line production. In this particular, they were setting the pace for the trade.

Yet their work had no more than begun. Once the company hit on the concept of lining up ever new combinations of machinery so as to give more and more continuity to the processes of production, it had to find ways and means of improving the flow of articles in production. For with the very best of floor plans, any part-in-the-making still made its way clumsily down the Ford line. It had to be carried or passed along from bench to bench by hand. The company finally eliminated this waste motion by making an original application of an old idea. It installed a continuous series of gravity-slides, leading from one bench to the next. Now the moment a worker finished his particular operation, he could turn to an inclined trough at his elbow and let go of the piece he had been working on; it slid down the incline and arrived at the next work-place automatically. This innovation, introduced sometime in 1910, brought a new tempo to the production line; it sped up particularly the processing of parts that were small and light.

co-workers—an original Taylorite—was employed by General Motors when automotive shop methods were still relatively primitive. Shortly before his death, Taylor had an even more direct effect on the growth of Detroit's technology. In 1909 he delivered a four-hour lecture before a group of technicians employed by the Packard Motor Car Co. He returned to Detroit again in 1914 at the invitation of the local Board of Commerce. On this occasion his audience consisted of six hundred foremen and superintendents drawn from all the leading automotive shops within the area.

Meanwhile, the idea of movement and specialization was carried over from the feeder lines and applied, little by little, to the processes of final assembly or to the last operation of all—putting the Model T together. By 1913 the company had outgrown the old method of stationary assembly. It hit on the device of laying out the chassis or the skeletons of the Model T in series, sixty to the row, with each chassis resting on a pair of wooden horses. Under the new arrangement men were no longer rooted to a given spot until they had built a complete car all by themselves. They were now required to move from one station to the next, and their jobs were growing ever narrower. The former general assembler had become a member of an "axle gang" or a "motor gang" or a "wiring gang." He moved from chassis to chassis, repeating his own particular set of operations over and over. As each "gang" moved down the line, a group of helpers and runners followed after. These auxiliary specialists had the job of keeping the assemblers stocked with tools and parts.

Even this procedure had its drawbacks. It could not begin to keep pace with the volume of Ford's orders or with the scope of his operations. The factory was growing by the hour; and the larger the layout, the worse the confusion. Thousands were working on the production floor where hundreds had worked before. On final assembly, conditions approached pandemonium. Men were still criss-crossing and back-tracking in every direction. Station crowded station. Supply trucks jammed the aisles. Stockpiles cluttered up the floors. Assemblers and stockboys were tripping one another. Despite its advances, the new technique was still time-consuming. Strain as they might up to the summer of 1913, Ford's men had never succeeded in putting a single Model T together in less time than twelve hours and twenty-eight minutes.

## 2

The chaos on the final assembly floor threatened to become all the worse because of the changes in technology which were being introduced in other parts of the plant by C. W. Avery* and William Klann, two of Ford's ingenious technicians. Klann and Avery had been assigned to the job of taking the kinks out of certain sub-assembly lines. In the course of time this pair had gone far beyond the best adaptations of the gravity-slide; they had rigged up a crude device

---

* Henry Ford hired Avery originally at the request of his son, Edsel. Avery had been Edsel's favorite high school teacher.

for keeping the work "in motion" or for "bringing the work to the men" by purely mechanical means. During the spring of 1913 the Avery-Klann technique was applied to three feeder lines: those concerned with the assembly of motors, axles and magnetos. The experiment was prodigiously successful. Yet its immediate over-all effect at Ford's was catastrophic. It only aggravated the problem of final assembly. For in giving a disproportionate lift to the sub-assembly lines, Klann and Avery succeeded in crowding the finish line as never before. The already hard-pressed assemblers of the Model T could now expect to be swamped with parts and supplies.

Then Ford and the men about him had their next inspiration. If "moving assembly" worked wonders on a feeder route, why not extend it to the finish line! The job of working up an answer to this common-sense question fell, again, to Klann and Avery and their corps of co-workers. After weeks of trial and error, these men came up with the needed innovation: they hit on a method of putting a car together from start to finish "in motion." They were prepared to demonstrate the feasibility of "moving final assembly" sometime in August, 1913.

In the presence of all the top officials of the company, the test car which began its experimental "run" as a bare chassis, ending up as a finished Model T, moved along a two-hundred-and-fifty-foot path. "In production" every inch of the way, it was dragged along the floor ever so slowly by a rope and windlass. Six assemblers had been drilled for the occasion. In the course of the demonstration, these hand-picked mechanics moved with their work, either by walking to keep pace with the windlass or, at times, by "riding the job." The question of supply had been carefully worked out in advance. The walking or riding assemblers were provided with materials without having to turn to runners or to wait on trips to the parts bin; they dipped into stockpiles that had been laid out at appropriate points along the way.

By the time this sample car reached the end of its turtlelike run, it had made industrial history; it set the mold for all future developments in automotive technology. Moreover, the new arrangement or something like it was precisely what was needed at Highland Park at the moment. It broke the bottleneck of final assembly. At one stroke the Ford technicians had succeeded in reducing the time required for the assembly of a complete Model T by more than 50 per cent. Ford was so impressed by the performance that he issued orders for the immediate construction of two permanent lines for moving final assembly.

Ford stumbled on his next major innovation. It was forced upon him, by accident, coming about as the result of an unforeseen break-down. On a certain day late in 1913 one of the finish lines was either overloaded or propelled at too fast a rate. In either case the crude assembly line broke under the strain; it buckled and certain cars in the procession reared up and toppled over, all but collapsing a section of the factory wall. It was this misfortune and the resulting search for faster and sturdier methods of production that gave birth to the next outstanding achievement in Ford technology.

What followed was the invention of the first continuous automatic conveyor of its kind in existence. It consisted of a moving belt long enough and powerful enough to take the entire process of final assembly "off the floor," from the first car in the line to the very last. The first complete endless-chain conveyor for final assembly was installed at Highland Park on January 14, 1914. Its effect on production was akin to magic. Three months later, the company could boast of a new world's record; it could assemble an automobile, complete to the last detail, in ninety-three minutes. A Model T could now be put together in only one-tenth of the time it had taken eight short months before.

Ford's production experts rapidly retraced their steps. They hurriedly worked back from the finish line to the sub-assembly lines on which they had had their first successes with the principle of moving assembly. Soon the mobile trunk line—or the finish line—was flanked on every side by moving feeder lines. Each of the auxiliary conveyors was constructed either to keep parts in motion in the course of fabrication or to deliver them in finished form to the final assemblers. Most of the new belts were of the overhead variety. Their installation instantly cut down the amount of factory congestion. Parts and materials that had formerly clogged the floor were now lifted into the air by overhanging endless belts. And while Ford was not the originator of the overhead conveyor, his staff applied it to hundreds of new situations.*

As the moving belts at Highland Park grew ever more complex and interrelated, the plant itself took on the appearance of a river and its tributaries. But the flow of final assembly differed from that of a river in that it became increasingly dependent on the smallest of its tributaries; it stopped the moment any of its feeder streams "went dry." Under Ford's evolving system, the whole was more and more at the

* Long before the Ford Motor Co. began to "lift its material off the floor," the Chicago meat packers had employed a continuous "disassembly" line. They had strung up carcasses on an overhead conveyor. Each butcher removed a certain cut and passed on what was left by returning it to the moving belt overhead.

mercy of its parts; a serious breakdown anywhere along the line could quickly bring the entire factory to a standstill. The problem reduced itself to one of flawless timing, so that this or that series of parts could arrive at the finish line in exactly the desired quantity and at precisely the right moment.

All this while, three outstanding young executives were forging to the front at Highland Park. They were near-geniuses at mass production. The first was Charles E. Sorensen, a Danish immigrant who had been responsible for some of the shop work on Ford's old racer, the "999", and had started out at the Ford Motor Co. as boss of the pattern shop in 1904. Growing up at Highland Park, Sorensen was destined to become the expediter-extraordinary of the Ford assembly line and the most favored of all Ford's subordinates, save one. Sorensen's closest rival on the production floor at this time was P. E. Martin, an equally gifted mechanic. Martin had been hired in 1903 by C. H. Wills, the chief designer of the Model T. The third production expert who was currently pushing to the top at Ford's was William S. Knudsen, a young shop boss whom Ford had hired some years before as a pig-in-a-poke.* During the great decade of technological change at the Ford Motor Co., from 1910 to 1920, it fell to Knudsen to set up any number of small replicas of the factory at Highland Park. Until the time he stepped out, shifting over to General Motors, he was the man who built and superintended most of Ford's outlying assembly plants.

3

Once Ford's finish line had reached grand proportions, it began to founder because it moved too fast; it was forever threatening to outrun the auxiliary lines on which it fed. Sub-assembly lagged behind because too many of the ingredients of the Model T still had to be machined by hand. All along the various feeder routes—wherever pieces of metal required bending, shaping, grinding, drilling, stamping, punching or cutting—manual methods of fabrication were holding

---

* Before joining forces with Ford, Knudsen had been a key man at the John R. Keim steel mill in Buffalo. Originally, the Buffalo concern supplied certain parts for the steering wheel that went into the Model T. More than that, its manufacturing methods were outstanding. Ford bought the entire plant in 1907 and moved its machinery and the cream of its staff, including Knudsen, to Detroit. The owners of the property had been anxious to sell and Knudsen himself had helped to clinch the transaction. He had heard of Ford's predilection for any shop that was spic-and-span. Just before Ford came to Buffalo to have a last look at the mill he hoped to buy, Knudsen hurriedly worked over the plant, applying a fresh coat of white-wash to every last surface that would take a paint brush.

up the work. Now the crying need at Ford's was for more and more machine tools to supplant hand-labor down at the roots of mass production. By the time this want reached a critical stage at Highland Park, no machine tool company in the world could offer Ford precisely what he needed. The division of labor at his plant had gone so far that he required thousands of highly specialized machines that were non-existent.

The breach was finally filled by Carl Emde, one of Ford's own men. Emde was a German craftsman and master-mechanic. It was his original work that closed the gap between the tempo of sub-assembly and that of final assembly at the Ford Motor Co., for as an inventor of new automatic single-purpose machine tools, Emde saved the day. In the course of time he designed and installed hundreds of such machines at Ford's. One of his first wonder-creations was an automatic multi-dimensional steel drill that could bore forty-five holes in a cylinder block, drilling in four directions simultaneously.

At the height of his powers, this German genius towered over every other technician in Ford's employ. Ideas welled out of his brain at such a pace that to get them on paper it took a staff of two hundred designers, working day and night. In addition to his labors of sheer creation, Emde supervised the installation of all his more intricate inventions. For this purpose he maintained a crew of thirty hand-picked mechanics whom he called his "finishers." If the act of setting up a particular machine was to take six weeks or so, Emde would lie low and "let the factory play with it" for three weeks; then his "shock-troops" moved in and finished the job his way.

Of Emde's many talented satellites, three were outstanding. One was Ben Waderlow. Once a new automatic tool took its place on the production floor, Waderlow tried it out, reporting back to the inventor. Another of Emde's intimate co-workers was Charles Morgana. Morgana was a Ford purchasing agent on a roving mission that took him into every parts plant in the industry. But more than that, this man had an intuitive feeling for machinery. On his rounds through the supplier plants, he could size up a new piece of equipment by merely glancing at it. All he had to do was to pass on what he had seen to Emde, and shortly a copy or an improved model of the same machine would appear at Ford's. By this means, the last word in machine tool invention anywhere was quickly channeled to Highland Park. Because of his gift for divining new techniques of production, Morgana came to be known at the time as the "outside eyes" of the Ford Motor Co. John Findlater was indirectly another Emde scout.

It was Findlater's job to sweep through the shops of Ford's suppliers to check on their costs of production. When it appeared in his judgment that a part was over-priced, Ford sometimes cancelled the outside order and began its manufacture at Highland Park. If the shift required special equipment, something not yet listed in the catalogues of the tool-building trade, Emde could design it on the basis of Findlater's reports.

Though he moved behind the scenes during his stay at Ford's, and though his name was to be passed over in Ford's published memoirs, Emde was unquestionably a factory magician. Without his work, the Ford assembly line would never have forged ahead so spectacularly. After having lived through the great days at Ford's, William S. Knudsen remarked years later that unheralded Carl Emde had done more to revolutionize the automobile industry than any man who ever lived.

But the driving force behind this uprush of "Ford methods" of production was Henry Ford himself. On the threshold of his fabulous career, Ford hardly looked the part of the empire-builder. In appearance and manner alone, he was anything but the "born" leader. He was shy; he had the rustic mien. Nor was youth or education on his side. In 1913, when the factory revolution at Highland Park had no more than begun, Ford was already a man of fifty. Of books and formal education, even in his special sphere, he knew next to nothing. His, for better or for worse, was the equipment of the shrewd, ingenious, persevering Yankee mechanic. It was this self-made, self-taught product of a mid-western farm and of the Michigan machine shop, nonetheless, who dominated the factory floor during the exciting, creative years at Highland Park.

As his company gradually took on stature, Ford proceeded to measure up on many counts to the great work that opened before him. He had a remarkable knack for judging men and performance at the bench, and he made the most of it. From the very start he was canny enough to fill in the gaps in his own equipment by surrounding himself with technicians like Wills and Sorensen and Emde. Fortune worked in his favor as he slowly assembled the personnel for which his company was to become famous. Fully 50 per cent of his ablest colleagues were drawn into the organization originally by Couzens, the business manager whom Ford had inherited sight unseen from his old partner and sponsor, Malcomson. Then, too, during the dynamic years of the industry, with the Ford Motor Co. in the forefront, many another mechanic who wanted to get in on the ground floor and who was to distinguish himself in Ford's service—Knudsen, for one—hurried to Highland Park of his own accord. But in the early recruiting of the top staff of the company, none played a larger personal role than Ford. And the end-effect was outstanding. From 1910 to 1920, the entire trade was ready to concede that the men who managed the Ford Motor Co., both in the shop and in the "front office," were the best in the business.

In these formative years, the Ford personnel, on the upper tiers, was fired and bound together by a camaraderie and a will-to-work that had no equal in the industry. Some of this morale was self-generated; it was a by-product of what was going on at Ford's. As the plant continued to expand and prosper, most of the men who filled its more important posts expected to make a killing; all were driven by the knowledge that they were part of a big thing, that opportunities for promotion were limitless. All were conscious of the fact that, in the shop, they were working beside some of the most talented production men in the world. Ford, with Couzens at his side, kept this state of mind at fever heat. The two men announced very early in the game that they intended to give employment to none of their relatives.* They took this action, they said at the time, as a means of eliminating "chair-warmers" and of serving notice that everyone on the payroll was to have an equal chance for advancement. In the meantime, Ford keyed up his force still more by acting the part of the fairy godmother of production. He was here, there and everywhere, showering special rewards on the men who came up with new ideas. Time and again he would quietly take this or that innovator aside, press a wad of bills into his hand, and tell him to "forget about it." So motivated, Ford's original executives and production men not only drove themselves on the job but they fraternized spontaneously after working hours as well. The good feeling "at the top" took the form of gay celebrations like the memorable early "Victory" dinner at the Pontchartrain Hotel. When the company was beginning to burst with prosperity, all its key men, including plant superintendents and branch managers, gathered at the "Pontch" for a feast, drinking endless toasts to Ford and Couzens. Fittingly enough, the edibles consumed during the celebration were served up on a conveyor belt. This miniature moving food line was driven by a bicycle chain. It was powered by a five-horsepower motor, rigged up by one of Ford's men underneath the banquet table.

* Edsel Ford was the one exception to the rule. Edsel entered the business in 1913, the year he finished high school.

When things started to move on a grand scale at Highland Park and the profits began to pour in, Ford took more chances, he "let go" with fewer inhibitions than almost any of his competitors. As a consequence, from 1910 into the early twenties, the company's boldness, its willingness to experiment with production techniques in a large way and to throw money around in the process, was the talk of the trade. None of Ford's counselors at the time would have dared to oppose any idea whatsoever on the mere grounds that "it has been tried before" or that the "books" said it was "impossible."

The drive which Ford brought to bear at Highland Park was the more intense by virtue of this same lack of wider learning. The fifty-year-old empiricist with a passionate fondness for machinery had been tied to the bench from early manhood; he had come into middle age without a single diverting outside interest. The rise of the Model T and of Ford assembly methods only raised this single-mindedness to the *nth* power. Throughout the sixth decade of his career, blessed with a physical energy that belied his years, the manufacturer gave every indication of being obsessed by the mechanical changes that were going on around him. He behaved as though driven by a fear that he might miss something. If big changes were in the wind, and his maintenance crews were working the clock around in order to revamp an important section of the line overnight, Ford would camp in the plant until the work was done. When he left the shop in the normal course of events, he would hurry back at seven in the morning. So insatiable was the man's curiosity that he found it impossible to stay put, inside the plant. No regular office could contain him. He had to keep his finger in every pie, on a daily itinerary that enabled him to hop, skip and jump from one department to the next.

The new industrialism at Highland Park so enthralled its chief architect that he gloried in it. Wedded to the machine heart and soul, Ford went so far as to declare in his fifty-ninth year that mankind had discovered a new deity. Mass production, he asserted, had become the "new Messiah." On still another early occasion, the manufacturer gave voice to his driving preoccupation with things mechanical. What made him tick? he was asked by a friend of Clarence W. Barron's. Ever since 1908 and the birth of the Model T, Ford answered, his "life desire" had been to produce cars at the rate of one a minute.[2] Living for the day, and giving his staff no rest in the meantime, Ford was able to fulfill his "life desire" on February 7, 1920. But there was no stopping the "new Messiah." On October 31, 1925, Ford was to turn out 9109 Model T's, a new car for every ten seconds of the working day, a performance unrivaled thereafter either by the Ford Motor Co. or by any of its competitors.*

All the attributes which fitted Ford for his early leadership at Highland Park—daring, ambition, mechanical genius, inexhaustible energy and a capacity for undivided attention—were capped by still another trait, a will of iron. How well he knew what he wanted he demonstrated first when he held out alone for the Model T. Once his plant, rather than the commodity he was turning out, began to obsess him, Ford began to drive his staff with an ever more imperial hand. He spurred on his top men, said Arnold and Faurote in their classic Ford book of 1915, by impressing one and all with the fact that to hold their jobs they were expected to step up production every living day. Ford knew what he had at Highland Park well before 1915. With this self-recognition, the humble mechanic from the farm country began to merge, little by little, into the conscious empire-builder. And the more he succeeded, the harder he pushed.

Even so, the captain of industry who came into being with the "new Messiah" remained thin-skinned, handicapped throughout his forties by shyness and social awkwardness. However set in his ways, he still hated to meet the unpleasant situation face to face; he had a need for a factotum at his side who was made of tougher stuff. The harder man on whom Ford leaned up to 1916 was his secretary-treasurer, James Couzens.

4

For the rougher chores of management from which Ford seemed to shrink, James Couzens was tailored to perfection. The man was made of nails. He reveled in the rough-and-tumble into which he was plunged as business manager of the rising Ford concern. Brusque of manner and often overbearing, vain, self-interested and brilliant, he won the deepest respect, but never the love, of all his co-workers at Highland Park. A self-admitted taskmaster and a believer in autocratic management, Couzens snapped at the men about him, exhibiting at the same time a pathological dislike for the fawner or the truckler. No salesman or manufacturer's agent who tried to ingratiate himself

* The Rouge plant, which began to operate in 1927, was more efficient and more brilliantly mechanized than the old works at Highland Park. Yet it never approached the production record of 1925. Nor could it do so. The older plant had the advantage of dealing with the Model T, which was easier to make than any of the Ford products that replaced it.

with Ford's business manager by resorting to flattery or presuming on friendship ever made the same mistake a second time. He could consider himself lucky if he was ever again admitted to Couzens' quarters.

Like most of the new industry's successful executives, Couzens was self-made; he had begun to shift for himself at an early age; at seventeen he was earning his living as a car-checker on the Michigan Central. He was nearly thirty, ten years younger than Ford, and a mere bookkeeper, when he was placed in the front office of the Ford Motor Co. at the insistence of the coal merchant Malcomson. By the time the Model T had come into its own, Couzens was Ford's buffer and his official spokesman. By sheer force of character, he had, in addition, stamped himself as the business genius of the Ford concern.

In the course of his rise, Couzens displayed an energy no less fierce and a passion for work no less intense than Ford's. He performed on a dozen fronts. He was the company's chief publicist, its foremost buyer, its super-salesman, its best known missionary in the small town and the canny keeper of the exchequer. His office was the nerve center through which all Ford dealers and shippers and suppliers had to clear. Over a period of thirteen years the firm's sales force and its executive and office personnel were selected and groomed under his personal supervision.

As the first promoter of the popular Model T, Couzens piled up the orders faster than Ford could fill them. He did this in part through an ingenious method of financing new dealerships in every crossroads American town of any consequence, at no cost to the Ford Motor Co. The man who took a chance, under the Couzens' plan, was the Main Street banker. In approaching the small-town financier, a representative from the company would first tell the story of the Model T as a money-maker. Did his listener care for a cut in the business? If so, the Ford Motor Co. would regard him as one of its "bankers," it would immediately place a substantial sum of money—opening a savings account—with his institution. In return, of course, the banker would be expected to "invest" in the Ford business by placing his credit at the disposal of some newly selected candidate for a Ford dealership in the community. Once the Model T had won a name for itself and once the Ford franchise had come to be regarded as a prize, the village banker was only too glad to oblige.

By 1912 Couzens had built up a sales force of 7000 dealers. The following year he had at least one Ford agency to superintend in nearly every town in the country that had a thousand or more inhabitants.

The mere speed with which he reared an immense worldwide sales organization gave the company a tremendous headstart over its competitors. It meant that the early car buyer often turned to the Model T quite apart from its intrinsic merits. To his way of thinking the Ford product was perhaps not only the best buy for the money. It was, in addition, the car which you could learn to operate or have repaired more easily than any other because the men who sold it, and their mechanics, were so numerous and so accessible in every corner of the land. Moreover, the holder of the Ford franchise had to hustle. For Couzens, the driver, believed in pressing the market. His capacity for "crowding" his dealers was notorious. In his later years with the company, he thought nothing of forcing cars on an agency until its owner either performed miracles of salesmanship or sank under the load. Try as he might, producer Ford could not keep pace with promoter Couzens. Through 1913, Ford spawned Model T's at the rate of one every three minutes. Yet at the end of the year, he had 100,000 unfilled orders on his books.

So large was his energy and his capacity for management that Couzens by no means confined himself to the creation of a gigantic, high-pressure sales organization. With characteristic drive he took upon himself the further job of watching over the affairs of the Ford purchasing department. In no other province of the business did he make a larger contribution. When the company had finally caught on and its volume of buying had reached staggering proportions, Couzens took quick advantage of the fact; he wrested special terms from the parts makers. So sharp and tough were his dealings that he succeeded in forcing most of Ford's suppliers into line. As a consequence, many a parts maker was eventually driven to the point where he made no money whatsoever on his Ford business, in the hopes of making a profit on whatever surplus he could sell to some other customer. In 1913, thanks to Couzens' ability to drive the hardest sort of bargain, the company was getting its tires at cost, its sparkplugs at less than cost.[3] A sizable fraction of the resultant savings was passed on to the ultimate consumer. Thus, in his capacity as chief buyer for the Ford Motor Co. from the beginning in 1903 up to 1915, Couzens played a role, second in importance only to Ford's, in bringing the price of the Model T within reach of the average man.

During these same years, Ford's secretary-treasurer asserted himself in yet another sphere. He was the dominating force within the Ford traffic department, and under his direction the mere act of transporting a Model T from the factory to the man who bought it was to become one of the touchstones of Ford's fortune. Here the "Ford" formula was not original; it hinged on the fact that all automobile producers, from the start, made a practice of collecting an "imaginary" freight charge from any of their customers who happened to be far removed from the point of manufacture. But well in the lead, Couzens managed to convert this source of unearned revenue into a virtual Eldorado. He did so very early in the game by aggressively cutting down Ford's "real" freight bill to a minimum. Whenever possible, he shipped out completed Model T's by water instead of rail. If the use of a land carrier was unavoidable, he took advantage of the lowest existing railroad rates by arranging with the factory to have the Ford product "knocked down" for shipment—stripped down, so that certain easily attachable parts, such as wheels or fenders, could be shipped separately in carload lots, and added to the chassis by the distributor or the dealer at the other end.

In time the company carried this pattern to its logical conclusion; it eliminated many of its higher, long-distance hauling costs altogether by shifting the last touches of final assembly more and more to the outlying branch factory. By 1912 Ford had a dozen of these smaller subsidiary plants in actual operation or under construction.

All in all, when Couzens stepped out of Ford's in 1915, he left behind him one of the most brilliant executive careers of the era. With his departure the company lost the genius who managed its business affairs so masterfully that Ford had been able to turn his back on the front office for thirteen years and bring his full energies to bear on the production problem. By this time the company's leadership was so secure that no rival could challenge it successfully. Ford's annual sales were grossing $100,000,000. His net earnings over the preceding dozen years had aggregated $110,000,000. Shortly after Couzens retired, two of his more prominent contemporaries at Highland Park took his measure publicly. John Anderson, the company's first counsel and one of its original stockholders, took occasion to say, in harking back to Couzens, that "it was due to his efforts that the company became a success." Neither Ford nor Couzens could have "done it" alone, he said.[4] From Frank L. Klingensmith, Couzens' successor in the Ford hierarchy, came a still weightier tribute. Speaking as Ford's new treasurer (and vice president), Klingensmith remarked in 1916 that as far back as he could remember, after having worked for Ford for years, "matters of importance" at the Ford Motor Co. had always been "decided in Mr. Couzens' office."[5]

5

But long before Ford and Couzens parted company, the two men found themselves up against a labor crisis which the "new Messiah" had brought in its wake. For the new machine techniques were doing violence to the accustomed ways of the Ford mechanic. On the one hand, Ford's radical technology was in a constant state of flux; it necessitated the boldest experiments with labor. In order to give the new machine processes a tryout, men had to be commandeered, uprooted, shunted from job to job at a moment's notice. As early as 1910 the man on the bottom at Ford's had come to feel that his status was gone, that he had no work he could call his own from one day to the next. At the same time even the fixed assignment had begun to lose interest for the Ford man who liked to think of himself as a skilled or semi-skilled mechanic. The rank-and-file Ford job was becoming increasingly dull and repetitive. It was falling into the pattern of a certain factory process at Highland Park, which once required the skills of a craftsman but by 1914 had been split up into thirty-four separate operations, with each of the new subdivided tasks assigned to a different set of robot-workers.

The less interesting and more routinized operations that remained had to be performed faster than ever. After inspecting the Ford shops in 1914, the efficiency engineers Arnold and Faurote told how one human automaton at Ford's had been taught to raise his daily quota of 7000 pieces of work, thanks to a time-and-motion study which showed that he had been making 70,000 waste motions per day. Ford's factory bosses, driven from the top and fired by the potentialities of line-production, had come to accept as a matter of course the act of speeding up a new machine or an experimental assembly line 100 to 200 per cent at a single lick. In pushing his machines, Ford of necessity pushed his men. Every Ford workman, said Arnold and Faurote in 1915, "is perfectly aware that he is under constant observation, and that he will be admonished if he falls below the fast pace of the department."

Then, too, the mere physical surroundings of many a menial Ford worker had steadily worsened from 1908 on. An ever growing body of operatives was required to work in cramped, set positions or under conditions that were uncomfortable or unnatural. None was more affected by this change than the ordinary machine-tender. So closely had Ford crowded the machines and benches along his various feeder lines by 1914 that Arnold and Faurote remarked that "there seems to be no room for the operators." Ford was to make the same observation. His machine tools, he wrote sometime later, were banked more tightly than in "any other factory in the world." They were bunched up to the point that outsiders, touring the plant, would have had to conclude, he said, that his machines had been "piled right on top of one another."[6]

The ordinary Ford mechanic of 1913—now a mere assembler or machine-tender—was doing duller work and more of it than in former years. But he now had less chance to catch his breath. He could count on fewer "spells," if any at all. His work was more continuous and unremitting, adding to the monotony of his labors at the bench or on the line a new wear-and-tear or a new element of grind and nervous tension. In their authoritative report on Ford shop methods, Arnold and Faurote asserted that the average Ford worker had to keep going through the same set of semi-automatic motions "four hours at a stretch" without a break.

To top it off, Ford's factory hands were subjected to a cut in wages in the summer of 1913. Before the advent of the assembly line, the company had made a general practice of dispensing more or less liberal bonuses in order to stimulate production and individual initiative. But the moment moving belt lines came into being, Ford did away with incentive pay. He reverted to the payment of a flat hourly rate of wages. The company had decided, said *Iron Age* in July 1913, to abandon its graduated pay scale in favor of "more strenuous supervision."[7] Once the new wage policy had been put into effect, the run-of-the-mine Ford employe could expect no more variation in his earnings than in the operations which he was called on to perform. His maximum wage was frozen, seemingly for good, at $2.34 per day, the rate of pay which was standard for the area.

As a consequence, the new technology at Ford's proved to be increasingly unpopular; more and more it went against the grain. And the men who were exposed to it began to rebel. They registered their dissatisfaction by walking out in droves. They could afford to pick and choose. Other jobs were plentiful in the community; they were easier to get to*; they paid as well; and they were less mechanized and more to labor's liking.

Ford's men had begun to desert him in large numbers as early as 1910. With the coming of the assembly line, their ranks almost literally fell apart; the company soon found it next to impossible to

* The plant at Highland Park was not centrally located. It lay several miles distant from the heart of the city. The Ford employe had to spend a disproportionate amount of time merely commuting to and from work.

keep its working force intact, let alone expand it. It was apparent that
the Ford Motor Co. had reached the point of owning a great factory
without having enough workers to keep it humming. Ford admitted
later that his startling factory innovations had ushered in the outstanding labor crisis of his career. The turnover of his working force
had run, he was to write, to 380 per cent for the year 1913 alone.[8] So
great was labor's distaste for the new machine system that toward the
close of 1913 every time the company wanted to add 100 men to its
factory personnel, it was necessary to hire 963.[9]

Ford and Couzens were thoroughly roused by this threat to their
burgeoning "new Messiah." They were concerned, first of all, by the
immediate costs of the mounting unrest within their shops. Every one
of their thousands of raw recruits had to be fitted into his proper
niche by degrees. Until he knew his way about, such a man required
expensive supervision; he was a drag on over-all efficiency. Each time
a new man was taken on, it cost the company fifty or a hundred
dollars, just to break him in. By 1913 Ford was losing, directly, two or
three million dollars a year, all because his workers were in no mood
to stay put.

But this ebb and flow of labor alarmed Couzens and Ford even
more because of its remote and long-term repercussions. It was a
telltale sign that their entire venture was endangered. By 1913 the
company had evolved the most elaborate factory methods in existence; its physical investment was the largest in the trade. More so
than any of his competitors, Ford had boldly reinvested his earnings
in bigger and better tools of production. Machines rather than men
or wages had become the great item in his costs of operation.*

Thus, in 1912-1913 as never before, it began to dawn on Ford
and Couzens that their vast enterprise and their remarkable technology
would never pan out unless labor could be induced to submit to the
assembly line. Only then, they began to realize, could they hope to
get their money's worth from their capital investment, to make the
most of their superiority in mass production, to press on toward the
conquest of the mass market, and to expand their machine system on
an ever grander scale.

* This shift in Ford's costs of operation was so rapid that Arnold and Faurote
called it "unbelievable." From 1912 to 1915, nearly every working day at Highland
Park was marked by the introduction of some new piece of labor-saving equipment
that ran into big money. All along the line the machine was becoming not only
the "expensive" factor in production but the open sesame to output and profits as
well. One of the cheaper mechanical innovations—the installation of gravity-chutes
between the benches of adjacent machine-tenders—increased the rate of production
from 30 to 100 per cent.

# Four

## FIVE-DOLLAR DAY

### 1

MEANWHILE, A POTENTIALLY powerful outside labor movement began mustering its forces at Highland Park. Organizers for the I.W.W. approached Ford's workers. The leaders of this colorful, loose-knit body had been filtering into Detroit for a number of years, propagating the gospel of "one big union" and transplanting a tradition of revolt that was native to the wheat fields and to the mines and lumber camps of the Northwest.

In 1913 the "wobblies" had a following of sorts at Highland Park. They had something to work on in the way of indigenous unrest. Nearly 10,000 Ford employes were recent European immigrants to whom the accent of the I.W.W. had a more or less familiar ring. To propagate their doctrine, the wobblies had seasoned organizers who could speak most of the foreign tongues that abounded at Ford's.

These elementary trade unionists had already demonstrated their capacity for mass organization in and about Detroit. They had toured the state, preaching the eight-hour day and waging militant battles for free speech, and they led the great strike of 1913 in the copper mines of the Upper Peninsula, where throngs of foreign-born miners had been exploited for a generation. In the automobile industry itself, during the summer months of 1913, the wobblies called a strike at the Detroit plant of the Studebaker corporation. Here their "one week rebellion" failed to achieve its end of winning an eight-hour day and weekly paydays, but the threat of what some of the city's industrialists chose to think of as a "red flag" uprising remained. In the course of their short holiday, the Studebaker strikers had marched in a body down the boulevard to the Packard plant.

Simultaneously, the insurgence of the I.W.W. took root among a certain number of the employes of the Ford Motor Co. In the summer of 1913, "wobbly" organizers began to concentrate their fire on Highland Park. Their papers, *Solidarity* and *The Emancipator*, started to focus on working conditions at the Ford Motor Co. They pilloried "Henry Ford, the Speed-up King," naming him as the proprietor of a "sweat-shop" which paid wages of twenty-five cents an hour, frequently discharging his men to rehire them at twenty cents. The "one big union" showered Ford's workmen with handbills. I.W.W. orators carried the slogans of organization and the eight-hour day to the very doorstep of the Ford Motor Co.

The Ford management tried to ward off this challenge first from the outside. After a few preliminary appearances in Highland Park, certain I.W.W. speakers were carted off to jail as soon as they mounted the soapbox at the plant gates. Then the company arrived at a more drastic formula. Before the wobbly penetration, Ford's workers had enjoyed the right to saunter out of doors at lunch time. But once the I.W.W. had put in its appearance, the outdoor lunch privileges were summarily withdrawn.

Thus far, Ford and Couzens were only dabbling with symptoms. Their men were still quitting at the appalling rate of 40 to 60 per cent a month.[1] Nor had the I.W.W. really been driven to cover. The dogged missionaries reappeared. The handbills continued to circulate, and the grapevine had it that the wobblies were planning to strike Ford in the summer of 1914.

Then James Couzens, Ford's business manager, came to the rescue. Confronted by a spontaneous labor insurrection from within and by the threat of union organization from without, Couzens late in 1913 conceived the Five-Dollar Day.* He announced it to the world on January 5, 1914, and he did so with consummate showmanship. He presented the plan in terms of a large and disinterested humanitarianism.

To the reporters assembled in his office at Highland Park, Couzens declaimed, "The Ford Motor Co., the greatest and most successful automobile manufacturing company in the world, will on January twelfth initiate the greatest revolution in the matter of rewards for its workers ever known to the industrial world." Cast in the idiom of a far-reaching social reform, his statement to the press continued, "We believe that social justice begins at home." One week later, and in the joint interest of capital and labor, said Couzens, the company planned to double the current wage-rate for common labor. It would institute, he said, a basic Five-Dollar Day from which no "qualified"

* The best informed witnesses are agreed that this bright expedient originated in Couzens' fertile mind. John R. Lee, a prominent early Ford executive, so testified in court.[2] John F. Dodge volunteered the same opinion in the course of another legal action.[3] So says the Rev. Samuel S. Marquis who accompanied Ford on the Peace Ship and served for a time as director of the Ford Sociology Department.[4] A similar account is repeated by Theodore MacManus in *Men, Money and Motors*. Finally, Couzens himself acknowledged that the Five-Dollar Day was his idea.[5]

Ford workmen would be barred, not "even the lowliest laborer and the man who merely sweeps the floor."

Over and above "profit-sharing," the plan would provide, he said, for a reduction in working hours, from nine hours a day to eight. Henceforth, the announcement read, the right of any Ford foreman to discharge an ordinary worker would be subject to appeal. In addition, the Ford shop was about to establish a transfer department under whose supervision men would be shunted about until they found the "proper niche." Furthermore, said Couzens, the company hoped to guarantee year-round security for its men, by putting them "down on the farm" in slack seasons.

In proclaiming the new policy, Couzens did most of the talking. But Ford had his say. Standing at Couzens' elbow, he gave the plan a hearty endorsement. Of the forthcoming wage increase, Ford said he much preferred to have twenty thousand "prosperous and contented" workers in his establishment rather than a "few slave-drivers" and "multi-millionaires." He then ventured to say that his reforms-in-the-making would be the point of departure for a "new industrial order."

While holding forth as champions of labor, Ford and Couzens had not thrown caution to the winds. Nor had either man overlooked for a moment the considerations of self-interest or of cold business expediency. In fact, after conceiving the Five-Dollar Day, Couzens had to fight for his idea. Certain other Ford executives considered the proposal, at first hearing, too "radical." What brought them around eventually was the very hard-headedness of Couzens' arguments—his insistence that high wages would mean large profits; that his proposal, if put into effect, would enable the company to "skim the cream" of the labor market, to lower operating costs, and to make the Ford factory really "pay off" for the first time in its history.*

2

If Ford introduced his new wage primarily out of consideration for labor per se, as was commonly believed at the time, he began it in a peculiar manner at Highland Park. For the first upshot of the Five-Dollar Day was a scramble for jobs so crudely handled that it could not have subjected labor to greater indignities. All Ford pro-

* This initial coolness to the Five-Dollar Day and the private discussions that led to the adoption of the Couzens' plan are reported by MacManus, who commands general respect in the trade.[6]

vided for the rush of applicants who responded to his call for 4000 new workers, was an open hiring lot. To be sure, no large plant in the area had, to date, provided an assembly point for prospective employes that was any better.

But this case was different. The tumultuous and quite unforeseen reaction to the Ford announcement, once it manifested itself, called for extraordinary measures. On the morning after the day on which Ford proclaimed the Five-Dollar Day and issued a call for new men, 10,000 applicants all but stormed his gates. Several days later, Couzens tried to stem the tide. He issued a warning that local residents were to get precedence. But that word of caution was heeded neither by the applicants themselves nor by the company's hiring agents. Although the chaos on Manchester Street became steadily worse, nothing came of a rumor to the effect that Ford planned to take over a nearby vacant farm as a temporary hiring site.

Newspaper reporters who sampled the crowd quickly discovered that Ford and Couzens had precipitated a migration of national proportions. Clerks, farm hands, lumberjacks, sailors and miners in every section of the country had thrown up their jobs in order to cash in on Ford's "profit-sharing." A fresh batch of recruits rolled in on every freight train that entered the city.

By the end of the first week, conditions were ripe for mob disorder in the neighborhood of the Ford hiring office. A crowd of fifteen thousand, crammed within a relatively small area, had already crushed the surrounding wooden fence. The weather was bitterly cold. Tempers were frayed. Many of the job seekers had stood in line for hours without food and without having seen signs of any substantial activity at the Ford Employment Office. The hiring proceeded at a snail's pace.[7]

Only the incident was lacking to bring on a riot. That detail was provided on the Monday of the second week of waiting. By 5 A.M. that morning, 2000 job-hunters were already lined up. A few had begun to collect as early as 10 P.M. the night before. At daybreak, 10,000 men, tense and numb with cold, were pressed against the Ford shops that fronted on Manchester Street, their ranks so tightly wedged that regular Ford employes on their way to work found the route impassable. The milling crowd had virtually walled off the entrances to the plant. When an effort was made to clear a path through this human barricade, the patience of the crowd finally snapped. One minor disturbance led to another, until workers and police were soon embroiled in a street fight that lasted for the better part of two hours. The police finally dispersed the crowd by drenching the hiring lot and its occupants with a stream of water from two fire hoses. Some of the job hunters then retaliated by hurling stones and bottles at the police. A good number of Ford's factory windows were smashed during the riot.

Under the headline, "Icy Fire-Hose Deluge Stops Twelve Thousand in Riotous Push for Ford's Jobs," the Detroit *Journal* described the scene in these words: "Three thousand men were soaked, it is estimated. With the temperature hovering close to the zero mark and a biting blast coming across the field from the Northwest, they were an unenviable lot as they hurried away to find some place in which to thaw out. Their clothes froze a moment after they encountered the business end of the hose."[8]

Chief of Police Seymour of Highland Park then told reporters that his men would not have needed to use such strenuous methods of dealing with the situation had the Ford management planned its hiring more efficiently.

The riot was hardly in keeping with what Ford and Couzens had propounded as labor's Magna Carta. It did serve one immediate useful end, however. For the next several weeks, the number of men who came to Ford's looking for work tapered off to manageable proportions.

But if several thousand workers were somewhat bewildered by their first experience with the Five-Dollar Day, their reactions were mild compared with the bitterness of organized capital. For having inaugurated so radical a policy, Ford was universally denounced by the financial community as a quack, a visionary and a glory-seeker. His action, said the metropolitan press, would induce a national epidemic of strikes. To the thoroughly aroused editors of the *Wall Street Journal*, the five-dollar wage was nothing short of an "economic crime;" it was likewise immoral—a misapplication of "Biblical principles" in a field "where they do not belong."[9] The New York *Times*, the country's foremost financial newspaper, was no less vehement. It damned Ford's plan as "distinctly Utopian" and "foredoomed to failure."[10] The New York *Globe* sized up the Ford wage a bit more realistically. It appeared to the *Globe* that the Couzens' scheme had "all the advantages and none of the disadvantages of Socialism."[11]

At its face value, however, it was the plan's proximity to Socialism that put dread in the heart of the large financier and industrialist. The sound captain of industry was up in arms. He and his kind vilified the sponsor of the new wage as a traitor to his class. In a club for rich men of which Henry Ford was a member but where he seldom put in an appearance, a cultured aristocrat who had fallen heir to one of the lumber fortunes of Michigan pronounced sentence on the Five-Dollar Day by declaring that it would undermine permanently the peace and contentment of the "lower classes." Flying in the face of the higher standards of living which the Ford wage would usher in for those who were to get it, this descendant of one of the state's most eminent families grumbled in the presence of his peers that, "Any man whose wife wants more than two calico dresses a week is married to an indecent woman." In the city of Houghton, in the Michigan copper country, the mine operators fell to cursing Ford with that eloquence which they would reserve in a later day for Franklin D. Roosevelt and the CIO. To this hard-bitten set of employers, Ford's concession meant that the copper miners of the state, who were already six months along on a bitter strike, would now be less willing to settle for small stakes. These industrial tremors to the north had their counterpart in Detroit proper. As a consequence of the Five-Dollar Day, more capital and a larger number of industries took flight from Wayne County, migrating to new fields of enterprise, than was to be the case a generation later upon the rise of industrial unions and the advent of the CIO.*

3

To the prophets of doom who had forecast that the Ford Motor Co. would ride to ruin with the Five-Dollar Day—taking others with it—Ford's financial reward for casting bread upon the waters must have seemed miraculous. These critics were about to witness a brilliant demonstration of the economy of high wages. Eyes that were blind to the meaning of the Ford wage could hardly decipher the figures which were soon entered in the profit ledger of the Ford Motor Co. For the period 1914-1916, the company's net income after taxes read, for three successive years, $30,000,000; $24,000,000; $60,000,000. To account for these enormous earnings, orthodox businessmen were ready to concede that large-scale mass production was working wonders with a salable piece of merchandise. What few of them could fathom was just how the Five-Dollar Day was able to make the profitable union of the machine-system and the Model T still more lucrative. What escaped most of these bewitched observers was that

* This comparison of the Five-Dollar Day (1914) and the events of 1937-1939 was published in the Detroit *News* on March 26, 1940. It was contained in a report on the industrial progress of Wayne County, submitted by Harvey Campbell, vice president and secretary of the Detroit Board of Commerce.

Ford and Couzens were practical businessmen first, and men of good will second.

The issue was not long in doubt. The Five-Dollar Day established itself as a sound business measure while some of its critics were still grousing over its threat to the established order. Within less than a year it became evident to all who looked closely that the new wage was coining money rather than losing any for the Ford Motor Co. The magic of the maneuver of saving-by-spending lay in the plain fact that, keyed by higher wages, Ford's men were producing more efficiently and *for less money per unit of work performed*. Man-for-man on the factory floor, the new increment of output was soaring to such heights that very shortly it was much more than canceling out the margin of the wage increase.

The Ford-Couzens' formula of economy-by-largesse could be broken down into several ingredients. First, as Couzens predicted, the company had taken its pick of labor. Second, the speed of the Ford line had been greatly increased. Third, Ford workmen had either geared themselves to the new demands of the machine unprotestingly, or were tossed aside. Fourth, the Ford management took its profit from this realignment of capital and labor at once, while many of Ford's employes were unable to qualify for the five-dollar minimum for the next five and one-half years.

The most candid economic interpretation of the Five-Dollar Day on record was Ford's own. It appeared in the manufacturer's autobiography. There, Ford said, "The payment of five dollars a day for an eight-hour day was one of the finest cost-cutting moves we ever made . . ."[12]

Yet despite the speeding up by which the company recouped many times over what it had added to its wage bill, the automobile worker still preferred to work at Ford's. At least for the next half decade he would continue to show that preference in any number of ways. The overt signs of unrest all but disappeared at Highland Park. The company's labor turnover dropped by 90 per cent. Absenteeism fell away almost immediately from 10 per cent per day of the entire working force to 3/10 of 1 per cent.

Proof that Ford had found a formula for pacifying his labor could be seen at the factory gate. Men fought for admission to his plant. Just as quickly, the ground went out from under the I.W.W. Ford saw this point before the five-dollar wage was a week old. In the Detroit *Saturday Night*, he was quoted as saying during the second week of January 1914, "There will be no more excitement in Detroit's labor circles."[13]

Labor's new willingness to submit to the rigors of the Ford line was not wholly a matter of eagerness to cash in on the Five-Dollar Day. It was that at the start and something more. Fear of the job began to operate alongside the scramble for more money. The Ford employe who rose to meet new standards of output did so not only to become eligible for a higher wage but to make sure of holding any job at all. He was quickly reminded of this double necessity. Before the Couzens' plan was a week old, the company moved with dispatch to penalize several hundred of its foreign-born workers who had taken a day off on their own to observe a holiday of the Greek Orthodox Church.[14] Back at work, these celebrants were immediately sent home as a hint to the rest of the personnel that a five-dollar wage meant five dollars worth of discipline.

The very knowledge that a purge was under way at Highland Park in 1914 and in succeeding years had the effect of spurring the efforts of the Ford men who survived. Their fear of the job, as well as their anxiety to make a decent wage, was soon heightened by social forces that began to operate outside the mill. The Ford wage increase had acted like a magnet. Drawn by its pull, thousands upon thousands of new workers continued to inundate Detroit, thereby helping to glut the local labor market, and raising the premium on employment everywhere in the area. Small wonder that Arnold and Faurote, after completing their exhaustive study of Ford methods in 1914, could remark, "Not one word of protest is ever spoken at Ford's, because every man knows the door to the street is open for any who objects in any way, shape or manner to instant and unquestioning obedience to any directions whatever."[15]

Although Ford could pluck the fruits of the Five-Dollar Day the moment it was initiated—getting the choicest workmen and the maximum output of men and machines—a good many of his workers never tasted the heralded early benefits of "profit-sharing" at all. All had to qualify as profit-sharers either by putting in time in the company's employ or by meeting certain arbitrary tests. Women workers, unmarried men under twenty-two, family men who were living by themselves or not supporting their dependents, married men involved in divorce actions, new employes with less than six months' seniority or any worker who in Ford's opinion was "living unworthily as a profit-sharer"—all these were excluded from the beginning.[16]

How large a portion of the personnel failed to qualify as immediate recipients of the five-dollar wage was reported in the company's financial statement of July 1916. From this source it appears that more than 14,000 Ford employes—or 30 per cent of the company's total working force—were earning less than five dollars a day.[17] Two and one-half years after its formal induction, therefore, the Couzens' plan proved to be one of delayed "profit-sharing" for a considerable body of its potential beneficiaries. Probationers at the plant still earned no more than $2.72 a day after the five-dollar minimum had been in force for almost three years.[18] Meanwhile, new recruits had come and gone. Many were dropped from the payroll at the end of six months, with a fresh contingent brought in to take their places at a starting wage of $2.72. During the year 1916 alone, some 7,500 men were struck from the payroll. Two-thirds of this number, said the journal *Machinery*, had less than six months' seniority and had, therefore, never participated in profit-sharing.[19] Such a cycle, of hiring new men at a wage that lay a dollar or two below the five-dollar mark, persisted until July 1919—five and one-half years after Ford had presumably conceded a universal Five-Dollar Day.[20]

Even though the company was paying better than average for its common labor, it was correspondingly less generous with its workers who were skilled or semi-skilled. This early peculiarity of the Ford wage scale was summarized in the issue of the Detroit *Saturday Night* for July 6, 1918. Long the most influential employers' journal in the city, the *Saturday Night* sized up the Five-Dollar Day in the fifth year of its operation in the following manner: for the first six months of employment, said this weekly, common labor was earning no more and probably less at Ford's than at other leading establishments in metropolitan Detroit. To his skilled men, said the *Saturday Night*, Ford was paying no more than the prevailing scale and definitely less than what the same talent could command elsewhere in the area. The over-all Ford wage for 1914-1918, the paper concluded, had never greatly exceeded the rates that prevailed in and about Detroit.

4

Certain groups of Ford workmen, probably never more than 5 or 10 per cent, were barred from profit-sharing between 1914-1919 because they failed to live up to the code of conduct propounded by the Ford Motor Co. To pass on the essentials of "thrift" and "character" required of all Ford men who were to be paid five dollars a day, the company inaugurated a separate department. This division, charged with the mission of standardizing the private habits of Ford employes, was christened the "Ford Sociology Department." Its staff consisted of some thirty investigators who undertook to visit the homes of Ford workmen and to pass on those who should and those who should not qualify for profit-sharing. By 1919 the corps of home visitors rose to 150. It was supervised for the most part by two of the most picturesque men in Ford history, each of whom was to leave a chronicle of his experience. The first director of the department was John R. Lee, a personnel man of talent. Lee's successor in office was the urbane, intelligent clergyman and intimate of the Ford family, the Very Reverend Samuel S. Marquis, then Dean of the Episcopal Cathedral of Detroit.

In what amounted to a brief reign of benevolent paternalism, these gentlemen and their house-to-house canvassers imposed on the recipients of the Five-Dollar Day a set of rules which blended good sense with Ford whim and petty Puritan virtues.

On the positive side, the men who worked under Lee and Marquis behaved like the home visitor of the modern public welfare agency. They doubtless helped to "Americanize" Ford's vast body of immigrant workmen. Their charges were encouraged to start savings accounts and to budget their incomes. They were given elementary lessons in hygiene and home management. The wives of many of the foreign-born were taught how to shop to the best advantage and how to distinguish between various cuts of meat.

At its worst, the new department was a mildly tyrannical instrument which sowed the seeds of inquisition at the Ford Motor Co. Its agents became, to some extent, collectors of tales and suspicions. Examined on their doorsteps, wives were called upon to testify against husbands, children against parents. Hearsay as well as fact found its way into a card catalogue where a record was kept of every worker's deviations. To avoid getting demerits in this index, the wily Ford employe sometimes beat the game by only pretending an interest in the rules. To some extent, prying induced lying. As Ford was to put it in his autobiography, his home visitors made an effort to break up "the evil custom" of taking in male boarders.[21] To get around this prohibition, certain of his workmen and their wives simply passed off their lodgers as "brothers" or "cousins."

Frittering away one's evenings "unwisely," taking in male boarders, sending funds to the "old country," or spending money "foolishly"— these things came to be regarded as earmarks of "unwholesome living." The use of liquor was forbidden to a "profit-sharer," as was marital discord that resulted in a separation or a divorce action.

The canons of eligibility thus invoked were not unusual for the age. They included as well certain attributes which make the factory

worker a healthier and more efficient being. At the same time, the
Ford code bespoke the prim, village mores of the Protestant Middle
West. What was distinctive about it was the fact that any employer
should ever have attempted to superintend the private morals of his
workmen and their families.

Once a Ford man was judged to have been "wasting his substance"
or "living unworthily as a profit-sharer," his rights to the Five-Dollar
Day were straightway suspended.[22] His pay was cut in half. He could
regain his former wage only by satisfying the investigators who revisited his home that he had fully recovered his "strength of purpose."
The Ford staff worked out a six-point scale for sizing up one's rate
of "rehabilitation." If a man was quick about it he could hope to win
back his five-dollar wage within thirty days. For each succeeding
month that he might require before reinstatement, the less he could
count on as a profit-sharer. Thus if five months passed on probation,
the reinstated worker was entitled to a mere 25 per cent "bonus." His
top wage had to stay at $3.01 a day.[23] Those who were still wanting
"in the ways of thrift" at the end of six months' grace were discharged.
Before certain offenders could make the grade, said Lee, their "lives
and habits" required "complete revamping."

As to the final merits of this effort, the judges disagreed among
themselves. Even those for whom the system was intended viewed
it dissimilarly. At the start, certain Ford employes undoubtedly accepted the work of the Ford Sociology Department as but one more
proof of their employer's charitable inclinations. Others came to resent
the institution as an affront to their personal liberties. Most Ford
workers probably took a middle position. Perhaps the majority put up
with this department because its restrictions were not particularly
oppressive and even these were more than counterbalanced for the
time being by the Five-Dollar Day. To the public at large the "social
work" among Ford's employes must have appeared to be every bit
as large-hearted as the new wage. Of all the critics of the Sociology
Department and its attendant paternalism, the Ford management
applied perhaps the most materialistic standards of evaluation. In
July 1916, *The Ford Times,* a company house organ, remarked that
Ford's "educational work" had fully justified itself "from the cold-
blooded point of view of business investment."[24]

Meanwhile, what Ford had conceded to his profit-sharers inflation
took away. Within a four-year span ending in December 1918, a rising
cost of living gobbled up at least one-half of the purchasing power
of the five-dollar wage. This decline in real wages was reported in a

survey of living costs published by the United States Department of Labor in the *Monthly Labor Review* for February, 1925. Of the nineteen major cities included in the survey, Detroit led the list, showing the sharpest rise in prices from December 1914, on through the following decade. By December 1919, the cost of living in Detroit had risen 108 per cent; in what it could buy, a five-dollar wage had dropped to a value of $2.40.

The merchant, the landlord and the real estate speculator had helped to bring on this steady decline in real wages. In fact, the Five-Dollar Day had whetted their appetites. Ford's workmen had a foretaste of all this when they drew their first pay under the Couzens' plan, in January 1914. Waiting to receive them at the gates of the factory when they bolted into the street with their first five-dollar checks, said the New York *Times*, was a small army composed of wives, book agents, salesmen, bill collectors, representatives of installment houses and constables with writs. The subsequent process of melting down what five dollars or any other wage could buy in the city of Detroit was a flourishing business.

In the main, this devaluation of his employes' real earnings was quite beyond Ford's control. It was part and parcel of a process of national inflation. It meant that Detroit, at the heart of a great young industry, had growing pains in the course of which new workers were tumbling into the city by the tens of thousands, without plan or order, and more were on their way. Professional labor recruiters hired by local employer groups, were in the South and Middle West, spreading the gospel of the high wages that could be expected in Detroit.[25] Handbills, pitched in the same key, had been scattered everywhere.[26]

Until 1919, Ford made no basic move to restore the wilted purchasing power of his own employes. But for one gesture, he was apparently content to stand by. As his working force gradually lost ground because of rising prices, the manufacturer did found a legal aid and real estate department to which his employes could come for free consultation. But this agency, however well-intentioned, was quite powerless to get to the root of the matter or to raise Ford wages.

For every factory worker or mill owner who had misgivings about the Five-Dollar Day, however, there were thousands who hailed the innovation as a landmark of the era. When Ford and Couzens arrived in New York City a day or so after they had announced the new wage, they were received not as little-publicized makers of an inexpensive car but as celebrities of the first water. They were fussed over, virtually commandeered by journalists and newspapermen. In his suite at the Belmont, Ford found a thousand personal letters waiting for him. To cut himself off from admirers and busybodies, he had to have the telephone in his room disconnected. The curious gawked at him in the hotel lobby. Another fat pouch of mail was piling up back home.

No sooner had "profit-sharing" proved to be profit-making than Ford and Couzens made a second flourish in the same vein. This time they promised to "share" their earnings with the car buyer. They announced in July 1914 that if the company succeeded in selling 300,000 cars within the next twelve months, every purchaser of a Model T would receive a rebate of $50. This gesture spread Ford's name still more widely in the public prints and by word of mouth. The customers who collected a rebate of fifteen and one-half million dollars in the summer of 1915 became his personal advocates as well as new missionaries for the Model T. Heralded as the first capitalist of modern times to operate a great business on the principle that mass consumption and mass production must go hand in hand, Ford was enshrined at once as an idol in the hearts of plain people everywhere. Small wonder that reformers and labor leaders began to sing his praises as a second and greater Robert Owen.

When the man in the street began to deify Henry Ford, the great impetus to beatification came from the fact that the Five-Dollar Day had two faces. Here was a device for making money and for making the most of mass production that had, at the same time, every appearance of largesse. Taken at his own word, as uttered in 1914 and 1915, Ford himself appeared to possess, indeed, two selves in one: he was the calculating businessman engaged in the pursuit of purely selfish ends, and he was social prophet and philanthropist.

During the first wave of reaction to the unprecedented wage increase, Ford repeatedly struck, on the one hand, the pose of the industrial democrat, of the defender of the little man. In the New York *World* for January 9, 1914, he was quoted as saying, "I can see no purpose in one man or a few men accumulating a great fortune. It can do no good and more often causes others much harm. . . . There is no reason I should leave a great fortune behind me. I have only a son and he is a worker in the factory." Whatever future wealth he might amass, Ford told reporters, he planned to turn over in the end "to the boys in the factory." Similar sentiments were echoed by Ford's associates. In his notable paper on the Five-Dollar Day, John R. Lee went so far as to claim that, "We are simply demonstrating over and over again the absolute truth of that ancient adage known as the Golden Rule."

Yet Ford was every bit as insistent that the bestowal of the five-dollar wage was pure business and nothing more. He scoffed at his friend, John Burroughs, the naturalist, who once made the error in Ford's presence of calling the Five-Dollar Day a "humanitarian" gesture. Ford told him, said Burroughs, that it had been "simply a good business move" and had given him "the pick of the workers."[27] Again, testifying before the Federal Commission on Industrial Relations in January 1915, the manufacturer said once more that the institution of the Five-Dollar Day had been solely "a business proposition." Again it was the fortune-maker rather than the improver of mankind who replied to a reporter who asked Ford what he thought of charity as a means of coping with unemployment. The tart reply to this question was, "I give nothing for which I do not receive compensation."[28]

## Five

### NO MORE PARASITES

### 1

ON SO RICH a diet of publicity and social acclaim, any ego might well have gorged itself; Ford's, in the year 1914 and after, was no exception. The manufacturer had been stunned by some of his earlier successes. Only six years had elapsed since he so underestimated his accomplishment that he had been willing to dispose of his holdings for something less than $2,000,000. Nor had Ford been quite up to the job of comprehending his achievement of the intervening years. Asked to account for his career, he had already asserted more than once that he only listened to his "hunches." Meanwhile, with a panorama of empire at his feet, Ford's assurance and his self-esteem had risen. It positively soared as a result of the ground-swell of approbation that greeted the Five-Dollar Day. Now as never before the Yankee mechanic who had "arrived" by rule-of-thumb became the man of destiny; he began to feel that the "inner guide" to which he alluded so often could never do him wrong.

The first to brush against this expanding sense of self-sufficiency on Ford's part, ironically enough, was James Couzens, from whose brain the plan for a Five-Dollar Day had issued. It was a trivial but heated argument on the subject of pacifism that drove Couzens to the point of offering Ford his resignation on October 14, 1915. Couzens took objection to the fact that Ford was about to circularize all the customers of the Ford Motor Co. with a pamphlet which came out against military preparedness and urged Americans to turn their backs on the current World War. During an angry interchange, Couzens threatened to step out for good unless such "stuff" was deleted from all of the company's advertising matter. Ford accepted his resignation on the spot.[1] Both men had been expecting such a showdown. The particular issue over which they fell out was incidental.

Ford had been nursing a number of more fundamental grievances against his treasurer and vice-president. Months earlier he had told his friend E. G. Pipp, then editor of the Detroit *News,* that Couzens was so interested in politics—with "an eye on the U.S. Senate"—that he was losing his usefulness to the company. To drive the point home, and disclosing incidentally that Couzens had been preying on his mind for some time, Ford then confided to Pipp that he had ordered "a check kept on Jim, and he has been at the plant only 184 days during the past year . . ."[2] Yet neither politics nor pacifism nor Couzens' "attendance record" was at the bottom of this estrangement.

For at least a year the two men had been at loggerheads over a much more crucial question of company policy. They differed in their estimate of what the future held in store for the Model T. Ford took the longer view. He could see no limit to the market. As a result, he favored bold expansion. He wanted to plow back into the business every cent he made, as fast as he made it. Couzens, on the other hand, had a more conservative outlook; he was fearful lest Ford should overreach himself. It was his idea to expand, but cautiously. However, if Couzens had stayed on, he would have had little actual say in the matter. He would have had to defer to Ford, because Ford held control; he owned 58½ per cent of the company's stock. Meanwhile, Ford was chafing at the mere thought of having to impose his will on that of his tough-minded vice-president. In January or February of 1916, he told John F. Dodge that Couzens' leaving had been "a very good thing for the company." Henceforth, he said, the brakes were off; he would be free to expand at will.[3]

Clashes of temperament had hastened the day of a final rupture between the two dominant personalities of the Ford Motor Co. Nor was the fault entirely Ford's. Couzens, for his part, had been anything but the adroit or politic administrator. Waspish, cranky, tough, austere and headstrong, he had begun to needle Ford. Ford often complained to others that his vice-president was too "stubborn." On his way to a conference with Couzens in 1914 or 1915, Ford used to approach the appointed meeting place on tiptoe, inquiring along the route if the "Old Bear" was "in his den."

The number two man at the Ford Motor Co. had found it difficult to share authority with anyone, even with Ford. In an autobiographical piece which he wrote for *System* magazine in September 1921, Couzens freely admitted to ownership of the very traits of character that he disliked in Ford; he made no bones about his own love of power. He expressed a wholehearted contempt for democratic management. For thirteen years none but Ford and himself, he wrote, had ever been permitted to touch the reins of authority within the company. At the same time, the former autocrat of the Ford Motor Co. was perfectly willing to sing Ford's praises, in retrospect. The conception of the Model T and all it stood for, he said, had been Ford's own. The author of the *System* article even minimized his own substantial contribution to Ford's success. For this journalistic effort of 1921 he chose the self-effacing title, "What I Learned about Business from Ford."

If Couzens had remained in a class by himself at Ford's, his retirement could have been put down as proof of his own egotism or of his inability to bow to the will of other men, and nothing more. But in reality his stormy departure from Highland Park was a commentary on Ford as well. It was in some degree a measure of Ford's ability to withstand success. Couzens said as much at the time. Shortly after he withdrew from the company, he complained to the advertiser Theodore MacManus, "I finally decided that I could not be carried along on that kind of a kite. I was willing to work with Henry Ford," he stormed, "but I refuse to work for him."[4] Moreover, this break was only the forerunner of a wider conflict of personalities into which Ford was about to plunge. Couzens was first to draw the lightning at the Ford Motor Co. for the reason that, next to Ford himself, he was the tallest tree in the woods. Next in point of size and next to be felled was John F. Dodge.

## 2

John Dodge and his brother Horace, whom Ford was to take on as adversaries in his next vault to power, were, apart from Ford and

Couzens, the most ambitious and most talented of the original Ford stockholders. The two men had never been content to sit by, waiting for their 10 per cent interest in the Ford Motor Co. to drop plums in their laps. After having assembled nearly all of the first Ford cars, this pair had continued to operate a factory of their own. They had amassed a fortune in the business of making Ford parts. By 1913 their plant equipment alone was valued at ten to fifteen million dollars. In assessing the worth of their services, meanwhile, the Dodges had charged Ford all that the traffic would bear. John Dodge once confessed as much. When a Ford executive in 1912 accused him of profiteering at Ford's expense, or of making on a certain part a clear profit of sixty cents apiece over and above what Ford would have had to allow anyone else, Dodge is supposed to have replied with characteristic bluster, "Hell, those things don't even cost sixty cents apiece."

Yet, aside from the earliest years of their association with Ford, neither of the Dodges had ever felt secure or needed at the Ford Motor Co. Neither man had ever been drawn into the inner circle of Ford management. One had been relegated to the status of silent stockholder, the other to the lot of board member called in on occasion, but only to ratify some action that Ford and Couzens had agreed on in advance. For John Dodge, the more forceful of the two brothers, the situation was intolerable. This co-founder of the Ford Motor Co. was a full-sized, aggressive, sharp-witted industrialist in his own right. Reputed to have been as keen a man in the factory as Ford and as sharp a businessman as Couzens, John Dodge was not modeled to tag along in the shadow of the Ford Motor Co. He was itching for something bigger when he groused to E. G. Pipp, then a Detroit journalist, in 1912 or thereabouts, "I am getting tired of being carried around in Henry Ford's vest pocket."[5]

Well before 1912 the Dodges had good reason to suspect that their lush days in the parts field were numbered. The business in which they had struck it rich was no longer so attractive. It was becoming strenuously competitive. Any number of feeder plants were now scratching for a Ford account, and the margin of profit on any Ford business at all was rapidly shrinking. Gargantuan buyers, Ford and Couzens were beginning to squeeze their suppliers, playing one parts maker off against the next. The Dodges had no desire to pass their handsome profits on to Ford. Nor was Ford bound to do business with them on any terms. The orders which they filled for the Ford Motor Co. were governed by an annual contract that was subject to renewal or cancellation at the will of either party. They could foresee the possibility of being cut off on short notice with a highly special-ized idle factory on their hands.

Unwilling to forego either their earnings or their independence, the Dodges moved out of the Ford periphery voluntarily before they were shaken out.[6] They had other plans for their own factory that was almost as up to date as Ford's, for their cash-in-hand that ran to twenty or twenty-five million dollars, and for the profits they could expect to reap from their Ford stock. After resigning as a member of Ford's board of directors in 1913, John Dodge announced that he and his brother intended to manufacture a car of their own. Their automobile, he said, would not compete with the Model T; it would cost three or four hundred dollars more than the current Ford car. John Dodge is supposed to have stated his goal with all the scorn and swagger at his command. *Fortune* magazine credits him with the taunt, "Think of all the Ford owners who will some day want an automobile."[7]

After they had been marketing their own excellent car for a year and a half, the Dodges had a shock that robbed them of some of their ready self-assurance. Henry Ford, accompanied by his chief engineer C. H. Wills, walked into their offices one winter morning in 1916 to explode a bomb on the premises. Ford bluntly told the Dodges that neither they nor their fellow-stockholders could look forward to any substantial future earnings on their investment in the Ford Motor Co. Henceforth, he said, he would declare an over-all annual dividend of $1,200,000 and not a penny more. Every cent he made over and above that margin would be plowed back into the business.[8]

The moment Ford had finished delivering this ultimatum, John Dodge then and there put his interests and his brother's in the Ford Motor Co. up for sale. "If you are going to adopt as radical a policy as that," he is said to have countered, "why not buy out all the holders and then do just as you please?" Ford replied that he had no intention of adding any shares to those he already owned. As for the plan to limit future dividends to a small, annual, fixed payment, he said, the minority shareholders could take it or leave it.*

Belligerent and thoroughly capable of defending his own, John Dodge immediately called Ford to book, playing a joke on his ad-versary in the process. On the evening of November 2, 1916, John Dodge and his wife were guests at the wedding of Edsel Ford and Eleanore E. Clay, the niece of J. L. Hudson, the department store magnate of Detroit. The bride and the Dodges had been neighbors of long standing. Before the city had digested this social event, as

* This conversation was later vouched for in a court of law by C. H. Wills.

reported in the society columns of the local press the following day, the Dodges filed suit against the bridegroom's father. They asked the court to compel the Ford Motor Co. to issue reasonable dividends to its stockholders and to enjoin any further business expansion on Ford's part until such profits were forthcoming. This legal action was to cost the Dodges $130,000 apiece.[9]

Into Ford's threatened moratorium on profits the Dodges could read no more than spite, a desire on Ford's part to hobble their own efforts as independent manufacturers. They had resented and mis-judged the Five-Dollar Day with the same feelings of persecution. In both instances, the two brothers were convinced that Ford was determined to stanch his dividends for the sole purpose of embar-rassing the Dodge Corporation. On one score their fears were well-founded. Were Ford to win his battle against profits, their venture would, of necessity, have to trim its sails. More than that, by the fiat of one man the true value of their previous investment in one of the most lucrative businesses in existence—to whose success they had themselves contributed—would all but evaporate. On Ford's terms the most the Dodges could hope to collect from their 10 per cent interest in the Ford Motor Co. was $120,000 per annum. They could expect a meal of crumbs from a feast which was currently heaping Ford's table with a clear profit of from thirty to sixty million dollars a year.

But the legal case against Ford did not turn on the issue of whether a few millions more or less in Ford dividends might make or break the Dodge Corporation. As this action at law began its deliberate course toward the Supreme Court of the State of Michigan, its implication gripped the attention of all the other minority share-holders of the Ford Motor Co. For although these co-investors were content to stand by as spectators, their interests were as much at stake as the Dodges'. Ford had defied stockholders in general and the very principle of corporate management.

When the Dodges decided to contest this challenge in the courts, Ford was still something of a Populist, despite his millions. He had begun to lunge at the "money-power" wherever it bared its face. Under his ownership the Dearborn *Independent* was about to take a stand on race and money that harked back to the ruralist's ingrained prejudice against organized capital in general. Ford was very much in character when his antipathy for rich men, as of this date, was turned on the profit takers in his own business. As a matter of fact, he had launched such an offensive within a week of Couzens' resignation. In November 1915, he had made the founding of Henry Ford and Son, a partnership in which he assigned the rights of the Ford tractor, an occasion for lambasting every one of the financial interests which had helped to bring the Ford Motor Co. into being. At least in his tractor business, he had proclaimed, there would be "no stock-holders, no directors, no absentee owners" and no more "parasites."[10]

In wanting to shake himself free of "unproductive" partners, Ford had common sense on his side. Of all the co-founders of the Ford Motor Co., he alone in 1916 was the one remaining "producer" of the lot. Couzens and the Dodges had been stricken from the active list. The remaining minority shareholders—Couzens' sister, the heirs of the Gray estate, and the two attorneys Anderson and Rackham—had con-tributed almost nothing to the business.* Yet between them, through the year 1915, the minority owners of Ford stock had garnered $25,000-000 in cash dividends.[12] Such fruits Ford may well have considered as adequate return on a $28,000 investment, in view of the fact that some of his co-holders had put up no money of their own whatsoever, and that all of them were now resting on the sidelines!

Against the claims of these absentee owners Ford could pit, on the other hand, a dream of industrial conquest which had, for him, no measure in dollars and cents. The decision of 1916 to reinvest in the business all but a fraction of his future earnings was, to some extent, the will of the empire-builder to get on with his work. It was part and parcel of Ford's realization that his factory was overturning the arts of mass production. Such a limitless undertaking, as he must have en-visioned it, would only be cramped by the necessity of having to share his profits with a group of hangers on and "non-producers." During his appearance as a defense witness in the Dodge suit, Ford gave the court some insight into the sweep of his interest in mass production as an end in itself. Asked by counsel if he was going to "experiment" with the funds of the company on a certain immense project, he snorted, "We are not going to experiment at all; we are going to do it." Again, prodded by Dodge's attorney to see if he meant to get on with another grandiose and breath-taking scheme of factory expansion, the manu-facturer snapped, "Oh, certainly. There wouldn't be any fun in it if we didn't."

Finally, in colliding with his stockholders, Ford was driven by sheer will-to-power. Other springs of action that impelled him toward

* Anderson would not be seen riding in one of the conveyances to which he owed his millions. When asked by a tax examiner in 1927 if he could list the characteristics of the Ford car, Anderson replied, "Never having driven the Model T in my life, I regret to say I cannot."[11]

such a course—the vision of the machine age, the contempt of the ruralist and the producer for "unearned" dividends, and the alleged desire to slip a halter on the Dodges—seem only to have fed and strengthened this central hunger for authority. At least it may be said that Ford was to overcome his aversion for profits as such. Once in possession of the entire holdings of the company, the Ford family— Henry Ford and his wife and son—were to withdraw cash dividends for their private use for the next seventeen years at the rate of more than $25,000 a day![13]

Nor were Ford's co-owners of 1916 in any position to hamper his scheme of pushing mass production to its logical conclusions. None could have challenged him, so long as he saw fit to part with reasonable dividends, for the reason that Ford held control; from 1906 on, more than 50 per cent of the voting stock of the company had been concentrated in his hands.[14] Now that Couzens and John Dodge had vacated their seats of influence at the Ford Motor Co., no minority Ford stockholder had the opportunity, the force of mind, the business judgment, or even the desire to take issue with Ford. But Ford was resolved to rid himself of his minority interests, nonetheless; pure temperament drove him in that direction. So said twenty-six-year-old Edsel Ford at the time. When the stockholder fight within the company was at its height, Edsel was quoted by the New York *Times* as saying that he had the feeling it was quite possible to "get along" and "do business" with the minority interests of the company, but that "father" was of the opinion that it was altogether "impossible."[15]

### 3

Whether or not Ford's designs on his stockholders were primarily self-seeking—and few Americans would have even suspected such a possibility in 1916—he proceeded to root out his minority interests with a plan of attack that was both rigorous and wily. At the outset, he seems to have preferred combat to mediation. By refusing to buy out his former partners at a fair price, once he decided to whittle dividends down to the vanishing point, he let himself in for three years of wrangling and litigation.

He came no closer to a compromise even after the Dodges had dragged him into court. When Ford finally had to submit to cross-examination on the witness stand, he flared up the moment the possibility of a sale was introduced by Elliott G. Stevenson, the brilliant attorney who represented the Dodges. "If you sit there until you are petrified," he snapped at Stevenson, "I wouldn't buy any Dodge brothers' stock, if that is what you are talking about . . . I don't want any more stock."[16] All this while, the Dodges had been anxious to sell. Couzens and the heirs of the Gray estate had been casting about for prospective buyers for some time. But Ford apparently clung to the idea that he could put his fellow-stockholders out to pasture empty handed and get away with it. At least, in telling a newspaper reporter years later what he thought of the claims of his former co-investors, he said, "Personally, I never would have paid them a cent."[17]

As the Dodge action wore on, meanwhile, the minority Ford interests were more than a little ill at ease. They found themselves in the ambiguous position of owning stock that was potentially worth scores of millions, but which few outside buyers would dare to touch under the circumstances. Ford, in control, had chilled the prospects of sale to any new outside investors by having declared a ban on profits.

On February 7, 1919, the lesser owners of Ford stock could once again breathe normally. For on that day, the state Supreme Court, affirming the position of a lower court, saw fit to rebuke Ford's "no-dividends" philosophy. After reviewing the tremendous earning capacity of the Ford Motor Co., the bench invoked a rule of reason; it ordered Ford to declare an immediate, delayed, special dividend of $19,000,000, with interest at 5 per cent from the date of the decision in the lower court. The court based its position on a reading of the company's financial statement for August 1, 1916.

This report had listed assets at $132,000,000, surplus at $112,000,000, cash and bonds at $54,000,000, and expected profits for the ensuing year at $60,000,000. The refusal of so prosperous a corporation to reward its owners with normal profits, the court ruled, had been illegal and "arbitrary." Justice Ostrander, the author of the majority opinion in the case, commented on this refusal by saying, "The record, and especially the testimony of Mr. Ford, convinces that he has to some extent the attitude towards shareholders of one who has dispersed and distributed to them large gains and that they should be content to take what he chooses to give them."[18] To close the issue once and for all, the court then enjoined Ford from applying such a policy to his investors at any time in the future.

Now, it appeared, the lesser shareholders of the Ford Motor Co. were free to pick and choose. They could hang on and wallow in Ford profits, or they could peddle their Ford shares wherever they chose. But before these equally attractive promises had a chance to materialize, Ford attacked from another direction. In one of the sharpest

strategic moves of his career, he plunged his stockholders into a state
of outright panic.

To the utter consternation of the men who had just bested him in
court, Ford threatened, with a flourish, to withdraw from the Ford
Motor Co. and leave his minority stockholders high and dry. He was
about to found, he said, a competing independent enterprise. His
first move in this direction, however, was little more than a feint. One
month in advance of the final decision in the Dodge case, Ford had
relinquished the presidency of the Ford Motor Co., though keeping
his seat on the board. At a loss to understand such behavior, the other
members of the board had accepted the resignation "with regrets" and
elected Edsel in his father's place at a salary of $150,000 a year. From
the public statements which the elder Ford released as he stepped
down in favor of his twenty-five-year-old son, none could have
guessed what was up. It appeared that the retiring president of the
Ford Motor Co. had other worlds to conquer. In his letter of resignation, dated December 30, 1918, he said, "It is my desire to devote my
time to building up other organizations with which I am connected."[19]

His new aim, he said, was to develop a separate tractor business
and "to become a newspaper publisher." The vehicle for each of these
projects was already at hand. The new partnership Henry Ford and
Son would see to the tractor interests, and for his medium as a publisher, Ford had just taken over the Dearborn *Independent*. Edsel's
continuing association with the Ford Motor Co. was explained by
*Automotive Industries* on the curious ground that it would assure for
his father within the next six months a circulation of one million
subscribers to the Dearborn *Independent*.[20] The only remaining interest which tied the senior Ford to the automobile business, it seemed,
was the hope that the Ford Motor Co. might serve, under Edsel's
management, as a soliciting agency for a newly acquired rural weekly!

But within a month of his defeat in the Dodge action, Henry Ford
had more to say. From California, where he had gone for a vacation
with his family, he threw an entirely new light on the activities he proposed to substitute for his "previous" work at the Ford Motor Co. It
was now his intention, he said, to market a "more up-to-date" popular
car at one-half or one-third the price of the current Model T. The new
super-Model T would be brought out, he said, under the auspices of
still another brand new company—a concern in which only he and
Edsel were to have a stake!

The first to break this news to the world, the Los Angeles *Times*,
on March 4, 1919, referred to the new car as already far advanced in

the mind of its creator. Ford had given birth to his "newest dream child," said the *Times*, while taking a short "rest" at Altadena, California. Before long, the stories of "something new in the way of an automobile," at a price as low as $250, began to depress sales at the Ford Motor Co. proper. Potential buyers of the Model T slackened off, in their excitement over the prospects of the forthcoming "dream child" car. Edsel Ford tried to quiet his dealers by saying that it would take two or three years to bring the new car into production and that one should not credit every "Dearborn" rumor.

Meanwhile, the elder Ford was only playing at cat-and-mouse. He was preparing the ground so that he could buy out his minority shareholders without having to come up against any stiff outside bidding. His nominal retirement from the Ford Motor Co. and his threat to compete with the Model T had simply walled off any independent purchasers of Ford stock. The moment Ford felt certain that outside financiers and industrialists were no longer interested in his ostensibly priceless shares, he began to feel out his co-holders for a sale, and on his own terms. But he did so indirectly. He worked through purchasing agents who were pledged to keep the identity of their principal a secret. As his brokers began to make their quiet rounds, Dearborn did its best to hush up the fact. Asked point-blank if all the publicity about forming a new company was not simply leverage for a "forced sale," Edsel Ford retorted, "We will not buy a share of anybody else's stock."[21] When reporters put the same question to Ernest Liebold, then Ford's confidential secretary, Liebold replied, "Mr. Ford never threatens."[22]

All but one of the minority Ford holders came to terms with Ford's agents, though none, with a single exception, was aware of the fact that he was selling to Ford. Only Couzens, the hardest and the shrewdest of the lot, was able to better the terms that Ford proposed. First of all, Couzens refused to sell at any price until the ultimate buyer agreed to show his hand. Tough to the last, he carried his point in demanding a thousand dollars a share over and above what Ford had to pay the others.

But Ford, thanks to adroit legal advice, had bargained sharply all along the line. On the whole, his former partners had to come to him, on his terms. Had they been able to sell their shares on the open market, they would have come off twice as well. Several years later a financial syndicate was to offer Ford $1,000,000,000 for his interests. By such a reckoning, the minority shares of his company were worth four times over what he paid for them in 1919.

Even so, none of his minority owners had cause to brood over his fate. With the solitary exception of Mrs. Rosetta V. Hauss, Couzens' sister, each went his way a multi-millionaire. Couzens got $30,000,000; the Gray heirs, $25,000,000. To each of the other substantial holders —John Anderson, Horace Rackham, John Dodge and Horace Dodge— Ford paid out $12,500,000. For her twenty shares that had cost her a mere $100 originally, Mrs. Hauss received $260,000.

If the retiring shareowners of the Ford Motor Co. were reasonably content, so were the Fords. When the negotiations for Ford's purchases were all but finished in the summer of 1919, four months from the day Ford had threatened to desert ship, the New York *Times* quoted Edsel Ford as saying, "Of course, there will be no need of a new company now."[23]

Ford's new status represented a real shift of power; it left him in undisputed command of his business. He signalized this change by making pronouncements that were reminiscent of the Five-Dollar Day. Now that "parasites" could no longer feed on the profits of his business, Ford felt free to denounce the ritual of ownership which the highest tribunal of the state had risen to defend at the behest of the Dodges. He rededicated himself to mass production for the masses. Once more he promised to cater to the needs of society at large. It was his "ultimate desire,".he proclaimed, to convert the Ford Motor Co. into a "co-operative." When that day came, he said, his employes would enjoy the privileges that had formerly been lavished on his partners. It was his heart's desire, reported *Automotive Industries,* to keep on "cutting melons" with his workmen.[24]

## 4

It was this declaration of independence from "unproductive" stockholders, presumably, that made it possible for Ford to startle the world once more by going the Five-Dollar Day one better. On January 2, 1919, just before he had finished off his minority interests, he announced that, henceforth, he would pay his labor a minimum wage of six dollars a day. Actually, the new scale and the earlier Five-Dollar Day were identical twins. A rising labor turnover was common to both. From 1915 to 1919, this index of unrest had risen three-fold at Highland Park; it was a sign that the Five-Dollar Day had lost its magic and that Ford was, again, unable to hold his men. His workers had cause, indeed, for grumbling in the post-war years. By 1918 a number of automotive employers had caught up with the Ford scale of wages; some had gone beyond it. Moreover, in five years' time, the cost of living had risen in the city of Detroit 108 per cent.[25] In terms of what money could have bought in the locality in December 1914, the six-dollar scale itself was no fat wage in 1919; it boiled down, comparatively, to a pay-rate of 36 cents an hour for an eight-hour day.

When Ford began to notice this new restiveness in his shops, he first tried to meet it with words. In 1918 he started to publish a house organ entitled the *Ford Man*, in which his workers were coaxed to settle down and advised by poet Edgar Guest to "stick to the job you've got." When the signs of labor's disaffection only multiplied, Ford returned to the Couzens wage formula of 1914.

Like its more famous prototype, the Six-Dollar Day immediately made money rather than lost it for Ford. It traded higher wages for greater speed-up, with the balance of the exchange in Ford's favor, according to Dean Marquis, who was then directing the Ford Sociology Department. To reimburse himself for the six-dollar wage, Marquis relates in his Ford biography, Ford simply stepped up his conveyor belt to a "six-dollar speed."[26] Thanks to the new tempo, he doubled his production of automobiles in 1919, with only half again as many men as he had employed the year before.[*27] Small wonder that in his autobiography, written some time later, the manufacturer remarked, "The payment of five dollars a day for an eight-hour day was one of the finest cost-cutting moves we ever made, and the six-dollar day is cheaper than the five."[28]

But despite the fact that the money came pouring in faster than ever before, Ford still had his financial worries. Shortly after he began to capitalize on the profitable Six-Dollar Day, he needed $75,000,000 in cash for the purpose of buying out his partners. Rich as he was, he had no such surplus sum on tap. In order to dispose of Couzens and the others once and for all, he went to State Street and to Wall Street. He borrowed the $75,000,000 from the Old Colony Trust Company of Boston and the Chase Securities Corporation of New York City. As late as April 1921, he still owed these bankers many millions.

To repay his loans, Ford had counted on simply dipping into the current earnings of the Ford Motor Co. Such a plan seemed plausible enough. In 1920 the net profits of the company, after payment of taxes, were averaging $6,000,000 a month. They fell off the following year to a monthly average of $5,500,000. Yet the closer Ford came to

* Another factor contributed to this rise in productivity. The company had geared itself for peace-time production in the meantime. Throughout the year 1918, it had been turning out war goods as well as cars.

the date on which he would have to meet his commitments—in April, 1921—the greater his anxiety. His fears were well-grounded. Sales declined sharply early in 1920, and they revived only slightly in the summer months of 1920, when he had dropped the price of his touring car, f.o.b. Detroit, from $575 to $440, selling the Model T for less than it cost him to make it.

The crisis towards which Ford was headed was registered in his financial statement for December 31, 1920. From this accounting at the year's end, it appeared that although Ford's largest obligations would not fall due for the next four and one-half months, his liquid assets fell short of his current and prospective liabilities by some $9,-000,000.[29] While this deficit was remote rather than imminent and while it might never have materialized in view of the stupendous current profits of the Ford Motor Co., the margin of safety was slender at best. Rather than take a chance on the outcome, Ford resorted to a financial tour de force.

He conjured up the funds that he needed by compelling his dealers, from coast to coast, to act as his bankers. He shifted his debt, and more besides, to them. This expedient was so successful that it promptly added $50,000,000 to the liquid assets of the Ford Motor Co.—five times over the amount that was required to balance the books.[30] To make such a feat possible, even though the market for the Model T was slow, Ford worked up every bit of stock on hand into finished cars. He had a backlog of $88,000,000 worth of parts and supplies to play with. This material went into the hurried production of 93,000 surplus cars, none of which had been either sold or ordered.*

In the midst of a national depression in January 1921, Model T's began to rain on every Ford dealer in the United States. They were freighted, as usual, at the receiver's expense. Ford collected cash at the point of delivery for the cars. As was the custom of the trade, sight drafts were attached to the bills of lading.

The average Ford dealer was at a loss to know what to do with his special, unordered consignment of cars, but he accepted it willy-nilly. He did so knowing that he was complying with an order rather than a request. The dealers who rebelled, said the *Commercial and Financial Chronicle* of July 30, 1921, had their franchises cancelled. A few Ford agencies were literally overwhelmed. The *Chronicle* told of a certain Ford dealer in Indiana who was already oversupplied with

---

* This is the number of units which the company subsequently reported to the Federal Trade Commission. Laurence H. Seltzer, in his authoritative *Financial History of the American Automobile Industry*, puts the number of cars involved in this particular operation at 125,000.

new, unsold machines, when he learned that he was supposed to accept immediate delivery of an additional trainload of Model T's. He survived the experience only because a well-to-do friend bought up the entire lot and "startled the countryside by advertising a bargain sale of Ford cars."

Whatever may have happened to his dealers, Ford emerged from this transaction wholly solvent. By common consent he was now held to possess the powers of a financial magician, in addition to his other sundry talents. A measure of luck helped to give luster to his new character. Business improved so markedly in 1921, and consequently the prospects of most of Ford's dealers, that for the first time in its experience the Ford Motor Co. was able to build and market more than 1,000,000 cars in a single year. More than that, the "deal with the dealers" enabled Ford to pay off his debts without a hitch; and it was a tribute to the prestige of the Model T. For, in the end, unless he had believed in the Model T, the village banker and the small-town businessman would never have advanced the cash which the dealers in turn passed along to Ford. Finally, this neat piece of financing was managed in such a way that it clothed Wall Street in the dress of Goliath and Ford in the garb of David.

## 5

The dealers of the Ford Motor Co. were not alone in making it possible for Ford to lift himself up by his bootstraps and to write off his debts so spectacularly. Later on, in his own words, Ford was to make it perfectly clear that in pulling money "out of the air" or in finding untapped resources within his own organization, he had prodded his factory workers and his executive personnel as well as his dealers.

In his autobiography Ford told how in 1921 he managed to wring the same number of cars from the labor of 40 per cent fewer men than he had employed the year before.[31] To the Detroit *Saturday Night*, he later submitted even more startling information on the same point,[32] disclosing that in the year 1921 he had 30 per cent fewer workers, yet was able to double the production of the preceding season. Some 50,000 men not only did the work that had required more than 70,000 workers but out-produced this larger working force of the previous year besides, by a margin of half a million cars. The upsurge is all the more striking because it occurred in a short year. The Highland Park plant lay idle for the better part of January, 1921. Ford furloughed his factory help for a full month without pay, while he himself marked time, taking inventory and waiting for his dealers to pay cash for the unexpected consignment of some 100,000 cars. Then his factory workers, recalled to the shop at 60 or 70 per cent of their former strength, proceeded to increase production by 100 per cent in eleven months' time.

This enormous hiking of output was not the first of its kind at Highland Park. It was Ford's third memorable attempt to meet a crisis by pushing his labor. The Five-Dollar Day of 1914 had marked the first effort of this sort; the Six-Dollar Day, the second. Other periods of factory speed-up, less severe, had been ushered in as a matter of course year by year. It was routine procedure for Ford to make his men "dig for it" each time he dropped the price of the Model T.[33] The company never made a price reduction, John Dodge had already noted, without "more than making up for it" by a corresponding drop in its costs of operation, as often as not at labor's expense.[34] But the great push of 1921 differed from its forerunners of 1914 and 1919. It was wider in scope, faster in tempo, more ruthless in its methods and achieved far more by riding roughshod over the human element within the Ford organization.

Men rather than machines carried the brunt of the speed-up of 1921. The upsurge of production that followed the adoption of the Five-Dollar Day was more a question of fuller utilization of a technology that had hardly started to function and that was undergoing radical change every working day. But things were different in 1921. Ford's plant was more mature; its really revolutionary days were over. Hence the heightening of production that helped Ford to triumph over Wall Street came that much less from machine-power and that much more from manpower.

The extraordinary "man" speed-up of 1921 was in a class by itself in its motivation. The minimum wages of 1914 and 1919 had been special inducements, held out when times were good and workers hard to please. But the extra exertions and the more intense pace to which Ford labor submitted in 1921 went unrewarded, except for the fact that only the quickest, the most willing or the most desperate employes could survive, while the slow and the ailing or the rebellious lost their jobs. In general, Ford's better men geared themselves to the new speed-up because they had to. They had no other recourse, because in 1921 the industry and the nation as a whole were gripped by economic depression.

Ford was so sure of his men in such a labor market that he not only increased their output by 100 per cent, but he put into effect the most drastic wage reductions simultaneously. In the summer of 1921, said the *Commercial and Financial Chronicle*, the company "adjusted" its wage scale "downward" by 20 or 25 per cent.[35]

At the same time that he began to give his men less pay for doing twice as much work, Ford put an end to what someone once called the "era of good will" at the Ford Motor Co. The symbol of this departing era was the Ford Sociology Department, which had given itself over to the cultivation of thrift, character, a Christian home life and a desire to "stick to the job." In 1921 the department had no economic reason for being, so waiving its other functions, Ford sheared it off, and with it his man of good will, Dean Marquis. The passing of the institution was impudently remarked by the Detroit *Saturday Night*. "The sociology department, which was supposed to be Henry's pride and joy," said the *Saturday Night*, "has been whittled down until it can hardly be seen with the naked eye."[36]

As he beat a retreat from his paternalistic past, Ford stated his position in unmistakable terms. He bade farewell to reform in his autobiography of 1922. Paternalism, he wrote, is out of date. "I am not a reformer," he proclaimed, adding that "there is entirely too much attempt at reforming in this world and . . . we pay too much attention to reformers."[37] Had Ford forgotten momentarily that he was the exemplar of industrial statesmanship? Was this an admission that now, as ever, the manufacturer from Dearborn was at heart no Robert Owen? If so, such a lapse was not accented subsequently by his department of public relations. At least Ford's attitude toward the 20,-000 or more men whom he cut off in the midst of a nation-wide depression was one of individualism unalloyed. Of the social costs of this lay-off, he remarked autobiographically, "This does not mean that six out of fifteen men had lost their jobs" at his plant in 1921. His disemployed workers, he said, had only "ceased being unproductive."[38]

While he was at it, during the great sweep of the broom, Ford decided to clean house up to the roof, to do some firing and wage-cutting on the upper administrative and supervisory tiers. In his autobiography, he boasted of the fact that before he finished in 1921, he had discharged or rehired as bench-hands 75 per cent of his foremen. "Too many foremen sit at desks," and most of his former foremen, he reported in 1922, had to start life all over again. They were back where they came from, he wrote, at the foot of the ladder, in overalls, working "at machines." Into the discard with the bulk of his foremen and the desks of his foremen, he said, he had tossed 50 per cent of his

office force, 60 per cent of his intra-plant telephones, and his statistical
department in toto. The purge continued on into the top managerial
brackets of the company. Out with the desks and telephone extensions went an uncounted number of the more important executives and
factory supervisors—key men who had helped to make Ford and his
works possible. The foremost lieutenant who remained was the company's production manager, Charles E. Sorensen. It was Sorensen,
Ford's new factotum and chief of staff, who flew about the plant at
Highland Park in 1921, remorselessly efficient, pushing the factory at
white heat and chopping off the necessary heads—all at Ford's behest.

What of the high resolve, enunciated six years earlier, to convert
the Ford Motor Co. into a "co-operative?" In the eyes of the general
public, Ford was as good as his word at the start of the 20's. No one
was doing a better job of catering to the mass market, selling a sound
little car at a price the average man could afford. What of the promise,
once he had cleansed his house of "parasites," to keep on sharing
profits with his workers? Of that, the people of Detroit—businessmen
as well as mechanics—began to have their doubts. In 1921-1922, Ford
made an absolutely clear net profit of $200,000,000. Yet if he so much
as recalled the idea of "cutting melons" with his "partner-workmen,"
he kept it to himself.

## PART TWO
# Off the Assembly Line

Mr. Ford has a twenty-track mind.—*W. J. Cameron*

# Six

## OUT OF THE TRENCHES BY CHRISTMAS

### 1

BEFORE THE STRUGGLE for power at Highland Park had run its course, Ford allowed himself to be diverted. He began to stray from the assembly line in order to give battle to certain outside forces. He rode afield from 1915 to 1920, like a modern Don Quixote, laying siege to the citadels of privilege. His self-appointed antagonists, meanwhile, were Wall Street and the Jews, a rich and conservative newspaper, the Republican machine in the State of Michigan, as well as the men and institutions whom he held responsible for the first World War.

In his first effort as knight errant, Ford ran up the standard of a militant pacifism. His debut in world politics began in the summer of 1915 when the European war was entering its second year. His first skirmishes over the new terrain were purely verbal. They took the form of statements to the press that were studded with passionate denunciations of war. Most of these bristling manifestos were, in reality, the work of Theodore Delavigne, a Detroit newspaper reporter, whom Ford engaged as his pamphleteer and "peace secretary." Issued in the name of his distinguished patron, Delavigne's broadsides were all the more noteworthy in that Ford was swimming upstream. Wall Street had already forged an alliance with France and Britain. Pro-British sentiment was deep-seated in America. The advocates of military preparedness were in the saddle. Against such a combination of social forces, Ford flung himself headlong.

His interviews and statements of 1915 read like socialist hand-bills. Hot with fervor, they branded Europe's war a capitalists' war. The instigators of the conflict, Ford said, were the money-lenders, the absentee owners and the parasites of Wall Street. At one press conference he exclaimed, "New York wants war, but not the United States."[1] In another broadside he characterized the professional soldier as either "lazy or crazy."[2] On the day that Couzens tendered his resignation at Highland Park, after having broken with Ford over this same issue, Ford released a statement on the causes of war that was the most trenchant thing he had yet uttered on the subject. This time he named names. With consummate scorn he denounced the Morgan firm for sponsoring a half-billion dollar war loan to the Allies. The Anglo-French bankers who were then negotiating with the Morgan syndicate, he said, "ought to be tin-canned out of the country."

Ford proposed a course of action. First, he castigated the war profiteers of America by saying what he would do in the event the conflict abroad were to spread to the United States. Under such conditions, he prophesied, before accepting a single order for cars that might be used for military purposes—even though he were offered three times the normal price—he would burn his factory to the ground.[3] Next he issued a call to "the people" to stop the war by taking things into their own hands. He offered in August 1915 to pledge his entire "life and fortune" to the cause of peace.[4]

Before long Ford's peace plans took more specific form, thanks to the persistence and colorful personality of Rosika Schwimmer, an American feminist of Hungarian origin. Brilliant, handsome and persuasive, Mme. Schwimmer was courting support for a movement to end the European war by mediation. It was her belief, shared by a number of notable colleagues, that the conflict in Europe could be halted through the intervention of a congress of peace delegates drawn from the neutral countries. The mediators whom she hoped to enlist were to convene continuously in some neutral capital until peace terms could be drawn up that would prove acceptable to the belligerents. Before they could hope to win recognition or any official standing, the proponents of the "Schwimmer" plan were well aware of the fact that they would first have to rally popular support in each of the participating neutral nations.

As the ablest and most energetic advocate of this proposal, Mme. Schwimmer went to Detroit in the hopes of enlisting Ford's aid. Her plan and the declarations of her prospective patron had much in common. Both were predicated on direct action and the will of the people. Both hoped to cut through the red tape of diplomacy and to do what no neutral nation either dared or cared to initiate officially. Nothing seemed more fitting to Mme. Schwimmer than an attempt on her part to solicit the support of America's most celebrated and most highly regarded millionaire. In November 1915, therefore, she proceeded to Detroit, determined to see Henry Ford in person.

On the alert, none of Ford's intimates, particularly the secretary Ernest Liebold, would permit any such interview. These social censors could readily identify Mme. Schwimmer as one of the "inadmissibles." The feminist was just about to give up in disgust when Liebold left the city on a business trip. Then she slipped through what remained of the protective cordon, with the aid of a newspaperman. Once admitted to Ford's office, Mme. Schwimmer made the most of her opportunity. She put her case so convincingly that Ford invited her to have lunch at his home the following day. This second engagement fell on November 17, 1915.

At the Dearborn luncheon, not all the guests gave a friendly ear to Mme. Schwimmer's eloquent pleading. Her sketch of the projected Conference of Neutrals struck a responsive chord in her host and in the mind of Louis Lochner, then a Chicago pacifist who had been included in the party, but it did not impress Ford's wife and two other important guests. The principal listeners whom Mme. Schwimmer was unable to sway were two intimates of the Ford family, William Livingstone, a local banker, and the Very Rev. Samuel S. Marquis, then Dean of the Episcopal Cathedral of the city of Detroit. Pulled this way and that in the table conversation, Ford was none too comfortable, Lochner reported later. He was ill at ease and seemed afraid to express any opinions of his own. When he spoke at all he took aim at "a certain banker" who he felt was responsible for the war. To Mme. Schwimmer, herself a Jewess, Ford offered the opinion that "the Jews" were the promulgators of the war. As he dropped this hint, he airily tapped one of his pockets and said he "had the papers" to prove it.

But despite the charged atmosphere of the reception at Dearborn, and despite the vagaries of her host, Mme. Schwimmer carried the day. Her triumph was complete and instantaneous. Ford was so impressed that he rushed pellmell to carry her scheme into execution. At her suggestion he leaped at the idea of financing a "Peace Ship" for the purpose of transporting a delegation of American pacifists to a projected Conference of Neutrals. At the same time he resolved to go direct to the President to solicit for the expedition either official sanction or at least the blessings of the United States Government. Moving with vigor and confidence, Ford left for New York several days later in order to prepare for the coming pilgrimage. Quartered at the Belmont in what a certain New York newspaper soon caricatured as "the nut suite," he chartered a private steamer, the *Oscar II*. Lochner, Mme. Schwimmer and their colleagues, meanwhile, were busy trying to give the *Oscar II* an impressive passenger list.

The quixotic voyage of the *Oscar II* could not have hoped for a favorable press, on any terms. The American economy was already deeply committed to the cause of the Allies. After having floated a $500,000,000 Franco-British loan in the United States, the Morgan firm was acting as purchasing agent for the beneficiaries of this credit. American corporations were about to reap a harvest of war orders. Adroit British publicists were winning American sympathies. Against so powerful a coalition of forces, Ford was now flaunting his wealth as well as his heresy. None of his current utterances was calculated to soften the blows that were about to rain down upon him. Shortly before putting out to sea, he suggested that the soldiers in the trenches should call a general strike.[5] No conscientious objector could have excoriated the cause of war in more vitriolic terms. In a previous statement to the Detroit *News*, Ford had exclaimed, "Do you want to know the cause of war? It is capitalism, greed, the dirty hunger for dollars. Take away the capitalist," he said, "and you will sweep war from the earth."[6]

Taking its bearings from such a compass, the Peace Ship was doomed before it lifted anchor. It set sail, moreover, in the face of an organized campaign of derision for which Ford himself unwittingly supplied the themes. His every gesture served to provoke a press that was only waiting for the kill. To Oswald Garrison Villard, then editor of the New York *Evening Post*, Ford averred, "All you need is a slogan." Villard said, "Yes, Mr. Ford, what kind of a slogan?" "Oh, something like—'We'll get the boys in the trenches home by Christmas.' What do you think of that?" Villard was one of the few editors in New York who was not scoffing at the expedition. He pointed out to Ford that the *Oscar II* was one of the slowest steamers on the Atlantic, and that if the war ended the moment this vessel docked in Europe, the feat of moving 10,000,000 soldiers back to their homes by Christmas would have to be over and done with within a period of nine days. Grateful for Villard's correction, Ford said, "Oh, I hadn't thought of that. Well, we'll make it, we'll get the boys out of the trenches by Christmas."[7]

Sheathed in innocence and self-assurance, Ford blithely set out for Washington to see the President. With Lochner, he arrived in the capital hoping to get an endorsement from the White House. The audience with Wilson was described some years later in *America's Don Quixote,* Lochner's memoirs of the Ford expedition. The President carefully refrained from making any commitments. He was polite but evasive. When his guests were finally dismissed, they left empty-handed. Most of the time, said Lochner, Ford had sat in Wilson's presence, swinging his leg back and forth over the side of an armchair. Irritated because of the President's noncommittal attitude, he had held his tongue until Lochner and he were alone outside on the steps of the White House. Then in a rage, Ford told his companion what he thought of Wilson. He snapped, "He's a small man."[8]

Graciously rebuffed by the chief executive of the nation, the two men repaired to a theater in Washington for the purpose of addressing a women's peace rally. Here Ford made his second appearance as a public speaker.* He managed to get out a single sentence. He said, "I simply want to ask you to remember the slogan, 'Out of the trenches before Christmas, and never go back,' and I thank you for your attention." Flustered by the applause, the manufacturer reddened and retreated to the rear of the stage.

Such artless behavior on Ford's part was rich material for a metropolitan press that was both cynical and pro-British. It was fodder for a merciless effort to make the peace mission sound like comic opera. For purposes of caricaturing the "rich fool" or the "rustic innocent," nothing was handier than Ford's own homely, unaffected speech. It was in the mouth of a rural oaf that hostile reporters at the Belmont put Ford's prophecy that when the war was over, Europe would "grow up as quick as an onion"[9] or his ingenuous remark, "The Lord is with us . . . and we are going to follow the sunbeam right to the end."[10]

Into the hodgepodge of reporting and editorial writing at Ford's expense went every bizarre incident that occurred at the Belmont. This patchwork-quilt of hostility included the reported visit of a woman who offered to contribute what purported to be a patent medicine guaranteed to heal wounded soldiers. Another reporter told of an odd character who wandered into the Belmont headquarters, flippantly greeting its principal occupant as "the champion bug hunter." No journalistic art was required to burlesque what happened when some practical joker forged an invitation from Ford and sent it to Dr. Charles G. Pease, then a notorious anti-nicotine crusader with a pen-

---

* Ford's first recorded public address was delivered in 1915 to the inmates of Sing Sing penitentiary. To the lusty cheers of his audience Ford sheepishly mounted a raised platform in the dining room of the prison, only to stammer, "Boys, I'm glad to see you here. I've never made a speech in my life and never expect to."[11]

chant for haunting public places and snatching cigars out of people's mouths. Pease never joined the Ford party, but he accepted the fabricated invitation and his acknowledgment was duly reported by the press.

Men of substance added their voices to the chorus of ridicule. Col. Theodore Roosevelt lambasted the peace ship as the "most discreditable" exploit in history. On the floor of the upper house, Senator Thomas of Colorado characterized Ford's delegation as "an aggregation of neurotics." Arthur Vandenberg, then a newspaper editor in Michigan, referred to the *Oscar II* as a "loon ship."

Mocked and pilloried on every side, Ford of necessity lost much of the support which might have graced his expedition with prestige and dignity. Most of the substantial liberals and intellectuals on whom Mme. Schwimmer had been counting, discreetly snubbed an invitation to book passage on the *Oscar II* at Ford's expense. Many distinguished Americans wired their regrets: Jane Addams, Julius Rosenwald, Zona Gale, Charles P. Steinmetz, William Dean Howells, Ida Tarbell, Thomas Mott Osborne, David Starr Jordan, Cardinal Gibbons, Morris Hillquit and Margaret Wilson, the President's daughter. From the roster of outstanding public figures, even Ford's closest friends refused to enlist as co-mediators of peace. John Burroughs, John Wanamaker, Luther Burbank and Thomas Edison respectfully declined Ford's invitation. Not a single college president would come forward, though nearly every one of consequence was invited. Of the forty-eight governors who were sought as guests, only Gov. Hanna of North Dakota saw fit to accept the offer.

On the final passenger list there were, consequently, few names of note. The guests included eighty-three peace delegates drawn somewhat at random from the tiers of the less renowned in public life. Outside of a determined minority, the passengers were by no means even agreed on the object of their undertaking as it had been projected by Mme. Schwimmer. The bulk of the delegates the New York *Times* characterized as "rainbow chasers," "crack-brained dreamers" and "tourists." For full measure, and all at Ford's expense, the formal delegation was accompanied by a body of fellow-travelers: eighteen college students, fifty clerks and technical attachés, and fifty-seven members of the press.

As the *Oscar II* prepared to sail on December 4, 1915, comedy continued to plague her. At the dock someone handed Ford a cage that enclosed within its wrapper two squirrels. Caviling newspaper reporters promptly christened the little animals "Henry F. Acorn" and "William H. Chestnut." When William Jennings Bryan came to see the boat off, he was kissed by an elderly woman who wore white streamers reading "Peace At Any Price." Edison's brief reception was every bit as droll. When the inventor put in an appearance, Lloyd Bingham, an actor and one of the passengers, installed himself on the deck, megaphone in hand, acting as unofficial master of ceremonies. At Bingham's command, the crowd of 10,000 on the pier first honored Ford with a "hip-hip, hooray" salute. The same tribute was repeated for Edison as the cheerleader called out, "Here's the fellow who makes the light for you to see by. Three cheers for Edison." A "hobo" poet and magazine writer who was an accredited member of the press corps boarded ship with his bride-to-be. They were wedded at once in the ship's salon, with the captain of the *Oscar II* officiating at the ceremony. Ford and Bryan signed the certificate of marriage. These solemn rites had to be repeated in mid-ocean because the first ceremony was illegal. The couple's marriage license had been issued by the State of New York and the first union, to which Bryan and Ford attested, had been consummated while the *Oscar II* was still moored at the port of Hoboken, New Jersey.

Still other grotesque events marred the sailing of Ford's vessel. A band concert alternated with hymn singing on shore. As Ford stood quietly acknowledging the cheers of the crowd, a dozen women gathered around him singing "America." When the steamer was a few hundred feet from the pier, Urban J. Ledoux, who chose to call himself "Mr. Zero," dived in after it. When the crew of a river tug fished him out of the Hudson, Ledoux explained that he had only wanted to swim after the *Oscar II* "to ward off torpedoes."

Up to the final moment of embarkation, Ford's wife and advisers tried every expedient at their command to keep the peace ship from sailing under Ford's auspices. Most of the night before he sailed, Ford spent in the company of his friends Livingstone, the banker, and Marquis, the Episcopal dean, both of whom had opposed Mme. Schwimmer's proposals from the start. Imploring their wealthy friend to desert at the last moment, neither of these family intimates had the least success.[12] Unmoved by their appeals, Ford the following morning assigned his power-of-attorney to his son, Edsel, to provide for any emergency that might arise while he himself was at sea. Blocked on land, Mrs. Ford and several frantic Ford executives carried the fight to the Atlantic. They delegated to Marquis the task of weaning Ford from his fellow-travelers while the *Oscar II* was in passage. This practical-minded minister was promptly quartered in the King and

Queen's suite of the *Oscar II*. He was to share this space with Ford and with Ford's bodyguard, Ray Dahlinger.

## 2

Marquis' assignment to bring Ford back to Dearborn at any price was simplified by the circumstances of the voyage. Differences of opinion soon began to drive a wedge between various cliques within the delegation. The press intensified its effort to lampoon the expedition. Clashing personalities tugged this way and that at Ford, supplying fresh material for caricature and mockery.

Admittedly sincere, Mme. Schwimmer herself had personal limitations that disrupted the inner harmony of the voyage. Even the newspaper correspondents who conceded her charm and brilliance and her vast knowledge of foreign affairs had to agree that her manner was frequently lofty and imperious. Much ado was made of the feminist's "Black Bag," a controversial collection of "state" papers which presumably indicated the readiness of certain belligerents to consider a mediated peace. For some reason, the feeling toward this woman seemed to leave little middle ground aboard the peace ship. Long before the coast of Norway was sighted, she had become to different delegates or reporters the object of either the warmest respect or the coldest dislike. Her sex and her training in European politics may not have been the best qualification for coping with the situation. Perhaps no living soul cast in the same role as Ford's "peace adviser" could have done any better.

Like its prelude on shore, the overseas passage of the *Oscar II* was a journalist's holiday. With ingenuity and insolence the correspondents who covered the voyage more than fulfilled the instructions from the editors back home. Their stories read like comic strips.

Fresh reportorial hash was dished up because of a factional dispute within the delegation. In mid-ocean the "Ark of Peace" supposedly rocked with discord over President Wilson's preparedness proclamation. Mme. Schwimmer's followers were so opposed to the presidential edict that they drafted and approved an anti-preparedness resolution. Marquis and another bloc of Ford's guests supported the President. In the news columns back home, the anti-Schwimmer faction became the "insurrectionists." War was being waged within the aching hull of a "peace" ship. The stories of "mutiny" aboard the *Oscar II* became so lurid that the officers of two passing vessels are supposed to have volunteered to come to the aid of the captain of Ford's ship.

Unaware of the figure they were cutting in the big eastern papers at home, the serious-minded delegates on the *Oscar II* held fast to their aims. They gathered in the ship's second-class dining room for earnest discussions that ranged over the whole field of liberal thought, from the single tax to mothers' pensions and women's suffrage. With common consent, the entire delegation addressed an appeal for a truce to the President of the French Republic and to each of the ruling heads of Europe.

Ford, meanwhile, fell more and more under Marquis' spell, keeping pretty much to himself. Most of the passengers saw him only at meal times, when it was his custom to chat with whatever group took his fancy. At odd intervals he called to task this or that passenger whom he discovered violating one of his own moral scruples. He asked one of his guests, an intelligent, mature woman, what her parents would think if they could see her smoking cigarettes. Her rejoinder was that both of her parents smoked. Shifting to different ground, Ford insisted that the nicotine habit was "bad for the bowels." Lochner maintained that to a permanent employe of the Ford Motor Co. who appeared to be rooted in the ship's bar, Ford remonstrated, "You cut out the booze or I'll have you fired when you get back to the United States."[13]

As to the actual mechanics of the mission to Europe, Ford seemed to be no clearer than he had been during the interview with Villard. In the judgment of William C. Bullitt, who covered the voyage for the Philadelphia *Public Ledger,* the industrialist remained the "tenderest of the tender and the vaguest of the vague, a comic, charming child." Only once on the voyage was Ford truly himself. He dropped out of sight only to be found down below, happily inspecting the ship's machine shop and the engine room.

On the last leg of the journey, Dean Marquis seized the big chance to turn Ford against the idea of lingering in Europe with his "pilgrims." Ford was closeted in his stateroom with a bad cold, feeling out of sorts and allowed to see no one but Dr. Marquis. During this interval of segregation, the persuasive clergyman finally managed to make Ford promise that he would start home the moment *Oscar II* touched Norwegian waters. On one occasion, during his illness, Ford was disturbed by some reporters who burst into his suite just to satisfy their curiosity. One of their number, a little more graceless than his fellows, exclaimed, "Mr. Ford, J. Pierpont Morgan was dead six hours before any newspaper knew about it. We won't be scooped that way this time. So we've come to see for ourselves whether you are still alive."[14]

When the *Oscar II* docked at Christiania, Ford was still very much alive, though cold-ridden. Under doctor's orders he was bundled off to bed at the Grand Hotel. Marquis superintended the rest cure. He stood watch over his charge as though entrenched in a sentinel box. His room lay between Ford's and the corridor. The clergyman meant to have no peace delegates upset the plan to spirit Ford back to New York on the next available boat. Meanwhile the patient became ever more anxious to quit the expedition. Left alone for hours in a gloomy sickroom, he grew increasingly restless and eager for action of any sort.

When he was finally out of bed and every detail for a quick departure had been prearranged, Ford and his bodyguard and Dr. Marquis slipped out of the Grand Hotel. They made their exodus at 4 A.M. of a bitter morning on the day before the Christmas when, according to plan, the soldiers were to have evacuated the trenches. In the excitement of the flight, the suave and meticulous dean had to brave the weather without socks or underwear. The temperature outside was twenty-two degrees below zero.

Anticipating the escape, certain delegates massed in protest in the lobby of the hotel. They hurled epithets at Marquis as Ford's party was whisked into a waiting automobile. To expedite the exit, one of Ford's conspirators had arranged to have on hand a flying wedge of employes recruited from a local branch of the Ford Motor Co.

Homeward bound, Marquis made the most of his intimacy with Ford for purposes of further indoctrination. He tried to convince his charge that the peace expedition was laudable, but in theory only. The clergyman then strove to implant in Ford's mind the maxim that the shoemaker should stick to his last. His temporary dominance over the manufacturer was not achieved, apparently, without a struggle. Ford had resisted the rector's personal magnetism and his skillful campaign to scuttle the peace ship. At the Grand Hotel, he had revealed this conflict to Lochner. Clutching Lochner's arm, Ford had said, "Can't you get me something on the Dean?"[15] Mme. Schwimmer reports a similar conversation. To her, Ford is supposed to have said, "I know Marquis is a liar. But give me some concrete facts. Get something on Marquis." Despite such wavering, however, the quixotic industrialist finally yielded to the clergyman.

Like a fish out of water, Ford was only too glad to get home. A day or so after he reached Dearborn, he admitted to some friends that he would sooner work at his desk for the next twenty-five years without a vacation than "go through this thing again."[16]

Nor had he returned a much wiser man. He was still convinced that "the Jews" had fomented the war. He told John Reed that the "wrong people" had made the trip to Europe, that if he were to sponsor a peace ship all over again he would take with him the "whole village of Dearborn" rather than the people who "went along before." In the talk with Reed, he also picked on alcohol as a primary cause of war. Liquor, he said, had helped to bring on the struggle by making Germans and Frenchmen "suspicious" of one another.[17] The only thing he learned from the peace expedition, he told his friend E. G. Pipp sometime later, was that he could probably sell a vast number of tractors to Russia.

Bereft of the company of their renowned patron, the stranded peace delegates were surprisingly well received in the Scandinavian countries and in Holland and Switzerland. Though most of the favorable reception in these countries was unofficial and nongovernmental, the response was far more serious and substantial than any backing which Ford's movement had elicited at home. Reputable members of the Swiss and Swedish parliaments came forward to endorse the Conference. These supporters were joined by a significant number of feminists, intellectuals and Social Democrats. The lower house of the Swedish parliament unanimously approved a resolution urging the government to call an official neutral conference. In the French tongue the term "Fordisme" was coined to denote the act of cutting through diplomatic red-tape by means of direct, popular intervention. From its headquarters at The Hague, the committee of delegates that hung on in Europe after Ford's departure issued an Easter "Appeal to the Belligerents" that antedated much of the letter and spirit of Wilson's fourteen points.

However, after Ford's withdrawal only a remnant of the original delegation carried on. Still subsidized from Dearborn, the survivors became attachés of what persisted for some months as the Neutral Conference for Continuous Mediation. Mme. Schwimmer severed her ties to the Conference in February, 1917. The skeleton that remained was left pretty much to the mercy of Plantiff, the Ford salesman, to whom the complete financial control of the expedition had been delegated. Plantiff lingered on, as Bullitt reported to the Philadelphia *Public Ledger,* just to give the "corpse a decent burial."

## 3

Though his expedition petered out in 1916, Ford's pacifism still flamed at home. He continued to harangue the "Wall Street Tories" and the "armor-plate patriots." In paid advertisements he charged that "imperialists" and "profiteers" were "arming both sides" for the purpose of exploiting "the common people" who would have to "pay the bills" in the end.[18] As a result of one of these burning epistles, he was sued by the Navy League. During the memorable interview with John Reed, Ford ridiculed flags as "silly rallying points" of use only to militarists, profiteers and "crooked politicians" just "to get people excited when they want to fool them." When the war was over, he told Reed, he intended to haul down the American colors over his factory and to hoist in its stead a "Flag of All Nations," to be designed by his own artists.

The last outward show of Ford's total opposition to the war fell away the moment the United States severed diplomatic ties with Germany. When America finally declared war, Ford proclaimed that move to be "the best thing that ever happened."[19] He urged the nation to "back our Uncle Samuel with a shotgun loaded to the muzzle with buckshot."[20]

But on one vital issue, where his most personal interests were involved, Ford still held fast to his anti-war convictions. That was when the name of his son was drawn for military service in August, 1917. Edsel was nearly twenty-four at the time. Despite parental objections, he had been willing to enlist and he had refused to accept a civilian "swivel-chair" commission. For understandable reasons, his mother opposed his going to war. The father took the matter to heart for reasons of his own. He later told his friend E. G. Pipp that had Edsel been included in the draft, "certain interests" who disliked "the Ford system" of doing business would "have seen to it" that his son never returned.[21]

To contest Edsel's eligibility under the Selective Service Act, the attorneys of the Ford Motor Co. first appealed the case to the local draft board. They contended that the son was indispensable to the Ford industries and largely responsible for filling the war orders which had been allocated to the Ford Motor Co. When counsel argued this appeal, Edsel was acting as the secretary of his father's corporation. The local board could find no ground for special exemption. Representatives of the Ford family then took the case to the White House. The President never ruled on the appeal. Edsel's case was eventually disposed of to his father's satisfaction under Army regulations which allowed for the exemption of key men in a war industry.

Because of the effort to spare his son from front-line service, Henry Ford again ran afoul of the press and the jingoists. Congressman Nicholas Longworth, the son-in-law of Col. Roosevelt, dropped the indelicate slur that of seven persons in the world who were certain to go through the war unscathed, six were the sons of the Kaiser and the seventh was Edsel Ford.[22] Ford's "unpatriotic" pre-war utterances were resurrected and flaunted, such as an alleged boast that he would "stand up and be shot" rather than fight "under any circumstances,"[23] and an earlier remark that no man could be blamed "for avoiding military service."[24] The rural press of Michigan was heartless. The Clare County *Cleaver* nominated Edsel as the leader of the "office-chair cavalry." "All his life," ranted the Ishpeming *Iron Ore*, "he will be singled out as a slacker and a coward." Much of this baiting was reprinted in full by the Detroit *Saturday Night* under the headline, "Concerning the Exemption of Edsel Ford."[25]

However, when the *Saturday Night* began to make an issue of Edsel's war record, it was giving expression to something more than pure love of country. Its editor was more concerned with the killing which many of his influential readers expected to make on war contracts. He had already said as much. Gloating in anticipation of these riches, he remarked on one occasion that no "enterprising American" in the city of Detroit would be "caught napping." Those Detroit manufacturers who put the pocketbook first were certain they had a traitor in their midst when Ford, the heretic, rose up to volunteer, in the event America should go to war, to place his industrial resources at the disposal of the federal government on a non-profit basis. The lance that grazed the son was intended for the father. With the gibes it threw at Edsel, the Detroit *Saturday Night* was, in reality, getting back at Henry.

Unperturbed by such treatment, the elder Ford began to fit himself into the nation's war program. His largest contract from the government called for the construction of a new type of submarine-chaser. The vessel he agreed to build was known as the "Eagle" boat. Naval engineers had designed it. Dated March 1, 1918, the Ford contract specified that 112 Eagles would be delivered within the next ten and one-half months.

The wizardry which Ford was expected to bring to this project was trumpeted as widely as the offer to serve the nation "for nothing." Early in February 1918, Ford laid the keel of the first "Eagle." This accomplishment called for a ceremony at which Secretary of the Navy Daniels prophesied that the mass production of Ford's "Eagle" would shatter "all previous records" for building similar vessels. Later in the same month it was announced that the Ford sub-chaser had already reached the stage of quantity production. As time went on, the story improved. In the spring, 10,000 employes of the Ford Motor Co. marched in a body down the streets of Highland Park, flaunting a banner that read, "An Eagle a Day Keeps the Kaiser Away." In mid-summer the New York *Times* reported under the headline, "Warships While You Wait," that "Eagles" were being hatched like "flivvers." The last of these claims was circulated in the fall of 1918, after Ford decided to run for a seat in the United States Senate. His campaign literature said that "Eagles" had been "launched regularly," exceeding "all expectations" of the Navy Department.

None of these appraisals seemed to fit the record of actual performance. Nine days after the Armistice was signed it came out that only one of the 112 boats that the Ford Motor Co. had contracted to build was actually in commission. Even this lone "Eagle" was still undergoing preliminary trial maneuvers. Such was the testimony of Rear Admiral Ralph Earle, chief of the Ordnance Bureau, before the House Committee on Naval Affairs.[26] So great was the excitement generated by this revelation in Washington that Senator Lodge of Massachusetts proposed a Senate investigation to determine whether or not Ford was entitled to the $50,000,000 that his contract stipulated.

Quite unjustly the Detroit *Saturday Night* classed Ford's short-comings on his naval assignment as the "biggest industrial scandal of the war."[27] So severe an indictment was groundless in view of the record of the automobile industry as a whole. Most of the automotive producers in the trade had had similar difficulties.[28] In aviation alone their fumbling had cost the taxpayers hundreds of millions of dollars.* Such a showing was simply proof that American technology, mighty as it was, could not have hoped to convert for war painlessly or overnight. Ford was no exception. If his struggles with a complex, unfamiliar commodity were in any way unique, they became so chiefly on the basis of the over-statements which emanated from Highland Park.

Ford bore two other brain-children during the war, proposals for American ordnance on land and sea, that in no wise enhanced his stature as an industrial superman. The first of these conceptions con-

---

* A subcommittee of the Senate Committee on Military Affairs brought out in August, 1918 that the initial war-appropriation of $640,000,000 for aircraft production had been "practically wasted." After being in the war for sixteen months, not a single chassis or complete combat plane of American manufacture had arrived in France. In the opinion of the subcommittee a major reason for this delay was that too large a proportion of the aircraft program had been assigned to the automobile producers of Detroit who were relatively inexperienced in the field of aeronautics.

cerned a "peewee" or "jitney" submarine. This invention was to have been a one-man submarine, powered by a standard Ford motor, weighing in all not more than three tons, and so contrived that its operator could direct and explode his bombs with a "pill" on a "pole." The pilot of the "mosquito sub" was to have attached his pill (or bomb) to the side of an enemy vessel by means of a pole.[29] Ford was reported by the New York *Times* to be willing to stake his reputation as a manufacturer on the success of the projected "U-flivver." A marine engineer advanced the opinion that Ford's "baby sub" would never go "beyond the conversational stage."[30] This forecast seems to have had reason on its side.*

Ford's thought for the land forces was somewhat more feasible. He proposed building a "flivver tank" which was to be nothing more nor less than a Model T, only one with a thicker hide and a different set of limbs. As described by *Automotive Industries,* this piece of equipment was to differ from a standard Ford car in having a shell of armor-plate and caterpillar traction instead of wheels. The chassis and the engine were to be carried over intact from the Model T. The first specimens of this light armored tank were not conspicuously successful. Their limitations were all too evident in a motion picture film which Ford prepared for the benefit of the military experts. One of the scenes showed a "baby tank" trying to cross a trench. The bouncing little vehicle simply plumped into the recess, landing on its nose. When the army men wanted to know how the "whippet" tank could ever get around such traps, Ford is said to have replied, "Send them over in droves. We'll have so many of them, the stranded ones can be used for the 'vast army' that follows to cross over."[31] Had the war continued, perhaps the engineering brains of the Ford Motor Co. might have developed their light, armored tank as a significant addition to the arts of warfare. As it was, their first specimens were not a conspicuous success.

Both the sub and the flivver tank demonstrated that Ford's mechanical talent, immense though it was, was not universal. On war orders where the products in demand were more familiar and more akin to the automobile, the Ford Motor Company acquitted itself with unimpeachable zeal and skill. Its vast program of military production included thousands of trucks and ambulances, 5000 Liberty motors,

* Ford's critic marshalled these arguments against the miniature U-boat: it would have been too small to navigate in open water or in heavy seas; with a projected speed of eight knots it could not have competed with battle cruisers that were capable of twenty knots; its ordinary gasoline motor, lacking an air supply, would not have run under water.

an immense quota of parts for the Liberty engine, 10,000 caissons and 2,000,000 steel helmets.[32]

The necessity of accepting any war orders at all at Highland Park forced Ford into a compromise of his own making. He had to go back on the boast of 1915 that rather than operate as munitions maker he would first raze his factory. But the shift from pacifist to purveyor of armaments was as adroit as it was unavoidable. The manufacturer covered this moral retreat by reiterating the pledge to remit to the federal government whatever profits he might derive by trafficking with war.

But in proclaiming his intention to manufacture munitions at cost, Ford had reckoned without his minority stockholders. Couzens and the Dodge brothers were then still on the scene. These men immediately protested, insisting that the company accept its government contracts on standard terms. Ford qualified his position. He owned 58 per cent of the company's stock. He promised therefore to keep his eye on a corresponding portion of the profits on all war contracts. These earnings—his own—he repeated, would be returned to the nation at the end of the war.[33] No "blood money" for him!

From that day to this, the public has been reminded over and over again of the purported benefaction. As each new commodity of war was added to the production schedule at Highland Park in 1918, an appropriate statement was fashioned to call to mind the nonprofit character of Ford's war effort. His attorney at the time, Alfred Lucking, advised the Senate Committee on Military Affairs that not a penny of profit would be charged on the "Eagle" contracts.

Here Ford's repudiation of the fruits of war rested for a time, breeding incalculable good will for the Ford Motor Co. Only the publication in 1922 of a biography entitled *The Truth About Henry Ford* disturbed the quiet rise of a legend. Sara T. Bushnell, the author of this volume, made the assertion that Ford had gone so far as to restore to the federal treasury the sum of $29,000,000 in war profits. In the preface of her work, Miss Bushnell acknowledges that most of her material was supplied by Mrs. Henry Ford. One Detroit weekly alleged that the finished manuscript had been gone over in the Ford home.[34]

The truth of Miss Bushnell's report was immediately contested by Secretary of the Treasury Mellon and by the Treasury's Undersecretary, S. Parker Gilbert. The Treasury Department, said these gentlemen, had no record of the alleged $29,000,000 refund or of any war refund whatsoever from Ford or the Ford Motor Co.[35] The War Department announced concurrently that for all transport units delivered to the government Ford had received the standard price. The Navy Department then said the same for the "Eagle" boat.[36] Miss Bushnell was soon advised by the heckling Detroit *Saturday Night* to give her work a new sub-title: "What we would like the world to think about pa."

The Fords waited for thirty days and then countered with an evasion. To Andrew Mellon, the senior Ford asserted that he had not seen Miss Bushnell's biography in print, that he was unaware of its content, and that he had never authorized its publication. Eighteen months later, when a Ford presidential boom was in the making, Ernest Liebold informed the press that the audit of Ford's war profits was a "huge job" and was still in progress. When it was finished, he said, Ford would "do as he said."*[37]

The story of the one American millionaire who would not be soiled by the lucre of the first World War was to be told and retold for the next generation. In one of its issues which the Detroit *Saturday Night* devoted in 1935 to a history of the Ford Motor Co., the statement appears that "Henry Ford turned back to the government every cent of profit he had made from war contracts."[42] The *Saturday Night* got its material for this claim and for the body of its Ford issue direct from the publicity department of the Ford Motor Co. A group of Lutheran ministers honored Ford on his seventy-fifth birthday in 1938 as the "only rich man of note who had an opportunity to coin money out of the blood of nations during the World War, and refused to do so."[43] The tale cropped up again in a pocket biography of Ford, *The Triumph of An Idea*, written by Ralph H. Graves. Free copies of this little volume were still being circulated by the public relations department at Dearborn as late as 1940. Other writers and journalists of repute have since attributed to Ford this same generous act.

* Just what Ford made on his war contracts is not a matter of public record. However, the Federal Trade Commission has computed the net "war-time" earnings of the *corporation*.[38] But only part of this income came from war work. At the Couzens' tax hearing, P. E. Martin, then Ford's vice president, testified that 60 per cent of the company's floor space had been given over to war production.[39] According to *Automotive Industries*, on the other hand, by September 1918, Ford was filling war orders and nothing else.[40] When Edsel's draft status was up for discussion, one of his lawyers contended that war contracts were being placed at Ford's at the rate of $40,000,000 a month.[41] At any rate, from the date the United States entered the war until December 1918, the Ford corporation reported a net profit after taxes of approximately $78,000,000. Its net earnings for the following year—some of which must have come from war receipts—were $64,000,000. Henry Ford's personal share in all this was close to $45,000,000 in 1917-1918; and from 1917-1919, approximately $82,000,000.

In reality, Ford never "did what he said." Neither upon the completion of the audit to which Liebold referred nor at any time subsequently could he bring himself to part with the profits that he had chosen to renounce voluntarily. At least the Treasury Department has denied receipt of any such reimbursement as recently as 1939. By the same token Ford could not bear to make a clean breast of the fact that he had broken his word. On the contrary, he was content to let the legend stand—even to foster it—with nothing out of pocket.

This conflict between fact and pretension may explain some of Ford's later views on war and peace. It may have helped to make memories of the peace ship that much more painful. At least when he published his autobiography in 1922, the manufacturer was content to devote no more than one hundred and fifty words to the episode. In one of his later publications, *Today and Tomorrow*, he made a complete about-face. Pacifists, he said in this work, are "specialists in sentimentality" concerned only with making a people "soft."*[44]

## Seven

### HISTORY IS BUNK

### 1

WHEN "INCIDENTS" along the Mexican border led Washington to muster out the National Guard in 1916, Ford was soon embroiled in yet another encounter that lured him from the assembly line. He bitterly opposed the idea of American intervention. In the course of airing this opposition, he was quoted as saying that he would never reemploy any of his workers who so much as volunteered for border duty with the national militia. His statement to this effect was first reported by the Chicago *Tribune*. The story appeared in the *Tribune* under the heading "Flivver Patriotism." The following day the "World's Greatest Newspaper" made bold to call Henry Ford, editorially, an "ignorant idealist" and an "anarchist." Ford promptly sued for libel. For damages he asked $1,000,000.

* Even the peace ship itself eventually went over to the enemy. Twenty years after its famous passage to Norway, the *Oscar II* was sold—over the bid of King Christian of Denmark—to the munitions makers.

After three years of preliminary fencing, the case finally went to trial in the summer of 1919 at Mt. Clemens, Michigan, a small county seat outside Detroit. The setting for the contest that was to follow smacked of the American hinterland. The jury included a road inspector and eleven farmers. The judge in the case decreed as one of his first acts that he would dismiss the panel every evening so that its members could return to their homes to tend "their livestock." In the corridor of the little red-brick courthouse in Mt. Clemens hung a wall sign that supplied the perfect rustic touch. The sign read, "If you spit on the floor in your own house, do it here. We want you to feel at home."

Barnum and Bailey's circus could have brought no greater excitement than Ford's trial to this sleepy village. Many of the defense witnesses were imported from the Texas border. Some indeed could have qualified as circus performers. A score of them were cattle ranchers who loitered about Mt. Clemens for a month in full regalia. They sported sombreros, embroidered riding boots and holsters for their six-shooters. Their function on the stand was to recite the horrors of "rape" and "massacre" along the Rio Grande at the time that Pancho Villa was riding over the mesas. (It was the *Tribune's* argument that such border incidents had given Washington ample cause for intervention.) Some of Ford's witnesses were quite as colorful. His legal staff had brought more than a hundred Mexicans to Detroit for cross-examination.

The citizens of Mt. Clemens were goggle-eyed over the scale of the litigation. To accommodate its principals and witnesses, Ford's staff commandeered a suite of twenty-five rooms in the Colonial Hotel. Equally grand, the forces of the Chicago *Tribune* engaged a rival hotel. At trial Ford was flanked by seven lawyers to the *Tribune's* eight. Each set of attorneys had its own battery of private detectives on the scene. When Ford took time out on one occasion to have his shoes cleaned, the shoe-shining parlor was surrounded by a group of operatives whom the Detroit *News* described as "the old-fashioned bouncer type." Before long Ford counsel accused agents for the *Tribune* of tapping telephone wires. But Ford's experts in espionage were no less ingenious. Each side had detectives and research workers who had scoured the country for all of three years.

If the jury ever drowsed in the stuffy, baking courtroom as the trial wore on, it was not the fault of counsel. No case in the history of the Michigan bar was ever prosecuted more acrimoniously. Distinguished opposing counsel hurled taunts and jibes across the table. They exchanged such epithets as "slimy" and "yellow." More than once the competing attorneys narrowly missed coming to blows. The 64-year-old judge who rode the storm for fourteen weeks is said to have been hastened to his grave. By the time each litigant had his say, the venerable jurist, thoroughly wilted, lamented, "I have been talked almost to death." Two million words had been entered in the record.

As is customary in a libel action, the *Tribune* set out to impugn the plaintiff's character and intelligence. To justify the epithet which had been flung at Ford, defense counsel sought to establish the widest possible definition of the word "anarchist." By such a tactic, the Chicago paper hoped to prove that Ford was stupid, naive, uneducated and unpatriotic, and *quod erat demonstrandum,* a dangerous "anarchist." Chief counsel for the *Tribune* was the late Elliott G. Stevenson, one of Detroit's best-liked and most brilliant lawyers. A master of invective, renowned for his capacity to worry a witness to death, Stevenson had already impaled Ford in a courtroom. He had represented the Dodge brothers in the Ford stockholder suit. It was such a mind that took Ford in hand for six consecutive days of cross-examination. Stevenson went to work almost sadistically.

Forewarned that the defense meant to dig into the recesses of his client's mind, Alfred Lucking, Ford's principal attorney, made a valiant effort to come into court forearmed. Up in Ford's hotel suite, he instituted a series of cram-sessions given over to the rudiments of American history. His tribulations as a coach were later recounted by E. G. Pipp, the journalist who was then about to take over the editorship of Ford's Dearborn *Independent*.[1]

"At the end of the day's trial in court, the attorney would get Ford in his room in the hotel and drill him in the early history of the country. The attorney would begin with, 'Now don't forget this; remember the evacuation of Florida . . .' But Ford would be out of his seat, looking out the window.

" 'Say, that airplane is flying pretty low, isn't it?' he would ask.

"Again the attorney would steer him to the chair, but Ford would hop to the window with, 'Look at the bird there, pretty little fellow, isn't it? Somebody around here must be feeding it, or it wouldn't come back so often.' "

Ford's failure to concentrate on the chore of swallowing so many pellets of miscellaneous information is not surprising. Any learner might well have resisted such a program of forced feeding. To Lucking's restive pupil, then in his fifty-sixth year, the experience was abnormally annoying and unprofitable. It was completely foreign to Ford's interests; it demanded a type of concentration which he rarely displayed even when his mind was functioning at its best on matters that concerned him.* Naturally, the manufacturer was somewhat humbled when his attorney resolved to "bring him up to date." "The moment Lucking concluded one of his drills," said E. G. Pipp, "Ford would slip out of that door like a child who had been made to stand in the corner for a time and just had been released from the punishment."

Then the day of reckoning arrived. Once on the stand, Ford was thoroughly in character. He tilted his chair back with his feet on the rungs, cupping his chin in either hand, crossing and recrossing his legs, or lolling back with a bony knee clasped between his fingers. As Stevenson closed in on the witness, the court was showered with objections. As often as not, Ford would answer without paying the slightest attention to the cross-fire of his own attorneys. Generally good-natured, but twitching occasionally under the sting of Stevenson's questioning, he was compelled to think aloud for a solid week. His performance was what anyone might have expected from a farmer or a mechanic of the Middle West who worked with his hands most of his life, so busy grubbing in machine shops that he had never found time for much schooling or self-education.

Stevenson borrowed a good deal of his ammunition from the dictionary. He began to harry the witness with words of more than one syllable.

*Stevenson:* Are you ignorant of the fundamental [principles] of this government?

*Ford:* I don't know what you mean by the fundamental principles.

*Stevenson:* You don't know what the fundamental principles of government mean?

*Ford:* Do you mean the Constitution?

*Stevenson:* Do you know what the fundamental principles of the government mean?

*Ford:* I don't understand it, Mr. Stevenson.[3]

Counsel for the *Tribune* was taking his cue from the sort of replies Ford had given during the Dodge litigation two years before,[4] such as:

*Question:* Do you know when the case was commenced?

*Answer:* What do you mean, "commenced"?

* At any business conference, Ford was characteristically quick and short, seldom verbose. In moments of self-analysis, he was given to describing his stream of thought as a series of "hunches" or "jumps." His business companions of the period say that as a listener Ford could never hold himself to any given topic under discussion for more than five or six minutes at a time. Much of his strength as a captain of industry rested on his ability to forget the irrelevant detail. He testified during the Dodge trial, "I don't try to recollect anything that I want to forget. I only try to touch the high spots."[2]

*Question:* Do you know what "commenced" means?
*Answer:* Not very much acquainted with technical terms.

Soon Ford was adrift in a veritable sea of words. He gave up altogether on "chile con carne." He defined "a large mobile army" as "a large army mobilized." Asked to give the meaning of "ballyhoo," he replied, "Oh, a blackguard or something of that nature."

Stevenson then moved on from vocabulary to history. The classic portion of the testimony that followed had to do with a story which every American schoolboy can repeat from memory.

*Q:* Have there been any revolutions in this country?
*A:* Yes.
*Q:* When?
*A:* In 1812.
*Q:* One in 1812, eh? Any other time?
*A:* I don't know of any others.
*Q:* Do you know that this country was born in a revolution?
*A:* Yes, in 1776.
*Q:* Did you forget that revolution?
*A:* I guess so.

*Q:* Do you know what forced us into the Revolutionary War?
*A:* No, I do not.

*Q:* Do you know of any great traitors?
*A:* No.
*Q:* Who was Benedict Arnold?
*A:* He was a writer, I guess.
*Q:* He was a writer, was he? You must be thinking of Arnold Bennett.

Sara Bushnell, the biographer who was misinformed about Ford's war profits, contends that Ford was wool-gathering so that he missed this question. All he caught was the word "Bennett," she says, because he was relaxing at the moment by whittling the sole of one of his shoes with an old pocket-knife.[5]

At regular intervals throughout the grilling, Stevenson tried to broaden the scope of the attack by asking the victim to "read something" for the court. As sly as his inquisitor, Ford parried the question more than once by saying he had left his spectacles at home. He also added what millions of his admirers would have confessed had they been as frank, namely, that he seldom read anything but newspaper headlines anyhow. Stevenson picked up the same trail for a final chase.

*Question:* Mr. Ford, I have some hesitation but I think in justice to yourself I shall ask this question: I think the impression has been created by your failure to read some of these things that have been presented to you, that you could not read. Do you want to leave it that way?

*Answer:* Yes, you can leave it that way. I am not a fast reader and I have the hay fever and I would make a botch of it.

This salty reply and others equally pert bear witness to the fact that Ford was far from bested in all the exchanges with his inquisitor. Anything but a pathetic figure, he spoke up tartly time and again, displaying something of a gift for short, clean, Anglo-Saxon speech.* He had a way of turning some of Stevenson's questions so artlessly that they fell infinitely short of their purpose. When his tormentor once asked him to explain, "What was the United States originally?" Ford said, "Land, I guess." Cornered by some other conundrum, the manufacturer got off the most intelligent sentence that was uttered during the entire trial. He snapped at Stevenson, "I could find a man in five minutes who could tell me all about it."

After fourteen weeks of wrangling, the prosecution and the defense finally rested. Had the designation of Ford as an "anarchist" been libelous? If so, what was the injury worth to the plaintiff in monetary terms? The jury debated the question for ten hours and found in favor of Ford. Their neighbor, they held, had in fact been libeled. The *Tribune* was then ordered to stand the costs of the case and to pay over to Henry Ford in token damages the sum of six cents! Both litigants claimed a moral victory. To achieve that satisfaction, each had spent something like $500,000. At the conclusion of the experience on the stand, Ford is said to have sworn that "never again" would he submit to a similar ordeal.

## 2

To forestall any comparable experience, a number of readjustments were effected immediately at Dearborn. Each of these expedients was to influence Ford's subsequent development.

* His own publicists were to conceal this faculty. Ford's own speech, as recorded by a court stenographer, and most of his formal statements, phrased by his writing men, are as unlike as two different dialects. On the Peace Ship, Ford suggested a number of strong, simple statements. But the intellectuals aboard the *Oscar II* reworked these offerings. Ford often sanctioned the stiffly worded substitutes admiringly.

First, the barrier that separated the manufacturer from the outside world at once grew thicker. Bodyguards and secretaries began to take up more and more space in Ford's private life. This screening soon made its subject as inaccessible as the Grand Lama. Next, Ford added a corps of publicists and writers to his personal staff. These new retainers were more than mere adjutants of the advertising department of the Ford Motor Co. They were to serve as extensions of Ford's personality. One of their number, W. J. Cameron, was promptly set aside as Ford's personal interpreter and word-man. With such a body of literary servitors to command, the witness who had been so ill at ease at Mt. Clemens was shortly to publish over his own name no less than four volumes of autobiography and social opinion, as well as a life of Edison, a manual on the dance, and a stream of shorter compositions too vast to catalogue. Finally, Ford proceeded to develop a newspaper of his own. In the event of any future conflict with the commercial press, he would now have a private apparatus for molding public opinion.

Although each of these protective devices was employed henceforth to help erase the record at Mt. Clemens, such precautionary measures were really unnecessary. Whatever men of breeding may have thought of the muffing of Stevenson's questions, most Americans who followed the trial had enjoyed the spectacle immensely. The masses liked Ford all the better for his slips. They preferred him without the varnish. In their eyes, that was America for you—where a hayseed and a greenhorn could become both rich and great if he "had it in him." Ford was not to be hauled down from his pedestal simply because he had not cut a smart figure as a thinker. His publicists may have winced when the New York *Times* remarked editorially, "Mr. Ford has been submitted to a severe examination of his intellectual qualities. He has not received a pass degree." At the same time Ford's advertisers must have realized that what the New York *Times* thought about Ford cut no ice on Main Street.

Americans as a whole were just as indifferent to the savage manner in which Elliott G. Stevenson took final stock of Ford's mental dimensions. "Gentlemen of the Jury," Stevenson concluded in the summation of his case for the *Tribune*, "they forced us to open the mind of Henry Ford and expose it to you bare . . . to disclose the pitiable condition that he had succeeded in keeping from the view of the public." On any terms such an indictment was too severe. The man who made it erred the more by insinuating that what he had come up with as a result of his digging was either original or something rare or altogether shameful.

On the contrary, what had really been on trial when Stevenson prosecuted Ford was rural America. The victim of the probing was a typical specimen from the American prairie country, one who had reached his majority in 1884 and had married a country girl with intellectual antecedents no different from his own. Far from being odd, Ford's illiteracy and cracker-barrel philosophy could have been duplicated in any crossroads store in the American hinterland or in the offices of countless self-made men of affairs. Stevenson's feat, not particularly difficult for an acute, sophisticated lawyer, had been only that of drawing out dramatically in the strained atmosphere of a courtroom a type of behavior which Ford and millions like him displayed habitually in everyday life.

From the same intellectual climate that fashioned his habits of speech, Ford had inherited many a provincialism. Coming from the Bible Belt, he was at the same time an anti-rum and anti-nicotine fanatic. In 1916 he had prepared for mass circulation a tract entitled "The Case Against the Little White Slaver." Stuffed with testimonials of no scientific value, this volume traced nearly every known human affliction to the cigarette: palsy, juvenile delinquency, crime, death, muddy thinking and feeble-mindedness. Edison contributed to the booklet the unsupported claim that degeneration of the brain cells is an invariable result of addiction to "The Little White Slaver."*

Ford waged war against alcohol as well. Twice in his career he threatened to make total abstainers out of his entire working force the world over. Only when they threatened to strike for their rights were his employes in Denmark permitted to continue a time-honored habit of drinking beer with their lunches. Ford once forced his workers in France to sign a pledge of abstinence, whereupon the French comic weeklies accused him of trying to "dry up France." On American soil the manufacturer had somewhat greater success as a prohibitionist. On several occasions he threatened to discharge any workman who so much as frequented a public bar or was known to keep liquor in his home.† In 1928 Ford published a defense of the federal prohibition

* Edison himself was an inveterate cigar smoker and tobacco chewer.

† When the Ford secret service tried to enforce this temperance mandate, the Detroit *Saturday Night* of September 16, 1922 facetiously proposed that the gargantuan task of "smelling 50,000 breaths" a day could be simplified by applying the techniques of mass production. The weekly suggested that as each employe checked in for work he should be made to exhale on a sheet of sensitized paper attached to his time-card. If equipped with special "garlic filters," said the *Saturday Night*, these cards could then be tested for evidence of alcoholic stains.

amendment. This pamphlet bore the title, "The Benefits of Prohibition." A year later he delivered his most famous last word in behalf of a "bone dry" America. "If booze ever comes back to the United States," he said, "I am through with manufacturing."[6] When Ford threatened to close up shop unless other Americans shared his views on abstinence, the rum-runners along the Detroit waterfront were in their heyday, profiting from an illicit commerce equal to that of Al Capone's Chicago rackets.

Ford's eccentricities on the subject of diet stamped him as a son of the American hinterland. He became a disciple of the Hay diet which inveighs against mixing starches, proteins and fruit acids at any given meal. He later saw to it that the youngsters at one of his trade schools were fed on this principle.[7] He publicized his recipe for digestion as akin to "the way power is developed in a gas engine."[8] His food fads once carried him to the point of attributing "all sickness and disease" and "most wrong acts" to "bad mixtures in the stomach."[9] When he began advancing such a panacea for human ills, he even called for a religious crusade to "cure crime with food." Ford once warned an acquaintance in a friendly manner that the cottage cheese on his salad plate was "rotten milk." In one of his uncensored, and more interesting, newspaper interviews he expressed the belief that milk is "all right before it strikes the air."[10] On another occasion the manufacturer asserted that pigs are notoriously lazy and that cows waste a great deal of time lying in the shade.[11] Both animals, he charged, are given to eating much "more than they are worth."[12] As a result of these ruminations he predicted in 1936 that "the cow must go" and that he expected to establish this fact within the next two years.* Over the years Ford brought one or another of his favorite nostrums to the attention of his staff at the Henry Ford Hospital. In the twenties he once called on an old acquaintance in Dearborn who

* An English columnist recommended that while he was at it Ford might develop a date-stamping attachment for hens so that chickens could both lay and stamp their eggs with indelible ink by making one simple contraction. The Detroit *Saturday Night* then enriched the discussion with a piece of verse:

"Said Henry, 'Better than the milk which children quaff so free,
Is scientific fluid drawn from pasture timothee;
The cow is but a middleman, a crude machine and dear,
So gently bury Bossy, with an orchid on her bier.'

"Said Henry, 'Mark the passing of the bloody age of meat.
Synthetic steak and onions our posterity will eat;
For concentrated energy will supersede the cow.
So dig a grave for Bossy, 'neath the weeping willow bough.'"

was bedridden with gastric ulcers. Advised of the nature of the ailment, Ford had the case diagnosed in a jiffy. "Too much roast beef and milk, eh?" he remarked. "It does it every time." He then told the patient he could cure himself by "swallowing a ball of butter right down whole, once daily."

It was this simplicity that so endeared Ford to the masses at the time of his joust with the Chicago *Tribune*. The chasm that separated the average citizen from the good things of life seemed less forbidding when it was learned that, at sixty, one of the richest men in the world placed so low an esteem on airs and dignity that he could still challenge ten-year-olds to a foot race and demonstrate proudly to his old friends that he was still lithe enough to kick the lower tip of a chandelier and still sufficiently supple to land on the top of a waist-high table with one agile step and without a running start. The aristocracy of wealth and position assumed a neighborly quality when plain Americans heard that, despite his millions, the industrialist of Dearborn was fond of pottering about his mansion, fixing hangers or clothesracks with his own hands, just as ready to don an old raincoat and sprint between rows of cornstalks after a summer shower.

Lawyer Stevenson was not the first to suggest that Ford was no swell. Five years before the trial at Mt. Clemens it was reported by a special writer for *Collier's* that the creator of the Model T had a habit of pitching hay for relaxation and a weakness for arriving at business conferences by crawling through the windows of his office. No highbrow when the world first discovered him, Ford could never bring himself to engage a valet. He told Dr. Marquis he despised having a servant stand over his shoulder at meal times. "I still like potatoes with the skins on," he said, and he had no intention of trying to peel off the jackets as some menial looked on, secretly amused.[13] The owner of a Model T could feel he knew "Uncle Henry" when the story got around that, decked out in his best clothes, the manufacturer once espied the boiler of an abandoned threshing machine and crawled inside to make an inspection, emerging like a chimney-sweep. Ordinary folk could find even greater satisfaction in the report that for years the wealthiest man in Detroit was seldom seen in fashionable circles and rarely put in an appearance at the exclusive clubs of his locality.

Along with the plain speech, the homespun notions and the unaffected manners that brought him so close to the common people of his day, Ford also exhibited the typical rustic's distrust of intellect and refinement. Providing smug amusement for the smart set of Detroit, he made the blunt assertion in 1914 that he would not "give five cents for all the art in the world."* The *Collier's* article which printed his homely confession was entitled "Detroit the Dynamic."[14] The thing that was growing so dynamically in Detroit was neither art, nor beauty, nor thought, but the automobile industry with its correlated wealth, its factories and its sprawling population of mill hands. *That* was what counted with the readers of *Collier's* and on that scale Ford was more "dynamic" than any of his social peers. The manufacturer's antipathy for experts developed as a corollary of the ruralist's traditional scorn for learning and the intellect. Thus it was that Ford came to favor the "raw man" as against the expert, on principle, in nearly every facet of his business. Moreover, in setting out to rely on horse sense and trial-and-error, Ford was, understandably, simply projecting his own image. His model was a rural jack-of-all-trades whose smattering of skills was enough to carry him to the top of a great new industry.

At about the time he became enmeshed in the *Tribune* affair, Ford took stock of his own mental circumference as revealingly as most of his critics. In answering a reporter who had asked him what he thought of "history," he replied, "History is more or less the bunk. We want to live in the present, and the only history that is worth a tinker's dam is the history we make today."[15] Ford was making it, indeed, despite his boastful contempt for the past. Yet so pronounced was his simplicity and so marked his ignorance of history that Dr. Marquis, his companion of the period, could not help remarking, early in the twenties, "The isolation of Henry Ford's mind is about as near perfect as it is possible to make it."[16]

### 3

It was Thomas A. Edison who molded the bulk of Ford's social and political attitudes. The friendship between these two began in 1895 when they met almost by chance and the inventor had expressed an interest in Ford's work with a gasoline buggy. The association ripened and continued on for the next fifteen years after the pair

---

* Here, as on a number of other counts, son Edsel was anything but a chip off the old block. Young Ford, unlike his father, had strong esthetic leanings which flowered at an early age. As a boy of twenty, Edsel pleaded with his father to give the contract for the family residence at Dearborn to Frank Lloyd Wright. He would have won but it happened that Wright was working or vacationing in Europe at the time. Ten years later, Edsel led the fight, against his father, to give the Ford car more tone and style. Still later the younger Ford became an art collector, the leading patron of the Detroit Institute of Arts, as well as an accomplished landscape painter.

initiated a series of summer outings in the summer of 1914. Until their death, Burroughs, the naturalist, and Harvey S. Firestone, the tire magnate, were admitted to an annual gathering of the "vagabonds," as Ford and Edison called themselves.

The first of this series of pleasure jaunts was devoted, under Burroughs' guidance, to a study of wild life in the Everglades of Florida. As time went on, the "gypsy" trips became less and less primitive. The caravan roughed it in 1921 in the Blue Ridge Mountains, with twenty tents and a fleet of trucks as part of their camping equipment. More and more, Ford and Edison came to appreciate the advertising value of their excursions. They began to include a photographer in the party.[17] Three Republican presidents—Coolidge, Harding and Hoover—were honored guests on one or another of these well-reported trips. When Edison, at eighty-two, finally grew too feeble for camping out-of-doors, Ford and he switched their reunions to Fort Myers, Florida. Here they made an occasion of Edison's eighty-second birthday by participating in ceremonies that were publicized over a national hookup of twenty-six radio stations.

Each of the annual jaunts also served as an opportunity for the disciples of Edisonia to gather at the master's feet. Ford worshipped Edison. He venerated the older man's inventive ability. Edison was sixteen years his senior. The inventor, like Ford, was a native son of Michigan. Curious, talkative and opinionated, Edison was the "intellectual" among these sojourners. Summer after summer he treated Ford and the rest of his fellow travelers to an education in the rudiments of Tom Paine, Bob Ingersoll and William Jennings Bryan. As a consequence, any number of Ford's key ideas can be traced to the "vagabond" from Menlo Park.

What Burroughs, Ford and Edison secured through one another's company, among other things, was a free-thinkers' congress. Both of Ford's noted, older companions were agnostics. Burroughs had exchanged books and letters with the skeptic Robert Ingersoll. Ingersoll's first speech, delivered at the age of twenty-three at a picnic in Shawneetown, Illinois, had been a tribute to Tom Paine. Edison held up his end in this free-thinking tradition by writing an introduction for the publisher who brought out Paine's collected works in 1925. More than that, the inventor time and again declared himself to be an unbeliever. On his eightieth birthday, he told a reporter for the New York *Times* that spiritualism was "bunk" and that in his opinion the word "God" simply had "no meaning."[18] He also went on record to the effect that "Man is not the unit of life." "He is as dead as granite," he averred.[19] Edison once shocked Henry M. Stanley, the African missionary, with an irreverent quip. Questioned as to whose voice he would most like to hear recorded, Edison said, "Napoleon's." When Stanley asserted that "the Saviour's" would have been a better choice, the inventor retorted, "Oh well, you know, *I like a hustler!*"[20]

When the influence of the master was at its height, Ford also began to give battle to established religion. "I have very little confidence in these professional schools of religion," he said in 1923. "By the time they get through with religion, it is a very thin product."[21] Sometime earlier he had averred that his motto was "one world at a time."[22] When he announced that he was about to break a habit of going to church once a year, he remarked, "The churches probably do good and are all right for those who want them."[23]

Yet in spite of his agnosticism, Edison seems to have allowed for the possibility of reincarnation. He spoke at one time of personality entering a "new cycle" and thus surviving after death. Ford in time took a fancy to the same theory. In his biography of Edison, he ventured the belief that his own first car was only part of an "accumulated experience" that he had inherited at birth.[24] As the years advanced, the manufacturer embraced the doctrine of personal survival more firmly than ever. He made the forecast in 1922 that "three worlds from now" the Ford product would be a "better car than ever before."[25] When he began to build his tri-motor airplane, the "tin goose," he hazarded the guess that air pilots, then "in the vanguard of progress," would be the first to return to earth after death.

Firestone credits Edison with having planted the seed of Ford's interest in developing waterpower sites and small village factories.[26] On a tour through California, which they made in an open car in 1915, Ford and Firestone were lectured for hours by Edison on the possibilities of industrial waterpower in the West. The inventor labored the subject again when he and his companions toured the Shenandoah Valley in 1918. It was one of Edison's dreams to envision the Orange Valley of New Jersey dotted with a chain of village factories similar to the string of plants which Ford built in southern Michigan in later years.

The eminent inventor's dominating drive had a bearing on Ford's own motivation. If one may take the word of his private secretary, Edison was a frustrated industrialist. His controlling interest lay there rather than in the field of invention. When he was allegedly pushed aside in the reorganization of Edison General Electric, he plunged into the ore milling business, hoping to develop something "bigger."[27]

His test of success was frankly material. He once confided to his secretary, "I measure everything I do by the size of a silver dollar."[28] From so revered a source, therefore, Ford could find a sanction for his own interest in wealth as such. What was good enough for the master was good enough for him.

From the same ideological father, Ford discovered, in addition, a confirmation of his own lifelong habits of work. Edison arrived at most of his inventions by rule-of-thumb. Short on theory, he worked by trial-and-error. One of his favorite maxims was, "Don't experiment with lead pencils." He resented it whenever anyone called him a "scientist." He hated mathematics and record-keeping. To avoid writing out records, he once devised a special blackboard in which he merely inserted and removed wooden plugs to keep track of a certain procedure. When someone jarred the board and the pins flew out, no harm was done because an assistant in the laboratory had been keeping a separate printed record surreptitiously. Ford's dislike of the written form was quite as intense. Like his tutor, Ford exalted trial-and-error. All that Edison could transmit on this score was the stamp of authority. The pupil had come by the same intellectual processes independently.

A common thread of prim morality bound the inventor to his disciple. Edison refused to allow the phonograph to be exploited in the field of popular music on moral grounds. Ford in turn inveighed against the "evils" of jazz. In the twenties he attributed the difficulties of youth to the influence of modern music. He advanced the notion that contemporary jazz, like the excesses of alcohol and finance capital, were the means by which international Jewry hoped to destroy mankind.

Teacher and student were kindred spirits, again, in their grasp of finance. Alfred O. Tate, Edison's former secretary, maintains that his superior was incapable of reading a balance sheet and would fly into a rage whenever anyone tried to teach him.[29] Ford showed something of the same ineptness for figures and financial detail.

Both members of this celebrated pair were devout Wall Street haters. Edison had supreme contempt for the promoter and the speculator. The outcome of his own financial adventures did nothing to relieve him of this feeling. He suffered the great reverse of his career when Edison General Electric was swallowed in a secret merger, with his name stricken from that of the surviving corporation. This experience deepened his hatred of capital and monopoly and soured his disposition for the rest of his life. From that point on, says his secretary, he began to lose interest in life and to freeze up in the presence of his co-workers. "His decisions became mandates," says his secretary.[30] It goes without saying that Ford's own ingrained hostility toward Wall Street grew no milder because of the wounds that had been inflicted on his idol.

In communing with his fellow-campers, all the great inventor could pass on by way of political theory was the panacea of easy money. Edison was the disciple of "Coin" Harvey, "Sockless Jerry" Simpson and William Jennings Bryan. His concept of "pumpkin" money, proclaimed in 1922, was lifted intact from the Farmer's Alliance of the 80's and from the national platform which the Populists put forward in 1891. The proponents of fiat money had been a force to reckon with in Edison's youth. When the embryonic inventor was twenty-three, the Greenbackers cast half as many votes as the Republicans in a Michigan state election. Ford in turn was serving his apprenticeship in Detroit when the police of the city resorted to force to dispel a mass meeting of Greenbackers in the main public square. One of Ford's adult cronies for many a year was a former Detroit judge who had been a lieutenant in Coxey's Army in 1891. Whenever the manufacturer went fishing for "Jews," or "war-makers," or "profiteers," he would invariably discuss his catch in the prairie language of money and banking.

As for Ford's feeling about the open shop, here again Edison and he saw eye to eye. The wizard of Menlo Park greeted the Five-Dollar Day with the remark that labor unions were "done for." In the volume *Edison As I Know Him,* Ford recounts with approval how Edison once managed to break a union.[31] Faced with an organization of his skilled workers, Ford's idol is said to have hurriedly invented a machine that eliminated most of the jobs in question. Consequently, Ford wrote, the union was successfully destroyed at birth.

It may be that Edison fathered Ford's slogan, "History is bunk." The phrase bears his touch. In the company of E. G. Pipp, the inventor once developed such a concept as he expounded at length on the familiar scientific maxim that "Nothing is permanent but change."[32]

The attachment between Ford and his eminent older friend finally became so strong that the two built adjoining homes at Fort Myers. The pair began to spend winter vacations in one another's company. This contact, together with the camping trips, was supplemented by periodic visits back and forth between Dearborn and Menlo Park.

From such a give-and-take, Ford seems to have run up a heavy intellectual debt. Both Edison and Burroughs said as much. Edison never tried to hide his admiration for Ford's industrial achievements. Yet according to Tate, a creditable authority, what the inventor really doted on in Ford was the sheer bulk of the man's fortune. Nor was Burroughs greatly impressed by Ford's mental stature. After returning from one of the summer sojourns, the naturalist remarked in his diary, "Ford has a big heart, but his head is not so large except in his own line. He's not a reader." Burroughs once urged him to study up on American history, noting again that the Dearborn industrialist was a "mighty good talker in his own field." But his "philosophic ideas," he added, were those of a man who had "turned his attention in that direction late in life." "Sometimes I thought he was a Christian Scientist," said the naturalist, "and sometimes I thought he was not."[33]

This intertwining of Ford's mind with Edison's was given artistic expression many years later by Diego Rivera, the Mexican muralist. In his fresco at the Detroit Institute of Arts, Rivera reproduced the faces of the pair in the form of a superimposed image. He blended the portraits of the two men into that of a single figure. What the artist doubtless meant to convey by such a symbol is the interdependence of the power age and the machine age. But another interpretation of the portrait of Ford-Edison or Edison-Ford is just as apt: the patron saint of Henry Ford was Thomas Edison—rule-of-thumb inventor, free-thinker, waterpower enthusiast, agrarian with a money bug, open-shopper, enemy of Wall Street, laboratory man who yearned to be a rich industrialist, and man of ideas who reveled in the conviction that "history is bunk."

# Eight

## FLIVVER POLITICS

### 1

IN THE MIDST of his quarrel with the Chicago *Tribune*, Ford struck out on a bypath that led him even further from his natural medium. He attempted to win a seat in the United States Senate in the fall of 1918. His senatorial aspirations had grander implications of which he was well aware. By now the manufacturer had a vision of the White House; local Republican groups had already suggested that he run for the Presidency. At the Republican National Convention of 1916, the Michigan delegation had proposed Ford as its candidate for the White House. The Nebraska delegation named him as its second choice for the Presidency. New York reporters asked Ford at the time what he thought of going to Washington as the country's chief executive. He was prepared to consider the post, he said, "if called." He assured his questioners that running a government was no different from operating a factory.[1]

Yet, when Ford finally filed for political office in 1918, he did it only after the White House begged him to do so. In urging Ford's candidacy, Wilson had two points in mind. In the coming struggle over the peace, it was to his interest to have a man on whom he could count in the upper house. Ford was an avowed supporter of the projected League of Nations. More than that, the President was Ford's debtor. When the state of California hung in suspense in 1916, during Wilson's campaign for re-election, Ford had rushed to the support of the Democratic candidate with a last-minute contribution of $35,000.[2] It was the feeling in Dearborn that this last-minute donation had "put Wilson across" in California and, therefore, back in the White House.

Two of Ford's closest friends tried to discourage his political debut. When Alfred Lucking, his personal lawyer, first heard of the impending contest, he protested at once, "No true friend of Mr. Ford wants him to accept any political office at this time."[3] Edison found the prospect amusing. Yet he spoke against it. "What do you want to do that for?" he asked Ford. "You can't speak. You wouldn't say a damned word. You'd be mum."[4]

Ford's two closest business associates, however, egged him on. Liebold, the secretary, and Sorensen, the factory superintendent, could hardly contain themselves. With their pushing and prompting, Ford soon declared himself as "the President's candidate" for the Senate. "I have been commanded to run for Senator," he said. "Now, well, now we shall see whether I can build anything but automobiles, tractors and ships."[5]

In the state's open primaries in 1918, it was Ford's hope to win the nomination of both major parties. This was much too much for the keepers of the Grand Old Party. The dominant Republicans of the state were in no mood in 1918 to underwrite a candidate who had laid a curse on war profits. Nor could they see themselves embracing the favorite son of a Democratic President. Under the circumstances Ford was compelled to switch parties. Nominally a Republican, he survived the primaries only as a Democratic nominee.

The Republicans then began to poke fun at the "overnight" Democrat who had seldom bothered to go to the polls in any previous election. Two years earlier, they recalled, Ford had boasted that he was a Republican for the same reason that he had ears, because he was "born that way."[6] Before that, he had once tossed off the remark that although he was fifty-two he had voted only six times in his life, and then only because his wife drove him to it.[7]

Ford's opponent in the general election was the Republican standard-bearer Commander Truman H. Newberry. A cultured multi-millionaire and scion of one of the oldest wealthy families of the state, Newberry was a career politician who had served in Theodore Roosevelt's cabinet as Secretary of War. No love had ever been wasted between this man and Ford. The name of Newberry, like that of the McMillans, the Joys, the Buhls and the Algers, had crowned the social register of Michigan a generation or more before the founding of the Ford Motor Co. The Commander and his friends were heirs to timber and mining fortunes and could have been counted among the eighty-two millionaires who lived in Michigan when Henry Ford made his first speed record on the dirt track at Grosse Pointe.

Ford and Newberry were also business rivals of a sort. A large portion of Newberry's inherited wealth was invested in the Packard Motor Car Co. Among rich men, Newberry was a symbol of gentility and conservatism; Ford was suspect. Most of Newberry's wealthy friends had never been able to decide which was the greater absurdity: the Five-Dollar Day, the heresy of the Peace Ship, or Ford's bold stand on war profiteering. Ford in turn had nothing but scorn for the "Grosse Pointe crowd," whom he regarded as mere wastrels and speculators. The set Newberry personified was just as wedded to the conviction that the Democratic candidate for Senator was no more than a gauche, unreliable upstart.

Neither candidate did much personal electioneering. Throughout the campaign, Ford made no public appearance. Commander Newberry remained at his military post, as commandant of the Port of New York and the Brooklyn Navy Yard. Some of the campaign pronouncements which Ford released to the press did add, however, to the merriment if not to the dignity of the contest. He well recalled, said the manufacturer at one point, his twenty-first birthday when he had gone to the polls in 1884, and on his father's advice had cast a vote for President Garfield.[8] The Republicans quickly reminded the electorate that Garfield had been assassinated three years earlier in 1881. As the campaign progressed, Ford made a prediction which sounded much like a confession of bewilderment. "I shall not go to Washington alone," he said. "If need be, I shall take my whole organization with me, the men I have about me who are used to working with me and with whom I have been able to do things."[9]

The Newberry faction, hard up for an issue, built their campaign on the motif of Americanism. They tried to impugn Ford's patriotism. They made what capital they could of Edsel's exemption from military service. How did it happen, the Omer *Progress* asked its readers, that the Ford Motor Co. could now spare Henry Ford when Edsel one year previous had been "indispensable"? "Henry is too old to be drafted," the paper continued, "and is therefore not needed at the plant as greatly as sonny is."

This ugly vein of propaganda found its most lurid expression in a paid advertisement which the Republicans inserted in the Detroit *Free Press* two days before the voters went to the polls to choose their senator. This broadside called Ford a "Hun-lover." It attributed to the Hon. Charles Evans Hughes the charge that the Ford Motor Co. was harboring German aliens and German sympathizers on its payroll.[10]

Republican editors made sport of Ford's fitness for the Senate. The Sturgis *Daily Journal* asserted that if the manufacturer actually had the talent required for the office he had managed "to keep his light well hidden under a bushel." Echoing conservative eastern opinion, the New York *Times* passed the blunt judgment that Ford's entrance into the Senate "would create a vacancy both in the Senate and in the automobile business." From the pen of Harry M. Nimmo, then editor of the Detroit *Saturday Night*, came the sharpest thrust of all. "Our neighbor, the Dearborn *Independent*, wants Mr. Ford to run for president," said Nimmo. "Mr. Ford can easily qualify under the Constitution, which requires only that presidents shall be native-born and thirty-five years of age."[11]

In their joint opposition to Ford, Newberry and Nimmo were allied twice over. Their affinity was social in that the Detroit *Saturday Night* catered to the smart set of Detroit, as well as to the rich and powerful. (Ford's Dearborn *Independent* later labeled Nimmo's paper "the avowed champion of the employer against the employe.") The two men had economic ties as well. Newberry had a financial interest in the *Saturday Night*. His investment amounted to $6000.[12]

Ironically, the party of the opposition began to question Ford's labor record. The New York *Times* tried to make something of the report that Ford of Canada had just locked out its employes in order to defeat some labor union.[13] A former Republican governor, Chase S. Osborn, charged that Ford had saved money on the Five-Dollar Day by driving his men. Osborn alleged, in passing, that the Democratic candidate broke a pledge which he had once given to the officers of Olivet College. The ex-governor deplored, finally, the "bad taste" which the Ford Motor Co. had shown during his term of office in Lansing, by having offered him at that time a free, nickel-plated Model T.[14]

In the Ford camp, on the other hand, were a few men of means, the American Federation of Labor and the two daily newspapers of Detroit. In endorsing the sponsor of the Five-Dollar Day, the AFL averred that the Michigan Car Co., under Newberry management, had sweated Polish immigrants at a wage of ninety cents a day.[15] Prudence rather than principle explained the support of the big city dailies. Neither the *News* nor the *Free Press* wanted Ford. But Hearst was about to invade the community. Rather than give him a heaven-sent opportunity to build circulation on the Ford issue, both of the existing papers refused to come out for Newberry. Insofar as the Democratic nominee had a platform, it in no way endeared him to the Right. It espoused fiat money, prohibition, government regulation of utilities and the League of Nations. It repeated the manufacturer's promise to give his war profits back to the people. The men of wealth who followed Ford into the Democratic fold were, therefore, few and far between. The apostates included George M. Holley, the manufacturer of Ford's carburetors; Fred W. Wadsworth, a manufacturer who was then making bodies for the Model T; and Harvey S. Firestone, Ford's tire-builder.

The outcome of the contest did not hinge, however, on the issues or the platform which either party had served up to the electorate. Ford lost the election for the reason that his moderate financial donations to the Democratic party and his amateurish electioneering were no match for the machine politics of his opponent. When the votes were counted, Ford carried his own community, Wayne County, by a margin of two-to-one but he lost the state by about 7500 votes. The New York *Times* made no bones about the cause of his defeat. He was defeated, crowed the *Times*, by "fat Republican pocketbooks."

Ford explained the results somewhat differently. He later confided to a former president of the Detroit Board of Commerce that his defeat had been contrived by "Wall Street" and an "influential gang of Jews." Newberry, he told his confidant, had been used as a mere "Jewish tool."[16] Moreover, Ford was stung by the insinuations that had been directed at Edsel's war record. On top of that, he had a feeling, fed by his racial bias, that "New York" and the "Jews" had made a fool of him. He was all the more put out because his advisors had inflated his hopes, having assured him that he was politically invincible. On the eve of the election and in anticipation of a victory, his friend Firestone had come on from Akron. At a pre-election banquet, the tire magnate in an expansive mood had offered to sacrifice half his fortune to put Ford in the White House. Dropped from such heights, the unsuccessful candidate for the Senate began to hunger for revenge. Some of his counsellors were quite as anxious, for self-protection, to harass the Republican candidate who had made their calculations go awry.

The first scheme of retribution to which the members of Ford's inner circle put their minds was criminal prosecution. Ford and Firestone started out by hiring about a hundred private detectives. These agents then combed the state for four months, grubbing for evidence that Newberry had bested Ford by fraud. By the time the Department of Justice sent its own men into the field, said E. G. Pipp, the former editor of the Detroit News, the detectives who were working on the case began to trip over one another.[17] The Ford decision to hound Newberry on the grounds of suspected election irregularities was reached at a council of war which convened, Pipp averred, a day or so after the election. One of Ford's men who attended the conference is said to have posed the idea of launching an investigation. Ford presumably cut him short with the jibe, "If we are to have an investigation? We are going to have one. Put a gang on 'em."

The undercover men, whom Ford engaged to take orders from Liebold, were as ingenious as they were indefatigable. One of the number later told Pipp how he had gone about the business of entrapping "the Newberry crowd." "We crawled under beds to listen to conversations," he said. "We tried to get into homes as roomers, posed as prospective purchasers of real estate, represented ourselves as agents of the whisky campaign and the dry forces, got girls to extract telegrams out of telegraph offices, and all to what avail?"[18] The private agents enjoyed liberal expense accounts. They were prodded to greater effort at frequent banquets and "pep" meetings.

Even employes of the Ford Motor Co. were drawn into the inquisition. John W. Smith, who later became mayor of Detroit, fell into the net while working for Ford as circulation manager of the Dearborn Independent. Smith had some information on the Newberry campaign which he preferred to keep to himself. Sorensen tried to shake it out of him. Smith still refused to talk, and when he was warned point-blank that unless he learned "to be loyal and absorb some of the Ford spirit," he might lose his job, he resigned.[19]

What Ford gleaned from such sleuthing he used, first, to prick the Attorney-General into filing criminal charges against Newberry and, second, to fortify the government's case once the principal defendant and his chief colleagues had been brought to trial. The strategy worked so well, with so much solid evidence to support it, that on March 18, 1920, Newberry and sixteen co-defendants were convicted in federal court on a charge of having dipped into "fat Republican pocketbooks" more liberally than the law allowed.[20] Under a statute which both parties had freely ignored in the past, all any candidate was entitled to spend in a primary election was $3750. The federal judge in the case estimated that altogether the Newberry group had spent anywhere from half a million to a million dollars. Twelve of Newberry's supporters were sentenced to prison. For his own alleged violations of the law, Newberry was fined $10,000 and sentenced to spend two years in Leavenworth Penitentiary.

With Charles Evans Hughes as chief defense counsel, Newberry hastily repaired to the United States Supreme Court. Here the appellant made no effort to deny his guilt, under the law. He fought and won his case on constitutional grounds. For in May 1921, the high bench ruled five-to-four that Congress had no power to regulate primary elections. It was this phase of the campaign on which the Department of Justice had based its case. The contrary decision of the lower court was automatically voided, thus freeing Newberry from both a fine and a stiff prison sentence.

## 2

Balked in the courts, Ford then shifted his attack to the floor of the Senate. His attorney at once filed an affidavit with the Senate Committee on Privileges and Elections, demanding a recount. In this document Ford charged that he had been deprived of his rightful place in the Senate by fraud. He brought the present action, he said, solely to uphold the honor of the United States Senate and to establish the fact that seats in that chamber "are not for sale to the highest bidder."*

* How much Ford spent on his own campaign was never investigated. The sum was probably small because his collaborators were convinced they could win without having to spend anything to speak of. They were also able to put Ford

As long as the Senate had a majority of Republicans, Newberry could cling to his seat. Approximately 425,000 ballots were dutifully recounted with the same results as before. The twice-victorious Newberry was even spared when the Senate, in a gesture to virtue, passed a resolution condemning the principle of large campaign expenditures. Such spending was said to be incompatible with "the honor and dignity" of government. But after placing its seal on this effusion, the body dismissed the Ford petition and voted to let Newberry keep his seat.

Ford then advanced from another quarter. He began to attack the Senators who had voted to seat his rival. Here the first victim was Senator Townsend of Michigan, who had risen to Newberry's defense. In the summer of 1922, the New York *Times* supplied the information that in order to prevent Townsend's re-election, Ford's men were disbursing "a steady golden stream," and that for the time being the political map of Michigan was completely eclipsed by "the shadow of the flivver."[22]

At last Ford had the satisfaction of seeing Newberry stripped of office. Townsend's defeat and the loss of other Republican seats in the Senate gave control of the upper house to the Democrats. Ford's case had been championed by those doughty liberals, George Norris and Robert M. La Follette, Sr. Just before the Senate convened for a special session in November 1922, La Follette announced that he meant to reopen the Newberry case without delay. To avoid the humiliation of an almost certain expulsion from the Senate, Newberry stepped down voluntarily four days before the special session was called to order. In a letter of resignation, addressed to the Governor of Michigan, he alluded to the "political persecution" that had dogged him from the day he was elected and to the "hundreds of agents [who] had hounded and terrified men in all parts of the State."[23]

To round out Newberry's unexpired term, the Governor appointed James Couzens. Ever since the old break with Ford, Couzens had been

---

dealers and employes of the Ford Motor Co. into the field as electioneers. Hundreds of Ford cars were used in Detroit to transport voters to and from the polls. Many of these hustlers were regular Ford employes who campaigned on company time. Even a truckload of boys from the Henry Ford Trade School had gone about the city tacking up posters. Ford did not adhere to his pre-election pledge that he would not "spend a dollar" to get elected. Pipp wrote all but one of the two dozen pieces of campaign literature that came out of the Ford offices. The printing bill for only one of his pamphlets, he said, ran to $16,000. According to him, the Ford people paid for this booklet indirectly. They transmitted $20,000 to the Democratic State Central Committee and then sent the Committee the $16,000 printing bill.[21]

cultivating a flair for public office. He had risen from the post of
Police Commissioner to the mayoralty of Detroit. His elevation from
the city hall to the seat that Newberry had vacated must have given
Ford double cause for satisfaction. If so, the new appointee was to
prove particularly disappointing. His presence in the Senate was destined to cause Ford more embarrassment than anything which the
ill-fated Commander Newberry might have engendered had he been
allowed to stay in office.

Retired to private life, ex-Senator Newberry consoled himself
by waging a ten-year social feud against the Ford dynasty. His icy
hatred of Ford did not thaw until the banks of Detroit began to totter
in the thirties, and until his son and heir, Phelps Newberry, and Edsel
Ford had become fast friends. As for Mrs. Truman H. Newberry,
until the peace was made this dictatorial wellborn woman would not
think of sanctioning or attending any social gathering to which an
invitation had been extended to "that man."

Just as the disconsolate Senator Newberry arrived at the point
of returning to Detroit as a private citizen, Ford was himself hoping
to move into the White House as President of the United States. That
hope began to soar when a meeting was called in Dearborn on May 23,
1922, at which some of Ford's employes and old friends founded a
Ford-For-President Club. With much talk of "honest currency" and
"taxing idle gold," the citizens who attended this gathering wore stove-
pipe hats made of placards reading, "We want Henry." William T.
Kronberg, then editor of the Dearborn Press, let it be known that Ford
was in a "positively receptive frame of mind" toward the movement
to draft him for the Presidency two years hence.[24]

Ford was indeed bitten by the Presidential bug. Six months
earlier he had indicated as much to the journalist Allan L. Benson.
Benson was then preparing a series of articles on the manufacturer's
qualifications for the White House. While entertaining this writer at
a lunch attended by other members of the Ford organization, Ford
pointed to a certain member of his staff with the remark, "There is
the kind of man I would appoint Secretary of the Navy."[25] These
political hopes were no less ardent the following year. For the August
8th issue of Collier's in 1923, Ford authorized the publication of an
article that appeared, over his own name, bearing the suggestive title,
"If I Were President."

Again it was Liebold and Sorensen, the omnipotent Ford executives of the 20's, who did most to fan the interest in the White House.
Yet both men must have appreciated some of their candidate's political

shortcomings. He was inept as a speaker. Late in 1923 some Kansas farmers wanted him to address them in person. Liebold prudently declined the invitation. Using Ford's name in the first person, he told the farmers, "Public speaking is out of my line."[26] No one could say by what alchemy Sorensen and Liebold hoped to have messages to Congress or salutations to the world delivered by a man who found it almost impossible to face an audience. Nor would their candidate— as he had demonstrated at Mt. Clemens not long before—find it easy, if elected, to digest all the complex written memoranda thrust upon a President. As his designs on the White House came to a head, Ford confessed to Benson, his biographer, "I don't like to read books; they muss up my mind."[27]

Some of the men who had most reason to respect Ford's industrial genius began to cavil at his political ambitions. Were Ford to be elected President, Couzens told the Detroit Republican Club in November 1923, he would suffer the greatest humiliation of his career. Ford's interest in the White House, said the Senator, only reflected a desire to even the score with Newberry.[28] Dr. Marquis, no longer a Ford attaché, then offered a witticism that alienated Mrs. Ford forever. En route to Washington, about to take over the Capital—the rector prophesied at a Detroit dinner table—all Ford would need in the way of Pullman accommodations for his Presidential staff was one lower berth and an upper. Mrs. Ford thought the jest was at her expense and Edsel's. What the Dean meant to imply, however, was Pullman space for Sorensen and Liebold. The humorist Will Rogers then entered the discussion by contending that one simple speech would give the Presidency to the merchant of the Model T. The candidate had only to say, said Rogers, "Voters, if I'm elected I'll change the front." Why not dispense with the two-party system for one term and hire Ford on a commission basis, the humorist added. Put the Ford factory "in with the Government," he wrote, and "instead of seeds, every Spring mail out Those Things of his. Mail Newberry one every morning, Special Delivery." If Ford won the election, *Collier's* ventured to predict, members of his Cabinet would have to page him "from one garage to another."

None of these thrusts dampened the ardor of the Ford entourage. W. J. Cameron, Pipp's successor on the Dearborn *Independent*, bubbled with confidence in the summer of 1922. Before a group of local businessmen he said, "The next President of the United States will be a man who can read a blueprint and who understands the problems of production and keeping men employed."[29] Cameron assured Mark

Sullivan that once in Washington all Ford would leave standing in the Capital would be the buildings.[30] The only forces that might cheat Ford of this opportunity, Cameron let it be known, were the power companies, the "fertilizer trust" and "Jewish propaganda societies."[31] By December 1922, according to Pipp, Ford began to act out his expected new role. His immediate associates started playfully addressing one another as "Mr. Attorney General" and "Mr. Secretary of State."[32]

Liebold, the thwarted Senator-maker, meanwhile was beating the bushes for his candidate. He had already made a close study of the laws affecting primary elections in nearly every state.[33] By 1923 he was prepared to flood the Ford dealer organization with free copies of a Ford biography specially prepared for the coming campaign.[34] The mailing list of Ford's 7000 dealers was made available to the Ford-For-President Club of Dearborn. The latter agency, claiming that one hundred and fifty similar clubs had been set up over the nation after its model, was soon bombarding the sales staff of the Ford Motor Co. with campaign material.

Ford agents then set up headquarters in Chicago. From this radius point, they distributed 50,000 Ford-For-President circulars in the summer of 1922.[35] The reaction was so encouraging, Pipp said, that thirty young men "who could talk" in Ford's behalf were quickly dispatched to other strategic political centers.[36] The Dearborn *Independent* rushed into the burgeoning campaign.

Ford then reminded the commercial press of his existence by announcing late in 1923 that for the first time in five years the Ford Motor Co. would sponsor a program of national advertising, with a budget of $7,000,000.*

## 3

If Ford had let well enough alone he would probably have ended in the White House. On the eve of the national campaign of 1924, he was all but demi-god to the West and Middle West. No other aspirant for the Presidency commanded so wide an appeal. Farmers, pacifists, factory workers, reformists, prohibitionists, anti-Semites, the labor unions, and all the amorphous forces of unrest would have rushed to his standard. The fight against Newberry had stamped him as a champion of clean government. His Five-Dollar Day and his casti-

* This departure was a necessary business move as well. Ford was forced to get back to advertising at this time because the Model T had started slipping.

gation of war and war profiteers were topics of household conversation. William Allen White made the forecast that Ford's anti-Semitism would clinch the Klan vote of the South and Middle West.[37]

Everything Ford stood for captured the fancy of those remaining voters who had once been moved by the populist ferment and the agrarianism of the prairies. Dearborn had fanned these lingering fires during Wilson's campaign for reelection in 1916. The advertisements which Ford paid for in the fall of that year advocated the eight-hour day for railroad workers, workmen's compensation, higher taxes on incomes, and inheritances, and government ownership and operation of the railroads. The effusions from Dearborn on the subject of money, Jewry and Wall Street were part and parcel of the same appeal. Such talk fascinated numberless farmers and mechanics who had challenged plutocracy in an earlier day. Ford's piece for *Collier's*, "If I Were President," had the same ring. In it he inveighed against liquor, against the soldier's bonus, and the "evils" of railroad management. He flayed those "Jew financiers" who organize labor unions and pick over the bones of businesses that have "decayed." He added, ironically, that he shouldn't wonder if industry would eventually absorb the political government."[38]

By July 1923, the Ford specter really roused the major parties. With the election a little more than a year away, *Collier's* magazine published the results of an opinion poll on the Presidential favorites of the nation. From a sample of 260,000 voters, more than one-third designated Ford as their choice for the office. The manufacturer was named twice as often as Harding and nine times as frequently as Herbert Hoover. Hearst made the flat prediction that Ford would sweep the country in 1924, on a third ticket. He sent Brisbane to give the Dearborn candidate a "gentle warning" not to go too far with the talk about "paper money," lest he alienate the business element.[39] Anticipating a frosty reception from the financial community, Liebold made no effort to court either Democrats or Republicans. He dealt instead with The Committee of 48, flirting with the idea of running his candidate on an independent ticket. The campaign he had in mind had its headquarters on Main Street.

Thoroughly frightened by such a prospect, the forces of the opposition grew more articulate as election time approached. Oswald Garrison Villard warned the readers of the *Nation* that if Ford were to land in the White House "almost anything conceivable" might happen. In half a lifetime of political reporting, said Villard, he had never encountered a candidate "so absolutely unfit" for the responsibilities of the Presidency.

None lashed at Ford more trenchantly than Arthur Vandenberg, then editor and publisher of the Grand Rapids *Herald*. If Ford were eligible for the Presidency, said Vandenberg, the office boy at his newspaper was by the same token fit to manage the Ford factories. "Ford has to his debit," the editor continued, "more erratic interviews on public questions, more dubious quotations, more blandly boasted ignorance of American history and American experience, more political nonsense, more dangerous propaganda, than any other dependable citizen that we have ever known. . . ." So said the New York *Times* in different words. Half in fear and half in jest, the *Wall Street Journal* said it would string along with Ford, though the man did seem a "little eccentric" at times. A pair of skittish business men actually insured themselves against Ford's possible victory at the polls. To cover such a contingency, they went to Lloyd's taking out two policies valued at $200,000 each.

Shrewdest of all and fearful lest his own election plans go awry was the "fill-in" President, Calvin Coolidge. This silent, calculating man soon began to make capital of the fact that Ford craved one thing far more than the Presidency.

What Ford coveted more than occupancy of the White House were the power sites and nitrate plants which Congress had developed as a war measure on the Tennessee River. At the close of the war, a number of private interests had begun to jockey over the right to acquire this property. But none had been able to make off with the treasure—thanks to Norris of Nebraska and a few like-minded federal engineers. This little group in Washington then envisioned—in the interest of flood control, public power and national defense—the gigantic project which we know today as TVA.

Ford's hankering for the watershed is understandable. Edison had given him a glimpse of the power age. There was every reason to suppose that a Republican administration in Washington was about to auction off the Tennessee reserve at bargain prices. Possession of the nitrate plants would help Ford in his business. He was a manufacturer of farm implements. He was advocating mechanized "pooled" farms after the Soviet pattern. The idle equipment at Muscle Shoals was a source of fertilizer; its operation would fit hand-in-glove with the tractor business. All in all, Ford told the biographer Benson, he wanted this property more than he wanted "another billion dollars."[40]

For sheer effrontery, nothing in Ford's career can compare with the terms of the bid which he straightway put up for Muscle Shoals. He offered to pay $5,000,000 for title to the nitrate works. This equipment had cost the government $106,000,000. On the unfinished Wilson Dam, Ford asked a one-hundred-year lease, absolute freedom from federal regulation, with a first option to renew his rights in perpetuity at the end of one hundred years.* On Ford's terms, the government was to finish the Wilson Dam at its own expense. This work would cost the taxpayers an additional $50,000,000.

Ford was to pay nothing at all on the principal. He suggested in lieu of such payment, an annual "rental" of $50,000. Then came the pearl. *Ford proposed that this insignificant yearly rental be set aside and allowed to accumulate compound interest at 4% for the next one hundred years. At the end of the century—by his reckoning—the government would have a fund of more than $50,000,000, or enough to meet the costs of completing the Wilson Dam.* Such financial hocus-pocus was too much for six members of the House Committee on Military Affairs. These gentlemen declared in a minority report, "This is indeed a very shrewd, if not an entirely unique way of paying a debt of $50,000,000 with the comparatively insignificant sum of $4,674,000."[41]

But Ford was not disposed to rest, once he had propounded this novel method of installment buying. He soon offered, in addition, a substitute for hard cash. Liebold suggested that the government could complete the Wilson Dam at rock-bottom prices by issuing a special "Muscle Shoals" currency.[42] Edison seconded the motion. The inventor urged the Treasury Department to issue greenbacks secured by farm surpluses and by power projects "like Muscle Shoals."[43] As this grand scheme of aggrandizement at the public's expense began to take flight with Edison's blessing, Ford blasted away at the gold standard and the "fertilizer trust." He accused the "interests" of a plot to defeat his plan to reclaim the Tennessee Valley.

The purported plans for working a miracle in the watershed were grandiose indeed. The corn belt was soon astir with rumors that Ford had in mind handing out a ton of fertilizer free with every Model T. William B. Mayo, then chief engineer of the Ford Motor Co., hinted to the Senate Committee on Agriculture that Ford had perfected a

---

* The request for exemption from regulation for a century ran counter to the law and to Ford's alleged principles. The Federal Water Power Act then on the books prohibited the national government from awarding power grants for any term longer than fifty years. In the Dearborn *Independent* and in his publicity for Wilson in 1916, the petitioner for Muscle Shoals had come out for government control and ownership of public utilities.

secret process which would cut the cost of fertilizer by one-half.\*[44]

Mere discussion of the project Ford had in mind touched off a migration which the New York *Times* compared to the gold rush of '49. The "pioneers" of 1922 swarmed into the Tennessee Valley—the future mecca of the electrical age. Ten to fifteen miles wide and seventy-five miles long, this projected power belt the *Times* soon christened the "city of Ford's dreams."[45] Promoters began to plant orchards and truck gardens. They auctioned off old family estates, laying out streets and home sites in the area. A "Muscle Shoals Land Corporation" with offices in Detroit, founded a whole city, calling it Highland Park, Tennessee. The officers of this organization advertised their new Eldorado as "a spot where spare dollars have a chance to start a fortune."[46] A group of Detroit newspapermen and some of their friends cornered a square mile of the "dreamland" for future speculation.

Ford now planned, said the New York *Times*, to teach every farmer in the Mississippi Valley how to harness the brooks on his place so as to "run the United States" by water power. Within fifty years, said the *Times*, the magician of Dearborn intended to give his super-power network back to the people as a non-profit enterprise. By such means, the *Times* continued, Ford hoped to "revolutionize the financial system" and to make the government of the United States permanently "self-supporting."[47] The Ford organization, it was said, stood ready to swing into action along the Tennessee "on a few hours' notice."[48]

Dazzled by such reports, the House of Representatives, the Senate Committee on Military Affairs, the American Federation of Labor, the Federation of Farm Bureaus and any number of other bodies went on record in favor of the Ford proposal. Senator Norris, on the other hand, diagnosed the basic Ford idea and all its legitimate and illegitimate offspring as the "most wonderful real estate speculation since Adam and Eve lost title to the Garden of Eden."

Three sons of Michigan spoke up in opposition to Ford's scheme. Vandenberg published a ruthless dissection of the offer. From the Senate, Couzens affirmed that on principle he was opposed to transferring public resources to any private interests whatsoever. E. G. Pipp brought out a special issue of his weekly with a cover spread which proclaimed, "Muscle Shoals—The Biggest GRAB Ever

---

\* One clause in the official offer did stipulate that the Fords were to make no more than 8 per cent per annum from the manufacture of fertilizer. Yet nothing in the proposal bound them to turn out this product in any quantity whatsoever.

Attempted in America." "If you make a contract with Henry Ford," said Pipp, "make it 'horse high, hog tight and bull strong;' so high he can't jump over it, so tight he can't crawl under it, and so strong he can't break through it."

But it was Norris, the father of TVA, who really gave the Ford snowball a melting down. If his colleagues in the Senate felt like submitting to Ford's terms, Norris exclaimed, why not throw in for full measure a warranty deed to the national Capitol. The Senator first pointed out that Ford was bound by the terms of his offer to provide neither cheap power nor low price fertilizer. He could do as he saw fit, Norris maintained. He could produce just enough power to meet his own needs or—if he chose—take the whole project to Wall Street ten minutes after he got it and turn it over for $200,000,000.

When it came to analyzing the proposition that a gift of $50,000,-000 be repaid by a series of minute installments spread over the next 5200 weeks, the Nebraska Senator could scarcely remain sane. He began by making a computation of his own, on the basis of Ford's arithmetic. For a round sum of $10,000,000, half of which was to be payable over the ensuing century, said Norris, Ford was about to acquire public rights worth $236,000,000 in "cold cash" at the drop of a hat. Put out at 4 per cent compound interest for one hundred years, to borrow Ford's idea, this jewel stripped from the public domain would be worth at the close of the century $14,500,000,000. Such a gift, Norris stormed, would mark the end of the fight in America for conservation and public power. And in this instance, he added, the people would be taxed for the next hundred years in order to make a fat original bequest still more profitable for its beneficiary.

At the apex of the drive on the White House and the quest for Muscle Shoals, Ford was summoned to Washington for a personal conference with Calvin Coolidge. The two men came together early in December 1923. Several days later, in a message to Congress, the President, without mentioning Ford's name, recommended the sale of Muscle Shoals to private interests. The Baltimore *Sun,* the New York *World* and the Detroit *News* all surmised that Ford and the President had struck a bargain. Senator Hiram Johnson of California drew the same inference from the White House talk.[49]

Almost too soon for the President's comfort, Ford told the world that the country was "perfectly safe with Coolidge." He renounced his own Presidential aspirations with finality and repudiated the "Decision Day" on which a three-day Ford-For-President convention was to have opened at the Tuller Hotel in Detroit. "Mr. Coolidge means to do right," Ford submitted. "I would never for a moment think of running against Calvin Coolidge for President on any ticket whatever."

Irrespective of Coolidge's alleged intentions in the matter, Ford was still cheated of the prize in the Tennessee basin. He could never budge the stubborn figure in the Senate who stood astride Muscle Shoals all the while that Harding, Coolidge and Hoover were inhabiting the White House. Decisive Senate action on the Tennessee reservoir was to be withheld for a decade, however, until the creation by Act of Congress in 1933 of the Tennessee Valley Authority.

Ford himself formally gave up the fight in 1924. "Wall Street," he alleged, had once more done him in. His followers in the corn belt, meanwhile, doubtless believed that Ford's defeat had been theirs as well. For in the midst of the battle for Muscle Shoals the manufacturer had declaimed, "We are not asking the government for a nickel."[50]

As for what Ford did ask for on the Tennessee, Norris put his finger on the heart of the thing. He found it difficult, the Senator told his colleagues at the time, to reconcile Ford's reputation for fairness with his continued silence in the face of the possibly exaggerated offers that were gaining currency in his name. Were Rockefeller, United States Steel or International Harvester to attempt a similar killing, Norris pleaded, they would be denounced and pilloried. "It is simply a play upon a name, Mr. President," the legislator from Nebraska concluded. "Have we reached the point of saying that we are going to permit good men to capitalize their virtue and to be paid a premium for it out of the Treasury of the United States?"

# Nine

## TWENTY-TRACK MIND

### 1

NUMBERLESS AMERICANS thought all the better of Ford's interest in Muscle Shoals and the White House because of his newly won reputation as a railroad genius and reformer. Many a farmer and small businessman expected big things from Dearborn shortly after the manufacturer bought up, in 1920, a dilapidated, vest-pocket railway known as the Detroit, Toledo and Ironton. Before Ford took it over the "Ironton" had been a chronic money-loser. Under his aegis, however, it quickly came to life. The little road was soon earning an annual dividend of 25 per cent on its common stock, and a railroad revolution seemed to be in the offing. Ford said it in so many words. He began to ridicule the professionals in the business. His new discoveries, he declaimed, were sufficient to transform modern transport. In 1921, one of the foremost journals of the trade publicized Ford's boast to the effect that he could operate the entire American railway system with ease.[1] All he had to do to accomplish this feat, he said, was to "send word to the D. T. and I. gang to extend their principles to all the other lines."

What were these magic principles? Ford unfolded them in the November 1921 issue of *Nation's Business* in an article entitled, "If I Ran The Railroads." This piece antedated by some months Ford's article that bore the more expansive title, "If I Were President." Much of the rolling stock of the standard carrier, he said, was cumbersome and antiquated. He proposed the substitution of streamlined light weight equipment. The old-line railroad official, he charged, was a mossback, wedded to the past and floundering in red tape. How had he managed to breathe life into the D. T. and I.? He had simply made short shrift, he said, of every form of bureaucratic waste. He gave as the pivotal reason for his success the elimination of railway "parasites." These wastrels and barnacles, he said, were fourfold: lawyers, the "unproductive stockholders," useless bookkeepers and other unnecessary employes.

The Ford pronouncements had a thoroughly radical tinge. They bristled with criticism of Wall Street and rate-gouging. They espoused socialism itself. The fundamental curse of the railroad system, Ford charged at one point, was private ownership. The major trunk lines, he said, should be socialized. Their operation for the benefit of the holders of stocks and bonds, he said, was no more than an arrangement which permitted certain "parasites" to avoid having to go to work for a living.[2] Once more Ford was talking the language of the grain belt. To the smaller shippers of the country, his attack on the existing schedule of freight rates indicated an over-all interest in the nation's welfare. The stunning achievement with the D. T. and I. seemed to promise a new day in transportation.

The "Ironton" succeeded, but not for the reasons Ford alleged. The tiny road under his management was rigorously efficient; none of its managers lolled in easy chairs. Ford began with a most thorough

housecleaning. He put most of the old employes of the line out to
pasture. He discharged all but one of its former executives.[3] Then
the manager of a Ford assembly plant took over. This executive had
never had so much as a day's experience in railroading. He rose to
the occasion with model efficiency nevertheless, but even so, superior
management methods by no means accounted for the money Ford
began to rake in as a railroad operator.

It remained for the transport journals to unfold the real secret
of the D. T. and I.'s sudden prosperity. Once Ford had his hands on
the Lilliputian road, these journals reported, the bulk of the immense
outgoing shipments of the Ford Motor Co. were immediately routed
over its trackbed. From the largest automobile plant in the world,
Ford began to feed to his own line a gigantic supply of the most
lucrative class of freight. By the middle of the twenties, the little
road was drawing one-half of its income from Ford's own shipments.[4]

This was only the beginning. In Ford's pocket, the D. T. and I.
could make super-profits because of its position on the map. Its roadbed ran north and south. It cut across the rights-of-way of fifteen
other roads—most of the big trunk carriers whose tracks ran east and
West. Because of this criss-cross arrangement, Ford could collect from
the larger lines what amounted to concealed rebates. He simply hauled
his own traffic for seventy-five or a hundred miles in a southerly direction to some terminal where the goods had to be transshipped over
the rails of one of the intersecting lines. After changing hands, the
Ford shipments might travel for hundreds or thousands of additional
miles, but Ford was automatically entitled to a division of the
"through" rate. He could lay claim to a certain percentage of the
total freight charge, sharing in the proceeds of the intersecting carrier,
inasmuch as his road had initiated the shipment.

Ford must have pressed this device for all it was worth. At least
Walker D. Hines, the former United States Director-General of railroads, contended in November 1921, that the Ford Motor Co. was
extracting a significantly larger division of the "through" rate than
the trade had usually taken for granted.[5] In addition, Ford saw to
it that one or more of the large east-west lines supplied the D. T.
and I. with reciprocal loads. The roads which failed to route return
trip tonnage over his tracks ran the risk of losing out on the business
of hauling outbound shipments from the Ford factory.[6]

Crowing over his accomplishments as a railroader, Ford finally
made the claim that he had succeeded in eliminating from seven to
fourteen days from the time required to haul one of his cars from

Detroit cross-country. Such an economy of shipping time did not come from any revolution on the D. T. and I., for Ford's miniature line, however well-run, was only seventy to one hundred miles in length. If his shipments were being speeded up to the extent alleged, said an authoritative contributor to *Railway Age*, it could mean only one thing: the Fords were wringing still another special favor from the major roads. They were compelling the big carriers, said this writer, to give Ford traffic preferential through-routing.[7]

Before his railroading days were over, Ford involved the D. T. and I. in another one of his mock wars with Wall Street. This brief encounter occurred during the coal strike of 1922, a labor disturbance which Ford promptly decried as the handiwork of "twenty sharpers down in Wall Street."[8] The New York speculators behind the strike, said the manufacturer, were only creating an artificial fuel shortage so that they might "gouge" the public with high prices. As a gesture of contempt for the "coal trust," Ford straightway closed his factory, throwing 100,000 employes out of work for one week. He next offered to supply fuel for the entire state of Michigan.[9] He could arrange to import all the necessary coal, he said, by tapping the non-union fields of Kentucky and West Virginia with the facilities of the D. T. and I.

This gesture had as much substance as Ford's reputation as a railroad radical. The Ford Motor Co. was in no position to stock the coal bins of Michigan. Traffic experts were unanimous in their judgment that the D. T. and I. was incapable of hauling fuel. The road's rolling stock was too light, its grades too steep.[10] Ford's stand was all the more curious inasmuch as his own factories seemed to have been in no acute danger of running out of fuel. No other automobile manufacturer had to suspend operations. When the strike was well along, a mine owner in West Virginia wired an offer to supply all the fuel requirements of the Ford Motor Co. at Ford's price. Ford, said the Detroit *Free Press*, ignored the telegram.

The abortive promise to convert the D. T. and I. into a coal carrier was not totally meaningless, however. The flourish cost Ford nothing. It gave him another opportunity to rant against the money power, and by at least offering to place his railroad at the disposal of the State of Michigan, he could pose once more as the advocate of the people against the vested interests.

Behind the scenes of this sham battle with Wall Street waged another struggle, a real one in which railroader Ford sought to dislodge the one lone stockholder who refused to part with his minority interest in the D. T. and I. This stubborn investor was Leon Tannenbaum, a former real estate dealer in New York City. Tannenbaum's obduracy was, in some degree, a matter of sentiment. The man had put his money into the original D. T. and I. in 1900. When the road was reorganized several years later, he invested fresh capital in the enterprise.

For such a long-suffering shareholder, Ford's purchase price held no particular attraction. Ford absorbed the road by paying its owners 1 per cent of the par value of the common stock and 5 per cent of the book value of the preferred.[11] Until 98 per cent of these holdings were gathered in, no one could identify the ultimate buyer. Ford stayed in the background, employing Joseph P. Day, a New York auctioneer, to act as his purchasing agent. When Tannenbaum finally discovered that Ford was the principal in this transaction, he became all the more anxious for advantageous terms.

The two remaining owners of the D. T. and I. continued at loggerheads for the next decade. Meanwhile Ford was in a dilemma. He wanted to flaunt the success of his road by declaring handsome earnings. Therefore D. T. and I. common stock was soon reporting a profit of 25 per cent a year. Tannenbaum was now thoroughly convinced that his securities were worth a higher price than any he had yet been offered. Ford was just as set against sharing his railroad earnings with an outsider. Still unwilling to compromise, he set out to erase his fellow-investor in a roundabout manner.

He had his attorneys organize a separate railroad that was 100 per cent Ford-owned. This corporate creature, the Detroit and Ironton, was even more diminutive than the D. T. and I. Its tracks extended a distance of only twenty miles. This dummy line was the property which Ford brought forward in two applications presented to the Interstate Commerce Commission. In each petition he asked that the new paper corporation, with its twenty miles of roadbed, be allowed to absorb the D. T. and I., whose physical properties were twenty-five times as extensive. In 1922 the dummy road asked for permission to lease the D. T. and I. for the next seventy-five years. In 1926 it proposed buying the "Ironton" outright.

Neither petition was granted. Alexander L. Strouse, counsel for Tannenbaum, argued before the Interstate Commerce Commission that Ford's proposals had been conceived for the sole purpose of depriving his client of dividends. As required by the provisions of the Cummings-Esch Act of 1920, Strouse asserted, neither the sale nor the lease of the D. T. and I. could be shown to be in the public interest. The railroad commissioners accepted this line of reasoning. Consequently they rejected both of the Ford applications.[12]

Already out of sorts, Ford lost patience altogether when another agency of the federal government took steps two years later to challenge the legality of certain other D. T. and I. practices. This time, in 1928, the managers of the line were convicted under the Elkins Act, a federal statute which prohibited rebates and rate discriminations. The "Ironton" officials were adjudged guilty on twenty counts and fined $20,000.[13] Thus buffeted by two federal bodies and still plagued by the thought of having to put up with a single unrelenting stockholder, Ford decided to retire from the business.

The following year he sold out to the Pennsylvania Railroad for $35,000,000. It was understood, as a condition of the purchase, that the "Ironton" would continue to enjoy the tonnage of the Ford Motor Co. The Pennsylvania in turn quickly came to terms with the Tannenbaum estate. Tannenbaum himself had died in the meantime. Owning approximately 1 per cent of the "Ironton" stock, the minority holders were content to accept Ford's own valuation of the D. T. and I. as a whole. They settled for a price roughly equivalent to 1 per cent of the millions which Ford collected from the Pennsylvania.

## 2

Several years before he tried his hand at transportation, Ford had added a medical institution to his private domain. For $400,000 he bought a new hospital which a group of citizens were unable to complete after failing to raise the necessary capital. The project was immediately renamed the Henry Ford Hospital. With this institution in his possession, Ford set out to give a lesson to the practitioners of medicine and philanthropy, much as he held up the D. T. and I. as an example to the professional railroaders.

Like the "Ironton," the hospital was a going institution when Ford took it over. The medical plant, like the railway, soon lost most of its old personnel, professional and otherwise. In no time at all, the heart of the professional staff which Ford had inherited was dismissed and replaced by a new set of physicians, imported in the main from Johns Hopkins. Ernest Liebold, Ford's secretary, was installed as manager of the reorganized institution.

Before long, the imprint of Ford discipline was as unmistakable at Henry Ford Hospital as it was in the shops of the D. T. and I. One industrial practice of the Ford Motor Co. carried over to the hospital intact. At first, each physician on the staff was required to punch a time-clock to record his every entry or departure at the institution. Not even the highest salaried surgeon was exempt. This ritual finally had to be dropped, however. For ingenious members of the medical staff made it meaningless, by punching Liebold's time-clock to death, perforating any card in the rack at random, ten or twenty times a day. The time-cards in the physicians' rack soon became so dog-eared they defied deciphering. The rules were then amended so that only maids, orderlies and staff nurses would have to register their comings and goings by mechanical means.

Nor did the idiosyncrasies of Henry Ford Hospital stop here. Governed by the same injunction that applied to all other employes of the Ford Motor Co., members of the staff were prohibited from smoking anywhere at all on the premises, even when off duty. The bolder doctors soon defied this taboo by smoking on the sly, in the toilets of the institution. In the beginning, the no-smoking rule was imposed on all alike—even on the ill who patronized the place. Later on the regulation was relaxed, but for patients only. Fire hazards may have hastened the granting of this concession. For contrary patients had defied the original code by smoking cigarettes under their bed clothes.

Along with the ban against tobacco, Henry Ford Hospital threw up another barrier. By an unwritten law, no Jewish physicians were, then or later, admitted to the staff.

Under Liebold's management, the hospital then began to advertise its wares. It did the job so brashly that the Wayne County Medical Society cited the institution in 1924 for conduct that was deemed unprofessional.[14] In its indictment of Ford's supposed infraction of "medical ethics," the Society surmised that when Dr. John Brown, a trained hospital superintendent, was displaced by Liebold, the trade of the institution had been developing "too slowly for a Ford industry."

The profession took particular objection to a handbill which agents of the Ford Hospital once circulated among the passengers of excursion boats along the Detroit waterfront. Commenting on this circular, the medical association remarked, "Business was not good. There was not enough 'zip'. Real business methods had to be intro-duced. The newspapers were made available, and publicity—wide-spread, flagrant and inaccurate—was given to the public. The Johns Hopkins staff was capitalized.

"Ordinary equipment found in any well-conducted hospital was glorified. The old-time stethoscope was described as a wonderful instrument for listening to the heart and lungs. The microtone, used in every laboratory for cutting specimens, was described as the 'tumor machine.' The public's eyes began to bulge.

"The great Henry Ford had manned his hospital with supermen and installed marvelous and intricate equipment!"

The hostility of the profession was so pronounced in 1924 that the Detroit Academy of Surgeons refused to sponsor a clinic at the Ford Hospital. In view of the institution's "past history and present operation," the officials of the society ruled, Academy members could not accept Ford's hospitality "with dignity and fairness to the general public."

Some of the medical practitioners of Detroit who took this stand toward the Ford Hospital were thinking, first and foremost, of their pocketbooks. These physicians looked askance at Ford's medical experiment because it seemed to be a threat to the established order.

For one thing, it appeared as if Ford might win over the type of patient who was capable of paying large fees. The hospital early introduced a flat-rate charge for its services. This schedule of prices bore no relation to a patient's income. The one fee was gauged solely by the complaint under treatment. Moreover, Ford's hospital patrons were entitled to a complete clinical check-up at no extra cost. On a difficult case, every specialist on the staff might be summoned for consultation. The extra service was fully covered by payment of the flat-rate charge, and because of such an arrangement it was possible for the wealthy patient to pay $150 at Ford's for diagnosis and surgery that might cost him ten times as much anywhere else. Thus, certain outside practitioners were fearful that Ford might pick off the plums of their clientele.

These and other physicians of Detroit were equally alarmed that Ford would launch a grand experiment in group medicine. This even greater threat to the private practitioner was implicit in Ford's remarks when he first announced his acquisition of a hospital. It was his intention, he had said, to run the institution as a "poor man's hospital."[15] Were he to inaugurate a plan of group medicine just for his own factory workers, he could withdraw 100,000 men, together with their families, from every other local agency of medical care. Such was the specter that haunted certain members of the regional medical society.

With the passage of time the Henry Ford Hospital made its peace with the profession. Liebold was replaced by a professional hospital superintendent, and the management of the institution, completely divorced from the operation of the Ford Motor Co., settled into the hands of the brilliant corps of physicians whom the Fords had drawn from Johns Hopkins. Before long the institution was to earn the distinction of being the first general hospital in the country to make a practice of treating psychiatric patients. This innovation was pioneered by Dr. Thomas J. Heldt. Meanwhile, a dozen or more of Dr. Heldt's colleagues were distinguishing themselves in other fields of medicine.* As a consequence, the Henry Ford Hospital was to emerge finally as one of the foremost medical institutions in the Middle West.

Nothing came of the scare which Ford threw into the ranks of the profession at large. Despite the attraction of the fixed fee for all, the Ford Hospital never effected any monopoly of the ailing rich of the community.

Nor did the institution in years to come live up to its promise of catering to the underprivileged, after the manner of a "poor man's hospital." To be sure, the privilege of operating a vast private medical establishment is a costly one. Ford had to meet huge annual deficits out of his own pocket. To that extent, the community was his debtor. Yet, at no time in its subsequent history did the institution ever operate as a philanthropy for those to whom it opened its doors.

Many would have it that during its lifetime the Henry Ford Hospital has dispensed systematic, large-scale medical service to the employes of the Ford Motor Co., free of charge. In her Ford biography of 1922, Sara Bushnell asserted that free hospitalization is given as a matter of course to all Ford workers stricken with tuberculosis.[16] A still more pretentious claim of the same character was later advanced by the Ford biographer James Martin Miller.[17] Miller's book was used in connection with the Ford presidential boom. As time went on, Ford's stature as a patron of the medical arts kept growing. In 1936 Hartley W. Barclay, the author of *Ford Production Methods,* asserted, "Ford employes receive special rates and treatment" at the Henry Ford Hospital.[18] The most sweeping claim of all came from Edwin P. Norwood, whose book *Ford Men and Methods* appeared in 1931. "No charge is ever made for examinations, nursing, medicines, operations or any of the attention given [to Ford employes]," wrote Norwood. "Whatever the cost," said this author, "Henry Ford will tell you that here there would be no better investment."[19]

But whatever Ford or anyone else may have said in the matter, none of the statements put forward by these contributors to Fordiana is true. Despite Ford's original large-handed declaration, and despite one or another biographical claim to the contrary, Ford employes as a class have never at any time enjoyed either free or preferential treat-

* Among the physicians whose work at the Henry Ford Hospital was to win them national recognition were Frank J. Sladen, in medicine; J. Janney Smith, in the field of cardio-respiratory diseases; Roy D. McClure, surgeon; John G. Mateer, gastro-enterologist; Irvine McQuarrie, pediatrician; Jean Paul Pratt, gynecologist; John K. Ormond, urologist; Everett D. Plass, obstetrician; Frank W. Hartman, pathologist; and Thomas J. Heldt, neuro-psychiatrist.

ment at the Henry Ford Hospital. In general the Ford factory man in 1914 and in every year to follow discovered that he would receive hospitalization or any other form of medical care at Ford's expense, only when he incurred an occupational disability that was compensable under the law. Otherwise, either he or members of his family, he learned from experience, had to pay the going rate for all services received at the Ford Hospital. In fact, to make absolutely certain that such patients would pay their bills, Ford instituted the check-off. As a prerequisite for admission to or release from his medical plant, his employes were required from the beginning to authorize the Ford Motor Co. to make regular deductions from their wages.

In the course of giving hospital care to some of his own factory workers, Ford once instituted a system of occupational therapy for which few close analogies can be found in medical annals. In January 1918, a group of bedridden workers who had broken their legs on duty at the Ford factory were subjected to a unique experiment. Propped up with headrests, their bed clothes protected by oilcloth doilies, the injured men were put to the task of screwing nuts on bolts by hand. This departure in hospitalized mass production was reported by Dr. J. E. Mead, then chief surgeon of the Ford Motor Co.[20]

The nut-and-bolt therapy was short-lived, however. But while it lasted it took its place in the folk-humor of Detroit alongside outright legends like the jest that expectant mothers at the Ford Hospital are placed on a conveyor belt for delivery *ad seriatum* as they pass through the operating room.

## Ten

### CHRONICLER OF THE NEGLECTED TRUTH

#### 1

ONE OF THE FORCES that all but swept Ford into the White House and into control of the Tennessee watershed was his own newspaper, the Dearborn *Independent*. This private weekly had first gone to press, under Ford's ownership, on January 11, 1919. It implemented and mirrored the personality of its owner for the next decade. In the act of setting himself up as publisher, the manufacturer was, in part, giving way to a conviction that—despite the performance at Mt. Clemens—his talents knew no bounds. Like many another mighty captain of industry, he was submitting to the urge to project himself and to remind society of the grandeur of his mission. Moreover, he could now gratify by the printed word the same feelings of self-importance that underlay the quest for political office and the struggle with his stockholders. The editors of the Dearborn *Independent,* therefore, knew what they were about when they built their first issue around a feature to which they gave the name "Mr. Ford's Own Page." In reality Ford had neither the time nor the equipment required for the composition of editorials. Even so, the column that bore his name was to appear for years to come, reflecting the spirit, if not the letter, of most of the whims and social opinions he felt obliged to communicate to the world.

The real author of "Mr. Ford's Own Page," and his editorial colleagues, went to work under somewhat novel conditions. They were required to punch a time-clock. Their headquarters consisted of some space in the Ford Engineering Laboratory, next to the tractor plant of the Ford Motor Co. Ford soon took to calling the favorites among his writing men "good mechanics." He urged the editor to apply "assembly line" methods to the preparation of the news. Why not have one writer fill in the facts of a story, he asked; another, the humor; a third, the editorial comment? The editor tactfully explained that in making up a newspaper, one could carry the division of labor only so far. In the field of journalism, he pointed out, the individual article is normally the smallest divisible unit of production. That satisfied Ford.

In its circulation department, the paper soon acquired some real earmarks of mass production. When Ford purchased the *Independent* it had no readers to speak of. It was a sleepy rural weekly with a scanty circulation limited to the village of Dearborn. Neither the standard methods of promotion nor the quality of the reading matter sufficed to give the *Independent* any appreciable new circulation, so Ford set out to manufacture a ready public by exerting pressure on his dealers. In repeated communications his general sales manager told the Ford dealers to think of the Dearborn *Independent* as a "standard Ford product." In time the dealer was expected to sell a subscription to Ford's paper to every buyer of a Model T. The average Ford salesman soon came to regard payments to the *Independent* as part of his overhead. He would send an occasional check for twenty-five or thirty dollars to the managers of the paper, just to keep on the good side of the home office. The mailing list that accompanied his check was, often as not, none too carefully compiled. Many a dealer either sent free subscriptions to friends and customers, without sounding them out in advance, or if pressed for time, he sometimes went to the telephone directory and chose a list of names at random. By such means Ford was able to endow his paper with what some of his editorial employes chose to call, before long, a "lead pipe" circulation, consisting at peak of some 700,000 readers.

Most of the general press acknowledged the debut of the Ford weekly without comment. The Detroit *Saturday Night,* on the other hand, was less generous in its estimate of this journalistic nestling. The *Saturday Night,* moved by rancor, at once submitted the opinion that the *Independent* was by all odds the "best weekly ever turned out by a tractor plant."[1]

But as the *Independent* began to function under Ford auspices, it had a staff well worth respecting. Most of the eight men whom Ford recruited from the daily newspapers of Detroit were able journalists. His first editor, E. G. Pipp, had served for twelve years as managing editor and editor-in-chief of the Detroit *News.* Himself a liberal and a believer in Ford's liberalism, Pipp had encouraged Ford's political ambitions in 1916 and 1918. During a brief period of service as a European correspondent for the Detroit *News,* Pipp had dropped a hint of the kind of cause which he hoped to promote when he went to work for Ford. The *News* sent him to England to cover the first World War, but no one would have guessed it from the substance of the first dispatch he cabled back to his paper. What Pipp submitted as his initial reportorial effort, written in the midst of an all-embracing war, was a rapturous account of the three-cent fare which he had encountered on the municipally owned street railway of the city of Glasgow.

Then second-in-command at the Dearborn *Independent* was William J. Cameron. Cameron's first assignment was to compose "Mr. Ford's Own Page." Ford's literary double was well chosen. During a period of service that lasted sixteen years, Cameron had established himself at the Detroit *News* as a facile writer, a columnist of capacity and something of a scholar. His colleagues had nicknamed him the "walking dictionary." When Cameron transferred his talents to Dearborn, he was forty-one. He brought to his new post both the gravity and the vocabulary of a moralist. His politics were on the liberal side. He had been a minister in his younger days. He shared a common enthusiasm with Ford and Edison. The idols of his younger days were

Robert Ingersoll and William Jennings Bryan.[2] And as the new job unfolded, Cameron was to fill it to perfection, finally, by learning to absorb Ford's central ideas like a sponge.

The revived Dearborn *Independent* distinguished itself overnight as one of the paradoxes of American journalism. On its pages one of the richest men of all time began to speak out like an organizer for the Knights of Labor. This Midas of the 20th century declared war on Big Business in the first issue of his paper. He boldly aligned himself with the common people against the "speculative capitalists" of Wall Street. He forged a confederacy with the proletariat by announcing at the outset that his weekly would accept no advertising. By such a gesture the Dearborn *Independent* was attesting, its editors asserted, "the absolute sincerity of its motive and the independence of its thought." Charging that most newspapers are instruments of reaction, Ford's journal styled itself "Chronicler of the Neglected Truth." "This paper exists to spread ideas, the best that can be found. It aims to furnish food for thought."

What followed in Ford's paper was, for the most part, as dated as it was radical and eccentric. For an inventory of the social ills they set out to expose, his writers turned the clock back thirty years. They thundered like old-fashioned agrarian rebels, like dyed-in-the-wool Populists. Under Ford's aegis, these purveyors of "food for thought" went back to the politics and the mores that had colored the American hamlet and countryside of the 80's and 90's.

In its crusade for "right living," Ford's weekly fell back on the idiom of the Bible Belt. It railed at sex and rum. It reported that Parisians were floundering after dark in a "Babylon of jazz and liquor." London, it seems, was "staggering to bed at night" and "reeling" to work in the morning. Ford's Jeremiahs addressed themselves to the conscience of the American business man who was becoming so "boozy" he was "slipping." They devoted turgid passages to the "orgies and bacchanalian revels" of Hollywood. One issue Cameron gave over to the confessions of a "prominent Hollywood producer." Before he would allow his own daughter to go to work on a moving picture lot, said this insider, he would rather see her dead. According to the scribes at Dearborn, Broadway, hard by "Jewish Wall Street," was even more degenerate. Here, the paper charged, the theater was taking its dramatic material from "the slums, the Orient and the lower animals." Cameron's collaborators flayed New York actresses for daring to expose their undergarments in "reeking" bedroom farces. They professed that women in general were submitting to "sexitis" and yielding to "a present tendency to undress." "What," lamented the keepers of Ford's press, "is the world coming to?"

It was the spoilers of Wall Street whom the "Chroniclers of the Neglected Truth" held chiefly responsible for sapping the morals of the nation. These reputed sharpers were the subject of a fervid Dearborn memoir entitled, "What I Found in Wall Street, By a Girl Who Spent Five Years in a Broker's Office." This tender flower lost her bloom, she said, in an atmosphere polluted by tobacco fumes, nickel cuspidors, and Turkish rugs worth $1000 each. Amid such surroundings, the young woman confessed, her "ideals" had been "hopelessly shattered."

By serving such cultural fare, Ford was harping on a tried rural theme. Traveling players in the 90's had nourished the corn belt with similar melodrama. As an antidote to the debauchery of city life, the Dearborn *Independent* advised solid Americans to go to church and to keep their boys down on the farm. Inasmuch as two-thirds of Ford's readers at the time were living in small towns or in the country, this counsel was well aimed. After all, the paper insisted, "The real United States lies outside the cities. When we stand up and sing, 'My Country 'Tis of Thee'," it said, "we seldom think of the cities."

The economic preachments of the paper were equally moving when read by lamplight down on the farm. As a pamphleteer, Ford was rekindling flames that had raged over the prairies during his youth. Like rebellious agrarians of an earlier generation, he thumped loudest against money and monopoly. His periodical railed at the gold standard, dubbing it a creature of "Jewish Wall Street." He called upon the "people" to substitute greenbacks and fiat money as an "honest" medium of exchange. In Ford's case, as in Edison's, this recurrent thesis amounted to an obsession. It was seldom that the Dearborn *Independent* intoned any other battle cry when it was storming at the "international bankers" and the sundry agencies of finance capital.

When Ford dropped his preoccupation with currency reform, as he did on occasion, he meandered into some strange byways of social doctrine. He came out for government ownership of the railroads and of the telephone and telegraph system.[3] As a "great step toward protecting in this country the Right of a Man to a Job," "Mr. Ford's Own Page" then urged the adoption of a permanent federal works program. This service, declared Cameron in Ford's name, is the duty of "our highest socialized institution."[4] It was Cameron, again, who poked fun at one of the most sacred tenets of American individualism. "Successful persons often say that opportunities are just as plentiful as they ever were," he wrote in 1919, "but they don't tell you what they are, where to find them, or how to use them. . . . They deal in glittering generalities that mean nothing."

There were moments when Ford's journal went so far as to champion the cause of organized labor. The paper sided with the union during the coal strike of 1922.[5] It threw its weight to the men who struck the steel industry in 1919. When Gary refused to confer with a delegation of his own striking employes, the Dearborn *Independent* accused him of acting as if he were "more important than the president of the United States." It was J. P. Morgan of Wall Street whom Ford's paper held ultimately responsible for dictating the labor policies of United States Steel and for allowing the conflict of 1919 to take a violent turn. Of this financial titan, the Dearborn *Independent* cuttingly remarked that although "his friends say he is a very kind and tender-hearted man," none of these character witnesses was working in a steel mill for his daily bread.[6]

The cartoons from some of the early issues of the Ford weekly were reminiscent of *Puck* or *Life* when these magazines were combating capitalism in 1885. One of these pictorial offerings portrayed the "Consumer," a frail little chap, prostrate and strangled by the hand of a bloated "Profiteer." "Uncle Sam" could be seen in the background, scurrying to the rescue, brandishing the club of "Regulation." Another of the liberal, if not radical, Ford cartoons appeared in 1919 before the great steel strike had run its course. The only figure here portrayed was a proletarian Gulliver shown in the act of stripping off his fetters. Sitting on the ground with his legs still bound, this giant was yawning and stretching his great arms. Broken strands of cord dangled from his wrists. The title given the picture was, "Labor of the World Awakening."

All in all, there was nothing really revolutionary about the precepts of the Dearborn *Independent*. The magazine was wedded so firmly to the formula of fiat money and plain living that its tilting at Wall Street rarely went beyond the point of calling names or making faces. The recipe was shrewd as well as barren. By its exposition Ford could humor the farmers and the small shopkeepers of the nation. Among the issues he raised, few indeed had the effect of clashing with his own profound challenge to the old order, or of embarrassing his own dramatic career of money-making.

Ford could fuse the theory of Populism and the practice of capitalism easily enough for the reason that what he carried forward from the old platforms of agrarian revolt, in the main, were the planks that were most innocent and least radical. Like many a greenbacker of an earlier day, the publisher of the Dearborn *Independent* was haunted by the will-o'-the-wisp of "money" and the bogey of "race." It was these superstitions that lay at the very marrow of his political thinking.

2

Ford laid siege to the Jews on May 22, 1920. He opened fire with a front page editorial printed beneath the strident caption, THE INTERNATIONAL JEW: THE WORLD'S PROBLEM. "There is a race," his paper asserted, "a part of humanity, which has never yet been received as a welcome part." This people, the journal continued, has ever been fouling the earth and plotting to dominate it. To gratify their desire to see mankind go to the dogs, the Jews were charged with maintaining a secret "international super-capitalist government." This racial problem, said the Dearborn *Independent,* is the "prime" question confronting all society. Thus began the publication of a serial that was to fill the pages of Ford's magazine for the next ninety-one consecutive issues.*

Jew-baiting loomed large in the culture that had molded Ford. When the great anti-monopoly crusades swept out of the West from 1880 to the end of the century, *Puck* and the *Police Gazette* were caricaturing the Jew week after week. These journals, scattered over the hinterland, were given to lampooning the Jew as the villain of modern capitalism. They depicted Wall Street in lurid cartoons as a gigantic Jewish pawnshop. The same argument infiltrated the political thinking of the grain belt. When Ford was fifteen, in 1878, the Central Greenback Club of Detroit issued a philippic that laid the American railroad scandals and the hard times that followed the Civil War to the "Rothschilds across the water." The racialism of the back-country had taken some of its temper from organized religion. It was "the Jews" whom the Protestants of the Bible Belt held accountable for the Crucifixion. More than that, Ford's native soil was Ku Klux Klan country.

Nor did Ford doubt for a moment that the race war which he

* Ford reprinted his Jewish serial in four small volumes. As issued by the Dearborn Publishing Company, the original offprints bore the following subtitles:
Vol.   I   *The World's Foremost Problem* (1920)
Vol.  II   *Jewish Activities in the United States* (1921)
Vol. III   *Jewish Influences in American Life* (1921)
Vol. IV   *Aspects of Jewish Power in the United States* (1922)

was about to wage in print was anything but holy. In fact, he fully expected to have his crusade endorsed by all the "good Jews" of the country. He gave expression to such a hope in the way he behaved toward one of his few Jewish friends, Rabbi Leo M. Franklin of Detroit. These two had been intimates and nextdoor neighbors for years. Ford had long since made a practice of presenting to Dr. Franklin every year a new custom-built Ford automobile, as a token of friendship. Franklin was stunned when the *Independent* began to rend the air with anti-Semitism. He was dumbfounded when, sometime later, a chauffeur appeared at the door with the customary gift from Ford—another new car. But this time Franklin declined the gift. He told the driver to take the car back to its donor. Several days later Ford called the rabbi by telephone and inquired, in all innocence, "What's wrong, Dr. Franklin? Has anything come between us?"[7]

But neither the mortification of a distinguished old Jewish friend nor any other deterrent could turn the tide. For by the time Ford felt impelled to lambast the Jews, he was gripped by a monomania, driven by a racial phobia. Norman Hapgood dropped in at Dearborn about this time, preparatory to publishing his incisive Ford serial in *Hearst's International*. It was his judgment that Ford was then suffering from an advanced "persecution complex." After making a close study of the racial facets of this complex, Hapgood went so far as to say that on many a subject, unrelated to industry, Ford's head seemed to be "full of wheels." As far as he could tell, said the journalist, Ford's mind, apart from his own line, was "that of a child."[8]

Two of the men who were closest to Ford at the time only added fresh fuel to the flame. They helped to inflate Ford's conviction of omniscience. They gave his racial bias teeth and direction. W. J. Cameron put Ford's phobia into words. Ernest Liebold directed the secret service ring that kept the anti-Semitic arsenal of the Dearborn *Independent* stocked with ammunition. During a libel suit that occurred sometime later, the attorney for the plaintiff attributed to Ford's secretary the boast that, "When we get through with the Jews there won't be one of them who will dare raise his head in public."[9]

Most of the newspaper men on Ford's staff had no stomach for religious bigotry. For this reason and others they began to desert the Ford Engineering Laboratory, one by one. By the summer of 1922 only two of the original eight remained. Pipp, who had begun as editor, was first to leave. Pipp was a liberal Catholic who despised Jew-baiting. His days at Dearborn had been numbered for other reasons as well. He resented the harassment of Senator Newberry, and his relations with Liebold had never been cordial. On his own once more, the departing editor founded a curious magazine of his own, *Pipp's Weekly.* For a time he pitted this journal against the Dearborn *Independent,* and during his years of dissidence, from 1920-23, the files of his little weekly were to become a mine of fact and commentary on the inner workings of the Ford Motor Co.

Cameron stepped in to fill Pipp's shoes. Before taking up newspaper work, Cameron had been a village preacher in Brooklyn, Michigan. He filled this pastorate for six years. His interest in religion was still alive. Well beyond the date on which he assumed the editorship of the Dearborn *Independent,* he would appear from time to time in some Detroit pulpit. For several years it had been his custom to deliver sermonettes once a week at a small mission which catered to the city's unemployed and migratory workers.

When Cameron was forced to choose between his assignment at Dearborn and his scruples as a scholar and a man of God, he did some squirming. He had been openly caustic and derisive, says Pipp, when Ford took the stand at Mt. Clemens. Then, after driving to work with Ford one morning, the author of "Mr. Ford's Own Page" lamented to Pipp, "Ford has been at me to commence writing on those cursed Jewish articles. I don't know what to write," said the former pastor. As Ford's complex became more and more unruly, Pipp recounts, "Cameron would dish out biting bits of sarcasm and give vent to expressions of utmost disgust."[10]

But before long Cameron was hard at it, brewing poison for the arrows in Ford's anti-Semitic quiver. The job still irked him. Sometime after he tossed principle to the wind, the gifted ex-minister confided to a friend that he dreaded it every time he had to write one of those "Jewish" articles.[11] Later, however, he became so cynical, or else washed his mind so clean of any guilt feelings, that he could assert unblushingly at a banquet of the Ford Training School, "We have too many 'trained seal' writers taking orders."[12]

As chief procurer of the racial matter that appeared in the Dearborn *Independent,* Ernest Liebold went in for mass production. To insure a ready supply of anti-Semitic fodder, this Ford executive founded a special detective agency in New York City. It was the function of the eastern bureau to pry into the private lives of known and suspected Jews. Ford poured thousands of dollars into this effort. A few of his expenditures were uncovered by Norman Hapgood. The chief of staff alone was paid a salary of $1000 a month.[13] His office expenses for the week ending April 30, 1921 ran to $678.[14]

Ford's agents, like actors in a melodrama, tiptoed in their prowling. Most of the principals involved disguised their identity by adopting secret code numbers. Liebold was 121 X; Cameron, 122 X.[15]

Fanatics, adventurers, amateur detectives and seedy White Russians began to buzz around Liebold. On the market for any raw nonsense that suited his designs, he was duped into buying a translation of the spurious "Protocols of Zion." This notorious document is a classic in the literature of anti-Semitism. It appeared in Russia in 1905 at a time when the Czar's empire was shaken by pervasive social unrest. Its reputed author, Serge Nilus, was a Czarist agent. Nilus forged the publication in the hope that the Russian court might counteract the popular cry for reform and social revolution by fomenting a wave of Jewish pogroms. This inspiration of the "Protocols" was exposed by the London *Times* in August, 1921.

Liebold picked up an edition of the forgery in New York City. The man who translated it for him into rough English was Boris Brasol, an eccentric Russian monarchist and former member of a reactionary, anti-Semitic secret society known as the Russian Black Hundred. Some thirty-seven different editions of the work were then floating about the world. White Russian officers living in Paris had long made a business of hawking the "Protocols." These emigrés usually passed off the forgery as a rare work that secret agents had only recently managed to smuggle from the Jews. Liebold knowing nothing of all this—and caring less—rushed back to Detroit to reprint his "discovery."

For Ford's purposes the "Protocols" were made to order. No manual on Jew-baiting had more to offer. Written so as to suggest that its authors were Jews, the book unfolds the essence of a supposed Jewish plot to conquer the earth. In this alleged conspiracy for world domination, seven unidentified all-powerful Jews—the "Learned Elders of Zion"—dictate to the rest of their race. It is the business of these "wise men," say the "Protocols," to destroy the "Aryan" world by aiding and abetting every social malady known to man, and thus to prepare the way for eventual Jewish dictatorship. Seen in such a light, war, class conflict, immorality and the decline of capitalism are all equally Jew-inspired, on an international scale, and are only the prelude to a grand Semitic seizure of power.

Without checking this fabrication or without consulting any experts in the matter, Liebold hurried to the presses of the Dearborn *Independent*. For the next year and a half the "Protocols" provided the theme on which Cameron improvised with variations. The text had to be edited for American consumption. Cameron merely polished the document, brought it up to date, and gave it a ring of conviction by filling in contemporary material. He improved on the forgery so skillfully that, in modern dress, it became one of the foremost existing brochures on anti-Semitism. The resulting Ford version of the "Protocols" stands to this day as one of the world's most widely read standard editions.

In their defamation of the Jew, Ford and Cameron antedated the propaganda ministry of Nazi Germany by a full ten years. The Jews, they asserted in an early issue of the Dearborn *Independent*, are "the conscious enemies of all that Anglo-Saxons mean by civilization."[16] Ford's paper then did obeisance to the myth of Nordic supremacy by drawing a distinction between Jews and "white men." Some time later Cameron proclaimed that Jesus was not a Jew "as commonly conceived."[17]

The paper went on to attribute every conceivable symptom of social degeneracy to the Jewish people and to their seducers, the "Learned Elders." To the culture group which can boast the lowest crime record in the United States, Cameron and his staff applied the terms "vile," "lewd," "nasty," "erotic" and "criminal." To soften Aryans for the kill, the Jews were said to have introduced chorus girls, cabarets and midnight frolics. They were accused of plying Americans with liquor and spreading disease by innoculation.[18] The "skunk-cabbage of American jazz," the crime waves of the United States, and the "corruption" of professional baseball into a species of "garbage"— these too were said to be part and parcel of the same hateful Jewish plot.

The "Elders," it seemed, hatched a conspiracy at the dawn of American history. One of their naval agents presumably sullied our virgin shore in 1492. The first foreigner to set foot in the North Americas, said the Dearborn *Independent*, was a Jewish interpreter who came over with Columbus.[19] Catholic Queen Isabella herself, Cameron charged, was a "Jewish front," the money for her expedition having been raised by three "secret Jews."

Two of Ford's pet complexes were woven into Cameron's anti-Semitic crazy-quilt. Three chapters of the "International Jew" were dedicated to the thesis that Benedict Arnold had served as a "Jewish front" in the pay of Semitic bankers and warmongers.[20] This is the American traitor whom Ford had confused with the writer Arnold Bennett, at Mt. Clemens. On another subject of special concern to Ford, Cameron alleged that the Jews dodged the draft during the first World War so that Gentiles might have a better opportunity to kill off one another.

In time the authors of the "International Jew" managed to sound bottom in nearly every well of ignorance. They went to press with the claim that Jews were filtering into the Masonic Order and into the Society of Jesus for the purpose of boring from within.[21]

Ford accused the "Elders" of dominating the labor movement of the country. In so many words he attributed the 1922 strike of the United Mine Workers to the "greed and avarice of Wall Street Kikes."[22] The Jews, he said, had already seized "control" in Washington.[23]

Political theory as well as social action, it seemed, had suffered from the Jewish taint. Great Jewish economists, said Cameron, were ensconced at "both ends of the movement"—Marx on the left and Ricardo on the right. In fact, it was made to appear as if none but Jews had ever so much as questioned the social order from any standpoint whatsoever. For according to the *Independent,* "The whole science of economics, conservative and radical, capitalistic and anarchistic, is of Jewish origin."[24] Before Ford's pamphleteers had done with their grotesque and incredible outpourings, they issued a call-to-action. They brought things to a head by scoring Americans for their "flabby tolerance" toward the Jews.[25] After reciting a lurid tale about some young Jew who was supposed to have murdered a girl in a Southern factory, the Dearborn *Independent* remarked editorially that it was "not without reason" that the Ku Klux Klan had been revived in Georgia![26] What the United States lacked in this racial crisis, the paper lamented, was the "gristle to attack."[27] The Ford paper then predicted that the day would yet arrive for the "exodus" of the Jews from America.[28]


# Eleven

## CHRISTIANS ONLY

### 1

WHEN THE ANTI-SEMITISM of the Dearborn *Independent* was finally challenged in a court of law, Ford beat a hasty retreat. By resorting to one expedient, he escaped the ordeal of having to defend his racial views on the witness stand. A somersault in another direction enabled him to pose as having been utterly innocent of the anti-Jewish activity that had prospered in his name and with his financial support for nearly ten years. This double act of face-saving was performed by Cameron, the editor of the Dearborn *Independent*, and by Harry Bennett, then Ford's chief private detective.

Both of these measures of defense were aimed at Aaron Sapiro, a Jewish lawyer and promoter. Sapiro had come into some prestige and a small fortune by organizing marketing associations among the farmers of the country. When the Dearborn *Independent* accused him of fleecing his clients, he filed a million-dollar damage suit against Ford. The case came to trial in Detroit in March 1927.

Ford was represented in the action by an imposing staff of seven attorneys. All but one of this galaxy of able counsel were members of the Detroit bar. The single outsider, engaged for psychological effect, was Senator James A. Reed of Missouri. Ford's advisers fully expected to find the plaintiff represented by a "Jew lawyer from New York." Much to their surprise, however, Sapiro walked into court with William Henry Gallagher, a prominent Detroit attorney who was an Irish Catholic.

At the trial, W. J. Cameron, the author of "Mr. Ford's Own Page" and the star witness for the defense, simply offered himself up as a sacrifice on the altar of public opinion. On the stand for five days and subjected to a merciless cross-examination, Cameron assumed full responsibility for every word the Dearborn *Independent* had ever printed. He strove, under fire, to absolve Ford of any complicity whatever in the attack on Sapiro or any other Jew by asserting that he alone, as editor of the Dearborn *Independent*, had the power to frame the paper's editorial policy.[1]

Under oath, Cameron contended that Ford had never read the Dearborn *Independent* in his presence. His own judgment in the management of the paper, he testified, had been final and absolute in all matters. No advance copy, he swore, had ever required Ford's personal approval. Cameron then professed that he had never discussed with Ford "any article" on "any Jew." He stated, finally, that he had never so much as talked with Ford about the stand taken by the Dearborn *Independent* on any public question.

Some of this testimony was the whole truth; the rest, half-truth or fabrication. In the first place it had never been necessary for Ford to keep close watch over his newspaper. Ernest Liebold had done that for him. It was Liebold rather than Ford who had dictated the paper's editorial policy and censored its content again and again. In so doing, Liebold had always moved with authority: he was Ford's personal secretary as well as general manager of the parent corporation, the Dearborn Publishing Co., under whose auspices the Dearborn *Independent* was issued. More than that, Cameron had never required close editorial supervision. By the time he took the stand in the Sapiro case, he had been fraternizing with Ford and Liebold off and on for seven years. He knew the foibles of both men by heart.

Nor was Cameron's declaration that he had never discussed "any article" on "any Jew" in Ford's presence the same as saying that he had never talked with Ford on the subject of Jews in general. In a narrow sense, this protestation may have been true. The facts belie any broader construction. Pipp has told how Cameron had to be prodded into writing any anti-Semitic pieces at all. Liebold, his immediate superior, would hardly have purchased the "Protocols" and placed this document on Cameron's desk without having had Ford's tacit consent. Moreover, years before Sapiro filed suit, Ford and Cameron together once spent an entire afternoon vainly trying to infect Dean Marquis with their racial virus. Several months after the termination of the Sapiro case, Cameron impeached his own court testimony by refusing at first to credit the news that Ford had authorized a public retraction of his alleged anti-Semitism.[2]

Other face-saving evidence found its way into the Sapiro record. Clifford B. Longley of Ford counsel informed the court that his client had never so much as heard of Sapiro up to the very day on which suit was filed. The plaintiff countered this claim by introducing as a witness James Martin Miller, a Ford biographer and a former employe of the Dearborn Publishing Co. Ford told him in so many words, Miller testified, of his intention to have Sapiro "exposed."[3]

Once Cameron had his say, Sapiro's counsel pressed for an opportunity to examine Ford in person. Ford's lawyers, on the other hand, were just as anxious to avoid such a contingency. In the event that their client was to take a seat in the witness box, he might repeat the performance he had given at Mt. Clemens. He could easily ruin the defense and endanger his reputation for integrity and fair play. His attorneys were quite content with the strategy of allowing Cameron to stand as the scapegoat. The ensuing struggle over Ford's availability as a witness gave the Sapiro action a really dramatic turn.

The act of serving subpoenas on Ford and Liebold had proved to be no mean feat. Agents of the court worked for months before they succeeded in slipping past the Ford bodyguard. Liebold was finally apprehended in the environs of his home. The process server who caught him had to chase him for a block.[4] It took even greater ingenuity to reach Ford. The magician who finally broke through was a clever young lawyer who went out to Dearborn for that express purpose during a celebration at the Ford Airport, posing as a reporter and offering his services when the manager of the airport called for volunteers to help keep the crowd in order. Adorned with a badge that read "Official," the court's agent soon spied Ford riding to the airport in an open Lincoln. He slid close enough to the machine to hear its distinguished occupant issue a command to the effect that all cigarette smokers should be instantly removed from the premises. Just as a plane left the runway and all eyes were fixed on it admiringly, a subpoena and a five-dollar witness fee dropped into Ford's lap. Ford heard the words, "I am serving a subpoena for the United States Circuit Court in the case of Sapiro versus Ford." The process server turned and fled. He heard the manufacturer exclaim. "No, no, no; take it away."[5]

Ford and his guards immediately gave chase to the man who had pierced their defenses. They quickly overtook him and the first to challenge him was Ray Dahlinger, the bodyguard who had traveled on the Peace Ship and was now managing the Ford Airport. "You think you're pretty smart, don't you?" said Dahlinger to the cornered lawyer. "Well, you didn't serve a subpoena on Mr. Henry Ford at all. You served it on Mr. Ford's brother, John Ford."

Meanwhile Henry Ford stood by at Dahlinger's elbow, without uttering a word. Not relishing a physical encounter with Ford's men-at-arms, the process server quietly replied, "Then what's all the fuss about?" He left the grounds without further molestation. In court six months later, Ford counsel denied that service had ever been been properly effected. The subpoena, he argued, had fallen through Ford's knees to the floor of the car.[6] Sapiro's attorney met this objection by moving to have the defendant cited for contempt. Whereupon the Ford legal staff promptly agreed to produce their client voluntarily.

At this point the court was cheated of its principal witness by the occurrence of an automobile accident. On the evening before his scheduled appearance in the witness box, Ford is said to have been the victim of a hit-and-run driver. Officials of the Ford Motor Co. first asserted that Ford's car had careened over an embankment, crowded from the highway by a mysterious motorist who had "lain in wait at the gates of the Ford plant." The accident, so this statement ran, had really been a "deliberate attempt to kill" the president of the Ford Motor Co.[7] Dahlinger quickly removed the wreckage of Ford's car and Ford was spirited into his private hospital. His physical state became the subject of daily bulletins issued from the Henry Ford Hospital. The diagnoses ranged from "strained back muscles" to "concussion of the brain."

In the course of these proceedings, Cameron made a curious public statement. No one had questioned the authenticity of Ford's mishap; yet, said the protesting editor of the Dearborn *Independent*, an accident really had occurred, even if some people did feel like drawing certain "unavoidable and unfounded inferences" from the fact.[8]

Several newspaper reporters then revisited the scene of the alleged wreck. Here, at substantially the same time and place where Ford had presumably come to grief the week before, the group conducted an unofficial traffic count. The reported accident or attempt at murder had occurred at 8:30 of a Sunday evening on Michigan Avenue, perhaps the city's busiest thoroughfare; yet no one apparently had witnessed it. From their own survey of the Sunday evening drivers at that point, the newspapermen were forced to conclude that any accident occurring at such a time and place would probably attract a crowd of passers-by, particularly if the casualty were so conspicuous a figure as Henry Ford.

It was Harry Bennett, then Ford's foremost detective, who volunteered the most illuminating comment on Ford's purported misfortune. Only spokesmen for the Ford Motor Co. had suggested the possibility of attempted homicide. But after conducting a private investigation of the circumstances of the accident, Bennett ruled out intended "homicide" altogether. "Our connections with the Detroit underworld are such," he said, "that within twenty-four hours after the hatching of such a plot we would know of it."[9] The Ford detective did not elaborate further on the nature of his "connections." He did proceed, however, to marshal a number of his own secret agents so astutely that Ford was able to put off the day of reckoning and to postpone what he feared most—another cross-examination before a jury of his peers.

Bennett took a hand in the Sapiro action two weeks after the occurrence of Ford's reported accident. He intervened when it began to look as if Ford would really have to take the stand after all. He moved just as attorney Gallagher announced his intention to ask the court to appoint a disinterested physician who could inquire into Ford's physical condition.

At this point the judge in the case was suddenly served with a mass of affidavits signed by fourteen of Bennett's operatives. These

legal papers preferred charges of attempted bribery and jury tampering. They alleged that Sapiro had engaged the services of a certain
"Kid" Miller for the purpose of corrupting one of the women jurors
in the case. This purported intermediary was described in the affidavits as having a "Jewish cast of countenance."*

By a slip of the tongue, the accused woman juror brought the
Sapiro trial to a sudden close. She was indiscreet enough to defend
herself in public. A reporter asked her to say what she thought of
the Bennett affidavits. The woman replied that, to her mind, Ford
counsel seemed over-anxious to keep the case from going to the jury.
Her injudicious statement appeared in the newspapers. Ford counsel
at once filed a motion for a mistrial and the motion was granted.
When the jury was excused, one of its members reported that he and
his fellow jurors were "almost unanimous" in feeling that the Ford
defense had collapsed.[10] The bench then set a date for retrial, six
months hence.

Sapiro's counsel vigorously opposed the motion for a mistrial.
Bennett had only contrived to save Ford's face, he argued, "probably on the realization that he is either not fit to come into court or
that he cannot face the examination on the charges which he has been
broadcasting to the world all these years."[11] In the same argument,
attorney Gallagher asserted that the Ford affidavits had been drawn
in such a manner as to prefer "other nasty charges" against his client.

As to the plausibility of Bennett's allegations, Gallagher reminded
the court that Ford agents had been haunting the courtroom and the
adjoining corridors from the day the trial opened. In fact, even the
New York *Times* observed that these operatives, fifty strong, had all
but "blocked traffic" in the Federal building.[12] The charge of jury
tampering was unreasonable on the face of it, said Gallagher, inasmuch as he and his client fully appreciated that on other occasions
"Ford agents had made a practice of tapping telephone wires, wiring
the private rooms of various persons and even the chambers of
judges, examining private letters and private baggage, employing
neighborhood merchants to spread propaganda, going into the homes
of jurors posing as salesmen, sending notes of warning to jurors, and
doing many other things of the kind."[13]

But such pleading was legally beside the point. In dismissing
the case, the judge expressly cleared Sapiro and the accused juror

* Two of Bennett's deponents played a still more important part in Ford's
life later on. One of these men, Carl Brooks, became chief of police in the city of
Dearborn in 1929. The other, Verlin C. (Verne) Doonan, managed the campaign
for candidates approved by the Ford Motor Co. in many a Dearborn election.

of any attempt at jury meddling. His ruling was necessary, he said, only because a juror had issued a public statement on a case that was still pending in court. The court had nothing to say about the half a hundred private detectives who had infested the courtroom.


2


Two months before the Sapiro suit came up for retrial, Ford called off his seven-year war against the Jews. He settled his libel action out of court, honoring Sapiro with a personal apology. To the Jewish people as a whole, he submitted a full retraction of all his alleged past anti-Semitism. The intermediary who negotiated with Jewry in his behalf was Joseph A. Palma, an intimate of Harry Bennett's and a former United States Secret Service agent who was about to take over the Ford dealership on Staten Island. Palma arranged the peace terms by dealing with representatives of the American Jewish Committee.

Had Ford disavowed his anti-Semitism for the principle of the thing? If so, the light dawned slowly. Up to this point, none had succeeded in catching his ear on moral grounds. Heretofore, most of the letters of protest sent to Dearborn from outstanding Jews had been rudely acknowledged or gone unanswered. When one hundred and twenty-one distinguished non-Jews sometime earlier forwarded a public protest to Ford, their manifesto counted for nothing although its signers had included such notables as President Wilson, ex-President Taft, Jane Addams, Archbishop Hayes, and William Jennings Bryan.

The apology to the Jews coincided with the debut of the Model A. With the decline of the Model T, Ford's sales had suffered their first serious slump. This loss of orders was most severe in the eastern metropolitan centers of the country. Gaston Plantiff, chief of sales in the New York area, and a few other influential Ford distributors were able to convince Ford that his racism was hurting business. By repudiating his anti-Semitism, therefore, the manufacturer was hoping to dispose of a difficult lawsuit and, at the same time, to regain his position in the trade. In the second interest, the Ford Motor Co. saw fit to place in December 1927, $156,000 worth of advertising in the Jewish and Yiddish press. These Jewish papers were the only foreign-language media to which Ford paid any great attention in the course of setting out to recapture his leadership in the mass market.[14]

In his formal proclamation of good will toward the Jews, Ford promised to see to it that no racial material would ever again circulate in his name. He made the further pledge to call in all undistributed copies of the "International Jew" at home and abroad. He then apologized for his past conduct by repeating in essence what Cameron had said in court.

Once more Ford allowed his editor to assume full guilt for his own past anti-Semitism. "Mr. Henry Ford," said the formal detraction, "did not participate personally in the publication of the articles and has no personal knowledge of what was said in them."[15] Because of the pressure of his business affairs, Ford alleged, he had not been familiar with the content of either the Dearborn *Independent* or the "International Jew." The subject matter of these publications, he said, had only recently been brought to his attention by "trusted friends." He was "greatly shocked" and "deeply mortified," he asserted, to learn that his publication had given currency to the "gross forgeries" and "exploded fictions" of the "Protocols of Zion." Joseph Palma, his negotiator, informed a member of the American Jewish Committee that the men in charge of the Dearborn *Independent* had simply "taken advantage" of Ford.[16]

Few sophisticated observers could credit such an avowal of innocence. "Mr. Ford's amazing unfamiliarity with what his own magazine has been doing all these years and his willingness to attempt to avoid responsibility at the expense of his subordinates," said the New York *World*, "are anything but impressive."[17]

Within six years, however, the publisher of the "International Jew" had sealed off his memories of this period so completely that he could assert, "I have never contributed a cent, directly or indirectly or any other way, to anti-Semitism anywhere."[18] In a very special sense, perhaps, this disclaimer was not altogether untrue. For in reality, Ford had tried to make the public foot the bills for his anti-Semitism. The Dearborn *Independent* was a money loser. Pipp put the deficit for the first year at a quarter of a million dollars. Ford made an effort to pass on as much of this deficit as he could to the taxpayers. From the corporate earnings which he reported to the Bureau of Internal Revenue, at this period, he had deducted the losses of the Dearborn Publishing Co.[19]

When Cameron first learned of Ford's retraction, he was thunderstruck. Correspondents for the New York *World* and the New York *Times* quoted him as exclaiming, "This is absolutely the first time I have heard of any such statement or intention on the part of Henry Ford. I most certainly will get in touch with Mr. Ford," he said, "and find out what is back of this. It's all news to me and I cannot believe it is true."[20]

The immediate cause of Cameron's bewilderment was the fact that the settlement with the Jews had been negotiated without his knowledge. He had never heard of the matter until he read of it in a newspaper. Ford went to the press with a retraction without taking either his editor or his legal staff into his confidence ahead of time. Besides that, Cameron may well have feared that his own stay at Dearborn was at an end. For as a token of his will to reform, Ford gave publicity to the report that the author of the "offensive" articles of the Dearborn *Independent* was "no longer in the employ of the Ford Motor Company."[21]

Cameron survived, however. The "Chronicler of the Neglected Truth" suspended publication early in 1928, but the editor of the suppressed weekly stayed on. In fact, he continued to hold status as one of Ford's chosen few, and he served, without portfolio, as acting public relations director of the Ford Motor Co. for many a year to come.

It was much less simple, however, to heal the social wounds left by the "International Jew." For thanks to Ford's zeal and fortune, this treatise had been scattered to the four corners of the earth. It enjoyed an enormous domestic distribution. Until removed by order of the authorities, the volume had been placed on sale in the Ford tent at the Michigan State Fair in 1922.[22] It had been hawked on the streets of Detroit and Chicago. In the early 20's said E. G. Pipp, the Dearborn Publishing Co. was reprinting the work in lots of 200,000 copies at a time.[23] Its market, even after the retraction, remained world-wide.

In Europe, where the fires of anti-Semitism have smoldered for centuries, the Dearborn *Independent* left its deepest imprint. Even well before the Munich "putsch," the rising Nazi legions took over Ford's "International Jew" as their own. An anti-Semitic German publisher reissued the work sometime before 1927 in a dozen different tongues, including the Arabic.[24] Still later, say the American editors of the unexpurgated American edition of *Mein Kampf*, Adolf Hitler, at work on his magnum opus, copied certain passages almost verbatim from the original text of the Dearborn *Independent*.[25]

Ford's effect on the early destinies of the Third Reich was remarked in the 20's by a number of America's leading newspapers. As German storm-troopers were beginning to raid union halls and Jewish places of business in 1922, a New York *Times* correspondent called at Hitler's spacious quarters in Munich. This is what he found: "The wall beside his desk in Hitler's private office is decorated with a large picture of Henry Ford. In the antechamber there is a large table covered with books, nearly all of which are a translation of a book . . . published by Henry Ford. If you ask one of Hitler's underlings for the reason of Ford's popularity in these circles he will smile knowingly and say nothing. In nationalist circles in Berlin, too, one often hears Ford's name mentioned by people who would seem the very last in the world with whom an American respecting the Republican Constitution would seek any association."[26]

To round out its foreign story the *Times* sent a representative to Dearborn. Liebold would neither affirm nor deny the truth of the German reports. He said he had no information as to Hitler's alleged interest in Ford. He professed surprise that the "International Jew" had become so popular in Nazi circles.

Meanwhile—despite the retraction of 1927—Ford had given irrevocable comfort to the doctrine that the world is made for Christians only. Such was one of the formidable contributions to modern times made by a Yankee millionaire who had once vowed that "history is bunk."

# PART THREE
# Folk Myth

Henry Ford does not find it hard to put principle before profit: it is his nature to put first things first.—*W. J. Cameron*

# Twelve

## SLEIGHT-OF-HAND

### 1

NONE OF HIS meanderings beyond the bounds of industry proper
ever went so far as to disturb the central core of Ford's career.
In fact, each of the collateral excursions on Ford's part had been
buttressed by the authority and self-assurance that were his by virtue
of his achievement as an industrialist. In the theater which absorbed
most of his energies the manufacturer again enhanced his claim to
eminence as a business genius with a social conscience by the manner
in which he took over the Lincoln Motor Co. in 1922. This conquest
occurred at about the time Senator Norris was branding Ford's overtures for Muscle Shoals as an effort to "capitalize on virtue." The
acquisition of the Lincoln concern and the bid for the Tennessee power
rights were indeed both masterpieces of the art of combining self-
interest with seeming virtue. In the lesser but more successful of the
two endeavors, the manufacturer was again the sharp Yankee trader,
masquerading as a social benefactor.

The principals with whom Ford dealt while negotiating for the
purchase of the Lincoln Motor Co. were the venerable Henry M. Leland and his son, Wilfred. This pair had a name for precision manufacturing as old as the industry itself. The Lelands, father and son, had
produced the Cadillac and the Lincoln. They sold their Cadillac interests to General Motors in 1909. For the next eight years they remained
as managers of the Cadillac Division of General Motors. When the
country went to war in 1917 the Lelands went into business for themselves as manufacturers of the Liberty motor. So secure was their
standing that when they decided to reenter the automobile field by
founding the Lincoln Motor Co., immediately after the war, their issue
of stock was snapped up within less than three hours. Most of the 3000

163

investors who advanced the capital for this post-war venture were
residents of Detroit.

The Lincoln car, high-priced and universally respected, was the
only product the new corporation placed on the market. But its producers failed to survive the depression of 1921. They were forced into
receivership. Their property was then scheduled for sale at public
auction.

When word got around that Wall Street was planning to put in
a bid at the forthcoming sale, Ford entered into hurried preliminary
negotiations with the elder Leland. During these talks, Leland, a
conscientious gentleman of the old school, told Ford how he hated
to see the original Lincoln investors go to the wall. Turning eighty
and oppressed by feelings of guilt, he asserted that in the years
remaining to him he hoped to reimburse these stockholders, if all went
well. Whereupon Ford is said to have exclaimed, "You let me buy it;
you let me buy it. You come in and run it for me," Ford suggested,
"and I'll pay all the creditors and stockholders right away. I can do
that right away. It would take you years."[1]

Carried away by so large-hearted a gesture, the Lelands promptly
entered into an unwritten contract with their benefactor. By acceding
to Ford's proposals, they felt confident they were protecting their
own interests as well as those of their creditors and stockholders. The
producer of the Model T seemed, once more, to be indifferent to the
canons of ordinary business prudence.

Ford added that if he succeeded in acquiring the Lincoln Motor
Co. he meant to pay off all the outstanding creditors of the old firm,
in full. More than that, he promised to redeem the now worthless
securities of the company, or at least such shares as were still in the
possession of the original buyers. Both of these commitments were
entirely gratuitous. The unsatisfied creditors who had furnished parts
and supplies to the old concern would, under ordinary circumstances,
have no redress apart from sharing in the proceeds of the forthcoming
receiver's sale. The shareholders of the defunct corporation could
hope to salvage nothing at all from their investment, but for Ford's
munificence.

What of the Lelands? Both of these men, Ford promised, would
carry on as though nothing had happened. The concern would continue to operate, he said, as an autonomous division of the Ford Motor
Co., under Leland management.

For their part the Lelands agreed to approach no other prospective bidder. This concession gave Ford the inside track. It enabled

him to show up at the auction with a detailed knowledge of what he was buying and with a monopoly on the good will of the former Lincoln managers—assets to which no competing bidder would have access. Meanwhile Ford made the most of his position. At his invitation the Lelands laid their cards on the table before a committee made up of some twenty Ford executives.

Fortified by an alliance with the former manufacturers of the Lincoln car, Ford let it be known that at auction he would offer an upset price of not more than $5,000,000. This basic bid was rejected, however, by Federal Judge Arthur J. Tuttle who was presiding over the receivership proceedings. Judge Tuttle, in conference with certain Ford officials, announced that he could entertain no starting bid lower than $8,000,000. In the opinion of the trade, the property was a bargain even at the revised figure. Among the company's assets were the Leland name, a trained personnel, a plant investment of some $16,000,000 and a car of recognized superiority. Offsetting these values was one additional liability that could not be liquidated under the auctioneer's hammer. The federal government still meant to collect an unsettled claim against the company for overpayment on war contracts. This debt was subsequently written off by the payment of one and one-half million dollars to the Treasury Department.

The Lelands went ahead confidently, content to take Ford's spoken word at its face value. They had operated successfully on the basis of an oral contract under somewhat similar circumstances once before, when dickering with W. C. Durant for the sale of their Cadillac interests in 1909. The terms of the present agreement seemed clear enough. They were arrived at in Ford's home, in the presence of Ford's wife and son. They were restated before the assembly of Ford executives. A Ford attorney repeated them during the talks with Judge Tuttle. On top of that, Ford indicated his good faith without further delay by writing a check to reimburse Henry Leland for the full amount of his own personal investment in the original Lincoln enterprise.

If the Lelands still felt that Ford's offer was too good to be true, any lingering doubts on that score were probably quieted by the publicity which began to issue from the Ford Motor Co. So that none might mistake his warm heart, Ford drew a parallel between his intended purchase of the Lincoln assets and the "Sermon on the Mount."[2] "I don't need the concern," he added, "but I don't want to see the company go to the wall."

It was James Sweinhart, then a reporter for the Detroit *News*, who gave Ford's statement of motives its loftiest exposition. Swein-hart's high-flown version of the forthcoming reorganization of the Lincoln Motor Co. was a little epic of promotional art. Its affirmation constituted a virtual covenant of good will. It was warmly received, and would be well remembered by the Ford Motor Co.°

"The Ford interest in the Lincoln Company," wrote Sweinhart, "is solely to see that the Lelands and others who originally put their money into the company to support it financially get a square deal." Thanks to Ford's generosity, he said, "Those stockholders who, in the opinion of the company, actually invested cash in Lincoln securities, with the idea of sustaining the project and making it a going concern, may hope for some substantial return on their investment."

Similar assurances were advanced in the name of Edsel Ford. At the conclusion of the conference held in the Ford residence at Dear-born, the younger Ford is reported to have sent the Lelands "away into the night with lighter step and faces beaming." Presumably in the company of his father and mother, Edsel had asserted, "The Lelands for a generation have done so much work and meant so much to Detroit, that it would be a shame, a blot on the good name of the whole community, if Detroit let the Leland Company go to ruin and the Lelands be put out of it. We do not need the Lincoln as an auto-mobile venture," the younger Ford continued, "but rather than see these people lose all hope for their money—in many cases all they have in the world—rather than see the great shame of the wrecking of this fine company come on Detroit, we will buy it at the receiver's sale and continue production of the Lincoln as a Ford unit."

The voice of Mrs. Henry Ford added still another salutation to virtue. It was she, wrote Sweinhart, who had first conceived the idea of relieving the Lelands and the Lincoln investors. Pleading with her husband, she said, reportedly, "It's a shame that all Detroit would stand by and see the Lincoln Company wrecked. If Detroit will stand by and see the Lelands and their men who put money into that con-cern lose everything they've got and not lift a hand to help them, there's something wrong with our public spirit. Can't you do some-thing to help them?" she asked her husband.

Moved by his wife's entreaty—so the story ran—Ford straightway volunteered to act as Good Samaritan. Money was certainly no object. For the year ending December 31, 1921, the Ford Motor Co. had

° For giving so high a polish to this jewel of public relations, and for other kindred acts, Sweinhart was well rewarded. Sometime later he became a highly paid specialist on the Ford advertising account, first with the N. W. Ayer firm, and after that with the McCann-Erickson Co.

earned a net profit of $66,000,000. Nor did selfish considerations of any sort seem to be operating in Ford's mind. On the eve of the auction, he declaimed, "We should leave cut-throat competition in the era that has gone."

No cut-throat competitor dared to contest Ford's bid at the receiver's sale on January 4, 1922. A day or so before the sale, Pierre Du Pont called from New York to say that General Motors was not interested in the property. Two of the three bidders who did appear at the auction were Ford's men. H. H. Emmons, an attorney, was Ford's recognized agent. George B. Judson came as a Ford dummy, under orders to act as Emmons' foil if the bidding became active.[3] One lone independent bidder put in a brief appearance—E. T. Berger. But Berger no sooner arrived on the scene than he was challenged by a Ford attorney on legal grounds. Berger quickly withdrew from the contest. His principals, he said, had no desire to buy a lawsuit with Henry Ford. Having cleared the field of competition, Emmons placed the one and only bid of the afternoon. He promptly bought in the property "for Henry Ford." The price was $8,000,000.

The purchase hardly caught the Ford Motor Co. off guard. The moment the auctioneer dropped the hammer, a brass band hidden in the crowd began playing "Hail to the Chief." An immense picture of Henry Ford was suddenly lowered over the façade of the Lincoln office building. Then Henry Ford appeared from nowhere, touching off a demonstration. Reporters, in a frantic effort to get the story to their editors, are said to have paid from twenty-five to eighty dollars a piece for exclusive rights to each of the telephone lines inside the Lincoln office.

Sweinhart's copy for the Detroit *News* was, again, a little master-piece of promotion. The auction, wrote this reporter, was nothing less than an "industrial wedding" that had joined "Ford as master manu-facturer in quantity production with Henry M. Leland as the master of the finest things mechanical." As a symbol of the new union, Swein-hart called attention to the statue of Abraham Lincoln on the front lawn of the Lincoln property. The fitting inscription at the base of this sculptured figure, he said, was "Let Man Be Free."

Only one note in this mellifluous passage was slightly off key. Sweinhart was compelled to add an announcement, attributed to Edsel Ford, to the effect that all former employes of the Lincoln Motor Co. could regard themselves as having been discharged, unless specifically recalled by their foremen. When their status as unwanted guests at the Sweinhart "wedding" dawned on them, some 1000 former

Lincoln employes who attended the receiver's sale came up, one by one, to say good-bye to Henry Leland.

## 2

Returning to work under new auspices, the Lelands had to wait less than twenty-four hours for their first disappointment. On the morning after the auction it was clear that Ford had no intention of investing them with any real autonomy. In fact, their management powers were at once belligerently contested by Charles E. Sorensen, Ford's adjutant and chief of production.

A dozen or more of Sorensen's lieutenants immediately commandeered the Lincoln plant. Without consulting either of the Lelands, this group of outsiders overran the factory. "Hell was . . . knocked out of the plant" on the first morning of Sorensen's invasion, John A. Bourne, the elder Leland's secretary, deposed some time later. The second morning, Bourne said, was a "damned sight worse."[4] Henry Leland was still the nominal head of the revived organization, yet one of the first acts of the Sorensen crew, without paying Leland the slightest heed, was to tear down the walls that partitioned off his private office.

With two sets of officials working at cross-purposes, the morale of the plant simply collapsed. Sorensen would issue one set of instructions; Leland, another. Each man began to countermand the orders of his rival. By telling an inspector that his pile of rejected cylinders would pass muster for motor assembly, Sorensen on one occasion threw the eighty-year-old Leland into a choking rage. Beside himself, after verifying the judgment of the inspector, the senior Leland picked up a sledge hammer and smashed the defective parts beyond recognition. On his own initiative Sorensen then discharged all the factory watchmen and substituted a fresh corps. Leland retaliated by dismissing the new guards and rehiring his own. Over the conduct of the time-keeping department—a realm in which Sorensen acknowledged no peer—the two men quarreled openly in the presence of subordinates.

Henry Leland, at his wit's end, finally went to Ford. He asked for a flat definition of his powers. Ford met the request by saying that although "his" men had no business interfering with the operations of the Lincoln factory, he hesitated to remove them for fear of "destroying their initiative."[5]

Meanwhile, Sorensen grew even bolder. The Lelands decided to end their troubles for once and all. But reaching Ford's person was something else again. Their memoranda went unanswered. For three days they were unable to trace Ford by telephone, or even to learn of his whereabouts, whereupon Wilfred Leland, the son, headed straight for Ford's home. Here, however, he was strangely received. The younger Leland had paid numerous earlier social calls at the Ford residence without molestation, but on this particular day his entry to the Ford estate was challenged by an armed guard.[6]

Ford received his visitor nonetheless. Seated in his host's study, Leland submitted two proposals. He suggested, first, that Ford keep his word on the question of autonomy. Otherwise, asked the caller, why not allow him and his father to buy back the Lincoln property at the price Ford paid for it, with interest and a reasonable margin of profit? To the latter question, Ford allegedly replied, "Mr. Leland, I wouldn't sell the Lincoln plant for five hundred million dollars. I had a purpose in acquiring that plant and I wouldn't think of letting it go."[7]

In truth, Ford had the best of reasons for wanting to retain his new possession. He had struck a bargain at auction that Wall Street itself could not have bettered. Made under his auspices, the fine Lincoln car was an answer to the critics who liked to poke fun at the Model T. On esthetic grounds, Edsel Ford's interest in the Leland product was far stronger than his father's. For of the two, Edsel rather than Henry Ford had begun to suspect that the Model T was something short of perfect. Moreover, in dispensing one of the world's best high-priced automobiles, the elder Ford could compete with Packard, the excellent car then in the hands of his social and political rivals, the Joys and the Newberrys.

But Ford must have prized his latest acquisition for reasons still more basic and personal. The Lincoln was a challenge. Its new owner may have envisioned the possibility, under mass production, of getting dividends from a concern which had been forced to close its doors. Above all, Ford was doubtless nursing an old wound in clinging to the Lincoln works. Twenty years before, when he lost his post as director of production at the Detroit Automobile Co., it was the Lelands who had been called in to take his place. Now the tables were turned. Finally, there was good will to be considered. The acquisition of the Lincoln firm had been heralded as a benign act. Any clean-cut backward step from the status quo would call for explanation.

Yet, while giving Leland his ear, Ford yielded to the demand for autonomy. Treating his caller with deference, he reiterated the original pledge. The Lincoln operations, he assured his visitor, would no longer be plagued by dual management. He would order the immediate withdrawal of the Sorensen forces. Ford then complimented the Lelands on their work. As a final token of good will, he volunteered to visit the Lincoln factory two hours every day.[8]

But from the date of this interview to their last hour in office, the Lelands never laid eyes on Ford again, though they later made repeated efforts to do so. Nor did Ford fulfill any of his reputed pledges. "On the contrary," Wilfred Leland subsequently wrote to Ford in a published open letter, "your lieutenants apparently began to 'build their fires' many times hotter. Their procedure became continuously more drastic. Your chief of staff, Charles E. Sorensen, became increasingly aggressive. He gave orders with absolute disregard of our authority. His actions seemed to confirm the statement of one (other than your chief engineer) high in authority in the Ford organization, that your chief of staff is retained by you largely for the purpose of applying drastic methods and making life unbearable for those whom it suits your purpose to eliminate, and to 'push walls out' and 'push roofs off' if necessary to accomplish the desired end."[9]

This bizarre struggle within the Ford fold came to a head in the summer of 1922. It ended on the morning of Saturday, June 10, 1922, with the outright eviction of the Lelands. In Ford's name the inventors of the Cadillac and Lincoln were told to leave the Lincoln plant for good the same afternoon and to take "their personal belongings" with them. The emissaries who delivered this ultimatum were Liebold, Sorensen and William Mayo, then Ford's chief engineer. On the following Monday a certain Ford man asked Henry Leland to affix his signature to a Ford-prepared statement to the press. In this release Leland was to attribute his "resignation" to old age. But the hardy manufacturer, who outlived this incident by ten years, refused. He issued a bristling bulletin of his own instead. "That statement is not true," said the octogenarian. "I have not resigned, nor do I desire or need to be relieved from any legitimate obligations pertaining to the conduct of the business. If I could be relieved from the malicious and harassing tactics which have been pursued, I could conduct a business four times the magnitude of this one without finding it a burden."

The papers scarcely mentioned the passing of the Lelands. The Detroit *Free Press* dismissed their departure as proof of the fact that the Fords and the Lelands could not "reconcile their administrative methods." The Detroit *Saturday Night* was more candid, however. It noted with asperity the dissolution of "The Ford-Leland Mutual

Friendship Society, Inc." *Pipp's Weekly* was caustic. In promising "to help out the Lelands, Ford was as good as his word," said Pipp. "He helped them OUT." Pipp, incidentally, had predicted this turn of events six months before it occurred.[10]

Whatever their limitations, the Lelands were men of proven ability. Henry Leland, despite the weight of years, was still a recognized mechanical genius. The younger Leland had just completed eight years of service as vice-president and general manager of the Cadillac Division of General Motors. To the extent that either of these men may have fallen short of their responsibilities at the Lincoln plant, it is singular that their deficiencies were discovered a day or so after the receiver's sale, and not before. With Ford's tacit consent Sorensen had challenged their powers from the very beginning. Their aptitude for management under the new regime never had a chance to prove itself.

Ford may indeed have thought of the two men he had "rescued" as craftsmen rather than production men, and, hence, unsuited for re-education in the factory methods of the Ford Motor Co. The Lelands very probably did leave something to be desired as specialists of line-production at high rates of speed. Nor was it feasible to apply such methods of manufacture to the Lincoln car. As Sorensen was to discover, Lincolns were not Model T's.

What riled Ford more than anything else perhaps was the failure of his new factory to show a quick profit. During a six-months' trial, under Ford ownership, the Lelands had forced up their production quota from 15 cars a day to 30. Even so, the division continued to lose money. At Ford's new scale of prices, the Lincoln subsidiary would have had to sell 50 or 60 cars daily in order to show a profit.[11]

But the Fords were to come no closer to reaching this break-even point themselves. On their own for the next three and one-half years, they were to fall considerably below the best Leland performance of 30 cars a day. Fifteen years later, in 1935, the Ford Motor Co. would be making Lincolns at the rate of 10 a week. And for two months running, this slender output would be assembled not in mass production, but by hand.[12] What Ford had inherited, with his purchase of the Leland rights, was a white elephant that was too much even for his superb methods of production. The Lincoln, as he would learn to his sorrow, was simply too expensive to sell in large quantities. That truism had made the Leland receivership inevitable. Nor could Ford escape it. His losses on the Lincoln car from 1929 through 1937 were to aggregate nearly $16,000,000.[13]

Out of office, the Lelands immediately set out to enforce the remaining terms of their supposed oral contract with Ford. They concentrated, first of all, on the obligation that Ford had assumed in behalf of the creditors of the original company. Fifty per cent of these claims had been paid off with proceeds from the receiver's sale. The unpaid balance ran, roughly, to $3,500,000.

Before Ford could bring himself to discharge this self-incurred obligation, one of his attorneys called on Wilfred Leland to report that the debt to the creditors would be written off in full, but only on condition that the Lelands would sign a written agreement promising to drop their case in behalf of the stockholders. This the Lelands refused to do. The Fords seemed content to let the matter rest there.

In February 1924, however, Federal Judge Arthur J. Tuttle made it appear that the old Lincoln creditors had a claim against the Ford Motor Co. that was legally enforceable. Judge Tuttle repeated in open court what Ford's agents had told him in his private chambers the year before. Ford's declared intention, the bench recalled, was to pay off all approved Lincoln creditors 100 cents on the dollar.[14] One month later, each of the outstanding creditors of the former Lincoln concern received a check from the Ford Motor Co. This act occurred thirteen months after Ford took possession of the Lincoln plant.

A good deal of fanfare accompanied the retirement of these obligations. To a correspondent for the New York *Times*, the settlement was proof of a desire on Ford's part to "play square" with those "who . . . helped to make the automobile industry what it is." Later, Edsel Ford described this particular transaction as an act of "pure generosity."

The Lelands moved heaven and earth in the interests of their former investors, but intercession with Ford counsel availed nothing. Written communications to the Ford Motor Co. were ignored. Wilfred Leland then wrote an open letter to Henry Ford which *Pipp's Weekly* and the Detroit *Saturday Night* published in full.[15] Finally, in desperation, the Lelands went to law.

They were subsequently joined in their action by 2400 other original Lincoln stockholders. The petitioners alleged that Ford had repudiated one of the terms of his oral contract with the Lelands. He was obliged by an unwritten agreement, the plaintiffs charged, to redeem the old Lincoln securities, valued originally at $6,000,000. For relief the court was asked to order an accounting of the investments in question, to create a trust for the benefit of the jilted investors, and to authorize the sale of the present Lincoln concern as a means of liquidating these old claims. The Lelands filed suit in 1927.

By way of counterattack, Ford three months later filed a nuisance suit against Wilfred Leland. This action was designed to recover a debt of $2500 which the defendant had supposedly incurred while working for Ford as general manager of the Lincoln Motor Co.[16] A bill of particulars itemized such charges as "rags for garage," $2.76; "repairs on coupe," $2.70; and "putting [Wilfred Leland's] boat in the water," $17.

As the major action began to take its course, process servers experienced the usual difficulties with Ford's bodyguards. One deputy of the court who tried to deliver a subpoena to Edsel Ford, said the Detroit *News,* had the door of his car torn from its hinges.[17] No one from the sheriff's office of Wayne County, another paper remarked philosophically, had succeeded in serving a subpoena on Henry Ford for the preceding six years. But Henry Leland's grandson, Wilfred C. Leland, Jr., finally managed to do the trick. This young man appeared as an uninvited guest at an old-fashioned dancing party held at the Dearborn Engineering Laboratory. On this particular evening Ford was acting as host to a party of Buchmanites who were encamped in the city. As young Leland laid a subpoena in Ford's palm he was a party to the following conversation:

"Good evening, Mr. Ford."

"Why, what's this?"

"That, sir, is a subpoena in which your company is involved."

"Take it back! Take it back!"[18]

On grounds that proved to be technically defensible, it was possible for Ford to deny ever having received service of this particular summons. A fortnight later the manufacturer then submitted to the court a most interesting deposition. This legal paper, drafted in Edsel's office, was summarized by the Detroit *News.*[19] The document averred that Henry Ford had never met with Wilfred Leland to discuss the affairs of the Lincoln plant. Nor could Ford vow, according to the affidavit, that the Lelands were reputedly manufacturers of high-grade automobiles or that it had been Henry Leland and his son who sired the Cadillac and Lincoln cars.

When the Leland action reached the State Supreme Court, it foundered because of a still more formidable technicality. Here Ford counsel pressed the point that Ford's offer to reimburse the Lincoln investors had expressly excluded all but the "original" stockholders of the company. This promise, it was argued, made no provision for any shareholder into whose hands such securities might have passed subsequently, perhaps at bargain values or in large blocks with an eye to "mere speculation."

It was Ford and not the Lelands who had interposed this restriction. Yet Ford's attorneys suggested to the court that by seeking to enforce such a contract the Lelands were, in essence, perpetuating a fraud on the "qualifying" investors. Counsel for the Lelands, William Henry Gallagher and Kenneth M. Stevens, parried this thrust by contending that if the Ford argument were true and that "this contract was created to effect a fraudulent purpose, then since the terms were of Ford's own invention," Ford was charging himself with having obtained the Lincoln property "under false pretenses."[20]

Moreover, try as they might, attorneys Gallagher and Stevens could not unearth the "speculating" shareholders of whom Ford complained. After a diligent search, defense counsel informed the bench that no Lincoln shares, currently or in the past, had ended up in the portfolios of any brokerage house. No known present minority holders, the lawyers argued, had bought their Lincoln securities for speculation under the circumstances prescribed by Ford counsel. Ford, on the other hand, insisted that prior to the time of his promise to redeem the stock and prior to the date on which the court named a receiver for the defunct concern, certain speculators had bought up Lincoln certificates at $3 a share. Of this much the Lelands were positive: their action had the support of 2400 "original" investors or of some 80 per cent of the outstanding shareholders.

It was this qualification of the Ford offer, however, that determined its fate in the Supreme Court of the State of Michigan. The oral contract with the old Lincoln investors, the bench ruled on two separate occasions, was "void" and "fradulent" because it failed to protect the rights of every shareholder "on an equal basis."

After losing two appeals to the State Supreme Court, Henry Leland in his eighty-eighth year gave up the fight. By letter he advised some 2400 "qualifying" stockholders that he had exhausted his legal remedies in their behalf. He died the following year, in 1932.

Through his counsel Ford never denied having made the pledge to repay a certain class of investors in the old Lincoln venture. In fact, the heart of his case rested on the admission that such a promise had been made. But what Ford volunteered, his lawyers contended, was "no agreement to pay but merely a promise to attempt at some time in the future to work out some plan by which somebody might hope for something."[21] "We can conceive," said Ford counsel in a final valuation of their client's unfulfilled pledge, "of nothing more indefinite, uncertain, vague, foggy and ephemeral than this . . . Hope alone," they said, "was promised."[22]

The Ford attorneys concluded their brief by quoting a maxim in equity: "It is to the vigilant and not to those who sleep upon their rights that equity lends assistance."[23]


## Thirteen

### VIRTUE AT 6%

#### 1

IN 1926, before he disposed of the Lelands once and for all, Ford introduced the five-day week. In so doing, the manufacturer became all but untouchable; he succeeded overwhelmingly in creating the impression that, at his instigation, principle had triumphed once more in the world of affairs. To be sure, other industrialists had made a similar innovation earlier than Ford, but none of them had applied it on so large a scale. Labor leaders acclaimed the news. Just as Samuel Gompers had rejoiced over the Five-Dollar Day, his successor in office, William Green, paid homage to the five-day week. The reform at the Ford Motor Co., Green predicted, would have a profound "moral effect" on the entire economy.

Drowned by the general chorus of approval, certain other voices were raised off key. That staunch opponent of the forty-hour week, Gary of the United States Steel Corporation, argued that shorter hours for labor were "not logical." A preacher in Highland Park took objection to the new policy on moral grounds. With so much surplus time on their hands, said the clergyman, Ford's employes would plunge into wanton "gambling and intemperance." A Jewish newspaper made the suggestion that by eliminating Saturday from the calendar of working days, Ford was doubtless preparing to celebrate the Jewish Sabbath.

In actual operation, however, the five-day week of the Ford Motor Co. fell somewhat below the immediate high expectations of the president of the American Federation of Labor. For the new concession, like the Five-Dollar Day, was a qualified gift. It was ringed with reservations. If the meaning of these qualifications had been clear at the time, capital and labor might well have interchanged their first appraisals of the innovation. What Ford's employes soon found they had traded for their Saturday holiday was speed-up, added insecurity on the job, and an immediate reduction in wages.

For his part, Ford made it appear that his men would now work fewer hours each week for the same money. But most of his employes were at once forced to submit to wage losses that averaged at least four dollars a week. More than that, they were made to dig in, faster and harder than ever before, on the five working days that remained. When the new policy had been in force for about two months, Ford announced, "We are today producing the same number of cars with the same number of men as we formerly produced in the six-day week."[1] In return for such a step-up in the rate of production, approximately 65,000 men at Highland Park received no proportionate wage increase.[2] On top of that, the skilled worker paid a price that was dearer still. For as a corollary of the shorter week, said the *Wall Street Journal*, Ford lowered the compensation of his best paid men from a daily wage of $10.80 to one of $7.[3]

To an indeterminate number of the older hands at Highland Park, the program of doing a full week's work in five days at a reduced weekly wage meant the loss of their jobs, for another general pruning of personnel accompanied the institution of the forty-hour week. Under orders to "cut out all the inefficient employes,"[4] Charles Sorensen began to dislodge what he called the "drones" and "those who don't want to work."[5] When the campaign to eliminate the resistant or slower employe was only starting, the *Iron Trade Review* carried a news item to the effect that the new Ford speed-up had already eliminated "one man in six."[6]

Behind the screen of an ostensible labor reform, Sorensen quickly achieved a new peak of efficiency by pitting old against young. This source of heightened productivity was indicated in November 1926, when Ford made it known that he was about to give employment at "men's work" and at "independence wages" to some 5000 boys between the ages of sixteen and twenty. It was his resolve, he said, to stop juvenile delinquency and to keep young men out of mischief.[7] Six months later, *Forbes'* magazine offered a somewhat different interpretation of Ford's "war on crime." Ford was replacing, said *Forbes'*, family men and veteran employes who had been earning seven or eight dollars a day, with boys and single men at a starting wage of $3.20.[8]

Many an employe of the Ford Motor Co. undoubtedly approved of the exchange of a longer weekend in return for greater speed-up. Others who survived the ensuing struggle for existence may have found themselves less fit to appreciate the new increment of leisure. To them, the longer holiday was not worth the additional nervous output. Such was the observation of a Detroit businessman who told *Printer's Ink*, the advertising journal, how Ford workers looked as they filed into a company grocery store in the spring of 1927. "When a shift comes out of the factory," wrote this observer, "the commissary immediately fills up with grim-looking, determined men who never smile or joke, but rush over and buy supplies in the most determined sort of way. No shopping, just speed; no unnecessary talk, no time wasted by either customer or clerk, just cold-blooded Ford efficiency."[9] Whatever Ford's men may have thought of their new and more exacting labors, none relished the idea of having to submit to smaller earnings.

The thing that made Ford's shorter week so notable in the eyes of the general public, however, was the belief that the concession had been granted without any reduction of wages. Ford fostered such an impression in an article which he published in *World's Work* on October 19, 1926, under the title, "Why I Favor Five Days' Work with Six Days' Pay." He repeated this theme by declaring in one of his later published works that the five-day week has no justification "unless it carries with it a six-day pay."[10] From such seed, two responsible journals, the New York *Times* and *Barron's Weekly*, finally reaped the fiction that Ford actually had conceded a forty-hour week along with forty-eight-hours' pay in 1926.[11]

What really happened, however, was that the Ford Motor Co. postponed any corresponding advance in its wage scale until, through speed-up, the shorter week had paid for itself over and over again. Ford was able to exact six days' labor from his men in five days' time almost immediately. He reached this goal in November, 1926. A wage adjustment to compensate the men for loss of their Saturday pay was withheld until February 12, 1928—or until the five-day week had been in force for nearly seventeen months.[12]

At bottom, it turned out, the five-day week at Ford's was part of a burial ceremony. The death of the Model T and the inauguration of a forty-hour week went hand in hand. The first entailed a changeover to the Model A—a program of retooling that was enormously expensive. The second made it easier for Ford to pay the bill. Whatever name it went by, the shorter week at Highland Park was a means of cutting costs during a merchandising crisis.

At the same time Ford could still remain the "workingman's best friend." In fact, the five-day week carried him over two awkward situations on the labor front. Retooling for the Model A, he had to lay off tens of thousands of employes. These furloughs or dismissals riled his men. Then, by coincidence, the American Federation of Labor planned to hold its annual convention in Detroit in the fall of 1926. There was talk of an attempt to organize the automobile industry. If the AFL had carried such a scheme beyond the verbal stage, Ford, with a restless labor force on his hands, would have been particularly vulnerable. However, when the manufacturer announced the plan to confer forty-eight hours' pay for forty hours' work, his employes were automatically immunized from any immediate union penetration. The *Wall Street Journal* put the essence of the five-day week at Highland Park in a nutshell. "Here is the Ford strategy," said this journal. "He has cut down his labor costs and has warded off the unionization of his men in one fell swoop."[13]

In later years, however, Ford's publicists spoke of the innovation of 1926 and of Ford's adoption of the five-day week as a milestone of industrial philanthropy. Ford's own contemporary comment had a slightly different flavor. With delightful candor, the manufacturer explained his behavior by insisting, in 1926, that the forty-hour week was a "cold business proposition." "In the purchase of labor as of any commodity," he acknowledged, "you must be sure you are getting your money's worth."[14] Reinhold Niebuhr, then a Detroit pastor, made the rejoinder that Ford's disavowal of philanthropic intentions in his institution of the five-day week was "like the assurance of an old spinster that her reputation as a flirt has been grossly exaggerated."[15]

2

While professing a beneficent attitude toward their employes, the Fords likewise owned up on occasion to observing the same selfless principles in dealings with their competitors. In the 20's they began to foster the belief that they preferred to share their trade secrets with all comers, with an utter disregard of the profit motive. Such was Henry Ford's boast in an article published in *Nation's Business* in 1921, and given over in part to a discussion of patents. All inventions of the Ford Motor Co., Ford wrote, "belong to the world."[16] Two decades later the young Ford took the same position. Appearing before the Temporary National Economic Committee of the United States Senate in 1938, Edsel Ford asserted that his firm had never tried to collect royalties on any patents. On the contrary, he said, his father and he had always made a practice of passing on their trade secrets to others, free of charge. Nor had the Ford Motor Co. the slightest intention of trying to secure any "exclusive control over the arts of the industry." Neither he nor his father, said Edsel, were "interested in making money that way."[17]

In point of time, such declarations of Ford policy were to extend over the better part of a generation. Henry Ford stated his views in the matter when the trade was still embryonic. Edsel covered the same ground twenty years later. To appraise the Fords' liberality with patentable ideas, one must retrace the history of the industry over the intervening years.

When Ford and Couzens broke the Selden patent early in the game, they unquestionably rendered a service to the trade, for as a result of this action, all but two of the major producers in the field hurriedly formed a patent pool. In so doing, the industry forestalled the occurrence of an endless series of costly patent actions. But so long as the Selden matter was up in the air, the readiness of the Ford Motor Co. to share its ideas with others was never at issue. What Couzens and Ford were fighting for, and what they succeeded in getting, was legal immunity from someone else's patent claims. And when Ford's competitors decided to minimize similar litigation in the future, only the Ford company and Packard Motor declined to join the pool.

Nor did generosity seem to condition Ford's later attitude toward original discoveries in the arts of production. In the days when automotive technology was in a state of constant flux, the production experts of the Ford Motor Co. merely followed the pack. They learned what they could—any way they could—of the factory methods of their competitors. Give-and-take was the rule of the trade.[18] While Ford's contribution in this interchange of ideas was immense, so was his debt to others. His engineers, like all others in the business, scoured the plants of hundreds of tool-building and manufacturing concerns, in search of novel shop methods. The Ford scouts learned from others, meanwhile, quite as much as they yielded in return.

Moreover, it was to Ford's self-interest to acclaim what his firm was contributing to the techniques of mass production. Such publicity, fully merited by the brilliant work of the Ford Motor Co., was a form of free advertising. Nor did this open-door policy on Ford's part incur any competitive risks at the time. In letting the world in on his manufacturing exploits, Ford had nothing to lose because his technology was then so dynamic that few could keep up with it. His factory methods were being revised so rapidly that by the time some of his less alert or poorer competitors could copy this or that novel process, the Ford Motor Co. had already passed on to something new.

Ford's technological "gifts to industry" were ephemeral, in chief, because of the great circumstance that gave him his initial advantage as a merchant. Having a head start in the low-price market for cars, he could cut costs and revise his equipment faster than his rivals because he commanded a greater volume of sales and was rolling up a larger aggregate profit than any other manufacturer in the field. So long as the Model T held its own, Ford's advantage was progressive and cumulative. Many another producer, meanwhile, was well aware of Ford's factory methods, but none could keep pace with him for economic reasons.

In the realm of product engineering, the Fords were in no position to speak of a liberal sharing of their patents and inventions, because they had so little to contribute. The Model T, frozen for eighteen years, had almost nothing to offer, at least in its later years, to the arts of automotive design. In fact, Ford dropped the model only when the more progressive engineering of his competitors forced him to. Such was the case with the T's successors. During the years of its dominance, Ford's famous little product did wonders for the trade. It made an enormous contribution to the science of manufacturing, but among its fortes were neither beauty, nor comfort, nor progressive design.

Then, after coming around to the policy of changing his models once a year, Ford behaved like every other producer: he began to keep the plans for each of his succeeding models strictly to himself. Up to the point of introducing a new model, he became every bit as secretive as any of his rivals; he tried to conceal the exact specifications of each forthcoming car, hoping to take the trade by surprise. After the liquidation of the Model T, such Ford secrets were so closely guarded, on occasion, that advance parts were perfected in working places concealed behind canvas drops. As at any other automobile factory, the pains taken to protect such confidential work were often so extreme that even the Ford foreman in charge of a particular project would not know in any detail exactly what he was working on.

The significance of Edsel's flourish before the Temporary National Economic Committee was further circumscribed by the fact that the Ford Motor Co., as of 1938, had no fundamental patents to give away. Neither had any other major automotive producer. All the basic patents of the industry had long since expired. Consequently, no automobile manufacturer could have hoped to effect what the younger Ford described as "exclusive control over the arts of the industry." As William S. Knudsen informed the same committee—

speaking much more to the point—those patents which still remain in force in the trade have to do with small refinements. They contribute, said Knudsen, only to the "style and pattern" of any automotive product.[19] These still live patents add next to nothing to the over-all cost of production. For royalties on inventions not included in the patent pool of the Automobile Manufacturers Association, General Motors Corporation was paying in 1938 not more than 35 or 40 cents per car.[20]

All in all, the history of the Ford Motor Co. in the field of patents and inventions is hardly distinguishable from that of many another large manufacturing establishment. But it was Henry Ford and Edsel who chose to stress the point that, with the arts of the trade, Ford policy was one of generosity beyond compare. Actually, the Ford claim to open-handedness with patentable ideas must be reckoned as only another way of saying that the gifts least painful to part with are those which are more imaginary than real.

## Fourteen

## FORD ALUMNI ASSOCIATION

## 1

LOOKING BACKWARD, sometime in the 20's, Ford made the boast that he was making men rather than automobiles. At that time his primary "made man" was his chief of production, Charles E. Sorensen. Sorensen, a capable, iron-fisted giant of Danish extraction, had come to work for the Ford Motor Co. as a pattern-maker in 1904. This was the man who emerged, shortly after the granting of the Five-Dollar Day, as Ford's favorite executive and prime minister.

As both his employer and his job required, Sorensen was no milk-fed administrator. He had made his reputation at Ford's as a fire-eater. The man could display his scorn for some performance in the factory by simply tipping over a worker's bench. He is known to have put a foreman in his place by crashing a stool over the man's desk. If production stalled somewhere in the plant, he would often jump into a car and drive over the factory floor at a furious pace, with Ford workmen scattering en route like a flock of frightened chickens on a country road. At the source of the trouble, Sorensen's verbal lashings could be so withering that those on whom they fell, whether they were lowly assemblers or divisional superintendents, could be counted on to toe the mark without requiring another chastisement for weeks or even months to come.

Proud of his faculty for driving men, Sorensen soon inspired a fund of local legends of his own. In the metropolis in which most of the world's automobiles are made, stories about this man once had as wide a circulation as the tales given over to Ford's reputed benevolence. "Sorensen stories" used to improve in the telling. Even those which were complete fabrications died slowly.

It was this executive who helped to refinance the Ford Motor Co. by superintending the great Ford retrenchment of 1921. For the next ten or fifteen years, Sorensen's authority at Ford's exceeded even Edsel Ford's or that of P. E. Martin, the company's vice-president in charge of production. Ford himself gave proof of this fact when he published an authentic (but now dated) *Who's Who* of the Ford Motor Co. in his autobiography of 1922, *My Life and Work*. Of all the brilliant co-founders of his business, and of all the men who shared in shaping his great success, he mentions only one (other than his son). That distinction, in the major official chronicle of Ford's career, is Sorensen's.

For Ford's purposes, at least in the 20's, this right-hand man was well endowed. One thing which Sorensen could satisfy better than any of his contemporaries in the Ford organization was his employer's driving passion for cheap quantity production of the Model T. This newcomer was unquestionably a factory genius with a gift for pushing men and materials in production. If machinery was the New Messiah, here indeed was one of the cult's chosen apostles.

Sorensen and his employer brought to their mutual labors an identical philosophy of human nature. The two men agreed to a "t" on the motives which impel men to work for a living. In conversation with Dean Marquis, Ford once put his own theory of motivation into words. Men work for two reasons only, he said—for their wages and for fear of losing their jobs.[1] Sorensen expressed the fullest concurrence with this thesis of human behavior. At least he distinguished himself in the 20's as a Ford specialist in the psychology of job insecurity, if not as a dispenser of high wages.

Working on the premise that job fear is a prime mover of efficiency, Sorensen soon succeeded in putting into practice what some of his associates chose to call the "boiling pot" theory of management.

He came to excel, before long, at the art of surrounding his fellow administrators with an atmosphere of chronic anxiety. Under the turbulent regime that followed, swift and arbitrary dismissals, with no explanation given, became the order of the day. With Sorensen's rise to power, job security went out at the Ford Motor Co.

The technique of these discharges, calculated to spur the firm's surviving executives, took on a peculiar flavor. Often, as the Lelands discovered, Sorensen or Liebold would make a point of doing away with an important official circuitously and gradually, rather than point-blank. Ragging a man at his work became an everyday substitute for clean-cut dismissal.[2] The method sometimes took the form of whittling away an executive's duties, little by little, until he was completely shut off and impotent. At other times, Dean Marquis recounts, a given department would begin to interfere with the work of another "under instructions to do so." Such an instance was reported by the New York *Times* in 1928.[3] A certain popular department head at Ford's rebelled, said the *Times*, because his decisions were being persistently overruled. The man took the matter to Ford in person, demanding an answer to the question, was he or was he not the manager of his department? Ford allegedly replied, "You haven't been manager for two years."

The ensuing purges, which either Sorensen or Liebold superintended and which Ford either ordered or tacitly approved, occasionally bordered on the sadistic. Marquis cites the case of eighty office workers who left their desks in a certain department of the Ford plant one evening, without having been given the remotest hint that their work was either unsatisfactory or unwanted. When they returned to work next morning, their office was bare. It had been stripped of every last piece of furniture. "They were left to find out as best they could that they had been fired."[4] Another group of salaried workers received a still stranger quit notice. They arrived at their place only to find that their desks had been chopped to pieces with an ax.[5] Without rhyme or reason, not a few Ford executives were dropped in such a manner that their professional standing was all but ruined.[6]

Small wonder that a certain Ford executive once made the proud boast to Marquis that what made him such a "whale" of an administrator at Ford's was that everyone despised him so.[7] Nor, on the basis of such reports, is there any cause for surprise in Ford's autobiographical utterance that a "great business is really too big to be human."[8]

In allowing Sorensen and autocracy to prosper within his company, hand in hand, Ford was doubtless compensating for the same feelings of insecurity that had once impelled him to lean so heavily on Couzens. Before thawing out a bit, after the advent of the Five-Dollar Day, the manufacturer had shrunk from any contact with the public; he was, characteristically, shy and ill at ease in the presence of other men. Marquis recalls the day that Ford refused to see a reporter, begging to be spared any personal publicity whatsoever.[9] These were the days when Couzens met the public and the press in the name of the Ford Motor Co. Ford's diffidence had not altogether disappeared eight years after Couzens' retirement, when W. J. Cameron began to hold forth as the manufacturer's "personal spokesman." With the completion of the Ford Engineering Laboratory in 1923, Cameron told Barron that, because of the architecture of the new building, Ford could no longer crawl out of the windows in order to avoid seeing people.[10]

Much of this shyness and reserve the manufacturer could shake off only with difficulty even in the most familiar setting. As a host in his own home, long after he had become both wealthy and famous, he clung to certain more or less solitary and unsocial ways. When some of his male guests would adjourn to the grounds about the Ford residence, it was often Ford's habit to slip away, keeping to himself or chatting with the kitchen help.

By the same token, this empire-builder who could arrive at quick and bold decisions often lacked what it took to put his mandates into actual operation. For the actual execution of such orders, he preferred to rely on deputies who, like Couzens, were tough by nature. The more unpleasant a particular piece of business, the more certain it became that Ford would shift the responsibility to some thick-skinned lieutenant. William S. Knudsen remarked this trait in Ford some time after his own abrupt exodus from the company. Speaking of his former employer at Highland Park, Knudsen told Barron, "He himself never discharges a man . . . other people always do his 'firing'."[11]

As Ford proceeded to give preference to Sorensen and other executives who were harder than himself, he was also allaying more than the uneasiness of the drawing-room. He was, at the same time, seeking relief from certain anxieties that gnawed at him. In his own mind, the manufacturer was beset, now by a harrowing fear of Wall Street, again by a race obsession. In each case Liebold and Sorensen and Cameron were the knights who were commissioned to slay the dragon of Ford's fears.

In deputies like Liebold and Sorensen, the motor magnate was likewise trying to find an answer for a haunting sense of insecurity that lay much closer to home. Plot-conscious and profoundly suspicious by nature, he could never bring himself to trust even the men who worked with him closely, and had done so faithfully for years. Eventually Ford came to resemble a feudal lord, ever doubtful of the loyalty of his subjects, actually going so far as to encourage disharmony and bickering among his more important retainers. By such means he expected each rival for his favor to act as a counterweight and an informer against every other member of the entourage. When an executive of the Ford Motor Co. once reported happily to Ford that he had just succeeded in patching up a misunderstanding between X and Y, two other Ford administrators, he was told to let well enough alone the next time he discovered "fleas on a dog's back." From so medieval a school of business administration, Liebold and Sorensen emerged simply as Ford's aptest pupils, as experts in the realm of stilling the suspicions and self-doubts that tormented Ford even in the conduct of his business affairs.

## 2

Flushed by the wine of the Five-Dollar Day, harassed by nervous shyness and a pervasive fear of other men, enveloped by intrigue, convinced of the efficacy of fear as the keystone of motivation, passionately devoted to mass production as an end in itself, and equipped with a full-blown formula for getting ever-richer and plumbing the mass market to its bottom—all these things were Henry Ford as he reached the heights. From 1915 till the death of the Model T, he proceeded to convert his empire into a twentieth century absolute monarchy.

No longer content to hide his light under a bushel, the manufacturer began to glory in self-aggrandizement. He became enchanted of his virtues. The old Couzens formula for personalizing the Ford Motor Co. soon paled before the new Superman copy. Every breath that was drawn in the gigantic corporation was soon so "personal" that Walter M. Cunningham, the former Ford publicist, relates that his office was instructed never to mention in its releases any name save Henry Ford's.[12] As of 1930, Cunningham asserted, even the use of Edsel's name was a departure that required special dispensation. Every advance at the Ford Motor Co. was reported to the world, said the former Ford advertiser, as an expression of the "guiding genius of Mr. Ford." That went, said Cunningham, for everything from soy beans in Michigan and rubber culture in Brazil to the treatment of burns with tannic acid at the Henry Ford Hospital.

As his self-esteem continued to soar, Ford grew more sensitive to criticism from any quarter. More and more of his key men found themselves backing into cactus beds. Dean Marquis describes this transformation. He tells of a certain official whom Ford summoned to a conference. The man began to take issue with one of the company's established policies, with some reason on his side. Ford cut him off with the taunt, "Get out and send me an optimist. I want to talk to an optimist."[13]

To every corner of the company, Sorensen and Liebold then began to apply in dead earnest Ford's own mandate, enunciated in 1922, to the effect that the "vast majority of men want to stay put. They want to be led and to have no responsibility . . . democracy has nothing to do with the question, 'Who ought to be boss?' "[14] The Ford executives who thought otherwise became steadily fewer or less vocal. One of their number, an anonymous engineer, submitted his opinion to a commercial weekly in 1927 that only the lambs would survive at Highland Park. The winnowing process, he said, had already left Ford surrounded by a "court of handclappers," by men anxious to "curry favor" or to avoid the "oft-wielded ax." Henceforth, said this engineer, most of Ford's men would keep their ideas to themselves; they had discovered it was "dangerous" to try to give advice at the Ford Motor Co.[15] Even John Ford, though not connected with the company, could see that his famous brother Henry had acquired the authoritarian manner by 1927. "He can be as 'contrary' as a mule. He insists on having his own way and he does have it," said the Boston *Post*, quoting John's opinion of Henry. "We didn't notice it in him so much," said brother John, "when he was a poor man."[16]

Sorensen's status, meanwhile, became the barometer of Ford's itch for power. Every time another Ford executive went down, this man went up. By the same token Sorensen gradually negated a good many of the virtues which his superior professed. As Ford was consolidating his reputation as a model employer and winning respect and affection wherever men sweat for a living, his production chief was, at the same time, making a name for himself as the most despised factory boss in the industry. In the eyes of many of the company's employes, Ford, as a result, simply added another self to his multiple personality. He took on the additional aura of the French landlord prince whose subjects were convinced their hardships would end automatically, if only the Good Master of the estate could be told what was going on.

In this drive toward absolutism, however, Ford was no innocent. True, he seldom attended executions. He could become quite inaccessible, both before and after a beheading. Nor was it possible for him, in so vast an enterprise, to command firsthand knowledge of all the actions of even his closest deputies. But on essentials, Liebold and Sorensen were only hewing to a line laid down by their superior. Ford was also, to a degree, aware of his own temperament. At least he confessed to Barron in 1924 that he had yet to meet anyone in his business life with whom he could agree.[17] As for a good share of the power politics in which his chief delegates were engaged, the manufacturer was informed to the nicest detail. Dean Marquis made the discovery that while Ford could bait a trap, marking out a certain victim, he was equally adept at shifting the blame, later on, to Sorensen.[18] In later years the manufacturer once explained to an old friend, with refreshing candor, what he meant when he denied with spirit that anyone had ever been "fired" at the Ford Motor Co. The friend began to name names, asking Ford to account for this or that leading man who was no longer in his employ. The manufacturer went on to say that none of his former executives had been discharged outright, straight-from-the-shoulder. "You know how it is," he explained. "Every now and then we did drag a dead skunk across somebody's trail."

Had there been any question of the turnover among his executive force, Ford and his old acquaintance could have continued the count of noses. For when the manufacturer avowed in his autobiography of 1922 that his corporation had "no organization, no specific duties attaching to any position, no line of succession or of authority, very few titles, and no conferences," his pronouncement was not far wrong as a description of what had happened to the bulk of his more important early personnel.[19] He had already rubbed out a good share of the key men who had had a hand in the evolution of the Ford Motor Co.

Before long the methods which Ford used to achieve his suzerainty were the talk of the trade. This fact alone is revealing, standing out as it does in an industry notorious for the rate of mortality among its brusque, hard-boiled, self-made executives. In January 1939, *Fortune* divulged the fact that within four divisions of the General Motors Corporation, plant managers in the preceding seventeen years enjoyed an average tenure of only four years. The turnover of GM's sales managers was even faster. Yet at Chevrolet, the GM division which drove the Model T out of business, *Fortune* took note of a "remarkable continuity of management." Ford's epidemic purges, on the other hand, excited a widespread interest because they differed, in both number and quality, from anything the trade had ever witnessed.

As the heads began to fly, the Detroit *Saturday Night* suggested that Pelletier's clever phrase, "Watch The Fords Go By," be changed to read, "Watch the Ford officials go by." Dean Marquis proposed the formation of a "Ford Alumni Association" open to the "postgraduate group who have taken the third degree" at the Ford Motor Co.[20] Of those eligible for admission, he observed, "The character of that scrap heap is such as to lend distinction to the man who is cast upon it."[21] By then, in truth, the "honor roll" had come to include the bulk of the managers and administrators who had elevated the Ford organization to its position as undisputed leader of the world's automobile trade.

Among the sales managers who joined the ensuing migration of Ford executives, the foremost name is that of Norval A. Hawkins. Hawkins was the first general manager of Ford sales. Under Couzens' direction, this man had carried the Ford gospel to the farmers and small towns. Couzens called him the "world's champion salesman." Hawkins was one of the "originals." Hired as an auditor, he opened the books of the Ford Motor Co. in 1903. Three years later he became Couzens' dynamo, a colorful and tireless missionary, admirably equipped to preach the virtues of the Model T in the hinterland. As chief of sales, Hawkins energized Ford's dealers for the next thirteen years. When he stepped out in 1919, he was watching more than 11,000 retail agencies. No man had done more to swell Ford's volume of sales from 15,000 units in 1905 to nearly 1,000,000 a year in 1919. But Hawkins was too independent of mind to last indefinitely at Highland Park. No pussy-footer, he was both a warm admirer of Ford and one of his most caustic critics. His fearless, outspoken manner proved his undoing. Dropped at Ford's, he became a General Motors sales consultant at a salary of $150,000 a year.

Hawkins' three successors in office were scuttled seriatim for a different reason. Each was sacrificed in the course of those engineering wars in which Ford steadily lost more ground to Chrysler and General Motors. The trouble in each case lay in the product rather than in the man who was trying to sell Ford's wares; yet every time Plymouth and Chevrolet bit a little deeper into Ford's market, the Ford Motor Co. shed a sales manager. The first victim in this succession after Hawkins' day was William A. Ryan. Ryan carried on until the collapse of the Model T. Then he was let out, after having served the corporation in various capacities for nineteen years.

Next to come under the guillotine was Fred L. Rockleman, an able, hard-crusted utility man who had served Ford for about twenty-four years before he was asked to sit in Ryan's empty chair. Starting out in Ford's employ as a mechanic in 1903, Rockleman had climbed to the managership of a branch plant. From there he jumped to the management of the Detroit, Toledo and Ironton Railroad. It was Rockleman's "magic" that gave the Fords their cause for pride in the D. T. and I. As Ford's sales manager, this executive lasted only three short years. He was dismissed for good in 1930. His leaving was a by-product of the obsolescence of the Model A. It was hastened by a dealer revolt. Ford had eased into the depression by ordering a sharp reduction in the discount rate which set the profit margin of his dealers. This drastic change of policy precipitated a rebellion throughout the Ford sales force. Most of the dealers focused their wrath on Rockleman, who had the unpleasant job of enforcing an unpopular decree. To mollify his salesmen, Ford hastily restored the previous discount rate. He fired his sales manager at the same time. Having lost out at the company for which he had labored twenty-seven years, Rockleman joined forces with the enemy. He promptly went to work for the Chrysler Corporation.[22]

The job of selling Ford cars then passed to W. C. Cowling. It was this executive's hapless assignment to grub for sales during the seven lean years. Upon the completion of a twenty-three year association with Ford, he was put out to pasture in 1937. Cowling's last season with Ford marked the second year during which Chrysler, the new-comer, had wrested second place from the Ford Motor Co., in point of sales. With progressive styling, Walter P. Chrysler was squeezing the Ford V-8. In so doing, he inadvertently crowded Cowling out of a job.

The sloughing off of three other brilliant Ford executives in 1919 —C. H. Wills, Charles Morgana, Jr., and John R. Lee—followed a somewhat different pattern. These three men resigned simultaneously. Their departure took place as Ford was beginning to pinch pennies, shifting the controls to Sorensen. Of this group, Wills was perhaps outstanding, as the metallurgist and product designer whom Ford once described as being one of the greatest living automotive engineers.[23] John Dodge, on the other hand, was guilty of overshooting the mark when he exclaimed during his suit with Ford that Wills was the "brains" of the Ford Motor Co.[24]

If Dodge put the case for Wills too strongly, he could have said with justice, however, that Ford's debt to Wills was a heavy one and of long standing. To Wills' ingenious mind Ford owed much of his success on the experimental cars that had led to the founding of the Ford Motor Co. Wills had had a hand in designing one mechanical feature of the Model T after another: the car's engine and its planetary transmission, and working up the alloy steels that gave the T its name for lightness combined with rugged performance. It was he who hired P. E. Martin, who was to become the firm's vice-president in charge of production.

Aware of his importance in Ford's early scheme of things, Wills had joined the company in the first place on the condition that Ford agree to give him, in lieu of any shares of stock, a fixed percentage of his own personal dividends. When the two men first entered into this unusual arrangement, neither could have foreseen the staggering future earning power of the Ford Motor Co. By 1919, however, this obligation had become, to Ford's mind, both onerous and unjustified. Designers and metallurgists could now be had for a song. Ford had frozen his engineering and he meant to keep it that way. He had his product; mass production was his new dominating passion. And yet in addition to a salary of $80,000 a year, Wills was still collecting, under the old side-arrangement, approximately 10 per cent of Ford's private income. What is more, the oral contract which compelled this extra payment was probably enforceable at law. Among other things, Ford had revealed its terms as a witness in the Dodge suit.[25]

Anxious to break off the old relationship by any means short of litigation, Ford resorted to a left-handed tactic. Sometime in 1919, Wills was frozen out of his job. No work passed over his desk. He continued to report for duty, but his functions were pared away as though he were dead. Burly, hard-fisted and already fretting inside his Ford collar, Wills could not abide such treatment. He stomped out. Sometime later, Liebold paid him off. In return for a signed release, Wills accepted Ford's personal check for something like $1,000,000. Then Charles Morgana and John R. Lee hastily submitted their resignations. Morgana was the machine-tool expert who had roved the industry as Ford's chief technological scout. The other man, whose forte was personnel, had directed the Ford Sociology Department before Marquis' time. During the first World War, Lee had functioned as Ford's political agent in Washington. When he broke with Ford, he was earning a salary of $60,000 a year. The man to watch at the plant, Lee and Wills then predicted, was Charles E. Sorensen.[26]

Rich, energetic and vindictive, Wills turned at once to a pursuit whereby he hoped to even the score with Ford. He strode into a

Detroit bank with his millions wrapped inside an old newspaper, bursting with plans for a car of his own. Lee and Morgana promptly joined him in the venture. Out of this combination of talents came the Wills-St. Claire, one of the finest cars of its day. But the excellent new product was destined to give Ford no real cause for regrets. It was born during the depression of 1921. More than that, it aimed too high. The car was priced at $3000. Wills was so intent on producing a "Swiss watch" that would put the Model T to scorn that rashness overcame his better judgment and the wiser counsel of his associates. The man had forgotten a lesson which he should have learned by rote at Highland Park—the laws of mass distribution. Craftsman Wills had his victory over merchant Ford, but only for a day. Then his company and his fortune were no more. After this debacle, Walter P. Chrysler added Lee and Wills to his staff at the Dodge plant. Until his death in 1940, Wills continued winning laurels as an ingenious, imaginative engineer.

The year of the great housecleaning at the Ford Motor Co., however, came later, in 1921. Then, in the course of refinancing his corporation and while passing the scepter to Sorensen and Liebold, Ford nearly gutted what was left of his administrative force. Yet in his autobiography, the ·manufacturer describes this purge as one of the master strokes of his career.

Editor Pipp and Dean Marquis were shed at the turn of the decade. Pipp withdrew from the Dearborn *Independent,* up in arms against Ford's anti-Semitism and the policy of hounding Senator Newberry. Marquis was relieved of his duties and a salary of $30,000 a year when Ford decided to throw the Sociology Department overboard. Marquis, moreover, had long been at odds with Sorensen, for as Ford's social worker, the Dean had become a one-man court of appeal. Workmen carried their grievances to his office, after failing to get satisfaction from a foreman or superintendent or from Sorensen himself. Stripped of his powers, little by little, Marquis finally stepped out, but not until he had been party to a stormy three-cornered altercation in the course of which Sorensen raged and Ford squirmed.

The maelstrom of 1921 swept away Charles A. "Dad" Brownell. Brownell was one of the early Ford publicists. He edited the *Ford Times* and specialized in the handling of delicate company correspondence. He had deified Ford and was a favorite with the dealers.[27] Falling in step with other Ford alumni, Brownell was quoted by *Automotive Industries* as saying that Sorensen and Liebold were "practically in control" of the Ford Motor Co.[28]

Klingensmith, Ford's treasurer and vice-president, was cashiered during the same flurry of dismissals. It was this man's province, as Couzens' successor, to select and train the company's office personnel. He was responsible for most of Edsel's business training. At a top salary of $75,000 a year, Klingensmith had served the company for sixteen years.[29] He was discharged precipitously for having dared to question the methods Ford used to write off his bankers' loans. It looked for a time as though no one would risk sitting in the chair which Klingensmith had vacated. W. R. Campbell, president of the Ford Motor Co. of Canada, was considered for the post, but declined it. This executive had seen so many "bigger or better men" summarily dismissed or forced to resign for differing with company policy, his friends reported to *Automotive Industries*, that he had no desire to "go along with the procession."[30]

Klingensmith, outward bound, was followed a month later by W. C. "Fuzzy" Anderson, the director of Ford sales in Europe. Anderson, a former bicycle racer, had worked for the company for sixteen years. He left Ford, according to one of his friends, convinced that the company's European market would suffer seriously, so long as the Dearborn *Independent* continued to rant against the Jews.[31]

More heads fell before the year was out. On a single day in 1921, Ford dropped thirty key men from the secondary managerial ranks of his factory staff. The 20's saw the passing of Carl Emde, the company's technological genius; of Ben Waderlow, Emde's right-hand man; of William Klann and C. W. Avery, two pioneers of moving assembly; and of John Findlater, one of Ford's metallurgical experts. All these men had given Ford years of distinguished service. Avery had risen to the post of assistant general plant superintendent at Highland Park and chief developmental engineer of the Ford Motor Co. Though jettisoned in middle life, most of this group—and others like them—managed to land elsewhere, feet first. Waderlow went to General Motors; Avery to the Murray Corporation; Klann to Hudson Motor. Findlater founded a successful business of his own.

Other names on the roster of the Ford Alumni Association soon became too numerous to catalogue. A few, however, stand out. The Lelands were displaced in 1922. At about the same time, Henry Bonner was dislodged as chief of production in the branch plants of the company. Bonner's certificate of graduation was unique, if nothing else. He was told to sell his home and prepare for a transfer to some other part of the country. Writing a year or so later, Marquis reported, "He sold his house, but the transfer has not yet come through."[32]

For a time Ford's lawyers were cut down quite as fast as his production men. Here the most notable name is that of the late Alfred Lucking. Like his former client, Lucking was once instantly recognized by the little Ford car painted red which he drove around Detroit. This man functioned for years as Ford's legal brain. He handled the defense in the Dodge case and the Chicago *Tribune* suit. It was his thinking that finally spelled defeat for Senator Newberry. Too strong-minded to tolerate the Liebold-Sorensen machinations, Lucking fell into disfavor sometime before 1926. For one thing he spoke out against Ford's anti-Semitism. He was openly opposed to Ford's sallies into politics. When Lucking died in 1929, his passing was acknowledged neither by any representative of the Ford Motor Co., nor by any gesture from Ford that might have been expected toward a leading citizen with whom he had enjoyed a long and intimate association.

The fitful tenure of Ford's attorneys persisted long after Lucking's removal. In one instance it was announced by the New York *Times* that, on his next pay-day, Ford intended to wipe out his entire legal department, dismissing its personnel in toto. The reason cited for this change of policy was that Sorensen preferred to engage temporary counsel from time to time, as the occasion might require.[33]

Of the many Ford alumni, perhaps the best known is William S. Knudsen. Knudsen was graduated at Highland Park, after clashing with Sorensen, in the class of '21. He had built fourteen of the company's branch factories. From Highland Park he took his superb talents to the Chevrolet Division of General Motors. Jovial and easygoing, with a knack for leading rather than pushing his subordinates, Knudsen was never moonstruck by his brilliant subsequent success. Reviewing his career, he once said, "None of us are wonder men."[34] He is said to be the one man whom Ford regretted having lost. Such feelings were understandable. For under Knudsen's management, Chevrolet wrested the leadership of the trade from Ford's grasp.

By 1927, the remnants of the Old Guard at the Ford Motor Co. were slim indeed. Of the many co-workers who had started out with Ford on a more or less fraternal footing, only a handful remained. The rest were Ford alumni, like the "eminent automobile executive" who confided to B. C. Forbes the year the Model T expired, "I was a Ford man years ago. . . . Only four of the many men throughout the country who had positions similar to mine are still with him today."[35] So far as he could tell, said Forbes' informant, the surviving Ford organization was a "hotbed of jealousy and intrigue," in which no man "however responsible his position" could feel secure. He himself had left Highland Park, said this former Ford executive—now the "president of a nationally known motor company"—to keep his "self-respect," convinced as he was that Ford's "loud protestations about being the greatest friend labor ever had were nothing but hypocrisy."

Nor could any of the more enlightened administrators who carried on at Highland Park into the 20's think of Ford any longer as the inspired leader of men. On the contrary, these survivors were on tenterhooks, plagued by a rule of caprice and by the heavy hand of Sorensen and Liebold. Even the counselors who were closest to the throne were badgered by perennial feelings of insecurity. During his day at Highland Park and Dearborn, Marquis recounts, the top men of the company were seldom at ease in Ford's presence. They were, said the dean, always on edge, ever on the alert for the unexpected.[36] This state of apprehension deepened after Sorensen's and Liebold's rise to power.

Yet the purge that nearly overturned the Ford organization at the start of the 20's was by no means all to the bad. As the operation proceeded, bad blood was let with the good. As long as the Model T remained in its heyday, the great trek of Ford alumni never so much as dented Ford's outward fortunes. In fact, it may have improved them, for the time being. For in Sorensen Ford had a brilliant co-ordinator and forcer of production. Sorensen in turn could count on the support of other men of no mean ability, some of whom—like P. E. Martin—were more temperate of manner than himself. At least while the casualties kept mounting in the Ford personnel, during the five or six years that led to the birth of the Model A, Ford was presiding over a wondrous money-making machine. His earnings during the last several years of the life of the Model T exceeded half a billion dollars.


## Fifteen

### DEATH OF THE MODEL T

### 1

FORD WAS OVERTAKEN in 1926 by the sudden extinction of his automobile. No one lamented the Model T's passing more than he, and no student of the trade was so ill-prepared to grant the inevitability of this event. Enamored of his product and out of joint with the times, the manufacturer refused to believe the worst until the last. The jolt that opened his eyes was a precipitous drop in sales.

What gave the coup de grace to the world's best-known car, and what its producer was reluctant to face, was a permanent shift in consumer demand from price to style. By the middle of the 20's, the American car buyer was asking for "class" as well as economy in his mode of transportation. Price alone had lost its charm. By the new standards, the bony T had finally become "too cheap." Its severe and simple form was not up to the cult of color-styling, four-wheel brakes, shock absorbers, balloon tires, gear-shift transmission, roominess, or smooth engine performance and streamlining. Nor did its rigid make-up allow for survival once General Motors had made a national habit of the desire for an annual change of model.

Both the face of the earth and the tempo of the period as well were conspiring against the apple of Ford's eye. The roadbeds of a horse-and-buggy age had now been crusted with macadam and harder surfaces. Over such highways the American liked speed. He yearned, at the same time, for social tone. In the decade that bred jazz, bootleg liquor, gaudy movie palaces, the bull market of 1929, the "New Religion of Success" and Main Street's hunger for conspicuous display, the Model T was a crotchety relic.

Meanwhile William S. Knudsen had his ear to the ground. General Motors had begun to give the public what it wanted, designing its product in the popular image, just as the Model T had been conceived in an earlier day. In contrast to Ford's resistance to change, GM was germinating new ideas at an ever faster pace, having pooled all its research facilities in 1923 for that purpose. Within the next few years, Knudsen's success as a poacher in Ford's preserve was the talk of the trade. Chevrolet was stealing up on the Model T in terms of price as well. The T, in the middle 20's, was still much the best buy on the market—but only if a customer could put up with its nakedness. Ford was selling his car bare, stripped to the bone. He imposed an extra charge for accessories which Chevrolet had adopted as standard equipment. No competitor could yet match the price of the Model T roadster that sold for $290, f.o.b. Detroit, in 1926. But the rock-bottom Ford price covered neither demountable rims nor a self-starter, to mention but two of the newer refinements. For these items alone the Ford Motor Co. levied an additional charge of $55. By the time a buyer had embellished his T with each of the gadgets which it lacked in the raw state, he was within 25 per cent of the price of a Chevrolet.[1]

To many a prospective car-owner, the over-all superiority of the General Motors' product was now worth the difference in total cost.

The competitor who did far more than easy credit or good roads or a demand for new automotive styles to rob the Model T of its mass-market was one whom neither Ford nor Knudsen could resist. This intruder was the dealer in second-hand cars. By 1926 there were 25,000,000 gasoline vehicles on the highways of the world. Each of these units, however new, was destined for eventual resale. At this point the used car preempted the province which Ford had dominated for a generation. Henceforth, no producer of a low-priced automobile could hope to match the bargains of the used car lot. The buyer of little means could now go as low as ten or fifteen dollars, if need be, in his quest for an "economy" car. Hence, in 1926, the T was all but dead because, quite literally, the bottom had dropped out of its market.

Another clue to the future was implicit in the folk-humor aimed at the Model T in the later years of its existence. At one time the ubiquitous Ford joke had been an asset to the Ford Motor Co. This sort of humor, up to a point, had been a builder of good will, and a means of advertising the Model T by word-of-mouth down on the farm and in the market-place. But when the Dodge and the Chevrolet started crowding the T, the Ford jokes began to change their temper; they became increasingly defensive and apologetic. Millions of commonplace Americans began laughing at themselves and poking fun at the Model T good-naturedly, but in dead earnest. Much of this humor put its finger on certain changes which Ford should have been incorporating in his product. In a characteristic Ford joke of the period, one person supposedly asked another, "What shock absorbers do you use on your Ford?" His friend replied, "The passengers."

No large imagination was required to discern the fact that in its mere mechanics the all-purpose model of the Ford Motor Co. had outlived its day. Any car dealer could have told Ford that shock absorbers would help the farmer get his eggs to market. It was just as evident that a water pump would cool the Ford engine better than the device of "lifting the hood and folding it under," a common practice which gave the T the "appearance of a hen with her wings akimbo." None of Ford's patrons really enjoyed testing his fuel supply by having to dip a ruler or a screwdriver into the gas tank that lay buried underneath the front seat. It was too much to expect the driver of a Model T to keep fussing with side curtains in an open car in the dead of winter, or to put up with flat tires that had to be wrenched from undemountable rims. No more palatable, in view of the competition from battery ignition, was the Ford magneto system which made the lights of a T glow or fade depending on the speed of the motor. On stormy nights or in strange places, Ford drivers were fed up with the maneuver of coming to a dead stop, racing their engines in order to see what lay ahead.

Of all the earmarks of Ford's tardy engineering, none was more extraordinary than the planetary transmission. It was to this organic peculiarity that one critic attributed the "clutch epilepsy" of the model T. For a definitive statement of the art of stopping and starting a T by manipulating three foot petals, in lieu of a standard gear-shift system, society is indebted to L. S. White, the author of that hilarious classic of Fordiana, *Farewell to Model T*. Ford's planetary transmission, said White, was "half metaphysics, half sheer friction." Under its mysterious control, the engine and the wheels of a stationary Model T always seemed locked and poised for precipitous action. ". . . Even if the car was in a state known as neutral, it trembled with a deep imperative and tended to inch forward," said this author. "There was never a moment when the bands were not faintly egging the machine on. In this respect it was like a horse, rolling the bit on its tongue."

Despite the catalogue of its acute and chronic ailments, the Model T, on its death-bed, left behind it millions of friends and a record of sturdy, economical performance which no other car of its class had been able to challenge for nearly two decades. On a still grander scale, Ford's universal car had a record just as proud. Before its expiration, the celebrated product had aggregated in gross sales the stupendous sum of $7,000,000,000. During the last ten years of its lifetime, Ford's car had accounted for one-half of the automobile production of the United States. With 15,000,000 sales to its credit, it had peopled the globe for eighteen years at the remarkable birth rate of 1.6 new specimens per minute. To proliferate Ford's pride and joy, there had sprung into being the most advanced technological apparatus yet conceived since the dawn of the Industrial Revolution. During its youth and in its prime, the Model T was indeed the wonder child of the magic city of mass production, a gigantic social force. Yet, as a catalyst of the machine age, the T was finally destroyed by the very instruments of change which it had helped to unloose upon the earth.

As the hardy but outmoded Model T made its last stand in a changing market, it was Ford against the world. No one could tell him what he refused to see until the very end. The manufacturer neither read the signs nor cared what other people thought about his conviction that the T was as perfect and timeless as Pike's Peak itself. Self-centered and bull-headed, he spurned the counsel of his dealers when they began to beg him to modernize his product. He sat in silence for two hours, at a national gathering of Ford salesmen in 1922, listening to pleas to the effect that the time had come for some radical changes in the Ford offering. Yawning to express his unconcern, Ford responded to these appeals by remarking, "Well, gentlemen, so far as I can see the only trouble with the Ford car is—that we can't make them fast enough."[2]

During the model's final hours, Ford grew increasingly petulant and sulky. He spoke out defiantly in July, 1926, "When some of the knickknacks drop off an automobile, people with good sense don't stop to pick them up. If you lose a part, and the thing still goes," he said, "why worry about it?"[3] That was the trouble! Gadgets and knickknacks were corroding the better judgment of the sensible, thrifty, home-loving, garden variety of Americans who had bought some 15,000,000 Model T's. Ford's misguided clientele could go to the devil. Until actually confronted by impending disaster, the manufacturer was so sure of himself he tossed off the boast that he had never made a mistake in his life.[4]

In this desperate, solitary battle against the trend, Ford was nonetheless forced to compromise. He first resorted to psychological treatment. Breaking a precedent of years' standing, he allowed the home office to sponsor a vigorous campaign of national advertising. However, mere auto-suggestion worked no cure. The next expedient was superficial surgery. All for $60, the company offered to recondition any Model T, to rebuild the engine, to furnish new upholstery, to apply a fresh coat of paint, with a three-month guarantee that the operation would prove successful. Face-lifting came next. Still not getting to the root of the trouble, Ford's engineers frantically cupped the fenders, slanted the windshield, lengthened the body several inches, lowered the T's center of gravity, rounded the corners of the radiator, took the gas tank out from under the front seat and tucked it under the hood. Finally, even the black dress was discarded. Like a renovated, ancient dowager on her last fling, the Model T appeared in fawn gray, gun-metal blue, phoenix brown and highland green.

Then Ford was compelled to go the full distance. If he had not wrenched himself from the car of his choice and gone over to the cult of knickknacks and gadgets, his career as an automobile manufacturer would have ended; Chevrolet and other more progressive models would have stolen his business.

## 2

Caught napping in the midst of a trade war, the Ford Motor Co. discontinued the Model T abruptly in May 1927. At this point two gigantic tasks descended on the company: the designing of a brand new car and the complete overhauling of the most gargantuan automobile factory in existence. Of the two requirements, the second was by far the more demanding. The Ford retooling of 1927-1928 was the most elaborate thing of its kind yet undertaken by anyone in so short a space of time. Nearly every piece of the company's monolithic equipment, laid out on the assumption that the Model T would linger on forever, had to be torn down and rebuilt. The staggering change-over necessitated the replacement of some 15,000 machine tools, the total rebuilding of another 25,000, as well as the redesigning and rearrangement of $5,000,000 worth of dies and fixtures.

For so vast an undertaking, Ford was ill-equipped. To be sure, he had two beavers in Sorensen and P. E. Martin. It was this pair who shouldered the bulk of the managerial load throughout the ensuing crisis. For twelve frantic months or more these two labored heroically. Until their mighty chore was finished, Martin and Sorensen slept in the plant. But even so talented a pair of executives were struggling against fierce odds. The change-over had been preceded by little or no advance planning. Moreover, Ford and his chief deputies were now, for the first time in years, wrestling with difficult new problems, severely penalized by the absence of the river of talent that had been sluiced off into the Ford Alumni Association. Top-heavy, the Ford organization could not help but meet the emergency ponderously.

Far from soliciting any new talent to speak of, in this hour of trial the Ford Motor Co. did not even conserve the ability which it housed within its own ranks. Jealous of authority and fond of showmanship, Ford could not resist his compulsion to leave a personal "thumb mark" on every part of the new program. This intervention was so thoroughgoing on his part, that a state of inertia cramped the entire undertaking. The Ford organization began to suffer from an attack of what the trade called at the time the most severe "dynastic constipation." The company's draftsmen and engineers felt they were sitting on pins and needles. Cunningham, then a Ford advertising man, asked a Ford technician why a certain simple defect could not be easily corrected by changing a few dies. The technician replied, "The way things have been going we are scared stiff and afraid to do a thing."[5] Designs, once approved, were changed according to whim. Eight months along, the whole brake system of the new model had to be redesigned and rebuilt because someone had failed to check certain traffic regulations that had long been in force in New Jersey and Washington, D. C., and in Germany.

Ford meanwhile forced any number of new graduates into the Ford Alumni Association. Again, the high fell with the low. At the head of the departing group was Ernest C. Kanzler, Edsel's brother-in-law. Kanzler had been one of the more persistent critics of the Model T.[6] The recessional began to rival that of 1921. Its marchers included Herbert L. Leister, the company's general auditor who had served Ford for sixteen years; V. D. Overman, service manager, whose association with the company went back about twenty-one years; William A. Ryan, general sales manager, let out despite nineteen years of seniority; and Fred H. Diehl, chief purchasing agent.[7] As far back as 1916, Ford had paid Diehl $37,500 a year for his services.[8] The parade was soon joined by A. E. Wilson, general employment manager. Wilson was superseded in his important office by one of Harry Bennett's assistants.[9] At this period Bennett was beginning to share some of the authority that had formerly been concentrated on Sorensen and Liebold.

Again, as in 1921, the extirpation cut deep down into the tissue of the company. Bosses were let out at every turn; others were told to apply at the employment office for a run-of-mine job on the production line. Some of the discharged "star" men—foremen and superintendents—never got back on their feet. Many shifted to other automotive plants. The loss of such men did little to expedite the delivery of the Model A. For in the course of discharging countless lieutenants who had proved their loyalty and competence in the past, Ford infected those who remained with anxiety feelings.

But the Model A arrived, for all of that, after twelve or eighteen months of strain and turmoil. In the meantime, "dynastic constipation" took a heavy toll. In terms of money alone, the change-over cost Ford something like $100,000,000. More than that, the attendant delays opened the door to General Motors. Before Ford could get back in the running, Chevrolet had captured a vast segment of his business. Finally, his procrastination had had serious repercussions throughout the trade. The times were relatively good, but other manufacturers and hundreds of thousands of automobile buyers had been somewhat immobilized by Ford's action, anxiously waiting for the long delayed arrival of the A. The effect on Ford's dealers and factory workers was something else again. The losses sustained by this body of employes, during a shut-down that lasted much more than a year, were incalculable.

When production on the Model T came to a complete standstill, Ford laid off about 60,000 men in Detroit alone for approximately a year. This social dislocation spread fanwise through the trade, even reaching into remote corners of the land. Merchants, professional people, taxpayers and suppliers of parts and materials were drawn into the vortex of Ford unemployment. In September 1927, the New York *World* estimated that the number of wage earners who were dependent on the Ford business for all or part of their livelihood ran to 500,000. The enforced idleness of 1927-1928, imposed on some 100,000 Ford employes throughout the country, must have jeopardized the employment of several hundred thousand other workers. Struck by the whim and market blindness of one industrialist who had precipitated the widest work stoppage ever known to the industry, the New York *World* commented, "That the business of one man thus should dominate the affairs of the fourth city in the United States . . . must hit the person not familiar with Detroit as remarkable."[10]

Thousands of Ford's men, shunted into idleness or part-time work, had to turn to the relief agencies of Detroit for support. Thomas A. Dolan, then Detroit's commissioner of public welfare, reported that the Ford shutdown was responsible for 45 per cent of the city's relief load in 1927.[11] To cope with the Ford emergency, the free clinics and child-placing agencies of the community had to expand their resources from 30 to 300 per cent. The taxpayers of Detroit in 1927 were compelled to increase expenditures for relief, over the previous year, by more than a million dollars. The Fords did something, to be sure, to help defray the costs of this expanded program of public welfare. In the fall of 1927 Edsel sent a check to the Detroit Community Fund for $175,000. But alongside the family's total private income, such a donation was trifling. For the year 1925 alone, the New York *Times* revealed, the Fords had withdrawn personal dividends, apart from salaries, to the amount of $14,670,000.[12]

Nor was Henry Ford seemingly much interested in the social disarrangement that followed in the wake of his remarkable one-man work stoppage. At least his verbal pronouncements on the subject indicated no such concern. Speaking of this unemployment among his workmen, the manufacturer told Paul U. Kellogg, the editor of *Survey*

*Graphic,* "I know it's done them a lot of good—everybody gets extravagant—to let them know that things are not going along too even always."[13] From a close study of the situation Kellogg gathered the impression that the supreme individualist of Dearborn had not "thought through his relations to his employes in a way that would distinguish between their households and his idle coal seams and his timber reserves or the used water that ran over his spillways." The self-made genius of the Model T had to sweat for his money. Others could do the same. Half-a-million men underwent various degrees of economic distress because of his own tardiness in sensing the market. But Ford was not moved. In fact, as he disembarked from an ocean liner in England in the spring of 1928—some time after the birth of the Model A—he tossed one of his pearls to the newspapermen who met him at the dock. "If there is any unemployment [in America]," he declaimed, "it is simply because the unemployed do not want to work."[14]

When the Model A was finally ready for mass production, Ford's own unemployed scarcely acted like ne'er-do-wells who preferred loafing to useful work. By and large these men strained for a chance to take up where they had left off. Most of them welcomed reemployment at Ford's because in the past the Ford Motor Co. had been noted for a full production schedule that was relatively steady and little affected by the seasonal shut-down. In addition to this old attraction, the thought of "getting back on" at Highland Park had a still more urgent appeal for some 60,000-odd employes whom Ford had laid off anywhere from six months to a year or more. Many of these men, by 1928, were either in debt or on the brink of economic distress. Consequently when Ford reopened his plant, the majority of his former employes reapplied for their old jobs. Those who could pass muster at the employment office were so eager for work that they submitted, perforce, to conditions of labor nowhere near so desirable as those that had prevailed before the shut-down. Demotions, speed-up, lower wages and a thoroughgoing uneasiness of tenure—all these greeted the men whom the Ford Motor Co. re-absorbed. For in striving to recapture a market which he had ceded for the time being to General Motors, Ford proceeded to cut costs ruthlessly, and at the frank expense of his working force.

As for wages, Sorensen only repeated the technique of 1921. Old and tried foremen and superintendents, earning salaries of 200 to 400 dollars a month, were again dropped to the foot of the ladder. Many of those who stayed on went back to the production line at beginners' rates of pay.[15] White-collar workers in the business offices of the company were similarly routed to the factory, or let out.[16] Old production hands whose wages had run to seven or eight dollars a day before the lay-off, were rehired to do the same work for 15 to 30 per cent less money. In any number of cases, new and younger workers replaced Ford's older men altogether, at lower rates of pay.[17]

By the time these operations were completed, little if anything remained of the alleged superiority of the Ford scale, by contrast with the prevailing wage levels of the trade. *Federated Press* reported a downward trend in Ford rates of pay in the latter part of 1925.[18] Six months before the Model T was retired, said the *Iron Trade Review,* one other automobile producer in Detroit was paying its skilled men wages that topped the Ford scale by 15 per cent.[19] When this estimate was made, Ford's program of retrenchment had only begun. For the year 1925-1926, according to the Michigan Department of Labor and Industry, the average daily wage for all males employed in the automobile industry of the state was $7.03 for the skilled, and $5.77 for the unskilled. Sorensen set the Ford rate under both figures during the crisis of the Model T in 1927-1928. But just as Ford was able to retain his standing as the advocate of high wages— once the Model A was in mass production—so Sorensen proved, again, to be the giver of wages not quite so high.

Those Ford men who were reinstated at their old posts not only manned the lines and tended their tools at reduced wages, but they worked more intensively as well. Their labors had never been casual. In May 1927, *Forbes' Magazine* published an unsolicited, anonymous letter from a Ford employe who described the tempo of the Ford shops as they were operating before the change-over from the T to the A had taken place. "It is nothing but a continual speed-up and driving from Monday morning to Wednesday or Thursday night," said this nameless letter writer. "The men and women on the way home from work slump down in the buses and street-cars so near dead that they often go half a mile beyond their destination."[20] Pipp and Marquis were then reporting the same phenomenon.

What Sorensen effected in 1927 and 1928, however, was only an exaggeration of what had gone before. The scope of the new speed-up was suggested early in 1929 by the *Wall Street Journal,* which asserted that within the previous six months the Fords had increased their Canadian output 16 per cent after discharging 2000 men, or some 22 per cent of the working force.[21] In Detroit proper, Walter Cunningham, the former Ford advertising man, offered a more subjective estimate of the accelerated Ford pace. After the retirement of the Model T, Cunningham took a job in the factory. One of the more widespread complaints among his fellow bench-hands, he observed soon after, was a nervous condition known as the "Ford stomach."

Ford's clientele, meanwhile, was bitten with curiosity, waiting for the first public showing of the Model A. The forthcoming car became a subject of nation-wide gossip. To add to the suspense, the company carried on its developmental work in utter secrecy. It put the new engine through trial runs under the hood of a Model T. Newspaper photographers tried to take snapshots of the Ford proving ground by working at long range with high-powered lenses. The first A's to leave Detroit were shipped out to the dealers carefully concealed in canvas bags. When the incubation of the new model was six months along, speculation on its progress and expected appearance became so general that the subject occasioned an editorial in the New York *Times*. "The new Ford is completed," said the *Times*. "It is on the verge of being completed. It is still in the trial stage. Mr. Ford is through with the new model and has gone back to Colonial furniture . . . Mr. Ford is driving about in the new model. Nobody has seen the new model . . . It is a two-door sedan. It will be for some time only a touring car. It will hang low and sell very cheap. It will hang not so low and sell not quite so cheap."

The currency of such rumors gave proof of the fact that Ford's good will, as one of the great merchants of the era, was still immense. Public confidence in the new product was so universal that six months before the Ford Motor Co. could resume volume production, 500,000 customers had made down payments on a Model A, without knowing its price and without ever having seen the car.

When Ford's dealers were at last in a position to exhibit the long-awaited vehicle, their showrooms were overrun. The mass of prospective buyers who flooded Madison Square Garden as Ford's guests in January 1928, broke all existing records for an indoor exhibition of any kind. Mounted police had to be called out to prevent sightseers from caving in the Ford show windows in Cleveland. More than 25,000 persons flocked to the Ford exhibit in St. Paul, despite sub-zero weather. Colorado newspapermen could recall only one previous event that equaled the excitement which a similar showing evoked in Denver, and that was the public's reaction after a sensational robbery of the Denver mint. To set the stage for these demonstrations in both Canada and the United States, Ford spent something like $2,000,000 for five days of intensive advertising.[22]

The Ford dealer was eager to embrace the Model A and all its trimmings—with four color choices, and some seventeen variations of body style. As standard equipment the new model carried most of the refinements that Ford's salesmen had been itching for: hydraulic shock absorbers, four-wheel brakes, standard gear-shift, battery ignition, theft-proof ignition lock, automatic windshield wiper, stop light, water pump, gas and oil gauge, foot throttle and speedometer. In one particular Ford had actually stolen a march on the trade. His car was the first in any price class to include safety glass in the windshield as original equipment. On the whole a worthy successor to the Model T, the A arrived, but tardily.

While waiting for deliveries of the automobile, hundreds upon hundreds of Ford's dealers had been forced into bankruptcy.

## Sixteen

## FORD'S FRANCHISE

### 1

THE MODEL A, once it arrived, was not a cause for unrestrained celebration among those whose business it was to sell it. Straining for a comeback, Ford overproduced and crowded his dealers with stock. Consequently many a Ford agency, subject to inordinate pressure from the factory, failed to make good the earnings it had to sacrifice over the preceding twelve or eighteen months. Such was the experience of a former Ford dealer who managed to hang on for a year and a half in a medium-sized factory town, waiting for the Model A. Flailed by the home office, this man was so overloaded later on that he was forced to close out the season of 1929 by disposing of 150 cars at a loss. His experience the following year was even more disastrous. He did a gross business of a quarter of a million dollars. Yet, saddled with surplus cars he never asked for, he lost $10,000 for the season.*

The long-suffering sales force of the Ford Motor Co. was then alarmed by the fact that Ford gave every indication of repeating the

* Many similar stories are to be found in the files of the Federal Trade Commission.[1]

Model T pattern all over again. Once more he promptly froze his engineering. The Model A, though a striking departure from its predecessor and an excellent car as far as it went, soon turned into another case of arrested development. It remained substantially unchanged for the next five years. It was immensely popular for a season or so, and then Knudsen pulled away in 1929 by converting the Chevrolet into a "six." Just as quickly, General Motors started advertising the Knudsen product as a "six for the price of a four." Because of its better appearance and smoother engine performance, Chevrolet began to eat into the business of the Ford Motor Co. for the second time.

Walter P. Chrysler, taking advantage of Ford's lapse, invaded the field with Plymouth. This Chrysler model, introduced in 1931, embodied the most aggressive engineering and stylization yet witnessed in the low-price field. The car came equipped with hydraulic brakes, improved body lines and "floating power." No other automobile in the same price class could approach it for smooth engine action. Proud of his innovation, Chrysler took the wheel of the third Plymouth that came off the line and drove it out to Dearborn. After demonstrating the car for the benefit of Henry Ford and Edsel, he made a present of it to the Fords, riding back to his own factory in a taxi. Chevrolet kept the pace the following year by introducing an all-steel top and synchromesh transmission. A laggard in the war of style and progressive engineering for the second time within five years, Ford was again compelled to modernize his product. He discarded the Model A, reluctantly, in 1932.

The gestation of his next offering—the Ford V-8—was almost as labored as that of the Model A. The arduous job of arriving at a new design and retooling lumbered along, once more, because of its scope and because of inexperience in the dexterous art of changing models. Whimsy and showmanship again hampered the change-over. Ford's old fondness for rule-of-thumb, and the resulting delays of production, prompted *Barron's Weekly* to remark, "Being an engineer of the old school, Ford proceeds by the empirical method. He builds, tries and approves or rejects without due regard for theory or science."[2]

This time the distraught Ford dealer was short of merchandise for approximately half a year. The Rouge and all the lesser plants of the Ford Motor Co. were closed for at least five months.[3] But neither the straits of his dealers nor the state of the trade which had forced the belated retirement of the Model A seemed to give Ford any qualms. In W. J. Cameron's office sometime in 1933, the manufacturer described his own peace of mind by telling a *Fortune* writer, "I don't care how many cars Chevrolet sold last year. I don't know how many they're selling this year. I don't know how many they may sell next year. And—I don't care."[4]

The Ford dealer, on the other hand, enjoyed no such composure. He was frantic. His business had already slackened long before the actual stoppage at the factory. Orders dropped off at the mere rumor that the company was thinking of a change of models. The five- or six-month layover, pending delivery of the Ford V-8, hit the sales force of the Ford Motor Co. even harder than the earlier delay with the Model A. For this time the disadvantage of having little or nothing to sell descended on a dealer organization which was already up against it—in the midst of a great depression.

If Ford didn't care, his dealers did. The lot of one of his agents in a small eastern city is typical of a fate that befell hundreds of others in the same boat. The dealer in question operated a Ford agency for some six or seven years, from 1926 through 1932. He had nothing much to offer his patrons, in any quantity, for substantially two years. The break in deliveries on the Ford V-8 finished him. Other dealers, big and little, gave up voluntarily, to avoid bankruptcy. The largest Ford agency in the country, De Lisser Motors, Inc., of New York City, went over to Dodge and Plymouth. As a result of his second major stoppage of production, Ford lost, in all, another thousand dealers.[5] Profiting at Ford's expense, Chrysler at the same time increased the number of his agencies by one thousand.

Meanwhile, Ford was losing customers as well as dealers. In fact, his engineering crisis of 1932 forced him to forfeit his position as the second-ranking producer of the trade. By December 1933, General Motors had already bested him in sales for three consecutive years. Then the lengthy change-over from the Model A gave Plymouth its great opportunity. The new rivalry proved so vigorous in 1933 that Chrysler, the late-comer, could forge ahead of the Ford Motor Co., second in volume of business only to General Motors. For operating in a vacuum twice in five years' time—despite his knack for mass production—Ford was designated by *Fortune* in December 1933 as the "world's worst salesman."

Halfway between the ponderous retooling for the A and the Ford V-8, Ford pricked his dealers by initiating one of the most shortsighted changes of policy ever conceived at Dearborn. Just as the holders of his franchise were getting back on their feet after the lean years of 1927-1928, he cut their commissions drastically. This reduction, put into effect in November 1929, coincided with the onset of the depression. It came about as part of a plan for lowering prices. On a Tudor Ford sedan selling for $525, the drop in price amounted to $25. What galled the Ford dealer was that 70 per cent of this reduction was squeezed from his commission. His discount rate was lowered from 20 to 17½ per cent. Yet Ford's margin of profit was scarcely touched.[6]

As a result, the Ford sales force rebelled. The resentment was particularly fierce in the South and Middle West. Any number of Ford dealers simply quit the business.[7] Somewhat alarmed, Ford hastily backed down. He first discharged the sales manager who had to enforce the unpopular decree. Then, two months later, in May 1930, he substituted a sliding scale of commissions in place of the straight 17½ per cent discount. The new discount rates calmed the larger agencies at least. But the little fellow, who sold fifty cars a year or less, was still stuck with the 17½ per cent arrangement.

The fact that Ford would concede anything at all to any of his salesmen was so unprecedented that the trade began to talk. *Barron's*, the financial weekly, remarked, "For the first time, it appears, the Ford dealer body has won a victory in a general protest over the Ford factory policy which, at times, has involved some unusual practices with relation to the selling organization." As a body, the journal added, Ford's agents were "badly demoralized." The scale of the uproar, said *Business Week*, was an indication that the rebels had risen at last after "years of absolute domination by the factory." As to what Ford had thought of his dealers long before this tempest over discount rates, this same weekly continued, "He consistently refused to cultivate them, to cater to their wishes, to ask their advice."

Both during and after the heyday of the Model T, the primary complaint of the Ford dealer organization had to do with unbridled factory forcing. In good times and bad, and all too often in complete disregard of local needs and conditions, Ford compelled thousands of his agents to submit to sales quotas that were excessive and arbitrary. For countless numbers of his men, the rule of factory forcing spelled ruin. Even his more successful representatives groaned under the load of having to accept more cars and parts than their territories seemed to warrant. But after crowding and overstocking his men, Ford, in such cases, was never out of pocket. For in keeping with one of the oldest customs of the trade, the dealer paid cash on delivery for whatever shipments the factory cared to send.

Unwanted merchandise was usually forced on the salesman by mere fiat. Dearborn's word was law. The dealer could either comply with the overloading or he could quit the business. Occasionally Ford began heaping goods onto an agency even without the formality of a direct command or any overt memorandum. All too often, his dealers had to accept extra cars or trucks which they neither wanted nor ordered, as a condition of getting delivery on models which they did desire. The superfluous "tied-in" shipment often arrived, studded with higher-priced units or with unpopular models which the factory was eager to unload.

What gave Ford the whip hand when his men finally began to grumble over stiff quotas or their product was the revocable, one-way Ford franchise. Some time after Couzens' retirement, the home office abandoned the practice of granting its agents enforceable one-year contracts.[8] In place of the earlier two-sided instrument, it substituted franchises which were mere permits to do business. The new relationship had neither temporal guarantees nor any legal status. It could be canceled at a moment's notice, at Ford's discretion.

Thus armed, the Fords could and did simply rub out the dealer who proved refractory or dared to stand up for his rights. The dismissal of such a man was often acknowledged as coldly as the forced retirement of a certain Ford agent whose sales were averaging from 300 to 500 cars a year up to 1939, and who had served the company for seventeen years. When the holder of this particular franchise was told to go, all he received from any one by way of recognition of his many years of service was a notice to quit, signed by an assistant secretary of the Ford organization, and reading, "In accordance with the provisions of Clause 9, section (c), notice is hereby given of cancellation, effective as of this date, of Ford Sales Agreement with you, dated . . ."

Yet, as Ford proceeded to ride roughshod over his dealers, pains were taken to conceal the fact. His field representatives or his regional sales managers made a point of transmitting their commands by telephone or orally, face to face. They left no written record of their mandates, or at least none that the Federal Trade Commission could discover.[9] Nor were any such written instructions necessary. The ever-present threat of franchise cancellation put teeth in any hints that were passed along from Dearborn.

Factory forcing by every conceivable means became particularly unbearable during each of the company's engineering crises. As the T and then the A started slipping, the Ford commodity was that much harder to sell. Meanwhile, roadmen, operating out of Dearborn, turned on the pressure, until the outdated models were finally taken off the market. The same redoubled compulsion for sales occurred each time the company reentered the market.

If their sundry grievances had resulted from the imperatives of mass production alone, many of Ford's dealers, past and present, could review the record less bitterly. As it was, they had reason to feel that more than one shortsighted company policy was solely a function of Ford's personal idiosyncrasies. The stubborn freezing of Ford's two best-known early models was the least of it. For over and above the practice of pushing products that no longer pleased the public, Ford saw fit to burden his retailers, at one time or another, with goods for which no effective demand existed whatsoever. It was items of this character, on which Ford doted for purely personal reasons, that imposed incalculable and wholly avoidable hardships on his agents.

The great white elephant of the Ford line turned out to be the Leland-designed Lincoln car. This otherwise fine automobile was simply too expensive for general sale. Ford insisted on making it, minimizing his losses meanwhile by passing a good share of them on to his dealers. As early as 1926, the company began setting up a single, separately incorporated Lincoln outlet in each of its market areas. The dealers in a given region were then summoned to a meeting at which they were told they would have to finance a new Lincoln agency for the area, out of their own pockets. The spokesman for the factory was seldom given to pussy-footing at such a gathering. Each dealer's expected donation was, as a rule, computed in advance, sometimes on a lump sum basis, at other times in proportion to sales for the previous year. In the latter case, the larger a man's success, the stiffer the tax. At one such meeting the company's man arrived with the checks already written out. The sheep were merely told to sign. Non-subscribers were forced into line by the crudest of methods. In one city a certain dealer whose donation had been set at $10,000 refused to participate. He was shortly thereafter forced to move from his old location where he had built up a strong following. He quit a year later after failing to make a go of things at the new, less favorably situated place of business.[10] Of such cases investigated by the Federal Trade Commission, the compulsory donations ranged from $700 to $10,000 per dealer. Certain Lincoln agencies, thus financed, failed to show a profit. The collectors for the factory then made the rounds all over again, levying brand new special assessments.

A kindred Ford offering to which the market was equally unresponsive was a Model A taxi, a creation which *Barron's Weekly* once described as being "low and rakish." For a time, beginning in 1928, the Fords issued their taxicab in quantity, calmly overriding an adverse dealer reaction. The effort to market this unpopular unit was perhaps briefer and less costly than the experience with the Lincoln, but its temper was the same.

Among other vast consignments of unprofitable merchandise that were foisted on the Ford agent was a copious outpouring of parts and tools.[11] When the Model T was in its heyday, this particular mode of factory forcing was usually accentuated at the moment a dealer could least afford it. It was an old Ford custom to ship out vast lots of unordered parts during the winter months. The normal quota called for one carload per agency. Such a procedure carried real advantages for the consumer and for the Ford factory worker. Off-season shipments helped to stabilize production. Thanks to year-around stocking, the Ford customer could enjoy optimal facilities for service and replacement. But the standing complaint from the dealer, to which the home office paid not the slightest heed, was that such consignments were usually padded and assembled "by guess and by gosh." As far as the typical Ford agent could tell, through 1930, the company made no effort to gauge its parts requirements scientifically.

It was still another poorly conceived plan—Ford's ardent advocacy of horseless farming—that drove even the most successful Ford dealer to despair, during the rosiest years. This marketing adventure involved the Fordson tractor, when Dearborn courted a trade war with International Harvester. The bitter struggle between these two combatants and General Motors was to persist for ten years. At first Ford held the upper hand. By 1920 he had marketed three-fourths of all the tractors sold in the United States; he had lowered prices on the Fordson from $750 to $395. But to break even at the factory, the company produced the unit in such volume that any number of dealers had found it impossible to dispose of their allotments at a profit.

The Fordson, in its prime, arrived at nearly every agency in quantity, irrespective of the dealer's wishes in the matter. One proprietor of a Ford agency, located in poor farming country where no call for tractors existed at any time of year, had to pay cash for eleven Fordsons delivered at his door in the month of November. In the words of another retailer, "Some six or seven thousand carloads of tractors . . . started rolling along to the dealers." Geography meant nothing to Dearborn, said this dealer, who disposed of his surplus Fordsons, on occasion, by giving trade-in allowances on "old, stationary, ready-to-be-junked gas engines." The average agent, he said, was overwhelmed with tractors; the location of his place of business—

whether it was situated in farming country or in a city or in "swamps and mountains"—made no difference.[12]

An important detail of engineering made the job of selling Ford's farm machinery no simpler. On hilly ground or under stress, the machine was given to rearing on its hind wheels and falling over backwards. On such occasions, many an operator crushed his chest or otherwise maimed himself. So common was the bucking trait that one of the farm journals finally suggested the precaution of having every Ford tractor inscribed with the warning, in red paint, "Prepare to Meet Thy God." Before the product was redesigned, *Pipp's Weekly* listed in a single issue the names of 136 drivers who had been either killed or injured in the act of grappling with one of the early models.[13]

In the clash with International Harvester, Ford finally lost out altogether. His machine was too light to cope with large-scale road work or with the giant mechanized farming operations that were opening up in the western grain country. In addition, his dealers were no match for the experts in the business. International Harvester carried the fight to Ford, spending millions in the process, by challenging his agents to take part in a competitive trial every time a Fordson buyer came within view. This tactic was crucial. Harvester's men were specialists. They knew their farmers. Spent by such competition, the Fordson died like a burnt-out meteor. General Motors went down in the same contest. Its tractor, the Samson, was withdrawn in 1922; its losses were written off at $33,000,000.[14] Ford was less ready to concede defeat. He hung on six years longer, incurring untold dealer deficits, forcing his agents to fight on in a battle that was already lost.

2

Among the many spears used to prick the Ford dealer, the sharpest of all came into being when Ford created his own finance company, the Universal Credit Corporation. When the U.C.C. opened its doors in 1928, its officers included several Ford executives: the parent company's secretary, its treasurer, its sales manager and general purchasing agent, and its chief auditor and leading counsel. The president of the new firm was Edsel's brother-in-law, Ernest Kanzler.

In essence, the U.C.C. was a replica of the General Motors Acceptance Corporation. The Ford subsidiary, like its prototype, was instituted for the purpose of financing time sales. Its function was to lend money at interest to two classes of installment buyers: the ultimate consumer and—of far greater moment to Ford—the Ford dealer.

By means of loans to the dealer, under an arrangement known as "floor planning," the U.C.C. promptly began to operate as the factory's most powerful weapon. With credit resources of their own, the Fords now had the final answer for the dealer who tried to resist factory forcing because of an "inability to pay." The factory advanced him the money. The circle was closed. U.C.C. agents were soon given each dealer's blanket power of attorney, vested with full authority to accept and pay for consignments without waiting for any dealer's consent. If the branch manager and the U.C.C. man saw eye to eye, any agent could be stocked up forthwith, to the bursting point. The U.C.C. paid the factory—that is, the factory paid itself—at the moment of delivery. The dealer could settle with the U.C.C. later on, or else.

Ford did his best to cloak some of these operations. His credit organization, he said in 1928, had not been founded for the "primary and sole purpose of profit."[15] But in actual operation, the U.C.C., to all intents and purposes, was indistinguishable from the competing affiliates sponsored by Chrysler and General Motors. Its facilities were forced upon the dealer by devious means. Its credit leverage was frankly exploited as a means of increasing sales, under pressure. For the first five years of its existence, the subsidiary of the Ford Motor Co. earned a reported net profit of $4,500,000.[16] The rates of interest charged against loans to the retail buyer were standard for the trade, The car buyer paid 11 or 12 per cent for his money. Yet the U.C.C., following in the footsteps of General Motors, advertised this arrangement as a "6 per cent plan." Anything but profit shy, Ford finally sold the U.C.C. to the Commercial Investment Trust Corporation in 1933, making an additional net gain of $7,000,000.[17]

Why could Ford bring himself to relinquish so valuable a property? He was hard up for cash. He had lost money as a manufacturer in 1931-1932 to the tune of $115,000,000.[18] Perhaps he was trying to depersonalize his banking ties or to erase any direct connection between his car and a financial affiliate that was, out and out, his own creature. This bond had worried him from the beginning, or so it appeared from the content of the first confidential bulletin which the U.C.C. released in 1928. The opening message to the employes of the new finance company had read in part, "It was considered inadvisable to call the corporation "The Ford Credit Corporation', because the ownership of the Ford Motor Co. being a personal matter, and the name being too personal a one to be used in connection with collection activities which the credit corporation will undoubtedly have to undertake . . ." By such foresight, Henry Ford the

banker was never easily compromised in the act of repossessing a car
on which some installment buyer had defaulted in his obligations to
Henry Ford, the manufacturer.

Yet when the Ford Motor Co. divorced itself from this channel
of the banking business, it experienced no change of heart on the
subject of dealer financing. For after changing hands in 1933, the
U.C.C. continued to operate as the primary lever of Ford factory
forcing. The only difference under the new arrangement was that the
Ford Motor Co. could now exert its pressure more subtly and in
someone else's name. Other finance companies were available, but
Ford's men were still dragooned into dealing with the U.C.C. The
story of this carry-over was finally unraveled by the Department of
Justice when the Ford Motor Co., along with GM and Chrysler, was
indicted at South Bend in 1938 for alleged violations of the Sherman
Anti-Trust Act. It was the government's contention that the Fords,
though no longer holding title to the U.C.C., were nonetheless still
actively engaged in a conspiracy to monopolize the financing of their
automobile sales.[19]

Their conspiratorial methods were devious, said the South Bend
indictment. The Ford Motor Co. proper had been known to cancel
dealers who dealt with any independent finance company, to penalize
such "offenders" by delaying their shipments, to refuse to transfer
the title to Ford cars to outside finance companies, to discriminate
against the recalcitrant agent "with respect to the number, model, color
and style of automobiles," and to procure information on the books
and accounts of its dealers "from servants and employes . . . secretly,
covertly, and without the knowledge of the dealers, and sometimes
by means of bribery and otherwise."

In the face of this action by a federal grand jury in May 1938,
the Fords chose to compromise. The factory quickly spread the word
that its agents were now free to use any credit facilities they chose.[20]
Then, in order to escape further prosecution by the federal government and to seal off this well of adverse publicity, Ford empowered
certain of his representatives, in November of 1938, to sign a consent
decree in which he promised to refrain in the future from any of the
practices alleged by the Department of Justice.[21]

Strained as they were, Ford's dealer relations over a score of
years were by no means unique. Every automobile dealer, no matter
what his wares, made the discovery sometime in the 20's that he
was enlisted in one of the most precarious callings in existence. In
this relatively prosperous decade, the economic death rate of the men
engaged in this business was averaging from 20 to 30 per cent a

year.[22] When the industry passed the saturation point, in 1926 or 1927, the dealer's struggle for existence became that much more deadly. Of the seventeen leading Ford agencies which functioned in Detroit alone in 1926, only five still had their doors open in 1939. At least ten had been swept off the boards in the meantime, for financial reasons. By 1938 the trade as a whole was rocking with dealer failures. In the month of June of that year, *Fortune* estimated that of 43,000 passenger-car agents then doing business in the United States, 10,000 would go under before the end of the season. The average automobile salesman was then earning less than $20 a week. So grave was the marketing crisis of the industry during the relatively good season of 1937 that the typical dealer was taking an actual net loss of $4.26 on the sale of every new car. The man who survived did so only if he ran into volume in service charges or in the sale of parts and supplies, or if he had the good fortune to be able to carry his own finance paper for those of his customers who bought their cars on time.

Inasmuch as none of the manufacturers, Ford included, seemed anxious to put his house in order voluntarily, the National Automobile Dealers Association finally began to clamor for intervention on the part of the federal government. This agitation for statutory relief from excessive factory domination came to a head during the second Roosevelt administration. Washington in turn responded by pursuing a double course of action. On one front the Department of Justice instituted criminal proceedings against the Big Three and their respective financial affiliates. Each was indicted in 1938 on substantially the same counts. The charges leveled at Ford's manipulation of the Universal Credit Corporation were much the same as those aimed at the practices invoked by GM and Chrysler.*

Then Congress, acting in its own right in response to the dealers' lobby, authorized the preparation of what proved to be the most exhaustive tome yet published on the history of the trade—the definitive dealer's bible, *Report on Motor Vehicle Industry*, issued by the Federal Trade Commission in 1939. This fat volume established beyond question that in market forcing and dealer coercion the rule of the trade had been "dog-eat-dog." In view of the tremendous earnings accruing to the manufacturers, the Commission concluded, the lot of the automobile dealer was an unhappy one; his occupation per-

* At South Bend, in exchange for suspended prosecution, Chrysler joined Ford in signing a consent decree. Both companies stipulated the intent to drop the coercive features of their factory-dominated finance companies. General Motors, on the other hand, chose to stand trial.

haps the outstandingly bad example of callous, high-pressure, competitive marketing in the entire American economy.

When Ford and the other automotive manufacturers granted a few dealer concessions in order to escape federal prosecution and in order to stave off internal calamity, the Ford dealers smarted with the knowledge that their employer had crowded his men harder than any producer in the business. Of all the automobile retailers canvassed by the Federal Trade Commission, the Ford agents headed the list of those who complained of having been chronically overstocked with merchandise, up to 1938. This charge was raised by 58 per cent of the Ford men. The proportion who reported the same pressure at Chrysler and General Motors was, respectively, 23 and 28 per cent.[23]

*Fortune* magazine had already passed a similar judgment on the Ford Motor Co. In December 1933, *Fortune* remarked that Ford's dealers were suffering at that time not only from the excesses that were universal in the trade but "also from the domineering attitude which we have already noticed at the Rouge plant and which appears to be characteristic of the Ford Motor Co. in all its contacts."

## Seventeen

### DETROIT'S DEPRESSION

### 1

AS THE YEAR 1928 was drawing to a close—and as the dealers of the Ford Motor Co. were about to go under for want of cars—Ford announced that he would employ 30,000 additional production workers at the Rouge. It was his plan, he said, to hire new men over the ensuing three months at the rate of 400 a day. This call for labor immediately set off another tumultuous migration toward Detroit. Labor's fervid answer to Ford's announcement was both proof of Detroit's reputation as the mecca of high wages and an omen of falling employment elsewhere in the nation.

On January 2, 1929, the day on which the hiring was supposed to start, 32,000 applicants stormed the Rouge. Among these seekers of employment who milled outside the Ford hiring office were southern sharecroppers, vying with Mexican beet pickers and unemployed coal miners from Kentucky and West Virginia.

The willingness of men to submit to Ford's hiring methods was in itself a sign of desperation. The applicants underwent the same experience that had followed the proclamation of the Five-Dollar Day in 1914. On the day before the hiring was to start, many of the petitioners stood in line the whole night through. By 4 A.M. the following morning, with the temperature at 14 degrees below zero, Ford's guards estimated the crowd at 5000. Some of the keepers of this all-night vigil suffered from exposure and had to be rushed to a hospital. The first man in line was wrapped in burlap from head to foot. Some of the applicants, stricken by the cold, spent the night in cheap restaurants near the plant. "The dingy little all-night 10-cent movie houses in Detroit did a rushing business," said the New York *Times*. "Men straggled in all through the night, not so much interested in the show as in keeping warm."

The physical management of the hiring was again inept, as it had been in 1914. The applicants were corraled in an open parking lot. When members of this throng began to fight for positions close to the employment office, the crowd was dispersed, once more, by the use of a fire-hose. Those who were admitted to the factory were selected by methods which a New York *Times* reporter compared to a "lottery." For a time the company's hiring agents resorted to a "10 in, 10 out" method of choosing nominees for inspection. The ten men closest to the door were brought in for examination, the second ten arbitrarily told to go away, the third ten admitted, and so on down the line.[1] The systematic rejection of every "even" ten cost many men, for no apparent reason, positions close to the gate which they had won by standing in the snow most of the preceding night.

The massing of workers at the Rouge gates continued for half a month in the bitterest winter weather. By the 10th of January, however, the crowd had thinned to a daily turnout of several thousand. Just before this event finally faded from the news, a reporter making his rounds discovered that the remaining Ford applicants were lined up "ankle deep" in mud and slush, "some of them shaking with coughing spells."

Behind the façade of this labor migration which seemed to augur hard times ahead, Ford was by no means merely adding new recruits to the payroll. On the contrary, he was once more cutting costs at labor's expense. Preparing for the ever sharper struggle with General Motors, Sorensen was reapplying the formula of 1921 and 1927. He was cutting off the skilled and semi-skilled workman, and rehiring him or replacing him at a lower rate of pay.[2] The throngs at the gate supplied the needed replacements at beginners' wages. The Ford man with any degree of skill or seniority to his credit could indeed consider himself lucky if he succeeded in "getting back on" on any terms. His fear of losing out altogether was heightened by a widely quoted statement, attributed to the employment manager of the Ford Motor Co., to the effect that "men between 30 and 50 years of age are the best for automobile work . . . after 50 most of them can't stand the pace."[3]

Nor did Ford swell his payroll, during the allotted first quarter of 1929, by adding the heralded complement of 30,000 new men. Four months after he issued the call for that much more labor, the Detroit *Saturday Night* reported that, over the intervening sixteen or eighteen weeks, total employment at the Rouge had increased by a margin of only 8000 men.

Why did the much-bruited hiring fail to materialize? Had Ford overestimated his labor requirements for the first four months of the year? Was the promise to hire 30,000 new men in three months' time no more than a gesture calculated to win friends in the course of a grim trade war? Or did Ford in fact take on the full number, but largely as replacements for the older men whom he dismissed? None could say, but an excess of workers came pouring into Detroit. As the season progressed, Ford may have tapped this labor pool more extensively. At least he produced 2,000,000 cars in 1929. That output was the third highest for any season in the company's history.

If Ford's countrymen were impressed by a call for 30,000 new workers during the relatively prosperous months of 1929, they were confounded by the proclamation with which the manufacturer greeted the onset of actual depression. This astonishing declaration was issued in Washington on November 22, 1929, at a White House conference to which President Hoover had summoned the leading industrialists of the nation. The stock market had collapsed. Signs of serious social dislocation were mounting in every corner of the land. In a state of panic, the President begged his conferees to fight off the catastrophe by freezing wages at existing levels.

Ford usurped the center of the stage. He went the President one better by announcing a $7 day. The new figure meant a flat $1 increase over the reported daily minimum Ford wage for common labor. Proportionate wage raises were promised for those Ford

employes who were earning more than this basic rate of pay. "Probationers" alone would remain on the old $6 scale.

Ford's gesture made the front page of every leading paper in
the country. Then, after enjoying two weeks of wide and gratuitous
publicity, the company announced its intentions all over again, by
issuing a more detailed, formal bulletin on the subject. Outlining his
father's one-man battle against depression, Edsel explained in the New
York *Times* of December 4, 1929, that he and his father hoped to
contribute "to a continuance of normal business conditions by putting
a bit more buying power into the pockets of workmen."

Put to the test, however, this laudable undertaking soon proved
to be more illusory than real. The $7 basic wage did remain in force
at the Rouge for the next two years, but serving all this while as a
shield behind which the Ford management succeeded in cutting its
labor costs to the bone. Behind the cloak of largesse, Ford officialdom
proceeded to lower its payroll with a ruthless efficiency.

First of all, while maintaining the $7 pay for unskilled labor, the
company pared down the wages of those of its employes who had
been more highly paid. This technique was quietly carried forward
from former years. In the fall of 1931, the New York *Times* could
report that Ford had already cut wages severely in the upper and
middle brackets. "For some time past," said the *Times*, the "Ford
Motor Co. has been paying off men in one department and rehiring
them in another at lower pay."[4] The *Wall Street Journal* made the same
observation, calling the process Ford's way of "quietly readjusting
[his] wage scale."[5]

Secondly, to all of Ford's surviving workmen the concession of a
$7 scale came as a storm signal and an omen of greater speed-up.
Robert Cruden, who was then employed at Ford's, described the new
regimen at the Rouge in an article for the *New Republic*. As Cruden's
foreman put it, it was a question of "Go like hell, boys. If you're gonna
get that raise you gotta increase production."[6] By such means the
company could dispense with thousands of employes. Just before and
immediately after the inauguration of the "depression-beating" wage,
according to the liberal and labor press, Ford laid off 25,000 or
30,000 workers.[7] Cruden, the *New Republic* author, was one of the
survivors. To get his $7, thus qualifying for a 17 per cent increase in
pay, his personal production quota was stepped up 47 per cent.[8]

But neither of the foregoing economies could compare with a
third—one which enabled Ford to pose as a champion of high wages
and, at the same time, to force a good number of the men who had

a hand in making his car to accept something less than subsistence pay. The manufacturer simply farmed out a larger fraction of his work to the sweatshops of the industry. In fact, the announcement of the plan to put a "bit more buying power in the pockets of workmen" and the act of closing the Rouge departments given over to the making of brakes, rear axles, shock absorbers and differential housings, went almost hand in hand. Contracts for the fabrication of these units were then placed with the low-wage parts shops of the trade.[9] The number of suppliers to whom Ford thus sublet his work rose steadily from 2200 concerns in 1929 to 3500 the following year, then to 5500 outside establishments in 1931.[10]

As an ever greater proportion of his work was jobbed out to outsiders, Ford hammered down supplier prices so drastically that his parts makers in turn were forced to slash wages. Other producers, to be sure, were bringing the same pressure to bear on their suppliers. But Ford policy toward the parts plants had this distinction: none was any tougher, if as tough; yet none was so two-faced. Ford was not only boasting of the high wages paid at the Ford Motor Co. proper, but on top of that he struck the pose of the Little Father who was watching over the rights of the men who contributed their labor to his car, under any and all auspices. He let it be known, as the depression deepened, that a number of his representatives had been specially charged with the mission of policing the wage scales of the 5000-odd supplier plants with whom he was doing business, in order to put a stop to any contemplated wage cuts.[11]

It was doubtless the depth of Ford's pretense that led Theodore F. MacManus, the respected advertiser and co-author of *Men, Money and Motors*, to insert a large advertisement in the New York ·Times of February 24, 1930, in which the true Ford policy towards the parts supplier was taken to task. Over MacManus' signature, the indictment read, "These numerous component parts are 'farmed out' to outside manufacturers for the very practical reason that they can build them more cheaply—and one of the elements of saving, of course, is a wage scale considerably lower than the one so widely advertised." While taking pains to acclaim the "wizardry" behind Ford's career as a whole, the advertiser remarked, "Someone paid all along the line to produce the net profit which built [his] colossal fortune."

Then came a fatal blow to the prestige of the self-anointed apostle of high wages during the lean years. It was Detroit's first major depression strike. This labor upheaval occurred in 1933 at the Briggs Manufacturing Co. and, ironically, on Ford property. It involved the Highland Park plant of the Ford Motor Co. which the Briggs concern had leased for the purpose of making bodies for the Ford V-8.

As the Briggs strike wore on, competent observers began a study of its origins. Justice Frank Murphy, then mayor of Detroit, sent a fact-finding committee into the field. One group of investigators soon came up with the discovery that, in contrast to the much-publicized basic wage of $4, certain Briggs men had been working a 14-hour day, when the work was there, for 10 cents an hour.[12]

The machinery at the Briggs shops was speeded up to such a point, said the mayor's committee, that the health and safety of the working force had been imperiled. The Briggs workers themselves, quite as conscious of this fact, had already begun to refer to their place of work, with grim humor, as the "butcher shop." This Ford supplier was further said to be evading the state's 10-hour law for women by making women workers check out at the end of a 10-hour shift and then return to their posts immediately, their second shift being recorded on a separate set of time cards.[13]

A labor irritant second to none was found to be the company's past practice of keeping its workers at their places for five or six hours at a stretch, or for an entire day, though they might be engaged in actual production for as brief a period as two hours, and would be paid only for their working time.[14]

What the strikers asked for in a bill of particulars was something approaching the conditions of employment that supposedly prevailed at the Rouge: a nine-hour day, compensation for "dead" time, and a daily wage of $3.60 for women and $4 for men. Besides that, they demanded less speed-up, and time and one-half for overtime. But neither their immediate superior, Walter O. Briggs, nor their ultimate employer, Henry Ford, was in any mood for compromise.

Briggs, who had been vacationing in Florida, rushed to Detroit by plane. He refused to consider mediation and he promptly instructed his foremen and superintendents to ostracize the mayor's investigating committee.[15] The Ford supplier offered the defense that the walkout was simply a product of "Communism." The Murphy investigators gave it as their opinion that the stoppage was aimed at the "correction of certain real grievances against the management."[16] Certain · local Communists had given the strike support and leadership. *Business Week* said, "It is doubtful if they [the Communists] have been more than the fuse to the powder."[17]

Ford, who could have dictated the terms of a fair settlement in a moment, moved with dispatch to break the strike. His top men proclaimed that unless production was resumed immediately in the struck plants, the Ford Motor Co. would at once take possession of the dies which it had loaned to the Briggs corporation.[18] Several days later, the mayor's committee reported that state troopers were conveying strike-breakers from Highland Park to Mack Avenue—from one Briggs shop where the strikers had more esprit de corps to a second where the union was much weaker. At both sites the police forbade mass picketing. Worn down, all the Briggs employes finally straggled back to work. They won a pittance in the form of certain minor concessions, but they lost the strike.

"The biggest surprise of my career," Ford protested, "was when I was informed that 6000 employes of the Briggs Company had walked out without giving any particular reason. I have had difficulties in my early career," he said, "but this was the biggest jolt of all."[19] A New York *Times* man sought him out for a statement on Briggs labor policies, but Ford refused to say a word.[20] After that, the manufacturer began to talk of the stoppage as the handiwork of "certain bankers." The London *Evening Standard* quoted him as saying, "Certain of my competitors are operating against me, supported by these bankers, with the object of preventing another Ford car from leaving the factory."

Ford's wider audience may have received such talk with respect. But the trade subscribed to quite a different explanation of the Briggs disturbance. As to the essential causes of the walkout, conservative business spokesmen saw eye to eye with the Communists. One of the more caustic of the former was B. C. Forbes, the financial columnist. "The Ford Motor Co.," wrote Forbes, "is about the worst offender in the whole country in compelling suppliers of materials to cut prices drastically. Ford's extremely hard bargaining compels those doing business with him to squeeze workers."[21] Certain manufacturers actually welcomed the strike, said Forbes, because it might serve as a brake on large buyers like Ford who were in the habit of "wringing the last penny of possible profit from suppliers." *Automotive Industries* restated the Forbes indictment in its own words.[22] In still another treatment of Ford's "share of responsibility" for the Briggs wage scale of 12 and 15 cents an hour, *Business Week* remarked, "Labor, considered coldly (if incorrectly) is a commodity. Like all commodities it has its bottom price. This first 'depression strike' is the beginning of a process which established the limit of pay and hours and treatment which men will stand."[23]

## 2

Apart from his attitude toward the wage earners of the parts plants, Ford was on trial in a far more pervasive sense when the pall of the great depression of the thirties finally blanketed Detroit. This crisis gave him an opportunity to look to the needs of his own unemployed workmen or to come forward with some challenging social doctrine. As a test of economic vision, the manufacturer could have asked for nothing more definitive than the scene which industrial collapse brought to America's fourth largest city.

By 1933 Detroit was the focal point of 70 per cent of the unemployment that gripped the state. One-third of the wage earners of Michigan had been partly or totally unemployed for four years in succession.[24] When the depression was only two years old, the army of 211,000 dependents on Detroit's relief rolls was equal in size to the entire population of Grand Rapids. An additional 150,000 persons had fled Detroit, trekking to the homes of relatives in other parts of the country, to the South, or back to the farm. In this catastrophe that called for industrial statesmanship, there were signs of acute social distress and breakdown. On January 13, 1932, Detroit's newly elected mayor Frank Murphy informed the Common Council that 4000 children daily were standing in bread lines. The suicide rate in the city, the mayor reported, had risen 30 per cent over a previous five-year average. During the following summer, according to the Board of Health, at least 18 per cent of the school children of the city were suffering from severe undernourishment. Simultaneously, fifteen private banks closed their doors in metropolitan Detroit, impounding the savings of 34,000 depositors. Children from the poorer sections, the *Nation* reported late in 1932, had taken to smashing store windows in after-dark robberies and snatching parcels from the arms of customers as they emerged from grocery stores. Less than a year after the stock market collapse, the city welfare department was getting calls for assistance in eviction proceedings at the rate of 7500 cases per month. As the depression deepened, the Detroit *Times* told of people found on the streets, unconscious, after eating out of garbage cans. Captain John F. Ballinger, Detroit's director of public welfare, completed a detailed report on the depression that was ravaging America's most prosperous manufacturing community. The document in question, dated May 31, 1932, was so disturbing it was suppressed by every newspaper in the city.

Meanwhile, the foremost industrialists of the community were making themselves inconspicuous. Captain Ballinger made the rounds, asking for remedial suggestions from each of the business leaders in the locality. Getting nowhere, he appended to the report of May 1932, "They seem to be rather cautious and secretive . . . about what they are doing. When we inquire as to the extent of their relief, or when we inquire as to their interpretation of their responsibility, they become very defensive." Mayor Murphy himself, a vigorous advocate of federal relief, was little more successful when he tried to plumb the consciousness of the area's industrial chiefs. Totally dissatisfied with the "dole and soup kitchen" stage of public welfare, the mayor appointed an Unemployment Committee to see what could be done to better the situation. The committee was soon torn by an inner tug-of-war. The first group to withdraw en bloc from this body were the industrialists. The retiring faction departed, issuing a broadside to the effect that federal aid for the unemployed was "inspired by Moscow."[25]

Such behavior was not unexpected on the part of the conventional man of affairs. But with Ford, as the masses understood him, it was different. Ford did not serve on the mayor's committee, although from his lips the workers of the land would have anticipated some probing answer to the conundrum of world depression. Dearborn was in the habit of enunciating The Word.

Ford did, in fact, deliver a series of depression manifestos. When The Word was spoken, however, during the world's most profound industrial crisis to date, it was mumbo jumbo:

*Moving Forward,* by Henry Ford, 1930.
". . . the very poor are recruited almost solely from the people who refuse to think and therefore refuse to work diligently."

Detroit *Free Press,* September 7, 1930. (New York City, embarking on the liner *Bremen* for a vacation tour of Germany)
"It's a good thing the recovery is prolonged. Otherwise the people wouldn't profit by the illness."

Detroit *News,* March 16, 1931. (Fort Myers, Florida)
"The average man won't really do a day's work unless he is caught and cannot get out of it."

Detroit *Free Press,* October 20, 1931.
A depression is a "wholesome thing in general."

*Pictorial Review,* October, 1932.
"If we could only realize it, these are the best times we ever had."

Detroit *Times,* December 18, 1933. (New York City)
"I think that the depression really taught a lot of people how to

love their fellowmen . . . we did find a blessing in economic misfortune. . . . There is no depression, really, now."

The unemployed of the nation gained a further insight into Ford's philosophy of the times through the reflections of W. J. Cameron, who made his debut in 1934 as commentator on the Ford Sunday Evening Hour. Giving a sophisticated dress to his employer's views, Cameron began to speak of hard times as "strengthening encounters with life,"[26] invoked by a "good Providence" as a means of atonement for "our former false prosperity."[27] What was bothering America, said Ford's spokesman, was a "payroll complex."[28] Millions of unemployed factory hands who lacked the cash to pay their gas and light bills were told to start little businesses on their own.

As for the reforms espoused by the New Deal, Ford's publicist distinguished himself as one of the most insistent voices of reaction. Federal relief for the unemployed and the very thought of national unemployment compensation he dubbed a "slight to community honor" and a "new form of permanent pauperization."*

Before the federal government came to grips with Detroit's depression, however, it was expected in certain quarters and demanded in others that Ford bear a fair share of the common burden of caring for the local unemployed. His responsibilities in that direction were unusual. In the first place, Detroit's economic breakdown, while only a part of a larger picture, had been aggravated by Ford himself. The delays with the Ford V-8 had induced the "crisis within a crisis." For when the Ford Motor Co. withdrew from the market for five months or more, the entire industry felt the shock. The shutdown at the Rouge reacted on the parts business and on the shops of other primary producers. In March 1932, the New York *Times* remarked that while 50 per cent of the inhabitants of Detroit were piecing out a "hand to mouth existence," a number of Ford's competitors had suspended operations altogether, pending the arrival of the new Ford model.[30]

Secondly, while he was acting entirely within the law, Ford stood by and let the surrounding community bear the brunt of providing local relief for thousands upon thousands of his own unemployed. He was not bound to contribute to the commonweal on a parity with other

---

* This advocate of laissez-faire is the same man who had met the issue of mass unemployment fifteen years earlier by prescribing on "Mr. Ford's Own Page" a permanent system of federal works. Such a plan for dealing with the problem Cameron asserted to be the "sacred responsibility of our highest socialized institution."[29]

comparable corporations, because of the physical location of his properties. His chief competitors had huge Detroit plants on which they were compelled to pay local taxes. But Ford's major operations, in a class by themselves, lay in Dearborn and Highland Park, well outside the tax limits of the city which housed most of the welfare clients of the area, including the bulk of the Ford unemployed. Only the Lincoln division, the least important unit of the Ford Motor Co., was taxable in Detroit proper.

There was one channel through which the Fords could have voluntarily siphoned off some of their wealth to help Detroit maintain, in its program of public welfare, what Cameron was calling at the time "community honor." That avenue was the city's Community Fund. Yet in 1931, when the relief policies of the Ford Motor Co. were a burning issue, Henry Ford contributed nothing at all to the fund. He had made no gift of this sort since the year 1924. Edsel, on the other hand, forwarded in 1931 a check for $140,000. This contribution, under the circumstances, was anything but munificent. It was less than 2 per cent of the family's income for the year. In 1931 alone, the three bona fide stockholders of the Ford corporation—Henry, Clara and Edsel Ford—withdrew for their personal use cash dividends amounting to $8,500,000.[31] Nor was Edsel's grant commensurate with the proportion of unemployed workers whom his company had shunted to the relief rolls of a city in which the Ford Motor Co. was largely exempt from taxes.

This matter of allowing the taxpayers of Detroit to foot the bill for "Ford relief" embroiled the Fords and the political administration of Mayor Frank Murphy in a bitter and protracted controversy. The city's relief authorities were agreed to a man that Detroit had been saddled, in 1931, with a disproportionate number of welfare cases drawn from the roster of Ford's unemployed. They differed when it came to estimating the extent of this shifted responsibility. Walter Bergman, a member of the mayor's Unemployment Committee, reported that 36 per cent of the city's welfare clients were "Ford cases."[32] The lowest estimate came from Thomas E. Dolan, Detroit's superintendent of public welfare. Of the city's total relief population, Dolan placed the number of Ford employes at 14 per cent.[33]

If the lower figure is the truer one, the care of Ford's unemployed in 1931 cost the city of Detroit at least $1,960,000. In that case, Edsel's donation to the Community Fund amounted to less than 10 per cent of the sum which the whole community in turn was called upon to spend for the partial support of the Ford employes who were out of work.

When the Fords' "community honor" was thus called to book, the Ford Motor Co. spoke up in self-defense. Edsel Ford, first of all, questioned the city's ability to recognize a "former Ford employe" when it saw one. With some point to his argument, Edsel contended that the mother plant of his company had employed more than 300,-000 different persons over the preceding seven years and that, as a consequence, a very large proportion of Detroit's working population could rightly advance the claim of having "worked at Ford's" at one time or another. For the fate of so vast an array of former employes, he said, the company could not now, in all fairness, be held accountable.[34]*

As a second line of apology, the Ford organization raised the cry of fraud. Harry Bennett, speaking for Henry Ford, charged that the relief rolls of Detroit had been padded with spurious cases. That mistakes had been made in defining the need and filling in the background of certain relief applicants, the city welfare agency readily admitted. The department also countered by saying that Bennett in turn had greatly increased this margin of error by repeatedly refusing to submit work records or answer inquiries as to a Ford worker's eligibility for relief. In such cases, the welfare people retorted, "We couldn't let the families starve" while waiting for a reply from the Ford Motor Co.[35] Mayor Murphy declared that no more than thirty or thirty-five cases of "grafting" relief applicants had been brought to his attention.[36] Captain Ballinger, the director of the welfare division, placed the percentage of fraudulent applications at less than 2 per cent of the total number of petitioners.[37]

Finally, said the Fords, they were seeing to it on their own that none of their laid-off employes was in dire need. "The Ford Motor Co.," Bennett asserted, "will continue to care for all worthy cases. This means all persons for whom we feel a responsibility."[38] The younger Ford declared, "Bona fide Ford employes already know where to apply if in difficulties."

Neither of these pledges did much to relieve the situation. The social agencies of Detroit were still at a loss to know just who qualified as a "bona fide" Ford man for whom the company felt "responsible." The city's welfare department was so accustomed to stony silence when it asked the company to report a Ford man's earnings for the preceding three months up to the time of his application for relief,

* Whatever impression this rejoinder may have made on the city officials, it at least offered interesting commentary on the labor turnover of the Ford Motor Co. It indicated that within a brief span of years, and quite apart from the purge of 1921, the Fords had gone through a labor replacement of 200 per cent.

that Mary K. Guiney, the supervisor of the city's case workers, remarked, "In no instance that I know of has the Ford Motor Co. said the applicant was eligible for Ford welfare aid. As a result, we don't know what Mr. Ford's [statement] means."[39]

When the Fords proclaimed that, in matters of relief for the unemployed, they were caring for their own, that large responsibility rested with Harry Bennett, chief of Ford's private police. As the Ford specialist at dealing with social unrest of every description throughout the crisis of the 30's, Bennett hewed to one major policy that was commonly in force at most other large industrial establishments. He spread the work. He scattered it among the largest feasible number of workers, holding more or less intact, at the same time, a skeletal force of key men. The Ford plan of on-and-off hiring was unquestionably flexible enough to allow for the reemployment (at the expense of someone else's lay-off) of those former employes who could prove special need or who knew where to go to press such a claim to the best advantage. The mere administration of such an in-and-out hiring arrangement was doubtless trying from the standpoint of management. According to Ford's own figures, 45,000 men were laid off at the Rouge in 1930-1931.[40] Two years later the number of Ford unemployed had doubled.[41]

The remaining devices by which Ford strove to appear as his brother's keeper during the depression were, for the most part, only variations of Ford showmanship. One of these instrumentalities was the institution in 1931 and 1932 of what the Scripps-Howard Washington *News* diagnosed as 50,000 "shotgun gardens."[42] Under Bennett's supervision, and on pain of discharge for those who failed to comply, every Ford employe was required to tend a vegetable garden.[43] If he had none of his own in his backyard or on some vacant lot, he was assigned a patch of soil somewhere on Ford's 4000 acres of Dearborn farm land. Each worker was first required to pay a fee of 50 cents to have his strip plowed. He then took over the care of a designated "thrift plot." Each spring Bennett's men combed through the Rouge, passing out registration cards, taking close note of every worker's name and badge number. Few escaped the recruitment. The remoteness of an employe's home from Dearborn was no item. (In its 1929 Ford study the Bureau of Labor Statistics had reported that 40 per cent of the Rouge force were living anywhere from ten to twenty miles distant from the plant.) To the bolder spirits who protested that, having no car, they would have to spend an extra two hours daily merely to get to and from their allotted patch, Bennett's inquisitors sometimes exclaimed, "Why don't-cha buy a car? You're making 'em, ain't-cha?" Once cultivation was under way, it soon reached Bennett's ears if this or that "shirker" was remiss in keeping his plot in order. Bennett's personal deputy and general overseer of the gardens was tough Norman Selby, the former boxer "Kid McCoy."[44]

Nor did any Ford employe necessarily relish this opportunity to hoe potatoes under duress. Food costs in the chain stores had reached an all-time low. Often enough these factory-gardeners ended the season with a loss, after subtracting the cost of seeds, tools and transportation. Some of the soil on Ford's acres was streaked with sand and clay. On top of that, the publicity to which this gardening effort gave rise rubbed any number of Ford dealers the wrong way. The plan sounded too much like competition for the car buyer in the farm belt.

And there was publicity. As the depression hit bottom, Ford ran full-page advertisements in the daily press, calling on the country to get back to its "roots," to "cultivate a plot of land" in the "good old pioneer way." These insertions bore the acknowledgment, "Prepared and Paid For by the Ford Motor Co. as a Contribution to Public Welfare."[45]

Ford incorporated another interesting venture within his sphere of "constructive" charity. He commandeered the entire village of Inkster for a localized experiment in "self-help" and rehabilitation. Inkster, adjacent to Dearborn, was a jerry-built community that had sprung up in past years to house Ford workers. Most of the inhabitants of the little colony were destitute Negro families. When Ford took over the community in November 1931, it had been shorn of electric lights and police protection. The local bank had closed. Inkster's storekeepers were heavily in debt. Among the 500 Negro families in the village there were ten cases of rickets. Ten or twelve speakeasies were flourishing in the little community.

All this was changed in a wink under the new management. The Ford people set up a public commissary. Other community services sprang to life. The 500-odd families in the drab, miniature city were decently housed and clothed. Their back bills were paid up. Inkster, in no time at all, became a shining little oasis, immune from the worst ravages of depression.

Not that Ford was out of pocket. In return for his communal services he hired every adult male in the village and put him to work at the Ford Motor Co. at a cash wage of 12 cents an hour.[46] This money wage of $1 a day was carefully budgeted to meet the food

requirements of every wage-earner's family. An additional $3 per
diem per man, subtracted from the prevailing $4 minimum then in
effect at the Rouge, was retained by the Ford Motor Co. as a check-off
to pay for Inkster's rehabilitation. If about 500 of the villagers were
so employed, Ford was reserving from their wages a daily fund of
$1500. With that revenue, he was paying Inkster's bills.

The plan was discarded in 1933, but the Ford Motor Co. continued to employ some of these same workers thereafter—for $1 a
day, still deducting $3 or three-quarters of the normal daily wage for
the settlement of past obligations. In February of 1934, Congressman
John Leşinski registered a complaint to that effect with the federal
government. Certain $1-a-day men at Ford's, said Lesinski, demanded
an accounting of their past debts and were promptly discharged for
"insubordination." The congressman supported his charges with
affidavits. He had in his possession, he said, a score of similar statements, but only two men had dared to place formal charges.[47]

The Inkster experiment had its merits. The rescue of the dismal
little village was timely and beneficial. It was commercially intelligent.
An eyesore to all who beheld it, the colony had been too close to the
Rouge for comfort. The program of rehabilitation gave rise to reams of
free publicity. It built good will for the Fords in the immense Negro
population of metropolitan Detroit, and it paid for itself, in part at
least, by means of the $3 daily check-off from the wages of the
beneficiaries.

In Dearborn proper, Ford dispensed a certain amount of private
relief with an eye to holding his local taxes at a minimum. With that
object in mind Bennett entered into an arrangement with Mayor
Clyde M. Ford whereby the Ford Motor Co. agreed to feed all the
city's dependents, if the Dearborn Council would remove from the
general election ballot in October 1932, a proposal to levy a special
welfare tax.[48] Consequently the resident Ford employe who was out
of work and on relief was shifted from the city's welfare rolls to a
system of private bounty administered by the Ford corporation. The
company distributed food orders that could be traded in at a special
Ford commissary. Some of the cost of this Ford relief was, again,
passed on to the recipients themselves. When previously indigent Ford
employes were later rehired, their "welfare" debts to the Ford Motor
Co. were deducted from their wages.

In all probability, the manufacturer's off-the-record contributions
to the public welfare during the depression were sizable. His deficits
at the Henry Ford Hospital alone, from 1929 to 1934, must have been

enormous. But on the record, the evidence of any such largesse is slim indeed. During the run-in with Mayor Murphy in 1931, Bennett made the boast that in the course of the preceding year the relief expenditures of the revived Ford Sociology Department had run to $75,000.[49] Such an expenditure was the equivalent of what 15,000 workers, at a $5 wage, could earn in a single day. If Bennett's figure was meant to signify openhandedness, one can only point out that it was three ten-thousandths of the $248,000,000 which the Ford Motor Co. reported in cash and marketable securities on hand at the close of the fiscal year of 1931.[50]

## Eighteen

### FORD HUNGER MARCH

### 1

BEFORE THE PRESS had finished heralding the news that Ford early in 1932 intended to "risk his all" for the general welfare, the Communists of Detroit and the jobless singled out the environs of the Rouge as an appropriate site for a demonstration by the unemployed. That this minority group was organizing marches in behalf of the unemployed was anything but unexpected. Similar demonstrations were taking place in many another large industrial center as a concomitant of depression. Nor was it surprising that one or another protest group could rally a following among the industrial rank-and-file of Michigan. When the Ford Hunger March was projected in March 1932, from 30 to 50 per cent of the wage-earners of the community were out of work, and no private or public relief agency had more than begun to cope with the problem.

The city of Detroit had already accommodated itself to repeated outcroppings of organized protest on the part of the unemployed. With the election of Mayor Frank Murphy, incipient unionists and outright leftists had been accorded the right to demonstrate in the public squares. Delegations of the unemployed had been received at City Hall or at various relief depots as a matter of course. From time to time the city had come to expect demonstrations at the scene of an eviction proceeding. But in the main, these efforts to organize the unemployed or to dramatize the issue of relief by mass action had been singularly peaceful. Only when the police forcibly suppressed a parade or a street corner demonstration—as on Cadillac Square and in Grand Circus Park in 1930, before Mayor Murphy's time—had such agitational activities been marked by disorder or violence.

Yet the plan to march on Dearborn did have a flavor all its own. For in a community filled with any number of great industrial establishments, the militant unemployed settled on the Ford factory alone as their objective. For the duration of the crisis, no other factory owner in the state witnessed any similar demonstration at his gates. In gravitating to Dearborn, the Left was pursuing a line which had been painstakingly laid down by Ford himself. It was Ford's wish to be known as the head of a corporation that was uniquely benevolent and "personal." His company alone was family-owned. Hence it was not unnatural that the leaders of the unemployed should think of submitting his self-declared "non-profit" stewardship to an accounting. Inasmuch as the man and the corporation were so indivisible, such resentment as the working community bore toward the Ford Motor Co. tended to be individualized. The unrest engendered by business retrenchment might remain impersonal and generalized at other automobile plants, but at Ford's these grumblings and anxieties could be directed toward a single person whom both ownership and a generation of assiduous propaganda had invested with sole responsibility for his actions.

Moreover, during the acute stages of Detroit's depression, the Communists and their sympathizers were not alone in electing Ford as an object of special concern. Before the crisis spent itself, subscribers to every school of political thought took issue with one or another facet of Ford policy. By March 1932, the reform administration of Frank Murphy had been publicizing for two years its annoyance at having to support the bulk of Ford's unemployed. At the time that the left wing conceived a march on Dearborn, the foremost financial journals of the country were bemoaning the labored gestation of the Ford V-8—a process, they said, which had brought on a "depression within a depression." Other reputable journals of the trade were likewise taking note of the disparity between Ford's flaunted theory of high wages and the practices which had induced an orgy of wage cutting in his parts shops.

A shapeless resentment against management was germinating, meanwhile, inside the Rouge. Little of this sentiment had been mobilized by outsiders. Much of it was common to all automotive workers, among whom economic distress was the order of the day. Some of these undercurrents of ill will, however, were peculiar to Ford's. No other employer of automobile labor had made bold to proclaim, when 50,000 to 60,000 of his employes were out of a job and close to hunger, that men are "too lazy" to work. Many a Ford man, at the same time, may have resented the loss of his $4-a-day job in order to make room for the residents of Inkster, who were imported to do the same work for $1 a day in cash. A still larger cross-section of the rank-and-file at the Rouge were harboring a grudge against a species of surveillance that seemed to give the Ford premises an air all their own. Other plants had their hard-bitten overseers and their tough personnel men who invoked depression measures that pleased no one, but none other was quite up to the standard set by Harry Bennett. The policing of Dearborn's compulsory gardens had been among the least irritating samples of Bennett's work.

What the Communist group of Detroit espoused late in February 1932, therefore, was neither entirely without reason nor wholly out of joint with a trend. Ford had set himself up as a special symbol by virtue of his pretensions. Even critics from the Right had felt free to call his hand. The plan to demonstrate in Dearborn was distinctive only in its auspices and in the fact that a loosely organized band of workers and unemployed meant to give their feelings tangible expression.

As the demonstrators formed their ranks within the city limits of Detroit, their bearing was hardly that of a belligerent or revolutionary mob. Their numbers were short of formidable. The participants in the procession ran, at the most, to several hundred. Nor was the make-up of the group predominantly "Red." Led by a handful of Communists, the band represented a cross-section of Ford workers, former Ford employes, and, above all, the miscellaneous unemployed.

The announced objective of the demonstration was to march to the Ford plant in order to present to the management a formal petition embracing the demands of the unemployed for jobs or relief. A fairly large section of the working population of the community would have underwritten these requests. In behalf of the Ford worker as such, the hunger marchers demanded jobs, the right to organize, reduction of speed-up, abolition of labor spies, elimination of "graft" in the hiring process, two daily 15-minute rest periods on the Ford line, a six-hour day without reduction in pay, an unemployment bonus of $50 per man, and free medical treatment for Ford men and their families.[1] The ring of the handbills and the banners which had been prepared for the occasion is familiar enough in the language of labor gatherings. One of the conspicuous streamers in the procession bore the slogan, "We Want Jobs;" another, "Come on, workers, Don't be afraid."[2]

There was nothing untoward or menacing in the demeanor of the marchers as they approached the Dearborn city line. As long as the men were trekking through the streets of Detroit, said the Detroit *Free Press,* their deportment was "orderly in the main." As far as anyone was ever able to ascertain, the marchers were totally unarmed. Most of the newspapermen on the scene asserted later that at Baby Creek Park, on the dividing line between Detroit and Dearborn, the leaders of the parade took special pains to warn their followers to refrain from the use of violence in any form.[3] Up to this point the procession was accompanied by an escort of Detroit police. Mayor Murphy had seen fit to grant a permit for demonstrating within the confines of Detroit proper.

The further course of the Ford Hunger March would seem to indicate that Harry Bennett, the man of the hour at the Ford Motor Co., was not disposed to receive any delegation of the unemployed, whatever their intentions. The route of march was barred at the city line, where 30 or 40 Dearborn police had taken up advance positions, armed with tear gas bombs. These officers warned the Ford petitioners that the moment they dared to cross the border into Dearborn, their ranks would be dispersed by force. After a brief consideration of the matter, the leaders of the unemployed insisted on marching to the Rouge in an orderly manner. The plant lay one mile beyond. Without further ado, the marchers continued into forbidden territory. True to their word, the Dearborn police pumped tear gas shells into the columns of the unemployed until their stock of ammunition was exhausted.

What had started out as a pacific demonstration quickly degenerated into a free-for-all. Goaded by the tear gas assault, some hunger marchers returned fire by hurling anything they could lay their hands on—bricks and stones or chunks of frozen mud. Others scattered pell-mell over the fields and roadsides. A few engaged the police in hand-to-hand encounters. Certain of the more intrepid demonstrators refused to retire from the field and call it a day, and the officers of the law who had provoked the riot were equally dogged. Running engagements broke out all along Miller Road, which leads to the principal Rouge gate. Before long the police were joined by firemen from the city of Dearborn. Two fire-engines lay in wait at the first intersection along Miller Road. But before the people who manned this equipment could couple the hoses to a nearby hydrant, they were driven off by a shower of rocks.

Eventually this violent give-and-take began to center around Gate 3, the main entrance to the Rouge. Here, as various spectators could plainly see, the participants in the struggle were inflamed and out of hand. No observer of the scene has ever maintained that the hunger marchers were bent on forcing an entry into the Ford plant. They were, however, tangling with the police in the street and in the fields adjacent to the overhead bridge that leads into the Rouge at Gate 3.

If Harry Bennett had wished to end the encounter at this point, he could have done so. Such a stratagem would have allowed the hunger marchers to retire as best they could. It would at least have shifted the responsibility for any further violence to the marchers.

But Bennett either preferred a more rigorous alternative or he simply lost his head. At any rate he made matters worse by throwing his plant watchmen and his private police into the fray. From a connection made inside the plant, two high-pressure fire-hoses were run on to the overhead bridge opposite Gate 3. From the vantage point of this overpass, icy streams of water were played into the crowd below.[4] The Detroit *News* later published a photograph of Ford's fire-fighting equipment in action.[5]

Then, with a flourish, Bennett dashed through one of the Rouge gates in a closed car and onto the field of battle. Most of the newspapers reported that Sorensen, the plant manager, was seated at his side. The moment Bennett stepped from his car, he was seriously injured. Few, if any, of the hunger marchers may have recognized him. But he was struck in the head by a flying brick and was rushed shortly thereafter to the Henry Ford Hospital.

As Bennett was being taken from the field, a newspaper photographer for the Detroit *News* alleged having overheard one of the policemen remark, "Get your gats out and let them have it."[6] It was at this point, apparently, that the Dearborn officers and Ford's own private police opened fire on the crowd point-blank. Ray Pillsbury, who was taking pictures for the Detroit *Mirror*, gave this subsequent account of the shooting as he had observed it from the overpass at Gate 3: "Then two guns *behind the gate* flashed. *Through its openings*, policemen and guards leveled their guns and pulled the triggers. I would guess that hundreds of shots were fired into the mob. I saw their leaders drop, writhing with their wounds, and the mob dropped back, leaving their casualties on the road . . . every gun *inside the grounds* crackled in a battering volley of shots that brought men rushing from their work in every part of the two-mile-long factory strung up Miller Road. *Outside,* members of the mob were pitching forward every few seconds and lying still. . . . The dead and wounded lay on the pavement. . . ."[7]*

It would appear from a consensus of the newspapermen on the scene that Ford's private guards took an active part in this triumph of arms. Before the ensuing blood bath drew to a close, four were shot dead and a score or more were wounded by gun-fire. All the dead were hunger marchers. All the gun-shot casualties were either demonstrators or bystanders.[8] Nor were any arms, other than those in the possession of the Ford and Dearborn police, found "either at the scene of the riot" or on the person of any hunger march "suspect."[9]

The supporters and friends of labor were quick to lay the guilt for this bloodshed and loss of life at Ford's door. Of such indictments, the most incriminating was an article written for the *Nation* by Maurice Sugar, whom the surviving demonstrators engaged as counsel; and an open letter drafted by Arthur Garfield Hays of the American Civil Liberties Union. The commercial press passed much the same judgment on the outcome of the Hunger March.

Drawing the moral that the encounter at Dearborn was the first major labor disturbance of its kind in two years of unprecedented national depression, the New York *Herald Tribune* attributed the violent nature of the proceedings to "wretched police work" and to "gross blundering" on the part of local authorities. "The reports from Detroit," the paper continued, "show that the trouble began when Dearborn police refused the unemployed entrance to the city of Dearborn and hurled a barrage of tear gas bombs when their orders were disobeyed." "The Dearborn police are to be condemned for using guns against an unarmed crowd, for viciously bad judgment and for the killing of four men," said the *Herald Tribune*. "Such action must arouse resentment among the unemployed everywhere and accentuate class antagonisms so alien to our American life."

Detroit's own newspapers took much the same position. "On one of the coldest days of the winter," said the Detroit *Times*, ". . . men who had been unemployed for months, some for more than a year, undertook a demonstration without, apparently, any thought on the part of the marchers of a collision with the authorities. Before sunset, four men were dead and many were wounded. Someone," the *Times* concluded, "blundered in the handling of the throng of hunger

* My italics.

marchers that sought to present petitions at the Ford plant in River Rouge. . . . The opposition offered by the Dearborn police evidently changed an orderly demonstration into a riot with death and bloodshed as its toll. . . . The killing of innocent workmen, innocent of any crime, is a blow directed at the very heart of American institutions."

Who were these demonstrators? asked the *Free Press*. ". . . for the most part . . . ordinary men and women out of jobs and out of the necessities of life." ". . . Nobody could look at the marchers themselves," said the Detroit *News*, "and accuse them of any destructive purpose. . . . Insofar as the demonstration itself had leaders present in the march, they appear to have warned the participants against a fight. The easiest thing," the *News* concluded, "is to shout 'Communism' and incite class hatred . . . a crusade against Communism will not mend matters."

The critical temper of the commercial and metropolitan press may have been sharpened by the rough treatment accorded some of the newspapermen. Pillsbury, the photographer who had stood on the overpass at Gate 3, managed to save his film only by making a forced escape in an automobile. "When it was all over," he said, "a Dearborn policeman rushed up to me and said I would have to give up my pictures . . . 'No pictures,' he said, 'or there will be trouble.' "[10] "Newspapermen and photographers were ordered from the scene," remarked the *Herald Tribune*, "all negatives of all cameras that could be seized were confiscated. Only a few of the pictures of the battle were saved." The photographer for the New York *Times* had his camera shot out of his hands.[11]

In the aftermath of the Hunger March, neither of the Fords had anything to say. Their disinclination to talk was, apparently, not a question of remoteness from the facts. Three Detroit papers averred that from a high point adjoining Gate 3, Edsel had witnessed the battle of the Rouge in the company of former Gov. Fred M. Green. Henry Ford's whereabouts during the riot is not known. However, according to the press, the elder Ford did show real personal concern over the welfare of at least one of the casualties of March 7th. He is said to have maintained a direct telephone connection to the hospital room in which Harry Bennett was recovering from his scalp wound. As a reward for valor, Ford dispatched a new Lincoln car to Bennett's home in Ypsilanti.[12]

As the Fords maintained a discreet silence, W. J. Cameron rose to the defense. Cameron began by blaming Mayor Murphy for having permitted the hunger marchers to assemble in the first place. He then dusted off the Five-Dollar Day. "We have no statement to make," his defense read. "The statement should come from Detroit where those hoodlums came from. . . . The papers should run some statement about the man who has paid higher wages and kept more men at work than any other man, if they really want statements."[13] This apologist for the Fords went on to say that "no plant police took part in the riot."[14] Cameron's word on this point, however, is contradicted by eye-witness accounts submitted by reporters to every local metropolitan newspaper and to out-of-town papers of the stature of the New York *Herald Tribune* and the *Wall Street Journal*.

The Ford case was finally buttressed by belaboring the threat of a "Red rising." To give substance to this bogy, Henry Ford in person later averred, in error, that none of the marchers had ever worked for the Ford Motor Co. and that none was a member of any recognized trade union.[15]

2

Meanwhile, the sponsors of the Hunger March buried their dead. The organizers of these somber rites again were Leftists. That fact and the mere sight of so vast an outpouring of mourners inspired the real dread in certain quarters of the city that the end of the world was truly at hand. In a cortege that proceeded down Woodward Avenue, from the Detroit Institute of Arts to Grand Circus Park, were 10,000 marchers. The sidewalks along the route of march were lined with spectators four-deep. At Grand Circus Park, where the procession reversed its course and began a five-mile march to the cemetery, the newspapers and the police put the crowd at 30,000. Here various leaders of the unemployed, liberals and radicals, raised their voices. Leftists exhorted marchers and spectators alike to join Unemployed Councils and the Communist party. Other speakers rose to extol the virtue of trade unionism. The auspices of the funeral parade were not at all disguised. Some of the mourners wore red arm bands; others, red berets. The four caskets were clothed in red. At the cemetery, with the smokestacks of the Ford Motor Co. in full view, the dead—Joe York, George Bussell, Coleman Leny and Joe DeBlasio—were lowered to their graves to the strains of the "Internationale."

Yet, as had been the case with the Hunger Marchers, the mourners were too many and too diffuse in make-up to be called "red" through and through. Again, if only for a day, the left wing was augmented by additional thousands: trade unionists, the foreign-born, the unemployed, and the merely curious. As the bodies of the four dead men lay in state in a workers' hall, the biers had been reviewed, said the *Free Press*, by 15,000 people who were "beyond any one single description."

Whatever the composition of the funeral crowd, its behavior remained orderly and impressive. The police of Detroit, under orders from Mayor Murphy, comported themselves with good sense. They took up positions along the seven-mile funeral route, without full equipment, having been instructed to leave their clubs behind. The mayor himself watched the proceedings from a point high above Grand Circus Park, in the presidential suite of the Hotel Statler.

The only strident note of the week that elapsed between March 7th and the date of the Hunger March funeral came from Ford's men-at-arms who busied themselves, in dead earnest, getting set for the expected "Red revolution." Armed guards patrolled the Rouge the clock around. High-powered floodlights played on the main gates of the factory the whole night through. As though a state of siege were about to engulf the community, tear gas reserves and machine-gun emplacements were hurriedly provided for on the private estates of Henry and Edsel Ford.[16] Then, on the day of the funeral itself, the Dearborn police issued a brash warning to the effect that if the cortege so much as crossed the Dearborn city line, it would be driven out, first with clubs, and failing that, with tear gas, vomit gas and revolvers.[17]

If Bennett or the Fords were the least ill at ease because of what the press had to say about the Hunger March, their embarrassment must have been short-lived. For the moral indignation of the newspapers flickered out, and in Harry S. Toy, then prosecutor of Wayne County, Dearborn had a dependable sheet anchor. During the summer of 1932, the county prosecutor's office proceeded to absolve the Fords, officially, by converting a grand jury investigation of the Hunger March into an anti-Red carnival.

Prosecutor Toy began sniffing at "Reds" before the first fact was in. When the Dearborn case was only a day old, Toy scoffed at the possibility that the marchers had even the slightest interest in jobs or relief. In the same breath, he threatened to prosecute the demonstrators who were still alive for "criminal syndicalism."[18] His authority for such action was the state's Criminal Syndicalism Act, enacted by the Michigan legislature in 1931. The statute in question had invested local police with a blanket power to disperse any "unlawful assemblies." Under this law, if congregants were killed resisting any such order from a policeman, the officers of the law could not be held accountable. Conversely, the act prescribed that, under such circumstances, if any police officer was killed or wounded, every assembler, as well as every spectator in the neighborhood, was answerable. The syndicalism statute, however, was none too appropriate for Toy's purpose, for on March 7th the Dearborn police had contributed, at least, none of the dead.

Toy made no effort to conceal his hand in the course of building his case. His deputies began to raid the headquarters of this or that labor or radical group, at random.[19] They placed some sixty men and women, all Hunger March "suspects," under arrest, including one youth charged with membership in a "John Reed Club."[20] Harry Cruden, a former Ford employe, and Robert Dorn—two of the demonstrators who had sustained serious gun-shot injuries—were chained to their beds at Receiving Hospital. With handcuffs attached to their wrists and ankles, both men were riveted to their hospital cots for one week. Then the two prisoners were transferred to the Dearborn police station for finger-printing and further detention.[21]

Meanwhile, the county prosecutor was anything but rigid in the standards of investigation which he imposed on the other party to the controversy. After the bullets had been extracted from the bodies of the dead and injured, ballistics tests were conducted in a most casual manner. Four days after the occurrence of the riot, the Detroit *News* reported that Bennett's private guards had not yet submitted their firearms to the authorities.[22] To explain this curious delay, and a similar failure to impound the riot weapons still in the possession of the Dearborn police, spokesmen for the prosecutor's office were quoted as saying, "We haven't had time to get them, but they will be turned over to us in a day or so." Toy seemed equally anxious to draw a veil over the inquest conducted by the county coroner. The families of the four dead men asked for permission to have a representative of their own choosing at the autopsy. But the prosecutor intervened. He insisted that the post-mortem be closed.[23] The coroner's report contained no information as to who had fired the shots.[24]

The grand jury itself became a sounding board for the prosecutor's pre-formed thesis that the Fords had been victims of a far-reaching "Red conspiracy." In such a legal atmosphere, Bennett and the Fords came off scotfree. The jury returned no indictments. It did find, however, that "no agent, employe or official of the Ford Motor Co. took any part in forcibly quelling the riot." That operation, it concluded, had been "entirely handled by the police and fire authorities of the City of Dearborn." The jury reprimanded the Dearborn police with the assertion that the tear gas charge and other violent acts "though well intentioned, might have been more discreet and better considered." But the basic finding of the law was pitched in Toy's key. The jury found that the majority of the demonstrators had been non-Communists. Even so, it urged the prosecutor and succeeding grand juries to pursue the "agitators" who had conceived the Hunger March so that their "criminal purposes" might be "curtailed and forestalled."

Toy's success in dismissing the Hunger March as a "Red threat" elicited some public censure. Most of the community accepted his procedure as a matter of course, but at least one of the jurors, Mrs. Jerry Houghton Bacon, expressed a vigorous personal dissent. From start to finish, charged Mrs. Bacon, the prosecutor's staff had shown "extreme prejudice" in playing down certain lines of evidence.[25] The Detroit *Times* took occasion to remark editorially that Mrs. Bacon's comment verified "certain ugly rumors" that had "emanated from the grand jury room."[26]

The lines of evidence to which the prosecutor had turned his back were indeed weighty. The attention of the grand jury never came to rest on the question as to why it was that Ford alone, of all people, had attracted the special notice of the unemployed. The court gave the public no concrete report on the tests which should have determined just whose firearms had been responsible for the shootings. Nor had the public prosecutor paused to explore the relationship existing between the Dearborn city administration and Harry Bennett of the Ford Motor Co. An inquiry of the latter sort would have uncovered the fact that the city of Dearborn was then one of the tightest company towns in the United States. The key figures who held office in the city on March 7, 1932, were Clyde M. Ford, the mayor; Carl Brooks, chief of police; and Verne Doonan, chairman of the Dearborn Safety Commission. Clyde Ford is a distant cousin of Henry Ford's. Brooks and Doonan were the former Ford detectives who had helped Bennett some years earlier to dispose of the Sapiro litigation. A candid prosecutor could have pursued the point that Bennett was given to shifting his private guards back and forth, at a moment's notice, from the books of the Ford Motor Co. to the rolls of the Dearborn police department, and vice versa. In fact, a sophisticated grand jury, trying to decide who did what on March 7, 1932, would have found it difficult to draw anything more than the finest legal line between the public authorities of Dearborn and the private police powers of the Ford Motor Co.

To the extent that the Hunger March itself had been, in reality, Communist-inspired and Communist-led, the defense—in which the Fords were ably joined by Prosecutor Toy—that the police of Dearborn acted as they did, only to put down a "bolshevik menace" is not without irony. For at the time the demonstration occurred, the Fords were fulfilling a highly lucrative contract with the Soviet Union. A large delegation of Soviet technicians were stationed at the Rouge, receiving instruction in Ford methods of production. None of them was ever even faintly implicated in the Hunger March or in its inspiration. But their presence at the Rouge added a touch of grim humor to the events of March 7th, for within the Rouge on that particular day, Ford was, among other things, schooling Soviet engineers in exchange for $30,000,000 worth of "red gold" from the U.S.S.R. Yet outside the walls, his guards and their accomplices saw fit at the same time to suppress a labor demonstration by wounding a score of men and killing four others on the pretext that some of these outsiders were being either steered or "paid" by Moscow.

## Nineteen

### BANK WITH HANK

### 1

WHEN THE LEADING bankers and speculators of Detroit began to run for cover for fear of prosecution by the federal government during the depression, there were reasons for thinking that the Fords could stand by with an easy conscience. For by repute this wealthy family was unique in having frowned on the orgy that precipitated the Michigan bank collapse of 1933. Henry Ford was the last person whom the average American would have expected to find doing business in 1929 on Griswold Street, the Wall Street of Detroit. Everyone was aware that Ford had made his money honestly in industry, building and selling automobiles. The layman may then have had only the haziest notion of the size of the Ford fortune. But of its origin, he was certain: Ford had not made his pile by playing the market or by manipulating other people's money as an end in itself.

To be sure, the Ford corporation had long since been rich enough to act as its own banker. Ford's penchant for keeping his till flush with ready cash was common knowledge. Throughout the 20's he carried on his books from 50 to 100 million dollars worth of government securities, in addition to cash reserves ranging from 100 to 250 millions.[1] Time and again, Ford had called attention to these vast liquid resources, in order to dramatize the fact of his freedom from banker control. Accordingly, it was assumed that the Fords had kept their surplus earnings at home, as an anchor to windward and as a means of insuring higher wages and lower prices. As far as the man on the street could judge, the substance of the Ford family was confined to its purely personal belongings and to the concentrated assets of the Ford business.

In 1933 the public had never stopped to think of Ford as one of the great industrial bankers of the age. In that capacity, however, the manufacturer had already crossed many a bridge into the world of money and finance. Like any other automobile producer, he had utilized the credit mechanisms of the trade to the full, working on the borrowed capital of his dealers and profiting by the 30- to 60-day credit extended by his suppliers. The Ford corporation had branched out into other financial channels as well. It did so in 1930 when the House of Commons passed a law levying a 22½ per cent tax payable on the profits which any British corporation might declare on its continental business. The statute would have applied to the Ford subsidiary in the British Isles, the Ford Motor Co., Ltd., of England.* But in order to evade this tax, the Fords went to Luxembourg, the "Delaware" of Europe, where they formed a holding company, known as the Ford Investments Corporation. The Luxembourg corporation in turn took under its wing all the continental interests of Ford of England, thus all these subsidiaries were placed beyond reach of the taxing arm of the British government.[2]

Once before the Fords had reorganized their English holdings. The earlier transaction enabled them to escape a 33⅓ per cent duty

* The parent company of the Ford Motor Co., in Dearborn, has other foreign subsidiaries. These additional affiliated companies did business, as of 1937, in Canada, Germany, Belgium, Denmark, Finland, France, Holland, Italy, Spain, Sweden, Australia and South Africa. The domestic corporation is entirely family owned. But some of the stock in most or all of the foreign companies is held by minority owners. As of 1937, the principal Ford factories abroad were operating in Ireland, England, Germany and France. The Fords maintained at the same time a number of assembly plants and service branches: in Argentina, Canal Zone, Cuba, Mexico, Uruguay, Brazil, Chile, China, Japan, Egypt, Belgium, France, Spain, Italy, Rumania, Denmark, Ireland, Finland, Turkey, Portugal, Sweden, Greece and Germany.

on imported cars. This time, in 1929, their British directorate was revised to make room for three of the richest operators on Lombard Street: Sir John T. Davies, director of the Suez Canal corporation; Lord Illingworth, director of one of England's "Big Five" banks; and Captain Roland Dudley Kitson, director of the Bank of England and of six coal and steel corporations.[3]

In that year Ford also fused his interests with those of certain German financiers. He came to terms with the German chemical cartel, I. G. Farbenindustrie.[4] Forty per cent of the shares of Ford Motor Co. A. C., of Germany, were sold in a closed block to that great German combine.[5] The contracting parties exchanged complimentary directorates. Dr. Carl Bosch, then the leading figure in the dye trust, was elected to Ford's German directorate. Edsel Ford in turn joined the board of I. G. Farben's American subsidiary.

Had any ordinary American of the early 30's been conversant with Ford's history as an industrial financier, he would have conceded that most of Ford's financial policies, as a manufacturer, had been forced upon him by circumstance. Such were the practices invoked by any great corporation; they followed from the nature of the trade and from the international scope of Ford's business. Moreover, it appeared that shrewd industrial finance had even contributed to Ford's primary goal of producing a car for the masses.

Furthermore, the layman who was bewildered or hurt by the bank crash of 1933, and who had no reason for believing that the Fords had ever strayed from the most conservative canons of industrial finance, could have pointed to Henry Ford's oft-spoken word. What American millionaire, other than Ford, had been lambasting the "Wall Street crowd" for a generation? When the country's financial system began to crack in 1930, the manufacturer rose to the occasion for the express purpose of denying that his family had touched so much as the fringes of the market. The first of two such disclaimers followed a report printed by the New York *Journal of Commerce* of May 10, 1930, to the effect that the Fords had just purchased a large block of shares issued by the National City Bank of New York. Several days later a spokesman for the Ford Motor Co. exclaimed, "The Fords are not buying any bank stock anywhere."[6] In the fall of the same year, Henry Ford in person went even further. Interviewed on the eve of a trip abroad, he declaimed, "We've got plenty of business now because we didn't go dabbling in stocks."[7]

But the facts in the case were quite the reverse. For whatever the public was given to understand in 1930, Henry Ford and his son had already succumbed to the Wall Street fever. At the peak of the boom, Edsel, with his father's blessing, became one of the country's leading speculative financiers. Father and son began to "dabble in stocks" waist-deep, by virtue of an intimate association with a financial holding company known as the Guardian Detroit Union Group, Inc. Ironically, it was the impending collapse of the Guardian structure that was to touch off the national bank moratorium of 1933.

When the country was assured that the Fords were "not buying any bank stock anywhere," only the insiders of the financial world, to be sure, could have challenged the statement. The facts came later. They were supplied first, in 1934, by the Senate Committee on Banking and Currency, on which Ford's former partner, Senator Couzens, was to play a central role, and subsequently in 1939 by Ferdinand Pecora's volume, *Wall Street Under Oath*. Pecora was the Senate Committee's brilliant counsel and chief investigator, later raised to the bench of the New York Supreme Court. All the evidence pointed to the Fords having capitulated to the mood of speculation.

The presence of the family on Griswold Street signified an acquiescence in the financial practices which Henry Ford had been excoriating for a generation. The Fords were identified with the Guardian Group from its inception in 1929. Edsel, with more than 50,000 shares of stock in his own name, was a co-founder of the institution. He was joined in this capacity by his brother-in-law, Ernest C. Kanzler, the top man in Ford's Universal Credit Corporation. Clifford R. Longley, of Ford counsel, was president of one of the Guardian's subsidiary units. When the entire Guardian edifice began to topple in 1933, Edsel was holding a seat on three directorates: one in the parent holding company, two others in the Group's most important operating divisions. Kanzler was then chairman of the coordinating board of directors. The investors in this promotional enterprise included none other than Edsel's father. For a time 1188 shares of Guardian stock were listed in the name of Henry Ford.[8] This block was later passed on to Edsel as a gift.

Only a driblet of the total Ford fortune was invested in the Guardian venture, but therein lay a point which contravened what Henry Ford had been repeating for half a lifetime. For with a pittance of their own funds, the Fords and their friends had effected control of half a billion dollars worth of other people's money, and as these immense communal resources were being sucked into the whirlpool of frenzied speculation, neither Henry nor Edsel Ford made a single effective move to check the process.

Actually, from the moment the Guardian Group began floating at high tide in 1929, the Fords tacitly played the game according to Wall Street standards. They embarked with others upon what Justice Pecora calls a "boomtime project conceived in a boomtime mood." Throughout the subsequent history of this great banking chain, Pecora writes, the "spirit of bold speculation was pervasively present."

Such a spirit infected a majority of the officers and directors of the Group. The assets of the institution were made available to most of these insiders, and to their friends, for the frank purpose of playing the market. Before the fever of 1929 slackened, those who belonged to the inner set borrowed millions for their personal use and additional millions in behalf of enterprises in which they were personally interested. When the banks finally closed in 1933, the directors of just one—the largest—of the Guardian's banking affiliates had received direct loans amounting to $4,400,000 and indirect loans approximating $3,300,000.[9]

As for collateral on the loans which they extended to themselves and their friends, the responsible officers of this combine had acted like anything but prudent bankers. Vast credit, inadequately secured, was placed at the disposal of favored judges and politicians.[10] Certain insiders were permitted to borrow at will by pledging shares of ordinary speculative stock. One of the Guardian units loaned out more than $1,000,000 to 122 junior officers and other employes, so that these functionaries in turn could protect their investments as the market began to slump in October 1929. The collateral for this $1,000,000 inside loan was later found to be worth less than $15,000.[11]

Bewitched by a bull market, certain Guardian directors (other than Edsel Ford) commenced to borrow extensively by putting up their Group stock as security. Ernest Kanzler, chairman of the board, secured some of his loans in this manner.[12] In 1934 a federal receiver, poring over the books of the Guardian's largest member bank, reported that about $10,000,000 worth of stockholder loans had been secured wholly or in part by Guardian shares. As far as the creditors of the bank were concerned, such collateral proved to be utterly valueless.[13] If the Guardian had been a national bank instead of a holding company when its affiliates were extending credit in this manner, someone might have gone to jail for violating a federal statute. As it was, says Pecora, the practice in question was "illegal in all but the technical sense."

Moreover, the directors of the Group with which Edsel Ford cast his lot plunged into the stock market in an even more direct and official capacity. Entrusted with the management of $500,000,000 worth of assets, they purchased a brokerage and investment firm. This non-banking affiliate was a purely speculative venture. It was, in the words of Justice Pecora, free to engage in "any kind of dangerous business it pleased."

The affairs of the Guardian were likewise intertwined with the real estate boom which came to a head in the late 20's in "Detroit the Dynamic." Some of the leading land speculators of the city were among the Group's high-ranking officials. Shortly before it had to close its doors, a certain Guardian subsidiary loaned out to Robert Oakman, one of its directors and a prominent real estate promoter, sums aggregating $1,650,000.[14] As a consequence of this investment and a countless number like it, the Group's portfolios were cluttered with millions of dollars worth of slow loans, secured by real estate that had trebled in value artificially during a decade or more of frantic speculation and over-expansion.

When the Guardian Group once started crumbling, beset by depression and softened up by internal excesses, its dissolution was then hastened by the nature of the stock holdings which controlled the institution from the top. These shares were listed on the Detroit Stock Exchange. They had conferred upon their owners dominance over twenty banks and thirteen other financial corporations. Hence, in order to buoy up confidence in the combine's sundry underlying companies, Edsel Ford and his fellow directors were forced to give first attention to the market rating of their bank stock. With that end in view, they put on as bold a front as circumstances would permit.

In certain instances the measures invoked for the sake of appearances only drew the Guardian closer to the abyss of insolvency. Instead of trimming their sails from 1930-1932, the directors of the Group declared $9,000,000 in dividends that were purely artificial. This yield, says Pecora, was "squeezed out of unit banks . . . against every dictate of banking prudence and caution." Again, to strengthen the whole by sacrificing some part, the parent company added to its own assets $2,500,000 worth of government bonds, removing this capital from a constituent bank whose depositors were never advised of the transfer.[15]

The Guardian insiders then formed a $27,000,000 stock pool in 1930 for the purpose of bidding in Group shares in order to tone up the market.[16] Edsel Ford was a member of the buying syndicate. But this operation only postponed the hour of reckoning, and meanwhile, it weakened the sagging edifice still further. For in order to participate in the pool, some of the stockholders had to borrow fresh funds from Guardian sources, and were permitted to secure such loans by putting up defaulted bonds.[17]

Busy at face-saving, the officers of the holding company contrived a bit of camouflage which Senator Couzens later denounced as a "fraud upon the public."[18] On the eve of anticipated visits from bank examiners, Group officials began to shift funds to member banks heavily in debt so that these units could report a favorable, though fictitious, showing to the Comptroller of the Currency. Justice Pecora labels one such transaction as a piece of "accounting magic" and "bare-faced juggling." The New York Justice refers to an occurrence in Flint, Michigan, where the indebtedness of a Guardian unit was written down $600,000, thanks to a temporary credit which was never actually transferred from Detroit. Yet in its annual report, the Flint bank went so far as to list the fictitious entry among its assets.[19]

Even the Ford Motor Co. was a party to this general technique of window-dressing. With the Fords, however, the deposits that brightened up the statement of this or that bank were actually shifted. On the stand in 1934, Edsel admitted that the Ford Motor Co. had farmed out such transitory credit to various Guardian Units. When asked if he regarded this financial procedure as "ethical and fair," the younger Ford replied, "No, I don't suppose it is."[20]*

When neither the stock pool nor the resort to unwarranted dividends and "accounting magic" seemed to stave off impending disaster, the officers of the Guardian continued to issue stockholder reports that glowed with optimism. In Pecora's judgment, these annual statements were drawn so as to "mask or conceal the profound weaknesses that actually existed." Yet, while exuding confidence in the stockholder reports, the Guardian insiders were acutely conscious of catastrophe ahead. In fact, behind the bravest of exteriors, they were anxiously beseeching the federal government for emergency loans.

Such was the merry-go-round of speculation and promotional banking on which the Fords had a seat in 1933, on the eve of Detroit's financial panic. Through stock-ownership, they had joined hands with

---

* Fashions change but slowly in the financial life of Michigan. A century ago, just before the state's bank crash of 1840, it was the custom of certain bankers to keep one another posted on the movements of the bank commissioner and to employ fast teams to rush bullion and coin money from one shaky institution to the next. The banks, in those days, stored their gold and silver in nail kegs. All went well, until a Commissioner Bacon began to drop in by surprise. In Jackson County, this commissioner burrowed into one of the kegs that seemed to be overflowing with bullion, only to discover that the bulk below the surface consisted of nails, spikes and "other hardware."[21]

the Guardian promoters in 1929. The bonds that tied them to the institution grew ever tighter within the ensuing three years. When the most speculative unit within the whole chain—the Guardian's brokerage and investment house—threatened to fall, the Ford family advanced a loan of $6,000,000 in cash and Liberty Bonds.[22] All told, during the first three years of the depression, the Fords put up $16,000,000 in a vain effort to keep the Group afloat.[23]

## 2

The panic broke late in 1932. It was then that the Union Guardian Trust Co., the Group's weakest unit, approached actual bankruptcy. Some of the company's largest depositors began withdrawing so-called smart money. Street runs were imminent. Were this unit to go to the wall, the entire Guardian chain and all its affiliates would, in all probability, come tumbling down.

Alarmed by such a prospect, Kanzler and other Guardian officials rushed to Washington. In the capital they frantically sought out Senator Couzens and various members of the Reconstruction Finance Corporation. The petitioners and the RFC finally agreed that the distressed Guardian division needed $50,000,000 in order to weather the storm. Of this amount, the government offered to stand good for an immediate loan of $37,000,000. This figure, however, was $13,000,000 short of the required sum. The RFC offered to make up the difference, on condition that the bankers of Detroit raise additional collateral.

In its insistence upon stronger collateral, the RFC was supported by the nation's highest executive authority. Its position was confirmed by President Hoover during a conference held at the White House on February 9, 1933. The president's conferees included Secretary of the Treasury Ogden L. Mills, RFC president Charles A. Miller, and the two Senators from Michigan, Vandenberg and Couzens. As for the consensus of this gathering, Vandenberg later reported, "All present agreed that the trust company would have to be supported by voluntary contributions to merit RFC aid. There was no disagreement on that point."[24] But the phrase that stuck in the minds of Detroit's financiers was the thrust attributed to Couzens during the White House talk. Ford's former partner is supposed to have told the President that if the full $50,000,000 credit were to be advanced, without the required collateral, he would "denounce it from the house-tops" as an unauthorized raid on the federal treasury.[25]

Henry Ford entered the picture at this point. It was hoped in

Washington that the Fords would assume some of the responsibility for making good the $13,000,000 deficiency in collateral. Edsel was the Guardian Group's largest stockholder and one of its directors. Kanzler was chairman of the board. Longley, the Ford attorney, was president of the underlying trust company that needed the loan. These ties to the Guardian were so clear, in fact, that certain RFC agents began to ask themselves just why the government should have to "bail out Mr. Ford."[26] Certainly Ford had the means to care for his own. The value of the needed security was only slightly larger than the personal dividends which the Ford family had withdrawn from their automobile business in 1931.[27] And on New Year's Eve in 1932, the Ford corporation could list on its books $174,000,000 in cash and government bonds.

But Ford sat tight. So did his fellow-millionaires. No one in Detroit came forward with what the RFC was asking as security for its loan. Nor was it the sum involved that concerned either Ford or the city's other financiers and industrialists. Half a dozen of these men, between them, could have raised the required amount without the least trouble. Yet, though the state's credit structure was about to crash over their ears, these automobile magnates who had risen from the bench in less than a generation were too close-fisted, too suspicious of one another, to sense a class interest that concerned them all. Rather than act in concert or make any personal sacrifice, each preferred to risk large-scale financial panic. Detroit's men of affairs were of one mind, however, in wanting to take their troubles to Washington. They stood united in the conviction that ultimate responsibility for salvaging the banks they had fathered lay with the federal treasury. It was that united stand which Henry Ford, the outstanding individualist of the lot, expressed when he exclaimed in this hour of crisis, "I think it is up to the government to save these institutions by making them loans—all of them."[28]

Then Ford aimed a blow at his rivals in the banking business—in case the RFC should fail to invoke the principle of government aid to private business, in order to save the holding company with which his interests were involved. The Guardian Group had a powerful local competitor known as the Detroit Bankers Co. This rival combine was unofficially aligned with Chrysler and General Motors. It was taken for granted in February 1933, that without federal intervention every Guardian unit would topple in short order. Under such circumstances, the Fords had every reason to fear that while their own holding company went to the wall, the GM and Chrysler chain might remain standing, at least for the present. Whereupon, Henry Ford, still unwilling even to discuss the government's terms, served notice on his banking competitors that his house would not fall alone. Were the ailing Guardian bank to go under, he announced on the eve of the crash, he intended to demand the immediate withdrawal of $18,000,000 in Ford cash on deposit in the largest bank owned by the Detroit Bankers Co.[29]

By February 1933, street runs were about to close in on the sinking branch of the Guardian combine. Meanwhile the RFC held fast to its original terms, and no voluntary collateral was forthcoming from the city in which one corporation alone, from 1925-1927, is said to have produced some eighty millionaires.[30] In a final effort to break the stalemate, Alfred P. Leyburn, the national bank examiner for the area, called a conference on February 10, 1933, to which he summoned the state's leading industrialists and financiers. Only the Fords absented themselves from this desperate council, sending in their stead Kanzler and Ernest Liebold. The Chrysler and General Motors people, on the other hand, were represented by their principals, Walter P. Chrysler and Alfred P. Sloan, Jr. The general spirit of this anxious assembly was embodied in the words of Leyburn, the bank examiner, who exclaimed at one point in the proceedings, "Gentlemen, we are in a hell of a mess."[31]

For a meeting place, the city's bankers could have selected no site that was a better symbol of their difficulties. These financiers convened in the palatial quarters of the Union Guardian Trust Co., Detroit's "cathedral of finance." Modeled after the style of an Aztec temple, this ornate skyscraper was a gaudy monument to the 20's, a very altar of High Finance. Hollywood could have done no better. The building's fiery mosaics and its stained glass windows offered a garish contrast to the dreary, anti-climactic sessions which brought a decade of boomtime finance to a close. The last scene of the drama was enacted in the skyscraper's pretentious "gingerbread" suite.

Here, shortly after midnight on the morning of February 14, 1933, after three days and nights of fruitless haggling, Governor William A. Comstock signed the proclamation that invoked the Michigan Bank Holiday. But before he issued this executive order, the governor later averred, the bankers tried to "strong-arm" him into depositing state funds in their tottering institutions "without any surety or bond that was worth anything."[32] To protect his own political future, Comstock refused to impose the moratorium until the Michigan Bankers Association requested such action, in writing.

Thus ended an era in which "Detroit the Dynamic" overreached itself. The suspension of any and all banking activity in the state of Michigan had national repercussions. Cleveland and Chicago and other great financial centers were passing through similar crises. Hence the Michigan Holiday precipitated a banking moratorium that was nation-wide, and in March 1933, the Secretary of the Treasury appointed federal conservators to take over the resources of the Guardian National Bank of Commerce and the First National Bank of Detroit. These institutions were the cornerstones of the city's giant banking chains.

The most adventurous of all Detroit's citizens, in the midst of panic, was Henry Ford. Just before the arrival of the federal conservators, the man who had held apart from every effort to save the banks of Michigan by voluntary means stepped forward with one of the most spectacular gestures of his career. When it was a question of keeping the banks open, Ford had kept his cash to himself, but once the house had fallen, he opened his purse.

Out of his own pocket Ford offered to buy outright both of Detroit's foremost banks, the Guardian National Bank of Commerce, of which Edsel was a director, and the first National Bank of Detroit. The purchase price he suggested was $8,500,000. His offer was conditional. It provided that the buyer would assume none of the liabilities of the two institutions. It was to confer upon Ford the sole right, after reorganization, to name the new directors and officers. To dramatize the plan the city administration of Dearborn sponsored a demonstration for which the streets of Dearborn were specially festooned. As though the Fords were about to deliver the state from the temple of the money-changers, a parade of 3000 persons marched down the main street of Dearborn, bearing aloft in the procession a banner reading "BANK WITH HANK."

The Ford coup almost succeeded. The directors of the two banks were desperate. At a joint meeting, they went so far as to accept Ford's offer. They emerged from this conference, however—according to the Detroit *Free Press*—wearing a "sad expression" on their faces.[33] Then their heads cleared. It dawned on these harassed financiers, particularly those at the First National whose ties were close to Chrysler and General Motors, that the Ford bargain was too shrewd. In the meantime, Senator Couzens condemned the plan. So did the banks' depositors. The offer was then reconsidered and officially rejected. In the words of the *Free Press*, the "public of Detroit" were not over-long in grasping the "unfavorable consequences of an arrangement of the sort proposed."[34]

Nothing came of the Ford scheme. But the invitation to "Bank with Hank" had all the earmarks of a financial scoop of the first order, for had the plan borne fruit, it would have crowded from the scene both Wall Street and many of the local elite whom Ford had scorned for years. When the idea was first proposed, the Detroit *Free Press* had exclaimed, "In this manner, Mr. Ford again dealt a deadly blow to his enemy of old, the financial group of Wall Street."[35] The proposal likewise called to mind Ford's bargaining for Muscle Shoals. Both plans entailed a subsidy from the taxpayers. In this case Ford expected the government to match his small investment with an RFC loan of $78,000,000.[36] And here again, as with Muscle Shoals, the anticipated returns were grandiose. Had Ford acquired the city's two largest banks, by expending a mere eight and one-half million dollars, he would have assumed control of $700,000,000 worth of assets.

This ambitious tour de force clothed itself, as a matter of course, in the garb of the Five-Dollar Day. Once more Ford was presented in the role of "rescuing" Detroit, envisioning "banks for the people" and a grand "evolution of the money system." Before the scheme was rejected once and for all, the *Christian Science Monitor* alleged that the Ford Motor Co. was working out a new bank code based on the Ten Commandments. The gesture was all the more palatable to the Ford Motor Co. in that it glossed over the fact that the Fords had been among those present on Griswold Street when the panic was in the making.

Few of the apologies which the Fords and their friends had furbished for self-protection managed to survive the hearings conducted by the Senate Committee on Banking and Currency in January, 1934. The roster of the committee included the formidable names of Couzens and Pecora. It was in deference to the sharp wit of the latter that many a member of the city's financial colony is said to have been stricken at this time with "Angina Pecora." But if Edsel Ford and other witnesses had reason to quail under the cross-examination by Pecora, what struck them as unforgivable was the line of questioning that came from Senator Couzens.

Before this definitive Senate hearing was actually under way, most of the wealthier men of Detroit would have been ready to concede that their senior senator was suspect. Couzens had already been labeled the "millionaire radical" of the United States Senate. He had opposed Ford's conquest of Muscle Shoals. He had gone on record in favor of higher taxes on the rich. His fellow-townsmen could recall that bizarre gathering of the Michigan Manufacturers Association in December 1929, at which time Couzens had spoken up in defense of labor unions and of an adequate federal program for the aged and unemployed. The bankers of the city knew in a general way, ahead of time, where they stood with Couzens. But to their way of thinking, when the Senate Committee began to dig into the financial history of Detroit, Couzens might have had the grace to tread softly. After all, the man had made his fortune in the city; he owed his former business allies and acquaintances some degree of loyalty. These former associates were now exposed to the double danger of public investigation and possible prosecution.

But if mercy was expected from this quarter, none was forthcoming. Throughout the ensuing inquiry, Couzens was unsparing in his zeal to get the facts, and he treated his witnesses roughly. His running comment and the temper of his questions was trenchant and stabbing. Such behavior on Couzens' part might have been foreseen. The man had never been long on tact. He had always liked a fight, and in this case he was dealing with hostile witnesses, with not a few men who were desperately afraid of landing behind prison bars. Only the sharpest instruments sufficed to force the evidence to the surface. In addition, the testy, brutal, normal Couzens' manner was aggravated at the time by poor health. The Senator was slowly dying of uremic poisoning. His deportment was also conditioned by his principles. Couzens was a confirmed advocate of financial reform. Nothing could have assured him of the rightness of his convictions any better than the loose financial practices that had contributed so heavily to Detroit's banking disaster.

As a consequence, the rich of Michigan, almost to a man, began denouncing Couzens as an outcast. With unconcealed hatred, the wealthy families of the community dubbed him the "scab millionaire" and "Jim, the traitor." One of the city's principal bankers expressed the mind of most of his colleagues when he remarked in a letter which he wrote at the time, "Frankly, I shudder when I consider our senior senator."[37] So thoroughgoing was this ostracism that when Couzens seated himself at a luncheon table in the exclusive Detroit Club two and one-half years later, the club members who were near at hand picked up their plates and removed themselves from the Senator's company.[38]

It became the fashion among Detroit's financiers to hold that it was Couzens all along who had "blocked" the Guardian loan from the RFC and who had, therefore, forced the largest banks of the state into receivership. Henry Ford was the hitching post for this rationalization. According to the new line, Couzens could have pushed through the RFC credit, despite inadequate collateral, but had objected only because of personal spite against Henry Ford. The Senator foisted financial calamity upon his constituents, the argument ran, simply to aggravate a banking crisis which had entrapped the Fords.

Such a post-mortem account of Detroit's financial ills doubtless served to discredit Couzens politically. It was unquestionably pleasing to those who needed a whipping boy. But the facts were something else. Senator Vandenberg had already told a grand jury that, under the federal statues of February 1933, it would have been illegal for anyone to have approved the unsecured RFC loan to Detroit.[39] Moreover, during the same hearings, Vandenberg came to his colleague's defense by saying that, before the onset of the bank holiday, Couzens had been "more outspoken than anyone else" in urging proper RFC aid for his community.

In making a scapegoat of Couzens, Detroit's bankers likewise failed to publicize the fact that, apart from the legal code which bound the RFC, it was their own weak leadership that had muddled the appeal to Washington. The city's banks, in February 1933 and earlier, had been a madhouse of conflicting interests. Rival cliques had countermanded one another's requests; government officials were tearing their hair, trying to decide just who had authority in Detroit's financial picture. Part of this chaos was an outgrowth of the mergers by which the two vast bank chains had been pyramided. The Guardian Group alone had a board of directors that resembled a small parliament. Its membership, at sixes and sevens, numbered 110.

Those who were now questioning Couzens' civic loyalty finally chose to forget who it was that came forward when the RFC had asked for additional security for the loan that might have "saved" Detroit. Couzens was the solitary volunteer. Yet the Senator had taken no part whatever in the city's boomtime operations. His millions were salted away in government bonds. Nonetheless, when the banks began to cry for federal aid in February 1933, Couzens promptly agreed to subscribe 50 per cent of the wanting collateral. He offered to co-sponsor a note for the full amount of the required security, on condition that Ford act as fellow-endorser. But Ford, whose money was involved in the pending crash and who had helped to produce it, refused to co-sign. Longley, one of his attorneys, later reported that the Couzens' proposal had "annoyed Mr. Ford."[40]

A still greater punishment lay in store for the rich heretic of the Senate, for the "traitor" whose skin was too thick to be pierced by social rebuffs or personal recrimination. That final retribution was political. Couzens stood for re-election in the fall of 1936. His enemies saw to it that he was defeated in the primaries. Couzens, a life-long Republican, had not enhanced his status in G.O.P. circles by reaching across party lines to endorse the re-election of Franklin Roosevelt. Two months after this defeat at the polls, Couzens died. As his body lay in state at the Detroit City Hall, the *Free Press* in an obituary editorial probably spoke the mind of the city's financial and industrial interests. The paper remarked the death of the state's distinguished liberal Senator by saying that Couzens "meant to be honest," although he suffered from a "highly combative nature" and was the "victim of ardent hatreds and a vengeful spirit."[41]

Henry Ford made no public comment whatever on the passing of his former partner who had led a brilliant attack on Detroit's madness in using money to make money. That silence on the part of a great productive capitalist who supposedly had nothing but contempt for the money capitalist may be explained by the fact that when Couzens undertook to probe the story of the city's financial orgy, the Ford family had been found trafficking in Griswold Street.

Under prosecution by the Department of Justice, the bankers of Detroit came off lightly. If the Guardian Group and the Detroit Bankers Co. had been national banks instead of holding companies, however, it might have been a different story. As it was, the government's case dragged on for four years. Thirty-four of the state's prominent financiers were indicted, but only one major officer was convicted. The latter was fined $5000. This man, a former vice-president of the Union Guardian Trust Co., was convicted of the charge that he had been responsible for making false entries in the books of the Guardian affiliate in Flint.[42]

During the preliminary stages of the prosecution, attorneys for the government unearthed a most interesting detail. All the resident federal judges of the city declined to participate in the case. Several weeks later Pecora, who was working up the facts independently for the Senate Committee, disclosed that from one of Detroit's largest banks personal loans totaling $600,000 were still outstanding against the accounts of more than forty judges on the Detroit and Wayne County bench, and on the Michigan Supreme Court.

# PART FOUR
# Looking Backward

It was an evil day when the village flour mill disappeared.—
*Henry Ford*

# Twenty

## GRANDFATHER'S CLOCK

### 1

FORD'S LIFE had a lighter vein. It was not consumed by the responsibilities of operating a great business. After laboring almost incessantly for three-score years, the manufacturer discovered old-fashioned dancing. He began to cultivate the dance forms which had been popular on the American frontier, and he took his avocation seriously. Dozens of shaggy, antiquated fiddlers were imported to Dearborn. Of such guests, the best-known was Mellie Dunham, a 70-year-old champion backwoods fiddler from the state of Maine. With appropriate fanfare, Dunham and his wife were transported to Dearborn in a private railroad car. Then Ford's agents began to scour the country in search of old steps and bygone dance tunes. They returned with a massive literature: such items as *Money Musk, Old Zip Coon, Arkansas Traveler, Speed the Plow, Two Dollars in My Pocket,* and *Paddy on the Turnpike.*

Ford himself soon became a master of the art. He engaged Benjamin B. Lovett, of Worcester, Massachusetts, to act as his full-time dance instructor, and like Old King Cole, he employed his own musicians—an orchestra consisting of dulcimer, cymbalo, violin and sousaphone. These private performers were provided with practice quarters in the Dearborn Engineering Laboratory, subject to instant call whenever their patron felt disposed to skip through the measures of some old-style dance step.

Ford hit on the dance as a favorite mode of recreation almost by accident. But his cultivation of the art soon became studied. The hobby was also simple and folksy. It symbolized a picture which the publicity department of the Ford Motor Co. had been crystallizing in the public mind for a good two decades, and it fitted Ford's private tastes to perfection. Ford's personal fondness for the medium was evident in 1926 when he published a dance manual entitled *Good Morning: After a Lapse of 25 Years, Old-Fashioned Dancing Is Being Revived by Mr. and Mrs. Henry Ford.* This publication was more than a valuable collection of the early dance forms. It was an effort to defend the hobby on moral grounds, to relate it to Ford's agrarian bent, and to make a cult of the diversion as well.

The tone of the manual was moralistic. The book condemned modern ballroom dancing as a promiscuous bodily relationship which occurs "mostly above the feet." "A gentleman should be able to guide his partner through a dance without embracing her as if he were her lover," the manual exclaimed. "His right hand should be placed at his partner's waist, thumb and forefinger alone touching her—that is, the hand being in the position of holding a pencil."

In its original edition, since revised, Ford's treatise on the dance included a brief note on the subject of race. With a self-conscious "Aryanism," the earlier text identified the "more athletic and less confidential" steps at Dearborn with those dance forms that had survived longest "among the Northern peoples." This passage was written sometime before the Dearborn *Independent* lifted the siege against "Jewish jazz." The unrevised text rested its claim to Nordic superiority on the thesis that dances partake of the "racial characteristics of the people who dance them."[1]

Before long this interest in the dance began to transform Ford's social life. The man started loosening up in the company of people whom he had hitherto avoided. For the first time in his career, his wife and he began to entertain and to court acquaintances among the city's socially elite. The pair widened their social circle by acting as hosts at private dancing parties. The first of these affairs were informal and spontaneous. Then, little by little, the Ford parties lost the folksy touch. They became, instead, solemn state occasions. A ritual came into being. Eventually the attendant ceremonies began promptly at 9 P.M. At that hour, Ford and his wife, Clara, stood at the head of a receiving line to exchange salutations with their guests. All the dancers were expected to arrive attired in evening clothes. By 1933, according to *Fortune*, the rites had acquired an all but regal air. Any executive of the Ford Motor Co. whose presence was desired on the dance floor, the magazine asserted, had come to consider his invitation a command.[2] Moreover, dancing in attendance, Ford's business associates were studiously punctual. They appeared in their employer's ballroom at the stroke of nine. Their observance of this point of etiquette became so forced and anxious, it seemed to belie the law laid down in the Ford manual to the effect that the older modes of dancing have a "tendency to allay nervous trouble."

Once the Dearborn parties were no longer so gay and simple, they acquired a physical setting that was still further removed from their beginnings. The sumptuous ballroom which Ford built to accommodate his guests was neither rude nor primitive, nor at all redolent of the American pioneer. The splendor of these quarters had little in common with the log cabin or the country barn which gave birth to the early American dance. The tone of the vast hall in which Ford elected to play host was set by a luxurious teakwood floor. This magnificent, glistening woodwork, laid down in an intricate, flawless, herring-bone design, covered a reputed surface of eight acres. Even the history of the material that went into the making of the floor fails to suggest the era when America was raw. The logs which provided the lumber for the flooring had been felled in Burma, and hauled at great cost to jungle rivers by elephants and East Indian natives.[3]

But the circumstance which next divested Ford's dancing parties of any lingering association with the rustic was the altered character of his guest list. Sometime before the depression the manufacturer began to act as host to the smart set of metropolitan Detroit. From then on, those to whom he issued cards of invitation were limited, in the main, to gentlemen born and bred, to the survivors and descendants of the city's older wealthy families. Such an alignment on Ford's part was indeed a sign of change. For these were the people who had once spurned the producer of the Model T as an erratic, ill-bred upstart. They were drawn from the world of polite society which Ford, in turn, had once held in contempt as the idle, namby-pamby aristocracy of the community.

The final reconciliation was effected one season when Mrs. Truman H. Newberry, the widow of the Senator whom Ford had hounded from office, saw fit to let bygones be bygones and attend one of the formal balls at Dearborn. The two houses then patched up their differences for once and all, when, to the consternation of the city's social colony, Ford in person and the formidable, slow-thawing Mrs. Newberry, over a gleaming teakwood surface, enjoyed the cadence of a square dance as one another's partner.

But the rhythmic arts were neither the only pattern of recreation nor the sole form of early Americana that arrested Ford's attention. The first diversion was paralleled by a second. When the manufacturer began exploring the dance, he took to collecting antiques. The birth of the latter interest was a thing of chance. In or about 1920 Ford decided to restore his boyhood home. His dealers heard of the project, and then began combing the countryside and rummaging through their attics, with the result that Ford was swamped by a mass of old relics and period furniture he could never hope to use. Knick-knacks and curios had been accumulating in Dearborn long before this. They arrived either as gifts from Ford's many admirers or as unsolicited shipments for which the senders had hoped to collect a price. The antiques and bric-a-brac that streamed in from every source so exceeded the demands of Ford's immediate project that the over-flow was stored in an empty factory building on the Dearborn estate. Because of its bulk, and after some chance discussion of the matter, Ford plunged into the pursuit that was to distinguish him as one of the leading antiquarians of his age.

For the next twenty years the manufacturer's second preoccupa-tion with the old continued to absorb a little of his money and a great deal of his time. The avocation resulted in the monument to early Americana known as Greenfield Village. This project was named after the little community in Michigan in which Mrs. Ford spent her child-hood. As it stands today, in near-completed form, Ford's immense antiquarian enterprise has three principal facets: the Edison Museum, which houses a formidable collection of antiques; the Edison Institute, a complete private school system; and Greenfield Village, which sur-rounds the other creations, and which purports to be in itself a detailed reproduction of a rural American community of the 19th century.

The favorite of those who have made the grand tour at Dearborn is Ford's vest-pocket village. The miniature community is running over with nearly every outward souvenir of the years of Henry Ford's youth. Plain gravel roads wind through the village. Gas street lamps stand at every corner. The only mode of transportation is provided by several horse-drawn hacks. An imitation New England chapel graces the far end of an immaculately tended village common. An original Cape Cod windmill stands on the premises—said to be the oldest relic of its kind in existence. Ford doted on its mechanism. He had the shaft remounted on ball bearings. Moored at the dock in an artificial lagoon lies an old stern-wheeler, long since retired from service on the Suwanee. The proudest specimens of the village are an ancient apothecary shop and an original old-time country store. Both are internally complete, with all the fixings. In quaint little shops, scattered here and there, hoary handicraft workers ply their trades full time. These artisans include a glass blower, a village blacksmith, a cobbler making shoes by hand and a wizened photographer at work in a tintype studio.

Nothing dates the village more fittingly than the outmoded crafts pursued by Ford's little band of imported artisans. The shops which house this activity lie within walking distance of Ford's greatest monument, the colossal Rouge, whose 80,000 or 100,000 workers are so conditioned to the modern mold and so dependent on the centralized and routinized industrial pattern of modern times that most of them would starve if they were forced to strike out on their own, to earn a living after the fashion of the hand-workers of Greenfield Village.

It is the Edison Museum in which one comes to the heart of Ford's endeavors as an antiquarian. Here lie the results of a 20-year quest for memorials of the past. This bursting cargo of antiques is encased within a hull which might well have overwhelmed the pioneers whose simpler values it aims to preserve. From without, the pretentious building is cast in the Colonial Georgian style. It is a telescoped reproduction of three early American landmarks: Independence Hall, Congress Hall, and the old City Hall of Philadelphia. Whatever may be said for the mementos inside, this astonishing three-in-one recreation is unmistakably a child of the 20th century. In fidelity to detail and in the scale of its imitation, the structure is as lavish and "colossal" as a pompous stage set in Hollywood.

In content the Edison Museum purports to reconstruct the history of American agriculture, transportation and manufacturing. That end is achieved by many souvenirs of merit. Among such items, Ford's assortment of primitive automobile models is choice. These pieces are matched by countless others of equal worth and fitness.

But while restoring a record of things mechanical, Ford has done much more. He has assembled, at the same time, a wealth of curios that defy classification by any criterion other than the one which he enunciated in his autobiography. In that work, written when his collectors were only beginning to turn the country upside down in search of the old, Ford said, "We want to have something of every-thing . . ."[4] As a result, the numerically overpowering collection is diffuse and scattered. The expansive floors and corridors are choked with an array of whatnots. Airplanes and steam engines compete for attention with dolls, churns, hearses, china, washtubs, muskets, bed-steads, zithers and music boxes, baby jumpers, sleigh bells, hoop-skirts and covered wagons.

It is this striving for sheer mass and for "something of everything" that sets off the Ford collection from such an institution as the great Deutsches Museum of Munich. The Deutsches Museum, a superb pre-Nazi enterprise built by the state of Bavaria in cooperation with German scientists and industrialists, tells a story. It provides a cohesive and magnificent history of science and technology. By contrast, the Edison Museum is a hodge-podge, despite its core of excellent restorations. It has the appearance of an Old Curiosity Shop, magnified 10,000-fold. Its disunity is as remarkable as the musical fare with which a group of children once entertained Ford in the Greenfield Village chapel, during a formal celebration of the manufacturer's 46th wedding anniversary. The musical program on that occasion called for the rendition of *Ave Maria, The Lord Is My Shepherd, The Last Round-Up, What A Friend We Have in Jesus* and *Happy Days Are Here Again.*[5]

Without benefit of a coherent plan of accumulation, Ford's immense potpourri of remnants includes a forest of scraps. It houses a mass of radio cabinets of so recent a vintage that the entire series could have been duplicated by any large (pre-war) distributor of second-hand furniture. In the same strange category falls another acquisition which is conspicuously on display (or was in 1939)—sixteen outmoded Eureka vacuum cleaners. One of the oddest exhibits in the village was acquired for sentimental reasons. Ford sent a crew of workmen to Menlo Park to dig up the yard surrounding Edison's old laboratory. The excavators returned with twenty-six barrels of refuse.[6]

The collection as a whole is presumably dedicated to the vestiges of our forefathers, yet among its multitudinous odds and ends is the paraphernalia of the professional magician, the late Howard Thurston. It was through no lack of zeal on the part of a Ford buyer that the Edison Museum was not enriched by a still stranger specimen. One summer not long ago, a collector from Dearborn made a desperate but unsuccessful effort to garner a Nantucket privy, dated 1750, and equipped with a robust stone base, topped off with an ironwood seat.

Nor have Ford's collectors even confined their interest to the symbols of Americana. Their additions include the replica of a jewelry store that was once a famous London landmark, a complete 16th century Cotswold cottage and surrounding wall—imported from England stone-by-stone—and a copy of a state chariot used by King Tutankhamen in the year 1360 B.C. Twenty-seven years ago the press reported that Ford was in the market for a flute that had once been the property of the German emperor Frederick the Great.[7] For this relic the proprietor of the Edison Museum is said to have been willing to pay $62,500.

The loose and miscellaneous quality of Ford's vast collection is reflected by its physical arrangement. The array of left-overs is utterly formless. The curators have made no apparent effort to arrange their

pieces functionally, according to the time and place of origin, or
according to any other canon. Life-sized railroad cars adjoin a prolific
display of dolls and trundle beds and a random series of cigar store
Indians. Various items recur with endless repetition. The floors are
stuffed with an acre of clocks. Tucked end to end, antique dressers
stretch as far as the eye can reach. Really choice specimens are
frequently smothered by a multitude of pieces that are second-rate.
One of Ford's striking acquisitions is a stunning 19th century steam
engine. This superb apparatus is beautifully mounted in a sunken
casement. Its huge power-wheel is surmounted by an overhead con-
trivance that resembles the top of an old four-poster bed. This remarkable machine needs floor space all its own. Instead, it is almost lost to
view, cramped and suffocated by a thick stand of baby buggies and
antique chandeliers.

2

That the Edison Museum lacks coherence or direction is scarcely
surprising in view of the qualifications of some of the men who have
been entrusted with its management. By and large the custodians of
the collection have been amateurs, fish out of water. For years the
over-all manager of the Ford farms, which take in Greenfield Village,
was Ray Dahlinger, the Ford bodyguard who went to Europe on
the Peace Ship. Among those who have been more directly in touch
with the problem of amassing and evaluating the collection are Ernest
Liebold, Ford's former secretary; Frank Campsall, who succeeded
Liebold; William A. Simonds, a former Seattle newspaperman; and
Charles T. Newton, once a real estate scout for the Ford Motor Co.
Self-taught at their side line, these buyers and critics of the old have
been anything but disappointing in their powers of mass production.
With a fat purse at their disposal and with some two hundred acres
to fill up, they seem to have striven for quantity, first and foremost,
as well as bargains.

The keepers of the collection have fallen into error on a number
of occasions. At Ford's second colonial shrine, at Sudbury, Massachusetts, they preserved a memorial of doubtful authenticity. Here,
they raised a plaque and restored a schoolhouse to memorialize the
famous verse "Mary Had A Little Lamb." The rehabilitated school
is alleged to be the landmark about which the "original Mary" and
her lamb once gamboled. In this case the Ford collectors identified
their find by accepting the spoken word of an elderly woman named

Mrs. Mary Sawyer Tyler. Fifty years after the nursery rhyme was first published, in 1830, this same Mrs. Tyler announced that she had been its inspiration and that its author had scribbled the verse for her benefit on a scrap of paper. "Ford's Mary" never produced the slip of paper or anything else to substantiate her claim.

This woman's recollection is challenged by the strongest evidence. The real author of the noted rhyme is the well-known American writer and editor Sarah Hale, who published "Mary and Her Lamb" in a book of children's verse that appeared half a century before "Sudbury Mary" ever identified herself. Moreover, Mrs. Hale, a writer of recognized integrity, told her children who were living when she composed the poem, that its characters were purely fictitious.[8]

When Ford settled with finality on his own version of the poem and his findings were at last inscribed in permanent form at Sudbury —without benefit of professional advice—Mrs. Hale's granddaughter submitted the following parody to the New York *Times*:

> "Sweet Mary long has passed away,
> The poet, too, is dead.
> The children no more laugh and play,
> Afar they all have fled.
> At teacher's cold, unfeeling words
> The lamb no more can quivver,
> But still the gentle creature serves
> To advertise a flivver."[9]

The classic controversy of the Ford collection, however, lies within Greenfield Village. It concerns the White Cottage, which is designated as the birthplace of Stephen C. Foster, the composer of American folk tunes. This dwelling—the one in Ford's possession— was discovered in Pittsburgh and carted off to Dearborn by Charles T. Newton, the former Ford real estate scout. It stands to this day at the crest of a rise overlooking the Suwanee stern-wheeler and the artificial lagoon in Greenfield Village.

When buyer Newton first identified the White Cottage in the Lawrenceville section of Pittsburgh, he took a neighborhood legend at its face value. To validate his "find," he collected affidavits from persons whose parents or grandparents did not move into the Lawrenceville district until forty years or more after the Foster family had migrated to other parts. These newcomers picked a cottage in which Foster was thought to have been born, a century earlier, in 1826. Their hearsay was corroborated by a statement from Stephen

Foster's only daughter. But when this woman was consulted by Ford's representative, she was eighty-four and at the point of death. She died five days after the White Cottage was dedicated at Greenfield Village. Without any further investigation, the house was bought and ticketed for removal to Dearborn.

Meanwhile, fresh evidence turned up. Other Foster relatives had reason to feel that Ford had the wrong place. They politely tried to intervene. Their efforts were coolly received by Ford's negotiators. The purchase had already been publicized. Frantic lest the authenticity of his piece be opened to serious question, the agent who supervised the transaction for Ford reminded his principal critic that "Ford was right" or he never would have become so deeply involved, that "Mr. Ford has never lost a lawsuit," that the custodians of the Edison Museum might lose their jobs if it could be shown they were in error. Moreover, said this agent, the mistake—if one had been made—was immaterial "so long as Mr. Ford is satisfied." Did his critic know that a nail extracted from the assumed Foster house had been dated by a "wonderful precision instrument" at the Ford Motor Co. as a product of the year 1812?

Ford backed up his subordinates. He came to Pittsburgh to superintend the dismantling operations. On the scene, he dismissed the least possibility of error. "Oh, the contract is already signed and sealed," he said. "We had the same trouble with the Lincoln court house, but we went right through with it." Still in Pittsburgh, hovering over his purchase, the manufacturer "found an old silver flute that had belonged to Foster in a niche in one of the walls." "Knowing that the flute was Foster's favorite childhood instrument," said the Pittsburgh *Press*, "Mr. Ford was as pleased with this discovery as Foster doubtless was when the flute was first brought to him." The latter touch was too much for one member of the Foster clan. This skeptic remarked, "The newspaper account does not tell us whether an 'affidavit' from the infant Stephen was attached to this valuable relic when Mr. Ford found it, or not. Perhaps that turned up the next week at the 'Dedication.'"[10] (The Fosters, incidentally, moved out of the neighborhood in which Ford unearthed his musical memento when the infant Stephen was in his second year of life. Foster was a precocious child. It seems unlikely, however, that he took to the flute at one or two years of age.)

One year after the White Cottage had been added to the collection at Greenfield Village, the question of its genuineness was settled once and for all by Evelyn Foster Morneweck, one of Stephen Foster's

nieces. Mrs. Morneweck published a privately printed, definitive
brochure, *The Birthplace of Stephen C. Foster As Recorded by His
Father, Mother and Brother, and Other Contemporary Authorities.*
This meticulous work availed itself of every existing, verifiable record
on the subject. In the course of her labors, the author examined city
directories, old newspaper files and maps dating back to 1816. She
was able to produce an 1828 painting of the "true" White Cottage, as
well as contemporary family manuscripts that antedate Ford's investigation by more than a century.

The upshot of the Morneweck digging seemed to prove that Ford
did indeed buy the wrong house. No Foster was ever born in the house
in Greenfield Village. No Foster ever lived in it. What buyer Newton
picked up by mistake, it seems, was the former abode of a carpenter
who built his place two years or so after Stephen Foster was born in
1826, on an entirely different site. On the true site of Foster's birthplace, the city of Pittsburgh maintains a Foster shrine. The authenticity
of this location was never questioned—until Ford's purchasers decided
to unmake history to suit themselves. The building which houses the
Pittsburgh memorial was once the residence of a former partner of
Andrew Carnegie, who tore down the original Foster homestead in
1865 and rebuilt on the same location.

All the experts agree with Mrs. Morneweck. They include the
staff of the Western Pennsylvania Survey.[11] Another of her corrobora-
tors is John Tasker Howard, Foster's biographer.[12] Howard rose to
Mrs. Morneweck's support by telling the story of Ford's purchase in
an article entitled "History Bunked."

Sometime before the counterfeit White Cottage was officially
dedicated at Greenfield Village, its doubtful authenticity was called
to the attention of W. J. Cameron and Clifford B. Longley, the Ford
attorney, but the installation ceremonies proceeded according to
schedule. The booklet printed for the occasion states that the preser-
vation of Foster's birthplace is but "an act of piety." It a radio speech
of dedication, Cameron remarked, "It seems to be at home on its
green slope overlooking the woods and water—and already it begins
to speak to its visitors of that honest time when America was in the
making."

To one of the shrine's visitors in the fall of 1935, Cameron
expressed a different opinion. He admitted privately to John Tasker
Howard who had come to Dearborn to lecture on the life of Foster
that no new evidence had been found to validate the supposed Foster
cottage that was still standing in Ford's village.[13] Ford's own confi-

dence in the restoration remained unshaken, however. He countered Howard's questions in 1935 by asserting, "No doubt about it. We've got the right place. I have experts." For the duration of Howard's stay in Dearborn, the expert in this particular case, Charles T. Newton, remained discreetly out of sight.

The Newton version of the White Cottage still lives in official Ford publicity. Just before John Charles Thomas sang "Old Black Joe" during a Ford Sunday Evening Hour in 1939, the program announcer alluded to the Foster cottage which Ford was preserving nearby. A year later the guides at Greenfield Village were still assuring the curious tourist that in the White Cottage by the lagoon "Mr. Ford has the right place all right." The 1941 edition of the Greenfield Village guide book refers, as ever, to the "Stephen Foster House." With sufficient repetition, perhaps, the claim that "Ford has the right place" may become, in this instance, quite as immortal as Foster's lovely melodies. Should this come to pass, the manufacturer will have succeeded—as John Tasker Howard puts it—in proving that "history is bunk" right in his own backyard.[14]

The third institution at Greenfield Village, complementing the museum and the re-created village, is the Edison Institute. This division is a private, self-contained co-educational school system, with a course of studies extending from grade school all the way up. The beginners' classes are conducted in an air-conditioned restoration of the one-room log cabin once occupied in the wilds of Pennsylvania by William Holmes McGuffey—the author of the readers that were the standard textbooks of America's common schools for more than half a century.

In what it teaches, the Institute was conceived in the image of its founder. The institution is essentially a school of engineering and domestic science. It offers the best of tuition in the technical sciences, with an emphasis on matters practical. Its male students, in their college years, spend four hours a day inside the Rouge. High school youths are put at factory work for an hour or two daily. There are misfits for whom the Ford course of studies makes no provision—boys who are not mechanically inclined and girls who would be more in their element at a finishing school. Working on the premise of yester-year that a woman's place is in the home, the Institute weights the curriculum for its women students in the direction of the domestic arts. Many of these young women, dissatisfied with the pabulum afforded by supervised housekeeping and kitchen science, drop out after completing the equivalent of a high school education.

Ballroom dancing is emphasized in the curriculum. As a concession to youth and the times, the old-fashioned forms of the dance are
supplemented by contemporary styles. Out of deference to the older
modes, however, the school's first entering class of thirty-two students
was hand-picked, with an eye to the age and sex requirements of a
"quadrille set."[15]

Ford's idiosyncrasies colored this educational experiment at still
other points. No effort was made to arrive at any exact division of
studies on the part of the teaching staff. Each member of the faculty
oversees a rather broad and general group of studies. The enterprise
is, likewise, thoroughly paternalistic. Members of the staff never
assemble democratically to discuss their teaching aims or methods.
Whatever the merits of their joint effort, they have no part in formu-
lating its objectives. One more carry-over from the Ford factory is
the mere physical construction of the class rooms. The walls inside are
of transparent glass. Thus new recruits to the faculty have been
momentarily embarrassed by standing, accidentally, face-to-face with
an instructor in an adjoining class room.

Advertising, for the Ford Motor Co., soon took its place among
the school's extra-curricular reasons for being. The student body began
to participate in a weekly broadcast from the chapel on the village
green. On special occasions, these radio programs were garnished by
the presence of personages like the late Will Rogers, ex-President
Hoover, and famous baseball stars or motion picture comedians.

But despite such modern touches, Ford liked to think that his
miniature school system was promoting the "art of rugged individualism."[16] In tune with that belief, he subsidized a private printing of
selections from the old McGuffey Readers. Five thousand copies of
this reprint, *Old Favorites from the McGuffey Readers* (1926), he
donated to the larger libraries of the country. The collection's classics
—*Try, Try Again, The Spider and the Fly* and *The Hare and the
Tortoise*—are presumably what the Institute has taken for a model in
nurturing the pioneer virtues of thrift, contentment, honesty, charity
and self-denial.*

In reality the Ford educational plant bears only the scantiest

---

* The introduction for the Ford-McGuffey collection was written by Hugh S.
Fullerton, a former sports editor on the New York *Evening Mail.* In the preface,
Fullerton avers that composing something appropriate for a McGuffey text requires
as much courage as writing an "introduction to the Bible." Fifteen years earlier,
the Dearborn *Independent* had alluded to some of Fullerton's newspaper stories
in an effort to prove that American baseball was being corrupted by "Reds,"
"aliens," and "too much Jew."[17]

resemblance to the little red schoolhouse of McGuffey's day. Except for the emphasis given to engineering and domestic science, the Institute takes after the conventional private academy that caters to the children of the rich. McGuffey's bare, frontier individualism scarcely provided for air-conditioned school rooms, newfangled ballroom dancing and private lessons from a riding master, or for the new cars which Ford used to bestow annually upon certain members of the entering class.

3

The antique collector and the patron of the old-fashioned dance began to cultivate still another facet of the past. He became an active supporter of a back-to-the-soil movement. In fact, Ford was a champion of getting-back-to-the-land even before he was an antiquarian. The Five-Dollar Day ushered in his first public pronouncement on this subject. It was then, in 1914, his announced intention to lay out small plots which his factory workers could till for subsistence, during slack seasons of employment, but nothing came of the plan. Ford was too busy for many a year to bother about any project for returning his men to the land.

Up to the death of the Model T, such a scheme had no point, in view of the relatively steady employment which the Ford Motor Co. could give its workers. Meanwhile, Edison had a hand in reshaping Ford's dream of combining industry and agriculture, or of pooling the present with the past. The inventor gave him the idea of projecting a string of village factories. Edison had been frustrated in his own wish to father such a development in the Orange Valley. But where the master failed, the disciple succeeded. Ford built the first link in his chain of rural plants in 1920. He made no further move in this direction for a decade, or until the onset of depression. Within the next several years after that, he became the proprietor of nine country mills, strung along the banks of various streams and rivers in southern Michigan.[18]

Externally these mill-stream factories developed into Greenfield Villages, brought up to date. In most instances they had been, until Ford picked them up, abandoned grist mills or deserted flour mills. The earmarks of age were preserved at one of the sites by retaining an overshot water wheel that served no function other than an ornamental one. The miniature plants soon began to operate as up-to-the-minute auxiliaries of the Ford Motor Co. They were retooled as Rouge feeder plants. The grounds, in every case, were dressed up spic-and-span and landscaped with 20th century finesse.

The new and the old, or the urban and the rural, were likewise blended in the economic life of the workers who were given employment at the village mills. Farm folk were brought in to tend the machines. At each of the establishments the employes were expected to cultivate private gardens in odd hours or during the off-seasons of the automobile industry. Before long the "little factories in the meadow" came to supply inexhaustible material for the sermonettes fashioned by W. J. Cameron for the Ford Sunday Evening Hour. Ford's country workers were pictured at their benches with "one foot in industry and one foot on the land," enjoying a "country living with a city income," amidst idyllic surroundings which augured the decentralization of our great urban factory centers and the eradication of the slums of the machine age.

But Ford's hopes to recapture the good old times by means of countrified modern industry carried a challenge only as an idea, and never as an accomplished fact. For alongside the total scope of the Ford Motor Co., the rural projects remained minute in scale. By 1939, they employed not more than 2000 workers.[19] At that time none of the basic operations of the company was undergoing decentralization. The rural production of the corporation was confined to a certain few processes that had normally been jobbed out to the parts makers of the trade—those having to do with the fabrication of light products like rivets, valves and tail lights.

Insofar as the plan embodied a provocative future trend, its benefits had been no more than contemplated for the regular production workers of the Ford Motor Co. Except for a handful of imported technicians, the working force for the village shops was recruited from the surrounding countryside. What Ford took into the country, therefore, was not his urban workers and their families, but rather certain restricted manufacturing operations. City workers were not returned to the soil. Farmers were taken from the land and placed inside the shop.

Whatever the upshot of these country factories as a new social form, and whatever the merits of Greenfield Village as a recorder of history, both hobbies offer a clue to Ford's personal make-up. They reflect the man.

The shrine at Greenfield Village bears the imprint of the empire-builder. Ford soon suffused the petty dominion of a museum with the same air that had long since clothed his conquest in the world of affairs. He reveled in his new-found power as a collector with a fat purse and a commanding temperament. The mode of acquiring the Foster memorial was indicative of the authoritarian manner, of the baronial touch. Certain other noteworthy landmarks found their way to Dearborn. Most of these relics were imported more quietly, however. The Village is ornamented with Edison's workshops, Luther Burbank's study, Steinmetz' river house, and cottages once inhabited by Walt Whitman, Noah Webster and Patrick Henry. These remains, divorced from their original framework, may have only the most artificial historic value. Their uprooting may bespeak a meaningless effort to preserve the husk, without the kernel. But such transplantations do symbolize the temper of Greenfield Village. The king commands. The thing is done.

In its paternalism Greenfield Village has the courtly and majestic air. Certain retainers in the village were the master's personal body-servants. A cobbler kept his patron supplied with new handmade dancing pumps. To indulge a hobby of his youth, Ford maintained five private watchmakers. By their ingratiating demeanor in Ford's presence, the student body of Edison Institute revealed an awareness of the fact that their patron headed the second richest family in America. Conversely, when the whim was right, the lord of the manor had been known to display his authority by declaring a recess at the Institute so that his charges might join him in a spin about the lagoon on the old "Suwanee."

As he proceeded to recapture the past, Ford was not unmindful of the present. He took pains to give his hobby the benefit of the latest techniques of modern advertising. Important additions to the collection were impressively celebrated through the media of distinguished visitors and radio broadcasts. Minor accretions at the village inspired a stream of press notices. In this or that historic fireplace burn a number of "perpetual" log fires, one of these blazes having been kindled by ex-President Hoover. Gossip has it that the flames must be re-kindled from time to time, but the thought of thermal perpetuity lives on.

As a device for molding public opinion, the village symbolizes, above everything else, the personality of its creator. It gives body to the concept of Ford, the rustic millionaire who ambled about a 19th century village in the folksy manner, calling his employees by their first names, and once again, through the medium of a semi-public institution, sharing his means with society. To the ineradicable portrait of the benevolent employer is added the role of patron of the arts, collector of historical treasures, custodian of the American tradition, and educator in the pioneer virtues.

From the vantage point of Main Street, this antiquarian achievement in Dearborn is an overwhelming success. By contrast with many another private, semi-philanthropic project, it has reached the people with far more immediacy and in much greater numbers. Greenfield Village, before the war, was Detroit's most flourishing tourist center. It was a mecca for the Sunday drivers. It demonstrates, all over again, the tremendous folk-appeal of Ford and all his works, as measured by the values of a middle-class America. The village attracts a million visitors a year, at 25 cents a head; its customers contribute some $250,000 annually toward its support.

Ford's motives as a deifier of the past are blended to perfection in his trim village factories. These country developments stand for everything that Greenfield Village bespeaks. They are rooted in the sentiment of a bygone era. They symbolize the reformer. They fulfill a dream that was dear to Edison, Ford's idol. The tidy, vest-pocket plants have advertising value. They, too, like the display at Greenfield Village, arrest the casual tourist, and in a commercial sense, the rural shops go a step beyond the collection at Dearborn, for they are direct and highly profitable operating agencies of the Ford Motor Co.[20]

Greenfield Village and the country shops doubtless register Ford's cognizance of the fact that he, perhaps more than any other single being, personified two epochs, that his name ranks as one of the foremost symbols of the transition from the agricultural age to the industrial, that his life was centrally identified with the great movements of his day that helped to efface the old order. Hence, as a means of contrasting the two areas, nothing could have been more fitting than the conception of Greenfield Village. Reckoned in such terms, the mastodon at the Rouge stands as a superlative token of modern times. Greenfield Village bespeaks the period which the machine age has brushed aside. Both monuments are significant memorials and masterkeys to Ford's personal history.

In the lesser work of reconstructing the past, the manufacturer was guided by the most natural ties of sentiment. All men cling to their origins with some degree of feeling and identification. And Ford was no exception. He doubtless enjoyed the role of basking amidst reminders of the day when he carried wood, milked cows, bedded down horses, and tinkered in old sheds. Anyone whose life-span had been as long and meaningful as his would have reveled in the same associations.

At the same time, Ford's leaning for the outward forms of a bygone epoch had the appearance of an effort to stop the clock or to order an about-face from the machine age. Such, it would seem, were the feelings of the manufacturer when he busied himself at Sudbury, Massachusetts, restoring an old tavern, the Wayside Inn, and recreating a miniature colonial oasis modeled after Greenfield Village. After the Sudbury shelter was completed, it failed to satisfy its creator. The sequestered air of the development was menaced by the whir of Ford cars and other vehicles, all too remindful of the century of gadgets. So Ford gave himself over to the process of divorcing Today from Yesterday. He settled the issue by re-laying the highway, the Boston Post Road, for a distance of two miles. The operation cost him a quarter of a million dollars. Pushed back far enough to leave his colonial sanctuary in peace the new stretch of road was then presented to the Commonwealth of Massachusetts for a consideration of $1. This act on Ford's part may have been ordered by mere whim. It was perhaps a millionaire's idle flourish. It may rank, in addition, as one more symbol of what Ford was hunting for among the vestiges of early America. The road-building at Sudbury, along with countless other acts much like it, may well connote the manufacturer's effort to flee from himself, to turn against the values of an uneasy age which he had helped to found.*

Here and elsewhere, Ford's predilection for the old is redolent of the 19th century mind half lost in the modern era, of a great pioneer who distrusted the fruits of his own discovery, of a creative figure whose colossal life-work lay in one age, his heart in another. That confusion and divided loyalty were implicit in a nostalgic lament which Ford uttered in his autobiography. Just as his own contribution to the present scheme of things was reaching grand proportions, the manufacturer felt moved to exclaim, "It was an evil day when the village flour mill disappeared."[21]

## Twenty-one

### FOLK HERO

### 1

IF FORD WAS suspicious of the modern temper, the age in which he moved accepted him in turn almost without reservation. It enthroned him during the first third of the century as an accredited

* John Dos Passos develops this symbolism in the brilliant thumbnail sketch of Ford that appears in *The Big Money.*

folk hero. The number of his contemporaries who scaled loftier heights of popularity or reputation was few indeed, and in this process of ennoblement and deification the industrialist and his times were well joined. The man advanced his age. The era made the man.

The manufacturer delighted and dazzled his contemporaries, first by the sheer magnitude of his personal success. He was esteemed great, among other reasons, because he personified to a superlative degree the art of getting on in an acquisitive society. Ford, the poor farm boy 'who made good, was a dream symbol of personal advancement. He was what the man on the street wanted to be. The fact that a plain mechanic could become the sole owner of a billion-dollar corporation made the great American gamble seem plausible. Every schoolboy had a model for his aspirations in the homely saga of Ford's conquest. Nor did most Americans begrudge Ford his success. Here, it appeared, was a man of plain speech and simple manners who was one of them, who had had his chance and made the most of it. Ford, for the multitude, was the colorful exception to the reverses and drabness of normal, everyday existence.

Mere distinction as a money-maker, however, was only one of the charms which the manufacturer embodied for his times. He was accounted great in far larger measure as the innovator who revolutionized an epoch by bringing the automobile to the masses. Ford's identification with this second achievement, coming in a period already enchanted by the spread of mechanical appliances, carried his eminence to the four corners of the earth. For a race that was hungry for gadgets the Ford Motor Co. proliferated some 15,000,000 copies of the Model T. This plainly dressed little commodity on wheels was a foremost emissary of Mechanical Progress. It made numberless friends for its creator, moreover, by its very soundness. Twenty-two years after its discontinuance at the factory, stray specimens of the Model T were still huffing and puffing over the sundry highways of the world.

The culture of the automobile, with Ford up front, did more than give pace and fresh expression to a pre-existing interest in things mechanical. It transformed the age. It opened up, simultaneously, a new world of values. For better or for worse the Model T and its competitors revolutionized factory methods. They drew hundreds of thousands of men into new fields of employment. They accelerated the rise of congested urban centers. The inventions which accompanied this change made mechanical men of numberless factory workers. They placed mankind as never before at the mercy of the business cycle. The new mode of transportation, first popularized by the Model T, was to revolutionize the arts of war; it would intensify the world struggle for oil and foreign markets. In traffic accidents in the United States alone, the automobile in 1940 would be taking an annual toll of more than 30,000 lives. By 1930 American taxpayers would be spending upwards of $1,000,000,000 a year for the betterment of their highways.

The motor car was even more arresting to the common man because of what it portended about the shape of things to come. Americans in particular were spellbound by the technology which had brought the automobile into being. In the feat of mass production, as the Ford Motor Co. had performed it, the masses could read the secret to their vaunted standards of living. This grand achievement, more gripping to the popular mind than the winning of the West, seemed to diagram the future, to mirror the promise of plenty, to foreshadow universal material prosperity. The new machine system became a point of national pride. It was magnified in the minds of men as the great American Adventure destined to issue mankind into the Promised Land.

Ford's stature as a revolutionary technologist was heightened by the fact that his corporation was family-owned. Thus the successes of the Ford Motor Co. could be more easily personalized or more easily represented as the achievements of a single being. The industrial advances at General Motors on the other hand—though equally dramatic and equally significant—were less amenable to the process of symbol building. These rival attainments, which outshone Ford's eventually, were received more impersonally. They were never presented to the world as the handiwork of a single inspired personality.

Additional luster was imported to Ford's name in that his production facilities came to be so concentrated, so much of a piece, at Dearborn. As a result, few industrial establishments in the world can touch the house of wonders on the River Rouge for sheer immensity. The behemoth of Dearborn stands out as one of the triumphs of the century. Few other symbols of the industrial revolution are more commanding or more overpowering. In the eyes of many a spectator, this monument of Ford's is more awesome than the mightiest sights of nature for the reason that it is man-made. It looks like the ultimate, even in an age that is accustomed to feast on the big and the spectacular. The sweep of the plant tends to obscure the fact that the technical marvels which it houses can be duplicated at every other major shop within the trade.

It was Ford's voicing of the doctrine of high wages and low prices, however, that finally crowned him as the greatest of the mass producers. Here, it seemed, was a builder of the modern world who practiced what he preached as he spread the creed that no mechanized civilization could survive unless it could absorb what it produced. The apostle of the New Messiah seemed to have hit on the answer to war, to the riddle of the business cycle, to the plague of over-production and the maldistribution of wealth. It was this claim to economic statesmanship that led Edward A. Filene, the Boston philanthropist, to nominate Ford in 1930 as a logical candidate for the Nobel Peace Prize. But years before Filene made this suggestion, the man on the street had come to revere Ford for the same reasons. To Ford's person the plain people of the world had long since projected the American dream of plenty. In him the masses had identified the benevolent hero of the capitalist saga, the capitalist who had the wit to make capitalism work.

In his rise to national sainthood, Ford won the hearts of men for the further reason that his career seemed to resolve the dominant moral conflicts of the age. This American millionaire, living under a code of Protestant capitalism in a society which venerates goodness and rewards success, appeared to be two-in-one. He was the empire builder who shared with others as he gathered in the sheaves for himself. He was reputed rich and good, shrewd and fair, acquisitive and generous, powerful and kindly, self-seeking and benevolent. This demi-god of the machine age had somehow stitched together the incompatibles of the struggle for existence. He was the idol of an American middle class which wants to eat its cake and have it too, the venerated symbol of a system under which people aspire to be neither so self-seeking that they lose caste nor so good that they must spend their days in poverty.

Once in motion, the process of beatification which set Ford apart from other men kept growing of its own accord. It began feeding on itself. Adulation of the man became infectious and cumulative. His fame waxed to heroic proportions under its own momentum. Labor leaders, university presidents and foreign dignitaries applauded him. He was decorated by three European governments. Among the ranks conferred upon him by more than one institution of higher learning were the titles of honorary Doctor of Engineering and honorary Doctor of Law. His recognition traveled far beyond the field of his achievement. One hall of fame after another opened its portals to this revered figure. In 1926, said one South American author, Ford ranked in public esteem in Brazil on a parity with Cromwell, Bacon, Columbus, Pasteur and Moses. A group of American college students once ranked the manufacturer as the third greatest figure of all time, surpassed in their judgment only by Napoleon Bonaparte and Jesus Christ. For years the newspapers of Detroit made a habit of referring to Ford as "the sage of Dearborn."

## 2

The mature Ford legend—a composite of fact and fiction—was never a wholly spontaneous growth. It emerged in part because of careful nurturing by the Ford Motor Co. itself. It was fed and canalized by a small body of publicists who were keenly aware of the spell they were working. These opinion-makers worked at the job of grooming the Ford legend. Much of what they told the public about the Ford achievement was grounded on a rock of fact. Not a little was the fabrication of myth makers. The finished product, however fashioned and however abused in certain quarters, was a mountain of good will that towers above any comparable effort, even in a society which glories in the arts of promotion and super-salesmanship.

The mainstay of Ford's personal coterie of advertisers for fifteen or twenty years was W. J. Cameron, the former editor of the *Dearborn Independent.** Most of the prevailing Ford lore was furbished by this word artist. For almost two decades the press was received at Dearborn with Cameron standing at his employer's elbow, serving as his master's voice. Meanwhile, this shepherd of the Ford legend censored not only what Ford said but the way he said it. Thus arose the distinction between the press release edited and issued at Dearborn and the unguarded, out-of-town interview with Ford—the latter studded much more frequently with colorful and oftentimes injudicious Ford whimsies. Consequently it came about that for years the manufac-

---

* In its public relations the Ford Motor Co. has differed from most American corporations chiefly in the prominence which it has given to Ford as an individual and in the close watch which Cameron used to keep over Ford's official stream of consciousness. Yet Cameron has insisted that "The Ford Motor Co. has no public relations department and employs no public relations counsel or 'spokesman.' "[1] Whatever his own official ranking may have been at Dearborn when he made this remark in 1937, Cameron was then discharging the duties which he said the corporation had delegated to no one. On the face of it, his salary, which *Fortune* put at $23,000 in 1939, was a public relations fee.[2] The man rendered no other known service to the company which was sponsoring his weekly broadcasts at the time.

turer could talk like himself for the public prints, only in the absence of his verbal alter-ego.

One of Ford's later hobbies, his interest in the soybean, was to call forth a wealth of overstatement. The soybean is one of the important sources of commercial plastics. Its by-products have been used for a number of years in the manufacture of the horn button and other incidental components of a Ford car. Where the genuinely stimulating work of Ford's soybean laboratory left off, it remained for Cameron to begin his word-painting in the realm of fancy. At a chemical conference held in Dearborn in 1935, Cameron reported Ford's prophecy that before long, "We shall grow most of an automobile." The copy desk at the Detroit *Free Press* graced this story with the caption, "Ford Envisions Cars Springing from the Soil."[3] Several years later Ford's prevision made way for still a further large order of rural magic. He foretold, with abandon, the manufacture of complete automobiles made of wheat.[4]

In addition to meeting the press as Ford's prompter and go-between, Cameron finally widened his audience through the medium of the Ford Sunday Evening Hour. He began to hold forth as a commentator on this weekly radio program in 1934. The *Nation* once described the Hour as a whole as a musical sandwich, for which the Detroit Symphony Orchestra supplied the bun, and Cameron the filling. Cameron's brief talks punctuated the concerts at their mid-point.

Graced by the appearance of outstanding guest conductors and musical virtuosi, the Ford Hour distinguished itself from the beginning as an adroit performance, ably staged. The program evoked an air. It was pitched on a pious, folksy plane. The program announcer exuded the ultimate in good will toward men. Cameron's own mode of speech was that of the earnest village parson. The broadcast ended on a reverent note, always closing with a hymn. The orchestra itself, in its programming, was enjoined to strive for the widest common denominator of taste. Its musical fare was weighted with familiar melodies and with the lighter masterworks. When the Hour came into being in 1934, the orchestra's apparent orders to play down to the masses drew a tribute from the Detroit *Free Press*. After remarking certain selections on the order of "The Last Rose of Summer," the *Free Press* acclaimed Ford's program building as a "victory for the common man" that would stand comparison with the mass production of the automobile.[5]

The Cameron sermonettes soon became little gems of propaganda.

Wrought to promote good will for their sponsor, they approached that end circuitously, pregnant with the magic of words. They first unsealed the mind of the listener by a manipulation of verbal symbols that mean all things to all men. A master of shibboleth, Cameron could fuse the names of Lincoln, Washington, Jefferson and Henry Ford into one perfect whole. His addresses were surcharged with respect for the democratic tradition, with plaudits for "the American way," with obeisance to the institution of the family, with accolades to neighborliness and good fellowship. The man had a talent for expatiating on the dearness of Christmas or Easter or Mother's Day. On occasion he would drop quaint allusions to the "private twitter of birds," to "life with its cradles and its green God's acre under the hill," or to our "long-suffering womenfolk."

Cameron's art had still other facets. This publicist made a habit of dressing his points in the language of the ruralist and of the middle class. He wove around the personality of his sponsor the articles of faith that are dear to the farmer and sacred to those within the white-collar fold. He breathed the spirit of boomtown optimism. He hailed the forward march to "new frontiers." His talks overflowed with salutations to the nation builders, to "the spirit of '76," to the Pilgrim Fathers and our proud "pioneer extract."

Yet, in the same breath, Ford's commentator made a point of preaching the devotion of the middle class to the status quo. He sang of the virtues of contentment. He suggested scapegoats to whom the ills of the world might be attributed. All would be well, he averred, if the body politic could only cleanse itself of radicals and labor leaders, foreigners and internationalists, financiers and social planners. The accents of laissez-faire underlay Cameron's affirmations that the dependent and the unsuccessful are the drones of society, that our woes will vanish like a mist when we are wise enough to "get down to work" and abide by the tried formulas of the past, that by contrast with men of affairs politicians are vicious as a class, and that everything will work out for the best, automatically, in the long run.

Ford's student of Main Street always left the door to social reform slightly ajar. At times he sounded the challenge of a 19th century liberalism; his speech was then weighted with the charges of a Jeremiah; he could lambast a world that is fraught with discord and predatory conflict; yet despite these brief exercises of the conscience, the prophet of the Ford Motor Co. seldom descended from the general to the particular. In pointing up this or that moral or putting meat on its bones, he never went so far as to abuse the sympathies or to tread on feelings of the prosperous or the reputable.

Part of Cameron's power as a publicist rested on a faculty for posing a problem without answering it. As between the hopes of the race and its pessimism, he frequently declared for neither. He could boast in ringing tones that the world belongs to men of action, that intellectuals and reformers are up to no good, that the supreme achievement of the age lies in its material fatness. He could decry with equal verve the lack of plenty and the want of morals. In certain moods this former minister would find the world too much for him. His radio talks then shifted to the theme that the good old times were best and that the simple ways of the pre-industrial order were beyond compare.

Thus by dealing in slogans that command universal homage and by modulating his speech to the temper of those who constitute the "backbone" of the nation, the tribune of the Ford Sunday Evening proceeded to put his radio audiences at ease. His listeners, relaxed by pleasing music and charmed by the arts of language, were thus transported into a mental state that was, for the most part, friendly, unguarded and receptive.

Onto the foreground of such a stage Cameron projected, above all, the personality of his sponsor. He proceeded to elaborate the authentic Ford legend. The portrait thus etched into the public mind reached far beyond the great figure of the legitimate folk hero. Henry Ford, Cameron gave the world to understand, was the kindly and unassuming millionaire with whom principle invariably triumphed over profit. He was the oracular, divinely inspired all-wise one and the self-made Genius with a capital G. More than that, he was the benevolent employer harassed by labor agitators on the one side and by Wall Street ogres on the other. He was, finally, the New Economist who would set the world aright but for the selfishness of evil financiers and small-minded politicians.

Whatever its limitations as a technique of business salesmanship, the time-honored Ford theme of accenting the talents and accomplishments of a single person seems to have pleased the man who paid the bill. Indeed, Ford has given many another indication of a passion for the limelight. As a savant without benefit of much formal schooling, he was the acknowledged author of several full-length books and of innumerable lesser publications. His name has appeared on the title page of works purporting to deal with pedagogy, pharmacology, anthropology, political economy, money and banking, domestic science, the history of the dance and the art of thinking.

The magnification of the folk hero to colossal proportions, therefore, was partly of Ford's own doing. At the height of his power the
man's conviction of his own genius was overweening. In fact when a
journalist once asked him to state the secret of his life work in a nutshell, the manufacturer replied in all seriousness that he was a 20th
century reincarnation of Leonardo Da Vinci.

## 3

On still other grounds, Ford was accounted unique among men
of fabulous wealth because of his fondness for plain living. The Midas
of Dearborn, says the legend, had no stomach for the life of luxury
which fortune placed within his grasp. With the world at his feet, he
is said to have preserved the common touch, to have clung to the
simple ways of Main Street, to have preferred humble folk to the
company of kings.

Such a picture of the world's richest industrialist has been cultivated with a fine hand by the publicists at Dearborn. Any number of
the company's press releases have been cast in the idiom of the self-
made man of the people who chose to remain a commoner. The Ford
Sunday Evening Hour was steeped with the flavor of the folksy and
the neighborly. To a radio audience which has accustomed itself to
the image of American millionaires who winter in Florida and indulge
the sundry amenities of the leisure class, Cameron could speak of the
humbler pleasure which Ford extracted from "just circulating 'round,"
rubbing elbows with plain people and calling his workmen by their
first names. This same publicist could tell a convention of Ford
dealers in 1935 to stop thinking of Henry Ford as a "rich man."[6]

Much could be said, in fact, for the manufacturer's attachment
for the simple life. Neither wealth and power nor unlimited opportunity for wide social intercourse ever succeeded in effacing the inner
substance of his personality. Many of Ford's tastes and attitudes did
remain unchanged and rustic. At the same time, by capitalizing on
Ford's genuinely simple propensities, the opinion molders at Dearborn
were guided by an acute sense of American values. These men leaned
over backwards to court good will in a social order that reveres the
democratic tradition. They strained the "plain folks" device to the
point of affectation. By the same token they glossed over the fact that
the plain liver of Dearborn was, in his mode of living, not quite so
plain as one might imagine.

For many years, as a matter of fact, the senior Ford enjoyed a way of life quite in keeping with his ownership of one of the largest private incomes in history.* His rural temperament still imposed certain limits on this handsome mode of existence. The manufacturer's shyness, as well as his ties to the past and his mooring in the shop, would never permit him to cultivate the delights of the table or the rich man's normal diversions of travel and varied social exposure. There was nothing in Ford's make-up of the latent cosmopolite, ready to bloom in the more leisurely later years of a busy career. The manufacturer's scheme of life would allow for no Italian villas, no brilliant dinner parties or schedule of sumptuous private entertainment. The ruralist could never accommodate himself to much of the ritual of social decorum, including the services of a private valet.

Yet within the limits dictated by his nature, Ford did manage to surround himself for a generation with most of the comforts that are taken for granted among the affluent. The scale of his private life was for thirty years or more quite as lavish as that of most other American millionaires. Not that the elder Fords ever displayed their means in the vulgar, ostentatious manner. These basically simple people, on the other hand, struck a compromise with wealth. They proceeded to live modestly within an expensive framework. Their design for living was patterned after neither the Gilded Age nor the garish 20's. It followed, instead, the quieter but nonetheless expansive mold of a native landed gentry.

The country squire who made his fortune in the automobile industry finally came to maintain four separate domiciles. These properties compared favorably with the accommodations of other American families of great means. The Ford residence at Dearborn, situated in the heart of a private estate that runs to 5000 acres, is valued at more than $1,000,000. It has thirty bedrooms.† Outside the state the elder Ford acquired two winter homes, one on the Gulf of Mexico, the other on his Richmond plantation in Georgia. The Georgia residence,

---

* From May 1, 1920—after eliminating their co-investors—through the ensuing 17¾ years the Ford family withdrew from the Ford Motor Co. for their private use stock profits approximating $25,000 per day.[7] Salary payments were extra. The Fords had the second largest family fortune in America. It was probably inferior in size only to the combined assets of the Rockefeller clan. The Ford motor holdings alone were assessed by the Ford Motor Co. in May 1944 at a total book value of more than $1,000,000,000.[8]

† When this dwelling was under construction in 1915, its specifications, as detailed in a lawsuit, called for the erection of a $21,000 greenhouse, a $37,000 boathouse, a $33,000 gate-keeper's lodge, a $69,000 garage, a $30,000 pipe organ, a $167,000 power plant, and an $18,000 tunnel connecting the residence with the garage.

overlooking the Ogeechee River, lies in the midst of a private holding of 100,000 acres. This estate was created by merging more than thirty plantations scattered over two adjacent counties. At a cost of $100,000, the manufacturer then built a summer place, a sixteen-room dwelling, on the shore of Lake Superior in northern Michigan, on the property of the Huron Mountain Club, an exclusive colony whose membership is drawn from the wealthy strata of Michigan and Illinois.

On leave of absence from his native habitat, Ford moved about for twenty-five years in a stately manner. No other American traveler had his itinerary policed by so large a retinue of guards and secret service men. For transcontinental travel the manufacturer for a number of years employed the *Fair Lane,* a private railroad car. When he acquired this conveyance in 1922, the New York *Times* described it as one of the most elaborate vehicles of its kind ever built. For transportation to and from the Huron Mountain retreat before the war, the manufacturer was in the habit of using the *Henry Ford II,* a lake freighter named after his eldest grandson. The *Henry Ford II* is an ore carrier. The master's suite on the vessel is commodious and luxuriously appointed. The ship carried a unique bit of cargo for its owner's summer outing of 1933. It transported, with pomp and ceremony, from Dearborn to the Huron Mountain resort a choice collection of early American furniture. At the conclusion of Ford's vacation of two or three weeks' duration, these distinctive furnishings were then restored to the museum in Greenfield Village.[9]

The ruralist of Dearborn became thoroughly urban and quite on a par with the smartly attired men of Wall Street in his choice of haberdashery. Sometime in the 20's the press began speaking of Ford as one of the country's most fastidious dressers. He was reported at that time to have engaged a private tailor. This personal attendant was said to be devoting full time to the task of fashioning Ford's custom-made suits from bolts of fine imported fabrics. The manufacturer's needs in footwear were supplied for some years by a private cobbler at work in Greenfield Village. Indulging good taste in excellent wearing apparel, Ford came to bear a quiet, but nonetheless real, resemblance to his more worldly former partner, John Dodge, who willed to his heirs in 1922, 10 overcoats, 18 suits, 100 pieces of underclothing and 109 shirts.[10]

Until he mellowed with the years, the elder Ford acquired his reputation as one of the "plain folks" by holding himself aloof from polite society in general. There were exceptions even to this earlier rule. The early Ford came out of his shell occasionally to attend some wedding or funeral of interest to the elite of his community. He enjoyed the ownership of a $600,000 yacht. He experimented briefly with golf in 1927, dropping that avocation after laying out a private course and founding his own country club.[11]

He exchanged social courtesies with the great and near-great on several occasions in the middle 20's. The most notable event of this character occurred in his 62nd year, in 1924, when he played host to the Prince of Wales, the present Duke of Windsor. On this occasion the elect of Detroit were allowed two glimpses of the royal presence, the first at a private reception in the Detroit Club before fifty guests personally selected by Henry Ford, the second at a dinner party and dance held at the home of Edsel Ford. Four years later the senior Fords were received in turn by the Prince of Wales at St. James Palace, and by King George and Queen Mary on Lady Astor's Cliveden estate.

On approaching his 70th year, Ford's personal ties to the wealthy and the smart set became definitely more cordial. The dancing parties at Dearborn took their place in the social ritual of the community. The manufacturer began dropping in here and there to pay his respects to J. P. Morgan, Samuel Insull and John D. Rockefeller, Sr. His interest in the affairs of high society lured him even further afield. He made a special trip to New York to attend the wedding of John D. Rocke-feller III, and to Cincinnati to take part in the marriage ceremony of Annette Wurlitzer, the daughter of the manufacturer of musical instruments.

## 4

It was as the New Economist, however, that Henry Ford acquired the greatest measure of his legendary fame. The celebrated mass producer capped his claim to greatness over the years by striking the pose of the humanitarian who defied the rules of the game, who was out for big changes in the system. That accent was the key to Ford's public relations strategy. It was what Cameron had in mind when he used to contrast "honest industry," as represented by the Ford interests, and the "impersonal corporations" which comprised, by inference, the remaining big business interests of the country; or when he had a mind to decry wealth and worldly power as false gods that appealed to no right-thinking person, least of all to Henry Ford, the arch-enemy of things as they are. In Cameron's words, the prophet of Dearborn who yearned for a new arrangement of the social system "does not find it hard to put principle before profit—it is his nature to put first things first."

The very fact that Ford could attain so high a place in the affections of ordinary men is in itself a token of cynicism and disillusionment. It meant that the average being could never stop rubbing his eyes at the spectacle of a multi-millionaire who got rich without hurting anybody. This feeling toward Ford revealed the instinct of the people that, under the existing system, the moral capitalist or the art of mixing virtue with selfishness is so rare that the occurrence of either is startling. Thus some of the multitude's adoration of Ford sprang, unwittingly, from a deep-seated psychological need for a benevolent symbol in a society whose major social forces and dominant personalities behave, all too often, malevolently.

Wall Street was first to size up the New Economist correctly. Sophisticated men of means, like everyone else, made the initial error of misreading the Five-Dollar Day. These controllers of wealth jumped to the conclusion that Ford was giving away something for nothing. They had their misgivings about the Peace Ship. These financial and industrial titans were relieved to note that in his pacifism Ford was a rebel only for a day. They readily grasped the point that when the manufacturer's talk about what he intended doing with his war earnings collided with his pocketbook, principle bowed to self-interest.

Reassured little by little that the commoner of Dearborn was, after all, one of those who looks after his own, the economic leaders of the nation were still suspicious of his views toward privilege in general. They looked askance at the language of reform and Populism that buoyed up his political activity of 1918 and 1924. These lingering doubts were finally washed away when Ford frankly and permanently identified himself with the G.O.P. The Republican vanguard then recognized a tardy bedfellow in the person of the automobile manufacturer who threw over his pretensions as an agrarian radical in order to endorse Coolidge, Hoover, Landon and Dewey. The reconciliation was complete when the Ford Sunday Evening Hour began to distinguish itself in 1934 as a rampart of defense against the New Deal.

Thus the affluent—who were first to learn the story of the Ford dealer and the Ford supplier and the make-up of the Ford Alumni Association—were likewise the first to see in Ford a familiar American type, no better or worse than his contemporaries, but far less challenging and far less heroic than he himself made out. Judged by their code, Ford's behavior was conventional; he introduced no fresh doctrine; he acted like any other successful Yankee bent on empire building; he was moved by the same acquisitive and ruthless temperament.

If Wall Street finally could not bring itself to think of Ford as an enemy, neither could it grant him sainthood. As a matter of fact, the financial district came to covet Ford's double standard—his capacity for getting what he wanted, while keeping his status as a man of good will. When the manufacturer was at the point of taking over Muscle Shoals for a song, *Barron's Weekly* lamented that Ford "can steal a horse, where Wall Street cannot look over the fence."[12] What successful men of cynical intelligence envied so in Ford was his ability to say one thing and do another, his talent for seeming to be what he was not, his genius for self-advertising, and his superb formula for spreading what Mark Twain once referred to as "soul butter." According to the *Nation*, two large Wall Street operators fell to discussing this industrial Barnum in 1923. " 'Ford talks like a Socialist,' said one. 'Yes, but he acts like one of us,' the other replied softly, 'and he gets away with it.' "[13]

Yet the man of affairs who added up the Ford legend realistically was no iconoclast. He let the illusion—of Henry Ford, the Robert Owen of the 20th century—stand undisturbed. This secretiveness was fitting in an era when business barons no longer disclosed their intentions with arrogance or in an age in which it had become the fashion to conceal the face of naked frankness behind the mask of social conscience. It was to Wall Street's interest to permit the Ford legend and the gospel of the New Economist to ripen into one of the great rationalizations of the century. The sleep of all rich men was the sounder because of the belief that the system was essentially good, that it would work to perfection—if only there were more Henry Fords. This function of the Ford saga, as an antidote for social criticism, was once remarked by a certain realist in the New York financial district who said that Ford or the belief in Ford was one of "Wall Street's shock absorbers."[14]

The folk hero managed to win, therefore, the honor of commanding tremendous loyalty at both ends of the poll of social opinion. Among fellow industrialists and the more discerning leaders of finance and industry, he could pass as "one of us." The man on the street who lacked the facts to check the legend could be equally certain that the New Economist was indeed a true folk hero. The Haves respected the reality. The Have-nots and the unsophisticated middle classes clung to the dream.

PART FIVE

# Modern Times

Tell me your associates and I will tell you what you are.
—*Goethe*, quoted in the *Ford Almanac*, June, 1937.

# Twenty-two

## MEN-AT-ARMS

## 1

A T THE CORE of the legend of Henry Ford lies the saga of Harry Herbert Bennett, the last and most remarkable of Ford's factotums. Short of stature and alluded to by many of his former subordinates as the "Little Fellow," Harry Bennett was the personification of his employer's passion for one-man management. Bennett is a former sailor who is said to have won the lightweight boxing championship of the United States Navy, fighting under the ring name of "Sailor Reese." After fifteen years of service at Dearborn, this picturesque character was invested with plenipotentiary powers at the Ford Motor Co.

Neither his reported salary nor his various titles were in keeping with the man's exalted station within the Ford organization. For years Bennett was referred to as the company's director of personnel, but this modest title failed to do him justice. His eventual authority in the handling of Ford's affairs was pervasive, almost limitless. Nor did his reported remuneration jibe with his actual importance in Ford's life. Bennett, said a contributor to the *American Mercury* in 1940, was earning no more than $1400 a month, "combined with bonuses."[1] If that figure represents anything like a true measure of Bennett's earning power, as of that date, the man was underpaid. At least when the *Mercury* estimate was published, Sorensen, P. E. Martin and Edsel Ford—all then somewhat removed from the seat of power at the Ford Motor Co.—were each enjoying an annual income in excess of $150,000.

Ford may have rewarded his chief aide-de-camp more handsomely. No one, outside the Treasury Department or the Ford organization itself, can say. As the New York *Times* reported in 1937, the

size of Bennett's salary was a tight secret at the Ford Motor Co.[2]
Bennett's income has never been divulged by the Treasury Department. Yet his scale of living was certainly out of proportion to the
modest figure reported by the *Mercury*. His estate near Ypsilanti was
fairly imposing. He owned a hundred-acre island in the Huron River.
At a summer place on Grosse Ile, he moored a 75-foot private yacht,
the *Estharr*. The Grosse Ile property alone—deeded to him in 1938 by
Henry Ford and his wife—is valued at $17,000.[3] He made a habit of
wintering at Palm Springs, California.

But despite the mystery of his salary and the unassuming sound
of the titles he carried at one time or another, Bennett ruled the roost
at the Ford Motor Co., nonetheless, for twenty years. For a really
important Dearborn story, Detroit's newspapermen did not call at
Henry Ford's office for nearly two decades, nor at Edsel Ford's or
Cameron's. They went to Bennett. So firmly was this man entrenched
at Dearborn sometime in the 30's—meeting the press and doing much
else in Ford's name, and with more authority than any Ford executive
since the days of James Couzens—that one or another newspaperman
in the vicinity started calling the corporation, in jest, the "Bennett
Motor Co."

Magazines and newspapers of the highest repute took note of this
star in the Ford firmament. Speaking editorially in 1937, the New
York *Times* remarked that the former sailor was "said to have more
authority in the company than any one except the Fords, father and
son."[4] *Time* magazine went a bit further by saying in 1941 that it was
father rather than son to whom Bennett owed his exalted position in
the company. "Son Edsel," said *Time,* was the corporation's president
and its "technical" head, but "Father Ford" was "boss, still the absolute ruler of this industrial domain."[5] *Time*'s dictum was borne out by
John McCarten, the author of an article which appeared in the
*American Mercury* in 1940 under the title, "The Little Man in Henry
Ford's Basement." Bennett had "the wary respect of every other Ford
executive," said McCarten. "His orders can be rescinded by no one save
Henry Ford, the only man in the world to whom he has ever deferred."

In fact, the exact role assigned to this extraordinary man has no
counterpart in any comparable corporation in American history. The
"Little Fellow" functioned for many a year as his master's all-in-all.
He served Ford all this while in the multiple capacity of friend,
adviser, spokesman, confidante, strategist, hiring agent, chief of personnel, production whip, political intermediary, informer, personal
body attendant, captain of the guards, commander of the household

troops, and, in a figurative sense, as prince regent and lord high executioner.

To fulfill so wide a mission, Bennett required a tool; he had to bring a machinery into being. There arose, therefore, that bizarre institution known as the Ford Service Department. This instrument, stamped by Ford's temperament and molded by Bennett's genius, was twenty years in the making. It constituted, when fully spun, a web of spies and private police which the New York *Times* designated in 1937 as the largest private quasi-military organization in existence.[6]

Yet Bennett was by no means a glorified private detective, concerned with nothing more than the protection of Ford's person or the policing of a factory. In fact, he personified by the middle 30's the totality of Ford's interests. With Ford's purse strings at his fingertips, and feeling free to conduct his personnel office as a patronage mill, Bennett had become one of the reigning political forces of the state of Michigan. His appointive powers had waxed to the point where he could name not only some of the important functionaries of the Ford corporation, but certain public office holders as well. The base of these operations, however, was the instrument of Ford Service.

In composition alone, apart from its functions, Ford Service won a unique place among the classical private police systems of history. At its peak, its official personnel and its allies-at-large comprised one of the rarest assortments of men-at-arms ever assembled near any seat of power, public or private. No condottieri employed by a warring Italian prince of the 15th century were more formidable than the retainers whom Bennett enlisted at the Ford Motor Co. The bravi of the Medici family were superior to the operatives of Ford Service, as of 1937, neither in numbers nor in the arts of aggression and self-defense. Certain members of the Ford staff of 20th century compradores were personable and suave. But for the rougher work which his mission seemed to require, Bennett turned to more primitive characters.

In the choice of his immediate co-workers, while coming into his own at Ford's, Bennett leaned to athletes of every caste, from smooth, clean-cut amateurs to the shoddiest of cast-off professionals. In the first category were former college football stars. His personal secretary, for several years, was Stanley E. Fay, captain of the University of Michigan's championship football team of 1933. Also admitted to the inner circle was Harry Newman, a former All-American quarterback at Ann Arbor—and one of the few Jews ever employed at Dearborn. Until drafted for army duty in 1941, the Negro Willis Ward filled one of the key posts in Bennett's office. Ward had distinguished himself on the college gridiron. More than that, he was probably the greatest track star ever produced at the University of Michigan.

It was Bennett's further policy for many years to give preference in summer employment to football players who were still listed as undergraduates at one or another of the neighboring universities. This practice was particularly in evidence when coach Harry Kipke was producing brilliant football teams at Ann Arbor. Bennett and Kipke became fast friends at the time. Finally, in the summer of 1937, Bennett hired en masse a good proportion of the men who would make up the University of Michigan football squad in the season just ahead. These young athletes were ostensibly employed as guards and errand boys. They were paid the regular Ford wage for an eight-hour day. Nearly one-half of their working time, however, was devoted to the practice of football. For this side activity, the squad was assigned locker space in the Dearborn police station. Freshly laundered uniforms were provided three times a week. Coach Kipke never put in an appearance on the practice field, but the football drills, subsidized by the Ford Motor Co., were attended by the team's captain. Inasmuch as the rules of the Big Ten Conference forbid organized practice sessions up to September 1st, the legality or propriety of Bennett's arrangement was taken to task by the Chicago *Tribune*.[7]

This particular violation of the Big Ten code is said to have been one of the grounds for the unanimous vote by which the Athletic Board of Control at Ann Arbor relieved Kipke of his duties as head football coach at the close of the season of 1937. After this action, Bennett quickly came to the rescue of his deposed friend. Stripped of his coaching job, Kipke was able to enter the automobile industry at a beginner's income said to have been five or ten times the size of his former salary at Ann Arbor.[8] From that moment on, various parts suppliers in the trade began dealing with the Ford Motor Co. through the offices of Harry Kipke, "manufacturer's agent."

With many a Ford Serviceman, nothing was more common than a background of pugilism or wrestling. Bennett's entourage came to be studded with boxers and wrestlers, active and retired. He chose as one of his mainstays Elmer S. DePlanche, a former professional fighter, who once held a welterweight title, fighting under the name of Elmer ("One Round") Hogan.[9] Equally prominent in the operations of Ford Service was Jim Brady, a leading fight promoter and once a lightweight boxing champion of the state of Michigan.[10] He was subsequently suspended as a fight promoter in the state of Illinois, for a

period of five years, and this punitive action was supported at the
time by the National Boxing Commission.[11]

One of the more colorful characters who graduated from the ring
into the Ford Service Department was Norman Selby, known in boxing
circles as "Kid" McCoy. A soldier of fortune who married ten times
and whose history in the ring was infamous, the "Kid" was paroled
to Harry Bennett after serving eight years of a 20-year sentence at
San Quentin for the murder of his sweetheart, Mrs. Therese Mors, of
Los Angeles. For the next eight years, until he committed suicide in
1940, McCoy's duties at the Ford Motor Co. included those of payroll
guard, overseer of Ford's "thrift gardens," and "athletic director" of
Ford Service.

When the depression set in, Bennett began building bridges to
the American Legion. The resulting *entente cordiale* between certain
veterans of the first World War and the Ford Motor Co. came into
being in the wake of the Ford Hunger March. Shortly after the occurrence of that event in 1932, the Wayne County Council of the
American Legion forwarded a vote of confidence to the Fords, pledging
the assistance of its membership "in any further emergency."[12] The
personnel office of the Ford Motor Co. reciprocated in the fall of
the following year by offering preferential employment on production
jobs to 5000 veterans of the A.E.F.[13] Applicants were instructed to
present their credentials at the Legion's Memorial Hall in downtown
Detroit. The ensuing scramble for jobs rivaled the Ford hirings of
1914 and 1929. A small army of war veterans, desperate for work,
descended on Detroit. Some of these newcomers spent their first night
in the city on open door fronts close to the designated hiring hall.
For a day or two the job seekers were so numerous they tied up traffic
for several blocks in a busy section of the city.

This depression hiring, coming when it did, benefited an indeterminate number of Legionnaires, while working an injury on an
equivalent number of Ford's regular employes. The placement occurred in 1933 when the active payroll at the Rouge had sunk to
40,000 or less, its lowest ebb in fifteen years. It was consummated in
the face of a little-advertised and futile expression of protest from
those Ford employes who had been without work for months or had
been laid off for the specific purpose of making way for the incoming
applicants. Scores of old Ford men who were themselves veterans of
the first World War complained to the NRA compliance board of
Dearborn that they had been displaced at Dearborn in deference to
the out-of-town Legionnaires then being enrolled at Memorial Hall.[14]

Other Ford men who had been idle for as long as one or two years reported to the same agency that they, too, had overseas records, but were not recalled during the placement of the ex-service men who were being added to the Ford personnel as total strangers. Many of these informants were too down and out, they said, to be able to keep up their dues in any veterans' organization.[15]

Ford and Bennett continued to court the Legion in other ways as well. In 1937 Ford donated thirty-eight acres of his Dearborn estate as a site for a veterans' hospital. Later on, he began to operate two summer camps for the sons of Legionnaires and Ford employes. These ventures were diminutive farming projects that gave gainful employment to a hundred or more adolescents. Both sites, Camp Legion in Dearborn and Camp Willow Run in Ypsilanti, were trim showplaces. Both were heralded by the Ford public relations department. At the same time the Fordson Post of the American Legion began to enjoy unusual favor with the hiring agents of the Ford Motor Co.

The manufacturer then appeared as an honorary guest of the American Legion during its 1939 convention in Chicago. He made this trip in Bennett's company. Speaking from the platform before the veterans of a World War which he had once decried from the housetops, Ford declared that the experience of being received as a special Legion guest constituted one of the "greatest moments" of his life.[16]

## 2

Among politicians, big and little, who joined Harry Bennett's official family, the most notorious is John Gillespie, the former Republican boss of Detroit and Wayne County. Before striking up an alliance with the Ford Motor Co., Gillespie was for years one of the state's outstanding symbols of corrupt machine politics.[17]

Gillespie's affiliation with the Ford Motor Co. was not the only omen of the political ambitions of Ford Service. As Henry Ford's emissary, Bennett came to power in Republican circles by distributing benefactions throughout the rank and file of the state's influential politicians. The principal plum at his disposal, for purposes of patronage, was employment at the Ford Motor Co. Until the coming of the union, Bennett could manipulate at Dearborn, without check or hindrance, a vast revolving fund of jobs that called for little special skill. Thus, as long as his powers were unfettered, the chief of Ford Service could always lend an ear to the appeal, "I want so-and-so put on." No request for preferment was any more common among politicians of influence within the state. Thousands upon thousands of Ford placements were ordered through such channels. Among those who availed themselves of the privilege of dipping into this pool of jobs were certain ministers, "nationality" leaders, judges and other holders of public office, politicians at large and all other persons of substance with whom Ford Service deigned to treat.

Before unionization gave Ford's men seniority rights, Bennett is said to have deployed more patronage over a given period of time than any governor of Michigan, Democratic or Republican.[18] The man succeeded in playing politics with the Ford payroll on a scale which no other corporation in the state has ever tried to equal. That authority, while it lasted, gave Bennett tremendous leverage in the country's fourth metropolis, whose electoral system is non-partisan. Neither of the major parties had an entrenched local machine that could give him a run for his money.

The prisons and the police courts of the nation had their day as recruiting centers for a certain personnel in which Bennett had an interest. From this source came many an operative or auxiliary of Ford Service, as well as large numbers of regular Ford factory workers.

Among the law-breakers who began to honeycomb Bennett's immediate staff and the general working force of the Ford Motor Co. could be found perpetrators of nearly every crime listed on the statute books. The gamut of their police records ran from rape and gross indecency to leaving the scene of an accident, carrying concealed weapons, forgery, embezzlement, burglary, robbery, violation of the Drug Act, felonious assault, murder and manslaughter.[19]

The hiring of former criminals was indeed a Ford custom that antedated Bennett. But the practice seems to have attained large-scale proportions only after Bennett's accession to power and during the lush years of the Service Department. In 1928, when Bennett was a relative newcomer, still bearing the title of chief of Ford's private police, the New York *Times* reported that the company was employing 2600 ex-convicts.[20] Six years later, after Ford Service had reached maturity, Henry Ford was quoted by the Detroit *Times* as saying that the number of former prison inmates on his payroll had risen to 8000.[21] Such a number would have represented anywhere from 10 to 20 per cent of the total working force at the Rouge.

Ford's recruitment of former penitentiary inmates was all the easier both because most business establishments are somewhat wary of hiring men with criminal records and because Bennett proceeded to exert his influence at the office of prison parole in the state of

Michigan. In 1935 the "Little Fellow" was appointed by a Republican governor to serve on the Michigan Prison Commission. The Detroit *News* acclaimed the appointment by remarking editorially that "Mr. Bennett has an intimate knowledge of convicts. He has handled hundreds of them, perhaps thousands."[22] While rounding out his two-year term on the commission, Bennett introduced a resolution which enabled prisoners to shorten their sentences by receiving credit for "extra good time." At this juncture, convicts discharged from the state's penal institutions were being paroled to the Ford Motor Co. at the rate of approximately five per week.

When Governor Frank Murphy took office in 1937, Bennett lost favor in Lansing. He was not reappointed to the prison commission and the state-wide paroling of ex-convicts to Dearborn was halted for the time being. Meanwhile, Murphy introduced a program of prison reform. He placed the penal offices of the state under civil service. One of his first acts was to remove Harry H. Jackson, the warden of Jackson Prison. Warden Jackson, a former policeman, was notorious for using the "punishment block," a close-fitting, medieval device in which recalcitrant prisoners are made to stand upright and motionless, until their confinement becomes intolerable. The inmates under his care had staged frequent riots. One of their favorite methods of retaliation was to flood portions of the prison by stuffing up the toilets and causing breaks in the plumbing.

The deposed warden found refuge at the Ford Motor Co. He was hired by Bennett to superintend a revived Ford Sociology Department. He was not long deprived of public office. When the Republicans defeated Murphy in 1939, Bennett quickly recouped his fortunes at Lansing. The octogenarian governor, Luren ("I have a pipe-line to God") Dickinson, restored the penal agencies of the state to the rule of patronage. Warden Jackson was shifted from the Ford Sociology Department back to Jackson Prison. This man's return to power was marked by the reinstatement of the "punishment block."

Innumerable former policemen and countless professional athletes, active or retired, have wended their way to Dearborn along still another route. These additions to Ford Service were, as a rule, men who had fallen from grace or who had been discredited in their previous callings, sometimes without ever having been legally convicted for the commission of any wrong.

On Bennett's payroll were any number of castaways from Detroit's police department. Such was the history of three city detectives—Stephen Merritt, John Colon and Hugh Turney—on whose guilt a

Detroit jury, in convicting the leader of an automobile theft ring, could not agree in 1936. Under a cloud of suspicion, however, these officers were suspended from the force. Bennett promptly hired all three.[23]

The least reputable of the retainers at Dearborn were not mere unfortunates who ran afoul of the law unwittingly, or on only one occasion. They were case-hardened criminals. These recipients of Ford patronage ranged from small fry to some of the most desperate characters of the American underworld. They included thugs and gunmen just emerged from jail, as well as criminal racketeers at large.

One such gangster was Joseph ("Legs") Laman, a former rum-runner and kidnaper. A creature of the prohibition era, Laman acquired the name "Legs" in connection with the kidnaping of David Cass, an abducted child whose body was retrieved from a gully along the Flint River. This gangster was caught by the police with $4000 in ransom money on his person. One of the officers who made the arrest later reported that Laman sprinted so furiously to escape apprehension that he seemed to be all "legs." The leader of a ring implicated in at least thirty kidnapings, Laman earned still another nickname by turning state's witness after he had been sentenced to prison for a term of thirty to forty years.[24] Because of his revelations, six other gangsters received long prison sentences. Laman was rewarded by having his own prison term commuted to six years. The Michigan underworld rechristened him, meanwhile, "Legs, the Squealer." Once more at large, Laman was paroled to the Ford Motor Co.[25]

At least two renowned racketeers have enjoyed the double privilege of holding a lucrative business concession from the Ford corporation, and of continuing their careers of crime simultaneously. One such character was the former boss of the Brooklyn underworld, Joe Adonis, variously described by the New York *Post* as "politician," "gang punk," "hijacker," "dope king" and "murder boss." "Without Adonis' approval," the *Post* charged in 1940, "no gang can operate in Brooklyn." According to the *Post*, the man's illegal traffic extended from dope peddling and gambling to counterfeiting, waterfront hijacking and the operation of racket unions and loan shark agencies.

His legitimate business, carried forward simultaneously, rested on ownership of the Automotive Conveying Company. To this concern, the Ford Motor Co. awarded an exclusive contract for trucking its finished cars from the Ford assembly plant at Edgewater, New Jersey, to adjoining states on the Eastern seaboard. Adonis disguised his relationship to the haulage company by employing for the purpose the alias "Joseph Doto." For this work, from 1932 to 1940, he is reputed to have received at least $3,000,000 from the Ford Motor Co.[26]

The biggest name in crime ever associated with the Ford business was that of Chester (Chet) LaMare, a gangster who at one time was the "Al Capone" of Detroit. During the prohibition era, LaMare came closer than any of his rivals to wielding absolute control over the down-river, Sicilian gangs which infested Detroit's 70-mile waterfront. The bootlegging enterprise which his men dominated was ranked by federal agents as the state's second largest industry in 1928. It was said to be collecting a gross revenue of $215,000,000 a year.[27] At the apex of his career, in 1931, LaMare was depositing money in the bank at the rate of $3500 a day.[28]

The manufacture and smuggling of illicit liquor, however, was only the cornerstone of this man's semi-monopoly in crime. His interests were reported by the police to extend to hijacking, dope traffic, freight car robberies and the operation of night clubs and houses of prostitution. His lieutenants were so fierce that no outside gang was long tempted to challenge his supremacy along the Detroit waterfront. Before sitting down to take a drink at their favorite night clubs, some of his henchmen made a habit of placing their firearms in full view. Poachers drifting in from other parts of the country were driven off by violent means. One of LaMare's lesser competitors is said to have been "dropped into Lake St. Clair through a hole in the ice. When he came to the surface, he had changed his mind."[29]

Although Detroit's "Capone" was subject to repeated arrest as a criminal suspect, he escaped with only one short prison sentence. On that single occasion, he was convicted in federal court in 1927 on a charge of violating a prohibition statute. However, the sentence was suspended. Instead of going to jail, LaMare was allowed to go to work for the Ford Motor Co. in an indirect capacity.[30] Thanks to Harry Bennett, his new privileges at Dearborn were two-fold. He became a co-partner in a Ford sales agency known as the Crescent Motor Sales Co.,[31] and he was given a concession which empowered him to supply fruit for the food wagons that service Rouge employes during their lunch period. His income from the second source alone is said to have approximated $100,000 a year.

But reputable employment in no way sidetracked the criminal inclinations of Bennett's new protégé. According to the Detroit *Times*, LaMare continued as of old to expand the scope of his unlawful, outside business, exploiting the Ford connection merely as a "cloak of respectability."[32] While "technically employed at the automobile plant," a reporter for the Detroit *News* wrote in 1931, LaMare's "principal activities during that period unquestionably were in connection with the bootlegging industry. Detectives knew that during last winter [his] racketeering took on another ramification—preying on handbook operators in Detroit."[33]

The presence of this unregenerate concessionaire at Dearborn was a source of embarrassment to certain Ford officials. Without explaining his association with the company at the time, they went so far as to announce in May 1929, that he was not employed by the "Ford Service Department."[34] The fruit concession itself was canceled some time the following year, but not until LaMare had been implicated in the so-called fish market massacre that cost the life of Gaspare Scibilia, "the peacemaker" of a rival gang. Shortly after the occurrence of the fish market murder, LaMare himself became a marked man. The aspirants to his throne openly spread the word that his days were numbered. Joseph Palma, a Ford dealer on Staten Island and a former federal secret service man, made an effort to mediate this dispute in Detroit's underworld. He came on from New York to meet with representatives of the opposed factions during a private conference held in the Book-Cadillac Hotel. But the intercession was futile.[35]

Finally, at the conclusion of a bloody year marked by eleven local gang killings, LaMare was assassinated in his own home. His murderer was never apprehended. When the police ransacked LaMare's home, they found on the premises 4000 rounds of ammunition and a small arsenal of fully loaded weapons and gas bombs.[36]

As the short, bull-necked, swarthy Sicilian lay at rest in a $5000, silver-mounted casket, the threat of gang recriminations or of surprise arrests was so imminent that his wife was compelled to hire professional pallbearers. Taken into temporary custody, pending further investigation into her husband's murder, Mrs. LaMare was represented by Emil W. Colombo, brother and law partner of Louis J. Colombo, Sr., then chief counsel for the Ford Motor Co.[37]

By retaining as counsel a member of the firm of Colombo, Colombo and Colombo, the widow of Chester LaMare was entrusting her fate to a legal family of Italian extraction which had distinguished itself before the criminal bench of Michigan. The three Colombo brothers—Paul, Emil and Louis—had argued in court a good number of the state's outstanding criminal cases. The elder member of the firm, Louis J. Colombo, Sr., was identified with counsel for the Ford Motor Co. from 1928 through 1940. He brought to Dearborn a competent, professional knowledge of the intricate vendettas and subterranean interlacings of the community's criminal population.

The late Joe Tocco operated on the outer fringes of Ford Service. Tocco, another Sicilian and former confederate of LaMare, was once the leader of a notorious gang of West Side rum-runners. After investigating his home on a search warrant issued in 1931, police officers reported their discovery of a residential fortress the walls of which were lined with brick and armor-plate. Arrested time and again, but never convicted on any criminal charge, Tocco participated in his last gang feud in 1938. He was ambushed and shot to death. For burial, his body was encased in a silk-lined casket made of copper and secured at the lid by means of a combination lock.

Tocco was a frequent visitor both at the employment office of the Ford Motor Co. and in the private quarters of "The Little Man in Henry Ford's Basement."[38]

The criminal connections which existed on the fringes of Ford Service in the 30's were discernible in the murder trial of Leonard ("Black Leo") Cellura. "Black Leo" is one of the few gangsters of Detroit before whom the crime squad of the local police department really quailed. After working as Chester LaMare's partner for a time, "Black Leo" founded his own gang on the city's East Side.[39] Up to 1930, his police record in the city included ten arrests and one conviction.[40] He was fined $1000 in 1929 for bribing an agent of the federal border patrol. In the following year, he committed a crime that eventually brought his career to an end. In downtown Detroit on July 3, 1930, he shot and killed a pair of Chicago gangsters.

For the next six years "Black Leo" was a fugitive from justice.[41] Toward the close of his hideout, however, he made overtures to the county prosecutor's office to learn what sort of treatment he could expect if he were to stand trial. The intermediary who made this cautious inquiry was his former aide, Joe Tocco. Though informed that a "fair and vigorous trial" was awaiting him, Cellura voluntarily surrendered to the police in July, 1936.

In June of 1937, Cellura was finally convicted of first degree murder and was sentenced to spend the rest of his life in a state penitentiary.[42] To prevent that outcome the court had been subjected to persistent pressure from the underworld at large and from retainers of the Ford Motor Co. In pronouncing sentence, Judge Arthur E. Gordon took official note of such tactics by informing the prisoner that "efforts have been made by misguided persons even in the precincts of this court building to interfere with the ordinary course of a trial for murder and [they] have not ceased with ycur conviction. If these efforts are continued I may find it necessary to expose the persons making them."[43]

While awaiting trial, Cellura had been visited in his jail cell by various members of Ford Service and by John Gillespie. Showing unusual deference toward a suspect indicted on a double murder charge, Judge W. McKay Skillman had released the prisoner on bond, before trial.[44] It was after argument on a motion to give Cellura his freedom, pending his prosecution, that Gillespie made his boldest effort to intercede in the case. Seated in the courtroom, he had heard Assistant Prosecutor William L. Brunner oppose the motion on the ground that "Black Leo" was a notorious "killer" and a dangerous enemy of the State. At the close of the argument, Gillespie followed Brunner into the corridor where he allegedly tried to assault him, shouting at the State's attorney, "You can't call my friend a 'killer' and live in this town."

The court house scuffle was not an isolated instance of the link between Cellura and Dearborn. Shortly after his release on bail and before his conviction, "Black Leo" was seen riding about the streets of Detroit in a Ford car registered at the Motor Vehicle Bureau in Lansing under his own name "In care of the Ford Motor Co., Dearborn, Michigan."*

When the case was still being tried, Sam Cuva, a Ford Serviceman, comported himself so abusively that the bench had him arrested and held for examination. Cuva had attended the trial, sitting among the spectators in the front row, armed and glowering at witnesses and members of the jury. He informed the court that he had forgotten to leave his weapon at home. Cuva is an interesting character in his own right. Not long after Cellura's conviction, Cuva was himself convicted on a charge of assaulting with intent to murder. He was sentenced to spend one to four years in prison for shooting his mother-in-law.[45]

In their heyday, both the operatives of Ford Service and their allies were noted for their brawn and for scientific skill in one or another of the arts of physical aggression. In the opinion of John O'Brien, a Detroit newspaperman who dealt with "Henry Ford's Commander-in-Chief" in the February 1938 issue of *Forum* magazine, many of the sub-leaders and a fair proportion of the flotsam and jetsam of Ford Service were no more than "simple, husky gentlemen, handy in a rough-and-tumble with no holds barred."

* Michigan license, 1936; number Y 99614; title number, X 281490; motor number, 3332523.

For a number of years these abundant natural talents were developed at the Ford Motor Co. under the tutelage of "Kid" McCoy. When McCoy first appeared at Dearborn in 1932, Harry Bennett was quick to proclaim the man's faculties as a teacher. "When I started boxing," Bennett said at the time, "I didn't know how to take care of myself. See these hands? I couldn't fight without breaking them. Then I met the 'Kid' and he taught me most of the boxing tricks I know."[46] In the ring itself, the "Kid's" style of fighting was notorious.* As "athletic director" of the Ford Motor Co. he had an opportunity to transmit his science to those members of Ford Service who still had something to learn.

The common run of Bennett's appointees had reason indeed for feeling beholden to their benefactor. Their sense of obligation was deeper and more personal than the ties that usually bind employer and employe. It partook of the gratitude felt by John Gillespie, the flattened ex-millionaire, who confided to an acquaintance some time after his rejuvenation at Dearborn, "I could die for Harry Bennett."

Moreover, as in feudal days, the vassals of Ford Service could count on far-reaching protection, so long as they kept within reasonable bounds in the service of their liege lord. The Ford Servicemen who were more reckless and criminally inclined, occasionally ran afoul of the law in their private pursuits. In the course of a proceeding before the National Labor Relations Board, Bert Gantner, chief of Ford Service at the Ford assembly plant in St. Louis, testified that it was his custom to furnish professional bondsmen and attorneys for certain of his employes who became involved in criminal prosecution. He had come to the aid of such men, he said, by signing "possibly 200" bonds in 1935 and 1936 alone. In at least one case he reported having paid a court fine imposed on one of his subordinates.[48]

Even the outsiders of good repute who took advantage of the opportunity to place their nominees on the Ford payroll were submitting to a subtle, if informal, two-sided relationship. For in dealing with Bennett, they were meeting a master of the uncompleted contract. They were bargaining with an astute politician who was guided by the rule that for every favor granted, a quid pro quo may be demanded in return.

---

* A number of his ruses are famous. He sometimes disarmed an opponent by pretending to shake hands at the beginning of an early round, or by drawing a victim's attention to the fact that his "shoe was untied." Some of his more naive opponents who took the bait and dropped their guard were then floored for the count.[47]

## Twenty-three

### JOB NEUROSIS

#### 1

ONCE PERFECTED, Ford Service began to impose upon the entire personnel of the Ford Motor Co. a scheme of things that was both military and feudal. Its main business, ostensibly, was personal supervision and "plant protection." It set out to guard Ford's property and to help preserve along Ford's assembly lines that degree of discipline and coordination which is indispensable for successful mass production. But because of its make-up and because of the theory of management it betokened, Ford Service cast a far longer shadow over the men whose lives it presumed to regulate. In practice the department evolved into an engine of repression and regimentation for which no exact contemporary parallel can be found in any comparable locality in the United States.

Thanks to Ford Service, the factory of the River Rouge became an ingenious, if imperfect, replica of the Model T utopia of Aldous Huxley's *Brave New World*. Huxley's fanciful world and Harry Bennett's real one were alike in crowning Henry Ford as deity of all the universe. The author dates the beginning of time from the year in which Ford introduced the Model T. He has his characters, on hearing the slightest reference to the patron saint of Dearborn, make "the sign of the T" on their stomachs. The Ford employe, driven by Ford Service, found it quite as irregular and every bit as dangerous to question his employer's infallibility.

Bennett's universe and Huxley's again had common ends in sharing the same philosophy of human nature. Each was a machine order in which ant-like beings were expected to enjoy the drudgery of existence. Huxley has his "Director of Hatcheries and Conditioning" grind out numberless sets of half-witted, identical twins who are tagged for their mean status from the moment of conception. Bennett's efforts to eliminate the human equation became almost as extraordinary. The novelist and the director of Ford Service arrived at their respective heavens or hells by different paths. The machine tenders of the *Brave New World* are congenitally subnormal, bred in test tubes and reared like guinea pigs. Bennett, on the other hand, had to deal with normal beings, brought to the work-bench relatively late in life. In a quest for robots, he turned not to magic or super-science, but to Ford Service.

For something like two decades the Ford worker was marshaled into submissiveness by his mere knowledge of Bennett's alliance with the underworld and by the appearance of the Serviceman whose profession was written into his face. It became a standing jest in Detroit during this era to designate any primitive or wolf-like being by remarking that "he looks like a Ford Serviceman." At the same time the Toccos and the "Kid" McCoys were freely mentioned in the street-talk of the city. Moreover, by engaging in public brawls, a number of Bennett's men-at-arms kept reminding the entire community of the composition of Ford Service.

It was inside the Rouge, however, that the Ford employe could see the workings of Ford Service at firsthand. On the job he was constantly exposed to members of this department who were insolent, untrustworthy, and often violently inclined.

For years after Bennett came to power, it was the proud, undisguised aim of the Service Department to blot out every manifestation of personality or manliness inside a Ford plant. Striving for such an end, Bennett's mercenaries finally mastered every tactic from the swagger of the Prussian drill sergeant to outright sadism and physical assault. On the night shift they would jolt an incoming worker out of his wits and take the starch out of his system by flashing a light in his face and shouting at him, "Where did you get that badge?" or "Who's your boss?" Another intimidating practice that came into being under Bennett's rule was the act of "shaking 'em up in the aisles." In this case a workman summoned to the employment office for any reason at all, even one that was totally unrelated to his work, would be shoved and pushed along the aisle by a pair of officious Servicemen, like a felon in the custody of the police.

Certain members of the Bennett guard were not averse to administering floggings on company property. In 1932, in the main tool and die room of the Dearborn plant, a foreman was "pushing a job" on an undersized forge machine with the result that a steel block shot into the air, killing the operator on the spot. After being penalized by a short layoff, the foreman in question was soon back on the job, pushing the same operation at the same old pace. The new tender of the machine, a high-strung Polish worker tormented by the memory of what had happened to his predecessor, finally turned on the foreman in a state of frenzy. Four or five Servicemen immediately intervened. After beating the Pole unmercifully, they removed him from the plant. Other thrashings on the job, some of them administered simply by way of example to the rank and file, are familiar in the experience of countless older employes of the Ford Motor Co.

Even the tool and die men—the "aristocrats" of the Rouge—have felt the rough hand of Ford Service. A notable experience of this sort occurred in 1932, when these artisans were considering affiliation with a small, outside craft union. After a brief shutdown for inventory, the tool and die men returned to work to find that their private tool kits had been smashed and sacked. Their micrometers and precision gauges were missing. The rest of their instruments were strewn over the floor helter-skelter. Only maintenance men and the operatives of Ford Service had the run of the premises during the shutdown. Inasmuch as Bennett prided himself on factory protection and inasmuch as the tools were never recovered and no formal explanation of the pillage was ever forthcoming, the sabotage was commonly interpreted in the tool and die room as a signal from Ford Service that union-minded employes, even though they be master-craftsmen, had best keep their necks in their collars.

Nor were Bennett's rougher subordinates able to hold themselves back in the presence of certain Ford workers who were ailing, or had been injured on the job. One of his more callous henchmen strode into a first-aid station in 1937, followed by two sheepish-looking Negroes who were suffering from a summer complaint that is common among foundry workers. Glowering at his companions, the Serviceman ordered the first-aid man in attendance to "give 'em a shot of bismuth and Jamaica ginger. These niggers," he said, "claim they have diarrhea and keep walking off the job. Bind 'em up so's they can work." During the same year another colored man at the Rouge had his skull crushed by a double crane hook. As the man's lifeless body was being carried out on a stretcher, one attendant Serviceman remarked to another, in the presence of a reliable auditor, "If this would happen to a few more of these brown sons-a-bitches, we wouldn't have so much of a labor problem around here." Again, an intelligent medical assistant, new to the Rouge, was treating his first case in 1936. He was dressing a hand wound. To be civil and to facilitate his work, he had offered the patient a chair. Before he had finished, one of Bennett's toughs strutted into the station. After a quick glance at the injured man, the intruder croaked in a tone of voice that was instantly heeded, "What's *he* sittin' down for? That chair is for guys that can't stand up." A little later, the first-aid assistant asked his medical superior privately if he had broken some rule. He was told, "Unless you want to take a chance with the Service boys coming in, let 'em sit only if it's a leg or head case."

But the disciplinary whip which caused greater dread than periodic bullying or an occasional show of force at Dearborn was the facility of Ford Service in exploiting fear of the job. This practice at Ford's was the talk of the trade. In an industry which was characterized by chronic job insecurity even in the 20's, the operatives of Ford Service made matters worse by invoking the right to fire without appeal. Answerable to no one but Bennett, they could override the judgment of factory foremen and superintendents. They asserted such authority on so many occasions that, eventually, no Ford employe had the least assurance that the quality of his work in the shop was in any way related to his chances of survival on the payroll. As a result, the distance which separates the operating management at the top from the worker on the bottom in any large corporation became all the wider at Ford's. Between these two poles, Bennett had inserted a super-management whose agents constituted not only the police arm of the corporation and its ears and eyes, but its central nervous system as well.

As long as Bennett held sway, the employe of the Ford Motor Co. was cowed by the further knowledge that only a fraction of the activity of Ford Service was visible and above-board. The rest was underground. The feeling spread, therefore, that no one at Ford's could afford to trust his neighbor. It came to be common knowledge that snooping at the Rouge carried over to the pettiest details of a worker's daily experience. Thus, according to an unsolicited letter published in *Forbes' Magazine* twenty years ago, Ford men were conscious then of being trailed even when they took time out to go to the toilet.[1] In 1937, Servicemen in search of union cards rummaged through the lunch boxes of Ford workmen.

Moreover, the cult of espionage that tinged the Ford shops was quite as oppressive among the white-collar employes of the company. It enmeshed even the top administrators of the corporation. In his *American Mercury* piece of June 1940, John McCarten asserted, "[Bennett] created a vast espionage network, which included hundreds of undercover agents whose identity he kept secret from even his fellow-executives . . . the atmosphere of the plant soon became so thick with intrigue that Bennett himself had difficulty deciding who was shadowing whom from day to day."

The higher ramifications of Ford Service were illuminated by an episode involving Ernest Liebold, Henry Ford's formerly omnipotent private secretary. After a period of intense preoccupation with Ford's banking maneuvers, Liebold disappeared. He left town without notifying even his family, driving his car aimlessly over the state. Twenty-four hours later he was traced to a hotel in Traverse City where he had registered under the assumed name of W. F. Sampson.[2]

Meanwhile, the dragnet which Bennett stretched to fish for the missing Ford executive was of the finest mesh. It included every Ford dealer in Michigan, as well as gas station attendants and railroad ticket agents. County sheriffs, village marshals and the police of the commonwealth were mobilized for the search. The reporters who responded to Bennett's call were so numerous that by the time the errant, careworn executive reached Traverse City, he had been spotted at six points along a 600-mile route. He finally reported his own whereabouts after seeing his name flashed in a newspaper headline. He called Dearborn by telephone to say, "Tell Bennett I'm all right. Tell Mr. Ford, too."

The two Servicemen whom Bennett sent north as Liebold's escorts for the return trip to Detroit were the former boxer Elmer Hogan, and Verne Doonan, then Bennett's overseer of Dearborn elections. In a statement carried by the press, Bennett announced that the missing official was found to have on his person at Traverse City $3000 in cash and a sheaf of traveler's checks. It would seem, therefore, that Liebold was either searched or minutely cross-examined by the Servicemen who took him in tow. Reinstated at Dearborn, the fugitive was no longer designated by the press as Ford's private or personal secretary. He dropped out of sight, to be referred to by the newspapers on rare occasions only as a Ford secretary[3] or in other dispatches as Ford's former secretary.[4] The reasons for Liebold's subsequent eclipse in the Ford fold are something of a mystery. But the nature of the chase following his brief disappearance in 1933 is proof of Harry Bennett's skill at playing fox-and-hounds with a fellow executive.

## 2

Once its tentacles were fully grown, the Ford Service Department bred a state of mind in and about Detroit that could be duplicated only in those localities which have written the darker pages of American industrial history. In Ford's case, however, an oppressive discipline manifested itself not in a provincial steel town nor in a backwoods mining community, but in one of the country's largest metropolitan centers. The strained air that became characteristic of the Ford organization was perhaps unique in exempting from its spell no one in the corporation, high or low.

The temper of the Rouge was exemplified, as of 1939, even by the air of the reception room in the company's Engineering Laboratory. The room itself—a small, cheerless cell in an otherwise spacious building—was an architectural reminder that on Ford property even the ease and comfort of the business caller were out of place. In Ford's waiting room, unlike the Packard lobby or the General Motors corridor, were no comfortable lounges or brass cuspidors arranged for the convenience of the guest. While waiting for an interview, the Ford visitor who wished to smoke had to step outside. If he was familiar with the traditions of the Rouge, he took the further precaution of driving to his conference only in a Ford car.

Admitted to the suite of a Ford executive, or to the publicity office of the corporation, the casual visitor was likewise struck by the tense, guarded manner of the employes. This uneasy demeanor seemed to be, first, a by-product of the cult of man-worship that had long prevailed at Ford's. It also savored of the chilling effect of Ford Service. These executive mannerisms at Dearborn had several variants. The Ford publicist who gave one an audience in 1939 was ready, as ever, to eulogize The Man. The Man's name, when it entered the conversation, was always, reverently, "Mr. Henry" Ford. The Ford spokesman appeared to his caller as though he were walking on eggs for fear some Tom, Dick or Harry—other than Ford or Bennett—might be taken for an entity in his own right. If any Ford subordinate was inadvertently singled out because of some noteworthy performance, the Ford publicist would, as often as not, instantly qualify that distinction with some such remark as, "Oh, just forget I mentioned that. So-and-so is just one of Mr. Henry Ford's men. He wouldn't want his name known. He wouldn't want to stick his neck out."

A General Motors man, on the other hand, was by common agreement at this period much less inhibited. In his shop talk with an outsider he was far less self-conscious and much less idolatrous. He would speak of *his* work or of the *corporation*. He could hold forth more freely on ideas or on the trends of the trade. Names, big or little, might come and go in his conversation. If he mentioned the "boss" at all, it was "Sloan" or, before the second World War, "Bill Knudsen."

The public relations man at the Ford Motor Co. during the
Bennett regime ran to type in still another sense. He seemed to be
parroting phrases committed to memory; he talked *at* his listener
rather than *to* him. He would say repetitiously, "Everyone knows that
Mr. Bennett is a man of unusual physical courage," or "Well, of
course, Mr. Ford has a twenty-track mind." Officials who filled similar
positions elsewhere in the trade, on the other hand, seemed less
forced, much readier to talk. Within limits they spilled out at will
whatever thoughts came to mind. Moreover, by contrast with their
peers at the Ford Motor Co., the head men at Chrysler's or General
Motors were not only easier to talk to, but a hundred times easier
to see in the first place.

Even among their familiars, Ford's administrators, hedged about
by Ford and Bennett, acquired a reputation for this same nervous
pulling-in. Under the Bennett regimen there was little of the inter-
office banter that the most casual observer could overhear in the
General Motors building on Grand Boulevard, and almost none of
the executive manner that looks like soldiering but is actually a method
of doing business.

The Ford dealer was likewise more constrained than most of
his competitors. He did not feel at liberty to unburden himself on
company policy, other than in the presence of his closest friends. One
of the firm's energetic Eastern dealers entered into such a discussion
with a stranger whom he had met through a mutual acquaintance in
1939 by remarking, with evident embarrassment, "I'd be perfectly
willing to go into this subject with you, if I could be absolutely sure
who you are. Harry Bennett has some pretty slick customers at work
around the country. As it is, I've stuck my neck out pretty far already."

Employes on every rung of the Ford ladder came to respond to
the eccentric, tight discipline and the catlike watchfulness of Ford
Service by showing every manner of job anxiety. This state of mind
at Ford's was a common subject of gossip in the trade. *Fortune*
magazine in its issue of December 1933, could observe that "Mr.
Ford's organization does show extreme evidence of being ruled
primarily by fear of the job." As a rule, Ford's managers, having
more to lose, came to watch their jobs more nervously than the man
at the Rouge who swept the floor.

On the lower tiers of the Ford organization, Ford Service gave
rise to any number of unmistakable industrial neuroses. These "shop
complaints" went all the way from mild states of anxiety to advanced
nervous symptoms that were fit material for a psychopathic ward. Thus

conditioned, the personality of many a Ford employe was subjected to a process of subtle and profound degradation.

Any number of idiosyncrasies bore witness to the stifling effect of regimentation within the Rouge. Chatting or fraternizing with work-mates during the lunch hour was taboo in the old days which lasted twenty years or more. It was then the rule during the noon-day spell to see a Ford employe squat on the floor, glum and uncommunicative, munching his food in almost complete isolation. The locked-in manner of the Ford worker supposedly at ease was remarked by Raymond J. Daniell who observed in the New York *Times* on October 31, 1937, "The visitor [at the Rouge] is struck by the restraint among the workers; even in moments of idleness, men stand apart from one another."

Ford men, before long, became noted for their ingenuity in circumventing the ironclad law against talking at their work. They developed an art of covert speech known as the "Ford whisper." Masters of this language, like inmates in a penal institution, could communicate in undertones without taking their eyes from their work. If Ford or Sorensen were about to tour the plant, even the plant foremen knew how to spread the word by resorting to the "grapevine."

Ford's tool and die men used to be governed by the same taboo, though their work by its very nature compelled them to move about. Long ago, these craftsmen invented their own brand of hidden talk. Their technique was to exchange small talk while gesticulating in mock earnestness at parts of a lathe, or while feigning interest in a blueprint. One highly intelligent artisan in this department invented a type of "Ford speech" all his own. He learned to talk like a ventriloquist. After spending ten years in Ford's service, this man became the laughing stock of his wife and friends, for the habit of talking out of the side of his mouth without moving his lips finally became ungovernable; he began to talk that way unconsciously, at home or in the most casual conversation with someone outside after working hours.

"Fordization of the face" was once the rule among all Ford men at work, inasmuch as humming, whistling or even smiling on the job were, in the judgment of Ford Service, evidence of soldiering or insubordination. John Gallo, a Rouge employe, was discharged in November 1940—caught in the act of "smiling," after having committed an earlier breach of "laughing with the other fellows," and slowing down the line "maybe half a minute." At a formal hearing on the case, a state labor referee gave it as his opinion that while a shop rule prohibiting the least show of levity may have been acceptable under the "Puritans" and in the day of the old "overseer," such a ban was hardly in keeping with the standards of "this enlightened age." Inasmuch as he could establish no demonstrable connection between "smiling" and efficiency in this case the referee ruled that Gallo was entitled to full benefits under the unemployment compensation act. The award was bitterly contested by Ford counsel.[5]

The taut nerves of a Ford employe snapped in public in the course of testifying at an inquest called to investigate a case of cyanide poisoning that occurred at the Rouge in 1935. The witness was a healthy, phlegmatic specimen of foreign extraction. He was reporting on the use of cyanide in his own department. His manner on the stand, up to a point, was frank, easy and uninhibited. Then all at once he swooned and nearly slipped to the floor. An attorney in the room later learned what had caused the fainting spell. The witness had been seated so that he could see the doorway at the rear of the hearing chamber. He fainted a moment or so after he saw the head of his department walk into the room.

En route to the Rouge on Christmas Day of 1936, a bright and personable white-collar worker tried an experiment in the psychology of Ford inhibitions. To each of the ten or twelve night-shift men whom he passed one by one on their way to a factory exit, the incoming worker extended a cheery "Merry Christmas." One of the passers-by mumbled a sheepish greeting in return. A second workman came to a dead stop. He was speechless and flabbergasted; he stared at the man who had greeted him, as much as to say, "What's eatin' the guy!" The rest passed by in silence without so much as looking the well-wisher in the eye.

## Twenty-four

### COMMUNITY NEUROSIS

### 1

BENNETT DID MORE than keep watch inside the Rouge. He stalked the Ford employe in his private life as well. Thus an 8-hour factory neurosis was transmuted into a 24-hour community neurosis, and many a Ford employe was sheared of some of his rights as a private citizen, after working hours. There were times when Bennett set himself up as an inquisitor-at-large in the act of enforcing one or another of Ford's periodic dry crusades. He mustered the resources of Ford Service for the purpose of putting teeth into the edict of 1930 which ordered every Ford employe, on pain of dismissal, to stop drinking liquor either in public or even in the privacy of his own home.*

To satisfy still another of Ford's whims, Bennett invoked the 1932 experiment in compulsory gardening. This was the program under which every man in the corporation was expected to hoe potatoes under the surveillance of "Kid" McCoy.

Poaching on still another private preserve, Ford at one time or another began to hound the men who worked for him into buying his own product. This means of grubbing for sales was characteristic in good times and bad. Bennett, as usual, did the squeezing. His men would start out by combing the company parking lot to identify the employe who drove to work in a car made by anyone other than Ford. After rounding up such potential customers, Ford Service would tip off an outside Ford dealer to the effect that such and such a Ford worker was "in the market." At the same time a foreman or Service-man would advise the "prospect" of his "availability." All this was known to the automobile finance men of Detroit, who invented a special term for the Serviceman or foreman who made a point of digging up prospective car buyers from within the Ford personnel. These informers came to be known in the retail trade as "Ford's bird dogs."

Before long all the reputable leaders of the industry were aware of the "bird dog" technique at Dearborn. When the financial district

---

* This ban, insofar as it applied to the Ford employe, was international. It had to be suspended, however, at Ford's rubber plantation in the Amazon Valley. In this South American colony, "Fordlandia," drinking was sanctioned among the white American overseers, but prohibited for the Brazilian rank and file. Where-upon the native laborers of the plantation called a strike. They were coaxed back to work only after being guaranteed their spot of rum.[1]

Ford had a perfect legal right to dictate the moral code of Fordlandia. His contract with the State of Para, covering an area of 4,000,000 acres of jungle strip, invested the Ford Motor Co. with autonomous police powers in perpetuity. More than that, the contract called for a 50-year exemption from taxes, an immunity from certain impost duties and a perpetual monopoly in the mineral, waterpower and surface rights of the area.

Founded in 1927, Fordlandia was Ford's answer to the price-gouging tactics of the international rubber cartel dominated by the Dutch and British. Any number of serious labor disturbances punctuated the development of the planta-tion. Even so, Ford had a better labor record here than most of his Dutch and British competitors.[2]

was still amusing itself at Ford's expense, the *Wall Street Journal* once tracked down the rumor of "forced sales" at the Ford Motor Co. It sent a reporter to list the makes of cars that were parked on the lot set aside for Ford employes. This check was made in 1926 when, in popular favor, the old Ford product was on its last legs. The count for the Model T was, nonetheless, 91 per cent.[3] The same pressure for "sales from within" was all the greater at Ford's six years later, despite the depression and despite the fact that most of Ford's men who were employed at all were working irregularly and on short shifts. At least so said R. H. Grant, a General Motors vice-president, on December 9, 1932, in the course of addressing the sales managers of the General Motors Corporation. After announcing that any GM employe who wanted to buy a General Motors product could take advantage of a special discount, Grant said, "We don't check cars in the yard. The reason I mention coercion is with particular regard to Ford."[4]

In response to such goading and to this watch over their taste in motor cars, Ford's men reacted variously. Many must have preferred the Ford car of their own accord. Others conformed so as not to become marked men. Others succumbed, buying Fords on time in the hope that their jobs would be secure as long as an unpaid balance remained outstanding. One evasion to which certain non-conformists retreated is said to have embarrassed the company. According to Walter M. Cunningham, the former Ford publicist, the firm once issued a formal order to the effect that the company parking lot would be open only to drivers of a Ford car. The ineligible motorists continued to drive to work, said Cunningham, but they began tucking their cars out of sight on side streets and vacant lots, within walking distance of the plant. The peripheral overflow, said the former Ford advertiser, had the effect of placing an impressive number of Chevrolets in public view within the immediate environs of the Ford shop; the ban was quickly lifted.[5]

But the "bird dogs" remained, though some of the prey fought back. The more resourceful, non-conforming Ford employe beat the game, after buying some other make of car, by never driving to work, or by registering the title to his automobile in someone else's name. Other Ford employes tried to slacken the pressure through publicity. During the second year of the depression, when browbeating Servicemen were scratching for orders on the Model A, which was about to be closed out, any number of Ford workers began to flood the Detroit *News* with anonymous protest letters.[6] Perhaps the majority of the men at the Rouge tolerated the imposition of being told what to buy in motor cars, and when to buy it, as one of the least of Ford's invasions of their privacy.

In trying to dictate how the Ford employe should spend his free time, Ford Service was perhaps most blatant in its management of the political conscience of the city of Dearborn. Dearborn, a suburb of Detroit, is the home of the Ford Motor Co. Most of its 50,000 or more inhabitants were beholden to Henry Ford for a living. Most of them also know that for many a year their municipality had all the earmarks of a private duchy over whose affairs they, as citizens and taxpayers, have had little or no say.

The chief cogs in the machine by which Bennett dominated the civic life of Dearborn for ten or fifteen years were Municipal Judge Leo J. Schaeffer and two former Ford Servicemen, Verne Doonan and the late Carl Brooks. For most of this period Brooks was the city's chief of police. He had graduated to that office direct from Ford Service. This earlier tie to Ford was first revealed in 1927 when Brooks' signature appeared on the mass affidavit that brought the Sapiro trial to a halt. Later the same year Brooks and a "fellow named Brady" were mentioned in court during Bennett's first divorce action. When the bench asked to have this pair identified, Bennett remarked, "They are a couple of fellows . . . I don't care to discuss that unless I have to."[7] Two years later, in 1929, Brooks was a full-fledged Ford detective. Under Bennett's command, he was directing the plant police at Highland Park.[8] He relinquished this post in order to become Dearborn's chief of police. Brooks remained in office for the next twelve years. He was suspended in May 1941, following his indictment in Circuit Court on a charge of having accepted bribes to protect the criminal element which had flourished in the community under his regime.[9]

Verne Doonan, like Brooks, was another product of Ford Service. Doonan was likewise one of the co-signers of the Sapiro affidavit. His connection with Ford Service was further revealed by the errand which took him and the former prize fighter, Elmer Hogan, to Traverse City in 1933 to retrieve the errant Ford executive, Ernest Liebold. From 1929 on, Doonan became Bennett's utility man in Dearborn politics. This assignment, at least in critical elections, involved the job of acting as campaign manager for candidates approved by Ford Service. In 1935, Doonan successfully supported for the mayoralty an aspirant for the office whom he advertised openly as the choice of the Ford Motor Co.[10] For the most part, this former Ford Serviceman ruled the roost ex officio, behind the scenes. He did hold local office, however, at one crucial period. He was the city's Safety Commissioner in 1932. Acting in that capacity, he was in a position to issue a formal apology for the Servicemen and the local police who had resorted to force to suppress the Ford Hunger March.

In the person of Municipal Judge Leo J. Schaeffer, who sat on the local bench consecutively for some fifteen years, Harry Bennett had a political ally of the first order. By virtue of his office Schaeffer could act, all this while, as one of the city's final arbiters of free speech and free assembly. He represented, consequently, the judicial arm of the police power of the city, the authority who was entrusted with the enforcement of any and all municipal ordinances. This judge, in whose court many of Bennett's machinations came to a jell, was leagued with the Ford Motor Co. financially as well as socially. He was one of Dearborn's favorite sons. His father was an old settler and a close friend of Henry Ford's. While holding court in Dearborn City Hall, the jurist was doing a remunerative business with the Fords on the side. His Schaeffer Lunch Co., a family-owned enterprise, enjoyed catering privileges similar to the fruit concession which Bennett once tendered to the gangster, Chester LaMare. Thanks to this sideline, which consisted of selling lunches to the Ford factory worker, the judge in 1937 was making a net income of $50,000 a year.[11]

To fortify the machine in which Doonan, Brooks and Schaeffer were top men, and to capture the city administration as a whole, Bennett utilized in the main a technique that came to be known in the locality as "sweetening the payroll." This device, applied by his deputies during an electoral contest, consisted of padding the payroll of the Ford Motor Co. with known supporters of the Ford slate. First-hand acquaintance with such a practice was admitted by Bruce Turrell, a former Ford employe, who testified in a government hearing in 1941 that his first assignment as a member of Ford Service was to work under Doonan, checking voters' lists to see that the "right" people got jobs at the Rouge.[12] Under cross-examination by Ford counsel in 1941, Turrell admitted having served a sentence in the state penitentiary on a conviction of burglary. His record also included a term of service as a professional labor spy.

For years Bennett's practice of "putting men on" at election time was enough to win the vote of Dearborn's West Side, the home of Ford bosses, old settlers, tradesmen and professional people. It usually gave him a comfortable majority in job-conscious South

Dearborn, the section of the town inhabited largely by men who worked at the Rouge with their hands.

The effect of a job scare on South Dearborn was demonstrated in 1929, when the voters of that area decided by popular referendum to come in with Dearborn and do away with their separately incorporated city, then known as Fordson. Before the merger, Fordson had elected an independent ticket time and again. The move for consolidation was a stroke of gerrymandering conceived by Ford's political strategists. When petitions calling for the referendum were circulated in 1928, Ford's signature led the list.[13] The vote on the issue was delivered by Bennett's electioneers, who took to the field under Doonan's supervision. The voters were given the traditional promise of a feast of jobs with a Ford victory or a famine of work with a Ford defeat. Put to the people in such a manner, the proposition for amalgamation carried. With the loss of its political independence, Fordson then became South Dearborn. Swallowed by Greater Dearborn, the uncontrolled vote of this workers' community was, until fairly recently, largely nullified.

Besides swinging Dearborn elections with the leverage of Ford jobs, Bennett sought to clinch his control by filling the community with informers the year around. The function of such undercover agents was twofold. They kept Ford Service posted on the activity of every conspicuous, dissident citizen in the locality, and they fostered a fear psychology which was in itself a method of molding the political temper of the city and of circumscribing the influence of its political freethinkers.

The spies whom Bennett detailed to Dearborn were usually disguised operatives of Ford Service. They were professional informers, employed by the Ford Motor Co. to nose about the city on company time. One of their number was Ralph Rimar, the ex-Ford spy whose serial "confessions" appeared in 1941 in the New York newspaper *PM*. Rimar asserts that, while directing a sub-section of secret agents whose business it was to shadow Ford workers and other residents of Dearborn from 1933 to 1935, he gave his reports not to Bennett, but to Bennett's political intermediaries, Brooks and Doonan.[14]

The content of such reports may be inferred from the thoroughness of the eavesdropping. In Rimar's words, "My own agents reported back to me conversations in grocery stores, meat markets and restaurants, gambling joints, beer gardens, social groups, boys' clubs and even churches. Women waiting in markets buying something might discuss their husbands' jobs and activities; if they did, I soon heard what they said . . ."[15]

For use against either townsmen or outsiders who still dared to think of Dearborn as an open city, Bennett forged a weapon that was even cruder than espionage or fear of the job. This extra sword, first unsheathed during the depression, was an auxiliary of Ford Service known as the Knights of Dearborn. The Knights were to operate, as the occasion might require, either as a pseudo-patriotic political machine or as a reservoir of middle-class as well as professional vigilantes. It was organized by Verne Doonan. Its later disposition is personified by the leader whom Ford Service placed at its command from 1937 to 1938. This later appointee was Sam Taylor, a Ford boss and strong-arm man. In addition to having been a heavy-weight boxer and one of Bennett's fellow sailors in the Navy, Taylor came to Dearborn as a renegade from the International Molders Union of the American Federation of Labor. He was hired by the Ford Motor Co. in 1936, one year after his official expulsion from the molders' union on a charge of embezzling strike funds.[16]

## 2

Any curious resident of Detroit—either Ford worker or citizen-at-large—who missed the import of Dearborn politics could have watched Ford Service in action on a larger political stage simply by reading his daily newspaper. By the late 30's he would have gathered from the public prints that Harry Bennett was a power and a past master in the state councils of the Republican Party.

Certain prominent Republicans went so far as to express public concern at this time when it was evident that Ford's director of personnel was taking a hand in the internal affairs of the state university at Ann Arbor. This invasion of an area so remote from the business of making automobiles occurred during the state elections of 1939. It was then that Bennett demonstrated the political authority of the Ford Motor Co. by placing his protégé, Harry Kipke, on the board of regents of the University of Michigan. Kipke is the former football coach who was discharged at Ann Arbor in 1937, and whose subsequent quick rise to affluence in the automobile business had demonstrated the scope of Bennett's patronage.

The campaign which gave the deposed coach a seat on the board of governors of his alma mater was directed from the headquarters of Ford Service. At Bennett's dictation, the Republican delegation from Wayne County came to the party's state convention of February 1939, pledged to Kipke in advance. That bloc of votes represented nearly one-third of the total strength of the full state delegation. When the nominating convention was called to order in the city of Flint, Bennett and his aspirant for the regency appeared together at the Hotel Durant where they could mix with delegates from other parts of the state. The former coach and his patron had just returned from a cruise in the Caribbean.[17] On the convention floor where the nomination won formal party approval, Kipke's most active lobbyist was Louis J. Colombo, Jr., the son of the lawyer who was then chief counsel for the Ford Motor Co.[18]

For tactical reasons Bennett took pains at election time to gloss over the fact that his nominee was a candidate of the Ford Motor Co. He was guided by the tradition that an open "Ford" endorsement is often fatal to a candidate's success in any state election. Dropping into the background, he delegated the active management of the Kipke campaign to Frank P. Nolan, a Ford lawyer and political go-between. At one point, however, Bennett was forced to issue a guarded, public statement. Prominent university alumni known to be conservative Republicans were too vocal to be ignored in their repudiation of Kipke's base of support and in their charge that university meddling on the part of any private corporation was undesirable and without precedent. When Bennett did speak up in self-defense, he did not disown his candidate. On the contrary, he aped the language of Henry Ford in such a manner that Kipke's sponsorship was unmistakable. To answer his critics, Bennett averred that the ex-coach's defeat was desired only by the "banking interests." Whatever the opposition, Kipke was elected. Although deserted by a distinguished minority from within his own ranks, his campaign had state-wide party support in an election year marked by a general Republican renaissance in Michigan politics.

The auspices to which the new regent owed his triumphant return to the Ann Arbor campus were verified by the character of the dinner which was held at the Hotel Statler to celebrate the victory. This social affair was unpublicized. Kipke took his oath of office during the evening. The most conspicuous celebrants at the banquet table were Bennett and his personal entourage. The guests included young Colombo and Charles Sorensen, the Ford production manager. The toastmaster for the evening was the Ford lawyer and political ally, former County Prosecutor Harry S. Toy. Surrounded by Stan Fay, Chuck Bernard, and Harry Newman—three members of his

personal staff who were All-American football players at Michigan—
Bennett, the regent-maker, was in high spirits throughout the ceremony. He strutted about the hall, very much the center of attention.
His cause for self-satisfaction was not dampened when Kipke was
called upon for remarks. In a formal speech of acceptance the former
coach, who was now vested with a measure of control over the educational life of the state, was frank in acknowledging a supreme debt to
his "close friend, Harry Bennett."

It was, however, during the Wayne County Republican convention of September 1940 that Ford Service gave the least camouflaged
demonstration of its mature political strength and slickness. This
party gathering was called for the purpose of naming delegates to a
forthcoming Republican State Convention. The proceedings in question were of more than local importance inasmuch as the Republican
forces of Michigan were balanced in such a way at this time that
whoever succeeded in controlling the Wayne County delegation would
automatically fall heir to party leadership throughout the state.

Harry Bennett set out to seize this control in the interests of the
Ford Motor Co. The field general whom he used for this purpose
was John Gillespie. Gillespie will be remembered as the once-powerful
local politician whom Bennett had restored to prosperity by setting
him up as an "insurance broker" and favoring him with a lucrative
Ford account.[19] From the outset Bennett and Gillespie were able
to name approximately a third of the delegates who were to attend
the critical 1940 county convention. The press was most explicit in
describing this group of delegates as the "Bennett faction" or the
"Ford bloc."[20] The so-called Ford delegation consisted for the most
part of employes of the Ford Motor Co.[21]

Two other mutually suspicious factions were to be represented
on the floor of the county convention in sufficient strength to be able
to block Bennett's intended coup. One of these competing delegations
comprised the supporters of Edward N. Barnard, the stalwart who had
dominated the Republican machine of the county for a decade. The
remaining bloc represented the followers of Fred M. Alger, Jr., a
descendant of one of the state's influential oldest families. The Alger
forces stood for nothing basically new in party doctrine. They were
simply a body of "Young Republicans" who were "anti-boss" or openly
pledged to unseat Barnard, the traditional party chieftain.

Before the convention was called to order, Bennett, working
through Gillespie, managed to come to terms with both of the non-
Ford delegations. Alger's workers and Alger's "anti-boss" literature

were placed at his disposal.[22] At the same time "Boss" Barnard was
induced to merge his forces with Bennett's with the secret understanding that Bennett would be allowed to name the chairman of the
convention and that one-half of the county representation at the party's
state convention would fall to the "Ford machine;" the other half, to
Barnard.[23] The nominee for the chair whom Barnard consequently
agreed to support was Henry G. Hoppe, a Ford politician and an
employe of the Ford Motor Co.[24]

The moment the power of the chair actually passed to the Ford
delegation—with Hoppe installed as presiding officer of the day—
Bennett went back on his word, cutting his would-be ally, Barnard,
out of the picture. Before most of the delegates to the Wayne County
Republican convention could collect their wits, Chairman Hoppe
announced the appointment of Harry S. Toy as a committee-of-one
to select the full delegation to the subsequent state convention. Toy
was another Bennett man.* Having dropped the plum of the convention in Bennett's lap, Hoppe arbitrarily declared that the convention
stood adjourned and, assailed from all sides as a "robber" and a
"horse thief," he then left the hall. Shortly thereafter the lights went
out in the auditorium and the Alger and Barnard delegations were
left to their own devices, raging and milling about on the convention
floor in darkness.[26]

The leaders of each of the Republican blocs which Bennett and
Gillespie had brushed aside by intrigue could hardly contain them-
selves. Barnard charged that he had been duped by the Ford machine.
"I'm not going to stand by," he said, "and let Gillespie and the
Ford Motor Co. take control of the Republican Party affairs in this
state."[27] In an acrid manifesto which he released to the press, young
Alger averred that he, as well as "Boss" Barnard, had received "the
double-cross and the triple-cross" from "Bennett and the Ford Motor
Co."[28] In his efforts to negotiate with Bennett and Gillespie, Alger
said, he had been "a novice dealing with past masters in the political
art of sleight of hand." Finally, in a blaze of anger this scion of one
of the first families of Michigan berated the principals of the convention by calling Chairman Hoppe a mere Ford "stooge;" Gillespie,
Bennett's "worn-out, discredited political plod-horse;" and Harry S.
Toy, "the front man for Bennett and Gillespie."

Because of the fact that Bennett's political upsurge was accom-

* Toy's connections with Bennett and the Ford Motor Co. were not new. The
man had been employed as legal counsel for the Ford Motor Co. In the primaries
of 1938 Toy had had Ford support in his unsuccessful candidacy for the governorship.[25]

panied by so much fanfare and controversy, the Ford worker who read the newspapers was in a position to round out the knowledge of Ford Service that was part of his daily experience. The party machinations of 1940 in particular gave him a wider insight into the character of the Ford executive whom he recognized as the principal force in the shop. No Ford worker of average intelligence could have missed the point that Bennett was a master of intrigue on the political front. Few could have failed to note the similarity between various industrial operatives of Ford Service and some of the agents who symbolized the authority, if not the name, of the Ford Motor Co. in the political life of the community.

To the minds of many a Ford employe the fact, as well as the style, of Bennett's political conquests of 1940 must have demonstrated the power of the man and the breadth of his operations. He may have appeared in their eyes as a force too big to oppose, either inside or outside the plant. He acquired part of his aura of invincibility by the very makeup of the "Ford" delegation which was leagued with Gillespie, the Ford politician, on the floor of the county convention. According to the papers, most of the state employes who were delegates to the convention had worked in concert with Bennett's scheme to seize the chair.[29]

If any mill-hand at Dearborn raised the issue as to whether or not the wide political authority of Ford Service would be devoted to the public interest, this question had occurred to others. It had been remarked by middle-class liberals and by conservative Republicans in the course of the Bennett-Kipke campaign for the university regency. On the eve of Kipke's election, Junius E. Beal, the retiring Republican regent whom Kipke replaced, asked the voters of the state to "rebuke" what he called an "irregular" procedure in the choice of a university director.[30] Simultaneously, an open protest letter was sent to the university's 30,000 alumni by James K. Watkins, a well-known Republican and former Rhodes scholar who had served under Frank Murphy as Detroit's commissioner of police. In an appeal to the voters, Watkins termed the Kipke candidacy "an affront to the present board of regents and the university." "We are likewise convinced," he said, "that the activities of Mr. Bennett cannot be beneficial to the public in general and the university in particular."[31] Over the same issue, even the Detroit News was less cautious than usual in its treatment of a "Ford" topic. What "worries the university's friends," said one of the paper's columnists, is whether Kipke will represent at Ann Arbor "the people of Michigan, or the Republican boss and the representative of the motor corporation to whom he is politically indebted."[32]

Bennett's regent-making, while successful, had been rejected most conspicuously by the university community itself. The student senate on the campus passed a unanimous resolution in which Kipke's election was condemned as "detrimental to the best interest of the university." In the judgment of the highest ranking student body at the university, the discharged coach was unqualified for the office of regent because of "his affiliations, his connection with machine politics, and his lack of training for the position."[33] Though he was elected on the basis of state-wide returns, Kipke made local party history by failing to carry Ann Arbor, the university seat, and the surrounding county of Washtenaw, where he and Bennett resided. But for its desertion of the "Ford" candidate for the regency, Washtenaw had voted the straight Republican ticket without interruption ever since the day of Abraham Lincoln.

New to some, but familiar to most observant Ford workers who had no part in the convention of 1940 was the fact that the majority of Bennett's delegates were Negroes who were working for a living at the Ford Motor Co. Bennett's chief Negro hiring agent and political boss was Donald Marshall, and the secret of this man's status as the acknowledged, if unofficial, "mayor" of Detroit's Harlem, was his power to reward hand-picked Negroes with "tickets to the gate" of the Ford Motor Co. The same authority in the local colored community was then vested in Willis Ward, Marshall's first assistant. But unlike his immediate superior, who was a former policeman, Ward had polish, education and the prestige of having been one of the state's greatest college athletes.

Bennett had crossed the color-line for a number of years to fill approximately one-tenth, or some 10,000, of the available factory jobs at Dearborn. Few colored men had been employed on the higher rungs, on jobs that are light and clean, or situated in the cooler portions of the plant. Most Ford Negroes were to be found in the foundry or on the loading platform, where the work is relatively dirty, heavy and dangerous.* Nonetheless, the Ford job had extraordinary lure

* When Joe Louis, the world's heavyweight boxing champion, was training for a match in Detroit in 1939, he put his finger on the type of work which is the Negro's usual lot at the Ford Motor Co. His pointed observation was made in the course of a formal interview with Don Marshall, the company's Negro boss. Knowing that Louis was a former Ford worker, as well as the idol of Detroit's colored colony, Marshall called at the training camp. He had his picture taken with the champion and advised him that his "old job" at Dearborn was "waiting for him"

in the colored belts of greater Detroit. It was sought after because
of the premium attached to Negro employment of any sort at all.
It worked like a magnet because at that time there was no other
large-scale employer of the race anywhere in the area.

Consequently, in his past relations with the Detroit Negro,
Bennett had been dealing with another desperate and dependent
social group. In this case the subjects of his preferment represented
the most acutely underprivileged cross section of the entire region.
The race reservoir into which he dipped for Ford labor comprised
only 10 per cent of Detroit's population, yet its people had contributed
one-third of the city's permanent relief clients and one-fourth of the
county's juvenile delinquents. Blackbottom and Paradise Valley, the
Negro sections of the city, were pools of chronic unemployment. The
wage earners of this stranded population of nearly 200,000 had been
job hungry.

For a considerable period of time, up to 1940, Ford Service had
exploited the economic plight of the local Negro by trading jobs for
votes. This bargain was implicit in an unwritten contract between the
Ford Negro and the men who employed him. Its terms were reiterated
publicly and repeatedly by the Ford lieutenants, Ward and Marshall.
The stakes of the game, from the standpoint of the Ford Motor Co.,
constituted control of the colored vote, or of one-eighth of the ballots
cast in a normal city election.

As his bargain counter—over which bread was exchanged for
ballots—Bennett used, at one interval, even the churches of the race.
This intrusion into the religious life of the community became so
flagrant in 1938 that an independent Negro clergyman in the locality
published a protest in the *Christian Century*.[35] His account of the
Ford practice appeared under the title, "Who Owns the Negro
Churches?"

At that time all amenable colored preachers were privileged to
name a certain number of their parishioners for placement on the
Ford payroll. Such a clergyman added to his religious duties, therefore, the appointive power of an unofficial hiring agent of the Ford
Motor Co., and the greater a given pastor's reputed influence with the
Ford employment office, the larger his congregation. The process was
contagious. Indeed, the local Negro clergyman could resist it only at
the risk of addressing empty pews. Once he was the debtor of the

any time he cared to come back. To this politic, if clumsy, gesture the prizefighter replied, "There's just one thing, though—I don't want to be lifting those
heavy old frames. I want something easier than that when I come back."[34]

Ford Motor Co., he had responsibilities as well as prerogatives. The price of his preferment was, in part, the delivery of the Negro vote as prescribed by Ward and Marshall.

It was the inability or the unwillingness of these religious shepherds to meet their obligations that moved Ford Service to discard their services in 1939. The Negro flocks simply refused to vote the straight Republican ticket. As canny as Bennett, they had managed to get Ford jobs, through church channels or, in other cases, independently, but they voted as they chose. In the Roosevelt campaign of 1936 and in the campaign of Gov. Frank Murphy a year later, the Negro preachers proved so ineffectual as Republican whips that Bennett threw them overboard. He founded his own Negro machine in the fall of 1939. Ward and Marshall built a tight neighborhood organization that they could control directly. For the next year and a half, colored applicants no longer went to church in search of the "word" that would open the gates of the Ford Motor Co.

Hence, the only novelty about the "Ford" delegation on the floor of the Republican county convention of September 1940, was the brazenness with which Bennett bared his bread-and-butter leverage in the city's colored community. His convention strength, mustered largely from the Negro element, was simply his most dramatic show of power. Emphatic enough in convention to catapult him into the highest ranks of party control, it served to remind the rank and file Ford employe who was on the outside looking in, that at bottom, it was jobs like his own and the practice of feeding them into a vast hopper of patronage that had given the Ford Motor Co. its preeminence in Republican circles. In his political designs, bartering "tickets to the gate" in exchange for influence was Bennett's masterkey, applicable to whites as well as Negroes.*

Such, in essence, was the Ford neurosis. The temper produced by Ford Service inside the Rouge was so like the morale of a Prussian army corps that the similarity was a commonplace of the trade, a truism among Detroit automobile workers, and the inspiration of a distinctive regional folklore. Bennett's field of action was state-wide and political, as well as plant-wide and industrial. Under such a regime, the traditional American freedoms were, in fact, less available

---

* Also, Ford money was being used to subsidize party activity in the orthodox manner. Edsel Ford made good the reported deficit of the Republican State Central Committee following the Michigan elections of 1938. He wrote out a personal check for that purpose, to the sum of $9918, after conferring with Bennett and the politician Frank D. McKay. McKay, at the time, was a Republican national committeeman for Michigan.[36]

to Ford men than to any other set of workers in the trade. All Ford employes were told, on occasion, how to live and what to buy. With some—Negroes and residents of Dearborn in particular—tenure in the mill was directly dependent upon political subservience. None of the rank and file in Ford's employ could be certain, from his work record alone, that his place would not be next in Bennett's brisk business of trading jobs for political preferment. It was this traffic, in particular, that made the Ford shop neurosis and the Ford community neurosis one and indivisible.

## Twenty-five

### EX-BOXER

### 1

T HE CONFLICT between Ford Service and the great Ford myth inspired three vigorous sub-legends at Dearborn. These subsidiary fables were furbished for a common end—to give face to the more disreputable element within Ford Service and to square the Ford dream with the harsh realities of the Ford neurosis. Most of these sub-myths are peculiar to Greater Detroit. They are as diverse in origin as the mother legend which they were thrown up to protect. Not a few have sprung from a will to believe on the part of ordinary Americans who understood a portion of the facts but never enough to doubt that Henry Ford, despite Ford Service, was warm and human and social, and distinguished among industrialists by his democratic respect for men as men.

One of the masks which Dearborn began to wear in order to camouflage the function of Ford Service could be called the fiction of rehabilitation. According to this defense, Bennett, in the choice of his rougher men-at-arms, was acting in the capacity of a reclaimer of fallen men. As a friend of the wayward and the down-trodden, he was purported to be observing the best tradition of the Five-Dollar Day.

Thus, in 1937, a national news bureau sent out a story to the effect that, at heart, the chief of Ford Service was a benefactor who hired down-and-outers and former convicts for "the highest social motive" of wanting to give them "another chance."[1] Bennett was frequently eulogized by the Detroit *News* as one of industry's Good Samaritans. On occasion the New York *Times* nourished the legend that the Fords, in addition to making cars, were running an asylum for reformed bad men. During the first bite of the depression, the *Times* ran a piece about a former burglar on the Ford payroll who rebelled because he found it impossible to support his family while getting work at the factory only three days a week. Unless he was given steadier work, this employe threatened to revert to his previous calling of professional robbery. The company found the man's case so "reasonable," said the *Times,* that his demands were granted.[2]

According to one apocryphal tale, Bennett's influence with the unfortunate orders of man seemed to border on the fabulous. Bennett was standing inside the gates of the Ford plant—so the story goes—when six carloads of gunmen whisked into the grounds with submachine guns, "hot after a quarter million dollar payroll." How any armed band, obviously bent on holding up the Ford paymaster, ever penetrated the defenses of one of the world's largest industrial bastions and yet lived to tell the tale is something of a mystery. But the saga holds nonetheless that Bennett stood up to these gangsters "single-handed," as well as empty-handed, and sent them on their way by giving them a lecture.

In the words of the old Detroit *Mirror:*

"Bennett stepped to the curb, raised a hand, and they stopped.

" 'You can't do this boys,' he pleaded—and he was unarmed in the face of these desperate characters—'you know it'll only cause bloodshed. You know it'll only mean jail for you.'

"He singled out the leader of the gang. He talked to him like a father.

"In a minute, the gangsters stepped into their cars again—and drove off the Ford grounds, as Bennett watched. The payroll was safe."

This extraordinary feat of moral suasion was reported in 1932.[3] It was printed two days after the occurrence of the Ford Hunger March.

Likewise, in the mold which Bret Harte employed to depict the bad men of the American frontier, it became the fashion to impute to Bennett and his harder condottieri, rough exteriors beneath which beat hearts of gold.

As reported by John McCarten in the *American Mercury,* "The Little Man in Henry Ford's Basement" once remarked, in characterizing the diamonds-in-the-rough who belonged to Ford Service proper,

"They're a lot of tough bastards but every goddam one of them's a gentleman."[4] Taking a somewhat different tack, Bennett was quoted by the New York *Times* as saying in 1937 that most of the former prison inmates under his jurisdiction were "physical wrecks."[5]

To the extent that Ford Service did dedicate itself to restoring the weak and errant, its efforts at reformation were singularly unsuccessful. Even before most of the facts were in, that failure was suspected by Paul Kellogg when he published his classic Ford studies in the *Survey Graphic*. Kellogg referred to Ford's expanding force of former convicts as "great big innocent kids from Atlanta." Actually, over the ensuing years many of Bennett's "gentlemen" enjoyed not reeducation, but an opportunity to indulge their anti-social impulses on assignments that had the sanction and legal protection of a great corporation. The two gangsters Chester LaMare and Joe Adonis never bothered to drop their outside racketeering as they fattened on their concessions at the Ford Motor Co. At the time that he was selling fruit to the Ford commissary, LaMare increased the range of his criminal activity. While monopolizing the haul-away business of the Ford plant in New Jersey for eight years, Adonis, until his conviction and imprisonment, showed no appreciable decline as king of the Brooklyn underworld. Furthermore, Ford's "rehabilitator" was unmistakably identified with acts of labor violence which occurred on other than Ford property and which involved outside, strong-arm men recruited from the followers of the late Joe Tocco. Tocco, at this time, was one of Bennett's familiars and admittedly one of the foremost, incorrigible desperadoes of the Detroit waterfront.

As an instrument for regenerating lost sheep, Ford Service made interesting history within the city of Dearborn itself. Not even this community, whose police powers were entrusted to a former Ford Serviceman for twelve years, could boast of clean government. In May 1941, Police Chief Carl Brooks was indicted in Circuit Court on a charge of perverting his office by having sold police protection to gamblers and the operators of a brothel known as the Little Brown House.[6] There was nothing new in this commerce of vice. It had persisted for years, reaping from Dearborn alone, under Brooks' protection, an estimated income of $500,000 a year.[7]

After conducting an investigation into the merits of Brooks' indictment, Prosecutor William E. Dowling said, "I found that no attempt was ever made to padlock a gambling or vice resort in Dearborn. No attempt was ever made to prosecute a gambler or a disorderly house operator under the state laws which provide terms in prison for the violator."[8]

The full story of Dearborn's corruption under the aegis of a former Ford Serviceman had to remain untold inasmuch as two of the principals were unable to stand trial. Shortly after learning of his indictment, Brooks had a heart attack. He died two weeks later. Brooks' second-in-command, Inspector Charles A. Slamer, who had become the state's star witness and had admitted his own complicity in the graft ring, soon followed his former Chief to the grave. Two months after the indictment, Slamer was found dead in a lonely clump of woods in an adjoining township. Pathologists attributed his death to a dose of "knockout drops"—a drug in common use in the underworld.

To others who wanted to believe the best, Ford Service at its worst appeared to be a creature of the kidnaping wave of the prohibition era and a mechanism for personal defense to which Henry Ford was obliged to submit in spite of himself. Its reason for being, according to this school, was the number of abduction and extortion threats directed at the Fords in general and at the Edsel Ford children in particular. Bennett forged an alliance with the underworld, therefore, only to insure the lives and property of the Ford family against the peril of imminent criminal attack.

Seen in such a light, the process of courting the lawless element was the price Ford had to pay for protection, and it was Bennett's tactic so to reward the criminally inclined that these characters would have a vested interest in safeguarding the freedom of his principal. This alliance, on the face of it, gave the Fords double indemnity. The former convicts or racketeers-at-large whom Ford Service befriended could be expected to be loyal to the source of their preferment. They could likewise be counted on to restrain, or help apprehend, any outsider who dared to move against the Fords with criminal intent.

Ford's "gang buster" did indeed achieve a measure of authority in the American underworld. His alliance with criminals and former prison inmates was attested by the composition of Ford Service. It was manifest, likewise, in the role which Bennett played outside of Ford Service, in the world inhabited by the racketeers who survived the prohibition era and the gun-play of the Detroit waterfront. In such circles, no public police official, state or federal, could match the power or prestige of the "Little Fellow." In fact, throughout the 30's, Bennett was esteemed by the criminal fraternity of the state as friend, arbiter, employer, benefactor and amateur detective-extraordinary. As John McCarten observed in the *American Mercury* in 1940, "Even the most powerful gangsters defer to him."

Bennett's familiarity with the ins-and-outs of organized crime also won the respect of the Detroit press. Most of the big crime stories which appeared in the Detroit *News* and the Detroit *Free Press* in the 30's were written by John M. Carlisle and Kenneth F. McCormick. These two reporters covered the "Ford beat" for their respective papers, and consequently were closer than any other local newspapermen to the sanctuary of Ford Service.

Several of Bennett's personal exploits in crime detection seemed to support him in the role of "protector" of the general welfare. He once succeeded in tracking down three criminals who were responsible for a "Torch Murder" in Ypsilanti. In the commission of this crime, two couples were slain and burned to death in an automobile. Several years later, Ford Service rounded up and turned over to the police Alphonse Vlemmick, an aged, half-witted creature who had destroyed a four-year-old child whom he mistook for his own allegedly incestuous daughter. In still another instance Ford's roving detective helped to recover "Jackie" Thompson, a Detroit child, from a band of kidnapers.

When "Jackie's" abductors were brought to trial in 1929, Bennett's connection with the case was hushed up. Defense counsel for one of the gangsters asked the court, Judge W. McKay Skillman, to explain if he would why the police and witnesses for the state closed up "like clams" whenever any of the witnesses touched on the mediating role of "Ford Motor Co. detectives."[9] One of the defendants in this case was defended by Paul P. Colombo, the brother and law partner of chief counsel for the Ford Motor Co.[10] It came out later that "Jackie" had been returned to his parents, unharmed, and that the ransom of $17,000 had been recovered in full—thanks to the intervention of Ford Service. The ransom money was remitted to the child's father in the offices of the Ford Motor Co.[11]

To all appearances, Bennett should have been honored by public acknowledgment of his services to the Thompson family. The immediate disposition of the case had been a happy one. Its wider implications, however, suggest why it was that various participants in the trial were so close-mouthed on the subject of "Ford detectives." Bennett had negotiated the recovery of the child and the ransom by dealing with Joe Marino, a confederate of Chester LaMare's. LaMare was then enjoying his remunerative fruit concession at Dearborn while plying on the outside, concurrently, an illegal trade alongside of which the "Jackie" Thompson kidnaping, despite its barbarity, was small pickings.[12]

The public at large shared the benefits of "Ford" protection, therefore, to the extent that while tolerating certain criminals, Bennett did hunt down others. Those whom he ferreted out for prosecution--notably the "torch" murderers, the Thompson kidnapers, and the aged sex pervert—were unquestionably dangerous social outcasts. Their conviction was all to the good. These men, however, were obscure little fellows. None represented the forces of organized, large-scale gang crime.

As a "protective" device, the institution of Ford Service did raise an impregnable wall about the persons of the Ford family. Beyond any question, the agency was "protecting" the Fords from something. For years it followed Henry Ford like a shadow. What harm might have befallen the subjects of this incessant vigil, had they moved about casually like most members of their class, no one can say. But insofar as such a guard was thrown up to fend off predatory gangsters, the precaution seemed out of proportion to the realities of the situation. The record fails to show that abductors or extortioners made a special target of the Fords as against any other family of great wealth. Nor was Henry Ford at the time a symbol of popular disfavor. On the contrary, any criminal who had preyed on his family would have raised a storm the world over.

Other facts suggest that Ford Service was more than a counter-weapon, born of the prohibition era. Many activities of the division, and its fundamental pattern, were already established in the conduct of the Ford corporation in the days before Harry Bennett had built his bridges to the underworld.

## 2

Of all the apologies for Ford Service, the most credible is the supposition that Henry Ford was basically unaware of what Bennett really meant to the Ford family and the Ford corporation. Those who subscribed to this thesis knew too much to be able to dismiss Ford Service as a means of reclaiming social outcasts or of securing Ford's personal protection from the underworld. Their case began with the admission that all was not well or that the worst was true in the conduct of Ford's men-at-arms. But whatever Ford pretensions were belied by Ford Service, these apologists imputed the blame, not to the folk hero of Detroit, but to his chief subordinate. Consequently, the excesses of Harry Bennett came to be reconciled with the virtue of Henry Ford by assuming that the principal was not answerable for the acts of his agent.

Thus regarded, things were done in Ford's name, and in his behalf, which Ford himself would never have condoned had he known the facts. The wool was pulled over his eyes, presumably, because he was old, because he was too far removed from the field of action to know the truth, because he assumed in all innocence that his subordinates were—like himself—men of good will, because his major advisers who had his ear told him what he wanted to hear or only what conformed to his reputation for humanity, or because he was duped by the men whom he had clothed with power. In this defense of Ford's conscience, Bennett in particular became the whipping boy. He was regarded either as the tail that wags the dog or as the Frankensteinian monster who swallowed his maker.

The claim that "Ford didn't know" is important, because of its plausibility. In fact, it is the only rationalization of Ford Service that demands a serious answer. Many of Bennett's actions must have escaped Ford's notice because of the size of his enterprise. With the best will in the world, any overseer of so vast a business could have hoped to follow, at most, only the high spots. Moreover, in trying to piece together the multifarious details of his business, Ford—like any other great industrialist—had to rely on the word of his subordinates. When it came to framing over-all policy, inside and outside his business, many of his trusted informants did shield him from unfavorable opinion. They went even further, on occasion, by trimming the facts to suit Ford's fancies.

It is logical to suppose, furthermore, that Ford's age helped to widen the gulf which separated him from the doings of his Service Department. When Ford Service reached its peak the manufacturer was in his seventies. He was engrossed in hobbies like the project at Greenfield Village. The presidency of the corporation had been passed on to his son, and then to one of his grandsons. Even before he lamented in 1933 that the Rouge "wasn't fun any more," his appearances in the shop had become less and less regular. These visits were so rare and so confined to special areas of the plant that only his older workers had ever laid eyes on him. By this time, presumably, Ford was an elderly industrialist who had shifted the burden of management to other shoulders and gone into a state of semi-retirement.

The habit of damning the agent and overlooking the principal in this relationship is doubly significant because of its popularity.

It is the fashionable method of resolving the paradox of Ford-versus-Bennett, and all but the wisest Ford men, past and present, who had their doubts about Bennett liked to think that Ford had been "taken over" by the toughest of his adjutants. The dealer or factory hand or topmost executive who underwent the most harrowing experience in the Ford organization was speaking for the lot when he said, "Oh, it isn't Ford! It's those so-and-so's he has working for him who are in control out there!"

To make the circle complete, even union organizers who eventually felt the edge of Bennett's sharpest weapons were often just as ready to rise to the defense of the folk hero. The frequent lament of these people, like that of the white collar workers who were soured by years of disappointment at Dearborn or Highland Park, was the cry, "If Ford only knew . . ."

In reality, Henry Ford could not have escaped knowing, for until 1945 he never yielded the control of his business either to his son, when Edsel was president of the corporation; to Bennett, his right-hand man; or to any other agent. As *Time* Magazine pointed out in 1941, Edsel was head of the Ford enterprise in name only; "Father Ford" was still "boss."[13] As of that date, "Father Ford's" authority was sealed by the fact that he still retained enough stock in the corporation to be able to outvote the rest of his family combined. His share of the company holdings was 55 per cent.[14]

Neither years nor hobbies prevented the senior Ford from utilizing his authority. In his seventh decade, he was blessed with unusual stamina, and while at that ripe age he no longer put in the hours or hovered over the shop as in bygone days, he remained close enough to his business to keep posted on all major questions of company policy and on the complexion of Ford Service. Cameron said that the Ford enterprise was the uniquely "personal" corporation within which neither jot nor tittle escaped the founder's all-seeing eye. Up until 1945 Ford inventions and new technical processes were still put forth as Ford's individual handiwork. If the man was that alive to the trend of events, he was surely able to follow the operations of Ford Service during an era when his company was locked in a national struggle with labor, and at a time when labor relations were foremost in the mind of every captain of industry.

Ford must have known, in the second place, because the newspapers of Detroit gave so much space to the maneuvers of Ford Service. No internal hushing up of the facts could have stood up against this pressure of news from the outside. At the city desks of the local press, Bennett ranked as important copy for twenty years. There was color in the story of a former sailor and pugilist who made good in industry. These journals based hundreds of columns on the ins-and-outs of Ford Service. They described Bennett's mercurial temperament, his gendarmes, his tilts with former Mayor Frank Murphy, his political intrigues, his clashes with labor, his dealings with criminals and former convicts. In the crisis of 1927, when Ford was not available as a witness in the Sapiro case and Ford Service assured the public that his injury was not the work of frustrated assassins, Bennett had candidly cited as authority for his findings the thoroughness of his "connections with the underworld." Ever since the "Little Fellow" came into prominence at Dearborn, his press alone would have fixed his associations and activities in the mind of anyone who had an interest in the Ford Motor Co.

The story of Ford Service was familiar to every knowing executive in the trade. It must have reached the ears of Bennett's employer by the same route. As a matter of fact, when *Time* Magazine in 1937 published photographs of Ford Servicemen caught in the act of beating Ford employes and union sympathizers, Ford was so well aware of this publicity that he withdrew his advertising from the pages of *Time, Life* and *Fortune* for the next seventy weeks.

If the founder of the Ford house was still unable to fathom Ford Service, despite his access to the newspapers and despite his close attention to affairs, he would have been compelled to grant some measure of recognition and understanding to the men-at-arms who closed in on his physical person. For twenty-five years or more Ford lived like an Italian noble of the 15th century, ringed about by swarms of *bravi*. He moved with as little personal freedom as the President of the United States. At home or at his place of business, in public or in private, inside or outside Detroit, wherever he set foot, his body-attendants seldom let him out of their sight. The mere number of such retainers, not to mention their outward bearing or their habit of popping up here, there and everywhere, should have told him that Ford Service was giving his private existence, if not his business as a whole, all the pomp and circumstance of a feudal court. The maneuvers of his bodyguard were notorious in Detroit.

In 1932 Ford underwent an emergency operation for hernia and appendicitis. His hospitalization called for intervention on the part of the Captain of the Guard himself. Bennett, in person, rushed to the scene and under his orders, so as to give the patient maximum isolation, one-half of the entire third floor of the enormous Henry Ford

Hospital was roped off as a restricted area.[15] When Ford merely entered or left Greenfield Village, his household troops put on a show that would do credit to the grenadiers who attend the royal presence of the King of England. It was ritual in 1939 for word of his entrance— "The 'Old Man' in Gate No. 2"—to be flashed to each of the many watching stations on the premises and to Service headquarters, where the report was picked up by an automatic recording device. The procedure was repeated as the "Old Man" made his departure. Moving in either direction, his own vehicle was usually trailed by a Service car.

Dearborn's pretorian guard gave perhaps its most ludicrous performance at a children's party held in the State Fair Coliseum of Detroit to celebrate Ford's 75th birthday. The guests of the day were 8000 underprivileged youngsters who had been rounded up from the public playgrounds of the city. Bennett's touch was conspicuous even here. It was evident not only in the number of secret service men whom photographers tripped over, but in the seating arrangements of the house as well. The huge arena was filled to capacity, except for one of its sectors. The deserted section consisted of a large V-shaped block of empty seats that fanned out directly behind the front row boxes set aside for Ford and members of his party. Evenly spaced across this roped-off sector, high enough to get a bird's-eye view of the rest of the house, were four bulky guards who stood rigid, on the alert. Although the guests were children who were engrossed in their helpings of free ice cream and fascinated by a circus performance down on the floor of the coliseum, the Ford guard was taking no chances with the prize once labeled by a Detroit journalist as "one billion dollars on the hoof."[16]

That Bennett plotted his course apart from Ford's knowledge or assent is unlikely for the further reason that the two men spent so much time in one another's company. Of all the former executives at Dearborn, Bennett enjoyed readiest access to Ford's person. That right of entrée appeared at times to have been his sole prerogative. Ford paid countless social and business calls at the headquarters of Ford Service. In these precincts no frequent visitor could have failed to sense Bennett's personality or the caliber of his aides. Bennett and Ford made trips together, such as their journey to Chicago to attend the 1939 convention of the American Legion. They fraternized socially. Bennett and his wife were regular guests at the old-fashioned dancing parties in Greenfield Village. Personal property passed between the two men, as in 1938, when Henry and Clara Ford deeded to Bennett the land which he used for his summer place on Grosse Ile.

On more than one occasion, Bennett was entrusted by his superior with responsibilities of a purely personal character. By their very nature, these man-to-man services touched on matters that Ford put store by. They were confidential charges which could not have been delegated indiscriminately to anyone whom Ford happened to know. When the senior Fords were on vacation at their Iron Mountain retreat in northern Michigan, a special Service car used to leave Dearborn daily, bearing supplies for the cuisine, including oil of black walnut for Ford's morning doughnuts. On another private errand, inspired this time by Mrs. Ford's personal fondness for the movie actress, Mary Pickford, a detail of Ford Servicemen arrived unannounced at the Detroit airport one morning at 4 A.M. to pick up Mary Pickford's husband, Charles (Buddy) Rogers, who was scheduled to fill a local theater engagement. Catching this young man quite unawares, Bennett's men whisked him to a hotel in style.[17]

Again, when Ford ordered that the homes of all his workers must henceforth become bone-dry, the enforcement of this edict was left to Bennett. Other personal errands for Ford carried many a Serviceman afield to make private investigations, to protect witnesses or to attend court trials and grand jury hearings.[18] Bennett took a hand, confidentially and at Ford's behest, in various private divorce actions. In the course of his own first divorce proceedings, he told the bench that investigating marital conflicts was one of his specialties. When a number of such cases were pending in court, he said, he had intervened "to stall them along."[19]

As familiars, the two men saw eye to eye on the Jewish question. Reading the weathervane of Ford's personal whim on that subject, Bennett once went out of his way to uncover what purports to have been original and confidential source material. Ford related in confiding to an acquaintance that although Booth is charged with Lincoln's assassination, the principals who egged him on to commit the crime were, in reality, a set of "Jews." When asked by his friend to document his findings, Ford said, "Oh, no doubt about the facts! Harry Bennett has made an investigation."

### 3

Few could have charted Bennett's course from a knowledge of his origins. The boy who later commanded the respect of the toughest Sicilian gangsters sprang from old American stock. His ancestors came over on the Mayflower. In Ann Arbor, the place of his birth, Harry

Herbert Bennett was a choirboy at St. Andrew's Episcopal Church. He was two years old when his father, a sign painter by trade, was killed in an accident. His mother, an artist and a woman of breeding, later married a college professor at the University of Michigan. As a youngster, Bennett, like most young Americans, picked his idols from the world of sports, and he lived in a college town where the aura of athletic heroes was, to him, all the more irresistible.

In 1909, at seventeen, young Bennett enlisted in the Navy. He filled out a four-year term in the service as a seaman, stoker and deep-sea diver. It was in the Navy that he took the ring name "Sailor Reese." This experience at sea was followed by adventures on the West Coast of Africa, where Bennett and a companion worked at deep-sea diving for the French government. "Sailor Reese" and his associate, bearing scars from an alleged encounter with a dangerous African native, eventually made their way to New York, taking passage on a Spanish tramp steamer.

The stage for Bennett's later career was set by Ford in person. In 1916, several years after his discharge from the Navy, Bennett was hired as a clerk in the photographic department of the Ford Motor Co. He was twenty-four at the time, about the age of Edsel Ford. He met the boss accidentally. Ford liked his looks and his jaunty air. He questioned him about his Navy record. "Sailor Reese" told him his story, and acting on instinct, Ford made him head watchman at the Rouge plant out in Dearborn. At this time the Rouge was nothing more than a blast furnace and a tractor factory. It was still a mere appendage of the works at Highland Park.

Ford's new watchman was the man for the job from the very beginning. Fresh from military service, he knew the meaning of discipline; he could carry out orders and ask no questions. Endowed with a bright mind and an active body, filled with the courage and combativeness of a seasoned athlete, flaunting the devil-take-it air of a young soldier-of-fortune, and smitten by a passion for devouring detective thrillers and murder mysteries, "Sailor Reese" had the makings of a policeman; he took to the work from the start. In addition, there was something in the grain that fitted him for the rough-and-tumble that was characteristic of the industry in general and of Ford's organization in particular; the young guard had a moderately thick skin. He was ambitious and loyal to boot. He was flattered by the sudden promotion from clerk to local chief of factory police in a corporation that was the talk of the world, and because he was grateful and because he was made that way, he applied himself to subordinating his own will to Ford's to a degree which no other Ford executive had ever equalled.

But the mold into which this man poured his talents was of Ford's design pure and simple. This fact is evident in the nature of his apprenticeship. During his first ten years at Dearborn, Bennett was no more than understudy to Liebold and Sorensen. He was drilled in the authoritative Ford tradition, therefore, by its masters, by the two men who were closest to Ford at the time, by the pair of executives who had escaped membership in the Ford Alumni Association because they were Ford's preeminent early favorites.

As Ford and Bennett began to fuse their personalities, it was Bennett and not Ford who had to change. In the process of coming together, agent rather than principal had to add steel to his temperament. Ford had demonstrated a will of iron when Bennett was still a youngster at Dearborn. The insides of the man who picked Sorensen and Liebold were anything but buttery. The Bennett of the mid-20's, on the other hand—according to those who were his intimates at the time—had to toughen up. In that formative period, say his old friends, his hardness was skin deep; he was a little man, affecting the Sorensen bluster without benefit of Sorensen's imposing physique. Ten years later, the imperious air was second nature. Meanwhile, the "Little Man in Henry Ford's Basement" had taken his cue from Ford, or from the men who stood highest in Ford's esteem.

Finally, Bennett was a homegrown Ford product from start to finish because of the rate and direction of his development. He did not descend on Dearborn out of the blue. Nor was power thrust upon him suddenly as the answer to Ford's kidnaping phobias, or for any other reason. It took Bennett two decades to become head man at the Ford Motor Co. When he began to make news as chief of Ford Service, he had been with the company for eleven years. Another decade passed before he emerged as Ford's director of personnel. He had grown all the while under Ford's nose. In proving himself on Ford's terms, it was not that Bennett did different things than Liebold or Sorensen had done before him. On the contrary, he did the same things. But in Ford's opinion, he did them better.

Thus, as production whips, Bennett and Sorensen were two of a kind but different in degree. Bennett in the end became the better disciplinarian; he had more policemen to work with; he could concentrate on the problem of regimenting men while Sorensen was looking after machines as well as men; and Servicemen inspired more dread than Sorensen's foremen and superintendents because so many of them worked under cover and because the right to hire and fire was eventually centered in the headquarters of Ford Service.

As an informer, Bennett was simply the artist or the scientist working in a field which Liebold had explored earlier as a novice and dabbler. Here the pupil surpassed the teacher only in thickening an atmosphere of stealth and suspicion that was already in existence. Whereas Liebold's spying was sporadic, informal and small-scale, Bennett in the same sphere went in for highly organized, permanent mass production. When Ford Service reached maturity, its eavesdroppers were more numerous and more skillful than their forerunners at Dearborn.

While intriguing in politics, Bennett may appear to have written an original page in Ford history. He was, beyond question, a virtuoso of the conspiratorial arts. But in this sphere, too, he merely improved on a technique which he had learned at Dearborn. Bennett attended the school of intrigue that produced the Ford Alumni Association in the 20's. As the foremost survivor of that course of tuition, he became a Ford specialist in the art of ruling a house by keeping it divided, by playing both ends against the middle. This tradition was so deep-seated at Dearborn that it ensnared even Edsel Ford, the nominal president of the corporation. Young Ford, long before his untimely death, even had to tolerate the discharge at Dearborn of able executives whom he regarded as "his" men. In such cases, the ax usually fell when his back was turned. He was taking a vacation in Europe when his brother-in-law, Ernest Kanzler, was dropped from the Ford organization.

Bennett seemed to cut a unique figure in Ford history by the frankness with which he flaunted his power. His efforts at self-dramatization were evident in his handling of public relations. He made no bones about the toughness of Ford Service. He passed off many of his own exploits outside the corporation with a flourish and with a sense of the dramatic. The effects of his office at Dearborn, including a formidable bodyguard in the waiting room and a microscope on his desk, suggested the stage properties of a "new-day Sherlock Holmes."[20] Bennett's enjoyment of the strong arm role was patent in the neat little speech which used to be parroted by the guides who showed tourists through the Rouge and Greenfield Village. These escorts were employes of Ford Service. If questioned about their chief, they replied like automatons, "Mr. Bennett is a man of great physical courage."

In many personal dealings with the press, it was this harder side of his personality that Bennett chose to put on display. He once explained to a newspaperman his preference for the bow tie. He spoke as the familiar of "bad men," as the self-conscious master of them all. A four-in-hand at the neck is risky business, he said, because it gives "tough customers" a handle for steadying a man, just before the punch.[21] For a time the "fearless one" worked at his reputation by raising lions and tigers. As the butt of a practical joke, a guest at his Huron River estate was "practically stripped naked" after having been closeted in a darkened room with an uncaged lion.[22]* When he strutted for the press, some of Bennett's gestures approached the ludicrous and the melodramatic. These antics were redolent of Wild Bill Hickock and his six-shooter. Using an air-gun that fired tiny lead pellets, the man used to entertain callers at the Ford Administration Building by shooting the tip off a lead pencil some distance away.[24] He delighted in such exhibitions of his "accurate and lethal" marksmanship. Kenneth McCormick of the Detroit *Free Press,* told a story that surpasses even the legend of William Tell. According to McCormick, a state boxing commissioner came into Bennett's office with a large, fresh cigar between his teeth. Because of the no-smoking rule at Ford's, Bennett told the visitor to put the cigar away. When the guest ignored the order and said with a laugh, "It ain't lit," Bennett reputedly drew a .38-caliber revolver and shot the stogie out of the offender's mouth.[25] While romancing about his youth for the benefit of another office caller, Bennett was quite in character when he bared his chest and peeled up his trouser leg to exhibit a collection of scars.

As intriguer, publicist, informer, labor autocrat, political tactician and Captain of the Guard, Bennett added nothing at Dearborn that was new in principle. He personified no more than an old tradition raised to the *nth* power. He stands out among Ford's other strong men only in having become the most potent of the lot, in having brought the tradition up to date, and in advertising more boldly than any of his predecessors exactly what he was up to. What brought him to the top, step by step, was not his divergence from Ford's personality in any essential quality, but rather the fact that he was the most perfect second self Ford ever produced. In the words of Kenneth McCormick, "This proud, rugged, impulsive bundle of dynamite

---

* Toying with ferocious game seems to have been a favorite sign of masculinity among Ford Servicemen. Elmer Hogan, one of Bennett's former boxers, tried to raise a lion in his garage. The late Carl Brooks repeated the experiment in the police barns of the city of Dearborn.[23] Bennett achieved the ultimate in this sort of thing when he expanded his staff in 1937 by adding Allen King, a professional lion-tamer.

[Bennett] was developed by Henry Ford just as surely as the motor that drives millions of Ford cars."[26]

Nor did Ford and Bennett make a secret of their temperamental affinity. They spread it on the record, independently, that they found their kinship mutually satisfying, that the younger of the two men was his master's double, and that as the ultimate creator of Ford Service, Ford's right hand was fully posted on the movements of his left. Bennett used to make a point of telling newspapermen he was "Mr. Ford's personal man."[27] According to an Associated Press story, dated March 22, 1939, "Ford is known to feel that he 'sort of raised' Bennett." One may take Ford's own word for the fact that he was proud of this man-of-all-work whom he felt he "sort of raised." In a Detroit newspaper which has always made a scrupulous effort to take down Ford's remarks correctly, the manufacturer was quoted as saying in 1935, "Let the police run the country. They know how to keep order. They have to go out and duck buckshot. For instance, if anything wrong is done here in the plant, the police take care of it. They can do the same for the whole country. And I don't mean federal, but local police."[28]

## Twenty-six

### MACHINE AGE

#### 1

THE WORST that was said about Harry Bennett, when Ford Service was making news, scarcely more than scratched the surface of the folk myth which holds that Ford's men for a quarter of a century had been the highest paid and the best treated in the world, and that his shops, since 1914, had been the model of the factory system. By common consent, it was agreed that Ford had no need for policemen or eavesdroppers; his employes were the most fortunate in the business; his factories, union-proof.

However, the labor tempest of the 30's did sweep into the Ford shops. In fact, in the struggle for self-organization, no mass production workers in the country were more resolute than Ford's. This protest movement at Dearborn suggests its own explanation. Either Ford's men were obstreperous, ungrateful and duped by outside agitators—despite high wages and model working conditions—or else Ford had not made the Rouge a workers' paradise and Ford Service rather than humanitarianism was the means which he had chosen to keep his men in line. His factory workers fought for union recognition for five years. Without knowing what was on their minds during this period, no one can gauge the "why" of Ford Service, nor Ford's legitimate place among labor's folk heroes.

The average outsider who gave any thought to the conflict that flared at Dearborn from 1937 to 1941 was wedded to the conviction that in wages alone, Ford's men had nothing to gain through union organization. This assurance was part of the American creed; it flowed as well from the prevailing belief that Henry Ford was as good as his word. Thus, when Ford vowed in November 1940, that he had always paid his men "well over the union scale," most of the nation took his statement on faith.[1] Likewise, in the midst of the struggle between the union and the Ford Motor Co., a certain number of his listeners took Ford seriously when he charged that once labor organizers got a grip on him, they would force him to pay low, un-American wages dictated by the "financial interests" of "Wall Street."[2] But if the average American had been pressed to establish the known fact of the superiority of the Ford wage scale, all he could have fallen back on, actually, was the Five-Dollar Day. Nor was he aware of the fact that even this celebrated innovation had been ringed about with qualifications. As to the history of Ford wages from that day to this, the run-of-mine believer in the Ford legend has virtually no knowledge at all.

To the extent that Ford's men wanted more money when they went out on strike in 1941, they had sized up their pay envelopes by using a standard often ignored by outsiders, to whom the "Detroit wage" of 75¢ or $1.00 an hour looked more than sufficient. Whatever Ford was paying at the time by the hour or by the day, the thing that mattered to his mill workers was the figure it added up to at the end of the year. Gauging his rate-per-hour in terms of what he hoped to get for his money and of what he had to show for his labors year in and year out, the Ford worker of 1937-1940 was less satisfied and less well off than the Ford man of 1914. He erred, of course, if he held the Ford Motor Co. alone accountable for this state of affairs. His seeming failure to get ahead in twenty-five years' time was chiefly attributable to the state of the trade and to the social system within which the trade was doing business. In fact, from the time of the

Five-Dollar Day up to 1941, three great social forces—all beyond the control of any single employer—had been thinning the purse of the Ford employe faster than he could fatten it.

In the first place, while his total yearly earnings stood still or went ahead by inches or actually decreased in the course of a ten-year depression, his wants had increased by leaps and bounds.

Second, even during the most prosperous peacetime era he could remember, the beginner at the Ford Motor Co. was poorer dollar-for-dollar than the man who had stood at the same bench in 1914. True, the newcomer of 1926-1929, by contrast with his predecessor, was making six dollars a day instead of five. But he had less to show for it because, from 1926 on, he had been working a shorter week, five days out of seven, in place of six. Thus, at least for beginners, the Ford wage of the boom years was just where it had stood a dozen years before. It was still $30 a week. Living costs, meanwhile, had soared. The boom was on in the country as a whole, and Detroit—whose great, central industry was still attracting tens of thousands of newcomers year by year, and whose landlords and merchants and real estate speculators were getting fat in the meantime—kept pace with the rest of the nation. According to the federal Department of Labor, the cost of living in Detroit by December of 1928 had risen in fourteen years' time by 77 per cent.[3] Hence, during the intervening years, the real wage of the new Ford man had shrunk to nearly one-half its previous size. The amount in the weekly pay envelope was the same, yet in terms of what it was worth at the grocer's or the landlord's, it had to be stretched almost twice as far. Even at the close of the ensuing decade of depression—before the war program was fully under way—a $30 paycheck in Detroit was worth less than $21 by contrast with what it had commanded in goods and services in 1914.[4]

Third, the Ford wage earner of the 30's had lost additional ground in that the day wage, which sounded so big to many outsiders, was his only when he got it, and for ten consecutive years he had been getting it fewer days per week and fewer weeks per year. In the slough of the depression, he earned nothing at all for weeks and sometimes for months. What work he did draw in the leaner years was fitful; it was confined, as a rule, to two or three, rather than five, days a week.

Moreover, acute general depression was not the only reason Ford men or other automobile workers were no longer so sure of actually pocketing the daily or hourly wage that may have looked so good on paper. As a matter of fact, the short year came to the automobile shops, seemingly for good, two or three years before the country had heard of a depression. As early as 1929, statisticians of the Department of Labor at Washington reported that, between the years 1923 and 1928, employment in the automobile industry was more seasonal and unstable than any they had studied.[5] From that date forward, the Ford job, which had been hitherto the steadiest in the business, had to follow the trend. Finally, between 1926 and 1928, all American automobile workers who worked for an hourly wage became permanent part-time employes; the seasonal lay-off—an annual furlough of two months or more without pay—made its appearance as a fixture of the trade. This shortening of the work year in all automotive plants signalized that the industry had reached its saturation point, that expansion had run its course, that henceforth—under the private enterprise system—automotive production would have to be trimmed to fit a more or less fixed replacement market, that the trade was committed to a policy of ordering annual shutdowns to retool for new models. Thus, for the rank and file of automobile labor, lay-offs lasting eight or twelve weeks a season had become so standard by 1938 that in that year a financial writer for the New York *Times,* in describing the trade, called the ten-month year a "trend toward normalcy."[6]

What these seasonal interruptions meant to production workers, in terms of wages, may be gathered from the data prepared by the NRA Research and Planning Division, under the chairmanship of Leon Henderson. The ordinary semi-skilled man in the trade, said the Henderson report, totaled between $800 and $1200 at the crest of the boom, in 1929.[7] The Ford worker unquestionably made a better showing than this, for 1929 was a year of enormous activity at the Ford Motor Co. His average income may have been no higher in 1927-1928, on the other hand, because these were the years when Ford shut down to retool for the Model A. In a list of automotive plants ranked in order of stability of employment for the twelve months ending in November 1928, the Department of Labor placed Highland Park 43rd from the top.[8]

Nor were automobile workers as a whole, at Ford's or elsewhere, doing so well in terms of the so-called American standard of living, in the recovery years following the low point of the depression. In his book *Detroit, Dynamic City,* Arthur Pound says that 45 per cent of the employes in the industry earned less than $1000 in 1934. For the following year, 1935, he puts the average income of automobile labor at $1150.[9] His estimate, like Henderson's, covers the wages of the parts shops. No one can say just where annual earnings stood

at the time at Ford's. Such a reckoning would require access to figures
that are not available.* It would involve, as well, a definition of what
constituted a Ford employe during this period. A fair determination
of Ford wages for 1933 might require summing up the income of
those workers who were making twelve and fifteen cents an hour
manufacturing parts on the orders which Ford had jobbed out to the
Briggs Corporation.

While all these factors—a general depression, the permanent
seasonal lay-off, the lag of wages behind prices, and the tug of new
and unsatisfied American wants—were working havoc with the income
of the Ford employe and of the factory worker everywhere, Ford was
given, meanwhile, a supreme opportunity to prove his labor statesmanship. Not that he could have stayed these vast, economic forces
as they influenced society at large, but it did lie within his power to
soften their effect as they squeezed the pocketbooks of his own men.
He had the money; his business was the foremost profit-maker of the
20's; and his reputation was at stake. If his apostleship of high wages
was anything more than words, this was the time for action.

However, beset by the recurring short year, Ford brought forth
no scheme for regularizing employment, nor any plan to which his
own employes could turn for assistance during their sustained, annual
holidays without pay. Further than that, he completely washed his
hands of the problem. He proclaimed that inasmuch as the laborers
of the trade had no just ground for demanding steady work, he had
no intention of acting as his brother's keeper. This statement of the
problem appears in Ford's book *Moving Forward*, published in 1930.
The declaration reads: "It may well be that some sections of industry
are better off working on the highly seasonal basis and that the
trouble is not with the industry but with the men who look for a
year's support from an industry which can give them only half a year's
support."[10] In this case, it is evident that Ford really meant what he
said, for it will be recalled that he was quite content in 1930-1932 to
let the taxpayers of Detroit assume the care of thousands of his own
unemployed.

While disclaiming any personal responsibility for the welfare of
the disemployed during fallow seasons, Ford went out of his way,
as well, to challenge the only remedial approach to the problem that
was forthcoming from any source at all. When the federal Social
Security Act was pending in Congress in 1934, he was one of the bill's

* The identity of any corporation is never revealed in wage data published
by agencies of the federal government.

most bitter opponents. His spokesmen tried to defeat its passage. In a
radio talk aimed at the proposed legislation, W. J. Cameron dubbed
federal benefits for the unemployed "a sop to the social conscience"
and "a new form of permanent pauperization."[11]

Nor did Ford's hostility to the principle of sharing responsibility
for the unemployed cease, once the Social Security Act had been
written into law in 1935. His tactics in the national election of 1936
were proof of his continued opposition to the measure. In this contest,
he campaigned for Landon by broadcasting the charge that the Security
Act was a worker's bugaboo. On the eve of the election, every Ford
employe found in his pay envelope a short, printed message which
stated, in effect, that in order to pay part of the costs of unemployment
compensation and old-age insurance, his wage henceforth would be
subject to a "hidden" tax exacted by the bureaucrats of Washington.*

When most of the major producers of the trade entered into
union contracts with their employes, from 1937 through 1940, the
facts on the Ford wage scale began to stream in. Every Ford worker
could read the trend with ease. He could gossip with his nextdoor
neighbor who worked at some other shop. He had access to union
handbills. The newspapers listed the hourly earnings of many of the
hundreds of Ford men whose detailed job histories were written into
the official record of the National Labor Relations Board. Meanwhile,
the wages paid at unionized plants were often posted in formal lists
that were available for public inspection. From this latter source
alone, it was evident by 1939 or earlier that even the Briggs shop,
which Ford had pushed into an orgy of wage-cutting during the
depression, was paying higher wages than the Ford Motor Co. By 1940,
Ford's men were convinced of the fact that their employer, far from
preserving his superiority as a payer of high wages, was actually trail-
ing the field. It was apparent that Ford's lag was chiefly a question of
paying his best men less than the prevailing rate.

Finally, owing to a slip-up in public relations, Ford himself resolved all doubts on the question. He admitted that, compared with
other wage earners of the trade, his men were standing at the foot of
the ladder, as of January 1940. This unintentional declaration appeared
in an advertisement published in the New York *Times* of January
28, 1940, in which the Fords announced that they paid their workers
on the average a fraction more than 90¢ an hour. Before the year was

* The working class voters of Dearborn registered what they thought of
their employer's philosophy of each-man-for-himself by giving Roosevelt a
plurality of ten to one.

out, the Department of Labor reported an average hourly rate of 95¢ for the whole industry, including all the parts shops.[12] Somewhat later, *Time* Magazine and the New York newspaper *PM* announced that Chrysler and General Motors men were averaging slightly more than $1 an hour.[13] Although these comparative checks did not appear until one year after the date of Ford's announcement, other events made it clear that there had been no significant upward revision of the Ford scale in the meantime.

Thus, at least throughout 1940, Ford by his own admission was the least liberal wage-payer in the industry. For that interval and probably longer, his average rate was 5¢ an hour behind the field, and below the Chrysler and General Motors standard by twice that amount. This variance from the mode may have been greater than it looks, for inasmuch as Ford was paying bottom rates, his claimed payroll of 130,000 workers was large enough to depress the over-all average of the trade. Moreover, it was the union's contention at the time that the announced Ford rate of 90¢ was an overstatement.

When Ford finally came to terms with the union in 1941 and agreed to meet the highest rates paid for similar work in comparable shops, his lag in wage payments was disclosed in full. There were two published estimates of what this concession meant in dollars and cents. One came from the union; the other from Kenneth McCormick, the Detroit *Free Press* reporter.[14] According to McCormick, the adjustment gave the Ford employe an average increase of $230 a year; according to the union, the annual raise per man amounted to more than $400. McCormick estimated that it would cost Ford $30,000,000 a year to close the gap that existed between his scale and the top rates of the trade. The union's estimate was $52,000,000.

When Ford gave battle to the union, therefore, his self-expressed fear of the "New York financiers" who were "conspiring" to keep him from paying high wages seems to have been relatively groundless. On the face of it, what he was really trying to protect, in resisting unionization, was a competitive position which enabled him to undercut the wage bill of two great Wall Street enterprises—Chrysler and General Motors—by a margin of from $30,000,000 to $50,000,000 a year.

## 2

While the wage question was a real one at Dearborn, it was not the key issue of the struggle between Ford and the union. As a matter of fact, when Ford's men began to organize, their demand for higher wages was as nothing compared with their insistence on the right to earn any wage at all. At bottom, their fight for a union was a fight for the job itself. It was a struggle for status at a business establishment where fear-of-the-job had eaten into the minds of the rank and file like a canker.

To appreciate this sense of insecurity on the part of Ford's men, one must grasp the position in which all automobile workers found themselves before the rise of a union. Job insecurity had been the rule at every automotive shop since 1927-1928. It was then that the industry stopped growing. At the same time the trade had settled once and for all on the program of promoting new annual models. This merchandising policy necessitated, in turn, the seasonal shutdown. Then, in 1929, the whole industry, already static and already operating on a short year, was engulfed by worldwide depression. Thus, for a period of at least ten years, no wage-earner in the automobile factory had a job that he could call his own; he was forced to take what he could get for his services; he was none too sure of his ability to sell his skills at any price.

In this glutted labor market, the men who were hit the hardest were the seasoned workers who had come up with the trade from the beginning. Their past loyalty or their sheer length of service counted for nothing in the ensuing scramble for employment. In fact, throughout the 30's or until the advent of the union, the longer a man had served his employer, the less his assurance of being able to hang on. Other things equal, the older man was first to go in slack times and last to get back when things picked up. As a result, men over forty had developed job neuroses; they had made a habit of lying about their age; they began to dye their hair if it was graying. The competition of age-versus-youth had become so fierce by 1935 that certain loan companies in Detroit refused to accept as a credit risk any unemployed automobile worker who was past the forty mark. These firms were convinced of the fact that even though such a client had a long record of steady employment, his chance of "getting back on" after the seasonal lay-off, was, within limits, only a gambler's risk.[15]

The skilled man, likewise, was clinging to his job catch-as-catch-can. Even though he succeeded in surviving the annual shutdown, he often lost ground in the process. Thousands of his kind, particularly in the slower years, were compelled to take beginners' jobs at beginners' pay, or were forced to go back to their old jobs at little more than starting wages. Toward the middle of the decade, all automotive employers were wiping the slate clean for any employe, irrespective of his age or skill, who had been laid off as long as six months.[16] Beyond that point, as a rule, every claim to seniority and every distinction between the new employe and the former employe was obliterated.

In treating their workers like robots to be bought at auction, employers of labor in Detroit were neither intentionally callous nor self-consciously sinister. On the contrary, they were sharp, orthodox businessmen who were manipulating the labor market in order to cut costs. The shops of the industry had always demanded speed and stamina from the operative. Caught in a ten-year depression, management turned as never before to young, green labor because it was cheaper; it would work for less money; it could be pushed faster on production; it could be quickly trained to handle tens of thousands of highly mechanized jobs. Wage-cutting became the order of the day for the same reason. In an open shop community overrun by surplus labor of every description, it was natural for management to drive hard bargains at the employment gate.

But whatever their motives and whatever their defense, Ford and his fellow industrialists were, by the same token, breeding unrest and resentment in the shop. They had stripped their men of status to the point where *Fortune* magazine, which speaks to and for management, had to remark the complete lack of job tenure in all automotive plants. After studying Ford policies in 1933, the magazine said, ". . . automobile labor . . . is labor with little dignity and less security."[17] Two years later, *Fortune* applied the same generalization to General Motors, saying, ". . . no [automobile] worker has any assurance that he will be working next year where he worked last."[18] By 1935, said Leon Henderson, job fear had reached the danger point along Detroit's assembly lines. Brought to the fore at last, under union auspices, the slogan of "seniority" had fighting value; it dramatized an issue that ran as deep as the struggle for life itself; it meant something to mass production workers whose jobs had been resting on quicksand for more than a decade.

When labor organizers began to force this issue at Dearborn, Henry Ford professed, once more, to be the exception that proves the rule. In December 1940, his advertisers proclaimed, "The Ford Motor Co. has no age limit for labor; and in fact deliberately attempts to keep older workers working."[19] This publicity called attention to the fact that in keeping with his esteem for the loyal older worker, Ford was carrying three octogenarians on his payroll. Visitors who toured the Rouge in 1939 were conducted to a conspicuous bench at which light assembly work was being performed at a sleepy pace by three veritable Methuselahs. The factory guides never hurried past this "seniority exhibit," this visual proof that the master lacked heart to turn a faithful servant out to pasture.

Ford's apologists produced figures to show that an inordinate number of Ford men were over forty, and the harder the union pressed the Ford Motor Co., the more this unchecked age count redounded to Ford's credit. In 1930, Ford had said that 33 per cent of his workers were forty or older. In 1937 Cameron raised the proportion by 10 per cent. The Ford advertisement of December 1940, maintained that the fraction of middle-aged or elderly workers had risen to "nearly one-half" of the total Ford payroll. Finally, when the struggle with the union entered the acute stage, the *Ford Almanac,* one of Ford's house organs, advanced the claim that 54 per cent of the company's personnel lay on the shady side of forty.[20]

Thus, by counting heads, by pointing up colorful examples, and by reiterating preachments, Ford made a determined effort to establish the claim that his men already enjoyed tenure without having to fight for it. At his plant, he told the world, life on the assembly line did not stop at forty; once a Ford man, always a Ford man.

But on this question, as on the wage issue, Ford was making out a case that the facts belied at every turn. To begin with, the same motives and the same competitive conditions that governed other mass producers in their past approach to the question of labor tenure had been compelling in his case as well. To lower his costs and increase his earnings, Ford had never hesitated to throw employe tenure overboard, to oust his older men, or to eliminate jobs that called for higher pay. In hewing to this policy, as long as his workers were unorganized, he had behaved like any other private employer who made a spectacular success of low-cost, high-speed, high-profit technology.

While job insecurity was characteristic at the Ford Motor Co. —particularly in 1914, in 1921, from 1926 to 1928, and throughout the depression—for the same reasons that employment was precarious at any comparable business institution, it had been intensified at the Rouge and at Highland Park by a purely personal factor. This additional source of job anxiety among Ford men grew out of Ford's familiar idiosyncrasies as an administrator. At least four major conditions of Ford insecurity could be attributed solely to the eccentricities of Ford management.

First, Ford was personally responsible for aggravating the job fears of his personnel because of his limitations as a merchant. Twice

in his history, first with the Model T and six years later with the
Model A, he had imposed unnecessary hardships on his men in failing
to anticipate a changing market.

Second, Ford had gone to extremes in disregarding labor's tenure
for the further reason that no other comparable employer was so sure
of his own self-sufficiency or so driven by the compulsion to cut costs
at the expense of his personnel.

Third, the practice of keeping men at sixes and sevens was an
essential part of the old Ford psychology of feudal management.

Fourth, workers and executives alike at the Rouge had been kept
on tenterhooks because of the instrument which Ford created to put
his principles of management into practice. Ford Service had undercut
the security and peace of mind of every employe on the Ford roster
by placing alongside the company's technical management a super-
management composed of spies and policemen and politicians, and
by substituting for a rule of reason at the company's employment
office the expediencies of machine politics.

All in all, when Ford spread the word in 1937-1941 that he alone
among the great mass producers had been the respecter of job security,
he was playing again at the game of make-believe. Here, as elsewhere,
some of his past practices had been no better or no worse than those
of the industry at large. Others had been beyond question the most
abusive in the trade. By the end of 1938, when all automobile workers
except his own had been successfully organized, the Ford job was
on every count the least dependable in the business. The time had
come when only the Ford Motor Co. was free to lower wages at will
or to discharge men without rhyme or reason. Ford's competitors, on
the other hand, were now bound to observe a code of seniority
whereby, other things equal, the oldest man in point of service was
last to be laid off and first to be rehired. Ford's men were all the more
anxious, therefore, to take the Ford job out of politics, to strip Ford
Service of its control of hiring and firing, to put an end to the tradition
of annual dismissals and seasonal wage cuts, and to make skill and
length of service the sole criteria of survival on the job.

What had loaded the wage and seniority question with a terrific
emotional charge in all automotive plants, however, was a third pre-
union condition of unemployment—the speed or "pressure" of the line.
On this primary issue—as to what constitutes a rate of production that
is tolerable as well as efficient—automobile labor had developed its
deepest rancor and its strongest antagonisms toward management.

This is not to say that the typical factory hand of Detroit was dead set against speed-up in any form, or that he was bothered by the feeling that he was "above" his work. It was clear to him, as to anyone, that if the machine is to be given a chance to do the work of the world, someone—in fact, millions of someones—must do the minute, routine, mechanical chores of line production; the endless, repetitive, high-speed sorting and bolting and screwing and assembling. At Ford's or at similar shops the average worker was probably content, and even anxious, to submit to a fast-moving line and to the necessary discipline of mass production—under certain conditions. All he asked (and nothing less could give meaning and dignity to his ant-like tasks) was that he should share, with others, the fruits of the machine economy, that his efforts be related to a common purpose. Up to a certain point, the man on the automobile assembly line could identify his own welfare with the great social gains of the machine order. He took pride in the fact that he was a part—if never a very secure one—of the workshop whose technology is the admiration of the world. Like most other members of society, he unquestionably believed in the machine system; he knew that only the miracles of line assembly could bring the automobile and other goods within reach of the common man.

Rebellion against the speed-up hit the industry like a tidal wave at the point where the man in the shop was convinced that the machine had failed to live up to its promise insofar as it affected him. The success of high-speed technology, in enriching its owners and managers and, more particularly, in widening the mass market for his own product, added to his feelings of resentment. Against these partial successes of the machine, he could contrast the hard fact of what factory speed-up had meant to him in twenty-five years' time; it had pushed him on production in most shops beyond the limits of human endurance; but it had not made his station in life proportionately better off or more secure. On the contrary, the pressure of the line had become, in a personal sense, the chief threat to his security and well-being.

The revolt against factory speed-up did not crystallize, however, until the depression. It came, finally, as a result of management's rigorous effort to retrench at a time when it was no longer possible to cut corners or to achieve great, new economies merely by rearranging the machinery of production. It came after all the major efficiencies of line production and all the revolutionary mechanical arts of the trade had been worked out to perfection, and after the machine as such had lost its cost-cutting magic of the 20's. By 1930, therefore,

354 THE LEGEND OF HENRY FORD

the only way to run this remarkable and almost perfect apparatus cheaper was to run it faster, just as it stood. On the line this meant additional pure man speed-up, or in the language of the shop, lowering costs by "taking it out of the men."

Under the stress of a depression market, that is exactly what automobile management did. The employers of the industry had the power to extort greater output from their men and they used it. Their leverage in the undertaking was the leverage of unemployment. Their agent, the line boss, had a ready answer for every assembler or machine tender who spoke up against the new "depression" pace. With a thousand variations and in a dozen languages his answer was the same on every conveyor belt in Greater Detroit. It was, in short, "If you don't like it, there're plenty waitin' at the gate outside who do. So get goin'!"

As a consequence, automobile labor was pushed to the breaking point. Prodigious new quotas of output were wrung from lines that had been fast and taxing in the 20's, and although the depression pace was more feverish than ever before, it was seldom, if ever, broken by periodic intervals of rest. As in the preceding decade, it was the rule of the trade to hold men to the line for four hours at a stretch without a pause. Nor were there adequate provisions in most automotive shops for "spelling" men even in emergencies. According to the Henderson Report, it was a common occurrence in 1934 for a worker who wanted to take time out for a drink, for a trip to the washroom, or even for first-aid treatment in the case of a minor injury, to have to wait at his station for hours before he could get a relief man to take his place.

No man who spent and drained himself on the assembly line during these years could have been expected to think of his job without bitterness and apprehension. As far as he could judge, the enormous factory speed-up of the 30's was neither voluntary—as in all-out production to win a war—nor beneficent. At the point where it touched him, line forcing undermined wages; it endangered health and safety; and it took away the last remnants of job security.

In depression speed-up, the man on the line saw, first of all, a threat to his earnings. It was as logical for him to call the effect of the stretch-out "a disguised wage cut" as it was for management to describe the same process as a means of "lowering costs." Earnings had withered; the trade was operating on a short year and with limited schedules of production. Under such circumstances it was a worker's natural, if selfish, reaction to feel that the faster he labored, the sooner he would "work himself out of a job" and the chance of earning any income at all.

In addition, when operated at abnormal rates of speed, the automotive belt was a man-killer. Its depression toll in accidents alone will never be known because many, if not the majority, of the lesser mill injuries of the period went unreported. A stiffer price for the speed-up was paid in terms of nervous and mental tensions that left no record of any kind. But the fact remains that the men who tended the lines at the time considered the pace more than their bodies could stand. They could feel the speed-up in their bones. They were convinced that standing up to such a pace was aging and debilitating.

Finally, speed-up was the key to the problem of job survival. If there was any one formula for hanging on in the pre-union days, particularly during the depression, it was an assembler's capacity to "take it." Hence the game of playing off the old against the young, a fierce struggle in which the older worker of the trade was competing against double odds. In countless instances, it made no difference how well he had performed in the past or what degree of stamina he could muster in the present; he was often dropped for good after a seasonal lay-off all the same, simply because age deadlines were drawn arbitrarily. On the other hand, if he managed to hold his own by matching the young, motion-for-motion, he was harassed by the knowledge that other men had sapped their energies to the point of burning themselves out on high-pressure line assembly. Among middle-aged automobile workers of the period no belief was more widespread than the conviction that it was only a question of time before the man who gave the best of himself and the best working years of his life to the line paid for it in the end by "working himself out of the mill."

Inevitably, therefore, automobile labor focused its hostility on this issue where the rub was sharpest, on the management practice which was the outstanding symbol, as well as the tangible and immediate cause, of job anxiety on every line. Management had ample opportunity to anticipate such a reaction. The speed-up was the focal issue of Detroit's wave of scattered and spontaneous depression strikes. This omen of labor insurrection was familiar to every employer in the business, though it was seldom mentioned aloud. No Detroit industrialist could have missed the point of the handbills and the shop papers that began to well out of the factories of the area. These contraband publications, appearing spontaneously or under left-wing auspices, were flaming indictments of the speed-up. Nor were they far wrong in their facts. Their charges were confirmed in essence by the Henderson Committee which surveyed the labor morale of the trade in 1934. In their report to the federal government, the Henderson investigators summed up the worker's feeling toward automotive speed-up by saying, "If there is any one cause for a conflagration in the automobile industry, it is this one."[21]

But despite the danger signals, Ford met this basic sign of labor disaffection by making the familiar flourishes. He talked, as ever, the language of moderation and benevolence. By various approaches to the subject he made it sound as though *his* men, at least, had been spared the abuses of line forcing. His argument on the issue could be reduced to three characteristic patterns.

First, it was Ford policy to rebut charges of speed-up by limiting the discussion to the virtues of mass production and by dismissing the critics of line assembly as enemies of the machine-order or of civilization itself. Thus, in one of his Sunday evening talks over the air, W. J. Cameron eulogized the regimen of the belt line as a miracle of "Christendom." "We say Christendom," he said, "for it is significant that there the machine has come to fullest flower."[22] In its specific effect on the conditions of labor, line production was extolled by Ford's propagandists for the reason that it had abolished any number of the "back-breaking" jobs of industry. From this acknowledged fact, the moral was drawn that the labors of the modern factory worker are safer, lighter and less tiring than the "brute strength" jobs of an earlier day.

Second, Ford and his spokesmen defended the status quo of the assembly line by imputing a special mentality to the men who drift into mass production. As Ford put the question in his book, *Today and Tomorrow* (1926), line assembly calls for the performance of many jobs that are, indeed, "exceedingly monotonous." But this is a fortunate state of affairs, he wrote, for dull work is a "boon" to the "many" factory hands who have "no brains."[23] Contrariwise, according to Cameron, the only people who object to the boredom or the drudgery of the line, under any conditions, are "bookmen" and "writers" whom nature never intended for factory work and "the pale, inactive critic [who] is out of touch with his times."[24]

Third, if one were to accept the publicity of the Ford Motor Co., Ford men had never had legitimate cause for complaint on grounds of factory pressure for the pace of the Ford line has been at all times humane and moderate. To quote Ford, we learn of "nervous exhaustion" on the part of workers who have been "driven" in mass production only from "books" or in the "library," but never from "the men" themselves.[25] Cameron in turn seldom, if ever, discussed the possibility of high-pressure production without edging away from the very term "speed-up" and penning it up inside quotation marks. But of all the denials of Ford speed-up, the most direct and sweeping was issued by Ford himself in the midst of his fight against the union. Carried by the Hearst press, this declamation appeared on November 16, 1940, in the body of an article in which Ford expressed at the outset his sentiments on various issues of world import.[26] Reviewing his career as a pioneer of line production, Ford was quoted as saying, "We see to it that our employes are never overtired in mind and body."

Of the several propositions that were advanced in order to set Ford apart as the humanitarian of the assembly line, not one holds water. The first is indeterminate; the second, a half-truth; the third, completely false.

In pointing up the recognized assets of a machine culture and in exalting the machine because it has eliminated jobs that require sheer manpower, Ford propaganda was talking around the issue; it was begging the question of speed-up. What Ford neglected to add, in this posing of the problem, was that under certain conditions modern industrial fatigue had taken on a new and exaggerated form because of the very nature of line assembly. This change in the quality of factory labor and in potential wear-and-tear on the part of the men followed from the fact that high-speed, flow-line production made it possible, and even necessary, to push and confine men in the automotive shops as never before in the history of the factory system. By his failure to come to the point or to discuss whether or not the modern factory hand could be, nervously or physically, more spent and worn than the worker of a previous generation whose labors had been heavier but more deliberate and less continuous, Ford's first answer to the question of speed-up was no answer at all.

Nor does it close the argument to contend with Ford that many men are content to do routine assembling because they are born that way, or to hold with Cameron that only intellectuals or outsiders who are "behind the times" take issue with the dullness of line production. Neither of these rejoinders met the question head-on, for the case against speed-up, as stated by labor itself or by "writers" and "bookmen," had been aimed for the most part not at the kind of work men do in mass production, but at the conditions under which they do it. The rebels of the line were protesting not against monotony, but against pressure, against the power of the belt to drive them to the point of wilting them. Moreover, to state that certain men take to factory work like ducks to water is no justification of the assembly line and no description of its operation. It is only a way of saying that, in meeting the requirements of the shop, men differ in their powers of adjustment; some work harder than others and give themselves to the line more fully than others, and for a variety of reasons, including the fact that certain top performers have, as Ford put it, "no brains." But here again, Ford was not clinching his case against speed-up. In describing the mentality of his workers, he failed to describe the requirements of his line, whether its demands had been harsh or lenient, whether its pace had been immoderate or humane.

When it came to saying out-and-out that "speed-up" is a fiction and that workers on the Ford line had never been "driven" or "over-tired," Ford was speaking as the myth maker. He was, again, throwing facts overboard for the sake of propaganda. Actually, the story of Ford speed-up simply repeats in miniature the story of speed-up in the industry as a whole, with the distinction that, as against the condition that prevailed in other automotive shops, line forcing and labor pushing at Ford's began earlier and lasted longer and was, in certain respects, more severe. Like most of his competitors, Ford used the device of incessant, cumulative man speed-up for a generation, both as an everyday procedure and as a means of working his way out of repeated business crises, and his workers reacted accordingly.

The speed-up that came with the depression and with the crisis of the Model A was so unrestrained that protest on the part of Ford's employes no longer represented the chafing of a bold or articulate minority. It was beginning to reflect, instead, majority opinion and an incipient, organized opposition. The signs of this shift were unmistakable. Ford's men were one of the first groups in the industry to start printing and circulating a militant, left-wing shop paper whose columns were given over chiefly to the subject of man pushing. Employes of the Ford Motor Co. were among the embittered witnesses who told their stories of speed-up to the Henderson Committee. At least once during the depression, the Rouge plant was the scene of a brief and unheralded "speed-up strike." Occurring on February 26, 1934, this localized stoppage was wholly spontaneous. The men who took part in it were acting on their own and without contact with any outside labor organization. They simply broke under the strain and walked off the job en masse.[27] Factory forcing was a central issue of two, similarly spontaneous, depression strikes which took place at Ford's assembly plants at Chester and Edgewater.

From 1937 to 1941, the standing complaint against Ford speed-up became more insistent because of the reforms which the union succeeded in wresting from Ford's competitors. During this interval, every leading concern in the field—with the single exception of the Ford Motor Co.—had agreed to recognize the rate of production as one of the accepted issues of collective bargaining. Ford, meanwhile, departed from his traditional practice of line forcing only insofar as temporary concessions served the purpose of combating the union and of countering the demand for any permanent reform. Thus, in 1937, when organizational efforts were at their height, the management at Dearborn instituted its own "slow down." But when the storm passed and it began to look as though the union either was unable to cope with Ford Service or was at the point of postponing its Ford drive indefinitely, the practice of man pushing returned to the Ford line unabated, and it persisted as long as Ford Service was able to best the union. The degree to which Ford speed-up differed from the general practice for the next three and one-half years was recognized throughout Detroit by workers and management alike.

Ford was now operating the only large plant in Detroit in which the men were never consulted about their rate of output and in which the standard of production for all, regardless of age or physical strength, was the most that management could squeeze from its employes. Under no obligation to observe the canons of seniority that were in force at competing shops, the Ford Motor Co. alone could hold the whip hand over its men by exploiting fear-of-the-job, and Ford made the most of his opportunity. Ford Service continued to push up production by the dog-eat-dog tactic of pitting young workers against the old, the normal against the handicapped, and race against race. When the old vocabulary of factory driving had gone out of circulation at most factories in Detroit, it was still an everyday experience at the Rouge to hear the Serviceman or the line boss bawl, "Better get goin', Buddy, or you'll be out on Miller Road pretty damn quick!" or "What the hell's the idea o' lettin' that nigger get ahead o' you!"

By contrast with conditions that prevailed at other automobile plants, the drive and tension enforced by the Ford line was distinctive from 1937 to 1941 for the added reason that the Ford Motor Co. was the only establishment in the field which had made no systematic provision for "spelling" its men. At a time when most of the workers of the trade had won morning and afternoon rest periods, varying in length from five to fifteen minutes, the men who worked for Ford either had no regular relief intervals at all or permission to take time out had been conceded to them in such a manner that the privilege was regarded with suspicion.

While Ford was fighting the union, the stress of a job at the Rouge was also unique because of plant regulations governing how the men should act during periods of mechanical breakdown. Ford discipline on such occasions may be contrasted with that of a unionized plant. At Chrysler's, for example, when the line was "down" for repairs and the men were waiting for the signal to start up, it was permissible for a worker to take a seat, to chat with his neighbor, or to munch a sandwich. During similar emergencies at Dearborn, however, it was a violation of company rules to leave one's station, to sit down, or even to lean against a post; any and all signs of "letting down" were strictly forbidden; the operator was expected to carry on as though nothing had happened.

By contrast with other automobile workers, Ford men from 1937 to 1941 had, in addition, fewer opportunities to unbend or to break the strain even while eating their lunches. Out of deference to Ford's personal inhibition against the use of tobacco, smoking was taboo at Dearborn between shifts, as at all other times, and because the mere act of two or more men collecting at a given point was viewed with suspicion by Ford Service, Ford workers, though supposedly "at ease," held themselves in, denied even the normal release to be found in passing the time of day with a co-worker who might have been close at hand. At most unionized mills, the men were free to "let down" between shifts by smoking or moving about socially and exchanging small-talk, or if they felt like it, squatting in a circle over a quick hand of cards. At this period the worker who had exercised such liberties at Dearborn would have courted instant dismissal. Hence, in contrast to the midday relaxation that was provided for in other automobile factories at the time, the noon-day "spell" at Ford's was, psychologically speaking, no "spell" at all.

When Ford speed-up, uncurbed for twenty-five years, finally produced a protest movement of major dimensions, the verdict of "the men" was borne out in Detroit both by members of the medical profession and by attorneys who were recognized authorities in compensation law. According to a substantial number of reputable local physicians who were engaged in the practice of industrial medicine, it was a common occurrence to find fatigue states and neurotic symptoms of every description in patients who had been long exposed to "the Ford pressure." In diagnosing what ailed innumerable Ford men,

at least some of these medical experts put their finger on the sheer
wear-and-tear of the Ford line, aggravated in its debilitating effect
by perennial feelings of insecurity and by a so-called Serviceman
phobia. Perhaps the weightiest evidence on this point came from
leading compensation specialists whose experience was state-wide,
covering all the shops of the industry. In the opinion of a number of
such observers, no assembly line in the history of the trade had ever
devitalized men or aged them prematurely more quickly than Ford's.
One of Detroit's leading figures in this branch of the law reported in
1939 that nothing was more characteristic of his "Ford clients" than
the person who looked sixty-five at fifty or the worker who at thirty-
five looked like a man of forty-five or fifty.

3

When the question of industrial safety and provision for the
disabled worker took its place among the issues that divided management and labor in Detroit, Ford's case was again put to the public
as that of the humanitarian without a peer. From the standpoint of
physical welfare, according to the widely published Ford advertisement of December 29, 1940, employes of the Ford Motor Co. had
always enjoyed conditions of work that were "the best in the industry."[28] In sanitation, safety appliances and "other health conditions,"
their working environment was said to be "far superior" to anything in
the trade, and by way of proving that "the chance of injury in a Ford
plant is much less than in the average automobile plant," the advertisement of 1940 stressed the point that the average American employer of
factory labor had an annual bill for workmen's compensation that was
relatively three times as high as Ford's.

This contention that no competitor could match Ford's safety
record is not amenable to proof in black and white. Comparative
accident rates within the trade are not a matter of public record, and
like most business establishments, the Ford Motor Co. has never aired
its own accident experience in any detail. Considering these facts,
the case for or against the proposition that Ford's "health conditions"
were "the best in the industry" was entirely circumstantial.

If one judged from externals alone, or from mere inspection of
the physical properties of the Ford Motor Co., everything that Ford
said about leading the field in accident prevention was true. The route
traversed by tourists who were taken through the Rouge was as
spotless as a Dutch kitchen. Nor was that all. In every branch of the

Ford business, cleanliness had been carried to the point of a fetish. There were a few notable exceptions to the rule, the Rouge foundry for one. But everything considered, no manufacturer in America had kept a neater, trimmer plant than Ford. More than that, the trade regarded Ford's mechanical safety devices by and large as up-to-the-minute and the best that money could buy.

But neither the polish of Ford's equipment nor the excellence of his safety appliances kept him from having his full share of industrial injuries. This judgment of the trade is convincing because of the number and credibility of the men who subscribed to it. For the most part, workers on the Ford assembly line had never felt that their chances of getting hurt on production were any less than those of assemblers at other plants in the area. The opinion that Ford's past accident rate was, at best, only average, was shared by a number of Detroit's ablest attorneys who had made a lifetime study of workmen's compensation. According to several of these experts, the "superiority" of Ford's "health conditions" would have been least evident in the old days, if it had been possible to make a case study of the more severe injuries of the trade, those to which workers were predisposed because of long-term, cumulative fatigue.

That Ford's quota of accidents was at least substantial was admitted inadvertently in 1938 by Serviceman Jim Brady, the boxing promoter and former prizefighter who was then one of Bennett's right-hand men. Brady's report on the subject was given to a newspaperman who was trying to locate a Ford worker who had been carried inside the Rouge for medical treatment after having been knocked unconscious by Ford Servicemen on Miller Road, outside the plant. When asked whether or not the victim in question had been cared for in a specified first-aid station inside the Rouge, Brady was quoted as saying, "So many people are treated there all the time, it is hard to check."[29]

There was, then, a contradiction between the "safe" and admirable outward appearance of Ford equipment and the preponderant feeling of the trade that accidents had been as common at Ford's as at any other comparable plant in Detroit. This meant, apparently, that in actual practice Ford's interest in accident prevention collided with his interest in low-cost production, and of the two drives, what seemed to matter most at Dearborn was production. This choice of ends is borne out by the indisputable fact that cost-cutting had been, almost without exception, the key to every Ford labor policy.

At bottom, therefore, there was no real coordination at the Ford

Motor Co. between the work of the safety engineer and the efforts
of the line boss. In fact, from most accounts, the two were working
at cross-purposes. By keeping the machinery clean and well-equipped
with protective devices, the one made the Ford shop a safer place
to work, and his efforts were noteworthy. The production boss
canceled out this advantage and increased the risks of injury by driving men and "pushing" the line. What damaged Ford's safety record,
consequently—despite the real superiority of his formal provisions for
safety—was the speed-up. Moreover, this condition of employment
persisted at the Ford Motor Co. in full force long after other companies in the area had revised their practices of man pushing. Thus,
if the chances of injury at the Rouge plant were never conspicuously
lower than average at any time, they were probably higher than
average from 1937 to 1941. During that four-year interval, Ford speed-
up was unique, and the Ford assembly line must have been, accordingly, one of the most hazardous in the trade.

At the same time that he was boasting of his safety record, Ford
professed to have shown special concern for the disabled worker.
Except for the carrier of contagious disease, he wrote in his autobiography in 1922, no employe of his had ever been dropped from
the payroll on account of his physical condition.[30] Even in the cost-
cutting 30's, according to repeated official accounts, the Ford Motor
Co. employed an army of 11,000 workers who were "blind, crippled,
or otherwise incapacitated for normal productive work."[31] Cameron
stated that in 1934, 20 per cent of the total Ford personnel was made
up of the physically handicapped.[32] This alleged treatment of the
"incapacitated" was pointed up, in turn, as one more proof of Ford's
effort in behalf of the underdog. Ford employes who were physically
under par, said the Ford advertisement of December 1940, had not
been selected "for their ability to build cars or to maintain the plant.
They are on the payroll because of Henry Ford's belief that the responsibility of a large company to labor goes beyond the point at which
the unfortunate worker can no longer produce profitably."

No test of Ford's regard for disabled workers is more illuminating
than his record of litigation in the field of workmen's compensation.
It is a commentary on the pretensions of the Ford Motor Co. that such
a record even exists. For if Ford had kept his word and made jobs
for all or most of "his own" incapacitated workers, none or few of his
men would have had occasion to sue him for damages. However,
denied regular employment after suffering disabling accidents at the

Ford plant, thousands of men had to go to law to win any recognition whatsoever.

In these innumerable instances of litigation, aggrieved employes prosecuted the Ford Motor Co. under the terms of the Workmen's Compensation Act of Michigan. This statute, passed originally in 1912 and subsequently amended, created a special agency of the state government for the settlement of accident claims. In addition, the act placed a statutory upper limit on the size of the disability grant for which any petitioner might qualify. According to law, the most an employer had to provide in 1939 for a worker who had been completely incapacitated for life was $9000, payable at the rate of $18 a week for 500 weeks. Smaller (maximum) awards were stipulated for temporary or lesser disabilities.

As the act stood and as it had been administered for many years by the state Department of Labor and Industry, it allowed wide scope to the industrialist who wished to contest the claims of his injured workers on principle. It was possible for the illiberal employer to make the most of technicalities that had been inserted in the law to prevent fraud and malingering. His legal representatives could oppose the spirit of the statute by challenging the credibility of the petitioner or by haggling over the size of the award. By invoking his rights of appeal and review, the close-fisted employer could, if he chose, make litigation in any given case almost interminable.

The corporation which was disposed to fight the law had an overwhelming advantage over the isolated worker in the caliber of the experts whom it could marshal for the purpose. It could muster foremen and co-workers to dispute the word of the petitioner. It could draw on the talent of a full-time staff of compensation specialists. The individual petitioner, on the other hand, usually came into court out of work and out of funds. Up against experts, he could speak for himself or he could hire a lawyer on a contingent basis. In the latter case, his legal representative was often neither as able nor as conversant with the law as counsel employed by the defendant corporation.

To the extent that medical testimony affects the outcome of compensation proceedings, Ford's position was particularly strong in that he owned the hospital which treated most of the men who had been seriously injured in his employ. No outside practitioners were admitted to this institution. Hence the opportunity to examine "Ford accident cases" immediately after injury had been limited for the most part to Ford's own physicians. Under such circumstances, the Ford doctor who took the stand to testify against a former patient had access to important evidence which the petitioner or the petitioner's counsel was in no position to duplicate.

Moreover, politics and jobbery had worked in favor of the employer who made a point of resisting compensation claims. This was particularly true when the will of the business community was largely unopposed in matters of state government. Thus, year in and year out, the Workmen's Compensation Act of Michigan was administered by Republican appointees. As long as labor was unorganized and politically impotent in the state, an undue proportion of these compensation referees were, consciously or unconsciously, management minded. They were "corporation" men by and large, because of their affiliations or their past obligations or their hopes of future preferment. It was a common practice, among other things, for the labor commissioners of the state to go direct from government service into private industry. A number of such office holders left their posts to become compensation consultants.

Implemented, then, with legal and political power which was beyond the reach of an individual factory worker, Ford had a "compensation history" that was both better and worse than that of his fellow industrialists. It was better in that the Ford Motor Co., in lavishing attention on a minority of its disabled employes, had gone to extremes. Ford's liberality, in such instances, had no parallel in the trade; no other corporation did as much for an injured man. At Ford's expense and quite apart from any legal obligation, disabled Ford workers had received long-term medical treatment that would cost the average patient thousands of dollars. More than that, after failing in an exhaustive effort to restore an incapacitated employe, the Ford Motor Co. had been known to go out of its way to assist the man's family by offering employment to one or more of his closest relatives. Many cases of this character were handled quietly. Others were highly propagandized. Nation-wide publicity was given in 1922 to the story of William Piso, an employe of the Ford Motor Co. who was disfigured for life while working on Ford's railroad, the D. T. & I. When Piso declared from a hospital bed that he had no intention of suing for damages, Ford rose to the occasion by volunteering to pay the man's hospital bills, to give him full wages and a bonus for his lost time, and to guarantee him a lifetime job.[33]

In the record as a whole, however, there was nothing to support the contention that Ford had ever recognized either the guarantee of employment or the payment of liberal compensation as one of his "responsibilities" to the disabled worker who could "no longer produce profitably." The Piso case and others like it are extraordinary. They were as rare as they were unpredictable. They occurred, apparently, when Ford or one of his intimates had been moved by whim. For the rank and file, Ford was as tough as they came in the field of workmen's compensation. In his dealings with the incapacitated employe, he was second to no industrialist in the state in his effort to drive a close bargain, to wriggle out of his legal obligations, to reduce compensation payments to a minimum or to oppose the concession of any disability award at all.

One index of Ford's real attitude toward the disabled worker is the past conduct of the legal department which handled his injury cases. The attorneys who represented the Ford Motor Co. at compensation hearings were generally able and personally fair-minded. But these men were agents rather than formulators of Ford policy. On occasion, they would lean over backward to treat a petitioner generously. As a rule, they would meet the claims of the Ford employe with spirited, if not bitter, opposition. Engaged in the cold business of saving money for the Ford Motor Co. at the expense of the individual worker, Ford counsel did not hesitate to take advantage of legal subterfuge. Examples of such procedure have been reported by the liberal and labor press for years.[34]

Nor is a vigorous prosecution in compensation proceedings the only technique which the Ford Motor Co. used to combat the legal rights of its disabled workers. To reach the same end, Ford management employed as well a strategy that was far more subtle and far more demoralizing to the handicapped employe. While by no means invariable, this further tactic was exploited often enough to constitute a familiar pattern in the past experience of many Ford men.

The process in question used to begin with a voluntary offer on the part of the Ford employment office to rehire a disabled worker as soon as he was able to get about and before he had reached the point of taking any legal action against the company. In cases of this sort it was a common practice to fit the man to the job, to give him light assembly work or to provide him with a "sitting" or "one-arm" job.

Few handicapped workers could afford to pass up such an opportunity. Nor was Ford's offer often, if ever, declined by any employe who was able to walk. If the mill was working full time, reemployment at suitable work meant a chance to regain one's footing while earning $30 a week or more, and it held out a promise that another "William Piso" case was in the making, that here was another fortunate employe to whom the company might show preference in the matter of status and tenure.

It follows that the injured worker who was taken back into the mill put aside any thought of "making a case" of his disability. Under this arrangement, there was no cause for litigation. The disabled employe had a job; his wages were higher than the top award which he could hope to win under the Workmen's Compensation Act, and under any circumstances, no injured man likes to go to law if he can avoid it. A compensation action costs money; it stamps the litigant as an "unemployable;" the petitioner's suit may prove unsuccessful; even if he wins it, the benefits are small and of limited duration; and in filing a compensation claim, the petitioner ran the risk—a very real one in Ford's case—of alienating his employer.

After accepting Ford's invitation to come back to work and after putting off an action for damages, many incapacitated factory hands learned to their grief that their reemployment was only the first stage of a tantalizing run-around. The reinstated man, in such instances, was "worked out of the mill;" sooner or later he lost his job either by drawing an outright lay-off or by getting transferred from light work to hard labor which he was unwilling or unable to perform, because of his physical condition. The Ford practice of shunting an injured employe to work that was beyond his powers of endurance or beyond his strength was documented in the "Report of a Thousand Examinations," an unpublished survey prepared for the automobile workers' union in 1938 by Dr. F. C. Lendrum, a former associate at the Mayo Clinic. Among the case histories recorded by Dr. Lendrum is that of a Ford employe who was offered light work at the Rouge plant before he had fully recovered from the effects of an operation for hernia. Two days after his reemployment, though he was still complaining of recurrent pain and other post-operative symptoms, the man was shifted to the job of lifting windshields on the Lincoln assembly line. Finding the new task too strenuous and getting no response to his request for a transfer, the worker walked out in disgust.

No estimate of Ford's concern for the disabled automobile worker would be complete without detailing, finally, the number of occasions on which the Ford Motor Co. refused to accept the preliminary findings of local deputy commissioners who ruled, at compensation hearings, in favor of the worker. In asking for a review in such cases, Ford was within his legal rights. He was empowered, like any other litigant, to take the matter to Lansing for a final determination by the Department of Labor and Industry. The worker, likewise, in order to pursue his claim had to bear the additional expense of buying a transcript of the original proceedings and of paying for further legal services.

In appealing compensation rulings that lay in favor of its employes, the Ford Motor Co. had an astonishing record. In 1937 and 1938, Ford was employing only one-fourth of the automobile workers of Michigan. Yet in that two-year period, *he carried more cases to Lansing than did all the rest of the automobile employers of the state put together.*[35]

It would appear, then, that propagandists for the Ford Motor Co. were broadcasting, at best, a half-truth when in December 1941, they cited a record of modest expenditure for compensation as proof of the "superiority" of Ford's "safety conditions." What they neglected to say was that these costs were low, in part, because Ford's policy of paying accident indemnities had been so hardboiled. In carrying his accident risks, Ford—like General Motors or Chrysler—was a self-insurer, and governed by the profit motive, he had operated his private compensation department by pressing his injured men harder and by challenging their rights more vigorously than any other leading automobile manufacturer in America.

When automobile workers the nation over began to league together to form a union, therefore, working conditions at the Ford Motor Co. were not what the public had been led to believe. Nor was Ford, as a handler of men, the lovable, human adventurer of modern capitalism or the enlightened patron of mass production at its best under private enterprise. On the contrary, the benefits of the machine which this great builder had done so much to extend to society at large were not conspicuous in the immediate lives of his own workmen. Most of the factory hands in his employ were assured of neither security nor self-respect, nor an American standard of living. What is more, the conditions of their labor over the preceding quarter of a century had not been bettered by a single, clean-cut industrial reform worthy of mention.

When all the leading manufacturers of the trade came to terms with the union several years ahead of Ford, there was a period when labor's status at the Ford Motor Co. was, on every score, the most backward in the industry. During that interval, the men at the Rouge could enumerate airtight grievances that held for their shop alone. Their wages trailed the field. Their speed-up had no parallel. Their jobs were the least stable in the business. If maimed at their benches, they were less assured of adequate protection than any other group of automobile workers in the state of Michigan. Nor was there at this time or earlier any plant in the community so spy-ridden as the Rouge or so drenched with a psychology that was calculated to break the spirit of men.

Ford more than once discussed men in general in terms that were quite in keeping with the facts of his labor history. On such occasions he gave it as his frank opinion that the man who works with his hands is a nobody. Most of the jobs in his mill, he asserted in one of his books, have no appeal for "men with brains."[36] According to his autobiography, the "majority of minds" are blessed by nature with a capacity to take the "drudgery" of mass production and like it.[37] Again, in his judgment, the man on the street is a congenital nitwit, doomed to failure. "It is evident," he wrote in the story of his life, "that a majority of the people in the world are not mentally—even if they are physically—capable of making a good living."[38]

Inasmuch as this contempt for the common man was made so evident by job conditions at the Rouge, feelings of unrest finally engulfed the Ford personnel. For a decade or more these feelings lay dormant and smoldering. Their existence was detected by the acute observer, however, years before they burst into the open.

As far back as 1927, B. C. Forbes, the financial analyst, expressed the conviction that if every employer in America were to take after Ford in his treatment of men, ". . . this country would be headed for the gravest trouble."[39] In arriving at this judgment, Forbes said he had received more unsolicited letters of complaint from Ford workers than from any other body of employes in the nation.[40] A year later, in 1928, in the course of gauging the morale of the Ford personnel, a reporter of the New York *Times* called Ford "an industrial fascist— the Mussolini of Detroit." This journalist cited Ford's organization as "the world's outstanding example of complete autocratic control of a vast industry."[41]

As the storm signs of unrest began to multiply at Dearborn during the depression, *Fortune* described the temper of the men inside the Rouge, "The atmosphere [at Ford's] is loaded with tension. You feel that if someone fired a cap pistol, 35,000 hearts would burst."[42]

When a vigorous national union of automobile workers finally took root in Detroit, there was nothing artificial or "manufactured" about its appeal to the Ford rank and file. As an organized mass movement, the union simply reaped the seed that Ford had sown. It offered a release for feelings of protest that had been long pent-up and long driven underground by Ford Service.

## Twenty-seven

### CALL-TO-ARMS

### 1

SURROUNDED by deep unrest within his own shops, Ford was not one to admit that his men had cause for complaint, nor was he disposed to deal with this discontent at its source or to disarm his opposition by granting concessions that went the union one better. Least of all did he relish the prospect of having to sit down with his men for purposes of collective bargaining. Moreover, to fend off these several eventualities, Ford was well equipped. In Ford Service he had an engine of suppression that had been twenty years in the making. This instrument had never failed him in the past. In his eyes, it seemed adequate for coping with the emergency at hand.

Therefore, in choosing to defend the status quo to the uttermost and to make the fight of his life against union recognition, Ford stated his position with supreme self-assurance. He was so confident of the outcome of the coming struggle that in April 1937, he proclaimed, "We'll never recognize the United Automobile Workers Union or any other union."[1] And while preparing to give that declaration force, Ford and Harry Bennett expressed open contempt for their antagonist. Labor organizations, said Ford at the outset of the struggle, are "the worst things that ever struck this earth."[1] In language that was identical in spirit but more forceful in content, Bennett—as quoted by the *American Mercury*—described the union he set out to crush as "irresponsible, un-American, and no god-dam good."[2]

As to the general character of Ford's effort to checkmate labor and to withhold the reforms which the union demanded, there is not the slightest room for doubt. Some of these maneuvers were recounted in the press. Others formed an integral part of Ford's official propaganda at the time. Most of the clinching details of the story were spread on the record as a result of nine separate legal actions which the federal government initiated against the Ford Motor Co. under the provisions of the National Labor Relations Act.* Ford's NLRB

* By November 1940, the NLRB had adjudged the Ford management guilty of engaging in unfair labor practices at nine of its plants, at the Rouge in Detroit and at eight of the company's branch plants—those located in Chicago, Buffalo, Dallas, St. Louis, Kansas City, Somerville (Mass.) and Richmond and Long Beach, California.

record alone is noteworthy both for its volume and for its content. Its exhibits and testimony run to tens of thousands of pages, and it documents the history of Ford's union resistance with a mass of evidence which only an agency of the federal government could have forced into the open.

The moment the union threat seemed imminent, Bennett girded himself for action by supplementing the permanent staff of Ford Service with a substantial force of fresh recruits. To one so familiar with the criminal colony and with former professional fighters, this process of enlistment was simplicity itself. How many men-at-arms he placed under his command in the course of raising the Service Department to full fighting strength is a matter for conjecture. John O'Brien, the Detroit reporter who wrote the *Forum* article on Bennett in 1938, put the number at 3000.* And this estimate seems to have hit the mark.

According to payroll records which the NLRB introduced in evidence, the Fords were maintaining at various plants from 1937 to 1939 a ratio of one Serviceman to every thirty production workers. In one instance, the proportion was much higher. At the assembly plant in Kansas City which employed more than a thousand men in 1937, there was one Serviceman on the job for every fourteen workers.[3] Ford Service reached its peak in manpower by the summer of 1937. It was then that the organization was designated by the New York *Times* as the largest privately owned secret service force in existence.[4]

But Ford Service, whatever its membership, was only one of a number of instruments which Bennett prepared for the coming struggle. He drew into his orbit, as well, underworld characters who had no official status as Servicemen. These outside colleagues were relied upon for assistance in espionage or for undertaking delicate assignments. During the Detroit hearing conducted by the NLRB, a former Serviceman took the stand to report, without contradiction, that while tracking down union members, he and another Serviceman made regular stops at a night club to confer with "Joe Tocco and his men."[5] Tocco was the gangster and former partner of "Black Leo" Cellura.

Placed on a war footing, the ranks of Ford Service and its outside allies were augmented in turn by agents whom the Ford management solicited en masse from the general run of its employes. Wherever

* In wages (at $6 a day), maintenance of 3000 Servicemen would have cost Ford four and one-half million dollars a year. These retainers earned their keep, however, insofar as their activity enabled the Ford Motor Co. to undercut the prevailing wage scale of the industry.

possible, foremen and workers on the line were induced to function
as auxiliaries of Ford Service.[6] Working undercover or in the open,
such operatives and assistants continued for the most part to perform
their normal factory duties. The men who engaged in this side activity
were impelled by varying motives. By some recruits in the Ford "sub-
service," the role of spy and strong-arm man was accepted, if not
relished, as the natural order of things. Thus, for his machinations at
the company plant in Dallas, Texas, Bennett segregated a group of
factory workers who were accomplished former boxers, wrestlers and
"muscle" men. He enrolled the bulk of his auxiliary agents, however,
by virtue of his authority in the personnel office of the Ford Motor Co.
Implemented with the power to hire and fire, he could, for purposes
of espionage and allied activity, dragoon candidates against their will.
Many of his aides from the rank and file were motivated, therefore,
either by the fear of losing their jobs or by the hope of winning
promotions or "easy" work.

While mustering his men-at-arms and their immediate satellites,
Bennett sought to insure the success of his contemplated operations
against the union by rallying still other supporters in the community
at large. He undertook, therefore, the task of mobilizing outside forces
that could be counted on to render aid to the Ford Motor Co. in its
hour of crisis. In such an effort, Ford's "personal man" could make
the most of his prestige as a long-time dispenser of patronage. Toward
many influential citizens in the area, he stood in the favored position
of a creditor calling in political debts which had remained, hitherto,
uncollected.

Among the outsiders whom Bennett began to court with renewed
vigor, though with familiar methods, were first of all politicians and
holders of public office. The Ford political machine performed as
never before in the municipal elections held in 1940 in the city of
Dearborn. Hunting bigger game, Ford Service surprised even the
business community with its bold and successful maneuvers within
the state and county apparatus of the Republican Party.[7] Insofar as
his efforts on the political front proved successful, Bennett hoped to
combat the union by influencing the use of the police powers in key
areas, by delimiting the rights of free speech and free assembly in
Ford communities, and by dealing with union organizers and union
members in his own way with little interference from the constituted
authorities of law and order.

Another outside agency which Bennett groomed for the emergency was the Knights of Dearborn. This organization had been

founded during the depression by former Serviceman Verne Doonan. It had functioned under the auspices of Ford Service as a vote-getting machine in Dearborn's municipal election of 1935. When the "Knights" were revived in 1937, they publicized their aim as that of "combating Communism" and "fostering true patriotism."[8] In private, they prepared to invoke vigilante methods for the purpose of converting the environs of Dearborn into a walled city.

Going still farther afield in their search for potential collaborators against labor, both Ford and Bennett made eyes at the war veterans of the nation. The two men, in the company of Detroit's chief of police, went to Chicago in October 1939, to attend a national convention of the American Legion. Appealing for the allegiance of men who had served in the armed forces during the first World War, Ford had remarked in October 1937, that Legion members comprise "the best police force in the country." While framing that tribute, he had made a point of reminding veterans of their debt to the Ford Motor Co. He called to mind the celebrated depression hiring when he had made jobs for 5000 Legionnaires.[9] Much the same sort of publicity had been issued in Bennett's name several months earlier, in June of 1937.[10] On the same day and on the same page that it carried this earlier statement of Bennett's, the New York *Times* published a separate story that helped to explain the meaning of Ford's studied effort to win a popular following among the country's former soldiers. According to the *Times*, anti-union forces in Michigan were recruiting at the time "a great army of volunteer strike-breakers," hoping to build this corps about a nucleus of Legionnaires and war veterans.

Among the camp followers who were eager to join hands with Ford Service or any other group in this fight against labor, there appeared in Detroit, finally, full-fledged American-Nazis. These volunteers were mentioned in the same issue of the New York *Times* that reported Bennett's appeal to the Legion. The *Times* of June 29, 1937, said, "The war veterans of Michigan who are being mobilized for strike-breaking duty are holding joint meetings with the 'Friends of New Germany.'" The latter organization was the immediate forerunner of the German-American Bund. The man who was then leading the "Friends" and who was to direct the destinies of the Bund until his imprisonment, was Fritz Kuhn, the "American Fuehrer." That the responsible heads of the Ford Motor Co. were not averse to forming a united front with this group of self-declared American-Nazis may be inferred from Kuhn's previous history. The American Fuehrer was listed on the Ford payroll as late as January, 1937.[11] Still earlier, while actually working at Ford's, Kuhn had been free to come and go, as necessity dictated, in his organizational work for the Friends of New Germany.

Wielding control or exerting influence over so wide an array of collaborators, Bennett set out to stifle the union at birth by dangling the threat of dismissal over the heads of its members who were employed at Ford's. In order to earmark the suspects who were destined for such intimidation, his informers embarked in 1937 on a head-hunt that went on, unabated, for the next four and one-half years. In ferreting out the identity of union members, Ford Service was not extemporizing on unfamiliar ground. On the contrary, its agents and auxiliaries were only enlarging upon techniques that were practiced and time-worn at the Ford Motor Co.

Inside the plant, this work of detection entailed a degree of skulking that was extraordinary even for Ford Service. Informers reported scraps of conversation overheard in the mill or on the approaches to the mill.[12] While at their benches, workers had their overcoats ransacked and their lunch buckets pried into. They were shadowed on their way to the drinking fountain and the lavatory. They were plagued by spies during the break between shifts. A key man in the local union at the Ford plant in Buffalo complained on the witness stand, without rebuttal, that at lunchtime he had been under the constant surveillance of Servicemen. As he sat down to eat his lunch on one occasion, he testified, two of Bennett's men closed in, one on either side of him, and remained seated at his elbows until the meal was finished.[13]

While stalking their prey inside the mill as never before, the emissaries of Ford Service extended the scope of the espionage which they carried on after working hours. They loitered as eavesdroppers in stores and taverns, in restaurants and hotel lobbies. They haunted the principal centers of union activity, endeavoring to tag the Ford men who appeared at labor gatherings. In May 1937, two Ford spies were apprehended by the Rev. John P. Boland in the act of shadowing a hall where members of the Ford union in Buffalo were about to hold a meeting. Father Boland was acting at the time as a regional director of the NLRB.[14] The favorite technique of identifying the Ford worker who participated openly in outside union affairs was predicated on the assumption that no body of informers could hope to recognize 100,000 men by sight. Hence, Bennett posted his agents near the chief labor halls of Detroit to record the license numbers of all the cars that were parked in the neighborhood day or night. He could then ascertain with ease the names of the car owners. The use he made of this information was later disclosed by Basil T. White, a former Ford clerk and a witness for the NLRB. Testifying under oath and uncontradicted by Ford counsel, White asserted that it had been his job to take the lists of names brought in by outside snoopers and to check them against the Ford payroll.[15]

In order to get to union membership lists at their source, operatives of Ford Service were detailed to spy on the enemy from within. With this object in mind, they tried first to corrupt union officials. Their second stratagem for sapping the union and bleeding its secrets from the inside was described by Bennett himself. Speaking out with the candor that set him apart from most Ford executives, past and present, Bennett boasted to the press in June 1937, that half the members of his personal Service staff, working undercover and posing as bona fide production workers, had taken out cards in the union.[16]

In thousands of instances that became a matter of proven record from 1937 through the early months of 1941, the Ford employe who was suspected of harboring union sympathies was promptly demoted or discharged. The first stages of meting out this form of punishment were described by former Serviceman William A. Stinson whom the NLRB summoned as one of its key witnesses in Detroit in 1941. Stinson testified that during his four-year term as a secret agent of the Ford Motor Co., he participated in daily meetings held in a first-aid station at the Rouge for the purpose of learning the names and badge numbers of newly discovered union suspects. Ford Service contrived forthwith, he said, "to get those men out of the buildings." To accomplish that end, according to the witness, Servicemen made the rounds of the factory, pointing out to the foreman in each department which of his men were to be "knocked off."[17]

Many of the dismissals that followed were straightforward and above-board.[18] In Ford plants throughout the country, men were openly advised at the time of their discharge that they had been seen at a union meeting, that they were "foolish" to try to "fight Ford," or that they had been "talking too damn much union."[19] Other employes of the company, packed off to the employment office to draw their last pay, were asked frankly, "How many handbills you been passing around the plant?" or "Wasn't you trying to give a fellow an application card to join the union, out in the parking lot?" Again, Ford foremen and Servicemen called at the homes of employes who had been laid off because of union activity, offering reemployment to those who would consent to drop out of the union and "play along

with Ford." Similar conversations stud the entire Ford-NLRB record.
Their credibility is enhanced, moreover, by the fact that much of
the Board's most impressive evidence on this point was volunteered
by former Servicemen and by former supervisory officials of the Ford
Motor Co.

In firing other workers, those in authority at Ford's indicated that
they were striking at the union. A few union suspects, immediately
before their discharge and for no good reason, were beaten up by
Servicemen on or near company property.[20] Similarly, the discharge
weapon was often invoked without delay as a means of retaliating
against Ford employes who were bold enough to come to work
wearing union buttons.[21] Such self-declared unionists were frequently
ordered from the plant or escorted to the street by squads of Servicemen. At the Ford factory in St. Louis in 1937, company guards and
watchmen denied the right of entry to employes who appeared at the
gate wearing union insignia. To these men who were turned away,
supervisory employes speaking with the authority of Ford management were frank: "If you want to go to work, you'd better take off
that button." Again, early in 1941, a foreman in the glass plant at
Dearborn went down the line and picked off the first forty men whom
he saw wearing pins that denoted union membership. Loaded in a
bus like suspects in a police wagon, this group on arriving at the
central employment office was discharged in a body.

With many of the men whom it wished to purge from the ranks
because of union affiliation, the Ford Motor Co. pursued a subtler
course. In such cases, Ford Service screened its real intentions by
"manufacturing" evidence against a victim. It was made to appear
that so-and-so was laid off because he had been "inefficient" or had
been late for work, or had been seen "loafing" or "singing" on the job
or "loitering in the toilet." In arriving at the opinion that the Ford
Motor Co. had built up a thin and artificial case against a multitude
of union members in its employ, the NLRB was supported by a mass of
incontrovertible evidence.

If Ford Service found a union suspect who was letter perfect in
his work and in his observance of all company regulations, it arranged,
time and again, to entrap him by resorting to devices from which
there was no escape. In the words of former Serviceman William A.
Stinson, one of the Board's witnesses in Detroit, "If we couldn't get
anything on a man that way, we'd frame him." Testifying under oath,
Stinson told how it was done. In one case, he told the Board, he had
someone dump pails of oil and scrap about a man's place of work.

The victim was then reported and discharged, he said, for "keeping dirty floors." The witness went on to describe how, on another occasion, he arranged to have a sweeper who was a former boxer "pick a fight" with a suspected union member. Whereupon the worker who had been goaded into defending himself was dismissed for violating a rule against fighting on company property. At the same time, according to Stinson, the aggressor—the company's *agent provocateur*—would be allowed to keep his job.[22] A still cruder instance of "picking fights" occurred in the Ford plant at Buffalo. There a production worker and active unionist who had a long and satisfactory work record was cast off in June 1937, the day after he had been assaulted on his way home from work. The attack was witnessed by two Servicemen who were standing nearby. His assailant, whom he had never seen before in his life, was later identified as a professional wrestler and an outside crony of Ford Service. Though the attack had taken place some distance from the plant, someone in the Ford Service Department falsified the termination record of the assaulted and discharged worker so that it read, "This employe caused disturbance with other employes in parking lot."[23]

Perhaps the most damaging admission of the depths to which Ford Service could stoop in framing union members was made from the witness stand by Elliott E. Murray, a former acting superintendent of the Ford assembly plant at Edgewater, New Jersey. This executive left Ford's employ in 1938. He served as a Labor Board witness in 1941. During his stay at Edgewater, Murray reported, it was a common practice to "pile up the work" so that a particular employe, already marked for the blacklist, would fall behind his co-workers and be able to catch up only if the entire line was stopped or slowed down. The "laggard" would then be fired for "inefficiency." Even lower methods were employed in order to "get" the unwanted Edgewater employe. A company spy would brush against a union man just before quitting time and slip a small wrench or gauge into his pocket. Immediately thereafter the unsuspecting workman would be searched by Servicemen. Then, accused of making off with company property and publicly branded as a thief, the "culprit" would be discharged forthwith.[24]

It was through no fault of Ford's that this thorough and underhand removal of union adherents failed of its ultimate purpose. While the fight was on, he was relentless in playing on the job fears of his men. From 1937 up to the summer of 1941, Bennett discharged more than 4000 Ford employes who were actual or suspected members of the union.* These 4000 dismissals, in turn, were held up to the rank and file by way of example. Their occurrence was pointed up in order to intimidate the employe who held back from the union because he was cautious and faint-hearted or because his mind was undecided. It was, therefore, a fundamental tactic of the Serviceman or the Ford straw-boss to broadcast warnings like, "You saw what happened to Joe! Better watch your step, or the same thing'll happen to you!"

In countering labor organization in this manner, Bennett timed his blows well. He struck early, picking off the leaders one by one, as soon as they showed their faces. Consequently, for the first two or three years of its existence, the Ford union was constantly drained of its bolder spirits, of its best campaigners, of its active members who had previous union experience elsewhere. Moreover, as long as it was cut down at infancy, the organization had no opportunity to prove itself or to win the confidence of the rank and file.

As a deterrent of the will to organize, the "Ford purge" of 1937-1941 owes much of its initial success to the strategic limitations of the union itself. For in making the job of "organizing Ford" the last of its original objectives, the national leaders of the United Auto Workers of the CIO unwittingly gave the Ford worker cause for watching his job with greater caution than ever. Because of this order of events, the employes of the Ford Motor Co. were stranded for three years or more on a non-union island; they were surrounded by organized shops whose operators, under union contract, were obliged to give preference to the hire and tenure of their own men. Under such circumstances, the ordinary Ford worker had a potent reason for lying low. If he exposed himself prematurely as a union man, he risked paying the price both of dismissal at Ford's and of unemployment everywhere else in the trade. That general fear continued to hamper the rise of a Ford union until 1940, when the United Auto Workers and the CIO finally brought their full energies to bear on the problem of bringing Ford into line with his competitors.

But long before the UAW could muster its strength for such an all-out engagement, its right to speak for the employes of the Ford Motor Co. was challenged by several labor organizations of the make-believe variety. Popping up at the Rouge or in Ford's satellite plants at about the same time in 1937, these mock unions, four in all, went by different names. There was the Liberty Legion of America,[26] the

* This figure is conservative and official. It was released in June 1941, when the Fords, after losing their battle against labor, agreed to rehire or to continue employing more than 4000 workers whom they had laid off because of union activity during the preceding four and one-half years.[25]

Workers Council for Social Justice, the Independent Automobile Workers Association, and the Ford Brotherhood of America. These "opposition" groups were, without exception, cut from the same cloth.

All were alike in making common issue against the CIO. All sprouted overnight. All made capital of the fact that they were "for the worker" but opposed to "radical activity" and "foreign isms." Each was adorned with a high-sounding name. Each was a puppet, tightly controlled from the top so as to prevent the infiltration of legitimate unionists. Not one had more than a paper membership, yet each—with one exception—was quick to boast that it, alone, was the qualified spokesman for Ford's workers.

Of these groups which set out to compete with the CIO, all were identical in purporting to have Ford's blessing. Only one was formally stamped by the NLRB as "illegal" and "company-dominated," yet all four were allowed to show their heads at all only because of connivance with Ford Service. Each was fostered by agents of Ford Service or by supervisory employes of the Ford Motor Co. The iron rule forbidding organizational activity at any time on company property was waived in the case of solicitors for one or the other of the "opposition" unions. These emissaries of "labor" were free to comb the mill during working hours, circulating pamphlets or application for membership cards. They made bold to caution the worker at his bench that he had better "join a thing Ford has a liking to," that "non-signers would find their names on the lay-off list," that only "saps" were joining the CIO. At the Ford plant in Long Beach, California, where a CIO organization was deeply rooted in 1937, the promoter who worked behind the scenes to instigate a rival union was A. G. Rogers, an assistant foreman. Rogers attempted to bribe one of the most popular shop stewards of the existing local union. He promised this man "some extra money" and a lifetime job if he would consent to switch over from the CIO and "go ahead with the company union organization."[27]

One or two of the "splitting" unions at the Ford Motor Co. could in truth flaunt a sizable membership, if only for a day. This support, however, was a product of the same technique that Bennett used in 1937 when he stampeded most of the production workers of the company into signing a "Vote of Confidence" in the labor policies of Henry Ford.[28] Signed by 98.3 per cent of the Ford personnel, these statements of satisfaction were circulated on company time in the presence of foremen and Servicemen. Signatures for the "loyalty pledge" were, in many cases, solicited by foremen. Non-signers were discharged or threatened with discharge.[29]

Both the "Vote of Confidence" and the reported membership of the Ford opposition unions had temporary propaganda value. Each was publicized in 1937 as an endorsement of Ford and a rejection of the CIO. The mere fact that the CIO had to compete with any rival organization at all at the Ford Motor Co. was exploited to create the impression that the Fords were unwitting victims of a "jurisdictional labor dispute" and that their employes were too divided to know their own minds.

Yet none of the make-believe unions at Ford's achieved its basic aim of weaning the rank and file from the CIO. They failed to pan out, in part, because they were too crude. Unlike the smooth, long-established "employe representation plans," which were once the rule in the American steel industry, the Ford organizations made no effort even to simulate collective bargaining. They failed to win a genuine following, furthermore, in having the open or covert approval of Ford Service. So, one by one, the competing "unions" defeated themselves.

Shortly after its founding in 1937, the Ford Brotherhood of America was discovered to be the handiwork of William S. McDowell, a professional organizer of company unions.[30] The Detroit *News* gave the death blow to the "Council for Social Justice" by reporting that two of its principal officers and full-time organizers were Ford foremen who had been granted leaves of absence.[31] Then, in 1938, the Michigan State Bar Association unmasked the auspices of the "Liberty Legion" by citing Judge Schaeffer of Dearborn for unprofessional conduct. The bar's Ethics Committee designated Schaeffer's work for the "Ford" union as "improper" and an attempt to "sell the prestige and influence" of judicial office.[32]

Finally, as a result of NLRB activity and of the efforts of organized labor generally, the company union movement petered out on a national scale. By 1939 it was finished, as an anti-union tactic, and Bennett, too intelligent to ride a dead horse, announced on January 20, 1939, that he was about to "dissolve" the "Liberty Legion," the most substantial of the Ford organizations.[33] He made this announcement, however, as part of a plot to capture the top leadership of the United Auto Workers of the CIO.

2

Bennett's scheme for rending the union from within revolved about Homer Martin, the United Auto Workers' first international president. In order to follow this line of attack, one must recall Homer Martin's history.

Martin began his adult life as a Baptist preacher. He left the ministry during the depression and went to work in an automobile assembly plant in Kansas City. He immersed himself in the CIO movement. Before long he became a full-time union organizer and the role seemed to fit him. Already an experienced public speaker, he developed rapidly into one of the ablest younger orators of the CIO.

It was the platform manner, more than anything else, that set Martin apart from his fellow unionists when the UAW held its first constitutional convention in 1936. At this early date none of the potential leaders of the organization had had adequate opportunity to prove his mettle. All were comparative strangers to the rank and file. In such a setting the UAW presidency went to the earnest young man who could "talk."

Within a matter of months, however, it was evident that the United Auto Workers had conferred its highest office on the wrong man. For apart from his forensic gifts, Martin proved to have few of the skills that his trust required. He lacked what it took to weather the storm of sit-down strikes, many of which were spontaneous and caught the UAW high command off-balance. Hence, the task of arriving at a strategy of organization and of steadying a membership drive that more than once got out of hand fell, of necessity, to his subordinates. When the union passed from the stage of agitation to that of collective bargaining, Martin was wanting as a negotiator. Despite his magnetism and self-assurance in the forum, he lacked force and presence of mind in the conference room. The basic practical job of coming to terms with employers for the first time had to be shunted, therefore, to men like Walter Reuther, Wyndham Mortimer and Richard Frankensteen.

Once the union had won most of its first dramatic battles for recognition, Martin had to meet a challenge within his own ranks. He was faced with a bitter factional fight that embroiled the UAW itself. This sapping struggle for power was largely a symptom of growing pains within a huge raw labor organization. The ensuing conflict pitted Martin against "unattached" leaders from the rank and file—most of whom were well-intentioned; others, careerists and opportunists. The Communists and the Socialists, though few in number, played a vigorous role in the struggle. Other participants in the fight were former labor spies who had not as yet been rooted out of the UAW. The largest number of all came from scores of spirited and powerful local unions that were often all too ready to value their own independence above any other consideration. Only a minority of these seekers of office had had any previous trade union experience.

Engulfed by union politics, Martin rapidly went from bad to worse. His every move only aggravated a situation that was already intolerable. By the end of 1937 he had himself become the arch-factionalist. The sharper the opposition and the deeper the crisis, the more he lost his head. His judgments on UAW policy and on questions of general interest to the CIO became increasingly erratic. All the while he was so sensitive to criticism that he brushed aside such counsel as was offered by interested outsiders like Philip Murray and Sidney Hillman. More and more he met the opposition within his own organization by calling it "Red" and ordering high-handed "expulsions."

Harry Bennett injected himself into the UAW's family quarrel in the summer of 1938. He began this intrusion by sending a confidential messenger to Martin to tell him that the Ford Motor Co. was ready to make peace with the union. Would the UAW president care to discuss the matter in private? The answer was "yes." Whereupon Martin held a series of secret meetings with John Gillespie, the former Detroit politician who was then functioning as one of Bennett's "labor fixers."[34]

When word got around that Martin was conducting backstairs negotiations with the Ford Motor Co., he was immediately suspect. He managed to save face temporarily only by insinuating that he was about to do the impossible—organize the Ford Motor Co. "from the top," single-handedly and without a struggle. When the truth was finally wormed out of Martin and his personal supporters, it appears that what the UAW president had listened to was a scheme for subverting his union.

If the proposals from Bennett had been accepted, there would have been concessions of a sort from the Ford Motor Co. For one thing, Bennett went on record promising to suppress one of his company unions. As a matter of fact, when he disbanded the Ford "Liberty Legion," he had done so, he said, at Martin's request.[35] The Fords were also said to be ready to submit to collective bargaining and willing to rehire all the NLRB complainants who had been discharged because of union activity.

Each of these gestures that emanated from Ford Service had a familiar ring. The promise to disestablish the principal Ford union was a flourish, no more. When Bennett decided to kill the "Liberty

Legion," it was already dead. The offer to reinstate NLRB complainants was equally empty. For, as matters stood during the period of the Martin-Gillespie talks, the federal government had already directed Ford to reemploy a large number of blacklisted workers and to make good their back wages. Similar relief was expected for hundreds of other Ford men whose cases were still pending before the NLRB. As for the pledge to recognize the union, all the UAW would have had to go on was promises; its only guarantee of performance was Bennett's reported oral word. In toying with Homer Martin, Ford Service would put nothing down in black and white.

All the concessions that Bennett expected in return, on the other hand, were real. They had teeth in them. As reported by Martin, the UAW was asked to drop its NLRB actions and to disassociate itself from all personal damage suits filed by union members who had been assaulted by Ford Servicemen. If the union had sanctioned this proposal, it would have thrown away its only legal leverage against the Ford Motor Co. It would have made it difficult for Washington to enforce the NLRA in Ford's plants. Another and even more basic demand from Ford Service was to the effect that the union withdraw from the CIO. Such a move, if effected, would have detached the UAW from the larger body that was giving it vigor and political direction. Finally, before he would consent to recognition, Bennett had insisted—or so the Martin faction alleged—that Martin retain the presidency of the union. "A sincere and honest champion of labor" were the words Bennett used in a press report to tell the world late in 1938 where he stood on Homer Martin.[36]

Once apprised of the "Ford Service deal," the UAW, however, saw Martin's character in a different light. All the opposition factions at last found a common issue. Spurred by the rank and file, the UAW executive board called a special meeting in January 1939, for the purpose of impeaching Martin. In the course of this hearing—which he refused to attend—Martin was "indicted" on fifteen counts; his "understanding" with Bennett was repudiated as "worse than a company union agreement;" his undercover negotiations, denounced as a "treacherous" attempt to "conspire with the enemies of the union." Then the board voted unanimously to strip Martin of his office and to read him out of the union. At a special delegate convention held two months later, the UAW presidency went to R. J. Thomas, a middle-of-the-roader.

Martin's next move was to form a union of his own. His group, he proclaimed, would be free of "CIO dictatorship" and "cleansed of

Red elements."[37] Wanting in prestige, he applied for affiliation with
the AFL. This body, which had never heretofore made any serious
effort to organize the industry, took him in to spite the CIO. Under a
new sponsorship and with money that seemed to come out of the air,
Martin then took his case to the NLRB, advancing the claim that the
UAW-AFL, and not the UAW-CIO, was the accredited bargaining
agency of the automobile workers.

All this was grist for Bennett's mill. He had nothing to fear from
Martin. As for the UAW-CIO, its funds were impounded, its bargaining machinery had all but fallen apart, its energies would be spent
in court actions and NLRB proceedings for months to come. Meanwhile a CIO drive at Ford's was out of the question. Ford Service
could, indeed, take pride in the fact that it helped to split the union
it had failed to capture. It was at this time, while speaking his mind
on the subject of labor organizations, that Bennett crowed, "Any time
I can't lick them, I'll join them."[38]

In the end, Martin's group lost by an overwhelming margin every
NLRB election of any consequence. Its leader retired from the field
for good in 1940. Before long, he reappeared as a manufacturer's
agent, working for a parts company that made its money doing business with the Ford Motor Co.[39] Simultaneously, he was often at the
luncheon table over which Harry Bennett presided in the Ford Administration Building.

When the UAW repudiated Martin and his dealings with Gillespie, it had surmised from past experience that Bennett was up to
trickery. It had already been duped by Ford Service at four Ford
assembly plants, those located in St. Louis and Kansas City and in
two California cities, Richmond and Long Beach. At all these branch
plants the UAW had a nearly unanimous following by the spring and
summer of 1937. The local management in each case began to fight
back. It was, of course, only following orders from Dearborn. For as
the NLRB was to discover later on, Ford's branch managers and
superintendents had received written instructions to the effect that,
"No representative of the Company shall talk with any person about
a labor dispute merely because such person claims he represents Ford
employes."[40] These orders were issued on April 27, 1937.

When the four local unions continued to flourish in the spring
and summer of 1937, Dearborn permitted what appeared to be an
about-face. It gave the union at each of these plants, and nowhere
else, de facto recognition. The local managements began to deal with
shop stewards, to see grievance committees, and to respect the union's

wishes on the question of seniority. This working agreement, relatively
frictionless, remained in force for the remainder of the summer. Meanwhile, union membership at these centers soared to the 90 per cent
point. Then, later in the summer, came the seasonal shutdown at
which time all the Ford factories were to be retooled for the 1938
model.

At this point Bennett disclosed what he had in mind when he
had allowed his subordinates to temporize with the union at the
plants in question. When the plants reopened for fall production, he
instituted a lockout. Only those who would renounce their union
membership were eligible for reemployment. Key union men, 94 at St.
Louis and 129 at Richmond, were not taken back at all. Almost the
entire working force was blacklisted at Kansas City, where 975 were
discharged at one blow.[41]

Classic methods were invoked to beat down the ensuing local
strikes. To give impetus to a back-to-work movement at Kansas City,
supervisory officials of the Ford Motor Co. were instructed to "scatter
the news" that Ford was about to move his Kansas City operations
to St. Louis. The police of Kansas City, taking orders from the Pender-
gast machine which then controlled City Hall, made mass arrests of
strikers and pickets.[42] At the same time they gave Ford Service free
rein. No arrests were made when a union organizer in the area was
cornered in a filling station and beaten so badly with hand billies
and a baseball bat that fifty-five stitches were needed to sew up his
wounds. Nor did the law take its expected course when a caravan of
strike-breakers en route to the Ford plant was searched by deputies
from the county sheriff's office and found to have in its possession
fourteen pistols, twelve loaded shotguns, a sawed-off shotgun and
fifty-five blackjacks.[43]

These isolated strikes were eventually beaten down. The four
local unions were obliterated; they lay dormant for the next three
and one-half years. In the meantime the story of Bennett's lockout
was painstakingly reconstructed by the NLRB, and the United Auto
Workers on a national scale had begun to pull itself together.

To the extent that Ford continued to fight the right to organize
after 1935, he automatically ran afoul of the federal government, and
like most industrialists over the country, he defied the NLRA from
the beginning. The moment the union set foot in Dearborn, the NLRB
had a case against the Ford Motor Co. This preliminary action before
the Board, based on Ford's allegedly illegal conduct at the Rouge
plant, was initiated in Detroit in 1937. It was followed in quick order

by similar proceedings in eight other cities where the Fords operate
assembly plants. In each of these separate actions, the government's
proof of the existence of unfair labor practices was irrefutable. At
four of Ford's outlying plants, the facts indicated that the union had
a following in 1937 that was all but unanimous.

Ford's workers were to be disillusioned, however, if they expected
to "organize Ford" merely on the strength of their NLRB charges or
if they looked to the government for a speedy settlement of their
differences with the Ford Motor Co. For at this point, Ford neither
changed his ways nor saw fit to let the Board's proceedings take a
swift or easy course. On the contrary, his Service Department continued to function as though the NLRA were nonexistent, and his attorneys embarked on a war against the act itself. That it was Ford's
intent to defeat or obstruct the union by legal maneuvering was
evident from the character of the defense which his lawyers raised in
their first dealings with the NLRB.

None of the nine Ford actions before the Board elicited greater
shrewdness from Ford counsel than those at Kansas City and St. Louis.
None of the other proceedings meant so much to either of the con-
testants, and in those cities, more than anywhere else in the country,
the union had a case that was air-tight. In both communities, it had
organized an overwhelming majority of Ford's employes. Nor was
there the slightest doubt of the fact that Ford had broken the law.

Caught in the awkward position of having to refute charges that
were in the main unanswerable, Ford's attorneys at Kansas City and
St. Louis fell back on the tactic of delay. They frankly played for
time by splitting hairs and by introducing copious testimony which
had no apparent object other than that of packing the record. The
maneuver of postponing an issue that could not stand on its merits
worked. It took the Board in Washington two and one-half years to
act on the St. Louis case. The Kansas City decree was held back for
three and one-half years. In both cases the sheer bulk of the record
compelled the government to move slowly. Bloated by the defense,
the St. Louis testimony ran to 21,000 transcript pages. The Kansas City
record was even fatter.

At the Ford-NLRB hearings in Detroit in 1937, and in Dallas in
1940, defense counsel followed an entirely different tack. For some
reason, Ford's lawyers made little show of resistance. They called
to the stand relatively few witnesses of their own. Their cross-
examination of the government's witnesses was neither intensive nor

sustained. At both hearings, consequently, the burden of a damaging NLRB record was allowed to stand, uncontradicted.

Ford counsel was discreet in failing to press the defense at Dallas. For this case resulted in one of the most sensational hearings ever conducted by the NLRB; it exposed to the public view the ugliest picture of Ford Service on record.[44] Again, the testimony introduced by the government was unassailable. In this instance, therefore, a spirited defense was pointless. It would have been futile, and from the standpoint of preserving the good will of the Ford Motor Co., the shorter the hearing the better.

In the case of the Detroit hearing, however, Ford's attorneys reconsidered their initial strategy of offering a lame defense and letting it go at that. They tried to reopen the case so that it might be heard all over again. The petition for a re-hearing, filed in the Circuit Court of Appeals in Cincinnati, was denied but it furthered Ford's cause nonetheless. It permitted yet another delaying action. By the time the bench acted to dismiss the Ford petition, it was December 1940, and the Detroit case had dangled in the courts for three and one-half years.

Despite anything that Ford counsel or Ford Service could do about it, the NLRB finally digested its voluminous record on the Ford Motor Co. Its first Ford decision, based on the Detroit hearing, was issued in 1939. Eight other decrees followed within the next two years. The Kansas City ruling, released in May 1941, came last in the series. In every instance, the Board found the respondent guilty of having committed varied and repeated violations of the NLRA. In giving this agency cause for nine valid actions, Ford set a precedent in American labor law. As a violator of the act which Congress had passed to protect the rights of labor, he was cited more frequently than any other employer in the nation.[45]

In these proceedings, the Labor Board was moved, likewise, to grant appropriate legal relief to the union. It ordered Ford to reinstate hundreds of blacklisted employes; it decreed that at four assembly plants* the union was entitled to full and immediate recognition; and finally, in order to stay the further use of unfair labor practices, the NLRB served the Ford management with nine cease and desist orders.

But rather than submit to any such mandates from the federal government, Ford began to litigate. He came into court forearmed. Anticipating an appeal, he had as early as 1937 retained the services of Frederick H. Wood, a brilliant member of the New York bar.

* Those located at St. Louis, Kansas City, Long Beach and Richmond (Cal.).

Nor was Ford's determination to fight the NLRA in the courts altered by the fact that the general validity of the act had been affirmed by the Supreme Court in 1937. The legal merits of his case were one thing. The bid for time was another. If his lawyers could put off the day of reckoning long enough, the NLRA might be repealed before Ford paid the price of his violations. If luck was with him, he might see the Republicans come to power (his hope in 1940) and scuttle the act through repeal or failure to enforce it.

Thus, with one of the country's foremost appeal lawyers mapping the way, Ford took the NLRB into court, making an issue of its Detroit case. The petition for a rehearing was carried to the Circuit Court of Appeals in Cincinnati. When this bench upheld the Board's decree on all but minor points, Ford tried his luck in the Supreme Court.[46] There, too, he was the loser. Acting in February 1941, the high court refused to review the case and it looked as though Ford's game was up. The NLRA was still on the books. The Democrats were still in Washington. Now, for the first time, the Board had leverage at the Ford Motor Co. At the Rouge plant, if nowhere else, it was in a position to have Ford cited for contempt if he persisted in violating an act of Congress.

But not even the word of the nation's highest court was enough to bring the Ford Motor Co. all the way around. The court's action effected no basic or immediate change in Ford's labor policies. At the Rouge plant, Ford Service continued to flout the law by ferreting out members of the union and punishing them with demotions and dismissals. As for the remaining Board orders which had not yet taken the long road to the Supreme Court, Ford management for the most part ignored their existence. Ford made no move to comply with the decree to start bargaining with his employes at the designated assembly plants. Nor were the majority of his men who had been discharged for union activity restored to their jobs, simply because the NLRB had gone the limit in winning one test case against the Ford Motor Co.

While offering this last desperate show of resistance and bringing the struggle between Ford and the union to a final climax in the spring of 1941, Ford Service did not lay aside even its crudest weapon. On occasion, it continued to beat off organization through the use of violence. Indeed, by 1941, Ford's men-at-arms, committed to the philosophy of force, had written one of the darkest chapters in American labor history. Except for the NLRB, whose authority Ford defied for five and one-half years, the pages of that chapter might have remained unopened.

## 3

A situation charged with all the potentialities of labor violence arose the moment the United Auto Workers announced its intention to come into Dearborn for the first time to distribute handbills at the gates of the Rouge. The day appointed for this initial attempt at pamphleteering was May 26, 1937.

Yet there were circumstances which led the union to believe that the act of propagandizing outside the Rouge would be uncontested. There was the NLRA and Roosevelt. By May of 1937, most employers in Detroit had, if unwillingly, begun to take the union for granted. Even the municipal authorities of Dearborn seemed ready to break with the past. After examining an advance copy of the "Ford leaflet," they issued a permit which made the forthcoming distribution legal. Thus, without any fuss or subterfuge, they all but opened the gates of the city and waved the union in.

On the other hand, the union's leaders must have known that their step was fraught with danger. They realized that bearers of CIO literature had been set upon in many another industrial community. They were posted on the make-up of Ford Service. They knew that Dearborn's chief of police was a former Ford Serviceman. It was common knowledge that of the last group of labor people who had walked into Dearborn in a body—the Hunger Marchers of 1932—four were shot dead and twenty others were wounded by gunfire. Moreover, the pamphleteers of 1937 represented a far greater threat to Ford than the relief petitioners of 1932. They could anticipate, consequently, that their presence in Ford territory was just as unwelcome.

Meanwhile, despite the permit from Dearborn City Hall, the union learned that word of its impending visit to the Rouge had touched off a flurry of activity within Ford Service. This report was verified by newspapermen who were sent to the scene by the three metropolitan dailies of Detroit.* Two days before the attempted circularization of Ford's workers, Arnold Freeman, a Detroit *Times* photographer, observed the fact that the approaches to the Rouge were alive with strong-arm men, wearing the insignia of Ford Service. He saw new faces in the group. Among the wearers of special Service badges, Freeman recognized hoodlums whom he had met before, either in the police courts or in the Detroit underworld. Out of curiosity, he asked one of the newcomers if he was "up to his old tricks,"

* For uncontradicted testimony concerning the Rouge riot of May 26, 1937, see the Ford-Detroit *Decision and Order* issued by the NLRB.

this time hiring out as one of Ford's "musclemen." Freeman's acquaintance answered that he had been on the job at Ford's for the past two weeks and that the old "down-river gang"—composed of former rum-runners and prohibition gangsters—had been "hired temporary for this union invasion."[47]

On the morning of May 26, the day of the proposed handbilling, Bennett's regulars and the men "hired temporary" were deployed about the Ford premises like members of a small mobile army. They were broken down into groups of from four to seven men each, with every sub-gang commanded by a separate "chief." They took up positions inside and outside every important plant entrance, on the bridges and overpasses leading into the Rouge, and in adjacent tunnelways. Driving about in compact cruising parties, they patroled the main thoroughfares of the neighborhood. For the benefit of an inquiring reporter, one of the Ford guards on the scene said, "We made a check and we got four to every union man that is coming out here."[48]

At this hour, furthermore, it was no simple matter to identify or photograph the men who were lying in wait for the union people, for many were wearing dark glasses. None was anxious to have his picture taken. When a photographer representing an out-of-town newspaper syndicate merely opened his camera on Miller Road—the highway which runs along the major Rouge exits—he was instantly surrounded and searched. One of the camera-shy intruders explained, "The boys wouldn't like their mugs in the papers" and if anyone wanted to take a shot of anything, he had better go inside and "talk to Harry Bennett."[49]

That same morning two other newspapermen, Fred Collins of the Detroit *Times* and a colleague, did hunt up Bennett, but for a different purpose. They went "inside" to find out what was going to happen "outside." After talking with Bennett and other Ford officials in Bennett's office, they got their answer from Everett Moore, then the nominal director of Ford Service.*

Asked for a direct statement of company policy, Moore said that "maybe some loyal employes might resent" the presence of the union delegation and that if these "loyal" people tried to put a stop to the distribution of leaflets "it wouldn't be the fault of the Ford Motor Co."[50]

Not deterred, however, by rumors of so extraordinary a mobilization on the part of Ford Service, the committee in charge of the

* Bennett was usually spoken of at this time as the Director of Ford Service. He was that and more besides. Officially, however, Moore was top man in Ford Service on May 26, 1937.

handbill project went ahead with its plans. At noon on May 26, its members held a meeting in Detroit proper. The leaders of the group were two of the union's national executives, Richard T. Frankensteen, a former Chrysler worker, and Walter P. Reuther, a former Ford employe. At this gathering, fifty to sixty people, two-thirds of whom were women, were selected to take part in the afternoon's proceedings. All the participants were cautioned against inciting the Ford gendarmerie. To reduce the chances of friction, the actual handbilling was delegated to the women. At the conclusion of the meeting, four union leaders, among whom were Reuther and Frankensteen, started for the Ford plant in an automobile. They were accompanied by the Rev. Raymond P. Sanford, a Chicago minister who came along as the representative of a civil rights organization. The other union people were to follow by streetcar.

The five members of the Reuther-Frankensteen group arrived at the Ford plant with more than an hour to spare before the afternoon change of shifts. They went at once to a point where they could command a view of the surrounding area. They mounted a large, semi-public overpass opposite Gate 4, the principal entrance to the Rouge.* Two other groups had preceded them to this point, a considerable corps of reporters and newspaper photographers and, in view of the hour, an unusually large number of men who appeared to be loitering near the sides and railings of the overpass.

At the request of the newspapermen, the four union leaders went to the center of the bridge to pose for a photograph. But the moment the cameras began to click, the union people were approached by three or four of Bennett's men, one of whom said, "This is Ford property. Get the hell off of here." According to every disinterested witness of this scene, Reuther and his companions heeded the command almost at once. Without making a reply or offering any show of resistance, they started walking toward the stairways.[51]

At this point, however, the "loyal employes" of Ford Service went to work. They sprang a trap on the departing unionists. The men who had been supposedly lounging in the background closed in. The open ends of the pocket were boxed off by a group of strong-arm

---

* This walk-way enables Ford employes to go in and out of the plant without having to cross Miller Road on the street level. Ford leases it to the Detroit Department of Street Railways. Vendors make regular use of the site. As a rule, there are no signs about to indicate that use of the bridge is restricted to Ford employes. However, on July 5, 1937, one day before the opening of the first Ford-NLRB hearing in Detroit, such a sign did appear. It read, "Private property, no literature to be passed out of any kind. Ford Motor Co." The sign was removed the following day.

men who had run out of Gate 4 on the street level, rushing up the stairways of the overpass. Trapped on the bridge, the unionists were brutally thrashed. Reuther and Frankensteen were singled out for particularly vicious treatment. Both men were alternately beaten, knocked down, lifted to their feet and beaten all over again.

Frankensteen's "going over" was the more "scientific." The four or five attackers who concentrated on him skinned his coat up his back and drew it forward over his face. Then two men locked his wrists and arms, while their accomplices slugged him in the face and torso. There is a photographic record of this incident. On the witness stand, Rev. Sanford described what happened to Frankensteen after he was knocked to the concrete floor of the overpass. ". . . A separate individual grabbed him by each foot and by each hand and his legs were spread apart and his body was twisted over toward the east, over to my left, and then other men proceeded to kick him in the crotch and groin, and left kidney and around the head and also to gore him with their heels in the abdomen. . . ."[52]

When they were able to stand up, the victims were allowed to leave. Reuther and Frankensteen were kicked and slugged as they staggered down the staircase.[53]

A few of the participants in the assault at Gate 4 were subsequently identified.[54] They were Sam Taylor, the Ford foreman who was then president of the Knights of Dearborn; Wilfred Comment, a Ford foreman who ran about most of the afternoon with a pair of handcuffs jutting out of his hip pocket; Oscar Jones, a boxer whose ring name is Jackie Young; Warshon Sarkisian, a professional wrestler; Ted Gries, a wrestling referee; Angelo Caruso; and Charles Goodman, an underworld character with a police record of twenty-one arrests and four convictions.

The union people who arrived near Gate 4 later in the afternoon were subjected to equally vicious attack. Laden with handbills, the women in the group were set upon the moment they stepped off the streetcar. Their attackers called them vile names and forced them to drop their leaflets by twisting their arms. Two of the women were kicked after being knocked to the ground; the others, relieved of their literature, were forcibly shoved back onto the street car: At the same time, William Merriweather, a union man who was walking by himself, headed in their direction, was struck down from the rear and beaten so violently—while one of his several assailants shouted "kill him, kick his brains out, stomp his face in"—that his back was broken.[55]

The attack opposite Gate 5 was no less savage. A corps of thirty or forty of Ford's strong-arm men, directed by a sub-leader who had white tape wrapped about the knuckles of his right hand, assaulted without warning a group of eighteen unionists, eight of whom were women. After being hit in the mouth, William McKie, a middle-aged former Ford employe as well as the spokesman of the union group, remonstrated, "We have a license from the city of Dearborn." But the Ford sluggers fell to, nonetheless, as one of their number replied, "That don't mean a damn here." One of the women who refused to give up her handbills was jabbed under the armpits.[56] Four of the attackers "worked over" a Negro unionist in the party, using their feet as well as their fists, picking up their man from time to time and throwing his body to the pavement "like they would throw a sack against a retaining wall."[57] All the while one member of this particular assault unit kept telling his aides to aim for the stomach because "you can't hurt a nigger or a black bastard when you hit him over the head." The man who was hurt the worst at Gate 5 was Tony Marinovitch, "that bastard with the union cap." Five or six men mauled and kicked Marinovitch until they had fractured his skull.[58]

Ford Service did not confine its operations to areas lying just outside the plant entrances. Its roving gangs hauled women off streetcars which had not yet made the loop inside the Ford loading zone. Other attacks occurred at points far removed from Ford property. Ralph Dunham, a handbill passer who was standing alone on a street corner a block from the plant, was beaten so severely that he suffered serious internal injuries and had to spend the next two weeks in a hospital.[59] Alvin Stickle, another union man, had the unique experience of the afternoon. Stickle was first dragged through Gate 4 into a sub-office of Ford Service. Then, inside the Rouge proper and in the presence of Everett Moore, the nominal director of Ford Service, he was beaten until his nose bled, and his face was cut and swollen. All Moore is reported to have said, as he watched the proceedings, is "Okay, boys" and "Get him out of here."[60]

The Dearborn police had every opportunity to intervene. They were present in large numbers. They witnessed assaults on the part of Ford Servicemen at more than a dozen points. But under orders from Carl Brooks, the former Serviceman, these officers of the law made no show of authority whatsoever. Their failure to act in connection with the handling of two women thrown to the ground near Gate 4 was later described on the witness stand by the Rev. Sanford. "One girl near me was kicked in the stomach, and vomited at my feet, right at the end of the steps there and I finally shot an imploring glance at one of the mounted policemen, to whom I had previously spoken and he dashed over on horseback to the west side of the fence and in a rather pleading tone, sort of 'For God's sake' tone in his voice, seemed to direct his remarks to this well-dressed gentleman in brown, and said, 'You mustn't hurt those women, you mustn't hurt those women,' and I was attracted to the manner in which he spoke, because he seemed to be pleading rather, not to injure the women."[61]

Not limiting its attack to unionists, Ford Service, again unimpeded by the police, turned its attention to the press as well. Throughout the afternoon, the Ford attackers bullied and harassed newspapermen by dropping hints like "Better get out of here, buddy, and not try to put anything in the paper. It isn't healthy."[62] Three reporters had their notes confiscated, wrenched from their hands. When certain members of the Ford gang at Gate 4 were assailing Reuther and Frankensteen, others rushed the newspaper photographers. Every photographer on the overpass who was slow on his feet had the plates ripped from his camera and exposed. On Miller Road, three cameramen who represented the New York *Times*, the Associated Press and the Detroit *News*, were forcibly relieved of their films.[63] After being spotted by a burly Ford guard who shouted, "There is a cameraman. Get that son-of-a-bitch. Break that camera," Frederick Arnold of the Detroit *Times* and his chauffeur made a getaway. Pursued by three men, they pushed their car to a speed of 70 or 80 miles an hour, crashing red lights and stop streets alike. Four or five miles distant from the Ford plant and still chased, Arnold and his driver took refuge in a suburban police station.[64]

In abusing the newspapermen who had come to Dearborn to see what they could see, Ford Service made its great tactical blunder of the afternoon. For instead of flinching under attack or acting like cynical bystanders, the reporters on the scene got their backs up. As a result, they outdid themselves; the pictures they salvaged and the stories they handed to their editors were, if nothing else, masterpieces of thoroughness. Incensed at having their own men pushed around, the three major dailies of Detroit held nothing back. Two months later, the same set of newspapermen told the story of May 26 all over again. They repeated their eye-witness accounts of the "Rouge riot," testifying against Ford for the NLRB.

More than that, the Detroit papers, their reporters who took the stand, and all other NLRB witnesses were in essential agreement as to what had taken place on May 26. Seen in retrospect, the story was completely damning. The attackers had not been regular production workers of the Ford Motor Co. They were either Servicemen or hand-picked Ford employes on special outside assignment. Their ranks encompassed gangsters, wrestlers and prizefighters who were serving Ford in the capacity of professional strong-arm men. The riot did not occur spontaneously. It was an organized and unprovoked assault during which an outnumbered and unresisting group of handbill distributors were ambushed by Ford's "musclemen" and drubbed by "gorilla" methods of combat that are used, ordinarily, only by gangsters and back-alley fighters. Likewise, according to the record, the attack was pre-planned; it was executed with the active knowledge of Ford Service and with the passive cooperation of the Dearborn police. Harry Bennett, the ultimate head of Ford Service and the man in the Ford organization who was closest to Henry Ford, was seemingly proud of the performance. Talking to the press late in June 1937, on the subject of unions, Bennett is supposed to have said, "They got a small sample of what they will get if they ever come out again."[65]

Having failed to kill the news at its source by subjecting reporters to personal abuse, the Ford Motor Co. tried its best to keep the story of the riot from spreading and to hush up all other forthright references to Ford Service. For as *Time* magazine observed, it looked as if the "brutal beatings" of May 26 "might hurt Henry Ford" as much as they hurt the people who had been set upon.[66]

Consequently, after the publication of a most candid report on the Rouge riot, *Time*, as well as its sister journals, *Life* and *Fortune*, whose relations with the Ford Motor Co. had already been strained, was placed on Ford's blacklist. All three magazines carried no Ford advertising matter for the next year and a half.

During the open hearing held by the NLRB in Detroit in July 1937, the defense did not jeopardize Ford's good will by making a spectacle of the men-at-arms who had participated in the assault of May 26. None of the attackers was placed on the stand to give an account of his actions. No official of Ford Service was called to testify as to what orders of the day he had issued to his men. Nor did Ford counsel even attempt to explain his willingness to keep these witnesses under cover. Moreover, when the hearing was in progress, the county prosecutor's office informed the Board that Angelo Caruso, one of the men who assailed Frankensteen, had skipped the country. Caruso was said to be hiding in Canada.[67]

The Ford organization met the adverse publicity with counter-propaganda. It harped on the familiar theme of Ford's benevolence. Thus, the same day the riot occurred, the New York *Times* reported the rumor that a bigger and better Five-Dollar Day was in the offing. All on his own, said the *Times*, quoting a "usually well-informed source," Ford had decided to institute a six-hour day and a minimum daily wage of seven dollars.[68] Several months later, the same appeal was sandwiched into the legal brief which Ford submitted to a federal court as part of his formal answer to the performance of May 26. "It is a matter of common knowledge," his counsel pleaded, "that the company and its founder have been pioneers in the payment of high wages, reduction in hours of labor and the improvement of working conditions."[69]

From the mouths of the three principal spokesmen for the Ford Motor Co., there issued, finally, point-blank comment on the events of May 26.

Harry Bennett for his part offered two apologies that were mutually exclusive. First, the morning after the riot, he charged that the newspapers had manufactured the violence of the day before, in order to drum up a "Ford strike story." The Detroit *News* dismissed this version of the facts by retorting, editorially, "utter nonsense."[70] Shifting his position a month later, Bennett acknowledged that "Ford men" had been involved in the fight, but "not a single Ford Serviceman," only "peaceable individual workmen" who had acted at all times in self-defense. "We don't tolerate," he added, "rough stuff or thugs in the Ford organization."[71]

Next to Bennett, W. J. Cameron came closest to making a frank admission that the union had been run out of Dearborn by force. But as he told his radio audience one Sunday evening in June 1937, it was a question of Ford against the "Reds," and "only timid citizens," he said, stand aside "when amateur revolutionaries say 'boo.'"[27] A month later, speaking before a convention of newspaper executives, Cameron changed his tune. On this occasion, he baldly implied that the riot had never taken place at all. "Henry Ford has not rioted," he said. "His representatives have not rioted. His employes have not rioted. As a matter of cold fact, there never has been any labor disturbance of any sort in the Ford shops."[73]

The grand gesture came from Henry Ford himself. Commenting on an NLRB complaint which gave a full account of what Ford Servicemen had been up to on May 26, Ford said in January of the following year, "Anybody who knew the Ford Motor Co. knew the things the Board charges never happened and could not happen here."[74]

On the rebound, the union decided to make another try at the Rouge in the early fall of 1937. This time it made an advance appeal to the city of Dearborn, asking for police protection. Its request was submitted in writing and was answered by James E. Greene, Dearborn city counsel and one of Ford's old political stalwarts.* Greene declined to act. He replied by letter that, inasmuch as the United Auto Workers was "a legal non-entity," he was "at a loss as to whom the city should afford the police protection you desire."[76]

The union went ahead on its own. The circumstances of its return visit to the Rouge on the afternoon of August 11, 1937, were embarrassing to Ford Service. On this occasion, the union delegation itself was imposing. Its "entity" was represented, not by fifty or sixty handbill passers, but by a body of volunteers one thousand strong. Throughout the afternoon, Ford Service was under the surveillance of an impressive group of outside observers. The spectators included the county prosecutor, newspapermen, representatives of the State Patrol, investigators for the NLRB, agents of the Senate Civil Liberties Committee, and Mrs. Cornelia Pinchot, wife of the former governor of Pennsylvania. Mrs. Pinchot said she had come to see if Dearborn was "still in America."[77]

When the day shift left the Rouge on August 11, therefore, Ford's Servicemen did no more than glower at the outgoing worker who grabbed or stuffed into his pocket the leaflet that some union man passed on to him. Consequently, tens of thousands of handbills found their mark; the afternoon was marred by not a single act of violence. Emboldened by this preliminary success, the union straightway announced that similar circularizations would become standard future procedure in the attempt to "organize Ford."

But the Ford machine in Dearborn had a different idea. Picking up where Ford Service left off, the Dearborn City Council built a wall around the Rouge so high that few could scale it. The Council passed a handbill ordinance which decreed that, henceforth, during designated hours it would be illegal to distribute any kind of printed matter within the "congested areas" of the city.[78] The areas of "congestion" took in all the approaches and all the walk-ways and thoroughfares leading to and from the Rouge. The hours specified by act of Council were the only hours of the day that had any significance

* Greene had been active in the movement to send Ford to the White House. As secretary of the Ford-For-President Club of Dearborn in 1923, he was preparing to blanket the nation with "Ford literature." According to the New York *Times,* Greene had access to the mailing list that had on it the name and address of every Ford dealer in the United States.[75]

for the union; they coincided with changes of shift at the Ford Motor Co.

What Ford Service had failed to effect by force of arms, the city fathers of Dearborn achieved by fiat. For many months to come, bearers of union literature who appeared at the forbidden time within the proscribed areas were placed under immediate arrest by Chief of Police Brooks. According to the New York *Times* of January 23, 1938, there were 906 such arrests after December 9.

There was, of course, the question of constitutionality, the chance that some judicial bench might decide that the handbill ordinance had set aside the Bill of Rights. Anticipating that contingency, the city hit on a clever device. For months on end, all the violators of the ordinance were temporarily locked up and then released without charge; none was held for trial.[79] As long as the city refused to prosecute and as long as neither of the two local justices of the peace took the overt step of actually trying and sentencing any of the people whom the police were packing into the city jail, the union had no legal grounds on which to base an appeal. *De facto,* the ordinance had teeth, but *de jure,* it had never bitten anyone. This state of affairs persisted for all of three years. From the fall of 1937 until the fall of 1940, the union was debarred from coming anywhere near the Ford plant outside of Detroit and, at the same time, cheated of an opportunity to state its case in a court of appeal.

Meanwhile, at one or another assembly plant where the Fords lacked the expedient to which they could turn in Dearborn, Bennett met the union with raw force. His tactics at Dallas, Texas, approached a degree of savagery that was extreme even for Ford Service. In this southern community the NLRB evidence is extraordinary.[80] It fills twenty-five volumes and it consists in the main of sworn testimony offered not by outsiders nor by union members, but by the agents of Ford Service itself. One of the men involved offered to take the stand for the government and most of his accomplices, preferring to tell their own stories, followed suit.[81]

For the work at hand in Dallas, Harry Bennett made use of a special undercover squad made up of rough, physically powerful production workers recruited from one local Ford plant, and a small corps of Ford Servicemen transferred from Detroit.[82] The members of this outside squad were told that they had been selected because of their physical strength and because they "wasn't scared to tackle anything they was put up against."[83] Supplied with pistols, black-jacks and lengths of rubber hose,[84] these men proceeded to "put the fear of God" into real or suspected union members or union sympathizers.

Their methods, the National Labor Relations Board later commented, were those of "organized gangsterism."[85] Their favorite procedure was to work over their victims with blackjacks or switches or wires covered with tape.[86] They began their operations on June 23, 1937, by ambushing and beating a visiting UAW organizer until his ribs were fractured and their victim lost sensibility.[87] Inasmuch as the UAW had no known members in Dallas, the outside squad decided to give its attention to anyone at all in the community who was suspected of harboring union sympathies. Its members began to shadow and tap the wires of W. J. Houston, a liberal Dallas attorney. Eventually, Houston was seized as he emerged from a drugstore in broad daylight and beaten so severely that he required hospitalization.[88] Next on the list was George Baer, who had no interest in automobile workers as such, but had been working in Dallas for a year and a half as an organizer for the millinery workers. Baer, subjected to the brutality of the outside squad, nearly lost the sight of one eye. As it was, he was beaten into a state of unconsciousness, losing several teeth and suffering severe head injuries.[89] Finally, the Ford squad set out to do violence to A. C. Lewis, a Dallas business man, who had confided to a neighbor that he believed in labor unions. Soon thereafter, on August 4, 1937, the suspected liberal business man was picked up and brutally thrashed. In this case, however, they got the wrong man. The person they manhandled was not their intended victim, A. C. Lewis, but Lewis' twin brother, Archie B. Lewis. Four months later the brother who was flogged died. The immediate cause of his death was a throat infection and an attack of pneumonia. Counsel for the NLRB did not allege that the beating by Ford's men was even a contributory cause of Lewis' death. But Lewis himself did level such a charge. On his deathbed and in the presence of his pastor he said he knew he was dying and he asked his brother to track down the men who had "killed" him and to "see they got justice."[90]

There is little reason to feel that Henry Ford was anxious to discountenance the tactics which Ford Service employed here south of the Mason and Dixon line. At least one of Ford's recorded social opinions is quite compatible with the happenings in Dallas. In the pages of the Detroit *Free Press* on July 22, 1934—two years from the date of the Ford Hunger March—the manufacturer was quoted as saying, "I remember when I was a boy seeing men arguing in the street and fighting with their fists over their ideas. I don't know how many years it is since I've seen that kind of a street fight. It would be a healthy sign to see them again."

## Twenty-eight

### COMPROMISE

#### 1

AS LONG AS the UAW had to spend its energies on a dozen fronts and as long as it suffered from internal division, it never had a chance against Ford Service, but the odds of the struggle began to shift in the winter of 1940. The union had come of age. It had put its own house in order and had wrested contracts from the entire industry. Among producers of any consequence, only Ford remained outside the fold. For the first time in its history, the UAW was free to focus on Ford Service. It made this job its chief order of business late in 1940.

This "Ford drive," unlike its forerunners, was no hit-or-miss affair. It drew on every resource which the UAW could muster for the purpose, including CIO support from coast to coast. Two consecutive CIO conventions had already resolved to back the campaign at Ford's, financially as well as morally. Counsel for the UAW—one of the ablest labor lawyers in America—was now in a position to give whatever time was necessary to the legal rights of Ford's workers. The new "Ford Organizing Committee" had topnotch personnel. Its director was a competent veteran labor organizer. Its subordinate staff was made up chiefly of former Ford employes who had been discharged because of union activity and were already schooled in the many subtleties of the "Ford psychology."

The methods which the UAW applied to the end of breaking Ford Service at its source were ingenious. For months the organizing committee held no public meetings; it kept its membership list under lock and key. To broadcast its case, the committee scattered handbills far and wide; it published a readable newspaper, *Ford Facts,* which was filled with up-to-the-minute information on Ford wages and working conditions. In order to penetrate the veritable Tower of Babel that Bennett had built at the Rouge, the committee sponsored a special series of foreign language radio broadcasts; it took particular pains to tell Ford's 10,000 Negro workers that without their help the job of organizing the Ford Motor Co. would be out of the question. Every CIO member in the Detroit area—of whatever race or creed —was asked to lend a hand; he was urged to "sign up" the Ford man who lived next door or went to the same church or was married to his wife's second cousin.

As the union was launching its first real push against Ford, the wall which had long sealed off the River Rouge plant began to totter. Lila Neuenfelt, one of Dearborn's two municipal judges, risked her political future by declaring from the bench in October 1940 that the Dearborn handbill ordinance was unconstitutional. The invalidation of this act of council by Judge Neuenfelt electrified Bennett and the Ford political machine. Two appellants rushed to the county circuit courts—the city of Dearborn which sought to have the Neuenfelt decision reversed, and the Ford Motor Co. itself, which asked the court to issue an injunction to forestall any future attempts at pamphleteering in the vicinity of the Rouge.

An injunction was granted, but not the one the Fords had counted on. On December 7, 1940, Judge James E. Chenot of the Wayne County Circuit Court decreed that the Dearborn ordinance, passed "under the guise of traffic regulation," was "unreasonable, arbitrary and discriminatory." It had made a "mockery" of the constitutional guarantees of free speech and free press, he said, and was therefore invalid. The court then granted an injunction which forbade future enforcement of the ordinance either by Dearborn officials or by any of their "associates or confederates."

Free at last to approach the Rouge without fear of assault or arrest, the union let no grass grow under its feet. It was at the gates of Ford's plant with 35,000 handbills within the next forty-eight hours. Once the ice was broken, the "Ford Organizing Committee" reappeared at the Rouge every two weeks with 50,000 copies of *Ford Facts*.

Six weeks from the time it became legal for the UAW to set foot in Dearborn, Ford's defenses against the union were breached by still another momentous court decision. After making the most of every loophole the law allowed, the Ford Motor Co. finally all but exhausted its legal remedies against the NLRB. It was called to book by the United States Supreme Court. This crucial action concerned the Rouge itself; it had to do with the Detroit case which the government had initiated in 1937 and which had already passed inspection by the

Circuit Court of Appeals in Cincinnati. On February 10, 1941, the Supreme Court put its stamp of approval on these earlier proceedings; it refused to review the case.

At this point the federal statute which Ford Service had flouted from the moment of its enactment began to take real effect. Now, at last, if Ford continued to defy the NLRB in his Detroit plant, he could be cited for contempt of court. The labor board had long since ordered the Rouge management to reemploy certain discharged union members with back pay, to call a halt to manifold violations of the NLRA, and to signify its intent to comply with the law by posting notices to that effect on the bulletin boards of the Rouge.

The Ford Motor Co. mended its ways at once, not completely, but enough to keep its distance from the federal bench in Cincinnati. The union men who had been discharged four years earlier were returned to their jobs, and on February 18, 1941, eight days after the Supreme Court had spoken, compliance notices were tacked up on the walls of the Rouge. They said, in effect, that Ford employes could exercise their right to organize without interference from the management. These bulletins gave the UAW the fulcrum it had been awaiting at Ford's for almost half a decade.

Fortified by the knowledge that their employer was no longer a law unto himself, Ford's men simply stampeded the headquarters of the "Ford Organizing Committee." The day after Ford posted the NLRB compliance notice, the UAW made capital of the event by having its members show their faces. Thousands of Rouge workers who had kept their union affiliations under cover did something they had never done before; they came to work wearing union buttons. One of their number had the temerity to call attention to his status as a union recruiter extraordinary; he worked at a bench with his cap entirely covered with red, white and blue buttons, each of which proclaimed, "I got my Ford member." As though placed there by magic, large pro-union signs began to appear on machinery and packing boxes in every corner of the giant works.

Within a matter of weeks, the Rouge chapter of the UAW— Local 600—had sent down its roots so deeply that it was ready to start functioning as an established institution. As soon as the membership warranted such action, the workers in each of the far-flung departments of the plant came together to elect shop stewards. These committeemen began to force Ford's hand. Loaded to the brim with grievances that had been piling up at the factory for forty years, they walked into the Ford offices and asked the management to start bargaining forthwith. Similar committees demanded hearings at the Lincoln factory and in the Ford plant at Highland Park.

Ford, with a wary eye on the Supreme Court and with the knowledge that a fever of organization had gripped his men, began to bargain. Moreover, he began to make concessions. He yielded now on this point, then on that. The Ford wage scale, still under par, was stepped up ever so little in one department after another. The Lincoln management and the company's top executives at Highland Park suddenly broke with one of Ford's oldest taboos: they conceded the right to smoke inside the factory at a designated time and place. Here and there Ford supervision was brought up short in accordance with the wishes of the union. In April, a well-liked foreman was removed, for no good reason, from the Rouge foundry; he was demoted to the foot of the line in another department. The union intervened and thirty minutes later the popular boss was back at his old job. Before long the company went so far as to provide a conference room in which the Rouge management deigned to hold meetings with the over-all grievance committee of Local 600.

On occasion, even Harry Bennett began to melt. In March, some shop stewards decided to beard the lion in his den. They called at Bennett's office to find out why two dozen union ringleaders in their department had been let out without notice or explanation. The visitors were dumbfounded by their reception. They were admitted to the inner sanctum of the Ford Administration Building at the drop of a hat. After hearing them out, what is more, Bennett was all apologies. In the committee's presence, he called in the mill superintendent and gave this man a dressing down; he ordered immediate reemployment of the discharged men who were under discussion. What all but robbed the complainants of their powers of speech was Bennett's ingratiating manner. He had opened the conference by passing around the cigars—on Ford property! While telling him what was on their minds, did the "boys" care to have a seat? Once outside, one of the union conferees gasped, "I've been working at Ford's for ten years and that's the first time anybody around here ever asked me to have a chair!"

As far as they went, however, these conciliatory gestures were only a cloak behind which the Fords resorted to one desperate measure after another in the hopes of cutting the union down at the eleventh hour. One of the counter-thrusts aimed at the "Ford Organizing Committee," which was a CIO agency, was a backdoor conspiracy to come to terms with the AFL, overnight if possible. Ford Service began courting this rival in January 1941, and the AFL hierarchy, which had never in its history done any serious campaigning at Ford's, stepped into the picture if only for the purpose of plaguing the CIO. The AFL organizers who set themselves up in opposition to the "Ford Organizing Committee" were all but feted by the Ford Motor Co. Their efforts were publicly endorsed by Harry Bennett.[1] Much of their work was done for them by Ford Service. In the colored communities of Detroit, Bennett's "Negro boss," Don Marshall, let it be known that the AFL had Ford's blessing.[2] Ford Service cracked the whip inside the Rouge. Foremen and other supervisory employes became AFL solicitors on company time. At one period an American Legion member who was an ordinary production worker devoted a good share of his working hours at Ford's to AFL recruiting. He was also the joke of the mill, because he came to work bedecked in full Legion regalia.[3]

This diversionary movement was mild by contrast with other last minute anti-CIO measures that Ford Service brought into play. Through February and March, Bennett attacked Local 600 head-on. His boxers and wrestlers redoubled their efforts at physical intimidation. Organized in raiding parties, they swooped down on this or that assembly line, accosting UAW members whom they could identify, wrenching union buttons from their hats or shirts.[4] Ford Service continued to weed out the more conspicuous supporters of the union. For every discharged employe who was reinstated at the insistence of Local 600, ten or a hundred other active union men were dismissed or demoted. In dealing with the shop stewards who had dug in throughout the mill, despite every obstruction from Ford Service, Bennett fell back on a strategy that was more subtle. He began to retaliate against such men by having them transferred from their regular departments to new ones. Once transplanted, the uprooted shop steward was temporarily done for; he was still a Ford employe, perhaps at his old rate of pay, but he was no longer a union committee man. Nor could he hope to regain such a status overnight; to his new co-workers he was a total stranger. By the same token, the department which he left behind had lost its union representation; its bargaining machinery, to a greater or lesser degree, had been disrupted.

At this late date, however, most of Bennett's frantic, anti-union expedients fell wide of the mark. They served only to hasten the day of a final reckoning. They made the union even bolder and less patient. For one thing, the "Ford Committee" exploited to the full the fact that Ford was playing with fire on legal grounds, that he was still voiding the NLRA at every turn though he had given his word in writing to the contrary. Local 600 swamped the regional office of the NLRB with affidavits, arming the government with massive proof of the company's continued defiance of the law. This approach had a sobering effect on Ford Service; it forced Bennett to be conciliatory now and then, if only for the sake of appearances. More than one union committee was able to get a hearing and to win some concession or other by merely threatening to initiate legal proceedings to have the Fords cited for contempt of court. Each of these minor retreats on the part of Ford Service added something to UAW morale; it brought new members into the union; it assured the rank and file Ford worker that his right to organize had legal sanction.

When Bennett continued to goad the union, even at the risk of inviting punitive action by the federal courts, he finally brought the roof down over his ears. He precipitated the first CIO sit-down strike in the history of the Rouge. Riled by the dismissal of several of their shop stewards, three thousand workers in the Ford rolling mill sat down on the job early in March. The strikers had only one demand —that their leaders be reinstated. They won their point and the mill resumed operations within an hour. Then the temper of the Rouge broke at a dozen points simultaneously. Defensive sit-downs spread from one department to the next like an epidemic. During the last two weeks of March alone, more than 15,000 men sat down to protest one or another provocation, bringing ten different sections of the plant to a brief but complete standstill.[5]

Such outbursts were neither inspired nor altogether welcomed by the directors of the "Ford drive." Each of the sit-downs was successful; it wrested immediate concessions from Bennett. Each was a union builder in the sense that it served to curb Ford Service and to give Ford's men esprit de corps. On the other hand, the new weapon had limitations that were all too apparent to the "Ford Organizing Committee." Any one of the demonstrations could have embroiled the union in a premature general strike. All were, at best, no more than holding actions which forced the Ford Motor Co. to maintain de facto relations with the union from one day to the next. None of them brought Ford and his men any closer to a lasting settlement of their differences. More than that, the UAW was convinced it could resolve these differences by peaceful means. Its strategy at the Rouge was to bring matters to a head through an employe election held under NLRB auspices. Early in December 1940, three months before the onset of the sit-down spasm, the national union had filed a petition asking for such an election at the Lincoln factory. Other petitions, appealing for similar action at Dearborn and Highland Park, had been filed in mid-February 1941. When the Ford rank and file, under Bennett's prodding, sat down spontaneously, the "Ford Committee," though committed to a non-strike policy, had no choice but to ride the storm.

The Fords made matters worse at this critical stage by doing their utmost to keep the issue from coming to an orderly decision. In conference with the NLRB, they refused to enter a stipulation agreeing to "consent" elections at their three Detroit plants.[6] This action only heightened the tensions within the Ford personnel, for although the three shops were seething with unrest, the NLRB was required by law, upon Ford's refusal to submit to an election, to conduct hearings to determine whether or not employe elections were warranted by the facts in the case. Such proceedings would take time. They would give Bennett that many more weeks or months in which to contrive ways and means of pulling the union apart before allowing the issue to go to a vote.

The company strained the temper of its men even more by making the boast that it would never come to terms with the union, irrespective of the outcome of any forthcoming election. Just before the great plant at Dearborn had its first CIO sit-down, Henry Ford proclaimed, once more, that nothing on earth could bring him to deal with the UAW.[7] Bennett, on the eve of the sit-down seizure, was as bold. If the government forced it on him, he said, he would make a pretense at collective bargaining, but nothing more. If the union won a Ford election hands down, *Time* quoted him as saying in mid-March, "we will bargain with it because the law says so. We will bargain till Hell freezes over, but they won't get anything."[8]

Aggravated by such expressions of policy and by unceasing opposition from Ford Service, the UAW finally turned in desperation to Lansing and Washington. It offered, in wires sent to the President and the Governor of Michigan late in February, to end the conflict at Ford's by using any methods of "conciliation and collective bargaining" which the government, state or federal, cared to invoke. The impasse at Dearborn could be broken overnight, said the union, if the company would at once go into conference for the purpose of arriving at a standard labor contract. The message to the President urged the holding of an NLRB election at the earliest possible moment.

If nothing else could keep Ford Service within the law and preserve the grievance machinery that was already in operation at the Rouge, the union announced that it would strike. In serving this formal notice of an impending walk-out, the UAW expressed its regrets, its conviction that strikes were out of date in "these days of national emergency," and its belief that the Ford Motor Co., even so, might not "understand" any other kind of "language."

Five weeks from the time the union's wire reached the state capital and the White House, the Fords removed any remaining doubt of their attitude toward conciliation. They made a sudden counter-move, the intent of which was to force the dispute with their men to a violent conclusion. Ford went to his Georgia estate. Then, on April 2, 1941, Bennett provoked the union as never before; he discharged the eight Rouge employes who had made up the over-all grievance committee of Local 600. These men were the accredited union spokesmen with whom he had conferred regularly in recent past weeks and to whom the company had granted unofficial recognition. In announcing their dismissal, Bennett made no effort to explain his action, other than to say that it was final. "They can bargain till Christmas," he said, "but we won't put the eight men back to work."[9] The truth was, however, that Local 600 or the "Ford Committee" could no longer bargain at all, for with the same stroke that stripped the union of its top leadership, Bennett broke off relations with the local's lesser representatives, with all its sundry shop stewards. In fact, he refused to see any union spokesmen or to discuss any labor issues whatsoever.

The UAW was now reduced to the choice of one of two possible alternatives. In either case it was obliged to fight Ford on Ford's terms. It could back down and ignore the total cessation of bargaining and the loss of its chief spokesmen at the Rouge. In that event the union would lose caste and membership; its failure to protect its key men would be construed by Bennett and the Ford rank and file as a confession of weakness; and Ford Service would capitalize on that weakness by the use of still other methods of making the right to organize a dead letter—all on the eve of a pending government election. The other course of action open to the UAW was to shut down the Ford plant and to risk having such action countermanded, short of its goal, by Ford Service, by government intervention, or by the force of public opinion. Of the two possible alternatives, the union chose the second. It quickly marshaled its forces at the Rouge for a general strike.

2

In the choice of a strategy that would have maximum effect at Ford's, the UAW had to consider the physical arrangement of the Rouge. Most of the huge plant is unapproachable from the outside. Only a few of its many buildings border on a public thoroughfare. The entire property is sealed off by formidable walls and fences, at that time closely guarded by armed defenders. Any prolonged sit-down action would have been doomed to failure in such a setting; its supporters, soon forced to capitulate because of hunger, if for no other reason. Thus the strike which the UAW launched at Ford's main plant in April 1941, was of necessity an outside affair.

The strikers and strike sympathizers who surrounded the property, outside its walls, plainly meant business. They deployed themselves so as to throw an impenetrable ring around the Rouge. This time, in contrast to May 26, 1937, it was the union rather than Ford Service which dominated the area. Thousands of pickets massed opposite the three principal gates of the plant. Smaller groups took up a station at the remaining gates and entrances. Still other bands were detailed to keep watch over tunnel-ways and railroad tracks and to patrol surrounding roads. At its local headquarters some distance away, the union held a thousand men in reserve, to be used day or night as replacements or as an emergency force.

During the first hours of the shut-down, certain strikers behaved as though Ford and his men were engaged in civil war. They set up barricades, making it impossible for outsiders to reach the main plant entrances by automobile. Miller Road was blockaded at key points by piles of railroad ties or by a double row of cars parked at right angles to the highway. When these barriers were removed the following day, normal traffic or easy ingress to the plant was still out of the question. Motorists, sightseers as well as strikers, began to cruise along Miller Road in such numbers that, except for its overpasses and its lesser gates, the plant was hemmed in on one side by an endless moving belt. Cars crept past the Rouge for the better part of two days, three abreast on either half of the road. They moved at a speed of seven miles per hour.

As for the conditions under which it would agree to settle the dispute voluntarily, the union raised three points. It insisted, first of all, on a return to the bargaining arrangements that had existed prior to the strike and on reinstatement of its eight key committeemen. More than that, it demanded an immediate government election, to be

followed, if the UAW won a majority at the polls, by formal recognition
and the signing of a union contract.

The company, however, had quite a different plan for bringing
the walk-out to a close. Having provoked the strike, Bennett meant
to make the most of it, to have it suppressed by force. His counter-
strategy, as he later revealed, was to smash the union in the field
before it could get to the ballot box at full strength, with its prestige
and confidence at high tide. But to do this, Ford Service alone was
insufficient. It was in bad repute and, for once, vastly outnumbered
by the opposition. What Bennett prepared to gamble on, therefore,
was outside intervention, the big chance that the strike which he had
precipitated would be broken for him by the state or federal government. Moreover, he had reason to feel that his scheme would work.
It was not for nothing that the Company had temporized with the union
and simulated collective bargaining. Among other things, they had
postponed the issue. Time now worked in their favor. With war imminent, the public and the government had had enough of strikes. What
the Company set out to trade on, when they called for help from
Lansing and Washington, was the national emergency.

Their appeal for outside assistance was a masterpiece of public
relations. It made headlines; it was taken to the White House by one
of Bennett's personal emissaries; it was couched in inflammatory
language. In a wire to the President, Bennett vowed that a paralyzing
"sit-down" was in progress, that the Rouge had been seized from the
inside by "communistic terrorists."[10] These "lawless" sit-down strikers,
he told the Detroit *Free Press,* had barricaded the doors, taking orders
from a dangerous "I.W.W. agitator."[11]

What of the patriotism of Ford's workers, their concern for the
national defense program? Those who had willfully laid down their
tools had none, Bennett advised the President. In addition, he charged,
there were saboteurs! Some of the Ford sit-downers, drunk with power,
he said, were careening about the plant on a spree of "wanton destruc-
tion;" they were "deliberately" wrecking tools and dies of vital importance for the manufacture of aircraft parts.

To meet the crisis, as they portrayed it, the Fords demanded not
an employe election or the services of a labor conciliator, but federal
troops and the state patrol. Chief of Police Carl Brooks professed
that nothing short of the state police could dispossess the "seven or
eight thousand" sit-down strikers who had captured Ford's property.[12]
Bennett went a step higher. Neither the local nor the state law enforce-

ment agencies, he wired the President, could cope with this "lawless sit-down."

The Fords had scarcely finished trumpeting these charges—alleging a sit-down, sabotage, and a serious interruption of defense production—before they were obliged to eat their words. For each of these claims was untrue. Each was immediately discredited by disinterested and unimpeachable observers.

That the plant had been occupied by someone during the first hours of the strike was certain. It remained for Thomas J. Dewey, the federal conciliator on the scene, and for James Sweinhart, the able, long-time Ford publicist, to disclose just who the "someone" was. Sweinhart, then representing the agency which had Ford's advertising account, had come out to the Rouge to lend a hand to out-of-town newspapermen who were covering the strike. Both observers, the conciliator and the advertiser, frankly admitted that the sit-downer who was in full control inside the Rouge was Bennett himself. More than a thousand men were bivouacked behind the plant's walls, but they were Bennett's own men! They were "make-believe" sit-down strikers, most of whom were total strangers to Detroit. They were, for the most part, colored men whom Ford Service and Bennett's Negro lieutenant, Don Marshall, had imported from the deep South.[13] All were wearing buttons that read "100% for Ford."

Meanwhile Bennett meant to keep this carefully planted inside force intact. Conciliator Dewey was allowed to speak to a thousand insiders who were assembled in the Ford foundry. He urged the men to quit the premises, promising them safe conduct through the picket lines. The union had already cleared the way at his suggestion, he said, by withdrawing its pickets from certain designated gates. But no one heard him. No one was permitted to hear him. Every time the conciliator opened his mouth, his Negro listeners, egged on by Ford Service, drowned him out.[14] Nor was it any easier for these "lawless sit-downers" of whom the Ford Motor Co. complained, to leave the property of their own accord. Those who tried it were manhandled. Some, said the Detroit *News*, were severely thrashed.[15] Sweinhart saw a few of the "sit-downers" try to force their way to the outside through one of the big plant gates. In each case, he said, twenty Ford Servicemen were on hand to "push them back" inside.[16] On April 3 still another strange touch was added to the alleged Ford sit-down. One of the company's lake freighters, the *Henry Ford II*, was reported by the Detroit *News* to have docked inside the Rouge with a cargo of food—enough to provision the occupants of the plant for at least two weeks. Had Ford decided to pamper the men whom he was begging the President to eject from his property? On the contrary, according to what Sweinhart could gather, the provisions were intended for Ford Service and the imported Negroes who "had been promised food and full pay if they remained" inside.[17]

The union had contended from the first that no actual sit-down was in progress. It so advised the governor. To strengthen its case, the UAW volunteered to go inside and to bring out its members, if any were to be found on the premises. The company received this offer in silence. Then the union appealed to the insiders directly; it rigged up a loudspeaker system over which it urged the men inside to vacate the plant. The occupying forces, largely Negro, were addressed from a sound car by Walter White, president of the National Association for the Advancement of Colored People. After White's appeal, two or three hundred men left the plant. The rest remained.

As for "sabotage," the Ford charges proved equally groundless. Five days later the company arranged a tour of inspection so that members of the press could see for themselves what the alleged saboteurs had been up to. For Bennett, the trip ended disastrously. The reporter whom the Detroit *News* sent on the hunt could find next to no evidence of what the Fords had publicized as $100,000 worth of "wanton destruction" of defense material. He did come up with something. He reported seeing half a dozen "blitz buggies" whose seats had been "slit." He saw a few defective testing machines which, in his opinion, could be readily repaired. But of the hundreds of production tools that he had inspected, said this reporter, "only one showed any visible sign of damage." As to who had been responsible for this flotsam of damage, the *News* man did not commit himself.[18]

The union, having been charged with sabotage, merely affirmed that if Ford or government property had been willfully destroyed in the course of the strike, Bennett should look to his own, for it was his men, rather than the union's, who had the run of the Rouge. R. J. Thomas, the UAW president, retorted further that the strikers had taken pains to safeguard company property. The furnaces had been tapped, he said, before the men walked out; if the company said the word, union workers would man the Ford power house. If actual sabotage had occurred and Bennett had not simply set a miniature "Reichstag fire," asked Thomas in a final challenge, why not give it a real investigation? Why not call in the FBI? Again, the Company chose not to reply.

Was the strike, as Bennett charged, a serious threat to national defense? The President was quoted as thinking otherwise.[19] The President knew whereof he spoke. The Ford bomber plant, under construction at Willow Run, was not affected by the stoppage. At the Rouge proper, Ford had not yet begun to convert for war on any considerable scale. In fact, only several weeks before the strike occurred, Cameron had gone to some length to explain why "premature" reconversion for defense at the Ford Motor Co. was unsound. The only actual war production which the strike had stopped at Dearborn, said the Associated Press, was the filling of a small though essential order of Army trucks and "blitz buggies."[20] The walk-out did interfere, however, with the construction of a new plant for the manufacture of aircraft engines at the Rouge, but to the forwarding of this really vital defense project during the strike, the Fords seemed strangely indifferent. The CIO agreed at the outset that AFL construction workers should stay on the job. The state police then asked the company to submit a list of the men who were essential for war work and who should be passed through the picket lines without delay. A list was provided, but it was no roster of defense or construction workers. The bulk of the names which Bennett turned over to the troopers were those of Ford spies, newly deputized police and private strong-arm men! Could it be, the union asked the Detroit News, that the Ford Motor Co. was using the issue of national defense as a "propaganda club"?[21]

Having failed to drive home the charge that radical trespassers and saboteurs were wrecking Ford property and causing a major breakdown in war production, Bennett tried another tack. Perhaps the state constabulary or the Army could be induced to take over on the grounds of maintaining "law and order." It was with such an end in view that Bennett informed the President on the second day of the strike that an unparalleled "reign of terror" had come to Dearborn.

Acts of violence had occurred at the Rouge from the beginning, on the side of the wall controlled by Ford Service—inside the plant. There, according to several eye-witnesses quoted by the Detroit News, existed pandemonium. After combing the grounds under orders to "give the works" to any stray CIO man found on the property, Bennett's insiders went berserk; they passed the time by gambling; they took to fighting among themselves. An old Ford employe who broke out of the plant after having spent two or three days inside reported that the docking of the Henry Ford II had touched off a riot. Rather than wait for the food ship to be unloaded, he said, a gang of two hundred of the insiders, brandishing "swords" and other weapons, had gone aboard to help themselves. In the pitched battle that followed on the deck and in the hold, he said, the pick of the food went to the stronger or the more vicious looters. Some of the less fortunate who came off empty-handed or were somewhere else at the time, had to buy their provisions from the "winners."[22] The Detroit *News* examined the matter further. It attributed to an "impartial source" the charge that a good many of Bennett's shut-in force, some of them under the influence of liquor, were cruising at random through the factory premises in new "blitz buggies" intended for delivery to the Army. The drivers, said the *News*, were armed with "iron bars, crudely fashioned swords and spears."[23]

The "mob violence" to which Bennett alluded—once he stopped calling the strike a "sit-down"—did not concern what went on within the Ford factory proper; it had to do, rather, with the conduct of the CIO pickets who were massed outside. Nonetheless, in charging that the "outsiders" had taken the law into their own hands, he had a point. The barricades athwart Miller Road obstructed traffic on a public highway. The air around the Rouge was fraught with potential violence. Though cautioned by their leaders not to make trouble, the Ford strikers had come prepared to meet it; they were ready, beyond a doubt, to use force, if need be, to keep their lines unbroken. Yet, on the whole, the strike began non-violently. The pickets, while in dead earnest, behaved at the start like a carnival crowd. They joked and sang to pass the time. Before long, they were being entertained, directly behind the "front lines," by speakers and baseball games and open-air movies.

In fact, apart from the road-block and the mere potentialities of violence inherent in militant mass picketing, the first hours of the strike were too quiet—from the standpoint of Ford Service. They by no means justified intervention by state guards or federal soldiers, so Bennett set out to create the sort of incidents that would make mass violence inevitable. The tool that he used for this purpose was the body of seven or eight hundred Negroes who were quartered in the plant and whom he had tried to pass off originally as "sit-down" strikers.

These insiders—just up from the South—began to function, under the command of Ford Service, as an assault force. One of their modes of attack was to make a sudden appearance on a roof of the plant or well inside an open gate and to shower the pickets outside with small lengths of pipe and other missiles.[24] On one occasion a man standing on the roof of a tall building adjacent to Gate 4 hurled a metal bucket and a wooden carpenter horse at the strikers in the street below. The horse struck a picket, knocking him unconscious. This act was reported by state troopers and newspaper photographers.[25] From the first day of the strike until the last, the insiders made periodic armed rushes at the picket lines, only to retreat back to the plant. Sweinhart witnessed the first of these sorties. The raiders, he was quoted as saying, carried steel rods and other metal objects.[26] According to several additional neutral bystanders, the "other objects" with which Bennett's men were armed consisted of clubs, crowbars, long iron pipes, makeshift swords and spears, and ice picks.[27] Forty of the insiders started out to taunt the strikers, driving up and down the picket line in cars. They were intercepted and searched by state police. The hecklers, said the police, were equipped with "clubs, files and other weapons."[28] The vital maintenance workers whom the CIO sent inside, with Ford approval, were subjected to repeated attacks and beatings on company property.

Thus provoked, the UAW strikers fought back, both with propaganda and with raw violence. Among other things, they offered the constant use of their sound car to prominent local Negroes and to Walter White of the NAACP. These respected Negro leaders broke the spirit of perhaps a third of the insiders; their very presence on the scene helped to forestall a race riot—the sort of thing which would have best served the ends of Ford Service. But aside from this appeal to reason, the union simply countered force with force. Every time the strikers were peppered with iron slugs or lengths of pipe, they picked up these missiles and returned the fire. The raiders who charged through the gates, armed with rods and other weapons, were hurled back into the plant by a counter-charge from the pickets. The CIO men, most of whom had started out empty-handed, according to witnesses who were not a party to the struggle, now armed themselves in self-defense. The baseball bat or the small iron bar soon became standard equipment on the picket line. Once aroused, the strikers were unquestionably in an ugly mood. More than one insider and more than one Ford Serviceman who fell into their hands, after leaving the shelter of the plant, was roundly thrashed.

In the course of this maneuvering by Ford Service, the Dearborn city police again looked on without asserting themselves. None of the armed attackers who sallied forth from the plant was placed under arrest by these officers of the law; none was even reprimanded.[29] The chief of the force, Carl Brooks, had met the emergency at the outset by adding new men to his staff. He had enrolled a body of

250 special police deputies. The failure of these temporary officers to pacify the men inside the Rouge may be accounted for, in part, by their origins. Many of them, said the Detroit *News,* were gate guards and Ford Servicemen, transferred direct from the Ford Motor Co. to the Dearborn city payroll.[30]

When the strike which had started out quietly took on a more and more violent complexion, the Fords could well report that disorder prevailed in Dearborn. In giving publicity to that fact, they were aided in no small degree by much of the nation's press. On the first and second day of the strike, the largest daily newspaper in the city of Seattle devoted to the event not so much as one line of news or commentary. It did manage, however, to give its readers the impression that "lawlessness" and the "CIO" were synonymous. Its sole treatment of the story was to publish under a vivid heading the picture of an unidentified non-striker who had been "laid out" on a railroad track after coming to grief at the hands of certain strikers outside the Rouge.[31] Confident that public opinion was on their side, the Fords reiterated their claim that armed intervention was called for. They went to the Detroit federal bench simultaneously to apply for a court order which would compel the union to take down the barricades on Miller Road.

Federal Judge Arthur F. Tuttle entertained the Ford petition when the Dearborn strike was two days old. The hearing in his court, during which the company produced only three witnesses, was brevity itself. It lasted less than two hours. Before the day was out, the bench issued a temporary restraining order which decreed that the Ford pickets would have to comport themselves peaceably and that the blockades on Miller Road should be removed forthwith.*

But neither the President nor the Governor seemed to give ear to the Ford contention that it was "up to the government" to suppress the strike by force. The President, said the Detroit *Free Press* on the second day of the strike, was not unduly alarmed by the reports that had come to him; he knew that Labor Conciliator Dewey had been in touch with the Ford problem for weeks; the Governor of Michigan had not appealed to the White House for aid. The President was

---

* Because of technicalities which Ford exploited to the letter, the law moved more deliberately in granting comparable relief to the UAW. Three years had passed before the union was able to establish the unconstitutionality of the Dearborn handbill ordinance. It took even longer—at least four years—to compel the Ford Motor Co. to recognize the legal validity of the NLRA. Nor did the Fords fully comply with the Wagner Act immediately after they had lost their appeal to the United States Supreme Court.

quoted as saying that he did not think he would reply to the Bennett telegram asking for "federal protection."

The Governor had already hurried to Detroit. But this officer was not the man whom Bennett had in mind for the state's highest office when the Ford machine had captured the county apparatus of the Republican party the year before. He was Murray D. Van Wagoner, a middle-of-the-road Democrat. Nor was Van Wagoner inclined to break the strike merely by making the Fords a loan of the state constabulary. The walk-out and the ultimate differences between Ford and the union, said the Governor, could and would be worked out by mediation. He had come to the city, he said, for the express purpose of arranging a temporary truce.

Bennett agreed to see the Governor and to explore the matter. He had no alternative. Neither troops nor any promising back-to-work movement were in the offing. Though Dearborn was relatively quiet and the barricades were gone, the strike wore on. A group of Ford representatives went into conference with the Governor and the federal conciliator. The personnel of Bennett's negotiating committee, however, commanded something less than the union's respect. At one or another of the subsequent meetings, the Ford delegation consisted of Frank Nolan, the Ford lawyer and politician; John Gillespie; James Brady, boxing promoter and Ford detective; and two "graduates" of Ford Service, Verne Doonan and Elmer DePlanche—the latter better known in veteran ring circles as "One Round Hogan."[32] Other corporations, exclaimed the union, sent their best men into critical labor conferences. General Motors had been represented by C. E. Wilson or William S. Knudsen; the Chrysler Corporation by the late Walter P. Chrysler. If the Fords meant business, asked the UAW, why should they delegate their negotiations to "members of their private espionage and police force or other minor employes"?

The Governor managed to get the contending parties into the same room and to arrive at a strike settlement, nonetheless. Five peace proposals brought the walk-out of ten days' duration to a close. Five of the eight union committeemen whose dismissal had caused the strike were to be reinstated immediately. The grievance procedures that had prevailed before the strike were to be resumed. Any unresolved disputes were to be referred to a mediation board. The current NLRB hearings which the government had already initiated in Detroit —because of Ford's continued non-compliance with the Wagner Act —were to be suspended temporarily. As a final condition of settlement, both sides agreed to expedite the holding of a government sponsored

employe election. When the truce terms were made public and all
the negotiators were leaving the conference room, "Bennett," said the
Detroit *Free Press*, "was one of the few about the Statler Hotel whose
face was not entirely cheerful."[33]

### 3

On May 21, 1941, 83,000 qualified voters went to the polls at
the three Detroit plants of the Ford Motor Co. They were given an
opportunity to register, by secret ballot, their choice of three forms
of representation: CIO, AFL, or none at all. Throughout the day,
company or union watchers occasionally exercised their right to
challenge the eligibility of this or that voter; only the bona fide Ford
production worker was entitled to cast a ballot. Of the two sets of
watchers, the union's was by far the more active. For nearly 6000
Ford foremen and Ford Servicemen, all of whom the law clearly
debarred from voting, calmly presented themselves at the polling
booths. When the votes were being counted, a company observer
raised a curious challenge. The board was about to discard a particular
ballot on which some crank or practical joker had made no mark, but
had written in, instead, the words "Jesus Christ." According to the
*New Republic,* a watcher for the company protested that the ballot
should be counted, for in his opinion the write-in "Christ" had perhaps
been intended as a vote for Ford.[34]

The election was a lopsided triumph for the United Auto Workers
of the CIO. Of the grand total of 80,000-odd votes, less than 3 per cent
were cast for "no union at all." A little more than 25 per cent voted
AFL. Seventy per cent, or about 58,000 of the eligible voters, declared
for the CIO.

When the count was known and the union announced its readiness to negotiate a contract with the Ford organization, Bennett made
a public statement. The election, he said, had been "a great victory
for the Communist Party, Governor Van Wagoner and the National
Labor Relations Board." The law forces one to "live" with such people,
said Bennett, "and we never violate the law."[35] I. A. Capizzi, the
company's chief counsel, said that the Ford Motor Co. would deal
with the "Communist-influenced and led" UAW but only "because the
law says it must." The Wagner Act, he averred, had stemmed from a
"dictatorial, European concept," its enforcement would compel "all
American industry to close down or be Sovietized."[36]

By way of reply, R. J. Thomas of the UAW called to mind that

Henry Ford had had more than two decades during which he could have won the good will of his workers. That he had failed to win it, said the UAW leader, had been demonstrated by the outcome of a secret election; 97 per cent of the production workers of the Ford Motor Co. had expressed a desire for some kind of union protection. As for "Communism," said Thomas, that charge so beloved of "reaction" had become "a pretty ragged scarecrow." Of the more than seven hundred business organizations already covered by UAW contracts, he said, all but a handful were still making money, most of them a great deal of money; none had, as yet, been "Sovietized."

The law was only one of the considerations which led Henry Ford to declare, through Bennett and Capizzi, that the time had come for getting together with the union on a permanent footing. Edsel Ford—the "moderate" in the Ford organization—on the other hand, might have arrived at such a decision voluntarily, quite apart from the company's legal position in May 1941. But in this case, as in countless others, it was the elder Ford and Bennett who determined basic Ford policy. Their motives, therefore, rather than Edsel's, were governing. When these two grudgingly admitted the necessity of "living" with the UAW, they were thinking not only of the law but of public opinion and of the state of the Ford exchequer as well.

On the one hand, they were mindful of the fact that Ford's immense good will was in jeopardy. Much of this precious business asset had already been frittered away. Ford's NLRB history—the longest on record and one of the most incriminating—had been skimpily reported in the general press, but it had been spread, with few omissions, on the pages of the labor press for the edification of six or eight million readers. Of perhaps greater danger to the repute of the Ford Motor Co. were the reports of its labor policy which had reached the middle class. *Time* Magazine had arrived at the point of calling Ford a "Model T tycoon." "Other automakers," *Time* had written just before the Ford strike, "look at Ford askance." They feel, said *Time*, that "he is bucking the tide, that so far as labor policy is concerned he is still rattling along in the Model T era."[37]

No threats to the good name of the Ford Motor Co., however, could hold a candle to what lay ahead in the Ford hearings which the NLRB had reopened in Detroit late in May. These proceedings promised to rock Ford's prestige to its foundations. For this time the government had at its fingertips, as fresh evidence against Ford Service, the case to end all labor cases. Into its preparation had gone six months of concentrated field work on the part of eighteen NLRB staff members, directed by a federal labor investigator of unusual brilliance. The actual hearings were to have started in April. They had been delayed at the frantic request of the Ford Motor Co. In fact, during the talks that ended the Ford strike, Bennett had insisted that, unless the NLRB first agreed to suspend its Detroit investigation, the Fords would entertain no peace proposals whatsoever. The dreaded government witnesses were now, at last, ready to take the stand. So shocking was their opening testimony, gathered in three days' time, that the Detroit papers had felt obliged to reproduce much of the record in full. What the country was about to read, if the proceedings went on to a conclusion, was the most sensational indictment in NLRB history.

The negotiations which followed the Rouge strike began none too auspiciously early in June. Once more the company was represented at the start by certain of its lesser lights—politicians Nolan and Gillespie, and ex-boxers Brady and DePlanche. Harry Bennett took a hand in the business, however, when it came to dealing with large issues and to affixing Ford's signature to the completed contract. At the end, Bennett arrived at the national headquarters of the CIO in Washington, vested with Ford's power-of-attorney.

The contract itself, drawn up in record time and announced on June 21, was all the union had ever asked for, and more besides. It encompassed, first of all, the tenets of a standard union agreement. Its written guarantees of collective bargaining, of seniority rights, and of overtime pay for work performed on Sundays and holidays or in excess of a forty-hour week, could be found in almost any UAW contract. Ford's men won nothing out of the ordinary when they were granted the right to take authorized leaves of absence without having to forfeit, as they had in the past, all accumulated seniority. The contract ran to type again in providing that in future periods of slack production no worker was to be laid off in any department until the average hours of employment at a given plant should fall to thirty-two hours a week or less. Still another clause was dictated by convention; it was one more attempt to bring Ford into line with general industry practice—a pledge that, henceforth, all employes who were to be charged with the duties of "plant protection" should be identified by wearing badges, uniforms or other conspicuous insignia.

However commonplace, all these provisions reduced to writing were notable departures at the Ford Motor Co. They clipped the wings of Ford Service and unhinged the Ford political machine at its base. Bound by a union contract, the Fords could no longer exploit their total payroll as a means of currying favor in the community or in the nation as a whole. Nor could they rely, as of old, on the services of the plainclothes spy. In fact, with the signing of the June agreement, Ford Service changed its name as well as its dress. What remained of the institution was referred to in the contract as the Division of Plant Protection. By the same token, these more or less conventional concessions were what Ford labor had been waiting for. They raised the average Ford man to a parity with his fellows in the rest of the industry; they gave him status and a measure of job security which he had never known heretofore.

Three remaining points of agreement were arrived at orally. Each was of cardinal importance to the union, yet all were, again, no more than any other employer in Ford's straits would have been compelled to allow. Both sides agreed man-to-man to expedite the settlement of a number of personal damage suits which various UAW members had filed against the company. To this unwritten promise Ford added a second, to the effect that such workers as had been discharged because of union activity would be rehired forthwith, and that in certain stipulated cases, their back wages would be paid without question; in others, after arbitration. Finally, the company committed itself by word of mouth to bring its wage scale up to date. It promised to meet the highest wage that any of its competitors were paying for every line of work within the industry.

Over and above its routine provisions, the written Ford agreement incorporated several additional clauses that were nothing short of extraordinary. These further items were all more than the union had bargained for; they represented remarkable concessions volunteered by the company itself. One had to do with "recognition." On this score, the most the union had yet won from any large corporation was exclusive bargaining rights, or the proviso that this or that employer would deal only with the UAW and with no other labor organization. But Ford, speaking through Bennett, went the full distance of his own accord. To the utter surprise of the UAW conferees and to the consternation of the trade, he advanced the proposal that every Ford factory should operate, henceforth, as a "closed shop;" that all Ford employes should be required to join the union as a condition of future permanent employment. To this radical departure, the company added still another. It volunteered the "check-off," offering to do what no other big automotive employer had ever dreamed of to date—to deduct union dues from the wages of each Ford employe and to transmit the income from this source to the UAW treasury. Quite overcome by such overtures, the UAW gave its ready assent when the company—now "100 per cent union"—then asked for authority to stamp its products in the future with the "union label."

Both parties to this unique labor contract emerged from the conference room in high spirits. The union, for one, was exultant. It had bested its toughest adversary; it had stormed Ford's feudal principality with success; it could well hail the new agreement as "a model for the industry." The Fords seemed to be no less pleased with the outcome. Their particular cause for satisfaction, they told the world in a formal press release, was to be found in the fact that once more, as ever in the past, the Ford Motor Co. was only trying to set an "example" for other industrialists and to address itself to "every problem from the viewpoint of its workingmen." The more substantial reasons for Ford's complacence were passed over. One in particular escaped public notice altogether. No longer at odds with Washington, the company could now rest assured of a vast collection of defense orders. Its fears of adverse publicity in the near future were at an end, for with the signing of a union contract, the deadly government hearing in Detroit and nine other pending NLRB actions as well were automatically quashed. Ford could find further comfort in the possibility that his own liberality might plague his competitors. Having posed the issue of the union shop and the check-off, he could now sit back, said the Detroit *News,* and watch the rest of the industry squirm, fully prepared to improve his own sales position in the event that any of his rivals in the business preferred to fight and to become strikebound rather than yield on these same fundamentals in days to come. Finally, Harry Bennett had private reasons for thinking that the union, rather than the company, had come off second-best. At least, before the ink was dry on the heralded agreement, he was assuring his confidants that it was the UAW people who had been "really licked," whether or not they were aware of the fact.

What Bennett meant to indicate privately, however, was his intent to exploit the Ford contract for all it was worth for the purpose of giving the UAW a "licking" in the future. His first step in that direction was crude and hastily contrived. It was an immediate, undisguised attempt to seize the union from within. The opportunity for such a coup presented itself when each of the Ford locals—one per plant—proceeded to the election of permanent officers and shop stewards. Hoping to capture this machinery at its birth, Bennett turned, in part, to the same Ford Servicemen whom the new contract had purportedly eliminated. Any number of these functionaries, still

THE LEGEND OF HENRY FORD

tied to Bennett's apron strings, were quickly shunted to the assembly lines. As production workers, they were eligible to compete for UAW office. They elbowed their way to winning nominations, concentrating on the shop steward apparatus whose conduct would subsequently make or break the union. But they failed to win any real support at the polls. Their successes occurred in certain branch factories where the Ford rank and file were still relatively unfamiliar with union procedures. At the Rouge the intended coup failed utterly. It did, however, raise a doubt. It served blunt notice on the UAW that Ford's latest "reform" was perhaps, after all, no more than skin-deep.°

The company's next move only clinched the suspicion that the leopard had not changed its spots. Once control of the shop steward machinery had slipped through his fingers, Bennett reverted over-night to still another plan of attack. This time his methods were more devious. He set out to "join" the institution which he had failed to storm by frontal assault. The UAW found itself tied to the Ford organization on a "honeymoon" of eight or ten months' duration. As long as this relationship persisted, nothing was too good for the union —or at least for the union's officialdom, high and low. On the bottom rungs of the ladder, Bennett began to make eyes at the shop steward and the local union official. His manner with such men became winning and deferential. He showered them with attention, bestowing little favors here and there. It was UAW higher-ups, however, to whom the Fords paid special court. R. J. Thomas and CIO President Philip Murray were entertained at lunch, and their hosts, Bennett and Henry Ford, were genial enough, except that Ford forbade the sort of publicity that might have been expected on such an occasion. He could not bring himself to the point of posing for a picture with his guests.

Throughout the honeymoon, Bennett catered to the top leaders of the UAW by playing first on their vanity, and then on their fears. His blandishments alone were enough to turn the head of any unprincipled youthful climber. On such a tack, Bennett once confided to one of the union's highest ranking officials that he had never met a young

---

° Ford labor policy in Canada, meanwhile, pointed in the same direction. For across the border, Ford continued to fight for many months the very union with which he had come to terms in Detroit. With variations, his propaganda techniques were the same. He had called the CIO movement of the United States an "un-American" thing of Soviet inspiration. In Canada, he maligned it as an "American" importation. Just before the company's Canadian employes took a vote on the question of union affiliation in November 1941, they were cautioned by the highest official of Ford of Canada to beware of the UAW in deference to the "Canadian way."[38]

man of greater promise. Why stop with mere leadership of a CIO union? he asked this UAW man. Why not go on to the governorship or to other high political office? There were ways and means of arranging such things, said the older man. But the trump card which Bennett played in the game of edging toward the UAW high command was the union shop and the check-off. Here was the prized concession, he never tired of reminding his more important UAW callers. Under certain circumstances, he indicated time and again, this plum could be withdrawn as easily as it had been given. It was, in short, he let it be known, a gift horse; it was the instrument by which he meant to hold the UAW in captivity.

But in trusting that manners alone would hypnotize the union's leadership or that the UAW would go to sleep for fear of losing its union shop at Ford's, Bennett made one basic slip. He forgot that the UAW, despite its normal quota of inner politics, is a democratic institution; that all its officials hold elective jobs and are answerable to the rank and file. Hence, the Fords were overcome with surprises. Bennett's first shock was the discovery that the UAW's top men were not for sale, at least on his terms. If they had so much as tried to make the Ford branch of their organization a "company union," not one would have survived a year in office. No one was interested in joining Homer Martin, the earlier UAW president who was now a show-piece in the Ford Administration Building. The effort to win over mere local union officers was no more successful. Indeed, a number of these lesser figures had been awed or misled by Bennett's attentions, so much so that they ceased to function as effective union men. They had met their reward for the most part by being promptly voted out of office.

After treading softly for nearly a year, Bennett learned to his dismay that the UAW leadership meant to keep the check-off and the union shop and at the same time to make Ford toe the line like any other employer. He saw, too, the vigor of Local 600. Instead of withering away, this key UAW chapter had dug in "for keeps;" it was housed in impressive modern quarters of its own; it was a force to be reckoned with on the assembly line; it was offering a vast program of healthy social services to which most Ford men had never before had access; and the leadership of the local was apparently not to be had. Bennett's high hopes foundered worst of all on the political front. He had lost his tight grip on the city of Dearborn. None of the union's up-and-coming young executives was interested in becoming a Ford candidate for public office, with Bennett as king-maker or with Henry Ford's purse as a bottomless source of revenue. Such was the outcome of the Ford plan to seduce the UAW with honey.

When he failed at the game of flattery and intrigue, Bennett changed his course. Once more he attacked the UAW and its sundry Ford branches head-on. This new policy came into being early in 1942. In the meantime, America had gone to war and the UAW had trimmed its sails accordingly. In fact, shortly before the Fords changed their minds and decided to make "living" with the union as difficult as possible, the UAW had earned the distinction of being the first major union in the country to read the times aright by vowing to countenance no strikes "for the duration." In announcing this action on March 17, 1942, UAW President R. J. Thomas declared, "We are at war and we must take the position that our country comes first. Without a democratic America," Thomas added, "there can be no labor movement; any strike now will weaken the war effort and will lay the labor movement open to attacks by its enemies." Bennett attacked nonetheless. For the next two years, until D-Day itself, the company's behavior toward labor seemed to be guided by a determination to strain the UAW's no-strike pledge to the breaking point, to discredit it before the public.

Such was Bennett's wartime policy toward collective bargaining of the most elementary form. He left no stone unturned in an effort to keep the grievance machinery at one or another Ford plant from functioning at par. His methods of blocking this process of give-and-take were manifold. He refused for more than a year to allow the company or the union to be represented for bargaining purposes by anything more than the barest skeleton. In all that time the union was rigidly held to the weakest clause in its contract; it was permitted only one shop steward per five hundred workers. The company, meanwhile, had provided for no recognized "grievance" officials of its own whatsoever! Fourteen months of wartime operation slipped by before Bennett could be made to concede either point—a wider election of shop stewards or the creation of a labor relations division of his own with authority to devote full time to the hearing of routine grievances.

Even then, collective bargaining seemed to exist at Ford's in name only. For the company's new labor relations people set out to plague the union all over again. At times they bargained willingly enough—as Bennett had once predicted—without ever "giving the men anything." Again, company representatives would refuse to see this or that qualified union committee on any terms. But the favorite technique was delay. As late as May 1943, Ford labor relations men were scheduling appointments with union officials, only to appear several hours late or the next day or not at all. So received, more than one shop committee won a hearing by trooping into an office somewhere in the Rouge and informing a clerk or a stenographer that they meant to "sit it out" indefinitely until the missing company executives put in an appearance.

All this while, the grievances which might have been winnowed out by conscientious bargaining, mounted steadily. Some concerned wages. In June 1941, the company had agreed orally to meet the highest rates in the industry, job for job. That meant, among other things, a thoroughgoing job analysis and an attempt to adjust various wage inequities *within* a given Ford shop. Bennett now chose to let this promise lie unfulfilled. In addition, the company made at least two major attempts to adjust its entire wartime wage level downward. At its Windsor plant, across the river from Detroit, Ford of Canada tried to introduce a plan for bringing in unskilled women workers at fifty cents an hour—a substantially lower wage than the men whom they replaced had received for doing identical work.[39] The second large-scale effort to cut wages occurred in Detroit proper. It took the form of shifting men from the Rouge to the company's two other plants in the city, and reducing their wages a dollar a day in the process. This practice was countermanded, but not until May 1944. Then, after investigating the matter, the War Labor Board decreed that such reductions had been uncalled for, and Ford was ordered to compensate 3000 men for the loss they had taken in back wages. The refund amounted to $1,000,000.[40]

On any number of other labor issues, all vitally related to war production and wartime morale and all presumably within the realm of collective bargaining, the company behaved almost as though Local 600 or the UAW were non-existent. For months it paid no heed to the union's insistence that Negroes should be hired without discrimination and that such colored workers as were added to the payroll should be assimilated by being placed alongside "experienced" Ford men who knew their "responsibilities" as well as their "rights." When failure to act on this suggestion, coupled with other short-sighted policies, helped to bring on a serious strike and a lamentable display of violence on the part of some segregated Negroes in a certain portion of the Rouge in May 1943, Bennett's remarks to the press only aggravated an already bad situation. Bennett went out of his way to stress the race of the offending workers and to impugn their motives as war workers. These Negroes, all recent employes, he said, had gone into war work in the first place only to escape the draft.[41]

Of the many wartime irritants of Ford labor, none could outrank the conduct of Plant Protection. The efforts of this division to impose "Ford discipline" were all too frequently pointless, over-severe and purposefully provocative. Like the Ford Servicemen whom they had replaced, functionaries of Plant Protection continued to rule the roost, to prowl about assembly lines and to pop into washrooms for the purpose of taking the violator of the pettiest plant rules by surprise. The taboo against smoking in company toilets was still rigidly enforced, as were other equally trivial regulations. Among the hundreds thus singled out for punishment were nine workers in the tank department at Highland Park who were "sent to the office" in April 1943, for having been caught matching quarters in a washroom during their lunch period.[42] On a par with their offense was the act of three Rouge steelworkers who were disciplined the following November for failing to "look busy" during a period of slack production over which they had no control.[43] All too many wartime labor disputes of every sort were settled on the production floor by Plant Protection and certain Ford foremen after the manner of Ford Service in times past—with the fist. On the other hand, production workers and members of the union were responsible for starting or aggravating their share of these violent encounters, and when such acts occurred, the UAW never contested the right of the company to penalize its employes accordingly. All Local 600 asked was that the rule against fighting on company property be enforced uniformly. But such was not the case. Time and again Bennett played favorites, invoking penalties for union men which were not applied with equal severity to Plant Protection or company foremen. In one outstanding case, a certain Rouge foreman who is said to have assaulted one or more of his subordinates on three separate occasions was not disciplined at all.[44]

When it appeared as though nothing short of strike action could induce the Fords to bargain in good faith, the UAW proposed the idea of referring all unsettled grievances to an outside umpire. It made this suggestion in the fall of 1942. General Motors had already submitted to such a procedure. The Fords, after some delay, agreed to follow suit. Then, despite the fact that their plants were aching with labor grievances, they proceeded to reject as a possible impartial umpire any and all of the men whom the union nominated for the job. When a candidate was finally agreed on—Dr. Harry Shulman, a former Yale professor of law—five more months had elapsed. By the time Shulman turned in his first official decision—only beginning to apply a rule of reason to the wartime labor policy of the Ford Motor Co.—it was March 1943; the country had been at war for two and one-half years and friction between the company and its men had long since passed the danger point.

For some of the wartime discord within the Ford plants, the union was responsible. Local 600 had its share of hot heads and of members who had never taken the union's no-strike pledge to heart. It had its impetuous shop stewards who promoted wildcat sit-downs for the most trivial of reasons or without bothering to consider the slower course of bargaining and negotiation. At times such offenders were not disciplined as they should have been either by local union officials or by the national office of the UAW. Yet where the same human frailties, the same inexperience and the same caliber of union leadership prevailed at many another comparable firm, wartime labor relations were, by contrast with the Ford experience, frictionless and uneventful. At Ford's the men were up against a management which was still determined to resist at any price a union that it had never accepted wholeheartedly in the first place.

The crowning indictment of Ford's wartime intentions toward labor took the form of a memorandum which a union committeeman spied on the desk and later retrieved from the wastebasket of one of the company's labor relations men. As reproduced in *PM* on March 12, 1944, this memorandum said in effect that only if production within the department could be "prodded" up to or ahead of schedule would it be opportune to "force the issue" and "pull a strike." Called before Shulman, the Ford umpire, the labor relations man in whose office the note had been found, admitted that the memorandum was in his handwriting. But he would say no more. He had come to the Shulman hearing escorted by two Ford lawyers. It was at this point that Local 600 addressed itself to the United States Attorney-General, asking that the wartime labor policies of the Ford Motor Co. be subjected to a thoroughgoing federal investigation.

As the war lengthened, an impressive group of outside observers concurred with labor in feeling that Ford's old regimen of autocracy was still very much alive. When Ford management and front office people were entertaining Eddie Rickenbacker at one of their plants in January 1943, their rudeness and lack of consideration for the newspapermen on the scene inspired a "press revolt." The Detroit *Free Press* singled out the incident for editorial comment the following day.[45] More than a year later, bad feeling between Bennett and

labor came to a head with a particularly shocking outbreak of violence
within the Rouge. Shortly after the occurrence of this deplorable
action, the author of the *Town Crier* column of the *Free Press* remarked that the "public relations chiefs" employed by other leading
corporations in the area were "frankly aghast" at the way the Fords
had handled the situation.[46]

Concurrently, early in 1944, a wave of bitter strikes engulfed the
Ford works in Windsor, Canada. After digging into the issues involved,
Mayor Arthur Réaume of Windsor gave it as his opinion that the
fault lay fundamentally with the management. Windsor would "never
have industrial peace," said Mayor Réaume, so long as the chief executive of Ford of Canada continued to vent "his hatred for the working
man."[47]

Of the many revealing criticisms of Ford's wartime labor policies,
the sharpest came from a source close to home—from Mayor Hubbard
of Dearborn. Mayor Hubbard felt obliged to speak his mind in connection with the same manifestations of violence that were discussed
in the *Town Crier* column of the *Free Press*. The Ford riot on which
he and others chose to comment occurred in March, 1944. It involved
a group of workers at the Rouge who gave expression to pent-up feelings of resentment against the management by invading a certain
labor relations office, wrecking various fixtures in the room, and
roughing up members of Plant Protection. When the riot subsided,
its perpetrators set up barricades in their particular shop, forcing
10,000 fellow employes who had no immediate interest in the dispute
to lose a day's work. Whatever their grievances, the rioters were
entirely in the wrong; they had ignored and ridiculed the advice of
their shop stewards; their action was decried in the strongest language
by Local 600; and all were severely disciplined. As a result of this
affair, and with the hearty approval of the union, twenty-six Rouge
men were permanently discharged.[48]

But before order was restored, the company had seen fit to chas-
tise Dearborn City Hall. By rights, said the general manager of the
Rouge, the Dearborn police should have commandeered the plant
during the emergency, but the city's chief official had been "unwilling"
or "afraid" to do his duty. It was this charge which spurred the
Mayor of Dearborn to offer his diagnosis of wartime labor problems
at the Rouge.

The Mayor's first observation was to say that he failed to grasp
why the Fords should ever complain of inadequate police protection.
"Most of our senior officers," he said, had been "hired, trained and

schooled in the police philosophy of a former Ford Serviceman." No informed person could deny, he added, that the Ford Motor Co. had always enjoyed, in the past and in the present, a "special super deluxe police service." Then the Mayor put his finger on what he considered to be the basic issue. Before blaming the Dearborn police for its troubles, he said, it would have behooved the company to "iron out the disgraceful and shameful mess" it had made of its labor relations and to learn something about the art of "getting along decently and peacefully with its employes," for the good of the war effort if for no other reason.

Bad as it was, this incessant conflict was never so serious that it prevented the Ford organization from making a stupendous contribution to national defense. The Rouge and other Ford plants, converted for war in 1942 and 1943, were among the nation's outstanding sources of a wide variety of superbly made war goods. Among the articles which poured from the Ford shops were jeeps, tanks, gun mounts, anti-tank weapons, aircraft engines, bomber parts, amphibious vehicles, armored cars, military trucks, and fire control instruments. Moreover, in their approach to wartime labor problems, the Fords were progressive on occasion. They were as openminded as any other large employers in the area—at least at the Rouge—when it came to respecting what their workers could suggest for the betterment of production. A notable example of such cooperation occurred in April 1943, when a number of Ford's steelworkers set a new production record. Their accomplishment was heralded in the union's paper. The mill superintendent sent a letter of congratulations to the Labor-Management Committee of the department.

## Twenty-nine

### WILLIT RUN?

### 1

MEANWHILE, at the great bomber plant in Willow Run, Ford management and Ford labor were engaged in another major effort to supply the armed forces of the United Nations. This project had been talked about in 1940. It was actually begun in January 1941, when Ford agreed to take a hand in the manufacture of the Liberator, or B-24, the four-engine bomber already designed and pioneered by Consolidated Aircraft. It was understood that Ford was to function at the start only as a subcontractor, or as a member of the B-24 pool. He was to begin by feeding parts to two western plants, one operated by Consolidated, the other by Douglas. Then as he got experience and his plant was in order, he was to make completed planes as well.

As the Willow Run program began to unfold, the publicity department of the Ford Motor Company outdid itself.[1] Henry Ford made the boast early in 1940, even before plans for the bomber plant had reached the drafting board, that in no time at all he would be making planes at the rate of a thousand a day. The nation buzzed at this pronouncement, and W. J. Cameron, Ford's veteran publicist, kept it buzzing. He gave the public his word for it in July 1940, that Ford would make good on the promise of a thousand planes a day. Then, endowed with the magic that has graced Ford propaganda ever since 1914, the Ford announcement snowballed of its own accord. A West Coast news commentator was soon quoting "reliable sources" to the effect that Ford had guaranteed to deliver not 1000, but 5000 planes a day!

These high hopes seemed to be borne out by the manner in which the Fords disposed of the preliminaries to production at Willow Run. The plant was built with astonishing speed. It was designed in January 1941. The first concrete was poured in April; the first machinery was installed five months later. Production began in short order. Willow Run was making bomber parts and subassemblies in May 1942.

The scope of the plant was a promise of big things to come. Designed by the late Albert Kahn, Willow Run was a mass production dream. It was conceded by everyone to be the most elaborately tooled aircraft factory in existence. A Detroit newspaper called it "the marvel of the industrial world." In point of size, nothing like Willow Run had ever been built before. Constructed at government expense at a cost of $65,000,000, the plant was the world's largest bomber factory operating under a single roof; it was a mile long and a quarter of a mile wide. The interior was equally grandiose. More than 30,000 parts were to go into the making of a single B-24. The program for the complete manufacture of such planes under one roof called for the setting up of seventy sub-assembly lines. Preliminary estimates of the size of the labor force required to man this mighty machine were enough to try the imagination. Willow Run issued a call for more than 100,000 aircraft workers.

But before the Fords could make the "miracle of Willow Run" come true, they had to solve a manpower problem of the first order. This problem, while common to all war industry, was peculiar at Willow Run, in view of the plant's location. With no vocal opposition from the Army or the government, Ford had elected to build his bomber factory out in the country, thirty-five miles from the center of downtown Detroit.

First of all, there was the question of living accommodations for the tens of thousands of aircraft workers who were expected to heed Ford's call. The communities adjacent to the plant could scarcely absorb such numbers. Nearby Ypsilanti was a sleepy college town; Belleville was no more than a crossroads country village. The homes of newly industrialized Ann Arbor, the seat of the State university, were already crowded with war workers. Outside of these centers, local housing was geared to the needs of a small, stable farming population. Nor was Greater Detroit bursting with vacant homes or apartments. Several months after Willow Run had gone into production, *Life* magazine reported that dwellings in Detroit proper were filled to the extent of 98.7 per cent, and that it was next to impossible to rent even a decent room within fifty miles of the city. It seemed likely from the beginning, therefore, that some of the thousands of aircraft workers whom Ford hoped to recruit would have to be housed, preferably close to the bomber plant itself, in brand new dwellings, built either by private or public agencies.

But until the plant was in actual operation, this point escaped the planners who had been responsible for the location of Willow Run. Ford, who owned extensive tracts of land in the area, had simply ignored the question. As his men were tooling up, he offered no housing plans of his own. Nor did federal agencies take any concrete action in the matter for nearly a year and a half after the plant had been designed and its location approved.

Finally, in the spring of 1942, the UAW and the Federal Public Housing Administration began to move independently. The union went to Washington. It asked the government to build a model city of permanent homes, large enough to house twenty or thirty thousand workers and their families. Meanwhile, the Detroit office of the FPHA started to function, without committing itself to the type of housing that was called for. Its engineers began to survey the land that surrounded the bomber plant, most of which belonged to Ford, the rest to small farmers.

But instead of welcoming the two agencies that wanted action on a manpower problem which he himself had passed over, Ford rose up to oppose both with all his might and main. Harry Bennett opened the fight by getting rough with the FPHA engineers. These surveyors became "trespassers," and were promptly evicted from Ford property and told not to come back to any of the vast potential Willow Run housing sites which belonged to Ford. Next, Bennett destroyed the work the engineers had left behind. His men tore up 700 stakes that had been laid out on Ford land. With much hullabaloo and the promise that "Mr. Ford would support all other landowners" who felt as he did, Bennett took to the field. His contact men began to rouse the farmers of the community. Up to this point, according to Col. F. Charles Starr, the regional liaison man of the housing administration, the farmers "knew who the surveyors were when they came around" and had raised no objections. But soon after "Ford objected" and Bennett had gone to work, the farmers followed Ford's example. They, too, began to evict FPHA men right and left.

In the meantime, the Ford organization took its case to Washington and to the press. This activity, guided by Ford's chief counsel, I. A. Capizzi, precipitated a state-wide revolt against public housing in general. All Detroit's standing enemies of federal housing made Ford's cause their own. The large, organized real estate interests of the area deluged Washington with telegrams and written communications. The chorus was joined by countless petty landlords who lived near Willow Run and were renting out spare rooms at premium rates.

Insofar as Ford's opposition to a housing development for his aircraft workers was directed against the idea of having the government build a city of *permanent* homes at Willow Run, in the midst of a war, well and good. As many of its critics contended, a permanent bomber city would have taken too long to build; it would have required vital war materials, and after the war was over, it might well become a ghost town, stranded in a cow pasture.

But such was not the crux of Ford's opposition to the project. If it had been, the Fords could have forced the issue by coming out strongly in favor of temporary war housing, as against permanent construction. Instead, they were content with inspiring a public movement that declared itself in opposition to any federal housing whatsoever. The high Ford official who was sent to talk to the national housing administrator at this time emphasized, for purposes of publication, that Willow Run had no housing problem of any kind. There were homes and apartments aplenty in nearby built-up areas, he said in May 1942, to care for all the "140,000 workers" who were needed at the bomber plant.[2]

The real reason for the Ford crusade against public housing was something else again. In their effort to hold off construction of a bomber city, Ford and Bennett were actually sparring politically; they were fighting for postwar control of Willow Run and the surrounding community. No one stated this fact better than James Sweinhart, the former Ford publicist. When Sweinhart put his finger on the Willow Run housing issue, however, he was no longer writing advertising copy for the Ford Motor Co.; he was back where he had started, at a reporter's desk at the Detroit *News*. In an incisive bit of writing, Sweinhart asserted that in jockeying about for postwar position at Willow Run, "the powers that control the plant and its environment" were apparently "unable to grasp the fact that WE ARE AT WAR . . . and to realize that the great, basic purpose of the plant is to help WIN— perhaps even DECIDE THE ISSUE of the war and act accordingly."[3]

War or no war, here were the facts that were governing Ford and Bennett as they first envisioned the possibilities of a bomber city. Willow Run is in Washtenaw County. Washtenaw, unlike the County of Wayne in which the Rouge plant stands, is rock-ribbed Republican. It was part of Bennett's job to keep it that way. Harry C. Mack, the sales manager of the Ford Motor Co., was a cog in Bennett's political machine in the area. Mack was a member of the Washtenaw Board of County Supervisors. What haunted the Fords, as they contemplated the rise of a bomber city, was the thought of what might happen to their compact Republican haven once 20,000 or more New Deal union workers established legal residence in the area and began to vote.

In fact, Harry Mack, the Ford sales manager, let the cat out of the bag. He condemned the proposed development by calling it an out and out "CIO plan" to which "Henry Ford was opposed." He frankly admitted entertaining "the fear" that a solid block of Democratic voting unionists might upset "the political complexion of Washtenaw County."[4] Mack must have known whereof he spoke. He was a social and political crony of Bennett's, as well as a top Ford executive. It was he whom Bennett had sent to interview the national housing administrator, and when Mack went to the root of Ford's campaign against public housing at Willow Run, the Detroit *News* was referring to him as "Ford's usual spokesman in Willow Run matters."[5]

Mack's candor and Sweinhart's revelations now made it clear why the bomber factory was put where it was in the first place; they also explained one of the oddities of the architecture of Willow Run. The very shape of the plant, like Ford's attitudes toward housing,

# 434 THE LEGEND OF HENRY FORD

had political significance. If Willow Run had conformed to the purest
canons of mass production, it would have been laid out in a straight
line. The original building plans called for such a floor plan. But when
Ford decided to expand the factory which already crowded the county
line that divides Washtenaw from Wayne, it threatened to sprawl
over into Wayne. Rather than permit such straddling, the new portion
of the plant was "bent." It was turned at an angle of ninety degrees
and two special turn-tables were installed on the production floor to
give the assembly lines a corresponding hook.

Both in choosing his original building site and in bending Willow
Run at right angles, Ford had placed himself out of reach of the tax
assessor and the police of Wayne County in which liberal-Democratic
administrations are frequently elected to office. All the advantages of
such an arrangement would be canceled or threatened, as he saw it,
if a well-housed bloc of factory-worker Democrats took root in Washtenaw County.

As a result of the anti-housing sentiment which the Ford people
abetted in Detroit, no immediate action of any sort was taken to
house the workers at Willow Run. Local housing officials and their
superiors in Washington had their necks in their collars. They were
afraid to move in any direction. Colonel Starr of the FPHA, who was
an exception, was getting nowhere. A month and a half after his
engineers were driven out of the Willow Run area, this officer said
that so many farmers had followed Ford's lead that "little progress
has been made on the local housing front." Nor would the Ford
Motor Co. even discuss the situation. In his efforts to reopen the
question with someone in authority at Dearborn or Willow Run,
Colonel Starr discovered what many have learned before him, that
"it is more difficult to see Ford than the President of the United
States."[6]

Circumstances finally brought the Ford Motor Co. around. When
it was more than certain that in the absence of some additional local
housing the bomber plant could never hope to get the labor it needed,
and when the federal government made it clear that its plans at Willow
Run called for the building of impermanent, emergency war housing
and nothing else, Ford backed down. He even provided the land for
the needed developments. He sold the government 295 acres of his
Willow Run property. This was in October 1942.

By April of the following year, 2500 FPHA family dwellings,
960 two-person units, 500 trailers, and dormitory space for 3000 single
workers were ready for occupancy. But the need for more Willow Run

housing persisted until January 1944. From then on, the community had an actual surplus of dwelling units. The government had over-built in the meantime, only because the labor force was one-half or one-third of the number Ford had stipulated originally.

## 2

After dropping the fight against public housing, the Ford Motor Co. was faced with the question of what to do with the workers who moved out to Willow Run while federal housing was under construc-tion or still in the blueprint stage. Perhaps a fourth, or even a third, of the 35,000 men and women employed at the bomber factory in the spring of 1943 fell in this category. Thousands poured into the region. They swelled the size of the population of the Willow Run countryside by 50 per cent.

Whole communities made up of bomber workers and their families sprang up in a matter of weeks. By February 1943, there were scores of trailer camps and shack towns in the immediate vicinity of the plant. All these sprawling little centers gave rise to an endless chain of acute social problems. They were overcrowded. They lacked fire and police protection. There were no stores or schools or centers of recreation anywhere about. The *Bombardier,* published by the union at Willow Run, kept a running record of the situation; it told of five of its members who were sleeping in an icy attic near the plant, of another group which was paying $250 a month for the privilege of renting a number of unheated cubicles in a converted chicken coop.

In the summer of 1943, a public report on living conditions in and about Willow Run was issued by the Metropolitan Defense Com-mittee whose members had been appointed by Mayor Jeffries of Detroit. The committee took note of the fact that recreational facilities in the Willow Run shack settlements were almost nil. It reported that large areas in the vicinity had neither sewers nor drainage nor a safe water supply. Most of the drinking water in the region was found to come from surface wells; and of the wells which were tested, 40 per cent showed the presence of typhoid bacilli. The committee informed the governor of the state that Willow Run was ripe for an epidemic.[7] The health commissioner of Washtenaw County had already char-acterized Willow Run as a "keg of dynamite" that might "explode" any minute.[8]

This state of affairs had a direct bearing on the number of bombers that issued from Willow Run. For, according to Mayor Jeffries' committee, lack of sufficient housing and "deplorable" conditions in existing housing were responsible for "a vast dissatisfaction and labor turnover" at the bomber plant. Half of the thousands who left their jobs at Willow Run, said the Jeffries' report, had done so because of poor living conditions. This diagnosis of the morale of Ford's aircraft workers was published by Mayor Jeffries fourteen months after Bennett had given chase to the FPHA surveyors.

Even so, the Fords continued to let the Willow Run community stew in its own juice. A local public health official who was working in the region in the spring of 1943 was quoted by *PM* as saying that "the Ford Motor Company is the chief block to getting social life organized in this area. When it does not actively obstruct, it pursues a negative policy of non-cooperation." After surveying the health and welfare activities of Willow Run, a professor of medicine at the University of Michigan remarked, according to *PM*, "Henry Ford thinks more of his machines than he does of the people who use them."[9]

When matters were at their worst, a committee of citizens from Ypsilanti called on a high Ford official. They asked for cooperation in providing for the social needs of resident Willow Run employes. *PM* described their reception. After listening politely to what the committee had to say, the Ford official replied, "Gentlemen, we are concerned with building the best bombers in the world. What our workers do outside the plant, or how they live, is no concern of ours. The community will have to take care of that."

When the job was done—within limits—it was the community, rather than the Ford Motor Co., that did it. The county health department, local dental societies, the United States Public Health Service and other outside groups took steps to safeguard the physical welfare of the area. Local 50 of the UAW undertook to organize the whole community on a self-help basis. It founded the Willow Run Community Council which in turn took the lead in health and welfare planning. Local 50 then sponsored an elaborate program of recreation and adult education. In fact, by converting itself in large part to a social service organization, the union did more than any other agency to meet the community problems which the Fords, for the most part, had ignored.

Long before the FPHA was able to finish its building program for Willow Run, the employment office at Ford's aircraft plant pursued a hiring policy that, to some extent, only added to the housing headaches of Greater Detroit. Badly in need of workers, the company sent labor recruiters into the South. This recruitment was limited almost entirely, if not exclusively, to white workers. It did, of course, help Ford to get men, for thousands of southerners moved north and became valued war workers at Willow Run.

Not all the migrants came to stay, however. Their willingness to stay depended, in part, on what they themselves expected to find "up north" and on what they had been told before they left Texas or Kentucky. According to stories that appeared in the *Bombardier* and the Detroit *Free Press*, many a newcomer from the South thought that Willow Run was in Detroit, or that upon his arrival, a private steam-heated apartment with bath would be ready and waiting. In some such cases, the disillusioned recruit, often accompanied by his wife and children, headed straight back for Texas.

While it was busy soliciting out-of-state workers whose arrival made a bad housing situation worse, the Ford Motor Co. passed over a large potential source of labor right at home. It withheld employment from available Detroit and Washtenaw County Negroes. This failure to tap an existing pool of resident workers was most evident at the bomber plant in the case of Negro women. Early in 1943 the UAW asserted that of the 10,000 women employed at Willow Run, only a handful were colored.

Not that the opposition to hiring Negroes was limited to Ford by any means, but as against other employers in the area, Ford's need for labor was the most critical, and the supply was there. Government manpower officials, speaking off the record in 1943, estimated that there were, all told, 20,000 potential Negro war workers in and about Detroit whom Ford could have hired, had he cared to.

Fifty per cent or more of the aircraft workers were never housed near Willow Run. These people lived where they could in Greater Detroit and commuted to work. This arrangement was inevitable in view of the lack of war housing and in view of the plant's location, but it did nothing to keep morale at a high pitch at Willow Run.

Like war workers everywhere, most of Ford's bomber workers drove to work in their own cars, sharing rides with others. On the whole, their rides were long and time-consuming. The *Wall Street Journal* said in the spring of 1943 that the average Willow Run worker had to make a daily round-trip of forty to seventy miles to get to and from work.[10] Little wonder that Senator Harold H. Burton, when he inspected Willow Run as a member of the Truman Committee, singled out this one fact for personal comment.

For the thousands of bomber workers who had to depend on other means of transportation, the daily trek to and from the plant cost even more in time and money. Two railroads led to the plant. But loaded down with war traffic, neither had any rolling stock to spare, so shuttle service between Willow Run and Detroit—suggested by the Truman Committee and by the union—was out of the question. That left the problem of transporting Ford's men up to two bus concerns, the Detroit municipal system and a private concern.

Just as Willow Run was getting under way in April 1942, a newspaper reporter sampled the service which the two transit companies were offering as of that date. He started from the center of Detroit. It took him two hours and twenty-three minutes to reach the plant. The round trip cost him $1.37.[11]

The service improved as time went on, but at best, running time from Willow Run to Cadillac Square in downtown Detroit was still sixty or sixty-five minutes. Arriving at this transfer point, the commuter then had to catch a city bus or street car to get to the part of the city in which he lived. Fares were reduced to seventy cents, round trip. At that, transportation alone continued to eat up nearly 8 or 9 per cent of what the average rider earned each day.

As far as the Ford Motor Co. was concerned, there was nothing basic it could do on the transportation front. What little the company could do to make commuting simpler or more convenient, it sometimes failed to do. In fact, by making things even more difficult than they were already, the Willow Run management on one occasion almost brought the roof down over its ears.

One day in March 1943, employes on the day shift in a certain department of the bomber plant were told that they would have to work beyond their usual quitting time at 4 P.M., in order to get in step with a new working schedule. This was the first that had been heard of the new hours. The word was passed around in mid-afternoon of the day the change was to be put in force. The men who reported for the night shift in the same department were told, on arrival, that their shift would begin, that day and in the future, at 5 P.M. instead of 4, and that they would quit at 1:30 in the morning instead of the usual time, 12:30 A.M.

The effect of this order was to disrupt the team arrangements of hundreds of ride-sharers throughout the plant. The department in question employed a thousand workers, many of whom shared rides with hundreds of men who worked in departments which were not affected by the new schedule. It was too late to get in touch with the riders or drivers in outside departments, for the change had been ordered without having warned the men in advance.

Boiling mad, the men whom the order did affect directly called no strike (for which action the *Bombardier* later commended them), but hundreds simply ignored the notice until they had time to rearrange their riding plans. The night shift men who stayed at their places got home as best they could. A few who tried to beg rides to Detroit or other communities at that time of morning waited, according to the Detroit *News,* "in vain and in zero temperatures."[12]

This piece of bungling or high-handedness was too much for Colonel George E. Strong, who was then representing the regional supply office of the Army Air Forces. In Colonel Strong's words, it was plain "stupid for a concern which is crying for labor to pull a stunt like this. You just can't treat people that way," the Colonel stormed.[13]

The incident that roused Colonel Strong was not peculiar in itself. It was, on the contrary, all too characteristic of the labor policies which were invoked by the company that was "crying for labor." The bomber plant had a union; under the terms of Ford's closed shop contract, all Willow Run workers were automatically members of the UAW. Their bargaining agent was Local 50. But from the day the factory first began to operate, it was apparent that along with giving the union recognition, the Ford Motor Co. was determined to give it little else.

It was Ford policy throughout this critical period at Willow Run to thwart Local 50 and the national officers of the UAW at every turn. The plant manager, steered by Harry Bennett, simply ignored as far as he could all the bargaining procedures that had become more or less accepted in the Detroit area. He steadfastly refused to admit any discussion whatsoever of certain basic issues which all unions take to heart and which most employers at this date had come to consider legitimate union business.

Even on issues which he did hold admissible to collective bargaining, this Ford executive contrived to make the union's grievance machinery as slow and inefficient as possible. He went out of his way to curb the more active union committeemen at the plant. His instrument for this purpose was the "three-day layoff," invoked for the flimsiest of reasons. For months Willow Run foremen had no real authority to settle grievances at their source. Instead, most union matters, however trivial, had to be referred to the plant manager's office where one man alone was supposed to sit in judgment on the complaints of 35,000 workers. Blocked at the level of the assembly line, the officers of Local 50 found the top management almost impossible to deal with.

Meanwhile, the methods of keeping discipline at Willow Run were every bit as arbitrary and provocative. These methods jeopardized morale all the more in view of the fact that many of the rules and regulations in force at the plant appeared to be petty and capricious.

One regulation, for example, required a division of the sexes at lunch time. For no good or apparent reason, there were separate cafeteria facilities for men and women. The two sexes were not allowed to mix in these eating places. This arrangement sat well neither with thousands of single men and women nor with the hundreds of married couples who worked at the plant.

For more than a year the UAW contended to no avail that Willow Run had too much Plant Protection *for the good of production.* Plant Protection men, the union said, were all too frequently over their depth, meddling with factory problems and overriding the technical judgment of trained production foremen and superintendents.

Again, the officers and members of Local 50 contended that Ford was going to extremes in pitting one shift at Willow Run against another. However good in principle, they said, the plan seemed to defeat itself in practice. In any number of instances, according to the union's report, one shift with extra time on its hands would stand around rather than start a job it could not finish for fear someone else would get credit for the work it had begun and was unable to finish.

Needless to say, Willow Run had no formal machinery for soliciting technical ideas from its rank and file workmen. Indeed the federal government finally singled out the Ford corporation and General Motors for failing to cooperate with labor on the production front. The director general of the WPB'S production drive in December 1943, called attention to the fact that 9000 first-rate "enlightened" corporations in Britain and the United States had found Labor-Management Committees "overwhelmingly" useful. This official went on to say that such committees, acting in a capacity that was "purely advisory to management" had been recommended by the Army, the Navy and the Maritime Commission. Yet thus far, he said, Ford (and GM) had given only "superficial attention" to the plan.

Ford's reply to the WPB was candid, if nothing else. Labor-Management Committees, said the Ford Motor Company, were out of the question, because "in the way of experience or ability along management lines, labor has nothing much to offer."

All in all, no other major war plant in the Detroit area had a history of labor relations that could compare with that of Willow Run. Throughout 1942 and most of 1943 the plant was choking with grievances. That Ford management was primarily responsible for this state of affairs, was not even questioned by qualified outside observers. Army supply officers, interviewed by *PM*, were said to have been "amazed and bewildered" by Ford's labor policy at Willow Run. Finally, in November 1943, the Detroit *Free Press*—no enemy of Ford's and no champion of organized labor—came out with the real explanation of what was ailing labor at Willow Run. "It is easy to believe," said the *Free Press*, "that if Mr. Bennett would use a little less sandpaper and a little more silk there would be less friction. . . ."[14]

Local 50 somehow managed to prevent its members from striking. What it could not do, on the other hand, was to keep them from leaving. Other war jobs paid as well; they were handier and more attractive all around. The number of Willow Run workers who quit to look for other work was legion. No other war plant in the area had so fantastic a quit rate. At its worst, in 1942, the turnover of workers at the bomber plant ran as high as 50 per cent a month.[15]

Convinced that this exodus from Ford's was, in part, the result of dissatisfaction with working and living conditions, the UAW made a study of the quit rate at the bomber plant. Its findings were published in March 1943. The union reported that 50 per cent of the terminations at Willow Run, as at most war plants, were military separations. The rest, said the UAW, represented for the most part workers who had no liking for the way Ford handled his manpower problem. Of the thousand who quit of their own accord in January 1943, five hundred were said to have left for reasons directly connected with inadequate housing and transportation. The *Bombardier* went on to say that countless hundreds, if not thousands, had left the job at Willow Run because they had spirit and found it impossible to knuckle under to the type of men whom Bennett had recruited for Plant Protection.

3

Ford had more than a manpower problem on his hands at Willow Run, however. He ran into self-made difficulties that were purely technological in nature. Some of these further problems stemmed from the fact that Willow Run was a somewhat unconventional aircraft plant.

When they planned their original layout, Ford's men were guided too much by their past experience with automobiles. They tooled up as though plane production was much the same as making Model A's or Ford V-8's. In so doing, they made a radical departure from existing methods of aircraft production.

The chief innovation at Willow Run was the extensive use of hard steel dies. Such dies, according to the trade, have their points: they hold up; they are ideal for getting big production runs. Their value is limited, presumably, to the extent that a manufacturer has to allow for frequent changes in the design of the thing he is making. Retooling with dies of this type is a slow, major operation. By the time Ford came into the field, old-line producers had taken this factor into consideration; they geared their plants accordingly, favoring soft, cheaper dies that could be changed over much more readily.

Experienced aircraftsmen tried to tell Ford what he was getting into from the outset; they warned him that some of his methods would make a hard and complicated job still harder and much more complicated. As early as July 1942, *Fortune* said that old hands in the industry were convinced that Ford was "spending time and energy on mass tooling" that would probably "never be fully utilized."

All this advice went unheeded, however. As the Truman Committee discovered later on, too few outside experts had been called in for consultation at Willow Run, and too few layout men and production engineers had been sent out to see how planes were made by Consolidated in San Diego.

Ford not only went ahead in his own way, but he ridiculed his critics as well. These old-line producers were just an "antiquated" lot, the Ford publicity department asserted in July 1942. "The bomber job," Ford boasted, was no different from "making auto bodies." Analogies were drawn between Ford's potential aircraft capacity and production of the jeeps which were "rolling off the assembly lines (at the Rouge) like cookies out of a cutter."[16]

The test came when the Army ordered hundreds of modifications of the B-24 design. Such alterations were inevitable. They were based on actual combat experience and dictated in the interests of safety and military necessity.

The result was what Ford's more experienced competitors had predicted. Change-overs at the bomber plant were much more painful and far more costly in time and money than at other comparable factories. Willow Run was bedeviled by retooling pains, swamped by what the Truman Committee termed wholly avoidable "waste and confusion."

Slow-downs, caused by laborious retooling operations, in turn demoralized the working force. Production schedules were thrown out of gear time and again in 1942 and 1943, and men were required to stand around because of insufficient work and slow-moving opera- tions. Such a state of affairs was common enough in all large-scale war plants that were getting the feel of a complex, new job. But it lasted longer at Willow Run. According to *PM*, many of Ford's aircraft workers were compelled to spend two out of three days "just looking busy"—there was not enough real work to keep them occupied—as late as January 1943.[17]

Moreover, when production ills began to harass Willow Run, their correction took over-long because of the status of the average worker at the plant. Creative ideas that might have come from the rank and file were, all too often, bottled up. By overemphasizing the functions of Plant Protection, and by opposing Labor-Management Committees, Ford had inadvertently built a wall between his engineers and the bright worker on the floor.

The cause of the technical bottleneck at Willow Run, which the trade had foreseen from the beginning, was eventually pointed up by one or another government agency. In February 1943, the Office of War Information announced that Ford could have started deliver- ing bombers months before he did if he had used "more flexible tooling methods."[18] One month later Charles B. Wilson, vice-chairman of the WPB, was said to be of the opinion that the Ford organization had not been "sufficiently receptive to the ideas of experienced aircraft manu- facturers."[19]

Ford's stiffness in the face of change in the B-24 program was all the more conspicuous inasmuch as he had had considerable past experience in the field of aviation. Fifteen years earlier a subsidiary of the Ford Motor Co., under the direction of the aeronautical engineer, William B. Stout, had begun the manufacture of the Ford "Tin Goose," a large all-metal, tri-motored transport plane. The technical difficulties that Ford ran into with this plane were much like those he encountered as a producer of the B-24. In both instances the manufacturer was loath to allow for progressive changes of design. The Tin Goose had appeared in 1926 and 1927. It was a dependable, if somewhat slow and heavy, ship to begin with. But from this point on, Ford's competi- tors continued to develop new models. The design of the Tin Goose meanwhile had remained basically unchanged. As a result, the Ford plane was rapidly outmoded. Its maker, having lost a great deal of money on this—his first—venture into the air, had apparently decided that he had had enough. In 1931, therefore, he had withdrawn from the field.

Just when Willow Run operations, planned the hard way, demanded the utmost in executive skill, the job was made still harder because of the fact that some of Ford's outstanding production men fell by the wayside. Part of this critical loss of management talent was an accident of fortune. The rest was of Ford's own doing.

Long before the bomber plant was functioning at its best, illness and death claimed two of the company's most capable executives. First, Peter Martin, Ford's vice-president in charge of production, was prevented from taking any part whatsoever in the Willow Run program. Martin had a heart attack in 1941 which forced him into permanent retirement. The removal of this man meant the loss of a mechanical genius who was the best liked of the few foremost executives who had lasted at Ford's from the time the company was founded. It was Martin, together with Sorensen, who had carried Ford through the tooling crises of the Model A and the Ford V-8.

Edsel Ford, unhappily, was next. The younger Ford died in May 1943, after making a substantial personal contribution at Willow Run. Edsel's grasp of aircraft production problems is said to have been excellent. His concentration on the Ford bomber program hastened his death. Insofar as he was able to bring his influence to bear, he had also tried to change Ford labor policy for the better. When Edsel Ford died, the union went out of its way to lament the fact and to say that he, more than any other high executive in the company, had made a notable effort to bring Ford labor relations up to date.

Then, when the job at Willow Run had no more than begun, mere whim on the part of Henry Ford was responsible for watering down the executive talent of the Ford Motor Co. still further. The company was facing a massive conversion program, both at Willow Run and at the Rouge. Ford had always used great retooling interludes as an occasion for dropping some of his higher paid executives. In the course of tooling up for war—indifferent, as ever, to the value of surrounding himself with an organization of men and convinced that he could buy new talent if any was needed—he fired key men right and left.

When General Motors heard of this latest large-scale exodus of management men at Ford's, it was overjoyed; it began to rub its hands, thinking in terms of post-war competition. It was GM's policy at the time to make work for its proven key men, both as an aid to war production and as a means of keeping its managerial force intact.

Consequently, when supervision of the herculean chore of building the world's largest bomber plant and operating it from scratch fell to Charles E. Sorensen, Ford's old production chief, Sorensen was shorthanded. Willow Run personnel was as competent as that of any other similar American war plant, down at the bottom. Its craftsmen and rank and file workers and many of its engineers and minor supervisors were as good as they come. The pinch came at the top, for Sorensen had to work without the aid of many expert administrators whom Ford had, quite rashly, thrown aside. But despite this handicap and despite the fact that he had everything to learn in the aircraft field, Sorensen made a brilliant job of it. He carried the colossal management load at Willow Run from 1941 into the fall of 1943. *Fortune* thought so highly of his performance and of his feverish energy at the age of sixty-one that it referred to him in 1942 as "the nation's No. 1 production man."

All this while Harry Bennett aggravated the management situation at Willow Run by staging another "palace revolution" at the Ford Motor Co., with Ford's tacit approval. This inner struggle, which enlarged Bennett's powers as never before, began even before the death of Edsel Ford. When the younger Ford was in the hospital having one of his several major operations, the "Edsel faction" in the Ford organization had been whittled away, piece by piece.

The turning point came in June 1943, following Edsel's death, when Bennett became a director of the Ford Motor Co. and took his seat on the board alongside Sorensen, Henry Ford, Mrs. Edsel Ford and Edsel's two sons, Benson and Henry Ford II. Simultaneously, Bennett acquired a title that was more in keeping with the power which he had enjoyed at Ford's for so many years. He became, officially, Ford's "Director of Administrative Affairs." Once his real authority at the Ford Motor Co. was outwardly recognized by virtue of an appropriate title, Bennett was the subject of a short biographical sketch, written by John Carlisle of the Detroit *News,* entitled "The Little Giant."

From this point on, apparently, the Little Giant decided that the Ford Motor Co. was too small for him and Sorensen both. In time, he carried his point. Sorensen was dropped from the Ford organization, officially, in March 1944. According to the automobile editor of the Detroit *Free Press,* he was "fired" after "clashing" with Bennett.[20]

Sorensen's removal, climaxing his near completion of the great management program at Willow Run, was interesting in itself. It was the last word on what insiders in Detroit had long taken for granted —that Bennett ruled the roost at Ford's. This discharge added to the roster of the Ford Alumni Association a name as illustrious in Ford history as that of Couzens, Knudsen and the Dodge brothers. Even the circumstances of the dismissal were unique. Some one other than Ford did the firing in most of the classic Ford purges. But in this case —a special one, perhaps, in view of what Sorensen had meant to Ford for a generation—the discharge order came from Ford himself. It reached Sorensen in Florida, by telephone direct from Ford's winter home in Ways, Georgia. When the call was put through, Bennett was reported to be wintering at Palm Springs, California.

The "palace revolution" spread. It claimed as victims other prominent executives who had served Ford long and well. A. M. Wibel, the vice-president in charge of sales and purchasing and a Ford man for thirty-one years, resigned in April 1943. Lawrence S. Shelldrick, Ford's chief engineer, walked out a little later. Shelldrick had worked at Ford's for twenty-one years. H. C. Voss was next. Voss was Ford's former general sales manager; he had served the company for twenty-seven years. Fred W. Black, long an able and popular member of the Ford executive staff, had been let out in 1942. All these men, incidentally, were immediately taken on by Ford's competitors. Sorensen was snapped up by Willys-Overland; Shelldrick went to General Motors; Wibel, Voss and Black, to Nash-Kelvinator.

Ford's wartime purge extended even to Cameron and Ernest G. Liebold, a pair who had long held sway at the Ford Motor Co. Cameron was retained but deprived of some of his time-honored functions. In June 1942, the company engaged the services of Steve Hannagan, a prominent public relations expert.[21] Charged with the task of supervising all press releases from the Ford Motor Co., Hannagan took over ground which had once belonged to Cameron.

Liebold barely survived Sorensen. Liebold was discharged outright in May 1944, after having served Ford in various capacities for thirty-four years.[22] Ten years had passed since he had been anybody at the Ford Motor Co. With his abrupt departure from Dearborn went Harry Bennett's prototype—Ford's earlier man-of-all-work, the organizer of the "Peace Ship" expedition, the manager of Ford's abortive campaign for the Presidency, founder of the Ford secret service, caterer to Ford's anti-Semitism, and court flatterer whom all the Ford personnel had once held in dread. In being dropped without notice or explanation, Liebold fell victim to a formula he had helped to perfect.

Three months after the Little Giant had disposed of Sorensen, a new and important face appeared in the Ford Administration Building. It belonged to John S. Bugas, former head of the Detroit office of the Federal Bureau of Investigation. Bugas, an intimate of Bennett's of five or six years' standing, left the FBI in order to fill the post of "chief aide" to Ford's director of administration. As a result, Ford's domain now had at the head of it, two policemen instead of one.

˙ But with so many factors operating against him, Ford found it quite impossible to bring off the miracle that the Army and the public were waiting for at Willow Run in 1942 and 1943. The first to publicize the fact that all was not well at the bomber plant was the UAW. Then *Life* and *Fortune* and journals as far apart politically as *PM* and the *Wall Street Journal* checked the facts independently and substantially confirmed what the union had been saying. By February 1943, Ford's troubles at Willow Run were a subject for gossip in all circles concerned with airplane production; *Fortune* said that aircraft manufacturers were of the opinion that the plant should have been named "Willit Run?"[23]

Ford's impending aircraft failure was not known in any detail, however, until Willow Run was investigated in the spring and summer of 1943 by the Office of War Information and the Truman Committee.[24]

The Truman Committee published its findings on the bomber plant in July 1943.

The Committee reported that Ford had failed the Army Air Forces in his least difficult aircraft assignment—in the making of a sufficient number of sub-assemblies for the B-24 pool. He was not able to supply the parts he had contracted to make for the Douglas plant at Tulsa or the Consolidated factory at Fort Worth. As a result, the Army switched the Tulsa plant to other work, and the factory at Fort Worth "proceeded far behind schedule."

As for the final assembly of completed planes, the record was even more startling. Willow Run had been functioning for more than a year. Yet until the period just preceding its investigation, the Committee reported in July 1943, Ford had not completed a single plane that was fit for combat duty at the front. Army men in charge of aircraft production had, in desperation, temporarily frozen the Ford model of the B-24 so that Willow Run could get production experience at any price. But such bombers, built without incorporating certain safety features and other new devices necessary for combat flying, were not equipped for service at the front. They had to be used for training purposes only.

The number of trainer planes which Ford had delivered to the air forces was disappointing. When the Truman report was in preparation, Blair Moody, Washington correspondent for the Detroit *News*, summed up the record for the entire year of 1942.[25] Ford officials, Moody wrote, had led the Army and the War Production Board to believe that Ford would turn out 500 bombers in 1942. The number actually delivered, according to Moody, had been "only a handful."

Ford's leading peacetime competitor, meanwhile, had made an excellent showing in the aircraft field. The Truman Committee in one of its aviation reports congratulated General Motors for its "splendid work" in converting an automobile plant for the manufacture of Grumman fighters and torpedo bombers. Still other bomber plants, no older than Ford's, began delivery many months before the first Liberator could take off from the Willow Run airport.[26]

Finally, as Senator Truman and his colleagues observed, the over-all production record at Willow Run had the effect of demoralizing the working force at the plant. After months of effort the workers there were all too conscious of the fact that they had not produced ships in quantity, or planes of the latest type that could be flown in combat. Senator Monrad C. Wallgren, the chairman of the Truman subcommittee that investigated Ford's aircraft problems, made a public address in March 1943, in which he characterized the employes of Willow Run as "aircraft workers who have never produced a plane."[27]

Such a showing, the Truman Committee concluded, was hardly conducive to building morale or to making a Willow Run worker feel that he counted or that his efforts were needed. Small wonder that, for this and other reasons, Willow Run had an appalling rate of absenteeism. The number of daily stay-at-homes at the Ford bomber plant averaged as high as 17 per cent of the total working force. This absentee record, according to the Under-Secretary of War, was the highest of any war production plant in the nation.[28]

Nor was the morale at Willow Run improved by the type of publicity that continued to stream from the Ford front office, in the absence of bombers. Shortly after the Truman Committee began making an oral report on the bomber plant, and three months before it issued its formal published report, Ford officials made bold to proclaim that if Willow Run production could be made public, Hitler would be "scared to death."[29]

Some months after Ford's publicists released this report of progress, however, it was Ford, rather than Hitler, who was "scared to death." For, according to Drew Pearson, the Washington columnist, the WPB let it be known that if Willow Run continued to founder, the government was prepared to commandeer Ford's plant and run it for him.[30]

Fortunately, several developments put Willow Run on its feet late in 1943.

Before his unseating in October 1943, Sorensen had finished the job of tooling up and making test production runs. In the meantime, all the Ford engineers and the entire labor force at Willow Run had gradually acquired the knack of plane building. They had mastered the hardest trick in the business—the art of making change-overs quickly and efficiently.

The job at Willow Run was also simpler at this time than it had been at the beginning, for the company had decentralized. It had farmed out the making of parts and sub-assemblies to other Ford plants and to subcontractors in Detroit. Many critics of the early Willow Run program, including Army men, had favored decentralization all along. Edsel Ford was apparently one of the first Ford executives to see the wisdom of such a plan; he is credited with having sold the idea to his father in the spring of 1943.

Then, too, the company had begun to ease the manpower problem that remained by hiring women in greater numbers.

Finally, Harry Bennett made some labor concessions. Among other things, he took a step which the union and certain Army men had been urging for eighteen months: he removed his director of labor relations at Willow Run. This unpopular executive was replaced in November 1943, by Colonel August M. Krech, a retired Army officer. This officer's first move augured well for improved labor relations at the plant. Colonel Krech left, almost at once, for the West Coast to see how other aircraft builders handled their workers and why it was that wartime labor relations at most aircraft plants, Willow Run excepted, had been relatively frictionless.

Buoyed up on many fronts, Willow Run finally caught on. Its rising output was reported in a statement which the Ford Motor Co. released in January 1944, with the approval of the War Department.[31] According to this more or less official reckoning, Willow Run was at last making a formidable contribution to the war effort. It was producing an average of 340 bombers a month. This volume was far from Ford's original prophecy of a thousand planes a day. It was closer to fifteen. But the plant had turned the corner. Its potentialities for production were limitless. Its production record improved so vastly in the spring of 1944 that the Army announced it would double Ford's bomber quota in the fall of the year. When the War Department discontinued production of Liberator bombers in the spring of 1945, the Willow Run plant had produced more than 8000 planes.[32]

Meanwhile, the Willow Run union had done an outstanding job of community and national service. Had the leadership of the UAW been other than it was, Willow Run would have been the most strike-bound aircraft plant in the country. As it was, the factory was remarkably strike-free.

It was equally evident from the near-tragedy of Willow Run that Ford and Bennett had learned next to nothing about labor.


# Thirty

## WORLD CRISIS

### 1

A S HE CARRIED ON his fight against labor and reform at home, Ford was inevitably drawn into the broader social struggle that gripped the world outside Detroit. Gigantic forces were setting the stage for the second World War. All men were being compelled to declare themselves for or against democracy.

Henry Ford, confronted by this crisis at home and abroad, turned for the second time in his career to racism. A new expression of Ford's old racial feeling soon became all too evident in some of the broadsides which the Ford Motor Co. aimed at labor and Franklin Roosevelt, helping to create the impression that the New Deal and all its parts was the handiwork of the Jewish "international money-lenders."[1]

This resurgence of anti-Semitism was likewise reflected in the views and actions of a number of the manufacturer's closest associates. It was during the years of Hitler's rise to power that Harry Bennett sought to prove to Ford's satisfaction that "the Jews" had plotted Lincoln's assassination. At the same time, William J. Cameron began picking up where he had left off ten years earlier, beating the drums of racism. Cameron openly identified himself in the late 30's with the pseudo-religious, anti-Semitic Anglo-Saxon Federation. He served this society first as its president and later as a member of its publications committee.[2] The commentator of the Ford Sunday Evening Hour became a frequent contributor to the Federation's monthly magazine, *Destiny*.[3] He began using the pages of this publication for the purpose of advancing some of the racial concepts that he had expounded in the Dearborn *Independent* during Ford's earlier war against the Jews.[4]

Shortly after Hitler's rise to power, Ford's old edition of the *Protocols of Zion*, *The International Jew*, began making the rounds all over again, winning converts to fascism. Spanish translations of the work made their appearance throughout Latin America. The document had its patrons to the north. It was actively sponsored in the United States by World Service, a Nazi propaganda bureau. In 1935 the Dickstein-McCormack Committee of the House reported that the Germans were trying to flood the country with the reprint. The work became one of the textbooks of the Silver Shirts led by William Dudley Pelley.[5] John Roy Carlson, gathering material for *Under Cover*, tripped over the *Protocols* and *The International Jew* at every turn.[6]

Two, if not more, of these newer imported editions of *The International Jew*, unlike the copies which the Dearborn Publishing Co. had distributed in the 20's, carried Ford's own name in large type on the title page. The Spanish language edition of 1936 and 1937, *El Judio Internacional, POR HENRY FORD*, went a bit further: it used the manufacturer's photograph for a frontispiece.

At least two attempts were made to call some of these facts to Ford's attention. After discovering thousands of copies of *The International Jew* crated up on the docks of New York, ready for importation to the United States, Congressman Dickstein wrote a personal letter to Henry Ford. Dickstein asked the manufacturer whether or not he had authorized the use of his name on the title page of these Nazi reprints and whether or not he would take any steps to prevent the continued circulation of the work in this country. Harry Bennett answered for Ford. Bennett merely told the Congressman what no student of the Dearborn *Independent* has ever questioned, that the person who actually wrote *The International Jew* in the first place was someone other than Ford.[7] Then Samuel Untermeyer, the New York lawyer, tried his luck. Untermeyer in 1937 sent a direct communication to Ford, repeating in essence the questions put by Dickstein. The response was much the same. Once more, Ford did not reply in person. One of his secretaries answered for him. The reply in this case, like the one that preceded it, again denied that Ford was himself the author of *The International Jew* and let it go at that.[8]

It was Adolf Hitler, however, who unwittingly set the stage for a later episode that proved to be the culmination of Ford's revived anti-Semitism. In the summer of 1938 the manufacturer saw fit to accept a high Nazi decoration. He received from the Chancellor of the Third Reich the Award of the Grand Cross of the German Eagle.[9] This honor differed from those which the Nazis were using to make eyes at men of power the world over only in that it was the highest of all possible awards from the German state.

Within a few months of the day that Ford had his picture taken wearing the Grand Cross on the breast of a special dress costume, his business in this country reached low tide; Ford sales in metropolitan New York alone had never been lower. What effect the Hitler medal had had on Ford's business, no one could say. It may have been that an undeclared boycott was on, that anti-fascist car buyers were turning to Chrysler and GM or to the independents and away from Ford, because of their political beliefs. At least the Ford organization suspected as much. It was so worried by this possibility that it decided to mollify the American liberals. Wheels began to turn which would permit Ford to recant in public as he had in 1927, to issue a social-minded statement that would remove some of the stain of anti-Semitism.

But instead of making this declaration through his usual channels, it was decided to have Ford speak through the medium of a prominent Jew. Such a gesture would highlight his statement. The recantation of 1938 was to have a sounding board. The man settled upon was Rabbi Leo M. Franklin of Detroit. None was better fitted to serve the purpose. Franklin was one of the city's outstanding civic leaders. He was a cultured and distinguished spokesman for American Jewry. His good works had been heralded in non-Jewish circles. He had long before received an honorary doctor's degree from the Jesuit University in Detroit. The Catholic scholars who conferred this degree had called the rabbi an "apostle of amity."[10] From the appearance of things, even sentiment entered into the plan to "make up" to the Jews with the aid of Dr. Franklin, for in days past, Ford and Dr. Franklin had been warm friends and next-door neighbors.

A wall had to be scaled, of course. Ford and Franklin had not seen one another for years. The rabbi had never recovered from the shock of Ford's first crusade against the Jews, and so two inter-

mediaries felt him out. The first was Moritz Kahn, the brother of the
noted industrial architect, the late Albert Kahn. Kahn, acting as go-
between, told Franklin that Ford wanted to see him, to discuss plans
for aiding German refugees. If the rabbi was willing, would he say
as much and ask for an interview in a formal letter addressed to Ford?

Franklin was more than a little mystified. But he agreed, confident
of Kahn's good will and convinced, as ever, that Ford for all his
errors was still "a good man at heart." He posted the requested letter
on November 26, 1938. Two days later the clergyman had another
caller—Harry Newman, the former All-American Jewish football player
who worked at Ford's. Newman again assured the rabbi that much
good would come of his seeing Ford, that Ford was deeply concerned
with the lot of German-Jewish refugees. The following day Bennett
called Dr. Franklin by telephone to arrange the time and place of
the conference.

The meeting took place in Bennett's office on November 29, 1938.
At the Ford Administration Building, Franklin was cordially received
by Henry Ford and three Ford employes, Bennett, W. J. Cameron
and Harry Newman. Ford began the interview by voicing his
sympathy for German-Jewish refugees. He declared himself ready to
give employment to as many of these people as possible. Would Dr.
Franklin collaborate in preparing a joint statement to that effect?
More than willing to oblige his host in such a cause, the rabbi, after
an hour or more of conversation, proceeded to reduce Ford's ideas
to writing. He was aided in this work by Cameron. When the joint
draft was completed, Ford gave it his unqualified blessing and called
in a photographer. The manufacturer and his distinguished Jewish
guest then had their pictures taken together. One final request: Would
Dr. Franklin be good enough to take Ford's authorized statement with
him and release it to the press? The rabbi agreed. It was understood
that he was to release the statement that same evening.

But no word of the meeting appeared in the papers that night
or the following morning. Bennett called the rabbi by telephone. Had
Dr. Franklin changed his mind? Had he decided not to go to press
with the write-up of the Ford interview? Not at all, the rabbi assured
him. He had, however, taken the liberty of making a few formal
and grammatical changes in the original draft of Ford's statement
and he wanted to clear it with Ford once more before going to the
newspapers. Franklin then read aloud the slightly revised text. Ford
and Bennett listened to the reading over separate wires. They
approved it warmly, word for word. Thus, before it went to press,

Ford's 1938 statement on the Jews had been checked and double-checked.

The statement itself was unequivocal. One group's hatred of another, Ford said, is un-American. He said in quotation marks that race persecution like that of Nazi Germany was anti-social and that it was not the will of the German people as a whole, but rather the will of a few war-makers at the top. It was the duty of the United States, he said, to make itself "a haven for the oppressed." For his part, Ford said, he intended to "do everything possible" to give "the oppressed Jew an opportunity to rebuild his life in this country."[11]

Up to this point Rabbi Franklin had every reason to feel that his renowned former neighbor had made a gracious gesture at a moment when all Jewry had cause for grief and alarm. It appeared, moreover, that Ford had atoned for his own past anti-Semitism by damning racism in general and by all but naming the foremost racial bigot—the man from whom he had just accepted the Grand Cross of the German Eagle.

Dr. Franklin's peace of mind was short-lived, however. The newspapers carried Ford's proclamation on Thursday, December 1. The following evening a member of the Franklin household received a telephone call from a stranger. The caller announced he had reason to suspect that Franklin would regret having "let himself in" for an interview with Ford. Why so? Because on Sunday next, the rabbi would be "double-crossed" by Ford and Bennett and the Rev. Charles E. Coughlin. After identifying himself as a "former Ford Serviceman" who knew what he was talking about, the anonymous caller hung up. Whoever this informant may have been, he called the turn.

The gist of Father Coughlin's radio broadcast the following Sunday evening was to the effect that Ford had been "taken" by a crafty Jew.[12] The "real author" of Ford's statement on the Jews Coughlin charged, was not Ford but Rabbi Franklin. The remarks attributed to Ford, said the priest, were "totally inaccurate;" they were pure invention on Franklin's part, "a gigantic attempt to put into the mouth of America's foremost manufacturer words he did not say."

What did Ford really say during the interview with Franklin? He had said, according to Coughlin, that "there was little or no persecution in Germany" and that such social injustices as did exist in that country had been caused by the "international bankers."

The whole object of the interview, the priest told his radio listeners, was to beg Ford to "assimilate Jewish refugees" in his factory; it was Franklin rather than Ford, he said, who had asked for the interview in the first place.

How had Coughlin come to know all this? Two of his reporters for *Social Justice* had called on Harry Bennett. His radio exposé, said the priest, was based on official Ford sources, on a statement bearing Harry Bennett's personal signature.

One local newspaper, the Detroit *Free Press*, made no bones about its choice between the two conflicting accounts of the Ford interview. It came out for Franklin. "The Doctor's reputation and standing in this community is such," the *Free Press* editorialized, "that when he issued the statement and said it was authorized by the motor manufacturer, no paper in this city had any reason to question it. Nor have they now." On the one hand, said the *Free Press*, there was the rabbi, "one of the great spiritual leaders of Detroit . . . so recognized by all denominations for almost half a century;" on the other, a priest well known for his "congenital inability to tell the truth."[13]

Coughlin promptly sued the Detroit *Free Press* for libel, asking $4,000,000 in damages. But as the court was about to set a date for the trial, the priest prudently withdrew his action. Counsel for the newspaper had been preparing a formidable defense in the meantime.

What was Bennett's explanation of the two rival reports of the Ford-Franklin interview?[14] He straddled the issue by making statements to show that each man—now the rabbi, now the priest—was in the right.

In support of the one, Bennett told the press that the original Ford-Franklin statement, as it was given to the papers, was "absolutely accurate." He admitted that the article was purposely prepared, with Ford's authorization, so as to highlight direct quotations attributed to Ford himself.

In support of the other, Bennett averred that Father Coughlin's charges as well were "substantially correct." He supported Coughlin in implying that the initiative for the interview had come from Franklin, rather than the other way around. He mentioned Franklin's letter and Ford's willingness "to see the rabbi any time." He did not reveal that the clergyman's letter had been written at Ford's virtual invitation.

Bennett supported Coughlin on another count by saying, without elaboration, that the Ford-Franklin statement which was attributed to Ford had been, in fact, "prepared" by Franklin. He neglected to add that most of Ford's remarks to the press were prepared by some-

one other than Ford. Nor did Bennett take the trouble to add that he
and Ford, listening in together, had approved every last jot and tittle
of the final statement that Franklin submitted to the newspapers.

Was it true, as Coughlin alleged, that Franklin had given a
distorted picture of Ford's remarks? Bennett insinuated as much. The
rabbi's quotations from Ford, he said, were "garbled" and incomplete;
they failed to report that Ford had indeed said that he knew of no
persecution going on in Germany and that if there was any, the
"international bankers" were at fault, not Hitler or the Nazi government.

Had a trap been set for the rabbi? Here, too, Bennett was
devious. Yes, he had signed the statement which gave Coughlin
ammunition for a broadcast. Yet the priest was guilty of a slight
falsification; Father Coughlin on his own initiative had added one
incriminating line to the statement and "crossed me up," said Bennett.
"I am going to get in touch with him and tell him so."

The butt of all this duplicity was the rabbi. Kindly, benevolent,
almost as old as Ford and quite unprepared for rough treatment,
Franklin was crushed by the experience. He was stung most of all by
the fear that, in seeing Ford on Ford's terms, he had done his own
people everywhere more harm than good.

All the while that Bennett and Coughlin were playing their game
at the expense of Ford's old friend, Ford himself stood by in silence.

Bennett's manipulation of the interview had been a masterpiece.
It cast Ford in a double image. To Jews and anti-Nazis and haters
of racial brutishness—and to potential boycotters of the Ford car—
the folk hero had been held up once more as the friend of the
oppressed, as the protector of the little man. But anti-Semites and
pro-Nazis and other assorted enemies of democracy had it on the
authority of Father Coughlin that the Ford-Franklin interview meant
nothing of the sort; it meant only that a wily Jew had put one over
on Ford. The reactionaries also had it straight from Bennett that, in
Ford's opinion, Germany's internal wrongs, if any, could not be laid
to Hitler or the Nazi system.

## 2

This was not the end of Ford's anti-republican expressions of this
period, however. As the emerging world conflict surged around him,
the manufacturer did not stop with his acceptance of a Nazi decoration in 1938, with his public humiliation of a prominent Jewish

religious leader, or with the act of permitting his spokesmen and representatives to engage in anti-Semitism.

Among other things, Ford aligned himself against democracy, from the time the Axis nations first began to execute their plan of world aggression, by keeping a number of known fascist sympathizers on his payroll. This bridge to reaction existed within the Ford empire both at home and abroad.

The war against China—or what the Japanese were then pleased to describe as the "China Incident"—was six months along when Ford's leading business representative in Asia declared for the aggressor. On December 28, 1937, Ford's chief agent in the Far East announced that he had just invested 1,000,000 yen in Japanese war bonds. "I have been here for thirteen years, ever since the Ford Motor Co. began to do business in Japan. During that time, the company has made profit . . . We thought we should do something for the land from which we have received much benefit, so we bought China Incident bonds."[15]

But the man in Ford's employ who was preeminent for the comfort he gave to the fascist cause at this time was the naturalized German-American Fritz Kuhn. Kuhn was listed as an employe of the Ford Motor Co. He used this Ford connection as a base from which he sallied forth for a number of years to organize the German-American Bund. In the course of doing the job for which he had been hired at the Ford Motor Co., the man had an eccentric history. As Harry Bennett felt obliged to inform the FBI some years later, Kuhn had been an indifferent worker; he was once caught during working hours "practicing speeches in a dark room."[16] He was finally discharged. Then the man was rehired as a metallurgist at the Rouge. He lasted on this job or retained such a classification for the next five and one-half years.

The responsible executives of the Ford Motor Co., meanwhile, had every opportunity for keeping abreast of the real nature of Kuhn's outside activities. Ford Service made a specialty of feeling out the political attitudes of the Ford employe. For such an accomplished espionage organization, the job of sizing up Fritz Kuhn was simplicity itself. Kuhn was conspicuous. He worked in the open. His thick German accent was unmistakable. The Friends of New Germany, his first political medium in this country, had direct and known Nazi connections, a fact which the McCormack-Dickstein Committee brought to light as early as 1935.[17]

At least one effort was made to bring these facts to Ford's personal attention. Samuel Untermeyer, then acting in his capacity as president of the Non-Sectarian Anti-Nazi League, asked Ford in writing to take a stand on Kuhn. This was the same note in which the manufacturer was asked to take a position on the revival of *The International Jew*. Ford failed to declare himself on either issue. But the spokesman who did reply to Untermeyer made it clear, without mentioning any names, that the Ford Motor Co. had no intention of disciplining Kuhn or any other Ford employe like him. This spokesman further implied that it would be up to Kuhn to decide whether or not he were to retain his listing as a Ford employe, inasmuch as "Mr. Ford has always extended to his employes the fullest freedom from any coercion with respect to their views on political, religious or social activities."[18]

After the letter to Untermeyer was published by the New York *Times,* however, the Ford people reversed themselves. They dropped Kuhn's name from the roster of active Ford personnel. A quit date was entered on the man's service card at the Ford Motor Co. on January 16, 1937. This act was unpublicized. It was reported to the FBI and made public later on, when Kuhn was having his day in court.[19] When the actual separation took place, however, Kuhn apparently had no inkling of the fact. Back in this country after having paid his respects to Hitler, he told reporters, "I was really on vacation when I left the [Ford] company's employ and I don't know when or whether I will return to my old job. I am a marked man now," Kuhn said, "and Mr. Ford might not want me."[20]*

In December 1939, Kuhn went to prison, convicted on a charge of having lined his pockets with money that was Bund property. As Kuhn's train, bound for Sing Sing, was about to leave Grand Central Station, Henry Ford appeared on the scene. According to the Detroit *News,* Ford had "chanced to be in the station. He peered into the train," said the *News,* "and walked away without comment."[21]

After dropping the Kuhn connection, Ford—thanks to Harry Bennett—proceeded to strike up an alliance with Gerald L. K. Smith, the super-salesman of reaction, American-style. Smith had not yet become the ranting "nationalist" or a spokesman for the country's

---

* The act of quietly dropping Kuhn from the Ford roster can scarcely be construed as a thoroughgoing repudiation of the man and his works, in view of later developments. Months from the day Kuhn's name was thus expunged from the Ford records, Ford saw fit to accept the Hitler decoration. In the meantime the character of the Nazi world movement had grown ever clearer and more ominous, and the movement's outstanding American proponent, Fritz Kuhn, had become notorious.

defeatists, for the war was still a year or two away. His past was already so notorious and dark, however, that only a confirmed antirepublican would have deigned to touch him.

By 1939 Smith had decided that Detroit was a likely market for his wares. He settled in the automotive capital at that time. Business prospered. Walter Davenport, writing in *Collier's* on March 4, 1944, made a guess that the "mysterious Gerald Smith, Detroit's rabble rouser," was collecting from his backers, off and on, as much as $5,000 a week.

In the bitterly contested election held in Dearborn in the fall of 1939, Smith was imported to buoy up the "Ford slate." He was the principal speaker at an election rally sponsored by the Ford machine in the Dearborn high school auditorium. The *Collier's* article went on to say that Smith had had a private audience with Harry Bennett in the pre-war period and that Bennett liked the man's bill of goods well enough to pay for three of his broadcasts over radio station WJR.

Finally, long after most supporters of the democratic cause had become convinced that Nazi-fascism was a threat to democratic institutions everywhere, Ford and Hitler, and Ford and the champions and appeasers of Hitler, continued to cement their ties or to exchange tokens of mutual esteem. The Franklin episode had revolved about Father Coughlin. When this incident occurred, in 1938, Coughlin had already been acclaimed in the party press of Nazi Germany.

Three days before the Wehrmacht overran Poland, Ford had nothing but kind words for the man whose name had become the symbol of Nazi appeasement. What did he think of Chamberlain, he was asked by a reporter. "One of the greatest men who ever lived," the manufacturer replied.[22] His chief enemies, Ford said, were the "war profiteers."

In this eleventh hour, moreover, Ford and Hitler were appraising one another in verbal terms that were anything but uncomplimentary. Ford accepted the Hitler medal in 1938. The following year an American edition of *Mein Kampf* made its appearance. In this work, the Fuehrer had words of adulation for "but one great man" in the United States. He so honored Henry Ford on the ground that Ford alone had succeeded in defying the Jewish money power of the Americas.[23]

Ford in turn told us what he thought of Hitler, while vacationing in Sudbury, Massachusetts. It was August 29, 1939. The war in Europe was three days away. Ford's publicists were not in attendance and a newspaperman asked him to express his opinion of the Reichfuehrer.

The manufacturer's reply was not unflattering. "I don't know Hitler personally," Ford said, "but at least Germany keeps its people at work."[24]

### 3

When events quickly demonstrated that Germany was indeed well on its way toward the conquest of all Europe, Ford joined forces in this country with the proponents of isolationism. He turned to the America First Committee. The America Firster with whom he chiefly consorted and to whom he gave direct aid was Charles A. Lindbergh. The circumstances surrounding this alliance did nothing to increase Ford's stature as a republican.

When America First finally reached its peak, speaking as it did for both pure pacifism and the neo-fascists, Lindbergh had become an American apologist for the invincible "Wave of the Future." By the same token, he had become the toast and idol of Nazi sympathizers everywhere. Such was his reputation in the spring of 1941, when Franklin Roosevelt took occasion to liken him to the Copperheads of the Civil War and the appeasers who had flourished during the American Revolution.[25]

In the summer of 1941, Lindbergh stopped off at Dearborn for approximately two weeks. What he and his hosts talked about, no one knows. The visit itself was unpublicized. It took place one month before the flyer delivered his anti-Semitic speech in Des Moines.[26]

Unlike General Wood and a few other wealthy patrons of the isolationist movement, Ford remained in the background.

One of the isolationist pronouncements which the manufacturer issued independently appeared in the form of a published article in December 1940. Insofar as this piece dealt with the issues of war and fascism, it stated, among other things, the case for defeatism; it offered an apology for two of the Axis dictators as well. Ford here predicted the defeat of the British. "The war," he said, "is going to end in a draw." He further introduced an argument already worn to rags by the German Propaganda Ministry; he attacked the "international bankers." He admitted that the men who were then leading Germany and Italy might not be truly representative of their people. But at bottom, he said, Hitler and Mussolini were only "puppets" at whose expense certain greedy financiers and profit-minded manufacturers had "played a dirty trick."

What made Ford's article important was not so much what it

said but rather the auspices under which it was published. It appeared in *Scribner's Commentator*. This journal, published at Lake Geneva, Wisconsin, had been taken over in 1940 by a small group of isolationists.[27] It identified itself in part by the character of certain members of its staff and by the affiliations of certain of its writers. Charles Lind, the business manager of the magazine, was then president of a corporation which was bringing out independently an anti-Semitic publication called *The Herald*. Ralph Townsend, who was later sentenced to prison, was a contributor to *Scribner's Commentator* while working in this country as an unregistered Japanese agent. In July 1942, the magazine was singled out by a federal grand jury as one of the publications which had been used in this country to promote sedition and disunity within the armed forces.[28]

## 4

By this time America was at war and the America First Committee had died a natural death. The vast majority of the committee's more active supporters had changed their tune. Some had changed their convictions. Others had simply gone into hiding. Henry Ford, for his part, made an about-face with the declaration of war by becoming one of the great industrial forces of the war economy. His gigantic properties were rapidly converted for their subsequent immense contribution to the war effort.

At the same time, the manufacturer seemed to carry his personal convictions into the fight against the Axis. The news of America's entry into the struggle was still warm when W. J. Cameron helped to erase old prejudices by speaking warmly of the U.S.S.R. The Russians, said Cameron in a radio broadcast, were fighting for their country like free men. All civilization, he said, owed a debt to the Red Army.[29] With its own rubber supply cut off, the Ford Motor Co. a few months later sold its huge tire plant lock-stock-and-barrel to the Soviets.

One month after the attack at Pearl Harbor, the manufacturer came forward with another public repudiation of anti-Semitism. Race hatred in general and antagonism toward the Jews in particular, he said in a letter addressed to the Anti-Defamation League, should "cease for all time." Those who manufactured ill will toward their Jewish "fellow citizens," he said, only wished to "divide our American community and to weaken our national unity."[30]

Two weeks later counsel for the Ford Motor Co. took steps to run down the old Dearborn product, *The International Jew*.[31] Ford's lawyer called the continued dissemination of this publication "the pernicious work of the German propaganda department." He begged the Mexican government to suppress a Spanish edition of the work that carried Ford's name on the title page. Another letter written in the same vein went to the imperial wizard of the Ku Klux Klan. In it the Ford attorney threatened to take legal action if the Klan continued to refer to Ford as the author of the newly condemned reprint.

On February 15, 1942, the cudgels against racial intolerance were taken up by W. J. Cameron, whose words on the subject, delivered during one of his last appearances as commentator of the Ford Sunday Evening Hour, were eloquent and trenchant. Anti-Semitism, said Cameron, is "scurrilous stuff, a vestige of tribal barbarism, the negation of humanity, intelligence and Christianity." In the long run, he said, this "deadly acid" consumes the "anti-Semite himself."

One month after he had renounced anti-Semitism, Ford made a place at the Ford Motor Co. for Lindbergh. Only the men who do the meanest work at Ford's—the foundry workers at the Rouge—had the temerity to protest the flyer's appointment. This group of Ford employes went on record to the effect that Lindbergh's past attitudes did not "speak for national unity" and that the man's presence at Dearborn would have "a demoralizing influence on the laboring man."[32] Harry Bennett, on the other hand, greeted Lindbergh with open arms. The flyer, he was quoted as saying, could "write his own ticket" at the Ford Motor Co.[33]

Lindbergh went to work at Willow Run. He made himself useful there, making studies of high-altitude flying. He also became one of Ford's and Bennett's social intimates. It was Ford's habit, said *Fortune* in February 1943, to pay a daily visit to the bomber plant and to call on Lindbergh before seeing anyone else. "Charles," *Fortune* quoted Ford as saying at this time, "in much of his thinking is not unlike me."

Much later, Ford gave even more dramatic proof of the point that, despite his great and steadily mounting contribution on the production front, and despite his latest call for national unity, some of his old feelings about the country's war effort were still very much alive. He demonstrated this fact by appearing in public and carrying on a discussion with his old enemy, Colonel McCormick, the most articulate and important of the die-hard isolationists. McCormick paid a visit to Detroit in December 1943. The publisher had already confessed that he was "horrified and outraged by the Government's conduct" in running down the thirty alleged seditionists who were up for trial.[34] He came to Detroit for the purpose of giving a talk at the Detroit Athletic Club. With all the world in flames and democracy fighting for its life, McCormick took occasion to tell his Detroit audience that the true enemies of the United States at the moment were the British and the "New Deal tyranny." It was America, he said, which brought on the Pearl Harbor attack, in having given the original impetus to Japan's career of conquest.

Shortly before he delivered himself of these opinions, Colonel McCormick had a caller. Henry Ford, with whom he had been at sword's points during the first World War, came to his rooms to pay his respects. The two men talked together privately for half an hour. In the course of their tête-à-tête, Ford is supposed to have expressed alarm at the severity of the punishment that American flyers and the R.A.F. were giving to the Nazis. He was quoted by his host as voicing the fear that "the relentless bombing of Germany will cause such havoc that an epidemic of disease will sweep the world."[35]

Thus ran this late chapter in the life of the former Michigan farm boy who richly deserved his rank as a giant of the machine age, and yet was so unworthy of his reputation as a respecter of men. Once more the mechanical genius of Detroit had cut a sorry figure in the social history of his age.

The ideas which Ford took to heart, and others which are of a piece with those beliefs, came close to carrying the day. Had history taken such a turn, the America which made Ford and his great works possible would have been no more. In that event, the social controls of the earlier New Deal, invoked by the elected representatives of the people, would have had to make way for mandates issued from a fascist Washington. Under those circumstances, perhaps Henry Ford himself would have found cause for taking issue with the regimented New Order in the dead republic.

# Thirty-one

## HENRY THE SECOND

### 1

THE FOUNDER of the Ford Motor Co. never came to grips with the New Order, however, for the republic survived. But before this triumph at arms had been won, Henry Ford was overtaken by a misfortune of a more personal nature. He was stricken in 1943 by the untimely death of his only son, Edsel. To prepare a successor, the octogenarian manufacturer turned in haste to the eldest of his three grandsons, Henry Ford II, then in the service of his country as a Navy ensign, who was released from military duty within a matter of weeks. This young man, along with his mother and Harry Bennett, straightway took a seat on his grandfather's board of directors. He was likewise promptly installed as executive vice-president of the Ford Motor Co.

Pushed to the top overnight, young Ford had many well-wishers. He had as well a number of assets which seemed to fit him for his role as heir apparent to the largest family-held corporation in existence. From all reports, Henry Ford II was something like his father, on the quiet side, easy and pleasant of manner. He was looked upon in industry circles as a moderate, or even a liberal, who would very likely prove to be "Edsel's boy" rather than a third-generation copy of his grandfather.

Edsel Ford, to be sure, had never had a chance during his lifetime to show his wares entirely on his own. This much was clear about his make-up, however. In his young manhood, Edsel had had no difficulty getting along with the partners whom his father shed.[1] He had never endorsed later on the school of management personified by Liebold, Sorensen and Bennett.[2] So long as his father remained in control, he had been unable to bring about any basic changes at the Ford Motor Co.

On a number of occasions, however, Edsel Ford had quietly pushed in that direction. He disapproved his father's anti-Semitism in the 20's. By contrast with his father who opposed charity in any form, the younger Ford had been for years one of the largest donors to the Detroit Community Fund. Had Henry Ford listened to his son, he would have avoided the languishing of the Model T and the subsequent outmoding of the Model A. The son had looked askance at the personnel policy which caused the loss of so many of the company's more talented executives. It was Edsel who had been primarily responsible during the war for the betterment of labor relations at the Ford Motor Co. and, along with Mead L. Bricker, for much of the eventual success of the great Ford undertaking at Willow Run.[3] By the time of his death, Henry Ford's only son was identified throughout the trade as the leader of the liberal wing within the Ford hierarchy.

The father of Henry Ford II had been at odds with the founder of the motor company in still another sphere of life. Unlike grandfather Ford who once said that all the art in the world was not worth five cents, Edsel had been an avid and cultivated patron of the arts. He was an accomplished landscape painter in his own right. His wife and he had been privately tutored by the noted art critic, Dr. W. R. Valentiner.* In his later years the younger Ford had served as President of the Detroit Arts Commission. He had also become the chief financial supporter of the Detroit Institute of Arts. It was during this phase of his career that Edsel commissioned Diego Rivera to paint the great murals which adorn the walls of the Detroit Institute of Arts. Rivera's patron and Dr. Valentiner had also courageously held their ground when a spirited minority in the city of Detroit attacked the frescoes and demanded their removal.[4]

As the son of Edsel Ford prepared to take over the vast responsibilities of managing the Ford corporation, he exhibited a refreshing degree of humility. He was frank to say that he had everything to learn, remarking after he had been in office for a number of months that he was still "green and reaching for answers."[5]

Young Ford could point to a three-year record in the Navy. Though assigned to land duty, just before his father's death the young ensign had applied for a transfer so that he could go to sea. Four years earlier, a month after his graduation from Yale University, he had married Anne McDonnell, the charming and vivacious daughter of an eastern broker. His bride was the granddaughter of the late Thomas E. Murray who had bequeathed to his heirs a fortune of $50,000,000.†

* This may have helped to allay some of Edsel's feelings of inadequacy. Even in his forties, the heir apparent to the Ford fortune is said to have continued to smart over the fact that his father had never permitted him to go to college.

† To consummate this marriage, young Ford, under the tutelage of Mgr. Fulton J. Sheen, forsook Methodism, the religion of his parents, and became a Catholic convert.[6]

At the same time, the new executive vice-president of the Ford Motor Co. had certain evident limitations. He was extremely young and had almost no industrial experience. Nor could anyone be sure that the young man's talents were equal to the task of managing the far-flung Ford empire. Up to this point, said *Life* magazine, Henry Ford's eldest grandson had shown "no pronounced aptitude" or given any indication to speak of that he "had one hidden."[7] Nor were his chances of "finding himself" particularly bright at the moment. As Henry Ford II stepped into his father's shoes late in 1944, grandfather Ford, with a tight grip on 58½ per cent of the voting stock, was still at the controls of the business, and as domineering as ever.[8] *Newsweek* could report that most "lesser Fordlings" still "stepped lightly and fearfully in an air of hushed intrigue."[9] Regardless of the title which the senior Ford had conferred upon his eldest male heir, the sycophants were in the saddle and Harry Bennett, newly rewarded with a seat on the board, was apparently still the man to reckon with at the Ford Motor Co.

Neither Henry Ford II nor his mother could have been expected to relish this state of affairs. Both mother and son had the best of reasons for not liking Bennett.[10] Eleanor Ford, Edsel's widow, made no secret of her feeling for the former pugilist who had harassed her husband and made his life miserable for fifteen or twenty years. Henry Ford II was no fonder of the "director of Ford administration" who had been leaning over backwards to court him in recent years. Young Ford, rumor had it, not only shared his mother's feelings but had sufficient reasons of his own for resenting the executive whom his grandfather had favored above all men. As a child, Henry Ford II had been hounded by operatives of the Ford Service Department. Reports on his comings and goings as a young man had reached his grandfather's ears through the channels of Ford Service. During the early months of his own tenure of office, "Edsel's boy" was confronted with the fact that grandfather Ford and Bennett still meant to run the show their way. Hence Eleanor Ford and her oldest son seemed to be caught in a situation which they disliked but were powerless to change. For the time being at least, it looked as though the lot of young Ford was no better than that which had befallen his deceased father. In taking over at the Ford Motor Co., Henry the Second was to all appearances head man in name only, another king without a scepter.

Meanwhile the job that confronted the 27-year-old vice-president of the Ford corporation was enough to try the most brilliant and seasoned of business executives. Every student of the trade was convinced that the house that Ford built was in a shaky state, that its postwar outlook was anything but bright. By contrast with General Motors or Chrysler, the Ford organization was badly managed.[11] The morale of its labor and executive personnel was at low ebb.[12] In point of sales the company had taken a back seat for years.* GM and Chrysler, the two alert corporations that had walked away with much of Ford's business and had proved themselves to be far more skilled than Ford in making change-overs, were now closing in for what they hoped would be the kill. Neither of these competitors was particularly disturbed over the arrival at Dearborn of Henry II, whose hands were more or less tied by Harry Bennett and a stubborn octogenarian.

Before many months had passed, however, the rivals of the Ford Motor Co. had reason to lose some of their complacency, and Henry Ford II lost some of the fetters that had kept him within bounds. This change came about when superannuation finally overtook the doughty founder of the Ford empire. Henry Ford, turning eighty-three, suffered the first sharp mental and physical decline of his career in the spring of 1945. From then on, he continued to fail so noticeably that any real participation on his part in the affairs of his business was out of the question. The Ford heirs proceeded to take up the slack in the reins that were slipping from the founder's grip. Eleanor Ford, with little experience outside her home and immediate social circle, started to make her presence felt at meetings of the Ford board of directors. Her son, now more or less on his own, began to breathe new life into the corporation. His initial successes in this direction were so emphatic that *Newsweek* took occasion to observe in a summer issue that one could already detect a definitely "brighter atmosphere" at Ford's.[14]

By early fall it was clear that the ailing grandfather would have to step aside for good. Thus in mid-September authority within the company passed to the heirs of the aged industrialist, and for the first time a Ford other than the original Henry became the dominant power at Dearborn, in fact as well as in title. Henry Ford II, now twenty-eight, was promptly elevated to the presidency of the corporation.[15] Benson, the grandson next in line, was quickly added to the board. William, the youngest of Edsel's three sons, would, it was announced, enter the business later on.

Thus entrenched and thoroughly assured of his grandfather's retirement, Henry Ford II did something which—some say—his father

* In 1941, the last full year of prewar production, GM alone had sold 47 per cent of the country's new automobiles.[13]

would have done, had he ever had a similar opportunity. Young Ford, with the energetic support of his mother, made a lightning move to have it out with Harry Bennett. The showdown occurred at a meeting of the board at which Eleanor Ford is reported to have taken the floor and flung at Bennett the accusation that she had watched him ruin her husband's life and had no intention of letting him do the same thing to her eldest son. Bennett was removed on the spot as "director of administration." It first appeared that he would stay on in an advisory capacity, keeping his seat on the board.[16] Henry Ford II was quoted as saying that he intended to make further use of Bennett because of the man's "excellent background and knowledge."[17]

Within the next ten days, however, even this remaining tie was broken.[18] It was now certain that the ex-boxer who had served the elder Ford for twenty-eight years was ignominiously trudging along the road onto which he had forced so many hundreds of other Ford men. By the middle of October the Detroit papers were making no bones of the fact that Bennett had been discharged and that most of his former friends at Dearborn had also undergone or were about to suffer a similar fate.[19] Bennett had set himself up in the meantime as a manufacturer's agent, forced for a change to eat humble pie.[20] Yes, he announced meekly late in October, he did have several accounts and he would "like" to continue to sell to the Ford Motor Co.[21]

Then, vested by the board with absolute powers, young Ford quickly went to the roots of the machine that Bennett had left behind.[22] The shake-up that followed was quite as thoroughgoing as any of the purges for which grandfather Ford is famous. But in this case it was more the deadwood and an inner political machine that was being pruned away. The grandson cut through his organization with a program of discharges and demotions that reached from the highest executive posts at the Rouge down to the foreman level, carrying over even to the branch plants and to the company's far-flung sales agencies in the field.[23] Before he was through, Henry Ford II succeeded in cleaning out the bulk of the men of any consequence who had been at all close to Bennett or were regarded as "Bennett appointees."[24] All this while young Ford moved at breakneck speed, guided by a blueprint that must have been quietly worked out to the last detail months ahead of time. The job was substantially finished by the end of October. The young president had been in office for slightly more than a month.

Among the few survivors of the Bennett regime was John S. Bugas, who at thirty-seven became Ford's director of industrial relations.[25]

The new overseer of Ford labor was reputedly capable. He had come into the corporation originally as Bennett's administrative assistant. Before this, he and Bennett had been social intimates and colleagues in crime detection. The new supervisor of labor relations, it will be remembered, had other ties as well. Prior to his first employment at Dearborn, Bugas served in the Detroit area for some years as regional director of the FBI. From young Ford's point of view, such a background may have been all to the good in Bugas' case. Perhaps no other candidate for Ford officialdom could have been better prepared for keeping an eye on any possibly disaffected members of the defunct Bennett machine.

As the purge proceeded, Henry Ford II began to bring in new faces to replace the old. He restaffed his executive and dealer roster.[26] For the first time in years the flow of talent reversed itself at the Rouge. The Ford organization began to import any number of competent outside specialists and administrators, cutting into the ranks of its competitors just as its own personnel had been repeatedly raided in the past. Many of the replacements came from within. They consisted of able and tried members of the Ford staff. Soon thereafter the grandson announced that in sundry sales and management policies he intended to bring the Ford organization up to date. In this realm, he candidly admitted, he had much to learn from his principal competitors, Chrysler and GM.

The weeklies and trade journals began to report, meanwhile, that Ford morale was soaring.[27] From all accounts, even the lowliest production worker at the Rouge could sense the change. Finally, young Ford took issue with his grandfather who had once exclaimed, as his sales were slipping from first position in the trade to third, that he "didn't care" how many cars he sold. From now on, said the grandson, every effort would be made to place Ford sales at the point where they had stood once upon a time—at the head of the list.[28]

All this came as something of a shock to Chrysler and General Motors. These organizations could now foresee some real competition from a rival they had all but given up for dead. Ford's main competitors "who haven't really feared the company in fifteen years," said *Life* magazine on October 1, 1945, "are watching it very closely now."

## 2

Not the least of the worries which beset the two leading members of the Big Three was how far, and in what direction, the Ford Motor

Co. intended to go on the question of postwar wages and prices. By the time young Ford finished the job of putting his house in order, this problem was the nation's Number 1 domestic issue; it was about to precipitate the bitterest tug-of-war between management and labor, with Washington uneasily in the middle.

Within the automobile industry proper, management as a whole, with GM and Chrysler in the lead, had already served notice of its intent to make a killing in the immediate postwar period. It took the offensive, first of all, against OPA.[29] With their eyes on a market that had seen no new cars to speak of in four long years, the motor manufacturers, moving in concert shortly after V-J Day, had long since requested price increases ranging from 6 to 60 per cent.[30]

In a determined effort to wrest concessions from OPA or to eliminate the agency altogether, the owners and managers of the automobile industry were not acting alone. They were joined by big business as a unit. The National Association of Manufacturers was pressing Congress and the Administration to do away with price controls at the earliest possible moment. The pressure for inflation was being brought to bear by what news commentators described as the largest and most powerful lobby ever seen in Washington. Among these petitioners for higher price ceilings, or no ceilings at all, was the National Association of Automobile Dealers.

The leading controllers and operators of American business, in and out of the automobile industry, also seemed generally ready to administer a setback to labor.[31] This turn of events would insure higher prices at the expense of wages. Not a few employers were envisioning a return to the 20's. Certain spokesmen for the automotive industry said as much at this juncture.

It was not until November 1945, however, that the automobile manufacturers were able to feel any real confidence in the success of their drive for postwar profits. Their doubts were stilled in that month when Congress passed its first important postwar tax measure. Thanks to this revenue act—with its carryback provision and its repeal of the wartime excess profits tax—the nation's financiers and industrialists now had the leverage they needed for the two-edged fight against OPA and labor.[32]

Meanwhile, the prime movers of the automobile industry, notably the directors of GM and Chrysler, became restive lest any of their number break ranks. More particularly, these colossi began to cast anxious glances in the direction of the Ford Motor Co. Here, as ever, was that anomaly of a monolithic, family-held corporation which had no strings attached to its earnings and could afford to go its competitors one better in wages or prices or in the caliber of its product. All the more unsettling, from the standpoint of GM or Chrysler, was the fact that the Ford corporation was no longer in the grasp of its founder. Henry Ford, the elder, was on the sidelines. His permanent retirement was announced early in December.[33] The wealth and productive power Ford left behind him—one billion dollars' worth—was now in the hands of a little-known young man who had majored in sociology at Yale and who was at this moment finishing a "palace revolution" that seemed to stamp him as a management liberal. Would "Edsel's boy" go on from here to make bold concessions to labor and the public? Would this stripling dare to take issue with a united front which included nearly the entire top hierarchy of American business?[34]

Then, by some of the things he said, Henry Ford II all but confirmed these fears on the part of his larger competitors. Throughout the summer of 1945, he had talked over Bennett's head, addressing himself to labor in language that was anything but combative or unfriendly. He was sure, said Henry Ford II in June, that the postwar labor problems of the Ford Motor Co. could be "amicably" worked out. "The majority of union men," he remarked, "are personable and anxious to cooperate for our mutual good."[35] On the eve of the clash between the UAW and the automotive employers, the youthful president of the Ford Motor Co. gave his business rivals real cause for concern. He minced no words, coming out in favor of the very things against which industry was generally up in arms.[36] He had a talk with Secretary of Labor Schwellenbach sometime in October. In the course of this conversation, it was reported, young Ford broke ranks. He averred that he was a confirmed believer in collective bargaining, that he had been planning to raise wages for some time, and that in his opinion some system of price control was still essential if the country were to avoid the calamity of inflation.[37]

Though heartened by this verbal heresy on the part of their youthful employer and by many real changes for the better which had already taken place on the Ford assembly line under his auspices, the employes of the Ford Motor Co. proceeded nonetheless to take a vote on the UAW's general demand for a 30 per cent increase in take-home pay.[38] The results of this poll were later announced. Ford's men by a margin of 11 to 1, it appeared, had authorized their representatives to call a strike in the event that the Ford management declined to discuss these and other terms with the union or declined to negotiate at all.[39]

At this point—much to the surprise of certain labor leaders and contrary to the forecasts of many journalists and newspapermen— Henry Ford II did an about-face.[40] His own negotiations with the union were to start within the week. The GM strike was still in the offing. All Detroit was tense with expectation. Whereupon young Ford, who up to now had been talking the language of conciliation and preaching his grandfather's doctrine of high wages and low prices, began to reverse himself. This was no time to tamper with wages, he announced on November 15, six days before the onset of the General Motors strike.[41] Were the UAW to present him with any demands for a 30 per cent increase in take-home pay, Ford said, he would not even deign to discuss the issue.[42] These sentiments were reinforced by a public statement from the Ford Motor Co. to the effect that the company's four-year relationship with the UAW had been a most "unhappy" one, owing to the union's complete irresponsibility.*[43]

But on November 21, General Motors rather than the Ford Motor Co. became the center of the mounting conflict over the country's reconversion policy.[45] The UAW, pressed by a restive rank and file and urged on by a powerful contingent of its leadership, took on its largest adversary. The union struck GM.[46] On the same day, Ford took a seat at the conference table with his employes. He began talking things over with the union.

As the Dearborn negotiations wore on, it became clear once more that Henry Ford II had no immediate intention of coming to terms with labor or of leaving strike-bound General Motors high and dry. To be sure, a lack of tension, even a spirit of good will, seemed to pervade the Ford negotiations.[47] But on fundamentals, the Ford Motor Co. stood pat from the outset; it fell in with the basic strategy of big business. For the next two months, young Ford and his advisers made no real moves to break the stalemate. They sat tight on wages. After bargaining with the union for nearly a month, John Bugas, Ford's new industrial relations chief, asserted that the company would be in no position to talk wage rates for the next 60 to 90 days.[48] A few

* Over in Canada, young Ford was already deeply involved in a labor dispute. He had also proved that he could be quite as stubborn as his grandfather. The employes of the Ford factory at Windsor had been on strike for nine weeks. These Canadian workers were asking that they be granted the same recognition and the same working conditions that had been conceded four years earlier to the men of the Rouge on the opposite bank of the Detroit River.[44]

days later the company changed its position. It offered to raise wages by slightly more than 12 per cent, but only under conditions which the union found "completely unacceptable." One of the strings which was tied to the offer was the proviso that the union must agree not to reopen the wage issue, should the company succeed in getting higher prices for its product through OPA relaxation of price control at any future date.[49] On other points as well the UAW soon discovered in Ford one of the hardest bargainers it had yet encountered.

On the other hand, though he seemed to have cast his lot with GM, Henry Ford II was suddenly being hailed in many quarters as the rising young labor "statesman" of the reconversion period.[50] The press was flooded with rumors to the effect that the Ford Motor Co. would at any moment throw over the traces.[51] The research director of the company let it be known that the idea of guaranteeing annual employment to all men was "an objective worth working for."[52] The following day a feature writer for the Detroit *News* advised his readers to "keep their eyes on Ford," for Dearborn was about to offer its employes a 30 per cent wage increase or something "equally spectacular."[53] From Eleanor Roosevelt's pen several days later came the word that Dearborn was the "one bright spot" in the domestic labor picture, and that among the "revolutionary" things which were currently expected from Ford was the offer of a guaranteed annual wage.[54] Finally, Henry Ford II in person helped to drive home the feeling that he alone among the automotive employers was still ready to meet labor and the public half-way. On January 9 Ford gave an address before the Society of Automotive Engineers, entitled "The Challenge of Human Engineering." The young man's remarks, which the company later circulated in a specially printed brochure, added up to an eloquent condemnation of the industrialist who could be charged with neglecting the "human factor" in his business.[55]

For two months, however, none of these hopes or promises implicit in what Ford or the men around him said, could be discerned in what Ford did. The union and representatives of the Ford corporation continued to meet off and on in a comparatively friendly atmosphere. But apart from that, the new and youthful overseer of the Ford interests rose to the defense of his fellow industrialists. When the UAW asked to "see the books" and offered to adjust its wage demands to fit GM's capacity to pay, and GM retorted that in wanting to "stick its fingers in the pie" the union was talking "socialism,"[56] Henry Ford II spoke up plainly for property and General Motors. There are certain things, Ford said at the time, which "management must manage;" they are none of labor's business.[57] Simultaneously, he joined with the many bitter enemies of OPA. He hit the roof when OPA announced in November that the only concessions it could allow him were a 2 per cent price increase on the over-all Ford line and a 22 per cent increase on one-ton Ford trucks.[58] On those terms, Ford exclaimed, his company would be forced to close out the year 1946 with a net loss of $35,000,000.[59]

President Truman seemed to think otherwise. His Office of War Mobilization had already estimated that industry could afford to raise wages 24 per cent without necessitating any price adjustments.[60] The OWM had gone further than that; it had issued a warning that unless such wage increases were forthcoming, the annual purchasing power of the country would suffer an immediate decline of 30 billion dollars.[61] The Administration was apparently dead set on "holding the line." Industry, on the other hand, was just as determined to have it otherwise. In fact, by December the franker trade journals and the financial news services had made it more than plain that big business meant, and could well afford, to sit down until it was sure of gaining its point at the expense of labor and the public. The *Christian Science Monitor* remarked in November that certain large sections of American industry were "holding back production for higher prices and lower wages."[62]

In such a setting, the grandson of Henry Ford went out of his way to gloss over industry's real intentions, as well as his own. Labor was lying down on the job, he complained in the course of his address on "The Challenge of Human Engineering." Man-hour productivity at the Ford Motor Co., Ford said, had declined by more than 34 per cent during the war years. "Irresponsible labor groups" were at the bottom of many of our reconversion difficulties, he asserted on December 2.[63] Here, the young industrialist seemed to be speaking for industry as a whole and not from his own experience. At any rate, two weeks after he offered this analysis of the situation the Detroit *Free Press* could report that Ford had had no reconversion labor problems to speak of in his own domestic plants. The Ford Motor Co., said the *Free Press* on December 17, had not had a single unauthorized strike from V-J Day on.

The bitter contest over wages, in which the Ford Motor Co. had consistently thrown its weight into the scales on the side of management, was finally eased by the Administration. The long-delayed compromise was embodied in the report on the General Motors situation, submitted by a special fact-finding board appointed by the

President.[64] After making a brief study of the union's demands and of GM's capacity to pay, the board recommended that General Motors should settle its differences with the UAW by sanctioning a wage increase of 18.5 cents an hour. The fact-finding committee had nothing to say on the companion issue of prices and OPA. Thus industry was given the kind of answer it had been fighting for—a formula that closed the wage issue for the time being, while leaving the question of prices open. The suggested wage increase of 18.5 cents was little more than one-half of what the CIO and the UAW had asked for originally. Moreover, industry could now give its full attention to the unresolved half of the economic equation. It began, therefore, to concentrate its fire on OPA. GM and the United States Steel Corporation, meanwhile, still refused to talk wages, holding out to the last for higher prices.

Any number of other corporations, however, hurriedly came to terms with labor. These concerns appeared to be satisfied with the President's suggested compromise on wages. They also seemed more or less assured that the OPA dike would yet be broken, thanks to the combined pressure of GM and United States Steel. Ford, as well as Chrysler, were among the great industrial establishments which promptly entered into wage agreements with this or that branch of organized labor. Ford and Chrysler signed their contracts on January 21. Countless other corporations quickly followed suit. General Motors, however, carried on the fight, fortified for the struggle, by the presence of U. S. Steel at its side and by the knowledge that its competitors would be forced to mark time because of the lack of metal. Consequently, the GM strike, then in its 67th day on January 21, continued.

This time the Ford contract contained no new basic provisions to distinguish it from any other major agreement in the field.[65] Both the Ford agreement and the Chrysler contract dealt solely with the question of wages. All other issues were postponed for later negotiation. In the specific hourly rates of pay agreed to, both contracts were likewise modeled after the report of the President's fact-finding committee. Chrysler accepted without change the recommended wage increase of 18.5 cents an hour. The Ford people settled for 18 cents, in view of the union's willingness to concede that the level of wages at Ford's was already somewhat higher than the scale at Chrysler's.

At this point Henry Ford II made his most important gesture in behalf of postwar profits. He was now in a position to speak up as the fair-minded industrialist who had been one of the first to meet labor half-way. With this aura about him, and again making the most of the great prestige of his grandfather's name, young Ford redoubled his attacks on OPA. Prices on consumer goods and services, as of 1946, had already risen by a margin of 33 to 50 per cent or more since January 1941.[66] The youthful manufacturer declared war on the government's efforts to check any further inflationary spiraling. He argued his case in the newspapers. He took it to Washington. In February Ford made a personal appearance before the House Banking Committee. He asked that body to support the policy of removing all price controls up and down the line in the automobile industry.[67] Young Ford then sent a wire to the White House. He remarked in this communication that even "a little Government price control" was a dangerous thing. At current OPA prices, he said, he was losing $300 on every car that left the Ford assembly line.

Two government officials felt obliged to answer Ford directly. President Truman replied on the 1st of February that he would have to oppose Ford's views and that he for one was still resolved to hold the line in order to stave off wild inflation.[68] Two weeks later Economic Stabilizer Chester Bowles took issue with the publicity of the Ford Motor Co. in a manner which left no doubt of the role Henry Ford II had been playing from V-J Day forward. Ford, Bowles charged, was guilty of making many "irresponsible statements."[69] The young man's contention that low price ceilings in the parts industry were holding up automotive production had no basis in fact, Bowles said. The coordinator of stabilization went on to explain that price controls had already been lifted for the parts plants and that he was "surprised" that Henry Ford II did not know this. More than that, Bowles said, the automobile manufacturers themselves, Ford included, were not producing anything to speak of. Without any normal production figures to back him, he asked, how could Ford speak of losing $300 or any other sum on each of his cars at current OPA prices? He knew of no "intelligent industrialist," said Bowles, who would think of using Ford's insignificant present volume as a fair long-term measure of pricing or of estimated future costs and profits. Yet such was the nature of the case that Ford was so vigorously prosecuting.

Moreover, Bowles said, the Ford Motor Company's eagerness to abolish price control was nothing new; it had manifested itself all along. When all the automobile manufacturers applied for price changes some six months earlier, he said, the Ford interests had made "outrageous" demands; they had asked for government permission to boost prices on the Ford line by a margin of 55 per cent. Thus, according to the Bowles disclosures, it would seem that Henry Ford II had been pushing for inflation from the beginning; he had hoped in 1946 to get 55 per cent more than he charged for his product in 1942, and his 1942 prices had stood well above the pre-war level. The selling price he requested for a Ford four-door sedan in the summer of 1945 was more than 100 per cent higher than the figure he had sold the same car for in 1938.[70] By contrast with such a policy, put forward in this instance in the name of Ford management, labor's subsequent demand for a 30 per cent increase in take-home pay seemed meek indeed.

The price administrator then went to the heart of the Ford post-war philosophy. He implied that by leaguing together with the defenders of property against the public interest, the principal heir to the Ford fortune had failed the first great test of his career. So judged, said Chester Bowles, Henry Ford II was deserting the tradition of high wages and low prices which the world had come to associate with the name of the first and more celebrated Henry Ford.[71]

Young Ford's deviation from the "Ford philosophy" was to continue after Congress had removed all price controls. In the fall of 1947 the Ford Motor Co. followed the lead of General Motors by raising prices on its entire line.[72] The increases ranged from $20 to $97 on Ford passenger cars and trucks, and from $86 to $229 on Lincoln and Mercury cars. They were significantly larger than the price reductions which Ford had put into effect the previous January. The increases were announced at a time when a different application of the Ford philosophy would have been particularly appropriate. The new schedule went into effect on August 25, 1947. By this date Henry Ford II was rapidly approaching, if he had not already passed, the break-even point. All along, like his grandfather before him, he had no outside stockholders who could have demanded the declaring of any profits at all. More than that, the rise in Ford prices took place at a point where the processes of inflation seemed to be well on their way, in the opinion of disinterested government economists, toward another catastrophic depression.[73]

At the same time, Henry Ford II gave further signs of departing from quite another set of tenets in the Ford philosophy. He continued to take issue with his grandfather's concept of feudal management. Acting on excellent advice, he finished the palace revolution that had begun with the removal of Harry Bennett and a thousand other Ford officials of greater or lesser importance.[74] In the course of revitalizing the Ford Motor Co. on the executive level, young Ford went on defying still another precedent that had guided his grandfather for

30 years or more. He continued to reach outside his own organization for the administrative talent so badly needed at the Ford Motor Co.

Among these outside recruits were any number of top-level men of unusual capacity.[75] Ernest R. Breech, a brilliant young GM executive, left the presidency of the Bendix Corporation to become Ford's executive vice-president. Breech had been regarded in trade circles as the probable future president of General Motors. To direct his planning and control division, Ford drew in Lewis D. Crusoe, inducing Crusoe to give up his position as controller of another key GM subsidiary. Albert J. Browning became the new vice-president in charge of purchasing at Ford's. Browning had had a vast experience in his field both as merchandising manager for Montgomery Ward and as the officer who directed all the purchasing for the United States Army during the second World War. Ford then dispensed with the services of his grandfather's old favorite, William J. Cameron, and engaged the highly intelligent firms of Elmo Roper and Earl Newsom and Co. Inc., to handle his public relations.[76] Finally, the alert young president of the Ford Motor Co. brought to the fore many capable, old-line Ford executives like Mead L. Bricker, who had never been able to make full use of their talents during the Bennett regime.

Within a matter of months the new group of Ford administrators succeeded in bringing the operations of Ford Motor Co. into line with the principles of modern scientific management. What these men inherited at Ford's, *Fortune* remarked in May 1947, was an "amorphous administrative mess." When *Fortune* made this comment, however, the Ford organization had already been transformed on the top levels; the company was making effective use of the best financial and executive procedures that had long been taken for granted in other great industrial establishments like General Motors or Standard Oil of New Jersey.[77] Modern accounting and budget methods were now the order of the day in the $900,000,000 corporation which had relied in the past on "a set of books that would put a country storekeeper to shame."[78] Henry Ford II was in a position to judge, for the first time in the history of his company, which operations were making money and which were not. With this information at his elbow he proceeded to dispose of the white elephants within his organization. The company let go of a score or more of its less efficient outlying plants.[79] It dropped a number of other unprofitable operations such as the soybean work at Dearborn and the Ford rubber plantations in Brazil.[80]

The new set of Ford officials did their most basic work, attacking the chief disease from which the top-heavy Ford Motor Co. had suffered for more than a generation. They decentralized and division-alized operations, rapidly bringing to a close the long period during which the Ford enterprise, like a feudal dynasty, had been governed by "an embittered, mutually distrustful group of executives—most of them without titles—with no clear lines of authority or responsibility anywhere delineated."[81]

Ably staffed and thoroughly reorganized at the top, Henry Ford II seemed equally determined, meanwhile, to usher in a new day in labor relations at the Ford Motor Co. His most striking success in this direction occurred in July 1947, during the Ford negotiations for a new two-year contract with the union. At this time the company was guided by an adroit sense of public relations, and the union agreed on a Ford pension plan, the cost of which was to be shared, as is the case with federal social security benefits, by both management and labor. This concession to a group of factory workers—a familiar one in a good many other large-scale corporations—was progressive for the automobile industry.[82] Everything else in the new Ford contract was, as *Business Week* observed, "insignificant."[83] The fact remained that in 1946 and 1947, under the aegis of Henry Ford II and John Bugas, the Ford vice-president in charge of labor relations, the labor policies of the Ford Motor Co. became unrecognizable. *Fortune* was probably close to the truth when it remarked in May 1947 that Ford's successes in dealing with his workers were "second to none in the tense Detroit area."

These sweeping changes at the Ford Motor Co. were interrupted by the death of Henry Ford, the elder. The ailing manufacturer died of a cerebral hemorrhage on April 7, 1947, at the age of 83. The value of the personal holdings which he bequeathed to his heirs and assigns, said the New York *Times*, lay somewhere between 500 and 700 million dollars.[84] When the body of this legendary American, whose career had symbolized for countless millions both the rise and fall of the American Dream, lay at Greenfield Village, a hundred thousand persons filed past for a last look. At a prearranged hour on the day of Ford's funeral, the workers in every industrial establishment in the state of Michigan were asked to stand in silence at their benches for one moment in his honor.[85]

The passing of Henry Ford made no sizable dent in the family fortune. The ownership of the Ford Motor Co., still the largest family-held corporation in existence, remained intact inasmuch as Ford bequeathed most of his Ford holdings to the Ford Foundation.[86]

The Ford Foundation is the non-profit organization to which Edsel Ford left the greater part of his personal investments in the Ford Motor Co.° Here, following a familiar pattern with the very rich, the entire family fortune—or the portion of it invested in the Ford Motor Co.—will eventually go into hiding from the United States Collector of Internal Revenue. Incorporated in 1936, the Ford Foundation is chartered to administer funds for "scientific, educational and charitable purposes, all for the public welfare."[88] The institution is now, and will probably remain for some time, tax-free.[89] It is subject to neither estate taxes nor income taxes. The present Ford family and their heirs will retain complete control of the operations of the Ford Motor Co. As things now stand, however, the bulk of the future declared profits of the company will be siphoned off to the coffers of the Ford Foundation. It will be up to Eleanor Ford and her four children to decide, with the advice of the court and a hand-picked, self-perpetuating board of directors, just what to do with the Foundation's income. To date, the Foundation has paid the expenses of operating Greenfield Village, the Edison Institute and the Henry Ford Hospital.[90]

If the Ford Motor Co. becomes a very profitable enterprise, as is likely, Henry Ford II and the other members of his immediate family will have at their command a vast accumulation of surplus wealth. They can, if they wish, arrange it so that the underlying Ford Motor Co. has only slight or moderate profits to pass on to the Ford Foundation. The Fords, in other words, may elect to share their earnings with the public at their source, by raising wages or lowering prices radically or by giving their customers the very best possible car for their money. In this event, as *Fortune* has indicated, Henry Ford II might "throw his weight around competitively."[91] He could become the pacemaker of the automobile industry as both employer and merchandiser.

On the other hand, the Fords may decide to make a more conventional use of the great means at their disposal. They may choose instead to make a large amount of money by standard methods, in which case the majority of their declared profits will go to the Ford Foundation. The custodians of this fund would then have enormous sums to dispose of. The Foundation is already the largest one of its kind in existence.[92] It is larger than the Rockefeller Foundation or the Carnegie Corporation. Its assets, which are those of the Ford

---

° Both men, father and son, willed all of their non-voting Ford stock to the Ford Foundation.[87]

Motor Co., may eventually run to $900,000,000.[93] On the double condition that Henry Ford II fulfills his promise as a business executive and that the Ford car sells as it should, the income available to the directors of the Ford Foundation may average anywhere from 20 to 30 million dollars a year, or more.

Up to now, the elder of "Edsel's boys" has not acted like a man who is bent on repudiating the canons of business-as-usual or of going over to the opposition of entrenched privilege. His term of office has been brief, however. No one can presume to chart his future course or to forecast with any assurance his ultimate role in the American economy. Time must decide whether Henry Ford II is, at bottom, a man of good will with a broad social outlook or simply a refined, contemporary copy of his grandfather.

## CHAPTER ONE—HORSELESS CARRIAGE

1. Theodore F. MacManus and Norman Beasley, *Men, Money and Motors;* Arthur Pound, *Turning Wheel;* George B. Catlin, *Story of Detroit.*
2. Arthur Pound, *Detroit, Dynamic City,* p. 288.

## CHAPTER TWO—BIRTH OF THE MODEL T

1. Detroit *News,* July 11, 1918.
2. James Couzens, "What I Found About Business From Ford," *System,* September, 1921.
3. Detroit *Saturday Night,* November 27, 1909.
4. Theodore F. MacManus and Norman Beasley, *Men, Money and Motors,* pp. 71-72, 103; Arthur Pound, *Turning Wheel,* pp. 120-21; Laurence H. Seltzer, *A Financial History of the American Automobile Industry,* pp. 34-35, 96-97; Federal Trade Commission, *Report on Motor Vehicle Industry,* pp. 421-22.
5. Theodore F. MacManus and Norman Beasley, *Men, Money and Motors,* pp. 55-56.
6. Chicago *Inter-Ocean,* February 11, 1910.
7. Henry Ford, *My Life and Work,* p. 63.

## CHAPTER THREE—THE NEW MESSIAH

1. C. W. Avery, "How Mass Production Came Into Being," *Iron Age,* June 13, 1929.
2. *They Told Barron,* p. 98.
3. Before the Board of Tax Appeals, Commissioner of Internal Revenue v. Estate of John F. Dodge, deceased, et al. Transcript, pp. 56, 1356-61.
4. Before the Board of Tax Appeals, *op. cit.,* p. 1333.
5. Dodge v. Ford, Transcript of the record, p. 618.
6. Henry Ford, *My Life and Work,* p. 113.
7. *Iron Age,* July 3, 1913.
8. Henry Ford, *op. cit.,* pp. 126-30.
9. *Automotive Industries,* March 14, 1918, pp. 539-41.

## CHAPTER FOUR—FIVE-DOLLAR DAY

1. John R. Lee, "The So-called Profit Sharing System in the Ford Plant," *Annals of the American Academy of Political and Social Science,* May, 1916, p. 307.
2. Detroit *News,* August 12, 1919, Chicago *Tribune* suit.
3. Dodge v. Ford, Transcript of the record, p. 511.
4. Samuel S. Marquis, *Henry Ford,* p. 21.
5. James Couzens, "American Industry and the Social Good," *Printer's Ink Monthly,* July, 1931.
6. Theodore F. MacManus and Norman Beasley, *Men, Money and Motors,* pp. 155-57.
7. Detroit *News,* January 9, 1914.
8. Detroit *Journal,* January 12, 1914.
9. Detroit *Free Press,* January 8, 1914.
10. New York *Times,* January 7, 1914.
11. Detroit *Free Press,* January 9, 1914.
12. Henry Ford, *op. cit.,* p. 147.
13. Detroit *Saturday Night,* January 10, 1914.
14. *Automobile,* January 22, 1914, p. 282.
15. Horace Lucien Arnold and Fay Leone Faurote, *Ford Methods and the Ford Shops,* p. 328.
16. John R. Lee, *op. cit.,* p. 307.
17. Detroit *News,* August 31, 1916.
18. *Automobile,* October 26, 1916, p. 685.
19. *Machinery,* June, 1917, p. 897.
20. Samuel S. Levin, "Ford Profit Sharing, 1914-1920. I. The Growth of the Plan," *Personnel Journal,* August, 1927; "The End of Ford Profit Sharing," *Personnel Journal,* October, 1927.
21. Henry Ford, *op. cit.,* p. 129.
22. John R. Lee, *op. cit.,* p. 307.
23. Samuel S. Levin, *Personnel Journal,* August, 1927, pp. 79-80.
24. *Ibid.,* p. 82.
25. New York *Times,* May 26, 1916.
26. Blanche Bernstein, *Hiring Policies in the Automobile Industry,* Unpublished W.P.A. research project, January, 1937.
27. John Burroughs, *John Burroughs Talks,* p. 331.
28. Detroit *News,* November 15, 1915.

## CHAPTER FIVE—NO MORE PARASITES

1. E. G. Pipp, *Henry Ford, Both Sides of Him,* pp. 13-16; Theodore F. MacManus and Norman Beasley, *Men, Money and Motors,* pp. 169-70.
2. E. G. Pipp, *op. cit.,* p. 18.

3. Dodge v. Ford, Testimony of John F. Dodge, p. 491.
4. Theodore F. MacManus, *op. cit.*, pp. 170-71.
5. E. G. Pipp, *op. cit.*, p. 18.
6. Before the Board of Tax Appeals, Commissioner of Internal Revenue v. James Couzens, et al. Testimony of Fred J. Haynes, chairman of the board of the Dodge Corporation, p. 957.
7. *Fortune*, December, 1933, p. 128.
8. Dodge v. Ford, Testimony of C. H. Wills, pp. 593-94.
9. Before the Board of Tax Appeals, *op. cit.*, John F. Dodge stipulation, Exhibit Q, p. 2.
10. Dearborn *Independent*, October 8, 1915; Detroit *Free Press*, November 22, 1915.
11. Before the Board of Tax Appeals, *op. cit.*, p. 1281.
12. Federal Trade Commission, *Report on Motor Vehicle Industry*, p. 634.
13. *Ibid.*, p. 646.
14. Henry Ford, *My Life and Work*, p. 52.
15. New York *Times*, July 12, 1919.
16. Dodge v. Ford, Testimony of Henry Ford, p. 295.
17. Detroit *Times*, February 15, 1927.
18. Dodge v. Ford, 204 *Mich.* 505.
19. Before the Board of Tax Appeals, p. 615.
20. *Automotive Industries*, November 28, 1918.
21. New York *Times*, March 11, 1919.
22. Los Angeles *Times*, March 5, 1919.
23. New York *Times*, July 12, 1919.
24. *Automotive Industries*, July 17, 1919.
25. *Monthly Labor Review*, February, 1925, pp. 68-69.
26. Samuel S. Marquis, *Henry Ford*, p. 95.
27. Detroit *Saturday Night*, June 15, 1935.
28. Henry Ford, *op. cit.*, p. 147.
29. Federal Trade Commission, *op. cit.*, pp. 640-41.
30. *Ibid.*, p. 642.
31. Henry Ford, *op. cit.*, pp. 174-75.
32. Detroit *Saturday Night*, *op. cit.*
33. E. G. Pipp, *op. cit.*, pp. 28-29.
34. Dodge v. Ford, Testimony of John F. Dodge, p. 505.
35. *Commercial and Financial Chronicle*, July 30, 1921.
36. Detroit *Saturday Night*, February 5, 1921.
37. Henry Ford, *op. cit.*, p. 3.
38. *Ibid.*, p. 174.

## CHAPTER SIX—OUT OF THE TRENCHES BY CHRISTMAS

1. Detroit *News*, June 18, 1915.
2. Detroit *Free Press*, September 5, 1915.

3. New York *Times,* April 11, 1915.
4. Detroit *Free Press,* August 22, 1915.
5. New York *Times,* December 1, 1915.
6. Detroit *News,* November 15, 1915.
7. Oswald Garrison Villard, *Fighting Years,* pp. 302-305.
8. Louis P. Lochner, *America's Don Quixote,* p. 25.
9. New York *Times,* December 4, 1915.
10. Detroit *News,* December 4, 1915.
11. John Burroughs, *John Burroughs Talks,* p. 330.
12. Samuel S. Marquis, *Henry Ford,* pp. 19-20.
13. Lochner, *op. cit.,* pp. 54-55.
14. *Ibid.,* pp. 63-64.
15. *Ibid.,* p. 87.
16. New York *Times,* January 4, 1916.
17. John Reed, "Industry's Miracle Man," *Cosmopolitan,* October, 1916, p. 66; Detroit *News,* May 6, 1919.
18. Detroit *News,* February 22, 1916; May 7, 1916; New York *Times,* April 23, 1916.
19. New York *Times,* October 17, 1917.
20. Detroit *News,* October 16, 1917.
21. *Pipp's Weekly,* July 9, 1921; E. G. Pipp, *Henry Ford, Both Sides of Him,* pp. 54-55.
22. New York *Times,* November 7, 1922.
23. Detroit *Saturday Night,* August 17, 1918.
24. Detroit *News,* May 22, 1919.
25. Detroit *Saturday Night,* August 3, August 24, and November 2, 1918.
26. New York *Times,* November 20, 1918.
27. Detroit *Saturday Night,* January 11, 1919.
28. *Automotive Industries,* August 22, 1918; New York *Times,* August 23, 1918.
29. New York *Times,* February 10, 1917.
30. *Ibid.,* September 28, 1915.
31. Detroit *News,* August 22, 1918.
32. *Ibid.,* July 11, 1919.
33. *Pipp's Weekly,* July 7, 1923.
34. *Ibid.,* May 6, 1922.
35. New York *Times,* March 3, 1922.
36. *Ibid.,* March 28, 1922.
37. Detroit *News,* October 13, 1923.
38. Federal Trade Commission, *Report on Motor Vehicle Industry,* p. 634.
39. Before the Board of Tax Appeals, Commissioner of Internal Revenue v. James Couzens, et al., Transcript, p. 872.
40. *Automotive Industries,* September 12, 1918.

41. Detroit *News,* November 8, 1917.
42. Detroit *Saturday Night,* June 15, 1935.
43. Detroit *News,* July 30, 1938.
44. Henry Ford, *Today and Tomorrow,* p. 253.

## CHAPTER SEVEN—HISTORY IS BUNK

1. E. G. Pipp, *The Real Henry Ford,* pp. 48-50.
2. Ford v. Dodge, Transcript, p. 219.
3. Detroit *Saturday Night,* July 26, 1919. Unless indicated to the contrary, Ford's testimony is reproduced verbatim from the file of the New York *Times.*
4. Ford v. Chicago *Tribune.* Argument on a motion to dismiss, p. 12. Ford's testimony entered on the record, December 11, 1917.
5. Sarah T. Bushnell, *The Truth About Henry Ford,* pp. 141-42.
6. Detroit *News,* August 22, 1929.
7. New York *Times,* April 13, 1930.
8. Detroit *News,* May 10, 1929.
9. *Ibid.,* January 4, 1928; May 10, 1929.
10. Detroit *Times,* July 16, 1936.
11. Detroit *News,* July 17, 1936.
12. Detroit *Times,* July 27, 1936.
13. Samuel S. Marquis, *Henry Ford,* p. 37.
14. *Collier's,* July 4, 1914.
15. New York *Times,* May 20, 1919.
16. Marquis, *op. cit.,* pp. 78-79.
17. John Burroughs, *John Burroughs Talks,* p. 350.
18. New York *Times,* February 12, 1927.
19. Detroit *News,* February 11, 1927.
20. Alfred O. Tate, *Edison's Open Door,* p. 164.
21. Detroit *News,* December 23, 1923.
22. New York *Times,* October 29, 1922.
23. Detroit *Saturday Night,* August 17, 1918.
24. Henry Ford, *Edison As I Know Him,* p. 12.
25. New York *Times,* October 29, 1922.
26. *System,* May, 1926.
27. Tate, *op. cit.,* p. 278.
28. *Ibid.,* p. 126.
29. *Ibid.,* p. 1.
30. *Ibid.,* p. 294.
31. Ford, *op. cit.,* pp. 52-53.
32. *Pipp's Weekly,* May 6, 1921.
33. Burroughs, *op. cit.,* pp. 326, 334.

## CHAPTER EIGHT—FLIVVER POLITICS

1. New York *Times*, April 23, 1916.
2. Detroit *News*, September 20, 1918.
3. Detroit *Saturday Night*, June 22, 1918.
4. John Burroughs, *John Burroughs Talks*, p. 337.
5. New York *Times*, June 23, 1918.
6. *Ibid.*, September 28, 1916.
7. *Ibid.*, January 3, 1916.
8. Detroit *News*, June 21, 1918.
9. *Ibid.*, September 5, 1918.
10. Detroit *Free Press*, November 3, 1918.
11. Detroit *Saturday Night*, August 3, 1918.
12. Detroit *News*, February 5, February 6, 1919.
13. New York *Times*, July 16, 1918.
14. *Ibid.*, June 15, 1918.
15. Detroit *Labor News*, November 1, 1918.
16. Spencer Ervin, *Henry Ford vs. Truman H. Newberry*, p. 301.
17. *Pipp's Weekly*, September 17, 1921.
18. *Ibid.*
19. Detroit *News*, February 4, 1919.
20. Ervin, *op. cit.*, pp. 56-57.
21. *Pipp's Weekly*, June 11, 1921.
22. New York *Times*, June 11, 1922.
23. Ervin, *op. cit.*, p. 101.
24. New York *Times*, May 24, 1922.
25. Allan L. Benson, *The New Henry Ford*, p. 347.
26. Detroit *News*, December 4, 1923.
27. Benson, *op. cit.*, pp. 352-53.
28. Detroit *News*, November 1, 1923.
29. New York *Times*, June 25, 1922.
30. *World's Work*, March, 1923, p. 492.
31. *Pipp's Weekly*, January 20, 1923.
32. *Ibid.*, December 16, 1922.
33. *Ibid.*, February 11, 1922.
34. New York *Times*, January 7, 1923.
35. *Ibid.*, July 4, 1922.
36. *Pipp's Weekly*, August 5, 1922.
37. *Ibid.*, August 25, 1923.
38. *Collier's*, August 4, 1923, p. 6.
39. New York *Times*, January 7, 1923.
40. Benson, *op. cit.*, p. 212.
41. New York *Times*, June 21, 1922.
42. *Ibid.*, April 19, 1922.

43. *Ibid.*, March 23, 1922.
44. *Ibid.*, May 2, 1922.
45. *Ibid.*, January 12, 1922; February 12, 1922.
46. *Pipp's Weekly,* March 28, 1925.
47. New York *Times,* January 12, 1922.
48. *Ibid.*, June 7, 1922.
49. *Literary Digest,* January 5, 1924, pp. 7-9.
50. New York *Times,* January 15, 1922.

## CHAPTER NINE—TWENTY-TRACK MIND

1. *Railway Age,* December 10, 1921, pp. 1137-38.
2. *Nation's Business,* November, 1921, pp. 7-9.
3. *Railway Age,* August 27, 1921, pp. 407-408.
4. *Ibid.*, August 14, 1926, p. 283.
5. *Ibid.*, November 26, 1921, pp. 1047-48.
6. *Ibid.*, September 3, 1921, p. 307.
7. *Ibid.*, November 26, 1921, pp. 1047-48.
8. New York *Times,* September 10, 1922.
9. *Ibid.*, August 4, 1922.
10. Detroit *Free Press,* August 30, 1922.
11. *Railway Age,* March 29, 1924, pp. 845-46.
12. New York *Times,* March 11, 1922; *Railway Age,* August 14, 1926, p. 283.
13. New York *Times,* July 20, 1928.
14. *Literary Digest,* May 31, 1924, pp. 23-24.
15. New York *Times,* June 10, 1914.
16. Sarah T. Bushnell, *The Truth About Henry Ford,* p. 217.
17. James Martin Miller, *The Amazing Story of Henry Ford,* pp. iii, 9.
18. *Mill and Factory,* January, 1936, p. 73.
19. Edwin P. Norwood, *Ford Men and Methods,* p. 82.
20. *Iron Age,* September 26, 1918, pp. 739, 742.

## CHAPTER TEN—CHRONICLER OF THE NEGLECTED TRUTH

1. Detroit *Saturday Night,* January 18, 1919.
2. *Radio Guide,* December 8, 1939. Kenneth F. McCormick, "Spokesman for Henry Ford."
3. Dearborn *Independent,* January 11, 1919.
4. *Ibid.*, March 22, 1919.
5. *Ibid.*, August 5, 1922.
6. *Ibid.*, October 4, 1919.
7. *Pipp's Weekly,* June 11, 1921.
8. *Hearst's International,* June, 1922, p. 14.
9. New York *Times,* March 26, 1927.

10. *Pipp's Weekly*, March 5, 1921.
11. *Ibid.*, July 2, 1921.
12. Detroit *Free Press*, October 29, 1933.
13. *Hearst's International*, Photostat, June, 1922, p. 16.
14. *Ibid.*
15. *Ibid.*, July, 1922, p. 15.
16. *International Jew*, Volume I, p. 6.
17. Dearborn *Independent*, October 6, 1923.
18. *International Jew*, Volume I, p. 111.
19. *Ibid.*, Volume I, p. 33.
20. *Ibid.*, Volume IV, pp. 67-69.
21. *Ibid.*, Volume II, p. 188.
22. Detroit *Free Press*, August 7, 1922.
23. *International Jew*, Volume I, p. 134.
24. *Ibid.*, Volume I, p. 123.
25. *Ibid.*, Volume I, p. 145.
26. *Ibid.*, Volume IV, p. 181.
27. *Ibid.*, Volume II, p. 244.
28. *Ibid.*, Volume I, p. 90.

## CHAPTER ELEVEN—CHRISTIANS ONLY

1. Detroit *News*, March 21, 1927; March 22, 1927; March 25, 1927; New York *Times*, March 25, 1927.
2. New York *World*, July 8, 1927.
3. New York *Times*, March 26, 1927.
4. *Ibid.*, April 13, 1927.
5. *Pipp's Magazine*, June 1927, p. 32.
6. New York *Times*, March 15, 1927.
7. *Ibid.*, March 31, 1927.
8. Detroit *News*, March 30, 1927.
9. New York *Times*, April 2, 1927.
10. *Ibid.*, April 22, 1927.
11. Detroit *News*, April 21, 1927.
12. New York *Times*, April 21, 1927.
13. Detroit *News*, April 21, 1927.
14. Detroit *Free Press*, December 7, 1927.
15. Dearborn *Independent*, July 30, 1927.
16. Statement by Henry Ford, American Jewish Committee, New York, 1927.
17. New York *World*, July 9, 1927.
18. Detroit *Times*, December 18, 1933.
19. United States Board of Tax Appeals, Washington, D. C. Henry Ford and Son, Inc., Petitioner, v. Commissioner of Internal Revenue, Respondent. Docket No. 24759. Exhibit "A".

20. New York *Times*, July 8, 1927.
21. *Ibid.*, January 17, 1928.
22. *Pipp's Weekly*, September 20, 1922, p. 2.
23. *Ibid.*, January 5, 1924, p. 3.
24. New York *Times*, July 10, 1927.
25. *Mein Kampf*. See Editors' comment, p. 929.
26. New York *Times*, December 20, 1922.

## CHAPTER TWELVE—SLEIGHT OF HAND

1. *Onlooker*, January, 1931, p. 6.
2. Detroit *News*, February 5, 1922.
3. Detroit *Saturday Night*, February 11, 1922.
4. Detroit *News*, December 27, 1929.
5. Detroit *Saturday Night*, April 5, 1924.
6. *Ibid.*
7. *Ibid.*
8. *Ibid.*
9. *Ibid.*
10. *Pipp's Weekly*, January 21, 1922.
11. *Automotive Industries*, June 15, 1922.
12. *Cram's Reports of the Automobile Industry*, September 28, 1935; October 5, 1935.
13. Federal Trade Commission, *Report on Motor Vehicle Industry*, p. 654.
14. *Pipp's Weekly*, February 3, 1922; Leland v. Ford, 245 *Mich.* 607, Amended bill of complaint, p. 91.
15. Detroit *Saturday Night*, April 5, 1924; *Pipp's Weekly*, April 5, 1924.
16. Detroit *Times*, February 19, 1928.
17. Detroit *News*, February 11, 1933.
18. *Ibid.*, January 21, 1933.
19. *Ibid.*, May 7, 1933.
20. Leland v. Ford, 252 *Mich.* 551, Reply brief of plaintiff and appellant p. 17.
21. *Ibid.*, Brief for defendants and appellees, p. 14.
22. *Ibid.*, p. 52.
23. *Ibid.*, p. 60.

## CHAPTER THIRTEEN—VIRTUE AT 6%

1. New York *World*, November 10, 1926.
2. Detroit *Free Press*, November 24, 1926.
3. *Wall Street Journal*, October 8, 1926.
4. Detroit *News*, November 14, 1926.
5. Detroit *Free Press*, November 14, 1926.
6. *Iron Trade Review*, November 26, 1926.

7. Detroit *News,* November 24, 1926.
8. *Forbes',* May 1, 1927, pp. 19-21.
9. *Printer's Ink,* March 31, 1927, p. 34.
10. Henry Ford, *Moving Forward,* p. 81.
11. New York *Times,* February 5, 1928; *Barron's Weekly,* November 7, 1932.
12. Detroit *News,* February 12, 1928.
13. *Wall Street Journal,* October 8, 1926; Samuel M. Levin, "The Ford Unemployment Problem," *American Labor Legislation Review,* June, 1932; Robert L. Cruden, "The Great Ford Myth," *New Republic,* March 16, 1932.
14. Detroit *Free Press,* November 14, 1926; New York *World,* November 10, 1926.
15. *Christian Century,* December 9, 1926, p. 1516.
16. *Nation's Business,* November, 1921, p. 8.
17. *Hearings before the Temporary National Economic Committee,* 75th Congress, Part II, Patents, Preliminary printing, 1939, pp. 155-58, 177.
18. *Ibid.,* p. 192.
19. *Ibid.,* p. 230.
20. *Ibid.,* p. 265.

## CHAPTER FOURTEEN—FORD ALUMNI ASSOCIATION

1. Samuel S. Marquis, *Henry Ford,* pp. 139-41.
2. *Ibid.,* p. 176.
3. New York *Times,* January 8, 1928; *New Republic,* November 14, 1923, p. 302.
4. Marquis, *op. cit.,* pp. 173-75.
5. *Ibid.,* p. 176.
6. *Ibid.,* p. 171.
7. *Ibid.,* p. 53.
8. Henry Ford, *My Life and Work,* p. 263.
9. Marquis, *op. cit.,* p. 9.
10. *They Told Barron,* November 23, 1923, p. 119.
11. *More They Told Barron,* pp. 307-308.
12. Walter M. Cunningham, *"J 8", A Chronicle of the Neglected Truth About Henry Ford, D. E., and the Ford Motor Co.,* p. 103.
13. Marquis, *op. cit.,* p. 51.
14. Henry Ford, *op. cit.,* pp. 99, 266.
15. *Forbes',* June 1, 1927, p. 14.
16. Boston *Post,* October 14, 1927.
17. *They Told Barron,* May 22, 1924, p. 122.
18. Marquis, *op. cit.,* p. 172.
19. Henry Ford, *op. cit.,* pp. 92-95.
20. Marquis, *op. cit.,* p. 119.

21. *Ibid.,* pp. 118-19.
22. *Business Week,* May 7, 1930.
23. Before the Board of Tax Appeals, Commissioner of Internal Revenue v. Estate of John F. Dodge et al., Transcript, p. 1018.
24. State of Michigan, *Supreme Court Records and Briefs,* Vols. 1070-1071, p. 663.
25. *Ibid.,* pp. 337, 409.
26. Detroit *Saturday Night,* February 5, 1921.
27. Marquis, *op. cit.,* p. 127.
28. *Automotive Industries,* January 6, 1921, p. 39.
29. State of Michigan, *Supreme Court Records and Briefs, op. cit.,* Testimony of Edsel Ford, pp. 530-31.
30. *Automotive Industries,* March 17, 1921, p. 624.
31. *Ibid.,* February 3, 1921, p. 243.
32. Marquis, *op. cit.,* p. 128.
33. New York *Times,* January 30, 1929.
34. *Fortune,* December, 1938, p. 180.
35. *Forbes',* June 1, 1927, p. 13.
36. Marquis, *op. cit.,* p. 160.

### CHAPTER FIFTEEN—DEATH OF THE MODEL T

1. *Automotive Industries,* June 20, 1931, p. 940.
2. Detroit *News,* November 24, 1922.
3. *Ibid.,* July 31, 1926.
4. *Forbes',* January 1, 1928, p. 10.
5. Cunningham, *"J 8," A Chronicle of the Neglected Truth About Henry Ford, D. E., and the Ford Motor Co.,* p. 96.
6. *Forbes',* May 15, 1927.
7. New York *Times,* December 12, 1927; Detroit *Free Press,* November 19, 1927.
8. Dodge v. Ford Motor Co., State of Michigan, *Supreme Court Records and Briefs,* Vol. 1070, Testimony of Edsel Ford, pp. 530-31.
9. *Automotive Industries,* July 6, 1929, p. 32.
10. New York *World,* September 11, 1927.
11. Paul U. Kellogg, "When Mass-Production Stalls," *Survey-Graphic,* 1928, Vol. 59, p. 683 ff.
12. New York *Times,* April 7, 1927.
13. Paul U. Kellogg, *op. cit.,* p. 684.
14. New York *Times,* April 7, 1928.
15. *Forbes',* May 1, 1927, p. 20; *Pipp's Magazine,* May, 1927, p. 22.
16. *Pipp's Magazine,* June, 1926, p. 16.
17. Robert L. Cruden, "The Great Ford Myth," *New Republic,* March 16, 1932; Robert W. Dunn, *Labor and Automobiles,* pp. 125-28; *Auto Workers News,* December, 1927, February, 1928.

18. *Federated Press,* December 30, 1925.
19. *Iron Trade Review,* November 18, 1926, p. 1296.
20. *Forbes',* May 1, 1927, p. 19.
21. *Wall Street Journal,* March 20, 1929.
22. *Barron's Weekly,* December 12, 1927.

### CHAPTER SIXTEEN—FORD'S FRANCHISE

1. Federal Trade Commission, *Report on Motor Vehicle Industry,* 1939.
2. *Barron's Weekly,* January 11, 1932.
3. Release of N. W. Ayer and Son, Inc., December 14, 1932.
4. *Fortune,* December, 1933, pp. 63-65.
5. *Sales Management,* November 15, 1932, pp. 432-45.
6. *Barron's Weekly,* May 5, 1930, p. 28.
7. *Business Week,* April 2, 1930.
8. *Automotive Industries,* September 27, 1917, p. 556.
9. Federal Trade Commission, *op. cit.,* pp. 201, 203.
10. *Ibid., op. cit.,* pp. 160-61.
11. *Ibid.*
12. William Pennypacker Young, *A Ford Dealer's Twenty Year Ride With the Old and New Model Ford Policies,* p. 76.
13. *Pipp's Weekly,* August 26, 1922, pp. 8-10.
14. *Fortune,* August, 1933.
15. Detroit *Times,* September 16, 1928.
16. Federal Trade Commission, *op. cit.,* p. 664.
17. *Ibid.,* p. 661.
18. *Ibid.,* p. 645.
19. United States of America v. Ford Motor Co. et al. In the District Court of the United States for the Northern District of Indiana, South Bend Division. Indictment returned May 27, 1938. No. 1041.
20. Federal Trade Commission, *op. cit.,* p. 286.
21. United States of America v. Ford Motor Co., Universal Credit Corporation, et al., Respondents. In the District Court of the United States for the Northern District of Indiana. Final decree, Civil No. 8, November 15, 1938.
22. *Automotive Industries,* February 18, 1926, p. 248.
23. Federal Trade Commission, *op. cit.,* p. 194.

### CHAPTER SEVENTEEN—DETROIT'S DEPRESSION

1. Detroit *News,* January 8, 1921.
2. *Christian Century,* January 31, 1929.
3. *Wall Street Journal,* July 4, 1929.
4. New York *Times,* October 30, 1931.
5. *Wall Street Journal,* October 29, 1931.

6. *New Republic*, March 16, 1932.
7. Detroit *Labor News*, September 13, 1929.
8. *New Republic*, March 16, 1932.
9. Henry Ford, *Moving Forward*, p. 74.
10. *Barron's Weekly*, May 4, 1931; Detroit *Times*, April 28, 1931.
11. *Barron's Weekly*, May 4, 1931; *Business Week*, February 22, 1933.
12. Detroit *News*, February 4, 1933.
13. *Ibid.*, January 30, 1933.
14. *Ibid.*, January 28, 1933.
15. *Ibid.*, February 12, 1933.
16. *Ibid.*, February 24, 1933.
17. *Business Week*, February 15, 1933.
18. New York *Times*, January 31, 1933.
19. Detroit *News*, January 28, 1933.
20. New York *Times*, January 31, 1933.
21. *Forbes'*, February 15, 1933, pp. 4, 13, 20.
22. *Automotive Industries*, February 18, 1933, pp. 185-87.
23. *Business Week*, February 8, 1933, p. 8.
24. Carroll R. Daugherty, *Labor Problems in American Industry*, p. 66.
25. Detroit *News*, January 3, 1933.
26. W. J. Cameron, *Ford Sunday Evening Hour*, February 17, 1935.
27. *Ibid.*, December 9, 1934.
28. *Ibid.*, June 16, 1935.
29. Dearborn *Independent*, March 22, 1919.
30. New York *Times*, March 13, 1932; New York *Herald-Tribune*, February 4, 1932.
31. Federal Trade Commission, *Report On Motor Vehicle Industry*, p. 649.
32. *The Unemployed*, Spring, 1931.
33. Detroit *News*, June 12, 1931.
34. *Business Week*, July 8, 1931.
35. Samuel M. Levin, "The Ford Unemployment Problem," *American Labor Legislation Review*, June, 1932.
36. *Literary Digest*, July 11, 1931.
37. Detroit *Leader*, February 11, 1933.
38. Detroit *News*, June 27, 1931.
39. *Ibid.*
40. Detroit *Saturday Night*, June 15, 1935.
41. *Fortune*, December, 1933, pp. 122, 125.
42. *Literary Digest*, September 12, 1931, p. 10.
43. Detroit *News*, August 23, 1931; Detroit *Times*, June 4, 1932.
44. Detroit *Free Press*, April 19, 1940.
45. *Ibid.*, June 1, 1932; June 3, 1932.
46. New York *Times*, December 17, 1931.
47. Detroit *News*, February 20, 1934; February 22, 1934.
48. *Wall Street Journal*, October 15, 1932.

49. Detroit *News,* June 12, 1931.
50. Federal Trade Commission, *op. cit.,* p. 649.

## CHAPTER EIGHTEEN—FORD HUNGER MARCH

1. Detroit *News,* March 9, 1932.
2. Detroit *Free Press,* March 8, 1932.
3. Detroit *News,* March 9, 1932.
4. Detroit *Mirror,* March 8, 1932.
5. Detroit *News,* March 8, 1932.
6. *Ibid.*
7. Detroit *Mirror,* March 8, 1932.
8. Detroit *News,* March 8, 1932.
9. Detroit *Times,* March 9, 1932.
10. Detroit *Mirror,* March 8, 1932.
11. New York *Times,* March 8, 1932.
12. Detroit *Mirror,* March 8-9, 1932.
13. Detroit *Times,* March 8, 1932.
14. New York *Herald-Tribune,* Detroit *Free Press,* March 8, 1932.
15. Henry Ford, *The Only Real Security,* p. 6.
16. Detroit *Mirror,* March 11, 1932.
17. Detroit *News,* Detroit *Times,* March 13, 1932.
18. Detroit *News,* Detroit *Free Press,* March 9, 1932.
19. *Federated Press,* July 5, 1932.
20. Detroit *News,* March 8, 1932.
21. *New Republic,* March 30, 1932.
22. Detroit *News,* March 11, 1932.
23. *Ibid.,* March 23, 1932.
24. Detroit *Free Press,* March 10, 1932.
25. Detroit *News,* July 3, 1932.
26. Detroit *Times,* July 4, 1932.

## CHAPTER NINETEEN—BANK WITH HANK

1. Federal Trade Commission, *Report on Motor Vehicle Industry,* p. 657.
2. *Barron's Weekly,* May 18, 1931.
3. *Wall Street Journal,* January 8, 1921.
4. *Ibid.,* May 9, 1929.
5. Henry Ford, *Moving Forward,* p. 262.
6. Detroit *Free Press,* May 14, 1930.
7. *Ibid.,* September 7, 1930.
8. Hearings before the Senate Committee on Banking and Currency, 73d Congress, Stock Exchange Practices, Part 10, *Guardian Detroit Union Group,* p. 4661.
9. Ferdinand Pecora, *Wall Street Under Oath,* p. 246.

10. Detroit *News,* January 3, 1933.
11. *Ibid.,* March 1, 1934.
12. Senate Hearings, *op. cit.,* p. 4607.
13. Detroit *News,* March 1, 1934.
14. Senate Hearings, *op. cit.,* pp. 4860-62.
15. *Ibid.,* pp. 5031-32.
16. Ferdinand Pecora, *op. cit.,* p. 243.
17. Detroit *News,* January 6, 1934.
18. Senate Hearings, *op. cit.,* pp. 4614-15.
19. *Ibid.,* pp. 5011, 5017-21.
20. *Ibid.,* p. 4668.
21. George B. Catlin, *The Story of Detroit,* pp. 361-62.
22. Senate Hearings, *op. cit.,* pp. 4664-65.
23. *Ibid.,* p. 4813.
24. Detroit *News,* August 25, 1933.
25. Senate Hearings, *op. cit.,* p. 4877.
26. *Ibid.,* p. 4627.
27. Federal Trade Commission, *op. cit.,* p. 649.
28. Detroit *News,* February 3, 1934.
29. Senate Hearings, *op. cit.,* p. 4695.
30. New York *Times,* February 13, 1927.
31. Detroit *Free Press,* August 16, 1933.
32. Detroit *News,* February 7, 1934.
33. Detroit *Free Press,* February 28, 1933.
34. *Ibid.,* March 2, 1933.
35. *Ibid.,* February 27, 1933.
36. New York *Times,* February 27, 1933.
37. Detroit *News,* February 3, 1934.
38. *New Republic,* September 30, 1936.
39. Detroit *News,* June 21, 1933.
40. Detroit *Free Press,* August 18, 1933.
41. *Ibid.,* October 24, 1936.
42. Detroit *News,* May 9, 1937.

## CHAPTER TWENTY—GRANDFATHER'S CLOCK

1. *Literary Digest,* January 2, 1926.
2. *Fortune,* December, 1933, p. 64.
3. *Christian Science Monitor,* May 16, 1934.
4. Henry Ford, *My Life and Work,* p. 228.
5. Detroit *News,* April 12, 1934.
6. Henry Ford, *Edison As I Know Him,* p. 110.
7. Detroit *News,* February 21, 1931.
8. Ruth E. Finley, *Lady of Godey's: Sarah Josepha Hale,* pp. 295, 302.
9. New York *Times,* January 18, 1927.

10. Evelyn Foster Morneweck, *The Birthplace of Stephen C. Foster as Recorded by His Father, Mother and Brother, and Other Contemporary Authorities*, p. 38.
11. *Guidebook to Historic Places in Western Pennsylvania*, Western Pennsylvania Historical Society, University of Pittsburgh Press, 1938.
12. John Tasker Howard, *Stephen Foster, America's Troubador*, Tudor, Fourth printing, 1939.
13. ———, "History Bunked," *Western Pennsylvania Historical Magazine*, March, 1937, p. 61.
14. *Ibid.*, p. 57.
15. William A. Simonds, *Henry Ford and Greenfield Village*, p. 40.
16. Detroit *Saturday Night*, June 15, 1935.
17. *The International Jew*, Vol. III, pp. 38, 49, 62.
18. *Ford News*, April, 1938.
19. Detroit *Times*, January 15, 1939.
20. *Wall Street Journal*, December 6, 1938; New York *Times*, May 21, 1937.
21. Henry Ford, *My Life and Work*, p. 205.

## CHAPTER TWENTY-ONE—FOLK HERO

1. W. J. Cameron, *Ford Sunday Evening Hour*, February 14, 1937.
2. *Fortune*, March, 1939, p. 109.
3. Detroit *Free Press*, May 9, 1935.
4. *Ibid.*, October 4, 1939.
5. *Ibid.*, December 3, 1934.
6. *Wall Street Journal*, September 6, 1935.
7. Federal Trade Commission, *Report on Motor Vehicle Industry*, p. 646.
8. Detroit *News*, May 22, 1944.
9. *Ibid.*, September 1, 1933.
10. Detroit *Free Press*, August 29, 1922.
11. New York *Times*, March 3, 1927.
12. Quoted by the Detroit *Saturday Night*, August 26, 1922.
13. *Nation*, January 24, 1923, pp. 92-93.
14. *Ibid.*

## CHAPTER TWENTY-TWO—MEN-AT-ARMS

1. John McCarten, "The Little Man in Henry Ford's Basement," *American Mercury*, May-June, 1940.
2. New York *Times*, June 14, 1937.
3. Deed from Henry Ford and Clara B. Ford to Harry H. Bennett, *Liber 5124*, State of Michigan, County of Wayne, December 12, 1938.
4. New York *Times*, July 4, 1937.
5. *Time* Magazine, March 17, 1941.
6. New York *Times*, June 26, 1937.

7. Detroit *Free Press,* December 13, 1937.
8. Detroit *Times,* September 12, 1939.
9. Detroit *Saturday Night,* June 15, 1935.
10. Detroit *News,* June 7, 1937.
11. *Ibid.,* July 13, 1938; February 24, 1939.
12. *New Republic,* March 30, 1932.
13. Detroit *Free Press,* September 16, 1933.
14. New York *Times,* September 26, 1933.
15. Philadelphia *Public Ledger,* September 26, 1933.
16. Detroit *Free Press,* September 26, 1939.
17. George B. Catlin, *The Story of Detroit,* pp. 672-73; Detroit *Saturday Night,* August 31, 1918; May 31, 1930; Detroit *News,* September 4, 1930; December 15, 1932; May 11, 1933; April 9, 1935; April 15-16, 1935; September 19, 1940.
18. John O'Brien, "Henry Ford's Commander-in-Chief," *Forum,* February 1938.
19. An extensive list of Ford parolees was published by *Friday* Magazine, issue of January 31, 1941, and by *Ford Facts,* organ of Local 600, United Automobile Workers, issue of November 18, 1940.
20. New York *Times,* May 9, 1928.
21. Detroit *Times,* August 19, 1934.
22. Detroit *News,* January 17, 1935.
23. *Ibid.,* March 27, 1936.
24. Detroit *Free Press,* October 15, 1933.
25. Detroit *News,* January 16, 1936.
26. Reproduced from the New York *Post,* in *Ford Facts,* organ of Local 600, United Automobile Workers, issue of November 18, 1940.
27. New York *Times,* May 3, 1928.
28. Detroit *Times,* February 7, 1931.
29. Detroit *News,* August 11, 1930.
30. *Ibid.,* December 2, 1927; Detroit *Times,* February 7, 1931.
31. Detroit *News,* February 8, 1931.
32. Detroit *Times,* February 7, 1931.
33. Detroit *News,* February 7, 1931.
34. *Ibid.,* May 11, 1929.
35. *Ibid.,* February 9, 1931.
36. *Ibid.,* October 11, 1930.
37. *Ibid.*
38. Detroit *News,* March 8, 1932; Detroit *Free Press,* March 8, 1932; *United Automobile Worker,* October 8, 1938.
39. Detroit *News,* July 29, 1930.
40. *Ibid.,* July 30, 1936.
41. *Ibid.,* October 21, 1936.
42. *Ibid.,* June 4, 1937.
43. *Ibid.,* June 25, 1937.

44. Detroit *Free Press,* November 1, 1936.
45. Detroit *News,* December 16, 1937; Sam Cuva v. The People, Recorder's Court of the City of Detroit, Docket No. A 15155.
46. Detroit *News,* July 20, 1932.
47. Royal Brougham, "The Morning After," Seattle *Post-Intelligencer,* December 8, 1941.
48. Matter of Ford Motor Co. and U.A.W.A., Local No. 325, N.L.R.B., Case No. XIV-C-145, Intermediate report, p. 14.

## CHAPTER TWENTY-THREE—JOB NEUROSIS

1. *Forbes',* May 1, 1927, p. 20.
2. Detroit *News,* Detroit *Free Press,* March 1, 1933.
3. Detroit *News,* December 15, 1938.
4. *Ibid.,* November 7, 1936.
5. *Ford Facts,* organ of Local 600, United Automobile Workers, issue of February 19, 1941; *CIO News,* February 17, 1941.

## CHAPTER TWENTY-FOUR—COMMUNITY NEUROSIS

1. Detroit *News,* October 16, 1929.
2. Howard Wolf and Ralph Wolf, *Rubber, A Story of Glory and Greed,* p. 268.
3. *Wall Street Journal,* July 19, 1926.
4. Federal Trade Commission, *Report on Motor Vehicle Industry,* p. 57.
5. Walter M. Cunningham, *"J 8," A Chronicle of the Neglected Truth About Henry Ford, D. E., and the Ford Motor Co.,* pp. 82-85.
6. Detroit *News,* May 27, 1931.
7. Harry H. Bennett v. Eileen C. Bennett, In the Circuit Court for the County of Washtenaw, State of Michigan, In Chancery. Transcript of testimony, December 1, 1927.
8. Detroit *News,* June 17, 1941.
9. *Ibid.,* May 27, 1941.
10. *Ibid.,* October 12, 1935.
11. *Michigan State Bar Journal,* February, 1938, Ethics Opinion No. 30, pp. 82-83.
12. Detroit *News,* May 27, 1941; *Ford Facts,* Organ of Local 600, United Automobile Workers, Issue of June 7, 1941. Transcript of NLRB testimony.
13. Detroit *News,* February 20, 1928.
14. Testimony reported during a hearing before the National Labor Relations Board, *Detroit Free Press,* June 3, 1941; Detroit *News,* June 3, 1941.
15. *In Fact,* July 21, 1941.
16. *Ford Facts,* Organ of Local 600, United Automobile Workers, Issue of April 23, 1941.

17. Detroit *News*, January 29, 1939; Detroit *Free Press*, February 19, 1939.
18. *University of Michigan Daily*, February 24, 1939.
19. Detroit *News*, September 20, 22, 1940. Detroit *Free Press*, September 22, 1940.
20. Detroit *News*, September 18, 20, 1940. Detroit *Free Press*, September 20, 1940.
21. Detroit *News*, September 19, 22, 1940.
22. *Ibid.*, September 22, 1940.
23. Detroit *News*, Detroit *Free Press*, September 20, 1940.
24. Detroit *News*, Detroit *Free Press*, September 20, 1940; Detroit *News*, September 22, 1940.
25. Detroit *News*, April 25, 1938; September 20, 1940; September 22, 1940.
26. *Ibid.*, September 20, 21, 1940.
27. *Ibid.*
28. *Ibid.*, September 22, 1940.
29. Detroit *Free Press*, September 19, 1940.
30. *University of Michigan Daily*, March 29, 1939.
31. Detroit *News*, March 23, 1939.
32. *Ibid.*
33. *University of Michigan Daily*, March 22, 1939; March 28, 1939.
34. Detroit *Free Press*, September 14, 1939.
35. Horace A. White, *Christian Century*, February 9, 1938, pp. 176-77.
36. Detroit *News*, November 27, 1940; April 21, 1941.

## CHAPTER TWENTY-FIVE—EX-BOXER

1. NEA Service, Inc., May 29, 1937.
2. New York *Times*, June 14, 1931.
3. Detroit *Mirror*, March 9, 1932.
4. John McCarten, "The Little Man in Henry Ford's Basement," *American Mercury*, Part I, May, 1940, p. 10.
5. New York *Times*, March 25, 1937.
6. Detroit *News*, May 27, 1941.
7. Detroit *Free Press;* May 26, 1941; Detroit *News*, May 27, 1941.
8. Detroit *News*, May 27, 1941.
9. Detroit *Free Press*, Detroit *Times*, November 29, 1929.
10. Detroit *News*, September 17, 1931.
11. *Ibid.*, September 26, 1930.
12. *Ibid.*, October 2, 1930.
13. *Time* Magazine, March 17, 1941.
14. "The Distribution of Ownership in the 200 Largest Nonfinancial Corporations," Temporary National Economic Committee, Investigation of Concentration of Economic Power, Monograph No. 29, Washington, 1940, pp. 433, 928.
15. Detroit *Free Press*, November 27, 1932.

16. J. H. O'Brien, "Henry Ford's Commander in Chief, Harry Bennett," *Forum,* February, 1938.
17. *Ibid.*
18. *Ibid.*
19. Harry H. Bennett, plaintiff, v. Eileen C. Bennett, defendant. State of Michigan, In the Circuit Court for Washtenaw County. In chancery. Action filed June 21, 1927. Transcript of testimony, p. 49.
20. *Fortune,* December, 1933, p. 203.
21. Detroit *Free Press,* March 5, 1930.
22. John McCarten, *op. cit.,* p. 206.
23. Detroit *Free Press,* January 15, 1936.
24. John McCarten, *op. cit.,* p. 203.
25. Detroit *Free Press,* February 8, 1942.
26. *Ibid.*
27. John McCarten, *op. cit.,* May, 1940, p. 7; NEA Service, March 22, 1939.
28. Detroit *Free Press,* June 14, 1935.

## CHAPTER TWENTY-SIX—MACHINE AGE

1. Detroit *Times,* November 16, 1940.
2. Detroit *News,* April 29, 1937.
3. *Monthly Labor Review,* February, 1929, p. 181.
4. Estimate of Bureau of Labor Statistics, Department of Labor, submitted by letter, March 16, 1942.
5. *Monthly Labor Review,* February, 1929, "Instability of Employment in the Automobile Industry."
6. New York *Times,* June 12, 1938.
7. *Preliminary Report on Study of Regularization of Employment and Improvement of Labor Conditions in the Automobile Industry.* Leon Henderson, director, Research and Planning Division, National Recovery Administration, January 23, 1934.
8. *Monthly Labor Review, op. cit.*
9. Arthur Pound, *Detroit, Dynamic City,* p. 315.
10. Henry Ford, *Moving Forward,* p. 68.
11. W. J. Cameron, *Ford Sunday Evening Hour Talk,* December 9, 1934.
12. *Employment and Pay Rolls,* Serial No. R. 1250, Department of Labor, 1941.
13. *Time,* March 17, 1941; *PM,* January 1, 1941.
14. Detroit *Free Press,* June 21, 1941.
15. Henderson — NRA report on automobile industry, *op. cit.*
16. *Ibid.*
17. *Fortune,* December, 1933, p. 125.
18. *Ibid.,* December, 1935, pp. 115-16.

19. Seattle *Post-Intelligencer*, December 29, 1940.
20. Henry Ford, *Moving Forward*, pp. 93-94; *Ford Sunday Evening Hour Talks*, March 3, 1935; April 5, 1936; October 31, 1937; Seattle *Post-Intelligencer*, December 29, 1940; *Ford Almanac*, June, 1937.
21. Henderson — NRA report on automobile industry, *op. cit.*, p. 9.
22. W. J. Cameron, "'Machine Bondage,'" *Ford Sunday Evening Hour Talk*, December 18, 1938.
23. Henry Ford, *Today and Tomorrow*, p. 160.
24. W. J. Cameron, *Ford Sunday Evening Hour Talk*, November 7, 1937; December 18, 1938.
25. Henry Ford, *Today and Tomorrow*, p. 5; New York *Times*, May 29, 1932.
26. Detroit *Times*, November 16, 1940.
27. Joe Brown, *Federated Press*, March 5, 1934.
28. Seattle *Post-Intelligencer*, December 29, 1940.
29. Detroit *News*, January 17, 1938.
30. Henry Ford, *My Life and Work*, pp. 106-107.
31. W. J. Cameron, *Ford Sunday Evening Hour Talk*, November 14, 1937; Seattle *Post-Intelligencer*, December 29, 1940.
32. *Ford Sunday Evening Hour Talk*, November 18, 1934.
33. New York *Times*, February 23, 1922.
34. *United Automobile Worker*, August 20, 1938; August 27, 1938; September 3, 1938; State of Michigan, Department of Labor and Industry, *Thomas Pytel v. Ford Motor Co.*, 1939; Pytel v. Ford Motor Co., *op. cit.*, *Reply Brief for Defendant and Appellant*; *Pipp's Weekly*, April 22, 1922; February 9, 1924.
35. State of Michigan, Department of Labor and Industry, *Hearings on Review*, 1937-1938.
36. Henry Ford, *Today and Tomorrow*, pp. 160, 183.
37. Henry Ford, *My Life and Work*, p. 103.
38. *Ibid.*, p. 77.
39. *Forbes'*, May 15, 1927.
40. *Ibid.*, May 1, 1927.
41. New York *Times*, January 8, 1928.
42. *Fortune*, December, 1933, p. 128.

## CHAPTER TWENTY-SEVEN—CALL-TO-ARMS

1. New York *Times*, April 8, 11, 1937.
2. John McCarten, "The Little Man in Henry Ford's Basement," *American Mercury*, June, 1940, p. 207.
3. Ford-NLRB, *Kansas City case*, Exhibit 122-a; *Richmond case*, Intermediate Report, p. 40; *Buffalo case*, Decision and Order, pp. 10, 22; *Dallas case*, Transcript p. 1474.
4. New York *Times*, June 26, 1937.

5. Detroit *Free Press,* June 6, 1941.
6. Ford-NLRB, *Detroit case,* Decision and Order, pp. 36-38.
7. Detroit *News,* September 18-22, 1940.
8. New York *Times,* June 29, 1937.
9. *Ibid.,* October 31, 1937.
10. *Ibid.,* June 29, 1937.
11. Investigation of the Federal Bureau of Investigation into Nazi Military Training Camps in the United States, Sub-section on Fritz Kuhn (Undated, 1939); also New York *Times,* April 4, 1939.
12. Ford-NLRB, *Buffalo case,* Decision and Order, p. 12.
13. *Ibid.,* p. 34.
14. *Ibid.,* p. 5.
15. Report on NLRB hearing in Detroit, Detroit *Free Press,* May 29, 1941.
16. New York *Times,* June 26, 1937.
17. Report on NLRB hearing in Detroit, Detroit *Free Press,* June 6, 1941.
18. Ford-NLRB, *Detroit case, op. cit.,* p. 31.
19. Ford-NLRB, *Buffalo case, op. cit.,* pp. 16-17.
20. *Ibid.,* pp. 7-10, 28-30.
21. Ford-NLRB, *St. Louis case,* Intermediate Report, p. 17.
22. Report on NLRB hearing in Detroit, Detroit *Free Press,* June 6, 1941.
23. Ford-NLRB, *Buffalo case, op. cit.,* pp. 28-30.
24. Report on NLRB hearing in Edgewater, *CIO News,* May 5, 1941.
25. Detroit *News,* June 21, 1941.
26. Ford-NLRB, *St. Louis case, op. cit.,* pp. 36-37.
27. Ford-NLRB, *Long Beach case,* Decision and Order, pp. 5-11.
28. New York *Times,* June 6, 1937.
29. Ford NLRB, *Detroit case, op. cit.,* p. 29; *St. Louis case, op. cit.,* pp. 12-16.
30. Detroit *News,* July 7, 1937; New York *Times,* April 25, 1938.
31. Detroit *News,* July 16, 1937; Detroit *Times,* June 13, 1937.
32. *Michigan State Bar Journal,* February, 1938, Ethics Opinion No. 30, pp. 82-83.
33. Detroit *News,* January 20, 1939.
34. Ford-NLRB, *Richmond case,* Intermediate Report, pp. 6-7.
35. Detroit *Free Press,* January 25, 1939.
36. Detroit *News,* October 14, 1938.
37. New York *Times,* March 7, 1939.
38. Detroit *News,* April 11, 1939.
39. *United Automobile Worker,* October 1, 1940.
40. Ford-NLRB, *Long Beach case,* Intermediate Report, pp. 5-6.
41. Detroit *Times,* April 19, 1942.
42. New York *Times,* October 30, 1937.
43. *Ibid.,* December 21, 1937.
44. Ford-NLRB, *Dallas case,* Decision and Order.
45. Detroit *News,* June 21, 1941.

46. NLRB, Petitioner, v. Ford Motor Co., Respondent. Sixth Circuit of the United States Circuit Court of Appeal. No. 8399. Decided October 8, 1940.
47. Detroit *News,* July 9, 1937.
48. *Ibid.*
49. *Ibid.,* May 27, 1937; Ford-NLRB, *Detroit case, op. cit.,* p. 20.
50. Ford-NLRB, *Detroit case, op. cit.,* pp. 21-22.
51. *Ibid.,* p. 9.
52. *Ibid.,* p. 11.
53. *Ibid.,* pp. 11-12.
54. *Ibid.,* pp. 20, 23; Detroit *News,* May 18, 1940.
55. Ford-NLRB, *Detroit case, op. cit.,* p. 13.
56. *Ibid.,* p. 14.
57. *Ibid.,* p. 15.
58. *Ibid.,* p. 16.
59. *Ibid.,* p. 19.
60. *Ibid.,* pp. 13, 24.
61. *Ibid.,* p. 12.
62. Detroit *News,* May 27, 1937.
63. Ford-NLRB, *Detroit case, op. cit.,* p. 19; Detroit *News,* May 27, 1937.
64. Ford-NLRB, *Detroit case, op. cit.,* pp. 17-18.
65. Detroit *Times,* June 30, 1937.
66. *Time,* June 7, 1937.
67. Ford-NLRB, *Detroit case, op. cit.,* p. 23.
68. New York *Times,* May 26, 1937.
69. *Ibid.,* January 4, 1938.
70. Detroit *News,* May 28, 1937.
71. Detroit *Times,* June 30, 1937.
72. W. J. Cameron, *Ford Sunday Evening Hour Talk,* June 13, 1937.
73. New York *Times,* July 22, 1937.
74. *Ibid.,* January 1, 1938.
75. *Ibid.,* January 23, 1923.
76. *Ibid.,* August 8, 1937.
77. *Ibid.,* August 12, 1937.
78. *Ibid.,* April 18, August 4, 1937.
79. *Ibid.,* January 22, 1938.
80. Ford-NLRB, *Dallas case,* Decision and Order.
81. Ford-NLRB, *Dallas case,* Transcript, pp. 273-77.
82. *Ibid.,* p. 1484.
83. Ford-NLRB, *Dallas case,* Decision and Order, p. 15.
84. Ford-NLRB, *Dallas case,* Transcript, pp. 186, 188-91, 636, 2093.
85. Ford-NLRB, *Dallas case,* Decision and Order, p. 49.
86. *Ibid.,* pp. 21, 25-33.
87. *Ibid.,* p. 13.
88. *Ibid.,* pp. 22-24.

89. *Ibid.*, pp. 34-36.
90. *Ibid.*, p. 34.

## CHAPTER TWENTY-EIGHT—COMPROMISE

1. Detroit *News*, May 17, 1941.
2. *Ibid.*, April 19, 1941.
3. *Ford Facts*, May 9, 1941.
4. Detroit *Free Press*, December 12, 1940.
5. *United Automobile Worker*, April 1, 1941.
6. Detroit *News*, January 18, 1941; February 18, 1941.
7. *Ibid.*, March 9, 1941.
8. *Time*, March 17, 1941.
9. Detroit *News*, April 3, 1941.
10. *Ibid.*
11. Detroit *Free Press*, April 2, 1941.
12. Seattle *Post-Intelligencer*, April 2, 1941.
13. *PM*, May 2, 1941.
14. Detroit *News*, April 5, 1941.
15. *Ibid.*, April 7, 1941.
16. *Ibid.*, April 10, 1941.
17. *Ibid.*, April 5, 1941.
18. *Ibid.*, April 10, 1941.
19. Detroit *Free Press*, April 5, 1941.
20. Seattle *Post-Intelligencer*, April 2, 1941.
21. Detroit *News*, April 5, 1941.
22. *Ibid.*, April 7, 1941.
23. *Ibid.*, April 5, 1941.
24. *The Antiochian*, "The American Scene: Impressions of the Ford Strike," October 3, 1941.
25. Detroit *News*, April 3, 1941.
26. *Ibid.*, April 10, 1941.
27. *Ibid.*, April 5 and April 7, 1941; *The Antiochian, op. cit.*
28. *Ibid.*, April 5, 1941.
29. Detroit *Free Press*, April 4, 1941.
30. Detroit *News*, April 3, 1941.
31. Seattle *Times*, April 3, 1941.
32. Detroit *News*, April 3, 1941; June 17 and 19, 1941.
33. Detroit *Free Press*, April 12, 1941.
34. *New Republic*, June 14, 1941.
35. Detroit *News*, May 23, 1941.
36. *Ibid.*, May 24, 1941.
37. *Time*, March 17, 1941.
38. Detroit *News*, November 10, 1941.
39. Seattle *Times*, November 24, 1942.

40. Los Angeles *News*, May 5, 1944.
41. Detroit *News*, May 1-3, 1943; *Ford Facts*, May 15, 1943.
42. Detroit *Free Press*, April 10, 1943.
43. Detroit *News*, November 19, 1943.
44. Detroit *Free Press*, April 27, 1943; Detroit *News*, November 9, 1943.
45. Detroit *Free Press*, January 26, 1943.
46. *Ibid.*, March 21, 1944.
47. Detroit *News*, April 24, 1944; May 6, 1944.
48. *Ibid.*, March 16, 1944; *United Auto Worker*, April 1, 1944.

## CHAPTER TWENTY-NINE—WILLIT RUN?

1. Detroit *Times* and Detroit *Free Press*, June 24, 1942; *Life*, August 17, 1942.
2. Detroit *News*, May 8-9, 1942.
3. *Ibid.*, March 22, 1943.
4. *Ibid.*, May 8, 1942.
5. *Ibid.*, May 9, 1942.
6. Detroit *Times*, June 25, 1942.
7. Detroit *News*, July 13, 1943.
8. *Bombardier*, June 15, 1943.
9. *Ibid.*
10. *Wall Street Journal*, March 15, 1943.
11. Detroit *Times*, April 22, 1942.
12. Detroit *News*, March 4, 1943.
13. *Ibid.*
14. Detroit *Free Press*, November 15, 1943.
15. Detroit *News*, February 20, 1943.
16. Detroit *Times*, July 13, 1942.
17. *Bombardier*, June 15, 1943.
18. Detroit *News*, February 14, 1943.
19. *Ibid.*, March 12, 1943.
20. Detroit *Free Press*, March 6, 1944.
21. Seattle *Times*, June 12, 1942.
22. Detroit *News*, May 24, 1944; Detroit *Free Press*, May 25, 1944.
23. Detroit *News*, February 14, 1943.
24. Special Committee Investigating National Defense Program. Aircraft Report, July 10, 1943. Report 10, part 10. 78th Congress, 1st session.
25. Detroit *News*, March 12, 1943.
26. *Ibid.*, January 16, 1944.
27. Seattle *Times*, March 8, 1943.
28. Detroit *News*, February 19, 1943; March 8, 1944.
29. *Ibid.*, April 7, 1943.
30. Radio broadcast of August 22, 1943.

31. Detroit *News*, January 16, 1944.
32. New York *Times*, April 8, 1944.


CHAPTER THIRTY—WORLD CRISIS

1. Detroit *Times*, September 19, 1935; Detroit *News*, November 2, 1936; April 29, 1937; New York *Times*, March 21, April 11, April 14, 1937.
2. *PM*, September 20, 1940.
3. Institute for Propaganda Analysis, July, 1938.
4. *The International Jew*, Vol. IV, pp. 45-51, 225, 236-39.
5. *Fortune*, February, 1936.
6. John Roy Carlson, *Under Cover*, pp. 25, 30, 33, 56, 86, 166, 194, 199-200, 205-206, 241, 284, 299, 327, 347.
7. McCormack-Dickstein Committee, *Investigation of Nazi and Other Propaganda*, 74th Congress, 1st session, House of Representatives, Report No. 153; February 15, 1935.
8. New York *Times*, January 7, 1937.
9. Detroit *Free Press*, September 10, 1938.
10. Detroit *News*, April 28, 1941.
11. Detroit *News* and Detroit *Free Press*, December 1, 1938.
12. State of Michigan, In the Circuit Court for the County of Wayne, Charles E. Coughlin, plaintiff, vs. The Detroit *Free Press*, a Michigan corporation, defendant, No. 211, 525.
13. Detroit *News;* Detroit *Times*, December 5, 1938.
14. *Ibid.*
15. New York *Times*, December 28, 1937.
16. *Ibid.*, April 4, 1939.
17. McCormack-Dickstein Report, *op. cit.*
18. New York *Times*, January 7, 1937.
19. *Ibid.*, April 4, 1939.
20. Detroit *Free Press*, March 12, 1937.
21. Detroit *News*, December 7, 1939.
22. Detroit *Free Press*, August 29, 1939; *Time*, March 23, 1942.
23. Adolph Hitler, *Mein Kampf*, p. 930.
24. Detroit *Free Press*, August 29, 1939.
25. Seattle *Post-Intelligencer*, December 30, 1941.
26. New York *Times*, September 12, 1941.
27. Seattle *Post-Intelligencer*, December 8, 1941.
28. Seattle *Times*, July 23, 1942.
29. Detroit *Free Press*, January 1, 1942.
30. Detroit *News*, January 12, 1942.
31. Detroit *Free Press*, February 1, 1942.
32. New York *Times*, April 11, 1942.
33. Detroit *Times*, April 4, 1942; April 17, 1942.

34. *PM*, January 7, 1944.
35. Detroit *Free Press*, December 16, 1943.

CHAPTER THIRTY-ONE—HENRY THE SECOND

1. New York *Times*, July 12, 1919.
2. *Fortune*, December, 1933, p. 132.
3. *Time*, February 4, 1946; *Business Week*, October 12, 1946.
4. Detroit *Times*, March 20, 28, 1933; Detroit *News*, March 18, 20, 22, 27; April 2, 12, 1933; Detroit *Free Press*, March 17, 20, 24, 1933; Bertram D. Wolfe, *Diego Rivera*, pp. 337-51.
5. *Life*, "Henry Ford II," October 1, 1945.
6. *Life*, July 29, 1940.
7. *Life*, "Henry Ford II," October 1, 1945.
8. *Ibid.*
9. *Newsweek*, June 18, 1945.
10. Drew Pearson, Los Angeles *Daily News*, October 30, 1945.
11. *Life*, "Henry Ford II," *op. cit.*
12. *Newsweek*, *op. cit.*
13. Detroit *Free Press*, November 20, 1945.
14. *Newsweek*, *op. cit.*
15. Detroit *Free Press*, September 30, 1945.
16. Detroit *News*, October 14, 1945.
17. *Ibid.*, September 28, 1945.
18. Detroit *Free Press*, October 26, 1945.
19. Detroit *News*, October 7, 14, 1945.
20. Detroit *Free Press*, October 13, 1945; Detroit *News*, October 12, 1945.
21. Detroit *Free Press*, October 26, 1945.
22. Detroit *News*, September 30, 1945.
23. *Ibid.*, October 7, 14, 1945; Los Angeles *Times*, December 2, 1945.
24. Detroit *News*, October 7, 11, 12, 14, 26, 27; November 10, 1945; Detroit *Free Press*, October 8, 14, 1945.
25. Detroit *Free Press*, Detroit *News*, September 28, 1945.
26. Detroit *News*, Detroit *Free Press*, October 11, 1945.
27. *Life*, "Henry Ford II," *op. cit.*
28. *Ibid.*
29. Samuel Grafton, Los Angeles *Daily News*, December 11, 1945.
30. Detroit *Free Press*, November 19, 1945.
31. Thomas L. Stokes, Los Angeles *Daily News*, December 24, 1945; Marquis Childs, Los Angeles *Daily News*, January 3, February 2, 1946.
32. Marquis Childs, Los Angeles *Daily News*, November 5, December 11, 1945.
33. Los Angeles *Times*, December 2, 1945.
34. Detroit *Free Press*, December 9, 12, 1945; Los Angeles *Daily News*, December 18, 1945.

35. *Newsweek, op. cit.*
36. Los Angeles *Daily News,* December 18, 1945.
37. *Ibid.,* October 30, 1945.
38. *Research Report,* Publication of the UAW-CIO, November, December, 1945.
39. Detroit *Free Press,* January 27, 1946.
40. *PM,* November 16, 1945; *Time,* November 26, 1945.
41. Detroit *News,* November 15, 1945; Detroit *Free Press,* November 16, 1945.
42. Detroit *Free Press,* November 20, 1945.
43. *Ibid.,* November 16, 1945.
44. *Ibid.,* November 13, 16, 17; December 20, 1945.
45. *PM,* November 25, 1945.
46. *Nation,* "G.M. Strike '46 Model," December 1, 1945.
47. Detroit *Free Press,* December 9, 12, 1945; January 11, 1946; New York *Times,* January 27, 1946.
48. Los Angeles *Daily News,* December 15, 1945.
49. Detroit *News,* December 18, 1945.
50. *Ibid.,* January 10, 1946; Detroit *Free Press,* January 13, 1946.
51. Detroit *Free Press,* December 12, 1945; Los Angeles *Times,* December 18, 1945.
52. Detroit *Free Press,* December 8, 1945.
53. Detroit *News,* December 9, 1945.
54. Los Angeles *Daily News,* December 14, 1945.
55. Henry Ford II, "The Challenge of Human Engineering." An address by Henry Ford II, President, Ford Motor Co. Annual meeting of the Society of Automotive Engineers. January 9, 1946. (Printed by the Ford Motor Co.)
56. Los Angeles *Daily News,* January 3, 9, 1946.
57. Detroit *Free Press,* November 19, 1945.
58. *Ibid.,* November 20, 1945; Los Angeles *Times,* December 2, 1945; Los Angeles *Daily News,* December 13, 1945; Detroit *News,* November 17, 1945.
59. Los Angeles *Daily News,* December 13, 1945.
60. *Research Report,* Publication of the UAW-CIO, December 1945.
61. *Congressional Record,* November 5, 1945.
62. *Christian Science Monitor,* Quoted by *In Fact,* December 3, 1945.
63. Los Angeles *Times,* December 2, 1945.
64. Los Angeles *Daily News,* January 12, 1946.
65. New York *Times,* January 27, 1940; Detroit *Free Press,* January 27, 1946.
66. *Monthly Labor Review,* "Income from Wages and Salaries in the Post-war Period," Bureau of Labor Statistics, September 1945; United States Department of Commerce, "Survey of Current Business," September 1945; Report of Presidential Committee on Cost of Living, November

17, 1944; Philip Murray and R. J. Thomas, "Living Costs in World War II," CIO publication.

67. Los Angeles *Daily News,* February 19, 1946.
68. Detroit *Free Press,* January 31, 1946.
69. Los Angeles *Daily News,* February 19, 1946.
70. *Research Report,* Publication of the UAW-CIO, November, 1945; March, 1946.
71. Los Angeles *Daily News,* February 19, 1946.
72. *Ibid.,* August 25, 1947; Detroit *News,* August 26, 1947.
73. Los Angeles *Daily News,* September 12, 1947.
74. *Fortune,* May, 1947.
75. *Business Week,* October 12, 1946.
76. *Fortune,* May, 1947; *Business Week,* March 20, 1946.
77. *Fortune, op. cit.*
78. *Ibid., op. cit.; Newsweek,* April 21, 1947.
79. *Business Week,* October 12, 1946.
80. *United States News,* April 18, 1947; *Inter-American,* January, 1946.
81. *Fortune,* May, 1947.
82. *Newsweek,* July 7, 1947; *Industrial Pension Systems in the United States and Canada,* Industrial Relations Counselors, Inc., 1936; *Designing a Company Pension Plan,* National Industrial Conference Board, 1944; *Trends in Company Pension Plans,* National Industrial Conference Board, 1944; Richard E. Wyatt, et al., *Employee Retirement Plans,* Graphic Arts Press, 1945.
83. *Business Week,* July 5, 1947.
84. New York *Times,* April 18, 1947.
85. *Ibid.,* April 11, 1947.
86. Detroit *Times,* January 19, 1936; New York *Times,* December 11, 1937; *Wall Street Journal,* December 11, 1937.
87. *Fortune,* June, 1944; New York *Times,* April 19, 1947.
88. *Fortune,* June, 1944.
89. *United States News,* April 18, 1947.
90. *Fortune,* June, 1944.
91. *Ibid.,* May, 1947.
92. New York *Times,* April 20, 1947.
93. *Fortune,* May, 1947.

# BIBLIOGRAPHY

## BOOKS

Arnold, Horace Lucien, and Faurote, Fay Leone, *Ford Methods and the Ford Shops,* Engineering Magazine Co., New York, 1915.

Barclay, Hartley W., *Ford Production Methods,* reprinted from *Mill and Factory,* January, 1936.

Benson, Allan L., *The New Henry Ford,* Funk and Wagnalls, 1923.

Borth, Christy, *Pioneers of Plenty,* Bobbs-Merrill, 1939.

——, *Masters of Mass Production,* Bobbs-Merrill, 1945.

Brooks, Robert R. R., *When Labor Organizes,* Yale University Press, 1937.

Burroughs, John, *John Burroughs Talks,* as reported by Clifton Johnson. Houghton Mifflin, 1922.

——, *The Life and Letters of John Borroughs,* edited by Clara Barrus. Houghton Mifflin, 1925.

——, *The Heart of Burroughs' Journals,* edited by Clara Barrus. Houghton Mifflin, 1928.

Busch, Jr., Niven, *Twenty-One Americans,* (Chapter, "Turkey in the Straw.") Doubleday, Doran, 1930.

Bushnell, Sarah T., *The Truth About Henry Ford,* Reilly and Lee, 1922.

Caesar, Irving, *Caesar's Commentaries on the Ford Peace Expedition.* Unpublished manuscript.

Catlin, George B., *The Story of Detroit,* Detroit *News,* 1923.

Chase, Stuart, *Men and Machines,* Macmillan, 1929.

Collected Papers by the Staff of the Henry Ford Hospital. First Series, 1915-1925. Paul B. Hoeber, 1926.

Copley, Frank Barkley, *Frederick W. Taylor,* Harper and Brothers, 1923.

Daugherty, Carroll R., *Labor Problems in American Industry,* Houghton Mifflin, 1933.

Dearborn Publishing Co., *The International Jew, Part I. The World's Foremost Problem.* A reprint of a series of articles appearing in the Dearborn *Independent.* November, 1920.

——, *The International Jew, Part II. Jewish Activities in the United States.* 1921.

——, *The International Jew, Part III. Jewish Influences in American Life.* 1921.

——, *The International Jew, Part IV. Aspects of Jewish Power in the United States.* 1922.

——, "*Good Morning.*" *After a Sleep of 25 Years, Old-Fashioned Dancing Is Being Revived by Mr. and Mrs. Henry Ford.* 1926.

Dos Passos, John, *The Big Money,* (Chapter, "Tin Lizzie.") Harcourt, Brace. 4th printing. August, 1936.

Dubreuil, H., *Robots or Men,* Harper's, 1930.

Dunn, Robert W., *Labor and Automobiles,* International Publishers, 1929.

Epstein, Abraham, *Insecurity: A Challenge to America,* Random House. 2nd revised edition, 1938.

Epstein, Ralph C., *The Automobile Industry, Its Economic and Commercial Development,* A. W. Shaw Co., 1928.

Ervin, Spencer, *Henry Ford vs. Truman H. Newberry,* Richard R. Smith, 1935.

Finley, Ruth E., *Lady of Godey's: Sarah Josepha Hale,* Lippincott, 1938.

Flynn, John T., *God's Gold. The Story of Rockefeller and His Times,* Harcourt, Brace, 1932.

——, *Security Speculation,* Harcourt, Brace, 1934.

Forbes, B. C., and Foster, O. D., *Automotive Giants of America,* B. C. Forbes Publishing Co., 1926.

Ford, Henry, *My Life and Work,* in collaboration with Samuel Crowther. Doubleday, 1922.

——, *Today and Tomorrow,* in collaboration with Samuel Crowther. Doubleday, 1926.

——, *My Philosophy of Industry,* an authorized interview with Fay Leone Faurote. Coward-McCann, 1929.

——, *Moving Forward,* in collaboration with Samuel Crowther. Doubleday, 1930.

——, *Edison as I Know Him,* in collaboration with Samuel Crowther. Cosmopolitan, 1930.

Glazer, Sidney, *Labor and Agrarian Movements in Michigan, 1876-1896.* Ph.D. dissertation, University of Michigan, 1932.

Graves, Ralph H., *The Triumph of an Idea. The Story of Henry Ford,* Doubleday, 1935.

Hitler, Adolf, *Mein Kampf,* Reynal and Hitchcock, 1939.

Howard, John Tasker, *Stephen Foster, America's Troubador,* Tudor Publishing Co., 4th printing, 1939.

Huxley, Aldous, *Brave New World,* Sun Dial Press, Garden City, 1932.

Lane, Rose Wilder, *Henry Ford's Own Story; How a Farmer Boy Rose to the Power That Goes With Many Millions, Yet Never Lost Touch With Humanity.* Jones, 1917.

Leonard, Jonathan Norton, *The Tragedy of Henry Ford,* G. P. Putnam, 1932.

Lochner, Louis P., *America's Don Quixote. Henry Ford's Attempt to Save Europe,* Kegan Paul, Trench, Trubner, 1924.

Loeb, Harold, *Production for Use,* Basic Books, Inc., 1936.

Lundberg, Ferdinand, *America's 60 Families,* Vanguard, 1937.

Lynd, Robert S., and Lynd, Helen Merrell, *Middletown,* Harcourt, Brace, 1929.

——, *Middletown in Transition,* Harcourt, Brace, 1937.

MacManus, Theodore F., and Beasley, Norman, *Men, Money and Motors,* Harper and Brothers, 1929.

Marquis, Samuel S., *Henry Ford,* Little, Brown, 1923.

McKenney, Ruth, *Industrial Valley,* Harcourt, Brace, 1939.

Merz, Charles, *And Then Came Ford,* Doubleday, 1929.

Miller, James Martin, *The Amazing Story of Henry Ford.* Privately printed, 1922.

Minnich, Harvey C., editor, *Old Favorites from The McGuffey Readers,* American Book Co., 1936.

Morneweck, Evelyn Foster, *The Birthplace of Stephen C. Foster as Recorded by His Father, Mother and Brother, and Other Contemporary Authorities.* The author, 1936.

Muste, A. J., *The Automobile Industry and Organized Labor,* Christian Social Justice Fund, Baltimore, 1935.

Norwood, Edwin P., *Ford Men and Methods,* Doubleday, 1931.

Palmer, Dewey H., and Crooks, Laurence E., *Millions on Wheels,* Vanguard, 1938.

Pecora, Ferdinand, *Wall Street Under Oath,* Simon and Schuster, 1939.

Pipp, E. G., *The Real Henry Ford.* The author, Detroit, 1922.

——, *Henry Ford. Both Sides of Him.* The author, Detroit, 1926.

Pound, Arthur, *The Iron Man in Industry,* Atlantic Monthly, 1922.

——, *The Turning Wheel. The Story of General Motors Through Twenty-Five Years, 1908-1933,* Doubleday, 1934.

——, *Detroit, Dynamic City,* Appleton-Century, 1940.

Raushenbush, Carl, *Fordism,* League for Industrial Democracy, October, 1937.

Rochester, Anna, *Rulers of America,* International Publishers, 1936.

Russell, H. M., *Oh, That Funny Ford!* Morris and Bendien, 1916.

Seltzer, Laurence H., *A Financial History of the American Automobile Industry,* Houghton, Mifflin, 1928.

Simonds, William Adams, *Henry Ford and Greenfield Village,* Stokes, 1938.

——, *Henry Ford,* Bobbs-Merrill, 1943.

Sinclair, Upton, *The Flivver King.* The author, 1937.

Smitter, Wessel, *F.O.B. Detroit,* Harper's, 1938.

Tate, Alfred O., *Edison's Open Door,* Dutton, 1938.

*They Told Barron.* The notes of the late Clarence W. Barron, edited and arranged by Arthur Pound and Samuel Taylor Moore. Harper's 1930.

——, *More They Told Barron,* Harper's, 1931.

Villard, Oswald Garrison, *Fighting Years,* Harcourt, Brace, 1939.

Walsh, J. Raymond, *C.I.O.: Industrial Unionism in Action,* Norton, 1937.

White, J. J., *Funabout Fords,* Howell, 1915.

White, L. S., *Farewell to Model T,* Putnam's, 1936.

Wilson, Edmund, *The American Jitters,* Scribner's, 1932.

Wolf, Howard, and Wolf, Ralph, *Rubber. A Story of Glory and Greed,* Covici, Friede, 1936.

Wolfe, Bertram D., *Diego Rivera*, Knopf, 1939.

Young, William Pennypacker, *A Ford Dealer's Twenty Year Ride With The Old and New Model Ford Policies*. The author, Pottstown, Pennsylvania and Hempstead, New York, 1932.

## MAGAZINE AND NEWSPAPER ARTICLES

* The author consulted the complete Ford files of the journals and newspapers marked with asterisks.

Adamic, Louis. "The Hill-Billies Come to Detroit." *Nation*. February 13, 1935.

Analysis of Muscle Shoals Bids. United States Treasury Department, 1926.

*Automobile.*

*Automobile.* "Weeding Out Inefficient at Ford Plant." May 21, 1914.

———. "Lest We Forget: New England's Pioneers Did Much To Put The Industry Where It Is Today." March 2, 1916.

Automobile Manufacturers Association. "Automobile Facts and Figures." New York. 1938 edition.

*Automobile Trade Journal.* Silver Anniversary Issue. December 1, 1924.

*Automotive Industries.*

*Automotive Industries.* "Ford Leaves Ford Motor." November 28, 1918.

———. "Ford Will Produce $250 Car." March 6, 1919.

———. "Ford Organization Shaken by Recent Resignations." March 27, 1919.

———. "Fords Buy Minority Stock . . . Co-operative Plan to Give Employes Former Minority Profits." July 17, 1919.

———. "Ford Shaken by Internal Strife." January 6, 1921.

———. "W. R. Campbell To Be New Ford Executive." February 3, 1921.

———. "Ford Reorganization Assumes Form." February 17, 1921.

———. "Ford Treasureship Is Left Unfilled." March 17, 1921.

———. Articles on Ford's war profits. September 5, 1918; May 15, 1919; July 3, 1919.

*Auto Workers News.*

Avery, C. W. "How Mass Production Came Into Being." *Iron Age*. June 13, 1929.

———. Address, Ford Motor Co. Dinner for 35-Year Employes. Dearborn Inn, Dearborn, Michigan. December 19, 1944. Unpublished.

*Bankers Home Magazine.* "Mr. Ford's Business Philosophy." December, 1916.

Barkley, Frederick R. "Says Kuhn's Bund Has 6,617 in 1937." New York *Times*, April 4, 1939.

Barringer, E. C. "Five-Day Week Reality With Ford; Six-Day Pay Total Being Restored." *Iron Trade Review*. November 18, 1926.

*Barron's.*

*Barron's.* "Why Ford Raised Dealer Discounts." May 5, 1930.

———. "Not Generally Known. Not Previously Told." (Report on first public reaction to the Ford Sunday Evening Hour.) June 22, 1936. p. 10.

Beeler, N. M. "How Thomas A. Edison Would Solve Farm Financing Problem." *Capper's Farmer*. April, 1925.

Benson, Allan L. "The Intimate Life of Henry Ford." *Hearst's International*. January-March, 1923.

———. "Mr. Ford and the Great Issues." *Hearst's International*. September, 1923.

Bent, Silas. "Ford's White House Bee Buzzing Far and Wide." New York *Times*. January 7, 1923.

Bergman, Walter G. "Henry Ford's Silent Partner." *The Unemployed*. League for Industrial Democracy. Spring, 1931, No. 3.

Bingay, Malcolm W. "Get a Horse!" *Saturday Evening Post*. June 29, 1940.

———. "The Motor Boys in Action." *Saturday Evening Post*. July 6, 1940.

°*Bombardier* (Publication of Local 50, UAW).

Borth, Christy. "Americana: On the Line." *Reader's Digest*. July, 1937.

———. "Henry Ford, Schoolmaster." *Forum*. September, 1938.

Botkin, B. A. "The Lore of the Lizzie Label." *American Speech*. December, 1930.

———. "An Anthology of Lizzie Labels." *American Speech*. October, 1931.

Bradford, Gamaliel. "The Great American Enigma. An Exploration of Henry Ford." *Harper's*. October, 1930.

Brown, Earl. "Detroit's Armed Camps." *Harper's*. July, 1945.

Bulletin of the Pan American Union. "Fordlandia, Brazil." Prepared by the Ford Motor Co. January, 1933.

Bullitt, William C. Dispatches to the Philadelphia *Public Ledger* from the Ford peace ship. Reprinted by the New York *Times*. January 31, 1916; February 1, 1916.

Burck, G. "Henry Ford II Takes Over the Presidency of Ford Motors." *Life*. October 1, 1945.

°*Business Week*.

*Business Week*. "Ford Dealers Rebel; Many Leave Ranks." April 2, 1930.

———. "Trouble in Detroit." February 8, 1933.

———. "Motor Body Blow." February 15, 1933.

———. "Ford's Year of Decision." October 12, 1946.

———. "Henry Ford's Death Will Leave His Empire Intact." April 12, 1947.

———. "Ford Becomes a Matriarchy." April 26, 1947.

Callahan, William C. "Auto Industry Keeps Going." New York *Times*. June 12, 1938.

Cameron, William J. "Jesus Christ Is a National Question: What We Stand For." Anglo-Saxon Federation of America. Detroit. Undated.

———. "Israel in the Streets of Today." *Destiny*. October, 1937.

———. "Is There a Chosen People?" *Destiny*. April, 1938.

———. "Interdependence of Farm and Industry." *Vital Speeches of the Day*. September 1, 1938.

———. "How Old Is This Anglo-Saxon Truth?" *Destiny*. March, 1939.

———. "The Servant Race." *Destiny*. June, 1939.

——. Testimony in the Ford-Sapiro case. Detroit *News*. July 8, 1927; New York *Times*. March 19-26, 1927.

——. Ford Sunday Evening Hour Talks. Ford Motor Co. Detroit. 1934-1941.

Carlisle, John M. "Detroit, Short of Cash, Buys Silks and Diamonds." Detroit *News*. March 9, 1933.

——. "A New Start for Gillespie." Detroit *News*. October 15, 1935.

——. "Police Sale of Policy Slips Bared in Dearborn Quiz." Detroit *News*. May 27, 1941.

Chasan, Will, and Riesel, Victor. "Keep Them Out." *Nation*. May 16, 1942.

Chase, Stuart. "Ford's Billion Breaks World Records." New York *Times*. February 13, 1927.

*Christian Century*. "Last of the Tycoons." April 23, 1947.

*Coal Age*. "Price Boosting Ford Rails Against What Was Practiced by Him Two Years Ago." September 14, 1922.

*Collier's*. "Speaking of Ford for President." December 8, 1923.

Colvin, Fred H. "Building an Automobile Every 40 Seconds." *American Machinist*. May 18, 1913.

*Commercial and Financial Chronicle*. "How Henry Ford Met Maturing Obligations of $58,000,000." July 30, 1921.

Commons, John R. "Henry Ford, Miracle Worker." *Independent*. May 1, 1920.

*Commonweal*. "Ryan-Coughlin Controversy." October 23, 1936.

Corey, Lewis. "Modern Machines and Tools." *Encyclopaedia of the Social Sciences*. Vol. 10, 1933. p. 24.

Couzens, James. "What I Found About Business from Ford." An interview with Samuel Crowther. *System*. September, 1921.

——. "Long Wages." *Survey*. April 11, 1930.

——. "American Industry and the Social Good." *Printer's Ink Monthly*. July, 1931.

Cruden, Robert L. "The Great Ford Myth." *New Republic*. March 16, 1932.

Daimler, Paul. "The Development of the Petroleum Automobile." *Engineering Magazine*. December, 1901.

Daniell, F. Raymond. " 'Vigilante' Army Forms To Aid Ford." New York *Times*. June 29, 1937.

——. "Ford Confidently Faces A Labor Duel." New York *Times*. October 17, 1937.

——. "Ford and Lewis: Foemen in a Duel of Titans." New York *Times*. October 31, 1937.

——. "Detroit—Our Laboratory of Social Change." New York *Times*. November 14, 1937.

Davenport, Walter. "The Mysterious Gerald Smith, Detroit's Rabble Rouser." *Collier's*. March 4, 1944.

°Dearborn *Independent*.

Dearborn *Independent*. Editorial, "Sapiro Case Settled." July 30, 1927.

Denny, Harold N. "Ford Takes Over 2 Detroit Banks; Move Ends Tie-Up."
New York *Times*. February 27, 1933.
——. "Ford Calls NRA a Step Toward An Era of Justice." New York *Times*.
January 11, 1934.
*Destiny*. Master Index. From May, 1937 through December, 1938. Haverill,
Massachusetts.
°Detroit *Free Press*.
Detroit *Free Press*. Article on Ford's war profits. November 3, 1918.
——. "Henry Ford and His Huns." Full-page political advertisement.
November 3, 1918.
——. Editorial, "Coughlin, the Demagog." March 27, 1933.
——. "Kid McCoy Ends His Life in Hotel Room." April 19, 1940.
——. "Poll Calls Ford Labor's Friend." May 29, 1940.
——. "Self-Styled Labor Spy Tells of Work For Ford Co." June 3, 1941.
°Detroit *News*.
Detroit *News*. Articles on Ford's war profits. February 5, 1917; February 9,
1917; April 19, 1917; May 14, 1917; November 17, 1917; August 22,
1918; September 5, 1918; February 22, 1919; May 24, 1919; June 26,
1919; July 14, 1919; January 27, 1920; October 13, 1923; July 30, 1938.
——. "Lelands Saved Whoever Buys." February 2, 1922.
——, "Ford Has 5,000 Jobs for Boys." November 24, 1926.
——. "Kuhn Denies Fascist Plot; 200,000 U. S. Germans Fight Reds."
March 12, 1937.
——. "Committee Questions Nazi Chief." August 16, 1939.
°Detroit *Saturday Night*.
Detroit *Saturday Night*. "The I.W.W. Gang Is Out to Get Detroit." June 28,
1913.
——. Articles on Ford's war profits. February 17, 1917; August 3, 1918;
August 17, 1918; January 4, 1919; January 11, 1919.
——. "What Michigan Thinks of Henry Ford and His Senatorial Candidacy."
June 28, 1918; July 13, 1918.
——. Article on draft status of Edsel Ford. July 13, 1918.
——. "Concerning the Exemption of Edsel Ford." November 2, 1918.
——. "Henry Ford on the Witness Stand." July 26, 1919.
——. "Flivver Anti-Semitism." January 1, 1921.
——. "The Ford Riddle." February 5, 1921.
——. "Henry Ford's Revenge." October 8, 1921.
——. By E. A. B. "Personal and Confidential: Henry Ford." May 20, 1922.
——. "Henry Ford, Prohibition Agent." September 16, 1922.
——. "Ford Publicity That Newspapers Missed." October 7, 1922.
——. "Lelands Demand Ford Pay Lincoln Stockholders." April 5, 1924.
——. By the Tenth Councilman. "The Gillespie and His Mayors." April 26,
1930.
——. "Drying Up Model A." April 26, 1930.
——. "Detroit Draws Nation's Jobless." May 3, 1930.

——. By the Tenth Councilman. "How Mayor Bowles Got That Way." May 31, 1930.

——. Ford Industries Number. June 15, 1935.

Dos Passos, John. "Detroit: City of Leisure." *New Republic.* July 27, 1932.

Dozier, Howard Douglas. "Henry Ford and Karl Marx." *Atlantic Monthly.* March, 1931.

Drake, J. Walter. "The Rubber Industry and the Automobile." *Annals of the American Academy of Political and Social Science.* Vol. 116. 1924.

Drucker, P. F. "Henry Ford: Success and Failure." *Harper's.* July, 1947.

Duffus, R. L. "Why We Consume the Most Autos." New York *Times.* July 24, 1927.

——. "Our Changing Cities. Dynamic Detroit." New York *Times.* April 10, 1927.

Duranty, Walter. "Talk of Ford Favor Thrills Moscow." New York *Times.* February 17, 1928.

Eiselen, Malcolm R. "Horseless Carriage." *Yale Review.* September, 1936.

Emden, Harold. "Barnum Never Did Better." Detroit *Saturday Night.* October 26, 1929.

*Engineering and Contracting.* "Henry Ford's Secret." October 15, 1919.

*°Federated Press* (Labor News Service).

Finney, Burnham. "Ford Blocks Path of C.I.O." New York *Times.* March 28, 1937.

——. "The Sun Never Sets on Ford's Empire." New York *Times.* August 8, 1937.

Fitch, John A. "Ford of Detroit." *Survey.* February 7, 1914.

Flynn, John T. "How Detroit Does It." *New Republic.* October 11, 1933.

——. "Michigan Magic. The Detroit Bank Scandal." *Harper's.* December, 1933.

——. "Public Dividends, Private Salaries, Secret Deficits." *New Republic.* January 10, 1934.

——. "Detroit Business Men Cheer Couzens' Defeat." *New Republic.* September 30, 1936.

——. "Watch the Ford Myths Go By." *New Republic.* August 4, 1937.

Forbes, B. C. "Ford Loses Motor Leadership. Amazing Facts." *Forbes'.* April 15, 1927.

——. "Slave Driving in Ford Factories Pictured by Ford's Own Workers." *Forbes'.* May 1, 1927.

——, "How Ford Dealers Are Treated." *Forbes'.* May 15, 1927.

——. "The Ford Worker." *Forbes'.* May 15, 1927.

——. "Can Ford Troubles Be Cured?" *Forbes'.* June 1, 1927.

——. "Why America Is in Debt to Ford." Detroit *Times.* July 29, 1938.

*Forbes'* Magazine. Editorial, "Ford Blamed for Strike." February 15, 1933.

Ford, Edsel. "Why We Employ Aged and Handicapped Workers." *Saturday Evening Post.* February 6, 1943.

Ford, Henry. Publisher. "The Case Against the Little White Slaver." 4 vols. Detroit. 1914-1916.

———. "If I Ran the Railroads." *Nation's Business.* November 7, 1921.

———. "If I Were President." An authorized interview reported by Charles W. Wood. *Colliers.* August 4, 1923.

———. "Henry Ford Expounds Mass Production." New York *Times.* September 19, 1926.

———. "Why I Favor Five Days' Work With Six Days Pay." *World's Work.* October, 1926.

———. "Machinery, the New Messiah." *Forum.* March, 1928.

———. "Let Prohibition Begin at Home." As told to Elizabeth Breuer. *Pictorial Review.* September, 1929.

———. "Henry Ford Says We Are in Revolution!" As told to Elizabeth Breuer. *Pictorial Review.* October, 1932.

°*Ford Times.*

"Henry Ford for United States Senator." Prepared and submitted by the Non-Partisan Ford-for-Senator Club. 1918. (Labadie Collection, University of Michigan Library.)

Ford, Henry II. "The Challenge of Human Engineering." Annual meeting of the Society of Automotive Engineers. Detroit. January 9, 1946. Ford Motor Co.

"The Ford Motor Interests in Brazil." *South American Journal.* August 6, 1938. Division of Financial and Economic Information, Pan American Union. August 31, 1938.

°*Fortune.*

*Fortune.* "Ford, Chevrolet, Plymouth." October, 1931.

———. "Brazil." November, 1931.

———. "Engineering Milestones." December, 1931. p. 43.

———. "Automotive Charivari." December, 1931. p. 43.

———. "Sales for Sale." January, 1933.

———. "Mr. Ford Doesn't Care." December, 1933.

———. "Chrysler." September, 1935.

———. "Success Story." December, 1935.

———. "Jews in America." February, 1936.

———. "Industrial War." November, 1937.

———. "The Used Car." June, 1938.

———. "General Motors." December, 1938.

———. "General Motors II: Chevrolet." January, 1939.

———. "General Motors III: How To Sell Automobiles." February, 1939.

———. "General Motors IV: A Unit in Society." March, 1939.

———. "Sorensen of the Rouge." April, 1942.

———. "The '43 Ford." February, 1943.

———. "Ford Heritage; Struggle for Its Control Approaches a Climax." June, 1944.

———. "Rebirth of Ford." May, 1947.

Garrett, Garet. "Edison's Idea for a New Kind of Money." New York *Times.* July 16, 1922.

General Motors Statement Before Fact-Finding Board. General Motors Corporation. Detroit. December 28, 1945.

Godwin, Murray. "The Case Against Henry Ford." *American Mercury.* July, 1931.

Guidebook for the Edison Institute Museum and Greenfield Village. Dearborn, Michigan. 1937.

Guidebook to Historical Places in Western Pennsylvania. Compiled by the Western Pennsylvania Historical Survey. University of Pittsburgh Press. 1938.

Hallgren, Mauritz A. "Grave Danger in Detroit." *Nation.* August 3, 1932.

Hapgood, Norman. "The Inside Story of Henry Ford's Jew-Mania." *Hearst's International.* June, 1922.

——. "The Inside Story of Henry Ford's Jew-Mania. Part II. On the Trail of the Sleuths." *Hearst's International.* July, 1922.

——. "The Inside Story of Henry Ford's Jew-Mania. Part III. The Strange Adventures of No. 25 H." *Hearst's International.* August, 1922.

——. "The Inside Story of Henry Ford's Jew-Mania. Part IV. Henry Swallows Old Bait." September, 1922.

——. "Henry Ford's Jew-Mania. Part V. Robbing the U. S. Censor." *Hearst's International.* October, 1922.

——. "Henry Ford's Jew-Mania. Part VI. Forcing Dealers to Spread the Poison." *Hearst's International.* November, 1922.

Hard, William. "Mr. Ford Is So Good." *Nation.* March 26, 1924.

Harris, Herbert. "Robot Revolt." *Current History.* April, 1938.

Harvier, Ernest. "Newberryism Chief Factor in Michigan." New York *Times.* June 11, 1922.

Haughton, R. A. "Ford's White House Bee." New York *Times.* June 25, 1922.

Hay, William Wren. "Ford's Future." *Barron's.* November 7, 1932.

——. "Financial History of Ford Motor." *Barron's.* November 7, 1932.

Hindus, Maurice. "Henry Ford Conquers Russia." *Outlook.* June 29, 1927.

Hines, Walker D. "Henry Ford Is Right—and Wrong." *Railway Age.* November 26, 1921.

\* *Horseless Age.*

*Horseless Age.* "Straws That Show the Wind." January, 1896.

——. "The Ford Gasoline Racer." November 20, 1901.

——. "How to Silence the Squeaks and Rattles in Used Cars." November 1, 1917.

Howard, John Tasker. "History Bunked." *Western Pennsylvania Historical Magazine.* March, 1937.

*Industrial Management.* "Ford's Mechanical Roustabouts." March 15, 1921.

*Institute for Propaganda Analysis.* "The Ford Sunday Evening Hour." July, 1938.

——. "The Public Relations Counsel and Propaganda." August, 1938.

*Inter-American.* "Ford Withdraws from Brazil." January, 1946.

Johnson, Oakley. "After the Dearborn Massacre." *New Republic.* March 30, 1932.

Kaempffert, Waldemar. "The Dramatic Story Behind Ford's New Car." New York *Times.* December 18, 1927.

———. "The Mussolini of Highland Park." New York *Times.* January 8, 1928.

Kahn, Dorothea. "Honors in His Home Town." *Christian Science Monitor.* May 18, 1938.

Kellogg, Paul U. "Henry Ford's Hired Men." *Survey Graphic.* February 1, 1928.

———. "When Mass Production Stalls." *Survey Graphic.* March 1, 1928.

*Labor Research Association (Labor News Service).

Lambert, George. "Dallas Tries Terror." *Nation.* October 9, 1937.

———. "Memphis Is Safe for Ford." *Nation.* January 22, 1938.

Leake, Paul. "Detroit, the Automobile Center of the World." Detroit *Saturday Night.* July 10, 1909.

Lee, John R. "The So-Called Profit Sharing System in the Ford Plant." *Annals of the American Academy of Political and Social Science.* May, 1916.

Leggett, E. S. "Henry Ford to Retire from Helm; Asserts He'll Devote Rest of Life to Philanthropy." Detroit *Free Press.* June 5, 1930.

Levin, Samuel S. "Ford Profit-Sharing, 1914-1920. I. The Growth of the Plan." *Personnel Journal.* August, 1927.

———. "The End of Ford Profit Sharing." *Personnel Journal.* October, 1927.

———. "The Ford Unemployment Problem." *American Labor Legislation Review.* June, 1932.

Levinson, Edward. "Detroit Digs In." *Nation.* January 16, 1937.

*Life* Magazine.

*Life* Magazine. "Detroit Is Dynamite." August 17, 1942.

———. "Henry Ford II." October 1, 1945.

———. "Father of the Automobile Dies." April 21, 1947.

Lane, Harold F. "More About Ford's Railroad Operating Methods." *Railway Age.* December 10, 1921.

Lindbergh, Charles A. "Aviation, Geography and Race." *Readers Digest.* November, 1939.

*Literary Digest.* "Figuring the Horse-Power of the Ford Endorsement." January 5, 1924.

———. "Henry Ford and the Detroit Doctors." May 31, 1924.

———. "Henry Ford Shakes a Wicked Hoof." August 15, 1925.

———. "Detroit's Duel Over Doles." July 11, 1931.

———. "Stirred Up By Henry Ford's 'Shotgun Gardens.' " September 12, 1931.

Littell, Robert. "Henry Ford." *New Republic.* November 14, 1923.

London *Daily Mail.* "Ford Party in a Wilderness; Nobody Wants Them." December 22, 1915.

London *Times.* Classic exposé of the "Protocols of Zion." August 16-18, 1921.

Lougee, E. F. "Industry and the Soy Bean." *Modern Plastics*. April, 1936.
Lucking, Alfred, et al. "A Synopsis of the Case Against Truman H. New-
    berry. The Issue—Are the Senate Seats for Sale?" 1921 (?).
Macfarlane, Peter Clark. "The Beginnings of the Automobile." *Collier's*.
    January 9, 1915.
*Machinery*. "Ford Motor Co.'s Profit-Sharing Plan." June, 1917.
MacManus, Theodore F. "Reducing the Price of Coffins Will Not Stimulate
    the Demand." An advertisement. New York *Times*. February 24, 1930.
Markey, Morris. "Young Man of Affairs." Profiles of Charles A. Lindbergh.
    *New Yorker*. September 20 and 27, 1930.
Marshall, Margaret. "The King Is Dead." *Nation*. December 14, 1927.
Martel, Frank X. "Is Father Coughlin a Friend of Labor?" Radio address.
    Station CKLW. Detroit, Michigan. May 1, 1939.
Martin, P. W. Editor. "365 of Henry Ford's Sayings." 1923.
McCarten, John. "Father Coughlin: Holy Medicine Man." *American Mercury*.
    June, 1939.
———. "The Little Man in Henry Ford's Basement." *American Mercury*.
    Part I, May, 1940; Part II, June, 1940.
McCormick, Kenneth F. "Attempt To Kill Harry Bennett in Auto Foiled."
    Detroit *Free Press*. March 31, 1937.
———. "Spokesman for Henry Ford." *Radio Guide*. December 8, 1939.
———. "Indicted Chief Is Suspended by Dearborn." Detroit *Free Press*. May
    27, 1941.
———. "Meet the Real Harry Bennett, Ford's Man." Detroit *Free Press*.
    February 8, 1942.
Mead, J. E. "Rehabilitating Cripples at Ford Plant." *Iron Age*. September
    26, 1918.
Michelson, Charles. On Ford's Offer for Muscle Shoals. New York *World*.
    July 9, 1927.
*Monthly Labor Review*. Bureau of Labor Statistics. Department of Labor.
    "Wages and Hours of Labor in the Automobile Industry in 1922."
    April, 1923.
———. "Training and Employment of Disabled Workmen in the Ford
    Plant." November, 1923.
———. "Index of Productivity of Labor in the Steel, Automobile, Shoe, and
    Paper Industries." July, 1926.
———. "Cost of Living. Changes in Cost of Living in the United States."
    Detroit, Michigan. p. 181. February, 1929.
———. "Instability of Employment in the Automobile Industry," February,
    1929.
———. "Age Distribution of Workers in a Small Group of Establishments."
    November, 1929.
———. "Standard of Living of Employes of Ford Motor Co. in Detroit."
    June, 1930.
———. "Age Distribution of Ford Employes." December, 1930.

——. "Wartime Wage Movements and Urban Wage-Rate Changes." October, 1944.

——. "Income From Wages and Salaries in the Post-War Period." September, 1945.

Mumford, Lewis, "American Taste," *Harper's*. October, 1927.

Murphy, Charles J. V. "Mr. Ford's Legacy." *Life*. April 21, 1947.

Murphy, Irene E. "A Study of Social Services Available for Handicapped Persons in the Detroit Area." Detroit Community Fund. July, 1936.

Mydans, Carl M. "Why Ford Workers Strike." *Nation*. October 25, 1933.

Nathan, Jacob. "Edsel Ford Seeks To Offset The Effects of His Father's Interviews." Detroit *Saturday Night*. March 29, 1919.

*Nation*. Editorial. "The Unveiling of Henry Ford." July 26, 1919.

——. "Henry Ford Goes Bargain Hunting." December 20, 1922.

——. "G. M. Strike, '46 Model." December 1, 1945.

*Nation's Business*. "The Case of the D. T. & I. By a Railroad President." November, 1921.

*New Republic*. "The New Flivverism." December 14, 1927.

——. "Mass-Production Poverty." March 7, 1928.

——. "Henry Ford, Individualist." September 13, 1933.

——. "Enemies At Home." April 20, 1942; June 1, 1942; June 22, 1942; July 13, 1942.

——. Henry Ford obituary. April 21, 1947.

*\*Newsweek*.

*Newsweek*. "Ford Shake-Up." March 13, 1944.

——. "Prince Henry." April 24, 1944.

——. "Young King Henry Ford II." April 21, 1947.

New York *Journal of Commerce*. "Ford Reported To Have Bought Into National City Bank." May 10, 1930.

New York *Post*. Biographical note on W. J. Cameron. April 29, 1938.

——. Documentary comparison of a speech by Paul Joseph Goebbels and a release by Charles E. Coughlin. December 30, 1938.

——. "Voice Is Coughlin's, But Words Are Nazis'." March 22, 1939.

*\*New York Times*.

New York *Times*. "The Evolution of the Motor Car Has Been Meteoric." January 4, 1914.

——. Editorial. "An Industrial Utopia." January 7, 1914.

——. "Henry Ford Explains Why He Gives Away $10,000,000." January 11, 1914.

——. Editorial. "A Success With a Weakness." June 20, 1914.

——. "Ford Describes His Labor Utopia." January 23, 1915.

——. "Humanity and Your Vote." Ford advertisement advocating the re-election of President Wilson. November 5, 1916.

——. Editorial. "Mr. Ford and the Senate." June 17, 1918.

——. Editorial. "Drafting Mr. Ford." August 29, 1918.

——. Editorial. "Legendary Mr. Ford." August 30, 1918.

——. Articles on Ford's war profits. September 28, 1916; August 16, 1917; March 3, 1922; March 28, 1922; April 20, 1922; April 21, 1922.

——. Ford's testimony at Mt. Clemens. July 16-19; 22-23, 1919.

——. Editorial. "A Derisory Verdict." August 16, 1919.

——. "Ford Plans a City 75 miles in Length." January 12, 1922.

——. "Rush for Muscle Shoals." February 12, 1922.

——. Comments by Senator George Norris on the Ford offer for Muscle Shoals. May 10, 1922; May 12, 1922; June 2, 1922; June 14, 1922; June 18, 1922; July 21, 1922; March 14, 1928.

——. "Ford to Market a Flour That Will Help Us All to Live 100 Years." May 20, 1922.

——. "Ford Offer Riddled in Senate Report . . . Norris Declares Muscle Shoals Profit Would Be $14,500,000,000 in a Hundred Years." July 21, 1922.

——. Comment by Senator James Couzens on the Ford offer for Muscle Shoals. December 6, 1922.

——. "Berlin Hears Ford Is Backing Hitler." December 20, 1922.

——. "Says Ford Aids Royalists. Auer Charges Financial Help To Bavarian Anti-Semites." February 8, 1923.

——. "How Magazine Started. First Editor of Dearborn *Independent* Tells of Original Plans." July 11, 1927.

——. "Ford Raises Wages $19,500,000 a Year . . . Minimum Goes Up to $7 a Day." December 4, 1929.

——. "Ford Manager Buys Japanese War Bonds." December 28, 1937.

——. "Henry Ford Is Dead at 83 in Dearborn." April 8, 1947.

——. "World Leaders in Tribute." April 9, 1947.

Niebuhr, Reinhold. "Ford's Five-Day Week Shrinks." *Christian Century.* June 9, 1927.

O'Brien, J. H. "Henry Ford's Commander in Chief, Harry Bennett." *Forum.* February, 1938.

O'Neill, Joseph Jefferson. Dispatches from the Ford Peace Ship. New York *World.* December 22, 1915; December 27, 1915.

*Onlooker.* "Leland's Plea." January, 1931.

Palmer, Dewey H. "Automobiles of 1939." *New Republic.* December 28, 1938.

Pierrot, George F., and Richardson, Edgar P. "The Diego Rivera Murals. A Guide to the Murals of the Garden Court." People's Museum Association. Detroit, Michigan. 1933.

——. "The Diego Rivera Murals. An Illustrated Guide." Detroit Institute of Arts. World Adventure Series, Inc. 1934.

Pipp, E. G. "Why." *Pipp's Weekly.* July 21, 1923.

*°Pipp's Magazine.*

*°Pipp's Weekly.*

*Pipp's Weekly.* "What About Newberry?" May 8, 1920.

——. "Facts About Edsel Ford." May 15, 1920.

——. "What Started Ford Against the Jews?" March 5, 1921.

——. "Answers to Questions: Was the Investigation That Resulted in the 'Newberry Case' Started by the Government or by Mr. Newberry's Political Opponents?" May 21, 1921.

——. "The Inside Story of the Newberry Persecution." September 17, 1921.

——. "About Ford and Benedict Arnold: Ford the Historian." October 15, 1921.

——. "Ford and That Leland Deal." February 18, 1922.

——. "The Biggest GRAB Ever Attempted in America—Muscle Shoals." July 15, 1922.

——. "More About Ford's Grab for Muscle Shoals." August 12, 1922.

——. "Essential Facts in the Newberry Case." September 2, 1922.

——. "Couzens and His Two Jobs." December 9, 1922.

——. Quotation from the Grand Rapids *Herald* concerning the Ford offer for Muscle Shoals. January 13, 1923.

——. "What Judge Tuttle Said." February 3, 1923.

——. Articles on Ford's war profits. March 25, 1922; April 29, 1922; May 6, 1922; September 16, 1922; September 30, 1922; February 17, 1923; May 12, 1923; July 7, 1923; October 20, 1923.

——. "The Ford-Lincoln Deal." February 10, 1923.

——. "Ford Men Get After Senator Norris." June 16, 1923.

——. Comment by Senator George Norris on the Ford offer for Muscle Shoals. June 16, 1923.

——. "Ford's Political Record." July 28, 1923.

Player, Cyril Arthur. "Gangsters and Politicians in Detroit." *New Republic.* August 13, 1930.

Pound, Arthur. "The Ford Myth." *Atlantic Monthly.* January, 1924.

Presto Publishing Co. "Funny Stories About Ford." Vol. I. Hamilton, Ohio. 1915.

Proceedings of the Dearborn Conference of Agriculture, Industry, and Science. Dearborn, Michigan. May 7-8, 1935. Chemical Foundation, New York.

Proceedings of the Second Dearborn Conference of Agriculture, Industry, and Science. Dearborn, Michigan. May 12-14, 1936. Under the sponsorship of the Farm Chemurgic Council and the Chemical Foundation, Inc.

*Railway Age.* "Ford Has Not Wrought Miracle with D. T. and I." August 27, 1921.

——. "Ford's Railroad Must Report Statistics of Employees." November 12, 1921.

——. "Ford Railroad Plan Disapproved." August 14, 1926.

*Railway Review.* "Ford and the Railroads." September 3, 1921.

Reed, John. "Industry's Miracle Man." *Cosmopolitan.* October, 1916.

——. "Why They Hate Ford." *The Masses.* October, 1916.

Reitell, Charles. "Machinery and Its Effect Upon the Workers in the Automobile Industry." *Annals of the American Academy of Political and Social Science.* November, 1924.

Rice, Willis. "The Decay of the Patent System." *Brooklyn Law Review.* May, 1936.

Richard, Gene. "On the Assembly Line." *Atlantic Monthly.* April, 1937.

Robinson, Helen Ring. "Confessions of a Peace Pilgrim." *Independent.* February 14, 1916.

Rogers, Will. "Slipping the Lariat Over." New York *Times.* December 31, 1922.

Russell, Frederick C. "Up From Cars of Yesteryear." New York *Times.* January 10, 1932.

Ryan, John A. "Anti-Semitism in the Air." *Commonweal.* December 30, 1938.

*Science News Letter.* "Rear-Engined Automobile Is Patented by Henry Ford." July 16, 1938.

*Scientific American.* "Some Early American Automobiles." January 12, 1907.

———. "The Rise of the Automobile." June 5, 1915.

———. "Trend of 1917 Passenger-Car Design." January 6, 1917.

Seldes, George. *In Fact.* November 10, 1941. Issue devoted to Charles A. Lindbergh.

Seldes, Gilbert. "Henry Ford's English." *New Republic.* September 23, 1925.

Seltzer, Lawrence H. Automobile Industry, United States, Manufacture and Sale, Social Incidence of the Automobile. Encyclopaedia of the Social Sciences. Vol. 2, 1930.

Shidle, Norman C. "Has Ford Lost His Big 'Sales Punch' in the Low-Priced Field?" *Automotive Industries.* October 29, 1925.

Shower, C. J. "Guiding the Workman's Personal Expenditures. Ford Reduced Turnover 350 Per Cent." *Automotive Industries.* March 14, 1918.

Shuster, George N. "The Jew and Two Revolutions." *Commonweal.* December 30, 1938.

Smith, A. M. "Ford Gives Viewpoint on Labor. Cautions Workers on Organization." Detroit *News,* April 29, 1937.

Smith, Rowland. "Gangsters and Petty Politicians Have Key to Jobs at Ford's." *United Automobile Worker.* October 8, 1938.

Spivak, John L. "Secrets of America First's Propaganda." *New Masses.* October 14, 1941.

Sprague, Jesse Rainsford. "Confessions of a Ford Dealer." *Harper's.* June, 1927.

Steiger, Andrew J. "Autos and Jobs." *Nation.* May 2, 1928.

Stidger, William S. "Henry Ford Tells His New Faith in America." *Liberty.* March 2, 1935.

Street, Julian. "Detroit the Dynamic." *Collier's.* July 14, 1914.

Sugar, Maurice. "Michigan Passes the 'Spolansky Act.'" *Nation.* July 8, 1931.

———. "Bullets—not Food—for Ford Workers." *Nation.* March 23, 1932.

Sullivan, Mark. "Democratic Presidential Possibilities. Henry Ford as a Conceivable Candidate." *World's Work.* March, 1923.

*Survey*. "Ford's Plan of Small Farms Near Detroit." July 25, 1914.

Sweinhart, James. "Lincoln Force Called by Ford." Detroit *News*. February 5, 1922.

———. "$300,000,000 Ford Program Announced." Detroit *News*. February 27, 1932.

———. "What's Really Wrong at the Willow Run Plant?" Detroit *News*. March 22, 1943.

*Time Magazine.

*Time* Magazine. "On the Overpass." June 7, 1937.

———. "Detroit Dynast." April 21, 1947.

———. "Last of an American; Europe's Picture of Him and of America." April 21, 1947.

Tolles, N. A., and LaFever, M. W. "Wages, Hours, Employment and Annual Earnings in the Motor Vehicle Industry, 1934." *Monthly Labor Review*. Bureau of Labor Statistics. Department of Labor. Washington, D. C. March, 1936.

Tunis, John R. "Why the Ford Man Fails." *American Mercury*. April, 1934.

Ulrich, Carl V. "Another Ford Story." *Machinists Monthly Journal*. October, 1931.

*United Automobile Worker.

*United Automobile Worker*. "Ford Man Tells of Job Selling." November 15, 1940.

United States Chamber of Commerce. "Survey of Current Business." September, 1945.

*United States News*. "Ford Empire: End of an Era." April 18, 1947.

———. "Labor Philosophy of Henry Ford II." May 9, 1947.

Verlaine, Ralph. "Soybeans: The Story of a Worker's Education in Economics." *The One Big Union Monthly*. December, 1937.

Villard, Oswald Garrison. "Why Henry Ford Should Not Be President." *Nation*. May 30, 1923.

———. "Issues and Men." *Nation*. April 24, 1937.

Walker, Charles R. "The Ford Way of Doing Business." *New Republic*. May 20, 1940.

———. "The Ford Way of Doing Business. Part II." *New Republic*. May 27, 1940.

*Wall Street Journal.

*Wall Street Journal*. "What's Behind Ford's Plan to Close Down?" Reprinted by Detroit *Saturday Night*. September 2, 1922.

———. On profits of the Ford Motor Co. May 23, 1935; May 26, 1936; April 6, 1937; May 27, 1937; May 28, 1938.

White, Horace A. "Who Owns the Negro Churches?" *Christian Century*. February 9, 1938.

Wilson, Edmund. "The Despot of Dearborn." *Scribner's*. July, 1931.

Woodford, Frank B. "C.I.O. Gets Upper Hand in Automotive Industry." New York *Times*. April 21, 1940.

Woolf, S. J. "Ford, at 80, Expounds His Faith." New York *Times*. July 25, 1943.

Zeisler, Karl F. "The Saga of Model T." *American Mercury*. February, 1939.

## PUBLIC DOCUMENTS

Deed from Henry Ford and Clara B. Ford to Harry H. Bennett. Liber 5,124. State of Michigan. County of Wayne. December 12, 1938.

Welfare Report to Mayor Frank Murphy, from Captain John F. Ballinger, Superintendent of Public Welfare. Detroit, Michigan. Dated May 31, 1932. (Detroit *News* Library.)

Reports to the Common Council. Report of the Mayor's Labor Committee to the Common Council, City of Detroit. Detroit, Michigan. January 7, 1930.

Investigation of the Federal Bureau of Investigation into Nazi Military Training Camps in the United States. Sub-section on Fritz Kuhn. Unpublished. (For a summary of this report see New York *Times*, April 4, 1939.)

*The Ford Plan: A Human Document.* Report of the testimony of Henry Ford before the Federal Commission on Industrial Relations. January 22, 1915. Prepared by John R. Anderson.

Federal Trade Commission. *Report on Motor Vehicle Industry.* 76th Congress, First Session. House Document No. 468. Washington, D. C., 1939.

Leon Henderson, Director, Research and Planning Division, National Recovery Administration. "Preliminary Report on Study of Regularization of Employment and Improvement of Labor Conditions in the Automobile Industry." January 23, 1935. Public hearings in Detroit, December 15-16, 1934.

Blanche Bernstein. "Hiring Policies in the Automobile Industry." Works Progress Administration, National Research Project on Re-employment Opportunities and Recent Changes in Industrial Techniques. January, 1937. Unpublished.

Hearings Before Temporary National Economic Committee, Congress of the United States. 75th Congress. "Investigation of Concentration of Economic Power, Part II. Patents." Preliminary printing, 1939.

Investigation of Nazi and Other Propaganda. 74th Congress, 1st Session. House Report 153. Washington, D. C. 1935.

Hearings Before a Special Committee on Un-American Activities. House of Representatives. 75th Congress, 3rd Session. Vol. II. Washington, D. C., 1938.

Hearings Before the Committee on Banking and Currency. United States Senate. 73rd Congress. Second session. Part 10. Guardian Detroit Union Group. January 5 to January 23, 1934. United States Government Printing Office. Washington: 1934.

Temporary National Economic Committee. Congress of the United States.

Monograph 29. "Distribution of Ownership in the 200 Largest Non-financial Corporations." Washington, 1940.

Special Committee Investigating National Defense Program. Aircraft Report. July 10, 1943. Report 10. Part 10. 78th Congress. First session.

War Labor Board. Report 24. July 15, 1944.

Hearings before a Subcommittee of the Committee on Interstate Commerce. United States Senate. 75th Congress. 3rd session. Part 20. January 5-7, 11-13, 1938. The Pennroad Corporation . . . Kuhn, Loeb & Co. United States Government Printing Office. Washington: 1939.

Statutes of the Corporation. Ford Industrial Company of Brazil. Filed in the Commercial Junta of Para under No. 271. Approved by public writ of October 10, 1927. Undated. (Translated from the Portuguese by Alcibiades Claudio.)

Report on Economic and Commercial Conditions in Brazil. Department of Overseas Trade. His Majesty's Stationery Office. London.

J. Garnett Lomax. December, 1930.

———. No. 506. December, 1931.

E. Murray Harvey and J. Garnett Lomax. No. 539. December, 1932.

—— and N. A. P. Sands. No. 630. September, 1935.

—— and W. G. Bruzand. No. 691. October 15, 1937.

## LEGAL AND QUASI-LEGAL ACTIONS

Parker Rust-Proof Co. v. Ford Motor Co. United States District Court. Eastern District of Michigan, Southern Division. In Equity. No. 424.

Antonio Felix Pajalich v. Ford Motor Co. In the Circuit Court for the County of Wayne. State of Michigan. In Law. No. 137,080.

Wire Wheel Corporation of America and Packard Motor Car Co. v. Ford Motor Co. District Court of the United States. For the Eastern District of Wisconsin. Under Patent No. 1,103,567.

Henry Ford v. The Tribune Co., and Sam Solomon, Max Solomon and Harry Solomon. In the Circuit Court for the County of Wayne. State of Michigan. No. 67,999.

John F. Dodge and Horace E. Dodge v. Ford Motor Co. State of Michigan. Supreme Court Records and Briefs. Vols. 1070 and 1071. April Term, 1918.

Dodge v. Ford Motor Co. 204 Michigan 459.

Wilfred C. Leland, et al. v. Henry Ford, et al. State of Michigan. Supreme Court Records and Briefs. Vol. 1191. June Term, 1928.

Leland v. Ford. 245 Michigan 599.

Wilfred C. Leland, et al., v. Henry Ford, et al. State of Michigan. Supreme Court Records and Briefs. Vol. 2209. June Term, 1930.

Leland v. Ford. 252 Michigan 547.

Ford Motor Co. v. City of Detroit. State of Michigan. Supreme Court Records and Briefs. Vol. 2673. April Term, 1934.

Ford Motor Co. v. City of Detroit. 267 Michigan 177.

Harry H. Bennett v. Eileen C. Bennett. In the Circuit Court for the County of Washtenaw. State of Michigan. In Chancery. Filed June 21, 1927.

Harry H. Bennett v. Margaret M. Bennett. In the Circuit Court for the County of Washtenaw. State of Michigan. In Chancery. May, 1935.

Charles E. Coughlin v. Detroit *Free Press*. State of Michigan. In the Circuit Court for the County of Wayne. Case No. 211,525. Declaration filed December 1, 1938.

Harry George Schlee v. Henry Ford. United States District Court. Eastern District of Michigan. Southern Division. In Equity. No. 488.

Hearings on Review. Department of Labor and Industry. State of Michigan. From January 1, 1937 through July 20, 1939.

Thomas Pytel v. Ford Motor Co. Department of Labor. State of Michigan. 1939. Also Reply Briefs for Defendant and Appellant.

United States of America v. Ford Motor Co., et al. In the District Court of the United States for the Northern District of Indiana. South Bend Division. No. 1041. Indictment returned May 27, 1938. Also Civil No. 8. Final Decree. Dated November 15, 1938.

The People v. Sam Cuva. Recorder's Court of the City of Detroit. Docket No. A–15155.

United States Board of Tax Appeals. Henry Ford & Son, Inc., Petitioner, v. Commissioner of Internal Revenue, Respondent. Docket No. 24759.

Before the Board of Tax Appeals. Commissioner of Internal Revenue v. Estate of John F. Dodge, deceased (Docket No. 4640), James Couzens (Docket No. 10438), et al. Hearings January 11, 1927 through February 25, 1927.

National Labor Relations Board. Ford Motor Co. and United Automobile Workers of America.
St. Louis case. Intermediate Report. Signed July 2, 1938.
Long Beach case. Intermediate Report. Signed August 12, 1938.
Richmond, Cal. case. Intermediate Report. Signed September 2, 1938.
Detroit case. Decision and Order. Decided August 9, 1939.
Buffalo case. Intermediate Report. Signed August 9, 1939.
Long Beach case. Decision and Order. Decided December 8, 1939.
St. Louis case. Decision and Order. Decided April 29, 1940.
Buffalo case. Decision and Order. Decided May 7, 1940.
Dallas case. Decision and Order. Decided 1940.

National Labor Relations Board, Petitioner, v. Ford Motor Co., Respondent. Petition for enforcement of an order of the National Labor Relations Board. United States Circuit Court of Appeals. 6th Circuit. No. 8399. Decided October 8, 1940.

# INDEX

535

540

Guardian Group, 245-253; and Hunger March, 237, 239; and labor, 418; and Lelands, 165-173; status of, 182, 185, 291, 292, 340

Ford, Mrs. Edsel, 67, 445, 464, 466, 467, 468, 480

Ford Engineering Laboratory, 141, 147, 173, 184, 259, 309

*Ford Facts*, 400, 401

Ford farms, 265

Ford-for-President Club (Dearborn), 123, 125, 397*n*

Ford Foundation, 479-480, 481

Ford, Henry, and anti-semitism, 85, 114, 146-160, 450-456, 460, 461; character of, 40-43, 106-108; and creation of Ford Motor Co., 16-22; and dealers, 72, 76-77, 204-216; and Dearborn *Independent*, 140-152; and depression, 223-242; early life, 9-10; and Edison, 110-115; and executives, 40-41, 73-74, 188-194, 309; Bennett, 290-341; Cameron, 106, 142, 148, 152, 279-282; Couzens, 44-46, 64-65; Dodges, 65-71, 79-80; Liebold, 85, 116, 123-125, 148-149, 183-186, 192-194; Marquis, 89-93; Sorensen, 116, 123, 168-174, 181-186, 192-194; and $5 Day, 51-58, 60-63; idiosyncrasies, 106-108, 113, 259-276; and Ford Service Department, 290-341; and labor, 47-61, 75, 77-80, 145, 175-178, 203, 217-222, 231-242, 305-308, 309-316, 341-429; and litigations: v. ALAM, 28-31; v. Chicago *Tribune*, 101-105; v. Dodge, 67-71; v. Lelands, 163-174; v. Newberry, 120-123; v. Sapiro, 151-157; and machinery, 9, 10, 91; and mass production, 32-40; myth of, 62-63, 109-111, 275-278; and pacifism, 64, 83-94, 100, 287; and philanthropies, 136-139, 262-276; and pioneering, 11-16, 19-20; and politics, 115-120, 123-130; and products: Model A, 200-205; Model T, 25-28, 194-205; Lincoln, 163-174; V-8, 206; and railroads, 131-136; and return to past, 259-275; and speculation, 242-256; and TVA,

127-131; and World War I, 83-100; and World War II, 449-463

Ford, Mrs. Henry, Sr., 10, 85, 89, 98, 117, 124, 165, 166, 226, 260, 261, 336

Ford, Henry II, 445, 464, 480, 481; and control of Ford empire, 465-469; and labor, 470-475; and management, 468-469, 477-479; and postwar profits, 475-477

Ford, Mrs. Henry II, 465

Ford Investments Corporation, 243

Ford, John, 154, 186

"Fordlandia," 314

*Ford Man* (house organ), 75

*Ford Men and Methods*, by E. P. Norwood, 139

Ford Motor Co., and dealers, 72, 76-77, 204-216; and depression, 223-242; and executives, 22, 44-46, 64-72, 79-80, 188-194, 309; Bennett, 290-341, 371, 377, 389-398, 410-417, 445-446, 468-469; Liebold, 116, 123-125, 148-149, 183-194; Sorensen, 168-174, 181-186, 192-194; and Ford Service Department, 290-341, 371-377, 389-398, 410-417; formation of, 9, 16-22; and Hunger March, 231-242; and labor, 47-61, 75, 77-80, 145, 175-178, 203, 217-222, 231-242, 305-308, 309-316, 341-429, 438-440; and litigations: v. ALAM, 28-31; v. Dodge, 67-71; v. Lelands, 163-174; and mass production, 32-40; and NLRB, 374-376, 379-380, 382-388, 394-399, 405-406, 416-419; and products: Model A, 200-205; Lincoln, 163-174; Model T, 25-28; 194-205; V-8, 206; and Rouge riot, 389-396; and Sociology Department, 58-60; and strike, 408-417; and UAW, 370-429; and Willow Run, 429-450; and World War II, 429-450, 475-478

Ford Motor Co. (subsidiaries), Buffalo, N. Y., 38*n*, 374, 377; Edgewater, N. J., 299, 377; Kansas City, Mo., 384, 385, 386, 387; Long Beach, Calif., 379, 387*n*; Richmond, Calif., 384, 385, 387*n*; St. Louis, Mo., 384,

## KEITH SWARD

Keith Sward is a clinical psychologist in private practice in Beverly Hills, California. Dr. Sward completed doctoral and post-doctoral studies in psychology at the University of Minnesota and at Stanford University.